WALT WHITMAN

COMPLETE POETRY
AND SELECTED PROSE

RIVERSIDE EDITIONS

RIVERSIDE EDITIONS

Under the General Editorship of

Gordon N. Ray

WALT WHITMAN

COMPLETE POETRY AND SELECTED PROSE

EDITED WITH AN INTRODUCTION AND GLOSSARY BY

JAMES E. MILLER, JR.

THE UNIVERSITY OF CHICAGO

HOUGHTON MIFFLIN COMPANY
Boston · The Riverside Press Cambridge

CONTENTS

BIRDS OF PASSAGE

DRUM-TAPS

WHISPERS OF HEAVENLY DEATH

FROM NOON TO STARRY NIGHT

SONGS OF PARTING

Contents • xiii

SANDS AT SEVENTY (First Annex)

OLD AGE ECHOES

REJECTED POEMS

SELECTED PROSE

INTRODUCTION

James E. Miller, Jr.

Fate has played a bad joke on Walt Whitman in decreeing that he be most popularly known by a poem which is not only among his weakest but also among his most uncharacteristic. "Oh Captain, My Captain" has been forced out of the throats of so many generations of school children that it is no wonder they feel a profound boredom when they see a portrait of the Good Gray Poet. It is tantalizing to speculate whether Whitman would excite more readers to greater curiosity were he more widely met, not in this undistinguished poem, but in, say, a poem like "A Sight in Camp in the Daybreak Gray and Dim," with such lines as

> Then to the third—a face nor child nor old, very calm, as of
>   beautiful yellow-white ivory;
> Young man I think I know you—I think this face is the face of the
>   Christ himself,
> Dead and divine and brother of all, and here again he lies.

Or, from "When Lilacs Last in the Dooryard Bloom'd,"

> Come lovely and soothing death,
> Undulate round the world, serenely arriving, arriving,
> In the day, in the night, to all, to each
> Sooner or later delicate death.

Such lines suggest some of the mystery and depth of the poet's multi-faceted work which lure the adventurous reader farther into his book.

Walt Whitman once wrote, "Do I contradict myself? Very well then I contradict myself." No remark seems more characteristic of the man or the myth. And we know infinitely more of the latter than we do of the former: Walt Whitman was a sexually obsessed individual; Walt Whitman was purity personified. Walt Whitman was an insufferable egotist; Walt Whitman was a great democrat. Walt Whitman praised the common man; Walt Whitman worshipped the hero of society. Walt Whitman was a socialist, a communist, a subversive; Walt Whitman was a snob, an aristocrat, a chauvinist. Walt Whitman was a great fraud, always posing to impress the public; Walt Whitman was America's great epic poet of democracy.

To get at the truth in this tangled mass of rumor, myth, and fact is a painstaking task, perhaps impossible of achievement. For truth, especially the truth of a man's life, is subtle and evasive, its essence most likely to escape the moment it appears apprehended.

But the task is well worth a try. For Walt Whitman has come to loom large out of the past, to cast a long shadow which mingles with and extends our own. As Americans trying to understand our past, and even our present and future, we need to understand Walt Whitman. As citizens of the world attempting to understand our place and our role, we should try to comprehend this man who styled himself poet of democracy. As human beings trying to understand ourselves, we should listen carefully to the subtle tones and muted melodies as well as the barbaric yawp of this poet as he sings the song of the self.

In fact, it should be a matter of simple pride for Americans to possess and know *Leaves of Grass*. If we neglect to read it, we shall be in the embarrassing and irresponsible position of permitting an important work of our cultural heritage to fall by default into the possession of others more sensitively perceptive than we. We Americans are by no means so rich in the arts that we can afford to give away this ambitious book. Its claim to be our epic deserves a sympathetic hearing.

I

A FEW FAINT CLEWS

(As if any man really knew aught of my life,
Why even I myself I often think know little or nothing of my real
    life,
Only a few hints, a few diffused faint clews and indirections
I seek for my own use to trace out here.)

All Whitman biographers have been mockingly confronted by this warning near the beginning of *Leaves of Grass*. It has been a commonplace of criticism to point out that Whitman's real biography is *Leaves of Grass* itself; and, as the poet confessed, even it offers only "a few diffused faint clews and indirections." What, then, can the biographer, sorting through the random and miscellaneous documents left by a life like Whitman's, hope to discover about the human being who was the poet? If Whitman, who lived his life, could convey so little of it, how can a biographer expect to convey anything except distortion?

The problem is even more complicated than it might at first seem A number of the "clews," many left by Whitman himself, are unreliable and sometimes deliberately misleading. An incident which occurred near the end of Whitman's life demonstrates some of the difficulties confronted by the biographer. John Addington Symonds, the British classical scholar, wrote to the aging Whitman probing and provocative letters attempting to draw him out on the "Calamus" cluster of poems — those poems of comradeship that have been psychoanalyzed and exposed so thoroughly in our own Freudian age that it is difficult to realize that during most of the Victorian period they were accepted as pure and innocent poems of the spirit. Although Whitman admitted privately to Horace Traubel, the young Boswell of his old age, that maybe he did not know all his meanings in "Calamus," the Good Gray Poet wrote to Symonds a startling reply: "My life, young manhood, mid-age, times South, etc., have been jolly bodily, and doubtless open to criticism. Though unmarried, I have had six children — two are dead — one living Southern grandchild — fine boy writes to me occasionally — circumstances (connected with their benefit and fortune) have separated me from intimate relations." So far as scholars have been able to determine — and they have searched diligently — this entire statement is pure fiction. The easiest conclusion, and one frequently met, is that Whitman lied in order to throw Symonds, near an uncomfortable truth, off the track. Probably the whole truth is more complex. But in any event Whitman's reply to Symonds offers the biographer a startling challenge while at the same time it infinitely complicates his task.

1

A Dreamy, Impractical Youth

Whitman was thirty-six years old when he published the first edition of *Leaves of Grass* in 1855. Each of these years, beginning with his birth in 1819, has been closely examined for some foreshadowing of the poetic genius to come. But when all is said and done, the few facts assembled do not throw much light on Whitman's sudden burst into magnificent song. If anything, the facts, by their very ordinary look, intensify the poetic mystery.

Whitman was born in West Hills, Long Island, on May 31, 1819.

His mother, born Louisa Van Velsor, from a long line of New York Dutch farmers, and his father, Walter Whitman, from a once-prosperous but declining Long Island farm family, were to present the world with nine heirs, two of them imbeciles. Except for its extraordinary contribution of the poet to American culture, the family is undistinguished. Indeed, it seems remarkable that a background so unpromising as two parents barely literate and an array of children simply ordinary if not sub-normal should turn out to be the breeding ground for poetic genius.

Whitman's attendance at school was limited to about five or six years. After working in a number of printing offices during his boyhood, he became a teacher at the age of seventeen. The mother of a family with which Whitman boarded during this period remembered him as a "dreamy, impractical youth, who did very little work and who was always under foot and in the way." After a short period during which he taught at several Long Island schools, Whitman abandoned the profession altogether and turned to journalism for a career. As contributor, as reporter, as editor, he was associated with a large number of New York journals and Brooklyn newspapers. His position as editor of the Brooklyn *Daily Eagle* through 1846-47 was no mean achievement for a young man of 27, and his resignation was precipitated by his support of the Free Soil Party in a paper which was conservatively Democratic on the slavery issue.

Whitman's first love during these early journalistic days in New York was the opera. His passion was easily gratified during a time when opera was widely popular and in a city which attracted the great singers of the day. It was a night at the opera which launched Whitman on his one extensive journey through America before the appearance of *Leaves of Grass*. Early in 1848, while strolling in the lobby between the acts of an opera, Whitman met and was hired by a representative of the New Orleans *Crescent*. This accidental meeting, probably not so casual as Whitman later described it, proved to be the beginning of an interlude in Whitman's life which is still shrouded in considerable mystery. It is too bad that Whitman himself cooperated with his early biographers in distorting the New Orleans episode, as current biography, going to another extreme, tends to minimize the importance of the experience. Leaving with his brother Jeff, then fourteen years old, Whitman traveled by train from Brooklyn to Baltimore, by train again from Baltimore to Cumberland, by stagecoach from Cumberland across the Alleghenies to Wheeling, West Virginia, by steamboat down the Ohio to Cairo, Illinois, where the

Ohio flows into the Mississippi, and on down the great continental river to the gulf and New Orleans.

As the trip by boat took twelve wearing days, it is no wonder that Whitman later recalled the entire journey with such amplitude of vision. He was gone from Brooklyn, however, only from February through May, returning via the Great Lakes. It is with some reluctance that Whitman scholars have given up the image of the young poet traveling far and wide through western America, absorbing and "tallying" the geography and the people for the poetry that was to come later. It is perhaps with even greater reluctance that the biographers have abandoned such a satisfactory myth as the New Orleans Creole romance. The myth clarified the central mystery in Whitman's life, the profound emotional awakening which became the source of his poetic inspiration. The only difficulty with the myth was that it was created wholly out of the imagination of the biographers, and although it seemed plausible and even necessary, it simply was not true. The impact of the New Orleans episode on Whitman may be plotted somewhere between the pedestrian facts we can verify and the fascinating legends that have been invented. Certainly Whitman did see a lot of the country and its people — enough, indeed, to fortify and even stimulate his vision of America and her destiny.

Details of Whitman's life from the 1848 New Orleans trip to the publication of *Leaves of Grass* in 1855 are scanty. He returned to editing for a while, took various newspaper jobs, did carpentering, sold houses, published a few conventional poems in scattered journals and papers. But we search in vain among the sometimes abundant, sometimes sparse, facts of Whitman's life for the experience that provided the chief nourishment for his imagination. Upon probing the soil in search of the taproot we do discover numerous branch roots — an indulged enthusiasm for opera, an intense interest in oratory, a passion for Homer and Shakespeare, respect for the Bible — but these are small roots indeed to support such luxuriant growth. The taproot is there deep down, no doubt, not in the form of a Creole romance in New Orleans or an unfulfilled, spiritually transfigured attachment to an anonymous individual, but in the form of a fusing and shaping genius that feeds omnivorously on all that life grants, that transforms scarcity into abundance, poverty into riches, fragments into wholes. Genius cannot be reduced to facts, measured and dated, but its presence can be felt. It is, perhaps, the central fact of Whitman's life which has remained so obscure precisely because it has been so plain.

2

An American Bard at Last

Although we now look back to 1855 as one of those signal dates in American cultural history, marking a beginning as well as an end, the truth is that the country largely ignored the birth of *Leaves of Grass*. But America seems to have no great talent for recognizing literary masterpieces. Only four years before, in 1851, Melville's *Moby Dick* went widely unnoticed, and just the year before, in 1854, Thoreau's *Walden* failed to attract significant attention. What was the country reading? A full answer is worth a book on the popular taste, but some idea can be gained from one or two examples. Harriet Beecher Stowe's *Uncle Tom's Cabin* appeared in 1852, and, as both novel and play, had such an impact on the American mind and conscience as to cause Abraham Lincoln later (and half seriously) to attribute the Civil War to it. As for poetry, it is ironic and symbolic that the same year that gave birth to *Leaves of Grass* saw also the introduction of Henry Wadsworth Longfellow's *Hiawatha*. Of the two books, both attempting to deal with native American material, *Hiawatha* was by far the more popular, not only with the public at large, but with the important literary figures of the time. This same year of 1855 gave birth to the Saturday Club, a Boston literary group which attracted as members the principal creators of the New England genteel tradition. The author of *Hiawatha* was a member, as were, among others, Ralph Waldo Emerson, James Russell Lowell, Oliver Wendell Holmes, and John Greenleaf Whittier. Although the Saturday Club has no great significance in our literary history, it symbolizes the solid front of respectability formed by the literary leaders of the time — a front which could easily intimidate or at least discourage brash, uncouth outsiders like Whitman.

Tradition tells us that *Leaves of Grass* appeared on July 4, 1855, and there is no good reason to examine too closely such a satisfactory legend. Whitman published the book, setting part of the type himself, and took care of distribution — there were few sales from the thousand copies that were printed. The format was in one way better suited to Whitman's poetry than that of any subsequent edition: the wide page gave a natural if dramatic look to the poet's long line. The famed 1855 Preface and twelve untitled poems appeared in the book's ninety-five pages. Among the poems were those ultimately entitled "Song of Myself," "The Sleepers," "I Sing the Body Electric," and

"There was a Child Went Forth." As any young author would, Whitman sent copies of his first book to the leading literary figures of the day. Whittier is said to have cast his copy into the fire. Many copies must have suffered the same fate, if not in fact at least in spirit. For to readers used to the measured, elegant, and restrained tone of the genteel tradition in literature, Whitman's uninhibited barbaric yawp must have seemed an indecent invasion of personal privacy.

But one New England reader's response was all that Whitman could have expected in his wildest dreams of critical acceptance. In 1844 in "The Poet," Ralph Waldo Emerson had drawn the portrait of the ideal poet and had announced at the conclusion: "I look in vain for the poet whom I describe." That day in 1855 when he opened *Leaves of Grass* for the first time, he must have felt that his portrait had come to life and that his search was ended. In the passion of his immediate response he wrote Whitman:

> I am not blind to the worth of the wonderful gift of "Leaves of Grass." I find it the most extraordinary piece of wit and wisdom that America has yet contributed. I am very happy in reading it, as great power makes us happy. It meets the demand I am always making of what seemed the sterile and stingy nature, as if too much handiwork, or too much lymph in the temperament, were making our western wits fat and mean.
>
> I give you joy of your free and brave thought. I have great joy in it. I find incomparable things said incomparably well, as they must be. I find the courage of treatment which so delights us, and which large perception only can inspire.
>
> I greet you at the beginning of a great career. . . .

There was more, in the same vein, in this most extraordinary letter in all of American literature. Whitman, the unknown poet, was naturally elated at the lavish praise from America's most distinguished man of letters. The only comparable commentary appeared in Whitman's own anonymous reviews of his poetry, in one of which he characteristically exclaimed, "An American bard at last!"

But neither Emerson's private letter nor Whitman's anonymous reviews could do much to help sell the first edition of *Leaves of Grass*. Whitman hurried the second edition through the press in 1856. There was good reason for the rush. Whitman wanted it to carry his reply to Emerson. Moreover, he was anxious to exploit Emerson's praise. He not only published Emerson's letter without his consent but extracted the sentence, "I greet you at the beginning of a great career," and stamped it together with Emerson's name on the spine of the 1856 volume. At the end of the book Whitman printed an extremely long and embarrassingly flattering reply to Emerson, addressed as a "dear Friend and Master." Such unauthorized use of his letter and such an ostentatious reply must have shocked the reserved New England essayist. In any event he never during his life made a public pronouncement on Whitman's poetry, in praise or blame. Nor, on the other hand, did he ever deny or modify the sentiments of his impulsive 1855 letter. But when in 1874 he edited an anthology of American poetry, he did not include a single poem by the Good Gray Poet.

The 1856 *Leaves of Grass,* much smaller in format than its predecessor, contained twenty new poems and all of the poems were given titles. The 1855 Preface was missing but much of it was used with very little change in the poetry, primarily in "Poem of Many in One" (final title, "By Blue Ontario's Shore"). Important new poems were "Broad-Axe Poem" ("Song of the Broad-Axe"), "Sun Down Poem" ("Crossing Brooklyn Ferry"), and "Poem of the Road" ("Song of the Open Road"). This second edition of *Leaves of Grass* gave ample evidence that Whitman was at the height of his poetic power and productivity; and the shifts and changes, deletions and revisions, all hinted at the intricate and painstaking process he was to go through over a thirty-year period to shape his masterpiece in accord with his expanding vision of himself, America, and his role in her destiny.

As the early biographers once believed that the 1848 New Orleans episode contained Whitman's key experience, more recent scholars have probed about in the 1856-60 period for the poet's spiritual crisis. They cite two sources for their conjectures: "Out of the Cradle Endlessly Rocking," written and published as "A Child's Reminiscence" in the *Saturday Press* during this period, and "Calamus," the cluster of poems of comradeship gathered together for the first time during these years for the 1860 edition. Both the individual poem and the cluster offer tantalizing "clews" to profoundly personal experiences that left, we may guess, deep marks on the poet. But we can only guess; for we have bare fragments of experience to deal with and they have passed through the poet's transfiguring imagination.

In its third (1860) edition *Leaves of Grass* found its first commercial publisher, Thayer and Eldridge of Boston. Whitman went to Boston to see the edition through the press and while there made one of the most difficult and most important decisions about his work. In a long stroll on Boston Common, Emerson attempted to persuade him to omit the sex poems from *Leaves of Grass*, even arguing at one point that because of the offensive poems the book's sales would be harmed. Whitman listened to all of the formidable arguments of his "dear Friend and Master" and when Emerson asked, "What have you to say then to such things," replied: "Only that while I can't answer at all, I feel more settled than ever to adhere to my own theory, and exemplify it." Emerson must have realized that Whitman was simply following the transcendentalist's own doctrine of self-reliance.

The 1860 edition of *Leaves of Grass* was by far the most impressive of the original three. For the first time Whitman's sweeping concept of his work became manifest: *Leaves of Grass* was not to be merely a collection of miscellaneous lyrics but an integrated, unified poetic vision, an epic that embraced the whole of life — and death. "Proto-Leaf" (later, "Starting from Paumanok") opened the volume with an introduction to the themes and imagery; "So Long!" closed the volume with a reiteration of major themes and a farewell to the reader. Within the volume, poems treating related themes were brought together under group titles. Most important of these clusters were "Enfans d'Adam" (later, "Children of Adam"), the poems of procreation, frankly and unabashedly sexual in nature, and "Calamus," the poems of spiritual love and comradeship. The greatest new single poem to appear was "Out of the Cradle Endlessly Rocking." Had Whitman published no more poetry during his life, it is likely that his reputation as a great, original talent could be largely supported today by the 1860 volume.

Some forty-two years of age in 1861 when Fort Sumter was fired upon, Whitman saw no service as a soldier in the Civil War. But when his brother George, a lieutenant in the Union Army, was listed as wounded in Virginia in 1862, Walt took over the family responsibility of going to the battlefront to find him. Shocked by the sights he saw not only near the front lines but in Washington, D. C., where the suffering of large numbers of sick and wounded was intensified by neglect, Whitman stayed on, after finding his brother, to help in the immense task of caring for the hurt and the maimed. Whitman the "wound dresser" regularly made the rounds of the hospitals, comforting those he could, writing letters home for the disabled, distributing scarce personal items such as note paper, stamped envelopes, reading matter. For his own support, a matter in which he seemed constitutionally careless, Whitman eventually took a clerkship in a federal office.

The massing of large numbers of young men for the war and the close, intimate association with the lonely young men of the hospitals must have seemed to Whitman both a national demonstration and a personal fulfillment of the complex emotion of comradely attachment which he had celebrated so eloquently in the "Calamus" poems in *Leaves of Grass*. Out of his sobering experiences during the war Whitman drew new substance for his poetry. In 1865 he published a volume of poems entitled *Drum-Taps*, later to be incorporated in the master volume. These poems ran the gamut of war emotions, from the first heady exhilaration and release to the tragic awareness of terrible waste. Abraham Lincoln's assassination in April, 1865, provided material for a poignant climax to Whitman's creative activity during this period. The poet discovered his finest poetic power intact as he shaped his restrained grief into one of the most moving elegies in the English language, "When Lilacs Last in the Dooryard Bloom'd." Whitman never met Lincoln, but he must have seen the President on numerous occasions when Lincoln was driven in his carriage through Washington's streets. Legend tells us that Lincoln had read and admired *Leaves of Grass*, and even that he had once seen Whitman in passing and had remarked, "He looks like a man." Whatever the actual relationship of the statesman and poet, it was far transcended by a spiritual affinity. Whitman found in Lincoln's life confirmation that democracy at its best could produce men who had both a touch of the common and much of the uncommon, who were of the mass yet capable of greatness.

In preparing a new edition of *Leaves of Grass* during this period, Whitman had gone through his personal volume marking many of the passages containing sexual imagery, perhaps with the intent of revision or deletion. His superior in the Department of Interior, James Harlan, happened upon the volume in Whitman's desk and apparently read the marked passages. Although the precise situation is obscure, it seems probable that Harlan decided to get rid of Whitman for writing obscene poetry. Although Whitman transferred to the Attorney General's office and suffered no hardship, his friends came vigorously to his defense. As a result, the entire incident must be recorded as advancing rather than obstructing Whitman's reputation. Two close Washington friends, in gestures meant to defend the poet's good name, claimed for themselves the honor of writing the first books on Whitman. William D. O'Connor, although a writer in his own right, is largely remembered for his outraged vindication of *The Good Gray Poet* (1866). John Burroughs, the naturalist writer, published the first biography, *Notes on Walt Whitman as Poet and Person*, in

1867. O'Connor's novel *The Carpenter,* portraying Whitman as a Christ-figure, followed in 1868.

In spite of the Harlan incident, the fourth edition of *Leaves of Grass* appeared in 1867. Only eight new poems appeared, none of any great distinction, but the volume showed signs of great activity in revision and rearranging. *Drum-Taps* and the *Sequel* (containing "When Lilacs Last in the Dooryard Bloom'd") were bound in the volume but were not integrated into the work. Probably the most important function of this edition was its serving as the basis for William Rossetti's English edition of *Selections* in 1868. Among the book's avid readers and promoters was the poet Algernon Swinburne. Although Swinburne seemed later to turn on Whitman, his earlier praise could not be entirely undone. Whitman's first female critic, Anne Gilchrist, who upon her husband's death had finished his important work on Blake, read and admired Whitman with an intensity rarely equalled. Her "An Englishwoman's Estimate of Walt Whitman" (1870) was the only slightly veiled opening of a prolonged but one-sided courtship which eventually brought Mrs. Gilchrist to America; but in the end her persistent pursuit failed: the Good Gray Poet was not of a mind to marry.

During the last years of the Civil War decade and the early seventies, there was no sign of decline in Whitman's creative activity. Indeed, in 1871 Whitman published two important works, *Democratic Vistas* and the fifth edition of *Leaves of Grass.* The first of these, which established Whitman's permanent claim as an important essayist, presented many of his poetic themes in a crabbed, convolute prose. To many who thought of the poet as a yawping chauvinist, Whitman's rigorous indictment of the materialism of money-getting America came as something of a surprise. The 1871 edition of *Leaves of Grass* gave evidence of Whitman's expanding vision of his life's work. The structure of the book was altered to incorporate the *Drum-Taps* poems as a natural part of the basic design. One of his greatest works, "Passage to India," appeared in an annex to this fifth edition. Like *Democratic Vistas,* this poem called on America to venture beyond material achievement into the realm of Spirit, to sail out daringly into the "seas of God."

3

A Batter'd, Wreck'd Old Man

The poet could not have known it, but by 1872 his basic work was largely done. During the year he began suffering spells of dizziness, which ended in paralysis in 1873, when Whitman was 54. The illness was naturally abhorrent to a man who had made health almost a fundamental virtue. And his condition was aggravated further by the death of his mother, to whom he was strongly attached, during this same year. His removal from Washington and return home in 1873 was a symbolic act of partial capitulation. The Washington years had been years of independence as well as service. Their termination drew to a close the period of the poet's greatest assertion of himself, the fulfillment of his most satisfying role, the "wound dresser."

These declining years, however, gave Whitman the time he needed to revise his poems and work over the basic structure of his book. The handsome sixth edition, the so-called Centennial Edition, appeared in 1876 in two volumes, the first bearing the title, *Leaves of Grass*, the second, *Two Rivulets*. The latter volume bound together a miscellany of publications that had earlier appeared separately, including the "Passage to India" pamphlet, but there were new poems, principally the "Prayer of Columbus" and "Song of the Red-Wood Tree."

Plans were made in 1881 for publication of the seventh edition of *Leaves of Grass* by a commercial publisher in Boston. When Whitman refused to delete certain lines designated by the Boston Attorney General as obscene, James R. Osgood and Company withdrew the book from publication. But Whitman obtained the plates and turned them over to a Philadelphia firm and the edition was published without further ado. In this seventh edition of *Leaves of Grass*, by incorporating the "Passage to India" poems into the main body of the book, Whitman finally achieved that structure which had been for a lifetime in evolution. Although he would add a few old-age poems later in "annexes," he ceased revising and shifting, satisfied that his work now "tallied" with his total vision. The eighth edition of 1889 merely added the Annex "Sands at Seventy" and the prose piece "A Backward Glance O'er Travel'd Roads" to the 1881 edition (these pieces had appeared in 1888 in *November Boughs*, a volume of miscellaneous prose and poetry); and the last lifetime (or "deathbed") edition included an additional Annex, "Goodbye My Fancy."

Whitman confessed in "Sands at Seventy" to moments of doubt if not despair during these declining years:

As I sit writing here, sick and grown old
Not my least burden is that dulness of the years, querilities,

Ungracious glooms, aches, lethargy, constipation, whimpering ennui,
May filter in my daily songs.

This complaint is a far remove from the heroic faith of the earlier
"A Prayer of Columbus" (1874), in which the "batter'd, wreck'd old
man" expressed his spiritual faith; but given the many moods of the
poet, no doubt the feeling in each of the poems is genuine. The finest
medicine for his ailments he found in the summers he spent at Timber
Creek, on a farm in New Jersey, and out of the many hours he loafed
and meditated in this "charmingly recluse and rural spot" grew a
collection of miscellaneous diary notes, which, together with earlier
bits and pieces, made up a sketchy autobiography in *Specimen Days
and Collect* (1882). The ailing poet was well enough to make an
extended trip west in 1879 as far as the Rockies; and in the following
year he journeyed to Canada and took a trip up the St. Lawrence.
During these last years he even made a number of public appearances, a belated fulfillment of his youthful ambition to become an
orator, to deliver lectures on Lincoln.

But a sunstroke in 1885 and a paralytic stroke in 1888 forced the
poet into fuller retirement and into greater reliance on his friends.
Of all the people Whitman came to know during his final years, he
was most firmly attached to a young man, Horace Traubel, who
turned up in Camden in the middle eighties to devote his life largely
to the role of Whitman's secretary and companion. As a result of
Traubel's records of his conversations and experiences with the poet,
published in four large volumes (*With Walt Whitman in Camden*),
we have a surfeit of information, valuable though sometimes unreliable, about Whitman's life, times, and opinions during these years.
When Whitman died in 1892, he seemed indeed prepared for the
end. He had managed to see through to publication the "deathbed"
edition of his masterpiece, leaving it at last to the world as he wanted
the world to know it. And he had given of himself, his mind, and
his memory to posterity through his young Boswell, Horace Traubel.

When all is said and done, when the known facts are carefully
placed upon the page, what, really, have we understood of Whitman's
life? There have been many who, frustrated by the scarcity of facts,
have soared beyond their pedestrian realm to create an image of the
poet to fit their fancy. Whitman has thus emerged, at one time or
another, as the vagabond poet, as the Christ-figure, as the wound

dresser, as the bewhiskered sage. And because of his all-embracing qualities and the largeness of his acceptances, he has been enlisted in every cause under the sun from socialism to free love.

Speculation as to the nature of Whitman's sexuality has rocketed high above the facts. The favorite charge of the nineteenth century, that Whitman was immoral, has given way to the frequent assumption of the twentieth century, that he was abnormal. The question of Whitman's sexual nature is by no means settled nor does the answer appear simple. Some contemporary critics have vigorously affirmed his homosexuality while others have as energetically denied it. The debate has revolved around the intimate male friendships in his life and the confession-like "Calamus" poems in his book. So little record remains of the former, and so much ambiguity exists in the latter, that no firm decision can close the debate. In this questionable controversy, Whitman at least has the comfort of distinguished companionship. The sexuality of a number of leading nineteenth-century American writers — Herman Melville, Henry James, Emily Dickinson among them — has recently been called into question. Perhaps this phenomenon is a more penetrating commentary on our own times than on theirs.

We may judge from Whitman's life and work that he was in a sense omnisexual, that he had a deep understanding of man's intricate sexual nature, and that he had sympathetic insight into sexual feelings in all their complex variety, auto-, homo-, or hetero-sexual. As Emerson discovered, sex was an inseparable part of Whitman's poetic program. And it seems that in this area, as in the rest, Whitman excluded none, embraced all. It is impossible to assert with assurance that one sexual nature dominated the others in Whitman throughout his life, though at particular times perhaps one or the other was in the ascendancy. It is, however, surely perverse to read homosexuality into Whitman's every mention of friendship, comradeship, or adhesiveness. But if, as the modern age seems to insist, such relationships inevitably have a residue of unconscious sexuality, Whitman was involved as deeply as any man. Though the question is never likely to be fully resolved, a sane and sober view, and one in line with the discoveries of modern psychology from Freud to Kinsey, is that the elements of Whitman's sexual nature were not far different from those of most men; but they seem to have been more delicately and fragilely balanced. In the ebullient act of poetic creation, Whitman permitted a public glimpse into depths of the unconscious that most men close even to private view.

As the new biographies of Whitman appear (and more seem inevitable), it is likely that the facts, but not our understanding, will increase. Whitman himself, were he to see the abundant facts and the elaborate guesswork about his life, would no doubt sceptically ask, "Is this then . . . what the author calls a man's life?" Whitman believed it self-evident that *Leaves of Grass* was his real biography. And it is surely true that there is more significant revelation of the man in the book than in all the accumulated facts and speculation. If the poet appears elusive even in the poetry, he asserts encouragingly:

> Failing to fetch me at first keep encouraged,
> Missing me one place search another,
> I stop somewhere waiting for you.

Where does the poet stop and wait? Perhaps if we look into our own spirit with the light cast by his bright, barbaric words, we shall at last find him lurking there. But in this pursuit we shall venture much too far out of the realm of fact into the realm of imagination. Just possibly, however, we shall venture far enough to discover the ultimate irrelevance to the significance of Whitman's permanent achievement of the list of dates, catalogue of events, inventory of surviving documents, the surmises and guesswork, which the baffled biographer assembles and calls a poet's life.

II

"My Omnivorous Lines"

> I know perfectly well my own egotism,
> Know my omnivorous lines and must not write any less,
> And would fetch you whoever you are flush with myself.

We need go no further than the opening poem of *Leaves of Grass* to discover that in Whitman's poetry we are meeting something new, something distinctly different from all the other poetry of the period — or from previous periods:

> One's-self I sing, a simple separate person,
> Yet utter the word Democratic, the word En-Masse.

The difference flashes out brilliantly in individual lines throughout *Leaves of Grass*. From "Song of Myself": "Only the lull I like, the hum of your valvèd voice"; "I am an acme of things accomplish'd, and I an encloser of things to be"; "Blind loving wrestling touch, sheath'd hooded sharp-toothed touch!"; "I find I incorporate gneiss, coal, long-

threaded moss, fruits, grains, esculent roots,/And am stucco'd with
quadrupeds and birds all over." In "When Lilacs Last in the Dooryard
Bloom'd," Whitman speaks of "the sure-enwinding arms of cool-
enfolding death." In "Song of the Exposition" he advises the muse,
"Placard 'Removed' and 'To Let' on the rocks of your snowy Parnas-
sus." Frequently in *Leaves of Grass* short passages startle by their
powerful and sudden impact:

> Smile O voluptuous cool-breath'd earth!
> Earth of the slumbering and liquid trees!
> Earth of departed sunset — earth of the mountains misty-topt!
> Earth of the vitreous pour of the full moon just tinged with blue!
> Earth of shine and dark mottling the tide of the river!
> Earth of the limpid gray of clouds brighter and clearer for my
>   sake!
> Far-swooping elbow'd earth — rich apple-blossom'd earth!
> Smile, for your lover comes.

Each enthusiastic reader of *Leaves of Grass* could make up his own
list of lines and passages, containing the essential Whitman, which
simultaneously mark his difference as they display his genius.

1

The New Poetry

Whitman's differences are more easily exemplified than defined.
First and foremost is his free verse, a form which we take so for
granted today that we sometimes forget its revolutionary impact at
the time Whitman wrote. No one had used free verse in quite the
same way before. In its elaborate and daring use Whitman appears
as one of the great, original literary innovators. That he received impetus from such diverse sources as nineteenth-century oratory, Italian
opera, the Bible, and Emerson's essays does not diminish his luster as a
great original voice. But he not only pioneered a new form; he probably remains its most impressive example. His defiance of restrictive
elements of form was so brilliantly welded to his democratic and
individualistic themes that the consequent unity of form and meaning
in his poetry has not been equaled by those who have taken up free
verse after him. But though Whitman broke away from stanzaic pat-
tern and measured line, he by no means abandoned all of the traditional poetic techniques. He used assonance, alliteration, repetition,
inverse word order, and many other conventional devices, all in

abundance. It is a triumph of his art that it remains largely concealed. The total effect of his free verse style is one of defiance of the traditional. Curiously this effect is reinforced by much that is quite strictly traditional.

But free verse is only a part of Whitman's newness, and achieves the fullest impact only in conjunction with other striking elements. While not really new, these ingredients are somehow transfigured by the individualistic stamp of Whitman's genius. Whitman hinted at one of these elements when he said (in *An American Primer*), "I sometimes think the *Leaves* is only a language experiment." The language of Whitman's poetry is like a breath of fresh air, especially when examined in the context of its time and place, alongside the language of Longfellow, Holmes, Lowell, and Whittier. As Whitman broke the metrical rules, so he violated the popular rules of poetic diction. He imported words from all kinds of unusual places — from foreign languages, from science, from opera, from carpentry, from the speech in the street and the talk in the country. Indeed, Whitman took the entire province of language to be also the province of poetry. And when he could not find the word he wanted, he was not averse to making one up or changing an old word around a bit to suit his need. Examples are abundant: "Me imperturbe, standing at ease in Nature"; "Allons! the road is before us!"; "Camerado, I give you my hand!"; "Shall we stick by each other as long as we live?"; "I know I shall not pass like a child's carlacue cut with a burnt stick at night"; "My foothold is tenon'd and mortis'd in granite"; "Having pried through the strata, analyzed to a hair, counsel'd with doctors and calculated close,/I find no sweeter fat than sticks to my own bones." Although Whitman's diction sometimes misfires, his successful language experiments far outnumber his mistakes. And one must point to the rich, varied vocabulary of *Leaves of Grass* as one of its finest original features.

But there are other elements which contribute to that sense of newness the book gives us. Not the least of these is an almost totally unselfconscious humor that is gently but frequently felt. As Whitman's language seems to bubble out of a melting pot, in a sense symbolic of the all-embracing democracy he writes about, so his jaunty, sometimes cocky perspective springs from a strongly individualistic and egalitarian feeling in which humor plays a natural role. The assertive democrat will not only poke a little fun at himself but at all that is ponderous and pompous. Whitman surely smiled, and hoped his reader would, when he wrote, "I too am not a bit tamed, I too am

untranslatable,/I sound my barbaric yawp over the roofs of the world."
And he was quite aware of the ludicrous incongruity when he portrayed the Old World muse transported to the New:

> By thud of machinery and shrill steam-whistle undismay'd,
> Bluff'd not a bit by drain-pipe, gasometers, artificial fertilizers,
> Smiling and pleas'd with palpable intent to stay,
> She's here, install'd amid the kitchen ware!

Although this quality of humor is elusive in *Leaves of Grass* (earlier
critics thought that Whitman had no sense of humor), and is closely
related to the "language experiment," it must be identified as one of
the elements contributing to the book's freshness of impact.

Another element, not so elusive but just as difficult to discuss, is
the sex imagery. Those protectors of the public morals, who would
have been satisfied had Whitman deleted a few poems and lines,
never realized how intricately woven into the whole fabric of *Leaves
of Grass* is the sexual imagery. The sex image appears not only as a
natural result of the poet's determination to be the poet of procreation
in the "Children of Adam" section, but elsewhere throughout *Leaves*
as a part of Whitman's pervasive theme celebrating the elemental and
primal, the life-force that infuses man and nature. Whitman asserted
in "Song of Myself":

> Through me forbidden voices,
> Voices of sexes and lusts, voices veil'd and I remove the veil,
> Voices indecent by me clarified and transfigur'd.

These voices might speak forth on any page of *Leaves of Grass,* in
such suggestive lines as, "Root of wash'd sweet-flag! timorous pond-
snipe! nest of guarded duplicate eggs!" or "Sprouts take and accumulate, stand by the curb prolific and vital,/Landscapes projected masculine, full-sized and golden." There are many extended passages
which could be cited, but the following from "The Sleepers" will
serve:

> I am she who adorn'd herself and folded her hair expectantly,
> My truant lover has come, and it is dark.

> Double yourself and receive me darkness,
> Receive me and my lover too, he will not let me go without him.

> I roll myself upon you as upon a bed, I resign myself to the dusk.

> He whom I call answers me and takes the place of my lover,
> He rises with me silently from the bed.

Darkness, you are gentler than my lover, his flesh was sweaty and
    panting,
I feel the hot moisture yet that he left me.

My hands are spread forth, I pass them in all directions,
I would sound up the shadowy shore to which you are journeying.

This scene from "The Sleepers" appears as a part of the phantasma-
goria of dream, with the dream's usual ambiguity and illogical flow
of images. Indeed throughout *Leaves* Whitman's technique appears
frequently to be an imitation of the state of the mind in sleep, with
image following image in pell-mell rush, many of them seeming to
surge up from the depths of the unconscious. The sexual image thus
becomes as natural in Whitman's pages as sexual symbolism in Freud's
dreams.

2

The New Poetics

These distinctive qualities are but some of the elements that force
us to acknowledge *Leaves of Grass* as an original work of powerful
impact. These qualities help us to understand but they do not explain
the genius of the book. Probably no entirely satisfactory explanation
will ever be found, but we shall not have exhausted all possibility of
discovery if we do not at some point turn in our search to Whitman's
poetic theory. In all of his prefaces as well as in *Democratic Vistas*
and in a number of miscellaneous pieces, Whitman wrote about
poetry, its origins, its nature, its consequences. All of his statements
together constitute a coherent concept of art, a poetics, that deserves
notice.

The Subject of Poetry. Whitman insisted on the poet's faithful-
ness to reality, and in his century and country saw that reality con-
sisted of science and democracy — science as the central truth of
the nineteenth century, democracy as the central truth of America.
But Whitman was far from demanding that all true poets should
choose as their subject matter astronomy, biology, and politics. He
asserted that the "construction" of science and democracy "underlies
the structure of every perfect poem." They are not, thus, offered as
the sole subjects for the poet but rather as the appropriate, even
inevitable, frame of modern reference; the poet who ignores or denies
this frame retreats to the past. Literary works of the past are not
inferior but rather are enclosed (and perhaps limited) by a different

frame of reference. But while the poet's genuine material exists in his own place and time, he still has the responsibility of striking through to the infinite and eternal. The mediocre poet will mirror the surface of reality. The profound poet will discover the "interior or spiritual life." Whitman asserted over and over again the transcendent importance of what he called the "religious" element in poetry. In insisting that science, democracy, and, above them, religion (or spirituality) must underlie the structure of modern poetry, Whitman was not limiting the possible subjects of poetry ("The Poetic area is very spacious — has room for all — has so many mansions") but was, rather, defining the nineteenth century's view of the universe and itself — a view in which the poet must be immersed if he is to be a poet of the modern, as Homer was immersed in his time in embracing Greek "mythology" and Shakespeare in his in reflecting "feudalism." Whitman did not ask the poet to propagandize but rather to embody or "presuppose" the modern "myth" of science, democracy, and, above all, spirituality.

The Poet. Whitman seemed at times to feel that if he could name the poet, find the right epithet for him, the people of his country would recognize him: "Their Presidents shall not be their common referee so much as their poets shall. Of all mankind the great poet is the equable man. . . . He is the arbiter of the diverse and he is the key. He is the equalizer of his age and land. . . . he supplies what wants supplying and checks what wants checking." *Referee, arbiter, key, equalizer* — the poet is all these and also more: "The known universe has one complete lover and that is the greatest poet." But the epithet which has proved most popular with Whitman's critics is *prophet:* "He [the poet] is a seer . . . he is individual . . . he is complete in himself . . . the others are as good as he, only he sees it and they do not." Those readers who have visualized Whitman's ideal poet as gazing studiedly into a crystal ball have mistaken metaphor for fact. Whitman's symbolic meaning for the term "seer" is suggested in such elaborations of the metaphor as: "What the eyesight does to the rest he [the poet] does to the rest. Who knows the curious mystery of the eyesight? The other senses corroborate themselves, but this is removed from any proof but its own and foreruns the identities of the spiritual world." The poet, endowed with a transcendental sight, serves as the spiritual eyes of humanity. But in Whitman's poetics, if the poet must be a prophet, he must also be a priest: "There will soon be no more priests. Their work is done. . . . Through the divinity of themselves shall the kosmos and the new breed of poets be interpreters of men and women and of all events and things." In "Passage to India" Whitman appears to elevate the poet from priest to Christ: "Trinitas divine shall be gloriously accomplish'd and compacted by the true son of God, the poet." Whitman, like Matthew Arnold, could view the poet in such high capacity because "serving art in its highest . . . is only the other name for serving God, and serving humanity." The poet, in this view, does literally take over the significant functions of the priest.

The Poem.   No doubt Whitman through his poetry contributed to the general belief that he viewed the poet as mere passive agent who wrote automatically, perhaps even in trance, what came from an external, divine source. When one becomes caught up in the hypnotic chant of the poet, and lost in his wild abandon, the automatic writing theory seems not only relevant but to have its finest example in Whitman. This effect of lawlessness, however, is not, as frequently assumed, achieved by the poet's real abandon; the effect is achieved only by his strictest artistic control. Genuine lawlessness could result in nothing but bad poetry. We have Whitman's own "confession" of this truth in a casual remark from an 1865 letter to William D. O'Connor: "It [*Drum-Taps*] is in my opinion superior to *Leaves of Grass* — certainly more perfect as a work of art, being adjusted in all its proportions, & its passion having the indispensable merit that though to the ordinary reader, let loose with wildest abandon, the true artist can see it is yet under control." This remark, with its clear assumption that the effect of "wildest abandon" can be achieved only through artistic "control," is perhaps more revealing about Whitman's poetics than any other remark he made. But of equal importance is his belief that the substance of poems must be derived from the concrete materials of the world. In his obsession with "sensuous objects," not only in theory but also in practice, Whitman may readily be acknowledged as a forerunner of the early twentieth-century imagists. His almost child-like ecstasy in sensuous contact with *things* is acknowledged in an 1860 poem finally placed among the "Inscriptions" of *Leaves of Grass:*

Beginning my studies the first step pleas'd me so much,
The mere fact consciousness, these forms, the power of motion,
The least insect or animal, the senses, eyesight, love,
The first step I say awed me and pleas'd me so much,
I have hardly gone and hardly wish'd to go any farther,
But stop and loiter all the time to sing it in ecstatic songs.

Although Whitman acknowledged a further function of the poet ("folks expect of the poet to indicate more than the beauty and dignity which always attach to dumb real objects . . . they expect him to indicate the path between reality and their souls"), he realized that first the poem, before it can exist at all, must engage vividly with the world we know through our senses.

The Reader. When, in the 1855 "Preface," Whitman said that the nation "may well go half-way to meet . . . its poets," and in "By Blue Ontario's Shore" that America "will in due time advance to meet them [her poets], there is no fear of mistake," he was visualizing not a passive but an active audience participating in and indeed creating the poetic experience. Whitman's demands on the reader of poems are similar to the strenuous demands made by the modern poet: "In fact, a new theory of literary composition for imaginative works of the very finest class, and especially for highest poems, is the sole course open to these States. Books are to be call'd for, and supplied, on the assumption that the process of reading is not a half-sleep, but, in highest sense, an exercise, a gymnast's struggle; that the reader is to do something for himself, must be on the alert, must himself or herself construct indeed the poem, argument, history, metaphysical essay — the text furnishing the hints, the clue, the start or frame-work." Few metaphors in contemporary criticism express so vividly, appropriately, and concisely, the current concept of the role of the reader in the poetic experience as Whitman's "gymnast's struggle." Readers of modern poetry, and especially the difficult stretches of Eliot, Auden, Pound, or Dylan Thomas, would instinctively understand and accept the figure as they perform mental acrobatics in order to keep up, developing agile, muscular minds in order to experience poetic pleasure. But the struggle of the reader in his encounter with the poem is not merely an aggressive effort to understand; it is also an attempt at imaginative creation. Whitman asserted, "The reader will always have his or her part to do, just as much as I have had mine. I seek less to state or display any theme or thought, and more to bring you, reader, into the atmosphere of the theme or thought — there to pursue your own flight." The gymnastic struggle, then, is not a mere display of brute force but an alert creativity through which the reader does indeed construct the poem. The poem comes to life only when read creatively. The poem's existence is made up of a series of such re-creations; in a very real sense it has many lives, as many lives as it has intelligent and perceptive readers.

3

Revision: Control of the Abandon

Whitman's theory of poetry, comprehensive in scope, offers some insight into the nature of his achievement. His practice, as revealed in his many revisions, offers still more. It is difficult to say just how extensive Whitman's revisions were, for we have little idea of how much he reworked his poems before they were published. But we do know that he revised a great deal from edition to edition of his work. It is a fascinating aspect of the study of Whitman to follow the growth of a poem, not from its conception (that lies back in the privacy of Whitman's conscious — or unconscious), but from its birth through its full maturity — or its abandonment by the poet. No aspect was too small for the poet's attention. For example, observe the changes in these lines from "Song of Myself":

> You villain touch! What are you doing?
> Unloose me, the breath is leaving my throat;
> Open your floodgates! You are too much for me.

becomes:

> You villain touch! what are you doing? my breath is tight in its
>   throat,
> Unclench your floodgates, you are too much for me.

This kind of tinkering with the individual lines of *Leaves of Grass* is the rule rather than the exception in the book's some thirty years of growth, from 1855 to 1891. The revisions generally reveal a poet moving with some assurance toward a more concrete, vivid diction and a less halting but purely felt rhythm. As we watch Whitman revise we have the feeling that we are observing a man working a melody out for himself by ear — but the touch is acutely sensitive and the ear very fine indeed. Who can doubt an instinct that transforms the undistinguished first line, "Out of the rocked cradle," into the title of one of the best poems in *Leaves:* "Out of the Cradle Endlessly Rocking."

Perhaps the best glimpse of Whitman's poetic instinct at work is offered by the poem, "A Noiseless Patient Spider." An early version of this poem was discovered in the notebooks:

> The Soul, reaching, throwing out for love,
> As the spider, from some little promontory, throwing out filament

after filament, tirelessly out of itself, that one at least may
catch and form a link, a bridge, a connection
O I saw one passing alone, saying hardly a word — yet full of
love I detected him, by certain signs
O eyes wishfully turning! O silent eyes!

For then I thought of you o'er the world
O latent oceans, fathomless oceans of love!
O waiting oceans of love! yearning and fervid; and of you sweet
souls perhaps in the future, delicious and long:
But Dead, unknown on the earth-ungiven, dark here, unspoken,
never born:
You fathomless latent souls of love — you pent and unknown
oceans of love!

This poem is easily recognizable as a "Calamus" poem, celebrating
"adhesiveness," or close and intense comradeship. The two basic
images, the spider and the ocean, are unequal in power, the first
growing organically with the basic impulse of the poem, the second
developed primarily by sheer repetition.

The revised version was finally to find its way to the "Whispers of
Heavenly Death" section, but only after it had undergone an astonish-
ing transmutation, a genuine conversion into poetic gold:

A noiseless patient spider,
I mark'd where on a little promontory it stood isolated,
Mark'd how to explore the vacant vast surrounding,
It launch'd forth filament, filament, filament, out of itself,
Ever unreeling them, ever tirelessly speeding them.

And you O my soul where you stand,
Surrounded, detached, in measureless oceans of space,
Ceaselessly musing, venturing, throwing, seeking the spheres to
connect them,
Till the bridge you will need be form'd, till the ductile anchor
hold
Till the gossamer thread you fling catch somewhere, O my soul.

An examination of the two versions of this poem reveals Whitman's
poetic genius at play — or at work. His astute imagination seized
the brilliant image of the spider from the original and gave it the
central position in his new poem. The blurred ocean-image is omitted
entirely. And brought into fine, sharp focus is the analogy between
the ceaselessly spinning spider and the roving, restless soul.

Although not all Whitman's revisions are this successful, most of them result in some improvement. And there is no better way to comprehend Whitman's method than to observe him in practice. A close scrutiny of the changes in *Leaves of Grass* gives a needed balance to Whitman's sometimes lofty if frequently acute generalizations about poetry. When we watch Whitman in the act of creation, we understand the honesty of his assertion to W. D. O'Connor in an 1865 letter: "I delight to make a poem where I feel clear that not a word but is indispensable part thereof & of my meaning." And we can respond with genuine feeling to the obsessed artist's cry, "[I] know my omnivorous lines and must not write any less." Whitman was the poet possessed, but his daemon was the desire for poetic perfection.

III

A BOOK I HAVE MADE

> . . . a book I have made,
> The words of my book nothing, the drift of it everything,
> A book separate, not link'd with the rest nor felt by the intellect,
> But you ye untold latencies will thrill to every page.

Although Whitman frequently wrote instructions for his reader, *Leaves of Grass* is quite likely to present a puzzle to the impatient seeker. There are two ways to approach the book. The reader can assume that it is the collected poetry of Whitman and can peruse and select and enjoy — and dismiss. Or he can assume that there is a comprehensive design, as Whitman frequently asserted, which bestows a significance on the work as a whole greater in scope and more powerful in impact than that of a mere collection of individual poems — and he can search on until he discovers that significance. The best approach is, of course, a judicious combination of the two. And the uninitiated reader might best begin, not with a straight-through reading of *Leaves of Grass* (that should come later), but with an intensive look at some individual poems.

1

Some Poems for Introduction

There are no doubt many good places to begin reading *Leaves of Grass,* and there is something to be said for developing one's own plan, even if it means stopping at random in the book and studying whatever the page chances to turn up. But there is, too, something to be said for assimilating as quickly as possible the critical discoveries that have been made, not merely to accept but to test and to pass on beyond. A reading of the opening cluster of short poems, "Inscriptions," will give some sense of the scope of Whitman's plan as well as the sweep of his vision; and a close reading of the group's central poem, "Eidólons," will bring one quickly to the heart of Whitman's transcendental view:

> The noiseless myriads,
> The infinite oceans where the rivers empty,
> The separate countless free identities, like eyesight,
> The true realities, eidólons.

It is perhaps best at the beginning to confront and penetrate whatever obscurity such a signal stanza as this presents. Its meaning, as well as the meaning of the entire poem, is rooted in the concept of a world of spirituality, counterpart to the world we know and embodying its ultimate significance. Whitman's images are all calculated to convey some idea of the nature of this "real" or spiritual world, where multiplicity and unity harmoniously coexist. Such a world is actually unknowable or even inconceivable except through metaphor. The basic concept underlying this poem is not only important to most of the great poems by Whitman but is crucial to the whole of *Leaves of Grass*.

Similar in structure to "Eidólons" but quite different in effect is "Pioneers! O Pioneers!" in the "Birds of Passage" section of *Leaves of Grass*. With this poem we are confronted not so much by apparent obscurity as a misleading lucidity. Many readers come to the poem with the image of Whitman as the poet of democracy fixed firmly in their minds. The title leads them to expect a celebration of the pioneering spirit which settled and civilized the American West. The opening stanzas seem to confirm the preconceived notion. And moreover, readers have a way of discovering what they already believe to be true. But in fact Whitman turns out in this poem to be more comprehensive in his embrace than one would expect from the poet of American democracy:

> Life's involv'd and varied pageants,
> All the forms and shows, all the workmen at their work,
> All the seamen and the landsmen, all the masters with their
> slaves,
> Pioneers! O pioneers!
>
> All the hapless silent lovers,
> All the prisoners in the prisons, all the righteous and the wicked,

> All the joyous, all the sorrowing, all the living, all the dying,
> Pioneers! O pioneers!

Whitman extends his celebration beyond the borders of the American West and, indeed, beyond the "Westering" spirit. The poet celebrates, as in some sense pioneering, all human life in all its variety and diversity. And further, he projects the pioneer spirit into the spheres:

> Lo, the darting bowling orb:
> Lo, the brother orbs around, all the clustering suns and planets,
> All the dazzling days, all the mystic nights with dreams,
> Pioneers! O pioneers!

This poet is the poet of cosmic democracy, celebrating the very human spirit itself as pioneering, and identifying it with the spirit which pervades the universe. "Pioneers! O Pioneers!" is less a poem about the American West than a poem of mystic vision. The most valuable lesson to be learned from this discovery is that *Leaves of Grass* is best comprehended — and most excitingly alive — only after we as readers have divested ourselves of our fixed notions of Whitman as the poet of this or that category. That he was simply a poet is surely enough for us to know at the outset. We can provide our own categories as we read.

Although their traditional stanzaic patterns and ballad-like refrains make "Eidólons" and "Pioneers! O Pioneers!" valuable as introductions to Whitman's ideas and subject matter, they do not rank among his best poems. Critical opinion seems in rather startling agreement on the greatest of Whitman's poetry. Any list of the finest poems would have to begin with "Crossing Brooklyn Ferry," "Out of the Cradle Endlessly Rocking," "When Lilacs Last in the Dooryard Bloom'd," and "Passage to India." Certainly not second to any of these poems, "Song of Myself" seems a unique achievement which must be judged alone. Poems of immense merit but whose inclusion might precipitate some controversy are "Song of the Open Road," "Song of the Broad-Axe," "By Blue Ontario's Shore," and "The Sleepers." All of these poems are of substantial length. Scattered throughout *Leaves of Grass* are many brief lyrics of brilliant quality — "I Hear America Singing," "Vigil Strange I Kept on the Field One Night," "The Wound-Dresser," "Sparkles from the Wheel," and many more.

2

Some Poems for Analysis

In continuing exploration of *Leaves of Grass*, it should be valuable to examine closely some of the great poems. "Crossing Brooklyn Ferry," "When Lilacs Last in the Dooryard Bloom'd," and "Song of Myself" may serve for brief analysis here.

The construction of "Crossing Brooklyn Ferry" is essentially dramatic. The two main characters are the poet and the reader. The opening section hints of the special relationship that is to be established between the poet and the reader in the course of the poem: "And you that shall cross from shore to shore years hence are more to me, and more in my meditations, than you might suppose." In the progress of the poem the reader is to move out of the shadowy realm of the poet's meditations into a quite substantial realm of being and into a direct and dramatically intimate relationship with the poet. This relationship reaches its greatest point of intensity in section 8 when the poet exclaims:

> What is more subtle than this which ties me to the woman or
>   man that looks in my face?
> Which fuses me into you now, and pours my meaning into you?

All of the poem has been focused in the direction of these two lines. Whitman has succeeded admirably in conveying the powerful impression of the fusion of poet and reader. All the barriers of time and space ("distance avails not, and place avails not") have for the life of the poem been transcended and Whitman becomes one with his audience. This feat, engaging the imaginations of poet and reader, is the great achievement of the poem. For Whitman meant this emotional identification or fusion to symbolize a spiritual unity — that which binds all men not only together but also to eternity. The "dumb, beautiful ministers" of the poem, those tangible objects of time and place which appear throughout and are excitedly catalogued in a final outburst of praise, furnish their "parts toward eternity" and "toward the soul" by playing central roles in the imaginative fusion which symbolizes the spiritual.

Although like "Crossing Brooklyn Ferry" in its essential dramatic quality, "When Lilacs Last in the Dooryard Bloom'd" offers a more intricate problem in symbolism. The two principal characters are the poet and Lincoln, though the latter is present only in a spiritual sense. Tension in the poem derives from the poet's state of shocked grief over the loss of the President. As the poem opens, the poet is burdened by the woe of this terrible loss; when the poem closes, he has become reconciled to the loss. The dramatic center of the poem resides in the alternating forces exerted on the poet, at one time by the overpowering memory of Lincoln alive, at another by instinctive knowledge of the spiritual significance of death. This powerful struggle between grief and reconciliation, although an internal affair of the emotions, is objectified in the poem by a set of symbols. In a very real sense the dramatic interest in "When Lilacs Last in the Dooryard Bloom'd" is centered in the interplay of the poem's vividly characterized symbols. The "powerful western fallen star" is Lincoln. The hermit thrush that calls the poet to the swamp cedars is the voice of the soul or the spiritual world. The lilacs symbolize the poet's powerful love. The "harsh surrounding cloud" which obscures the star is death. By the time, however, that we have listened to the "lilac and star and bird twined with the chant" of the poet's soul, we are convinced that our symbolic equations are too restrictive. We have placed the poem's drama in too narrow a context. And perhaps the best way to break out of this imposed confinement is to introduce "Chanting the Square Deific," a compact poem in which Whitman has attempted to distill the essential truth of all myth. The four sides of the Deific Square are identified as Jehovah (Time), Consolator (Affection), Satan (Defiance), and Santa Spirita (Soul). If we explore the relationship of the four dominant symbols of "When Lilacs Last in the Dooryard Bloom'd" to the four sides of the square (star-Jehovah, lilac-consolator, cloud-satan, bird-santa spirita), we discover one way of escaping the limitations imposed by a narrow interpretation of the symbolism. Indeed, we find the terms for discussing the poem's significance not only as it deals with Lincoln's death but also as it dramatizes the motive-forces of the universe.

Even more than "Crossing Brooklyn Ferry" or "When Lilacs Last in the Dooryard Bloom'd," "Song of Myself" presents a problem in poetic order. In many ways "Song of Myself" is the foundation poem of *Leaves of Grass*. Its position near the beginning of the book suggests its importance as the fundamental poetic proposition on which all that comes after solidly rests. "Song of Myself" does seem to contain, at least in embryo, all the basic themes of *Leaves of Grass;* but it is, too, one of the poems that have very full lives independent of the parent volume. On first reading, "Song of Myself" may seem like chaos, uncontrolled vigor and energy, a sustained barbaric yawp. But repeated reading of the poem, a penetration in depth, will convince the reader of a latent order which now and then reveals itself.

As with other Whitman poems, it is useful to conceive of "Song of Myself" as a drama with the poet himself assuming the central role.

The poem may be read as a dramatization of a mystical experience. The poet portrays his entry into the mystical state, his progression through its various stages, and, finally, his emergence from the state. Indeed it is useful, if one does not attempt too rigid an application, to outline the poem in terms of the traditional mystical experience:

I.	Sections 1-5:	Entry into the mystical state
II.	Sections 6-16:	Awakening of self
III.	Sections 17-32:	Purification of self
IV.	Sections 33-37:	Illumination and the dark night of the soul
V.	Sections 38-43:	Union (emphasis on faith and love)
VI.	Sections 44-49:	Union (emphasis on perception)
VII.	Sections 50-52:	Emergence from mystical state

Viewed in this way, the poem reveals its order in the successive emotional states of the mystic as he passes in his experience toward his goal of Union with the Transcendent. The order of the poem is primarily emotional rather than logical or philosophical. Once this basic point is grasped, the reader may go on to a detailed examination of the emotions represented in the various sections of the poem to find for himself the inapplicability of any rigid scheme. For example, Whitman departs widely in sections 17-32 of "Song of Myself" from the conventional mystic's methods of purifying the self. Indeed, Whitman celebrates those very same senses that the traditional mystic would mortify if not annihilate. But in a sense Whitman's aim is as surely purification as is the mystic's. All in all, if the reader maintains a balanced perspective, he can come to a fuller and richer understanding of "Song of Myself" by viewing it through the frame of the mystical experience.

3

The Design of the Book

After looking intensively at a number of the major poems of *Leaves of Grass*, the serious reader will want to come to terms with the whole work as constituting a sustained and integrated poetic vision. Whitman once wrote, "My poems when complete should be a *unity*, in the same sense that the earth is, or that the human body, (senses, soul, head, trunk, feet, blood, viscera, man-root, eyes, hair,) or that a perfect musical composition is." Just before his death, Whitman requested that his final arrangement of the poems be respected in any future editions: "In the long run the world will do as it pleases with the book. I am determined to have the world know what I was pleased to do." Although the world has come to know what Whitman was pleased to do, it has not yet fully assimilated the nature or scope of his achievement.

A brief review of the several lifetime editions of *Leaves of Grass* will assist us in comprehending the book that Whitman finally left to the world. The two years 1861 and 1873, crisis years for the nation and the poet, divide Whitman's life into three separate parts. These three periods have their own distinct literary activity: the first three editions of *Leaves of Grass* (1855, 1856, 1860) appeared in the first; the next two editions (1867, 1871-72) appeared in the second; and four editions (1876, 1881, 1889, 1891-92) appeared in the last. The significant point, however, is that these three periods mark distinctive steps in the growth of *Leaves of Grass*. The 1860 edition represented the culmination of the first flush of poetic activity, a considerably bigger, more varied, and more complexly organized book than the 1855 edition, which contained only twelve untitled poems, and certainly less rushed than the 1856 edition, which was probably hurried through the press in order to publish as well as answer Emerson's enthusiastic letter praising the 1855 volume. There is abundant evidence that Whitman considered the 1860 edition as final and did not plan extensive revisions. A second burst of creative activity was brought about by the Civil War and culminated in the publication of *Drum-Taps* in 1865. It was not until the edition of 1871-72 that *Drum-Taps*, having appeared merely as an annex in the 1867 edition, was integrated into the structure of *Leaves of Grass*. There is, again, considerable evidence that Whitman considered the 1871-72 version of *Leaves of Grass* final and complete and regarded the cluster of poems accumulating around "Passage to India" (published as an annex to the 1871-72 edition) as the material for a new volume of poetry. Even in the 1876 edition the "Passage to India" group was published in the second volume, *Two Rivulets*, and was not integrated into the structure of the master work until the 1881 edition, the volume in which Whitman finally arrived at a form that was to remain essentially unchanged through succeeding editions. The three periods of heightened creative activity correspond to the three biographical segments of Whitman's life, and this activity in each case culminates in major revision of form or structure, at the time considered final, of *Leaves of Grass* in the editions of 1860, 1871-72, and 1881.

Our knowledge of the evolution of *Leaves of Grass* together with an analysis of the "deathbed" edition enables us to propose the following structure:

Leaves of Grass: Prototype personality for the New World

I. Introduction to themes and greetings

> Inscriptions
> "Starting from Paumanok"

II. Gigantic embryo or skeleton of personality

> "Song of Myself"
> Children of Adam   } the self and others
> Calamus
>
> Songs (Eleven individual poems)   } the self and the world (place)
>
> Birds of Passage
> "A Broadway Pageant"   } the self and history (time)
> Sea-Drift
> By the Roadside

III. This time and land we swim in

> Drum-Taps   } national crisis
> Memories of President Lincoln
> "By Blue Ontario's Shore"   } rehabilitation
> Autumn Rivulets

IV. The resistless gravitation of spiritual law

> "Proud Music of the Storm"
> "Passage to India"
> "Prayer of Columbus"
> "The Sleepers"
> "To Think of Time"
> Whispers of Heavenly Death

V. Review of themes and farewell

> "Thou Mother with Thy Equal Brood"
> From Noon to Starry Night
> Songs of Parting

Afterthoughts: the Annexes

> Sands at Seventy
> Good-Bye My Fancy
> Old Age Echoes

This outline is not meant to impose a rigid scheme on *Leaves of Grass* but rather to suggest the breadth of the poet's vision and the impressive measure of his achievement. But the structure is not a mere grouping of poems in accordance with subject matter. It is, rather, an ordering of the poems and groups of poems in accordance with the shifting focus of the pervading thematic purpose — delineation of the prototype personality for the New World. The groups defined by the outline are not independent entities, to be shuffled around at will, but exist in an appropriate order embodying a complex network of relationships. It is necessary that the "gigantic embryo or skeleton of Personality" (Whitman's phrase) be first introduced, defined, and related to the world and time in general before it is plunged into this specific "Time and Land we swim in" (again, the poet's phrase). And it is inevitable that this prototype personality be given birth, identity, and relationships with a certain century and country before primary attention is focused on his relation to death and immortality. There is not only a "poetic" sense to this order; but, throughout, the basic poetic intent is gradually but designedly fulfilled: the articulation of the archetypal New World "hero."

4

The Book and the World

But, ultimately, each reader of *Leaves of Grass* must bring the scope of the book within the focus of his own insight. Fortunately for us all, there is infinite variety in human vision, especially of the inner eye. The structures presented above are intended to provoke thought rather than command agreement. Throughout the history of *Leaves of Grass*, readers have agreed only on the difficulty of ignoring the work. Emerson's writing the impulsive letter of praise and Whittier's thrusting the work into the fire have in common their instantaneous recognition of a disturbing voice of powerful impact. Although Whitman never attracted the wide popular audiences that he desired (as Longfellow or Whittier did in the nineteenth century or as Sandburg or Frost in the twentieth), he always commanded the attention of significant literary or intellectual figures, if quite frequently in a negative sense.

Oliver Wendell Holmes, that genial dictator who jealously presided over the genteel tradition in Boston, passed down his judgment from his Olympian height: "[Whitman] takes into his hospitable vocabulary words which no English dictionary recognizes as belonging to the language. . . . He accepts as poetical subjects all things alike, common and unclean, without discrimination. . . . I shrink from a lawless independence to which all the virile energy and trampling audacity of Mr. Whitman fail to reconcile me." But Holmes at least read *Leaves of Grass.* Others passed judgment — the cruel judgment of neglect — without looking into the book. Emily Dickinson remarked once in a letter to Thomas Wentworth Higginson: "You speak of Mr. Whitman. I never read his book, but was told that he was disgraceful."

In a more recent time the major poets have felt at one time or another impelled to pass judgment. T. S. Eliot publicly confessed that in order to read Whitman he "had to conquer an aversion to his form, as well as to much of his matter." Ezra Pound wrote a curious poem compounded of the elements of both repulsion and attraction:

> I make a pact with you, Walt Whitman—
> I have detested you long enough.
> I come to you as a grown child
> Who has had a pig-headed father;
> I am old enough now to make friends.
> It was you that broke the new wood,
> Now it is time for carving.
> We have one sap and one root—
> Let there be commerce between us.[1]

This reluctant acceptance may be set beside the poetic tribute in Hart Crane's *The Bridge:*

> Our Meistersinger, thou set breath in steel;
> And it was thou who on the boldest heel
> Stood up and flung the span on even wing
> Of that great Bridge, our Myth, whereof I sing![2]

Like Crane, the poet's poet Dylan Thomas looked to Whitman as both model and inspiration, an attitude summarized best by his placing Whitman's picture above his study desk. Numerous contemporary novelists have felt and exhibited Whitman's influence: Thomas Wolfe in America, D. H. Lawrence and E. M. Forster in England (the title of Forster's masterpiece, *Passage to India,* derives from Whitman's poem). With many of the newer poets, such as Randall Jarrell and

---

[1] Copyright 1926 by Ezra Pound. Reprinted by permission of New Directions.

[2] From *The Collected Poems of Hart Crane.* Copyright: 1933, Liveright, Inc. By permission of Liveright Publishers, New York.

Karl Shapiro, acknowledging and even insisting on Whitman's poetic achievement, it appears that the judgment of the literati is no longer in major conflict with academic opinion, which over the years has awarded Whitman more and more space in the literature anthologies and an ever higher position among the American poets. But though Whitman seems to have won the day over many of those who scorned him, he still does not have the great mass audience of which he dreamed. Ironically, his best friends today are those *he* frequently scorned — the professional poets, professors, and critics.

Can the measure of Whitman's achievement now be taken? For some idea of what he wanted to achieve we may turn to his plea in *Democratic Vistas:* "Never was anything more wanted than, to-day, and here in the States, the poet of the modern is wanted, or the great literatus of the modern. At all times, perhaps, the central point in any nation, and that whence it is itself really sway'd the most and whence it sways others, is its national literature, especially its archetypal poems." There can be no doubt that Whitman himself set out in *Leaves of Grass* to write America's archetypal poem. And moreover, there seems room for little doubt, now, some one hundred years after its first appearance, that *Leaves of Grass* is one of the archetypal poems of these States — indeed, it may well be the only poem that may claim such a distinction. In simultaneously embodying and creating the prototype New World personality, Whitman was claiming for himself a relationship to America not unlike Homer's to Greece, Vergil's to Rome, and Milton's to England. The hero delineated in *Leaves of Grass* is the epic hero of the new world — "a simple separate person," yet uttering "the word Democratic, the word En-Masse." We may surely now grant Whitman his own title, "the great literatus of the modern." In another hundred years we may be ready to acknowledge his *Leaves* as America's epic, written in the dawn of her history when her people were vigorous and naïve and their faith fresh and bold.

RECOMMENDED READING

For biography: Gay Wilson Allen, *The Solitary Singer* (New York, 1955). For criticism: James E. Miller, Jr., *A Critical Guide to Leaves of Grass* (Chicago, 1957). For scholarship: Gay Wilson Allen, *Walt Whitman Handbook* (Chicago, 1946).

COMPLETE POETRY

All of the poems which Whitman wrote and published as *Leaves of Grass* appear in the following text, including the poems he rejected from edition to edition.

The text for *Leaves of Grass* here reprinted is that variously called the ninth, the 1891-92, or the deathbed edition. But included are the last poems which Whitman's literary executors, following his wishes, gathered into a third annex under the title, "Old Age Echoes," and published in the 1902 ten-volume *Complete Writings*.

The rejected poems, some twenty-nine in all, are the poems that for one reason or another Whitman discarded from *Leaves of Grass* as he revised the work over a thirty-year period. They are reprinted here in the order of their first appearance. In some instances these poems reveal attitudes — such as the extreme bitterness of "Respondez!" — which are not easily discovered in the final edition of *Leaves of Grass*.

All footnotes and headnotes in the text are Whitman's, except for the note introducing the third annex, written by his literary executors. Words and phrases, some Whitman's own invention, which might present difficulty are defined in a Glossary of Difficult Terms, beginning on page 503. Terms included are identified by asterisk (*) in the text.

Some eccentricities of language-use might here be noted. Whitman frequently substituted *K* for *C*, as in *Kanada* and *Kosmos*. He usually deleted the *e* in past participles, as in *fail'd* and *conquer'd*. And he used the Quaker system of referring to months, as in *Ninth-month* for *September*.

With these brief explanations, you might now heed Whitman as he beckons with his book: "O to haste firm holding — to haste, haste on with me."

AUTHOR'S NOTE FROM 1891-2 EDITION

As there are now several editions of L. of G., different texts and dates, I wish to say that I prefer and recommend this present one, complete, for future printing, if there should be any; a copy and fac-simile, indeed, of the text of these 438 pages. The subsequent adjusting interval which is so important to form'd and launch'd work, books especially, has pass'd; and waiting till fully after that, I have given (pages 423-438) my concluding words.†

W. W.

†The work referred to, "A Backward Glance O'er Travel'd Roads," appears among the selected prose in this edition.

COME, SAID MY SOUL,
SUCH VERSES FOR MY BODY LET US WRITE, (FOR WE ARE ONE,)
THAT SHOULD I AFTER DEATH INVISIBLY RETURN,
OR, LONG, LONG HENCE, IN OTHER SPHERES,
THERE TO SOME GROUP OF MATES THE CHANTS RESUMING,
(TALLYING EARTH'S SOIL, TREES, WINDS, TUMULTUOUS WAVES,)
EVER WITH PLEAS'D SMILE I MAY KEEP ON,
EVER AND EVER YET THE VERSES OWNING—AS, FIRST, I HERE AND NOW
SIGNING FOR SOUL AND BODY, SET TO THEM MY NAME,

Walt Whitman

LEAVES OF GRASS

INSCRIPTIONS

ONE'S-SELF I SING

One's-self I sing, a simple separate person,
Yet utter the word Democratic, the word En-Masse.*

Of physiology from top to toe I sing,
Not physiognomy alone nor brain alone is worthy for the Muse, I say
    the Form complete is worthier far,
The Female equally with the Male I sing.

Of Life immense in passion, pulse, and power,
Cheerful, for freest action form'd under the laws divine,
The Modern Man I sing.

AS I PONDER'D IN SILENCE

As I ponder'd in silence,
Returning upon my poems, considering, lingering long,
A Phantom arose before me with distrustful aspect,
Terrible in beauty, age, and power,
The genius of poets of old lands,
As to me directing like flame its eyes,
With finger pointing to many immortal songs,
And menacing voice, *What singest thou?* it said,
Know'st thou not there is but one theme for ever-enduring bards?
And that is the theme of War, the fortune of battles,
The making of perfect soldiers.

Be it so, then I answer'd,
I too haughty Shade also sing war, and a longer and greater one than
    any,
Waged in my book with varying fortune, with flight, advance and
    retreat, victory deferr'd and wavering,
(Yet methinks certain, or as good as certain, at the last,) the field the
    world,

For life and death, for the Body and for the eternal Soul,
Lo, I too am come, chanting the chant of battles,
I above all promote brave soldiers.

IN CABIN'D SHIPS AT SEA

In cabin'd ships at sea,
The boundless blue on every side expanding,
With whistling winds and music of the waves, the large imperious
    waves,
Or some lone bark buoy'd on the dense marine,
Where joyous full of faith, spreading white sails,
She cleaves the ether mid the sparkle and the foam of day, or under
    many a star at night,
By sailors young and old haply will I, a reminiscence of the land, be
    read,
In full rapport at last.

Here are our thoughts, voyagers' thoughts.
Here not the land, firm land, alone appears, may then by them be said,
The sky o'erarches here, we feel the undulating deck beneath our
    feet,
We feel the long pulsation, ebb and flow of endless motion,
The tones of unseen mystery, the vague and vast suggestions of the
    briny world, the liquid-flowing syllables,
The perfume, the faint creaking of the cordage, the melancholy
    rhythm,
The boundless vista and the horizon far and dim are all here,
And this is ocean's poem.

Then falter not O book, fulfil your destiny,
You not a reminiscence of the land alone,
You too as a lone bark cleaving the ether, purpos'd I know not whither,
    yet ever full of faith,
Consort to every ship that sails, sail you!
Bear forth to them folded my love, (dear mariners, for you I fold it
    here in every leaf;)
Speed on my book! spread your white sails my little bark athwart the
    imperious waves,
Chant on, sail on, bear o'er the boundless blue from me to every sea,
This song for mariners and all their ships.

TO FOREIGN LANDS

I heard that you ask'd for something to prove this puzzle the New
    World,
And to define America, her athletic Democracy,

Therefore I send you my poems that you behold in them what you
wanted.

TO A HISTORIAN

You who celebrate bygones,
Who have explored the outward, the surfaces of the races, the life that
has exhibited itself,
Who have treated of man as the creature of politics, aggregates, rulers
and priests,
I, habitan* of the Alleghanies, treating of him as he is in himself in his
own rights,
Pressing the pulse of life that has seldom exhibited itself, (the great
pride of man in himself,)
Chanter of Personality, outlining what is yet to be,
I project the history of the future.

TO THEE OLD CAUSE

To thee old cause!
Thou peerless, passionate, good cause,
Thou stern, remorseless, sweet idea,
Deathless throughout the ages, races, lands,
After a strange sad war, great war for thee,
(I think all war through time was really fought, and ever will be really
fought, for thee,)
These chants for thee, the eternal march of thee.

(A war O soldiers not for itself alone,
Far, far more stood silently waiting behind, now to advance in this
book.)

Thou orb of many orbs!
Thou seething principle! thou well-kept, latent germ! thou centre!
Around the idea of thee the war revolving,
With all its angry and vehement play of causes,
(With vast results to come for thrice a thousand years,)
These recitatives for thee,—my book and the war are one,
Merged in its spirit I and mine, as the contest hinged on thee,
As a wheel on its axis turns, this book unwitting to itself,
Around the idea of thee.

EIDÓLONS

I met a seer,
Passing the hues and objects of the world,
The fields of art and learning, pleasure, sense,
To glean eidólons.*

Put in thy chants said he,
No more the puzzling hour nor day, nor segments, parts, put in,
Put first before the rest as light for all and entrance-song of all,
    That of eidólons.

Ever the dim beginning,
Ever the growth, the rounding of the circle,
Ever the summit and the merge at last, (to surely start again,)
    Eidólons! eidólons!

Ever the mutable,
Ever materials, changing, crumbling, re-cohering,
Ever the ateliers,* the factories divine,
    Issuing eidólons.

Lo, I or you,
Or woman, man, or state, known or unknown,
We seeming solid wealth, strength, beauty build,
    But really build eidólons.

The ostent* evanescent,
The substance of an artist's mood or savan's* studies long,
Or warrior's, martyr's, hero's toils,
    To fashion his eidólon.

Of every human life,
(The units gather'd, posted, not a thought, emotion, deed, left out,)
The whole or large or small summ'd, added up,
    In its eidólon.

The old, old urge,
Based on the ancient pinnacles, lo, newer, higher pinnacles,
From science and the modern still impell'd,
    The old, old urge, eidólons.

The present now and here,
America's busy, teeming, intricate whirl,
Of aggregate and segregate for only thence releasing,
    To-day's eidólons.

These with the past,
Of vanish'd lands, of all the reigns of kings across the sea,
Old conquerors, old campaigns, old sailors' voyages,
    Joining eidólons.

Densities, growth, façades,
Strata of mountains, soils, rocks, giant trees,
Far-born, far-dying, living long, to leave,
    Eidólons everlasting.

Exalté,* rapt, ecstatic,
The visible but their womb of birth,
Of orbic tendencies to shape and shape and shape,
 The mighty earth-eidólon.

All space, all time,
(The stars, the terrible perturbations* of the suns,
Swelling, collapsing, ending, serving their longer, shorter use,)
 Fill'd with eidólons only.

The noiseless myriads,
The infinite oceans where the rivers empty,
The separate countless free identities, like eyesight,
 The true realities, eidólons.

Not this the world,
Nor these the universes, they the universes,
Purport and end, ever the permanent life of life,
 Eidólons, eidólons.

Beyond thy lectures learn'd professor,
Beyond thy telescope or spectroscope observer keen, beyond all mathe-
  matics,
Beyond the doctor's surgery, anatomy, beyond the chemist with his
  chemistry,
 The entities of entities, eidólons.

Unfix'd yet fix'd,
Ever shall be, ever have been and are,
Sweeping the present to the infinite future,
 Eidólons, eidólons, eidólons.

The prophet and the bard,
Shall yet maintain themselves, in higher stages yet,
Shall mediate to the Modern, to Democracy, interpret yet to them,
 God and eidólons.

And thee my soul,
Joys, ceaseless exercises, exaltations,
Thy yearning amply fed at last, prepared to meet,
 Thy mates, eidólons.

Thy body permanent,
The body lurking there within thy body,
The only purport of the form thou art, the real I myself,
 An image, an eidólon.

Thy very songs not in thy songs,
No special strains to sing, none for itself,
But from the whole resulting, rising at last and floating,
A round full-orb'd eidólon.

FOR HIM I SING

For him I sing,
I raise the present on the past,
(As some perennial tree out of its roots, the present on the past,)
With time and space I him dilate and fuse the immortal laws,
To make himself by them the law unto himself.

WHEN I READ THE BOOK

When I read the book, the biography famous,
And is this then (said I) what the author calls a man's life?
And so will some one when I am dead and gone write my life?
(As if any man really knew aught of my life,
Why even I myself I often think know little or nothing of my real life,
Only a few hints, a few diffused faint clews and indirections
I seek for my own use to trace out here.)

BEGINNING MY STUDIES

Beginning my studies the first step pleas'd me so much,
The mere fact consciousness, these forms, the power of motion,
The least insect or animal, the senses, eyesight, love,
The first step I say awed me and pleas'd me so much,
I have hardly gone and hardly wish'd to go any farther,
But stop and loiter all the time to sing it in ecstatic songs.

BEGINNERS

How they are provided for upon the earth, (appearing at intervals,)
How dear and dreadful they are to the earth,
How they inure° to themselves as much as to any—what a paradox
appears their age,
How people respond to them, yet know them not,
How there is something relentless in their fate all times,
How all times mischoose the objects of their adulation and reward,
And how the same inexorable price must still be paid for the same
great purchase.

TO THE STATES

To the States, or any one of them, or any city of the States, *Resist
    much, obey little,*
Once unquestioning obedience, once fully enslaved,
Once fully enslaved, no nation, state, city, of this earth, ever afterward
    resumes its liberty.

ON JOURNEYS THROUGH THE STATES

On journeys through the States we start,
(Ay through the world, urged by these songs,
Sailing henceforth to every land, to every sea,)
We willing learners of all, teachers of all, and lovers of all.

We have watch'd the seasons dispensing themselves and passing on,
And have said, Why should not a man or woman do as much as the
    seasons, and effuse* as much?

We dwell a while in every city and town,
We pass through Kanada, the North-east, the vast valley of the
    Mississippi, and the Southern States,
We confer on equal terms with each of the States,
We make trial of ourselves and invite men and women to hear,
We say to ourselves, Remember, fear not, be candid, promulge* the
    body and the soul,
Dwell a while and pass on, be copious, temperate, chaste, magnetic,
And what you effuse may then return as the seasons return,
And may be just as much as the seasons.

TO A CERTAIN CANTATRICE*

Here, take this gift,
I was reserving it for some hero, speaker, or general,
One who should serve the good old cause, the great idea, the progress
    and freedom of the race,
Some brave confronter of despots, some daring rebel;
But I see that what I was reserving belongs to you just as much as to
    any.

ME IMPERTURBE

Me imperturbe,* standing at ease in Nature,
Master of all or mistress of all, aplomb in the midst of irrational things,
Imbued as they, passive, receptive, silent as they,

Finding my occupation, poverty, notoriety, foibles, crimes, less important than I thought,
Me toward the Mexican sea, or in the Mannahatta* or the Tennessee,
or far north or inland,
A river man, or a man of the woods or of any farm-life of these States
or of the coast, or the lakes of Kanada,
Me wherever my life is lived, O to be self-balanced for contingencies,
To confront night, storms, hunger, ridicule, accidents, rebuffs, as the
trees and animals do.

SAVANTISM

Thither as I look I see each result and glory retracing itself and
nestling close, always obligated,
Thither hours, months, years—thither trades, compacts, establish-
ments, even the most minute,
Thither every-day life, speech, utensils, politics, persons, estates;
Thither we also, I with my leaves and songs, trustful, admirant,*
As a father to his father going takes his children along with him.

THE SHIP STARTING

Lo, the unbounded sea,
On its breast a ship starting, spreading all sails, carrying even her
moonsails,
The pennant is flying aloft as she speeds she speeds so stately—below
emulous* waves press forward,
They surround the ship with shining curving motions and foam.

I HEAR AMERICA SINGING

I hear America singing, the varied carols I hear,
Those of mechanics, each one singing his as it should be blithe and
strong,
The carpenter singing his as he measures his plank or beam,
The mason singing his as he makes ready for work, or leaves off work,
The boatman singing what belongs to him in his boat, the deck-hand
singing on the steamboat deck,
The shoemaker singing as he sits on his bench, the hatter singing as
he stands,
The wood-cutter's song, the ploughboy's on his way in the morning,
or at noon intermission or at sundown,
The delicious singing of the mother, or of the young wife at work, or
of the girl sewing or washing,
Each singing what belongs to him or her and to none else,

The day what belongs to the day—at night the party of young fellows,
      robust, friendly,
Singing with open mouths their strong melodious songs.

WHAT PLACE IS BESIEGED?

What place is besieged, and vainly tries to raise the siege?
Lo, I send to that place a commander, swift, brave, immortal,
And with him horse and foot, and parks of artillery,
And artillery-men, the deadliest that ever fired gun.

STILL THOUGH THE ONE I SING

Still though the one I sing,
(One, yet of contradictions made,) I dedicate to Nationality,
I leave in him revolt, (O latent right of insurrection! O quenchless,
      indispensable fire!)

SHUT NOT YOUR DOORS

Shut not your doors to me proud libraries,
For that which was lacking on all your well-fill'd shelves, yet needed
      most, I bring,
Forth from the war emerging, a book I have made,
The words of my book nothing, the drift of it every thing,
A book separate, not link'd with the rest nor felt by the intellect,
But you ye untold latencies will thrill to every page.

POETS TO COME

Poets to come! orators, singers, musicians to come!
Not to-day is to justify me and answer what I am for,
But you, a new brood, native, athletic, continental, greater than before
      known,
Arouse! for you must justify me.

I myself but write one or two indicative words for the future,
I but advance a moment only to wheel and hurry back in the darkness.

I am a man who, sauntering along without fully stopping, turns a
      casual look upon you and then averts his face,
Leaving it to you to prove and define it,
Expecting the main things from you

TO YOU

Stranger, if you passing meet me and desire to speak to me, why
    should you not speak to me?
And why should I not speak to you?

THOU READER

Thou reader throbbest life and pride and love the same as I,
Therefore for thee the following chants.

STARTING FROM PAUMANOK

1

Starting from fish-shape Paumanok° where I was born,
Well-begotten, and rais'd by a perfect mother,
After roaming many lands, lover of populous pavements,
Dweller in Mannahatta° my city, or on southern savannas,
Or a soldier camp'd or carrying my knapsack and gun, or a miner in
    California,
Or rude in my home in Dakota's woods, my diet meat, my drink from
    the spring,
Or withdrawn to muse and meditate in some deep recess,
Far from the clank of crowds intervals passing rapt and happy,
Aware of the fresh free giver the flowing Missouri, aware of mighty
    Niagara,
Aware of the buffalo herds grazing the plains, the hirsute and strong-
    breasted bull,
Of earth, rocks, Fifth-month flowers experienced, stars, rain, snow, my
    amaze,
Having studied the mocking-bird's tones and the flight of the moun-
    tain-hawk,
And heard at dawn the unrivall'd one, the hermit thrush from the
    swamp-cedars,
Solitary, singing in the West, I strike up for a New World.

2

Victory, union, faith, identity, time,
The indissoluble compacts, riches, mystery,
Eternal progress, the kosmos,° and the modern reports.

This then is life,
Here is what has come to the surface after so many throes and con-
    vulsions.

How curious! how real!
Underfoot the divine soil, overhead the sun.

See revolving the globe,
The ancestor-continents away group'd together,
The present and future continents north and south, with the isthmus
    between.

See, vast trackless spaces,
As in a dream they change, they swiftly fill,
Countless masses debouch° upon them,
They are now cover'd with the foremost people, arts, institutions,
    known.

See, projected through time,
For me an audience interminable.

With firm and regular step they wend, they never stop,
Successions of men, Americanos, a hundred millions,
One generation playing its part and passing on,
Another generation playing its part and passing on in its turn,
With faces turn'd sideways or backwards towards me to listen,
With eyes retrospective towards me.

3

Americanos! conquerors! marches humanitarian!
Foremost! century marches! Libertad!* masses!
For you a programme of chants.

Chants of the prairies,
Chants of the long-running Mississippi, and down to the Mexican sea,
Chants of Ohio, Indiana, Illinois, Iowa, Wisconsin and Minnesota,
Chants going forth from the centre from Kansas, and thence equi-
distant,
Shooting in pulses of fire ceaseless to vivify all.

4

Take my leaves America, take them South and take them North,
Make welcome for them everywhere, for they are your own offspring,
Surround them East and West, for they would surround you,
And you precedents, connect lovingly with them, for they connect
lovingly with you.

I conn'd old times,
I sat studying at the feet of the great masters,
Now if eligible O that the great masters might return and study me.

In the name of these States shall I scorn the antique?
Why these are the children of the antique to justify it.

5

Dead poets, philosophs, priests,
Martyrs, artists, inventors, governments long since,
Language-shapers on other shores,
Nations once powerful, now reduced, withdrawn, or desolate,
I dare not proceed till I respectfully credit what you have left wafted
hither,
I have perused it, own it is admirable, (moving awhile among it,)
Think nothing can ever be greater, nothing can ever deserve more than
it deserves,
Regarding it all intently a long while, then dismissing it,
I stand in my place with my own day here.

Here lands female and male,
Here the heir-ship and heiress-ship of the world, here the flame of
    materials,
Here spirituality the translatress, the openly-avow'd,
The ever-tending, the female of visible forms,
The satisfier, after due long-waiting now advancing,
Yes here comes my mistress the soul.

6

The soul,
Forever and forever—longer than soil is brown and solid—longer than
    water ebbs and flows.

I will make the poems of materials, for I think they are to be the most
    spiritual poems,
And I will make the poems of my body and of mortality,
For I think I shall then supply myself with the poems of my soul and
    of immortality.

I will make a song for these States that no one State may under any
    circumstances be subjected to another State,
And I will make a song that there shall be comity* by day and by
    night between all the States, and between any two of them,

And I will make a song for the ears of the President, full of weapons
    with menacing points,
And behind the weapons countless dissatisfied faces;
And a song make I of the One form'd out of all,
The fang'd and glittering One whose head is over all,
Resolute warlike One including and over all,
(However high the head of any else that head is over all.)

I will acknowledge contemporary lands,
I will trail the whole geography of the globe and salute courteously
    every city large and small,
And employments! I will put in my poems that with you is heroism
    upon land and sea,
And I will report all heroism from an American point of view.

I will sing the song of companionship,
I will show what alone must finally compact these,
I believe these are to found their own ideal of manly love, indicating it
    in me,
I will therefore let flame from me the burning fires that were threaten-
    ing to consume me,
I will lift what has too long kept down those smouldering fires,
I will give them complete abandonment,
I will write the evangel-poem of comrades and of love,
For who but I should understand love with all its sorrow and joy?
And who but I should be the poet of comrades?

7

I am the credulous man of qualities, ages, races,
I advance from the people in their own spirit,
Here is what sings unrestricted faith.

Omnes!* omnes! let others ignore what they may,
I make the poem of evil also, I commemorate that part also,
I am myself just as much evil as good, and my nation is—and I say
    there is in fact no evil,
(Or if there is I say it is just as important to you, to the land or to me, as
    any thing else.)

I too, following many and follow'd by many, inaugurate a religion, I
    descend into the arena,
(It may be I am destin'd to utter the loudest cries there, the winner's
    pealing shouts,
Who knows? they may rise from me yet, and soar above every thing.)

Each is not for its own sake,
I say the whole earth and all the stars in the sky are for religion's sake.

I say no man has ever yet been half devout enough,
None has ever yet adored or worship'd half enough,
None has begun to think how divine he himself is, and how certain the
    future is.

I say that the real and permanent grandeur of these States must be
    their religion,
Otherwise there is no real and permanent grandeur;
(Nor character nor life worthy the name without religion,
Nor land nor man or woman without religion.)

8

What are you doing young man?
Are you so earnest, so given up to literature, science, art, amours?
These ostensible realities, politics, points?
Your ambition or business whatever it may be?

It is well—against such I say not a word, I am their poet also,
But behold! such swiftly subside, burnt up for religion's sake,
For not all matter is fuel to heat, impalpable flame, the essential life of
    the earth,
Any more than such are to religion.

9

What do you seek so pensive and silent?
What do you need camerado?
Dear son do you think it is love?

Listen dear son—listen America, daughter or son,
It is a painful thing to love a man or woman to excess, and yet it
    satisfies, it is great,
But there is something else very great, it makes the whole coincide,
It, magnificent, beyond materials, with continuous hands sweeps and
    provides for all.

10

Know you, solely to drop in the earth the germs of a greater religion,
The following chants each for its kind I sing.

My comrade!
For you to share with me two greatnesses, and a third one rising in-
    clusive and more resplendent,
The greatness of Love and Democracy, and the greatness of Religion.

Melange* mine own, the unseen and the seen,
Mysterious ocean where the streams empty,
Prophetic spirit of materials shifting and flickering around me,
Living beings, identities now doubtless near us in the air that we
    know not of,
Contact daily and hourly that will not release me,
These selecting, these in hints demanded of me.

Not he with a daily kiss onward from childhood kissing me,
Has winded and twisted around me that which holds me to him,
Any more than I am held to the heavens and all the spiritual world,
After what they have done to me, suggesting themes.

O such themes—equalities! O divine average!
Warblings under the sun, usher'd as now, or at noon, or setting,
Strains musical flowing through ages, now reaching hither,
I take to your reckless and composite chords, add to them, and cheer-
    fully pass them forward.

11

As I have walk'd in Alabama my morning walk,
I have seen where the she-bird the mocking-bird sat on her nest in the
    briers hatching her brood.

I have seen the he-bird also,
I have paus'd to hear him near at hand inflating his throat and joyfully
    singing.

And while I paus'd it came to me that what he really sang for was not
    there only,
Nor for his mate nor himself only, nor all sent back by the echoes,
But subtle, clandestine, away beyond,
A charge transmitted and gift occult for those being born.

12

Democracy! near at hand to you a throat is now inflating itself and
joyfully singing.

Ma femme!* for the brood beyond us and of us,
For those who belong here and those to come,
I exultant to be ready for them will now shake out carols stronger and
haughtier than have ever yet been heard upon earth.

I will make the songs of passion to give them their way,
And your songs outlaw'd offenders, for I scan you with kindred eyes,
and carry you with me the same as any.

I will make the true poem of riches,
To earn for the body and the mind whatever adheres and goes forward
and is not dropt by death;
I will effuse* egotism and show it underlying all, and I will be the bard
of personality,
And I will show of male and female that either is but the equal of the
other,
And sexual organs and acts! do you concentrate in me, for I am determin'd to tell you with courageous clear voice to prove you
illustrious,
And I will show that there is no imperfection in the present, and can
be none in the future,
And I will show that whatever happens to anybody it may be turn'd
to beautiful results,
And I will show that nothing can happen more beautiful than death,
And I will thread a thread through my poems that time and events
are compact,
And that all the things of the universe are perfect miracles, each as
profound as any.

I will not make poems with reference to parts,
But I will make poems, songs, thoughts, with reference to ensemble,
And I will not sing with reference to a day, but with reference to all
days,
And I will not make a poem nor the least part of a poem but has
reference to the soul,
Because having look'd at the objects of the universe, I find there is no
one nor any particle of one but has reference to the soul.

13

Was somebody asking to see the soul?
See, your own shape and countenance, persons, substances, beasts, the
trees, the running rivers, the rocks and sands.

All hold spiritual joys and afterwards loosen them;
How can the real body ever die and be buried?

Of your real body and any man's or woman's real body,
Item for item it will elude the hands of the corpse-cleaners and pass to
     fitting spheres,
Carrying what has accrued to it from the moment of birth to the
     moment of death.

Not the types set up by the printer return their impression, the
     meaning, the main concern,
Any more than a man's substance and life or a woman's substance and
     life return in the body and the soul,
Indifferently before death and after death.

Behold, the body includes and is the meaning, the main concern, and
     includes and is the soul;
Whoever you are, how superb and how divine is your body, or any
     part of it!

14

Whoever you are, to you endless announcements!

Daughter of the lands did you wait for your poet?
Did you wait for one with a flowing mouth and indicative hand?

Toward the male of the States, and toward the female of the States,
Exalting words, words to Democracy's lands.

Interlink'd, food-yielding lands!
Land of coal and iron! land of gold! land of cotton, sugar, rice!
Land of wheat, beef, pork! land of wool and hemp! land of the apple
     and the grape!
Land of the pastoral plains, the grass-fields of the world! land of those
     sweet-air'd interminable plateaus!
Land of the herd, the garden, the healthy house of adobie!
Lands where the north-west Columbia winds, and where the south-
     west Colorado winds!
Land of the eastern Chesapeake! land of the Delaware!
Land of Ontario, Erie, Huron, Michigan!
Land of the Old Thirteen! Massachusetts land! land of Vermont and
     Connecticut!
Land of the ocean shores! land of sierras and peaks!
Land of boatmen and sailors! fishermen's land!
Inextricable lands! the clutch'd together! the passionate ones!
The side by side! the elder and younger brothers! the bony-limb'd!
The great women's land! the feminine! the experienced sisters and the
     inexperienced sisters!
Far breath'd land! Arctic braced! Mexican breez'd! the diverse! the
     compact!
The Pennsylvanian! the Virginian! the double Carolinian!

O all and each well-loved by me! my intrepid nations! O I at any rate
   include you all with perfect love!
I cannot be discharged from you! not from one any sooner than
   another!
O death! O for all that, I am yet of you unseen this hour with irre-
   pressible love,
Walking New England, a friend, a traveler,
Splashing my bare feet in the edge of the summer ripples on Pauma-
   nok's sands,
Crossing the prairies, dwelling again in Chicago, dwelling in every
   town,
Observing shows, births, improvements, structures, arts,
Listening to orators and oratresses in public halls,
Of and through the States as during life, each man and woman my
   neighbor,
The Louisianian, the Georgian, as near to me, and I as near to him
   and her,
The Mississippian and Arkansian yet with me, and I yet with any of
   them,
Yet upon the plains west of the spinal river, yet in my house of
   adobie,
Yet returning eastward, yet in the Seaside State or in Maryland,
Yet Kanadian cheerily braving the winter, the snow and ice welcome
   to me,
Yet a true son either of Maine or of the Granite State, or the Narra-
   gansett Bay State, or the Empire State,
Yet sailing to other shores to annex the same, yet welcoming every
   new brother,
Hereby applying these leaves to the new ones from the hour they
   unite with the old ones,
Coming among the new ones myself to be their companion and
   equal, coming personally to you now,
Enjoining you to acts, characters, spectacles, with me.

15
With me with firm holding, yet haste, haste on.

For your life adhere to me,
(I may have to be persuaded many times before I consent to give my-
   self really to you, but what of that?
Must not Nature be persuaded many times?)

No dainty dolce° affettuoso° I,
Bearded, sun-burnt, gray-neck'd, forbidding, I have arrived,
To be wrestled with as I pass for the solid prizes of the universe,
For such I afford whoever can persevere to win them.

16
On my way a moment I pause,
Here for you! and here for America!

Still the present I raise aloft, still the future of the States I harbinge*
   glad and sublime,
And for the past I pronounce what the air holds of the red aborigines.

The red aborigines,
Leaving natural breaths, sounds of rain and winds, calls as of birds
   and animals in the woods, syllabled to us for names,
Okonee, Koosa, Ottawa, Monongahela, Sauk, Natchez, Chattahoochee,
   Kaqueta, Oronoco,
Wabash, Miami, Saginaw, Chippewa, Oshkosh, Walla-Walla,
Leaving such to the States they melt, they depart, charging the water
   and the land with names.

17

Expanding and swift, henceforth,
Elements, breeds, adjustments, turbulent, quick and audacious,
A world primal again, vistas of glory incessant and branching,
A new race dominating previous ones and grander far, with new con-
   tests,
New politics, new literatures and religions, new inventions and arts.

These, my voice announcing—I will sleep no more but arise,
You oceans that have been calm within me! how I feel you, fathomless, stirring, preparing unprecedented waves and storms.

18

See, steamers steaming through my poems,
See, in my poems immigrants continually coming and landing,
See, in arriere,* the wigwam, the trail, the hunter's hut, the flatboat,
   the maize-leaf, the claim, the rude fence, and the backwoods
   village,
See, on the one side, the Western Sea and on the other the Eastern
   Sea, how they advance and retreat upon my poems as upon
   their own shores,
See, pastures and forests in my poems—see, animals wild and tame—
   see, beyond the Kaw, countless herds of buffalo feeding on
   short curly grass,
See, in my poems, cities, solid, vast, inland, with paved streets, with
   iron and stone edifices, ceaseless vehicles, and commerce,
See, the many-cylinder'd steam printing-press—see, the electric telegraph stretching across the continent,
See, through Atlantica's depth pulses American Europe reaching,
   pulses of Europe duly return'd,
See, the strong and quick locomotive as it departs, panting, blowing
   the steam-whistle,
See, ploughmen ploughing farms—see, miners digging mines—see,
   the numberless factories,

See, mechanics busy at their benches with tools—see from among
        them superior judges, philosophs, Presidents, emerge, drest in
        working dresses,
See, lounging through the shops and fields of the States, me well-
        belov'd, close-held by day and night,
Hear the loud echoes of my songs there—read the hints come at last.

19

O camerado close! O you and me at last, and us two only.
O a word to clear one's path ahead endlessly!
O something ecstatic and undemonstrable! O music wild!
O now I triumph—and you shall also;
O hand in hand—O wholesome pleasure—O one more desirer and
        lover!
O to haste firm holding—to haste, haste on with me.

SONG OF MYSELF

1

I celebrate myself, and sing myself,
And what I assume you shall assume,
For every atom belonging to me as good belongs to you.

I loafe and invite my soul,
I lean and loafe at my ease observing a spear of summer grass.

My tongue, every atom of my blood, form'd from this soil, this air,
Born here of parents born here from parents the same, and their parents
　　the same,
I, now thirty-seven years old in perfect health begin,
Hoping to cease not till death.

Creeds and schools in abeyance,
Retiring back a while sufficed at what they are, but never forgotten,
I harbor for good or bad, I permit to speak at every hazard,
Nature without check with original energy.

2

Houses and rooms are full of perfumes, the shelves are crowded with
　　perfumes,
I breathe the fragrance myself and know it and like it,
The distillation would intoxicate me also, but I shall not let it.

The atmosphere is not a perfume, it has no taste of the distillation, it
　　is odorless,
It is for my mouth forever, I am in love with it,
I will go to the bank by the wood and become undisguised and naked,
I am mad for it to be in contact with me.

The smoke of my own breath,
Echoes, ripples, buzz'd whispers, love-root, silk-thread, crotch and
　　vine,
My respiration and inspiration, the beating of my heart, the passing of
　　blood and air through my lungs,
The sniff of green leaves and dry leaves, and of the shore and dark-
　　color'd sea-rocks, and of hay in the barn,
The sound of the belch'd words of my voice loos'd to the eddies of the
　　wind,
A few light kisses, a few embraces, a reaching around of arms,
The play of shine and shade on the trees as the supple boughs wag,
The delight alone or in the rush of the streets, or along the fields and
　　hill-sides,

The feeling of health, the full-noon trill, the song of me rising from bed
and meeting the sun.

Have you reckon'd a thousand acres much? have you reckon'd the
earth much?
Have you practis'd so long to learn to read?
Have you felt so proud to get at the meaning of poems?

Stop this day and night with me and you shall possess the origin of
all poems,
You shall possess the good of the earth and sun, (there are millions
of suns left,)
You shall no longer take things at second or third hand, nor look
through the eyes of the dead, nor feed on the spectres in books,
You shall not look through my eyes either, nor take things from me,
You shall listen to all sides and filter them from your self.

3

I have heard what the talkers were talking, the talk of the beginning
and the end,
But I do not talk of the beginning or the end.

There was never any more inception than there is now,
Nor any more youth or age than there is now,
And will never be any more perfection than there is now,
Nor any more heaven or hell than there is now.

Urge and urge and urge,
Always the procreant urge of the world.

Out of the dimness opposite equals advance, always substance and
increase, always sex,
Always a knit of identity, always distinction, always a breed of life.

To elaborate is no avail, learn'd and unlearn'd feel that it is so.

Sure as the most certain sure, plumb in the uprights, well entretied,
braced in the beams,
Stout as a horse, affectionate, haughty, electrical,
I and this mystery here we stand.

Clear and sweet is my soul, and clear and sweet is all that is not my
soul.

Lack one lacks both, and the unseen is proved by the seen,
Till that becomes unseen and receives proof in its turn.

Showing the best and dividing it from the worst age vexes age,
Knowing the perfect fitness and equanimity of things, while they discuss I am silent, and go bathe and admire myself.

Welcome is every organ and attribute of me, and of any man hearty
and clean,
Not an inch nor a particle of an inch is vile, and none shall be less
familiar than the rest.

I am satisfied—I see, dance, laugh, sing;
As the hugging and loving bed-fellow sleeps at my side through the
night, and withdraws at the peep of the day with stealthy tread,
Leaving me baskets cover'd with white towels swelling the house with
their plenty,
Shall I postpone my acceptation and realization and scream at my eyes,
That they turn from gazing after and down the road,
And forthwith cipher and show me to a cent,
Exactly the value of one and exactly the value of two, and which is
ahead?

4

Trippers and askers surround me,
People I meet, the effect upon me of my early life or the ward and
city I live in, or the nation,
The latest dates, discoveries, inventions, societies, authors old and new,
My dinner, dress, associates, looks, compliments, dues,
The real or fancied indifference of some man or woman I love,
The sickness of one of my folks or of myself, or ill-doing or loss or
lack of money, or depressions or exaltations,
Battles, the horrors of fratricidal war, the fever of doubtful news, the
fitful events;
These come to me days and nights and go from me again,
But they are not the Me myself.

Apart from the pulling and hauling stands what I am,
Stands amused, complacent, compassionating, idle, unitary,
Looks down, is erect, or bends an arm on an impalpable certain rest,
Looking with side-curved head curious what will come next,
Both in and out of the game and watching and wondering at it.

Backward I see in my own days where I sweated through fog with
linguists and contenders,
I have no mockings or arguments, I witness and wait.

5

I believe in you my soul, the other I am must not abase itself to you,
And you must not be abased to the other.

Loafe with me on the grass, loose the stop from your throat,
Not words, not music or rhyme I want, not custom or lecture, not even
the best,
Only the lull I like, the hum of your valvèd voice.

I mind how once we lay such a transparent summer morning,
How you settled your head athwart my hips and gently turn'd over
upon me,
And parted the shirt from my bosom-bone, and plunged your tongue
to my bare-stript heart,
And reach'd till you felt my beard, and reach'd till you held my feet.

Swiftly arose and spread around me the peace and knowledge that
pass all the argument of the earth,
And I know that the hand of God is the promise of my own,
And I know that the spirit of God is the brother of my own,
And that all the men ever born are also my brothers, and the women
my sisters and lovers,
And that a kelson* of the creation is love,
And limitless are leaves stiff or drooping in the fields,
And brown ants in the little wells beneath them,
And mossy scabs of the worm fence, heap'd stones, elder, mullein and
poke-weed.

6

A child said *What is the grass?* fetching it to me with full hands,
How could I answer the child? I do not know what it is any more
than he.

I guess it must be the flag of my disposition, out of hopeful green
stuff woven.

Or I guess it is the handkerchief of the Lord,
A scented gift and remembrancer designedly dropt,
Bearing the owner's name someway in the corners, that we may see
and remark, and say *Whose?*

Or I guess the grass is itself a child, the produced babe of the vegetation.

Or I guess it is a uniform hieroglyphic,
And it means, Sprouting alike in broad zones and narrow zones,
Growing among black folks as among white,
Kanuck, Tuckahoe, Congressman, Cuff, I give them the same, I
receive them the same.

And now it seems to me the beautiful uncut hair of graves.

Tenderly will I use you curling grass,
It may be you transpire from the breasts of young men,
It may be if I had known them I would have loved them,
It may be you are from old people, or from offspring taken soon out
of their mothers' laps.
And here you are the mothers' laps.

This grass is very dark to be from the white heads of old mothers,
Darker than the colorless beards of old men,
Dark to come from under the faint red roofs of mouths.

O I perceive after all so many uttering tongues,
And I perceive they do not come from the roofs of mouths for nothing.

I wish I could translate the hints about the dead young men and
women,
And the hints about old men and mothers, and the offspring taken
soon out of their laps.

What do you think has become of the young and old men?
And what do you think has become of the women and children?

They are alive and well somewhere,
The smallest sprout shows there is really no death,
And if ever there was it led forward life, and does not wait at the end
to arrest it,
And ceas'd the moment life appear'd.

All goes onward and outward, nothing collapses,
And to die is different from what any one supposed, and luckier.

7

Has any one supposed it lucky to be born?
I hasten to inform him or her it is just as lucky to die, and I know it.

I pass death with the dying and birth with the new-wash'd babe, and
am not contain'd between my hat and boots,
And peruse manifold objects, no two alike and every one good,
The earth good and the stars good, and their adjuncts all good.

I am not an earth nor an adjunct of an earth,
I am the mate and companion of people, all just as immortal and
fathomless as myself,
(They do not know how immortal, but I know.)

Every kind for itself and its own, for me mine male and female,
For me those that have been boys and that love women,
For me the man that is proud and feels how it stings to be slighted,
For me the sweet-heart and the old maid, for me mothers and the
mothers of mothers,
For me lips that have smiled, eyes that have shed tears,
For me children and the begetters of children.

Undrape! you are not guilty to me, nor stale nor discarded,
I see through the broadcloth and gingham whether or no,
And am around, tenacious, acquisitive, tireless, and cannot be shaken
away.

8

The little one sleeps in its cradle,
I lift the gauze and look a long time, and silently brush away flies with
    my hand.

The youngster and the red-faced girl turn aside up the bushy hill,
I peeringly view them from the top.

The suicide sprawls on the bloody floor of the bedroom,
I witness the corpse with its dabbled hair, I note where the pistol has
    fallen.

The blab of the pave, tires of carts, sluff of boot-soles, talk of the
    promenaders,
The heavy omnibus, the driver with his interrogating thumb, the clank
    of the shod horses on the granite floor,
The snow-sleighs, clinking, shouted jokes, pelts of snow-balls,
The hurrahs for popular favorites, the fury of rous'd mobs,
The flap of the curtain'd litter, a sick man inside borne to the hospital,
The meeting of enemies, the sudden oath, the blows and fall,
The excited crowd, the policeman with his star quickly working his
    passage to the centre of the crowd,
The impassive stones that receive and return so many echoes,
What groans of over-fed or half-starv'd who fall sunstruck or in fits,
What exclamations of women taken suddenly who hurry home and
    give birth to babes,
What living and buried speech is always vibrating here, what howls
    restrain'd by decorum,
Arrests of criminals, slights, adulterous offers made, acceptances, re-
    jections with convex lips,
I mind them or the show or resonance of them—I come and I depart.

9

The big doors of the country barn stand open and ready,
The dried grass of the harvest-time loads the slow-drawn wagon,
The clear light plays on the brown gray and green intertinged,
The armfuls are pack'd to the sagging mow.

I am there, I help, I came stretch'd atop of the load,
I felt its soft jolts, one leg reclined on the other,
I jump from the cross-beams and seize the clover and timothy,
And roll head over heels and tangle my hair full of wisps.

10

Alone far in the wilds and mountains I hunt,
Wandering amazed at my own lightness and glee,
In the late afternoon choosing a safe spot to pass the night,
Kindling a fire and broiling the fresh-kill'd game,
Falling asleep on the gather'd leaves with my dog and gun by my
    side.

The Yankee clipper is under her sky-sails, she cuts the sparkle and
  scud,°
My eyes settle the land, I bend at her prow or shout joyously from
  the deck.

The boatmen and clam-diggers arose early and stopt for me,
I tuck'd my trowser-ends in my boots and went and had a good time;
You should have been with us that day round the chowder-kettle.

I saw the marriage of the trapper in the open air in the far west, the
  bride was a red girl,
Her father and his friends sat near cross-legged and dumbly smoking,
  they had moccasins to their feet and large thick blankets
  hanging from their shoulders,
On a bank lounged the trapper, he was drest mostly in skins, his luxuriant beard and curls protected his neck, he held his bride
  by the hand,
She had long eyelashes, her head was bare, her coarse straight locks
  descended upon her voluptuous limbs and reach'd to her feet.

The runaway slave came to my house and stopt outside,
I heard his motions crackling the twigs of the woodpile,
Through the swung half-door of the kitchen I saw him, limpsy° and
  weak,
And went where he sat on a log and led him in and assured him,
And brought water and fill'd a tub for his sweated body and bruis'd
  feet,
And gave him a room that enter'd from my own, and gave him some
  coarse clean clothes,
And remember perfectly well his revolving eyes and his awkwardness,
And remember putting plasters on the galls of his neck and ankles;
He staid with me a week before he was recuperated and pass'd north,
I had him sit next me at table, my fire-lock lean'd in the corner.

11

Twenty-eight young men bathe by the shore,
Twenty-eight young men and all so friendly;
Twenty-eight years of womanly life and all so lonesome.

She owns the fine house by the rise of the bank,
She hides handsome and richly drest aft the blinds of the window.

Which of the young men does she like the best?
Ah the homeliest of them is beautiful to her.

Where are you off to, lady? for I see you,
You splash in the water there, yet stay stock still in your room.

Dancing and laughing along the beach came the twenty-ninth bather,
The rest did not see her, but she saw them and loved them.

The beards of the young men glisten'd with wet, it ran from their long
    hair,
Little streams pass'd all over their bodies.

An unseen hand also pass'd over their bodies,
It descended tremblingly from their temples and ribs.

The young men float on their backs, their white bellies bulge to the
    sun, they do not ask who seizes fast to them,
They do not know who puffs and declines with pendant and bending
    arch,
They do not think whom they souse with spray.

12

The butcher-boy puts off his killing-clothes, or sharpens his knife at
    the stall in the market,
I loiter enjoying his repartee and his shuffle and break-down.

Blacksmiths with grimed and hairy chests environ the anvil,
Each has his main-sledge, they are all out, there is a great heat in the fire.

From the cinder-strew'd threshold I follow their movements,
The lithe sheer of their waists plays even with their massive arms,
Overhand the hammers swing, overhand so slow, overhand so sure,
They do not hasten, each man hits in his place.

13

The negro holds firmly the reins of his four horses, the block swags
    underneath on its tied-over chain,
The negro that drives the long dray of the stone-yard, steady and tall
    he stands pois'd on one leg on the string-piece,
His blue shirt exposes his ample neck and breast and loosens over his
    hip-band,
His glance is calm and commanding, he tosses the slouch of his hat
    away from his forehead,
The sun falls on his crispy hair and mustache, falls on the black of
    his polish'd and perfect limbs.

I behold the picturesque giant and love him, and I do not stop there,
I go with the team also.

In me the caresser of life wherever moving, backward as well as for-
    ward sluing,
To niches aside and junior bending, not a person or object missing,
Absorbing all to myself and for this song.

Oxen that rattle the yoke and chain or halt in the leafy shade, what is
    that you express in your eyes?
It seems to me more than all the print I have read in my life.

My tread scares the wood-drake and wood-duck on my distant and
    day-long ramble,
They rise together, they slowly circle around.

I believe in those wing'd purposes,
And acknowledge red, yellow, white, playing within me,
And consider green and violet and the tufted crown intentional,
And do not call the tortoise unworthy because she is not something
    else,
And the jay in the woods never studied the gamut,* yet trills pretty
    well to me,
And the look of the bay mare shames silliness out of me.

14

The wild gander leads his flock through the cool night,
Ya-honk he says, and sounds it down to me like an invitation,
The pert may suppose it meaningless, but I listening close,
Find its purpose and place up there toward the wintry sky.

The sharp-hoof'd moose of the north, the cat on the house-sill, the
    chickadee, the prairie-dog,
The litter of the grunting sow as they tug at her teats,
The brood of the turkey-hen and she with her half-spread wings,
I see in them and myself the same old law.

The press of my foot to the earth springs a hundred affections,
They scorn the best I can do to relate them.

I am enamour'd of growing out-doors,
Of men that live among cattle or taste of the ocean or woods,
Of the builders and steerers of ships and the wielders of axes and
    mauls, and the drivers of horses,
I can eat and sleep with them week in and week out.

What is commonest, cheapest, nearest, easiest, is Me,
Me going in for my chances, spending for vast returns,
Adorning myself to bestow myself on the first that will take me,
Not asking the sky to come down to my good will,
Scattering it freely forever.

15

The pure contralto sings in the organ loft,
The carpenter dresses his plank, the tongue of his foreplane whistles
    its wild ascending lisp,

The married and unmarried children ride home to their Thanksgiving
   dinner,
The pilot seizes the king-pin, he heaves down with a strong arm,
The mate stands braced in the whale-boat, lance and harpoon are
   ready,
The duck-shooter walks by silent and cautious stretches,
The deacons are ordain'd with cross'd hands at the altar,
The spinning-girl retreats and advances to the hum of the big wheel,
The farmer stops by the bars as he walks on a First-day loafe and
   looks at the oats and rye,
The lunatic is carried at last to the asylum a confirm'd case,
(He will never sleep any more as he did in the cot in his mother's
   bed-room;)
The jour° printer with gray head and gaunt jaws works at his case,
He turns his quid of tobacco while his eyes blurr with the manu-
   script;
The malform'd limbs are tied to the surgeon's table,
What is removed drops horribly in a pail;
The quadroon girl is sold at the auction-stand, the drunkard nods by
   the bar-room stove,
The machinist rolls up his sleeves, the policeman travels his beat, the
   gate-keeper marks who pass,
The young fellow drives the express-wagon, (I love him, though I do
   not know him;)
The half-breed straps on his light boots to compete in the race,
The western turkey-shooting draws old and young, some lean on their
   rifles, some sit on logs,
Out from the crowd steps the marksman, takes his position, levels his
   piece;
The groups of newly-come immigrants cover the wharf or levee,
As the woolly-pates hoe in the sugar-field, the overseer views them
   from his saddle,
The bugle calls in the ball-room, the gentlemen run for their partners,
   the dancers bow to each other,
The youth lies awake in the cedar-roof'd garret and harks to the
   musical rain,
The Wolverine sets traps on the creek that helps fill the Huron,
The squaw wrapt in her yellow-hemm'd cloth is offering moccasins
   and bead-bags for sale,
The connoisseur peers along the exhibition-gallery with half-shut eyes
   bent sideways,
As the deck-hands make fast the steamboat the plank is thrown for
   the shore-going passengers,
The young sister holds out the skein while the elder sister winds it
   off in a ball, and stops now and then for the knots,
The one-year wife is recovering and happy having a week ago borne
   her first child,
The clean-hair'd Yankee girl works with her sewing-machine or in the
   factory or mill,

The paving-man leans on his two-handed rammer, the reporter's lead
    flies swiftly over the note-book, the sign-painter is lettering with
    blue and gold.
The canal boy trots on the tow-path, the book-keeper counts at his
    desk, the shoemaker waxes his thread,
The conductor beats time for the band and all the performers follow
    him,
The child is baptized, the convert is making his first professions,
The regatta is spread on the bay, the race is begun, (how the white
    sails sparkle!)
The drover watching his drove sings out to them that would stray,
The pedler sweats with his pack on his back, (the purchaser higgling*
    about the odd cent;)
The bride unrumples her white dress, the minute-hand of the clock
    moves slowly,
The opium-eater reclines with rigid head and just-open'd lips,
The prostitute draggles her shawl, her bonnet bobs on her tipsy and
    pimpled neck,
The crowd laugh at her blackguard oaths, the men jeer and wink to
    each other,
(Miserable! I do not laugh at your oaths nor jeer you;)
The President holding a cabinet council is surrounded by the great
    Secretaries,
On the piazza walk three matrons stately and friendly with twined
    arms,
The crew of the fish-smack pack repeated layers of halibut in the
    hold,
The Missourian crosses the plains toting his wares and his cattle,
As the fare-collector goes through the train he gives notice by the
    jingling of loose change,
The floor-men are laying the floor, the tinners are tinning the roof, the
    masons are calling for mortar,
In single file each shouldering his hod pass onward the laborers;
Seasons pursuing each other the indescribable crowd is gather'd, it is
    the fourth of Seventh-month, (what salutes of cannon and
    small arms!)
Seasons pursuing each other the plougher ploughs, the mower mows,
    and the winter-grain falls in the ground;
Off on the lakes the pike-fisher watches and waits by the hole in the
    frozen surface,
The stumps stand thick round the clearing, the squatter strikes deep
    with his axe,
Flatboatmen make fast towards dusk near the cotton-wood or pecan-
    trees,
Coon-seekers go through the regions of the Red river or through those
    drain'd by the Tennessee, or through those of the Arkansas,
Torches shine in the dark that hangs on the Chattahooche or Altama-
    haw,

Patriarchs sit at supper with sons and grandsons and great grandsons
 around them,
In walls of adobie, in canvas tents, rest hunters and trappers after
 their day's sport,
The city sleeps and the country sleeps,
The living sleep for their time, the dead sleep for their time,
The old husband sleeps by his wife and the young husband sleeps by
 his wife;
And these tend inward to me, and I tend outward to them,
And such as it is to be of these more or less I am,
And of these one and all I weave the song of myself.

16

I am of old and young, of the foolish as much as the wise,
Regardless of others, ever regardful of others,
Maternal as well as paternal, a child as well as a man,
Stuff'd with the stuff that is coarse and stuff'd with the stuff that is
 fine,
One of the Nation of many nations, the smallest the same and the
 largest the same,
A Southerner soon as a Northerner, a planter nonchalant and hos-
 pitable down by the Oconee I live,
A Yankee bound my own way ready for trade, my joints the limberest
 joints on earth and the sternest joints on earth,
A Kentuckian walking the vale of the Elkhorn in my deerskin leggings,
 a Louisianian or Georgian,
A boatman over lakes or bays or along coasts, a Hoosier, Badger,
 Buckeye;
At home on Kanadian snow-shoes or up in the bush, or with fishermen
 off Newfoundland,
At home in the fleet of ice-boats, sailing with the rest and tacking,
At home on the hills of Vermont or in the woods of Maine, or the
 Texan ranch,
Comrade of Californians, comrade of free North-Westerners, (loving
 their big proportions,)
Comrade of raftsmen and coalmen, comrade of all who shake hands
 and welcome to drink and meat,
A learner with the simplest, a teacher of the thoughtfullest,
A novice beginning yet experient of myriads of seasons,
Of every hue and caste am I, of every rank and religion,
A farmer, mechanic, artist, gentleman, sailor, quaker,
Prisoner, fancy-man, rowdy, lawyer, physician, priest.

I resist any thing better than my own diversity,
Breathe the air but leave plenty after me,
And am not stuck up, and am in my place.

(The moth and the fish-eggs are in their place,
The bright suns I see and the dark suns I cannot see are in their place,
The palpable is in its place and the impalpable in its place.)

17

These are really the thoughts of all men in all ages and lands, they
are not original with me,
If they are not yours as much as mine they are nothing, or next to
nothing.
If they are not the riddle and the untying of the riddle they are
nothing,
If they are not just as close as they are distant they are nothing.

This is the grass that grows wherever the land is and the water is,
This the common air that bathes the globe.

18

With music strong I come, with my cornets and my drums,
I play not marches for accepted victors only, I play marches for conquer'd and slain persons.

Have you heard that it was good to gain the day?
I also say it is good to fall, battles are lost in the same spirit in which
they are won.

I beat and pound for the dead,
I blow through my enbouchures* my loudest and gayest for them.

Vivas to those who have fail'd!
And to those whose war-vessels sank in the sea!
And to those themselves who sank in the sea!
And to all generals that lost engagements, and all overcome heroes!
And the numberless unknown heroes equal to the greatest heroes
known!

19

This is the meal equally set, this the meat for natural hunger,
It is for the wicked just the same as the righteous, I make appoint-
ments with all,
I will not have a single person slighted or left away,
The kept-woman, sponger, thief, are hereby invited,
The heavy-lipp'd slave is invited, the venerealee is invited;
There shall be no difference between them and the rest.

This is the press of a bashful hand, this the float* and odor of hair,
This the touch of my lips to yours, this the murmur of yearning,
This the far-off depth and height reflecting my own face,
This the thoughtful merge of myself, and the outlet again.

Do you guess I have some intricate purpose?
Well I have, for the Fourth-month showers have, and the mica on the
side of a rock has.

Do you take it I would astonish?
Does the daylight astonish? does the early redstart twittering through
  the woods?
Do I astonish more than they?

This hour I tell things in confidence,
I might not tell everybody, but I will tell you.

20

Who goes there? hankering, gross, mystical, nude;
How is it I extract strength from the beef I eat?

What is a man anyhow? what am I? what are you?

All I mark as my own you shall offset it with your own,
Else it were time lost listening to me.

I do not snivel that snivel the world over,
The months are vacuums and the ground but wallow and filth.

Whimpering and truckling fold with powders for invalids, conformity
  goes to the fourth-remov'd,
I wear my hat as I please indoors or out.

Why should I pray? why should I venerate and be ceremonious?

Having pried through the strata, analyzed to a hair, counsel'd with
  doctors and calculated close,
I find no sweeter fat than sticks to my own bones.

In all people I see myself, none more and not one a barley-corn less,
And the good or bad I say of myself I say of them.

I know I am solid and sound,
To me the converging objects of the universe perpetually flow,
All are written to me, and I must get what the writing means.

I know I am deathless,
I know this orbit of mine cannot be swept by a carpenter's compass,
I know I shall not pass like a child's carlacue* cut with a burnt stick
  at night.

I know I am august,
I do not trouble my spirit to vindicate itself or be understood,
I see that the elementary laws never apologize,
(I reckon I behave no prouder than the level I plant my house by,
  after all.)

I exist as I am, that is enough,
If no other in the world be aware I sit content,
And if each and all be aware I sit content.

One world is aware and by far the largest to me, and that is myself,
And whether I come to my own to-day or in ten thousand or ten
    million years,
I can cheerfully take it now, or with equal cheerfulness I can wait.

My foothold is tenon'd and mortis'd° in granite,
I laugh at what you call dissolution,
And I know the amplitude of time.

21

I am the poet of the Body and I am the poet of the Soul,
The pleasures of heaven are with me and the pains of hell are with
    me,
The first I graft and increase upon myself, the latter I translate into a
    new tongue.

I am the poet of the woman the same as the man,
And I say it is as great to be a woman as to be a man,
And I say there is nothing greater than the mother of men.

I chant the chant of dilation or pride,
We have had ducking and deprecating about enough,
I show that size is only development.

Have you outstript the rest? are you the President?
It is a trifle, they will more than arrive there every one, and still pass
    on.

I am he that walks with the tender and growing night,
I call to the earth and sea half-held by the night.

Press close bare-bosom'd night—press close magnetic nourishing night!
Night of south winds—night of the large few stars!
Still nodding night—mad naked summer night.

Smile O voluptuous cool-breath'd earth!
Earth of the slumbering and liquid trees!
Earth of departed sunset—earth of the mountains misty-topt!
Earth of the vitreous pour of the full moon just tinged with blue!
Earth of shine and dark mottling the tide of the river!
Earth of the limpid gray of clouds brighter and clearer for my sake!
Far-swooping elbow'd earth—rich apple-blossom'd earth!
Smile, for your lover comes.

Prodigal, you have given me love—therefore I to you give love!
O unspeakable passionate love.

22

You sea! I resign myself to you also—I guess what you mean,
I behold from the beach your crooked inviting fingers,

I believe you refuse to go back without feeling of me,
We must have a turn together, I undress, hurry me out of sight of the
      land,
Cushion me soft, rock me in billowy drowse,
Dash me with amorous wet, I can repay you.

Sea of stretch'd ground-swells,
Sea breathing broad and convulsive breaths,
Sea of the brine of life and of unshovell'd yet always-ready graves,
Howler and scooper of storms, capricious and dainty sea,
I am integral with you, I too am of one phase and of all phases.

Partaker of influx and efflux I, extoller of hate and conciliation,
Extoller of amies* and those that sleep in each others' arms,
I am he attesting sympathy,
(Shall I make my list of things in the house and skip the house that
      supports them?)

I am not the poet of goodness only, I do not decline to be the poet of
      wickedness also.

What blurt is this about virtue and about vice?
Evil propels me and reform of evil propels me, I stand indifferent,
My gait is no fault-finder's or rejecter's gait,
I moisten the roots of all that has grown.

Did you fear some scrofula out of the unflagging pregnancy?
Did you guess the celestial laws are yet to be work'd over and rectified?

I find one side a balance and the antipodal side a balance,
Soft doctrine as steady help as stable doctrine,
Thoughts and deeds of the present our rouse and early start.

This minute that comes to me over the past decillions,
There is no better than it and now.

What behaved well in the past or behaves well to-day is not such a
      wonder,
The wonder is always and always how there can be a mean man or
      an infidel.

23

Endless unfolding of words of ages!
And mine a word of the modern, the word En-Masse.*

A word of the faith that never balks,
Here or henceforward it is all the same to me, I accept Time abso-
      lutely.

It alone is without flaw, it alone rounds and completes all,
That mystic baffling wonder alone completes all.

I accept Reality and dare not question it,
Materialism first and last imbuing.

Hurrah for positive science! long live exact demonstration!
Fetch stonecrop* mixt with cedar and branches of lilac,
This is the lexicographer, this the chemist, this made a grammar of
the old cartouches,*
These mariners put the ship through dangerous unknown seas,
This is the geologist, this works with the scalpel, and this is a mathe-
matician.

Gentlemen, to you the first honors always!
Your facts are useful, and yet they are not my dwelling,
I but enter by them to an area of my dwelling.

Less the reminders of properties told my words,
And more the reminders they of life untold, and of freedom and extrication,
And make short account of neuters and geldings, and favor men and
women fully equipt,
And beat the gong of revolt, and stop with fugitives and them that
plot and conspire.

24

Walt Whitman, a kosmos,* of Manhattan the son,
Turbulent, fleshy, sensual, eating, drinking and breeding,
No sentimentalist, no stander above men and women or apart from
them,
No more modest than immodest.

Unscrew the locks from the doors!
Unscrew the doors themselves from their jambs!

Whoever degrades another degrades me,
And whatever is done or said returns at last to me.

Through me the afflatus* surging and surging, through me the current
and index.

I speak the pass-word primeval, I give the sign of democracy,
By God! I will accept nothing which all cannot have their counterpart
of on the same terms.

Through me many long dumb voices,
Voices of the interminable generations of prisoners and slaves,
Voices of the diseas'd and despairing and of thieves and dwarfs,
Voices of cycles of preparation and accretion,

And of the threads that connect the stars, and of wombs and of the
     father-stuff,
And of the rights of them the others are down upon,
Of the deform'd, trivial, flat, foolish, despised,
Fog in the air, beetles rolling balls of dung.

Through me forbidden voices,
Voices of sexes and lusts, voices veil'd and I remove the veil,
Voices indecent by me clarified and transfigur'd.

I do not press my fingers across my mouth,
I keep as delicate around the bowels as around the head and heart,
Copulation is no more rank to me than death is.

I believe in the flesh and the appetites,
Seeing, hearing, feeling, are miracles, and each part and tag of me is
     a miracle.

Divine am I inside and out, and I make holy whatever I touch or am
     touch'd from,
The scent of these arm-pits aroma finer than prayer,
This head more than churches, bibles, and all the creeds.

If I worship one thing more than another it shall be the spread of my
     own body, or any part of it,
Translucent mould of me it shall be you!
Shaded ledges and rests it shall be you!
Firm masculine colter° it shall be you!
Whatever goes to the tilth° of me it shall be you!
You my rich blood! your milky stream pale strippings of my life!
Breast that presses against other breasts it shall be you!
My brain it shall be your occult convolutions!
Root of wash'd sweet-flag! timorous pond-snipe! nest of guarded dupli-
     cate eggs! it shall be you!
Mix'd tussled hay of head, beard, brawn, it shall be you!
Trickling sap of maple, fibre of manly wheat, it shall be you!
Sun so generous it shall be you!
Vapors lighting and shading my face it shall be you!
You sweaty brooks and dews it shall be you!
Winds whose soft-tickling genitals rub against me it shall be you!
Broad muscular fields, branches of live oak, loving lounger in my
     winding paths, it shall be you!
Hands I have taken, face I have kiss'd, mortal I have ever touch'd, it
     shall be you.

I dote on myself, there is that lot of me and all so luscious,
Each moment and whatever happens thrills me with joy,
I cannot tell how my ankles bend, nor whence the cause of my
     faintest wish,

Nor the cause of the friendship I emit, nor the cause of the friendship
I take again.

That I walk up my stoop, I pause to consider if it really be,
A morning-glory at my window satisfies me more than the metaphysics
of books.

To behold the day-break!
The little light fades the immense and diaphanous shadows,
The air tastes good to my palate.

Hefts* of the moving world at innocent gambols silently rising, freshly
exuding,
Scooting obliquely high and low.

Something I cannot see puts upward libidinous prongs,
Seas of bright juice suffuse heaven.

The earth by the sky staid with, the daily close of their junction,
The heav'd challenge from the east that moment over my head,
The mocking taunt, See then whether you shall be master!

25

Dazzling and tremendous how quick the sun-rise would kill me,
If I could not now and always send sun-rise out of me.

We also ascend dazzling and tremendous as the sun,
We found our own O my soul in the calm and cool of the day-break.

My voice goes after what my eyes cannot reach,
With the twirl of my tongue I encompass worlds and volumes of
worlds.

Speech is the twin of my vision, it is unequal to measure itself,
It provokes me forever, it says sarcastically,
Walt you contain enough, why don't you let it out then?

Come now I will not be tantalized, you conceive too much of articula-
tion,
Do you not know O speech how the buds beneath you are folded?
Waiting in gloom, protected by frost,
The dirt receding before my prophetical screams,
I underlying causes to balance them at last,
My knowledge my live parts, it keeping tally with the meaning of all
things,
Happiness, (which whoever hears me let him or her set out in search
of this day.)

My final merit I refuse you, I refuse putting from me what I really am,
Encompass worlds, but never try to encompass me,
I crowd your sleekest and best by simply looking toward you.

Writing and talk do not prove me,
I carry the plenum° of proof and every thing else in my face,
With the hush of my lips I wholly confound the skeptic.

26

Now I will do nothing but listen,
To accrue what I hear into this song, to let sounds contribute toward
  it.

I hear bravuras of birds, bustle of growing wheat, gossip of flames,
  clack of sticks cooking my meals,
I hear the sound I love, the sound of the human voice,
I hear all sounds running together, combined, fused or following,
Sounds of the city and sounds out of the city, sounds of the day and
  night,
Talkative young ones to those that like them, the loud laugh of work-
  people at their meals,
The angry base of disjointed friendship, the faint tones of the sick,
The judge with hands tight to the desk, his pallid lips pronouncing
  a death-sentence,
The heave'e'yo of stevedores unlading ships by the wharves, the re-
  frain of the anchor-lifters,
The ring of alarm-bells, the cry of fire, the whirr of swift-streaking
  engines and hose-carts with premonitory tinkles and color'd
  lights,
The steam-whistle, the solid roll of the train of approaching cars,
The slow march play'd at the head of the association marching two
  and two,
(They go to guard some corpse, the flag-tops are draped with black
  muslin.)

I hear the violoncello, ('tis the young man's heart's complaint,)
I hear the key'd cornet, it glides quickly in through my ears,
It shakes mad-sweet pangs through my belly and breast.

I hear the chorus, it is a grand opera,
Ah this indeed is music—this suits me.

A tenor large and fresh as the creation fills me,
The orbic flex of his mouth is pouring and filling me full.

I hear the train'd soprano (what work with hers is this?)
The orchestra whirls me wider than Uranus flies,
It wrenches such ardors from me I did not know I possess'd them,
It sails me, I dab with bare feet, they are lick'd by the indolent waves,

I am cut by bitter and angry hail, I lose my breath,
Steep'd amid honey'd morphine, my windpipe throttled in fakes of
    death,
At length let up again to feel the puzzle of puzzles,
And that we call Being.

27

To be in any form, what is that?
(Round and round we go, all of us, and ever come back thither,)
If nothing lay more develop'd the quahaug in its callous shell were
    enough.

Mine is no callous shell,
I have instant conductors all over me whether I pass or stop,
They seize every object and lead it harmlessly through me.

I merely stir, press, feel with my fingers, and am happy,
To touch my person to some one else's is about as much as I can stand.

28

Is this then a touch? quivering me to a new identity,
Flames and ether making a rush for my veins,
Treacherous tip of me reaching and crowding to help them,
My flesh and blood playing out lightning to strike what is hardly dif-
    ferent from myself,
On all sides prurient provokers stiffening my limbs,
Straining the udder of my heart for its withheld drip,
Behaving licentious toward me, taking no denial,
Depriving me of my best as for a purpose,
Unbuttoning my clothes, holding me by the bare waist,
Deluding my confusion with the calm of the sunlight and pasture-
    fields,
Immodestly sliding the fellow-senses away,
They bribed to swap off with touch and go and graze at the edges
    of me,
No consideration, no regard for my draining strength or my anger,
Fetching the rest of the herd around to enjoy them a while,
Then all uniting to stand on a headland and worry me.

The sentries desert every other part of me,
They have left me helpless to a red marauder,
They all come to the headland to witness and assist against me.

I am given up by traitors,
I talk wildly, I have lost my wits, I and nobody else am the greatest
    traitor,
I went myself first to the headland, my own hands carried me there.

You villain touch! what are you doing? my breath is tight in its
    throat,
Unclench your floodgates, you are too much for me.

29

Blind loving wrestling touch, sheath'd hooded sharp-tooth'd touch!
Did it make you ache so, leaving me?

Parting track'd by arriving, perpetual payment of perpetual loan,
Rich showering rain, and recompense richer afterward.

Sprouts take and accumulate, stand by the curb prolific and vital,
Landscapes projected masculine, full-sized and golden.

30

All truths wait in all things,
They neither hasten their own delivery nor resist it,
They do not need the obstetric forceps of the surgeon,
The insignificant is as big to me as any,
(What is less or more than a touch?)

Logic and sermons never convince,
The damp of the night drives deeper into my soul.

(Only what proves itself to every man and woman is so,
Only what nobody denies is so.)

A minute and a drop of me settle my brain,
I believe the soggy clods shall become lovers and lamps,
And a compend* of compends is the meat of a man or woman,
And a summit and flower there is the feeling they have for each other,
And they are to branch boundlessly out of that lesson until it becomes
    omnific,*
And until one and all shall delight us, and we them.

31

I believe a leaf of grass is no less than the journey-work of the stars,
And the pismire* is equally perfect, and a grain of sand, and the egg
    of the wren,
And the tree-toad is a chef-d'œuvre* for the highest,
And the running blackberry would adorn the parlors of heaven,
And the narrowest hinge in my hand puts to scorn all machinery,
And the cow crunching with depress'd head surpasses any statue,
And a mouse is miracle enough to stagger sextillions of infidels.

I find I incorporate gneiss, coal, long-threaded moss, fruits, grains,
    esculent roots,
And am stucco'd with quadrupeds and birds all over,
And have distanced what is behind me for good reasons,
But call any thing back again when I desire it.

In vain the speeding or shyness,
In vain the plutonic rocks send their old heat against my approach,
In vain the mastodon retreats beneath its own powder'd bones,
In vain objects stand leagues off and assume manifold shapes,
In vain the ocean settling in hollows and the great monsters lying low,
In vain the buzzard houses herself with the sky,
In vain the snake slides through the creepers and logs,
In vain the elk takes to the inner passes of the woods,
In vain the razor-bill'd auk sails far north to Labrador,
I follow quickly, I ascend to the nest in the fissure of the cliff.

32

I think I could turn and live with animals, they're so placid and self-
    contain'd,
I stand and look at them long and long.

They do not sweat and whine about their condition,
They do not lie awake in the dark and weep for their sins,
They do not make me sick discussing their duty to God,
Not one is dissatisfied, not one is demented with the mania of owning
    things,
Not one kneels to another, nor to his kind that lived thousands of
    years ago,
Not one is respectable or unhappy over the whole earth.

So they show their relations to me and I accept them,
They bring me tokens of myself, they evince them plainly in their
    possession.

I wonder where they get those tokens,
Did I pass that way huge times ago and negligently drop them?

Myself moving forward then and now and forever,
Gathering and showing more always and with velocity,
Infinite and omnigenous,* and the like of these among them,
Not too exclusive toward the reachers of my remembrancers,
Picking out here one that I love, and now go with him on brotherly
    terms.

A gigantic beauty of a stallion, fresh and responsive to my caresses,
Head high in the forehead, wide between the ears,
Limbs glossy and supple, tail dusting the ground,
Eyes full of sparkling wickedness, ears finely cut, flexibly moving.

His nostrils dilate as my heels embrace him,
His well-built limbs tremble with pleasure as we race around and
    return.

I but use you a minute, then I resign you, stallion,
Why do I need your paces when I myself out-gallop them?
Even as I stand or sit passing faster than you.

33

Space and Time! now I see it is true, what I guess'd at,
What I guess'd when I loaf'd on the grass,
What I guess'd while I lay alone in my bed,
And again as I walk'd the beach under the paling stars of the morning.

My ties and ballasts leave me, my elbows rest in sea-gaps,
I skirt sierras, my palms cover continents,
I am afoot with my vision.

By the city's quadrangular houses—in log huts, camping with lumber-
    men,
Along the ruts of the turnpike, along the dry gulch and rivulet bed,
Weeding my onion-patch or hoeing rows of carrots and parsnips,
    crossing savannas, trailing in forests,
Prospecting, gold-digging, girdling the trees of a new purchase,
Scorch'd ankle-deep by the hot sand, hauling my boat down the
    shallow river,
Where the panther walks to and fro on a limb overhead, where the
    buck turns furiously at the hunter,
Where the rattlesnake suns his flabby length on a rock, where the
    otter is feeding on fish,
Where the alligator in his tough pimples sleeps by the bayou,
Where the black bear is searching for roots or honey, where the
    beaver pats the mud with his paddle-shaped tail;
Over the growing sugar, over the yellow-flower'd cotton plant, over
    the rice in its low moist field,
Over the sharp-peak'd farm house, with its scallop'd scum° and slender
    shoots from the gutters,
Over the western persimmon, over the long-leav'd corn, over the
    delicate blue-flower flax,
Over the white and brown buckwheat, a hummer and buzzer there
    with the rest,
Over the dusky green of the rye as it ripples and shades in the breeze;
Scaling mountains, pulling myself cautiously up, holding on by low
    scragged° limbs,
Walking the path worn in the grass and beat through the leaves of
    the brush,
Where the quail is whistling betwixt the woods and the wheat-lot,
Where the bat flies in the Seventh-month eve, where the great gold-
    bug drops through the dark,
Where the brook puts out of the roots of the old tree and flows to the
    meadow,
Where cattle stand and shake away flies with the tremulous shudder-
    ing of their hides,
Where the cheese-cloth hangs in the kitchen, where andirons straddle
    the hearth-slab, where cobwebs fall in festoons from the
    rafters;

Where trip-hammers crash, where the press is whirling its cylinders,
Where the human heart beats with terrible throes under its ribs,
Where the pear-shaped balloon is floating aloft, (floating in it myself
    and looking composedly down,)
Where the life-car* is drawn on the slip-noose, where the heat hatches
    pale-green eggs in the dented sand,
Where the she-whale swims with her calf and never forsakes it,
Where the steam-ship trails hind-ways its long pennant of smoke,
Where the fin of the shark cuts like a black chip out of the water,
Where the half-burn'd brig is riding on unknown currents,
Where shells grow to her slimy deck, where the dead are corrupting
    below;
Where the dense-starr'd flag is borne at the head of the regiments,
Approaching Manhattan up by the long-stretching island,
Under Niagara, the cataract falling like a veil over my countenance,
Upon a door-step, upon the horse-block of hard wood outside,
Upon the race-course, or enjoying picnics or jigs or a good game of
    base-ball,
At he-festivals, with blackguard jibes, ironical license, bull-dances,
    drinking, laughter,
At the cider-mill tasting the sweets of the brown mash, sucking the
    juice through a straw,
At apple-peelings wanting kisses for all the red fruit I find,
At musters, beach-parties, friendly bees, huskings, house-raisings,
Where the mocking-bird sounds his delicious gurgles, cackles, screams,
    weeps,
Where the hay-rick stands in the barn-yard, where the dry-stalks are
    scatter'd, where the brood-cow waits in the hovel,
Where the bull advances to do his masculine work, where the stud to
    the mare, where the cock is treading the hen,
Where the heifers browse, where geese nip their food with short
    jerks,
Where sun-down shadows lengthen over the limitless and lonesome
    prairie,
Where herds of buffalo make a crawling spread of the square miles
    far and near,
Where the humming-bird shimmers, where the neck of the long-lived
    swan is curving and winding,
Where the laughing-gull scoots by the shore, where she laughs her
    near-human laugh,
Where bee-hives range on a gray bench in the garden half hid by the
    high weeds,
Where band-neck'd partridges roost in a ring on the ground with
    their heads out,
Where burial coaches enter the arch'd gates of a cemetery,
Where winter wolves bark amid wastes of snow and icicled trees,
Where the yellow-crown'd heron comes to the edge of the marsh at
    night and feeds upon small crabs,
Where the splash of swimmers and divers cools the warm noon,

Where the katy-did works her chromatic reed on the walnut-tree over
the well,
Through patches of citrons and cucumbers with silver-wired leaves,
Through the salt-lick or orange glade, or under conical firs,
Through the gymnasium, through the curtain'd saloon, through the
office or public hall;
Pleas'd with the native and pleas'd with the foreign, pleas'd with the
new and old,
Pleas'd with the homely woman as well as the handsome,
Pleas'd with the quakeress as she puts off her bonnet and talks
melodiously,
Pleas'd with the tune of the choir of the whitewash'd church,
Pleas'd with the earnest words of the sweating Methodist preacher,
impress'd seriously at the camp-meeting;
Looking in at the shop-windows of Broadway the whole forenoon,
flatting the flesh of my nose on the thick plate glass,
Wandering the same afternoon with my face turn'd up to the clouds,
or down a lane or along the beach,
My right and left arms round the sides of two friends, and I in the
middle;
Coming home with the silent and dark-cheek'd bush-boy, (behind me
he rides at the drape of the day,)
Far from the settlements studying the print of animals' feet, or the
moccasin print,
By the cot in the hospital reaching lemonade to a feverish patient,
Nigh the coffin'd corpse when all is still, examining with a candle;
Voyaging to every port to dicker and adventure,
Hurrying with the modern crowd as eager and fickle as any,
Hot toward one I hate, ready in my madness to knife him,
Solitary at midnight in my back yard, my thoughts gone from me a
long while,
Walking the old hills of Judæa with the beautiful gentle God by my
side,
Speeding through space, speeding through heaven and the stars,
Speeding amid the seven satellites and the broad ring, and the
diameter of eighty thousand miles,
Speeding with tail'd meteors, throwing fire-balls like the rest,
Carrying the crescent child that carries its own full mother in its belly,
Storming, enjoying, planning, loving, cautioning,
Backing and filling, appearing and disappearing,
I tread day and night such roads.

I visit the orchards of spheres and look at the product,
And look at quintillions ripen'd and look at quintillions green.

I fly those flights of a fluid and swallowing soul,
My course runs below the soundings of plummets.

I help myself to material and immaterial,
No guard can shut me off, no law prevent me.

I anchor my ship for a little while only,
My messengers continually cruise away or bring their returns to me.

I go hunting polar furs and the seal, leaping chasms with a pike-
pointed staff, clinging to topples of brittle and blue.

I ascend to the foretruck,*
I take my place late at night in the crow's-nest,
We sail the arctic sea, it is plenty light enough,
Through the clear atmosphere I stretch around on the wonderful
beauty,
The enormous masses of ice pass me and I pass them, the scenery is
plain in all directions,
The white-topt mountains show in the distance, I fling out my fancies
toward them,
We are approaching some great battle-field in which we are soon to
be engaged,
We pass the colossal outposts of the encampment, we pass with still
feet and caution,
Or we are entering by the suburbs some vast and ruin'd city,
The blocks and fallen architecture more than all the living cities of
the globe.

I am a free companion, I bivouac by invading watchfires,
I turn the bridegroom out of bed and stay with the bride myself,
I tighten her all night to my thighs and lips.

My voice is the wife's voice, the screech by the rail of the stairs,
They fetch my man's body up dripping and drown'd.

I understand the large hearts of heroes,
The courage of present times and all times,
How the skipper saw the crowded and rudderless wreck of the steam-
ship, and Death chasing it up and down the storm,
How he knuckled tight and gave not back an inch, and was faithful
of days and faithful of nights,
And chalk'd in large letters on a board, *Be of good cheer, we will not
desert you;*
How he follow'd with them and tack'd with them three days and
would not give it up,
How he saved the drifting company at last,
How the lank loose-gown'd women look'd when boated from the side
of their prepared graves,
How the silent old-faced infants and the lifted sick, and the sharp-
lipp'd unshaved men;
All this I swallow, it tastes good, I like it well, it becomes mine,
I am the man, I suffer'd, I was there.

The disdain and calmness of martyrs,
The mother of old, condemn'd for a witch, burnt with dry wood, her
    children gazing on,
The hounded slave that flags in the race, leans by the fence, blowing,
    cover'd with sweat,
The twinges that sting like needles his legs and neck, the murderous
    buckshot and the bullets,
All these I feel or am.

I am the hounded slave, I wince at the bite of the dogs,
Hell and despair are upon me, crack and again crack the marksmen,
I clutch the rails of the fence, my gore dribs,* thinn'd with the ooze of
    my skin,
I fall on the weeds and stones,
The riders spur their unwilling horses, haul close,
Taunt my dizzy ears and beat me violently over the head with whip-
    stocks.

Agonies are one of my changes of garments.
I do not ask the wounded person how he feels, I myself become the
    wounded person,
My hurts turn livid upon me as I lean on a cane and observe.

I am the mash'd fireman with breast-bone broken,
Tumbling walls buried me in their debris,
Heat and smoke I inspired,* I heard the yelling shouts of my com-
    rades,
I heard the distant click of their picks and shovels,
They have clear'd the beams away, they tenderly lift me forth.

I lie in the night air in my red shirt, the pervading hush is for my sake,
Painless after all I lie exhausted but not so unhappy,
White and beautiful are the faces around me, the heads are bared of
    their fire-caps,
The kneeling crowd fades with the light of the torches.

Distant and dead resuscitate,
They show me as the dial or move as the hands of me, I am the clock
    myself.

I am an old artillerist, I tell of my fort's bombardment,
I am there again.

Again the long roll of the drummers,
Again the attacking cannon, mortars,
Again to my listening ears the cannon responsive.

I take part, I see and hear the whole,
The cries, curses, roar, the plaudits for well-aim'd shots,

The ambulanza* slowly passing trailing its red drip,
Workmen searching after damages, making indispensable repairs,
The fall of grenades through the rent roof, the fan-shaped explosion,
The whizz of limbs, heads, stone, wood, iron, high in the air.

Again gurgles the mouth of my dying general, he furiously waves with
    his hand,
He gasps through the clot *Mind not me—mind—the entrenchments.*

34

Now I tell what I knew in Texas in my early youth,
(I tell not the fall of Alamo,
Not one escaped to tell the fall of Alamo,
The hundred and fifty are dumb yet at Alamo,)
'Tis the tale of the murder in cold blood of four hundred and twelve
    young men.

Retreating they had form'd in a hollow square with their baggage for
    breastworks,
Nine hundred lives out of the surrounding enemy's, nine times their
    number, was the price they took in advance,
Their colonel was wounded and their ammunition gone,
They treated for an honorable capitulation, receiv'd writing and seal,
    gave up their arms and march'd back prisoners of war.

They were the glory of the race of rangers,
Matchless with horse, rifle, song, supper, courtship,
Large, turbulent, generous, handsome, proud, and affectionate,
Bearded, sunburnt, drest in the free costume of hunters,
Not a single one over thirty years of age.

The second First-day morning they were brought out in squads and
    massacred, it was beautiful early summer,
The work commenced about five o'clock and was over by eight.

None obey'd the command to kneel,
Some made a mad and helpless rush, some stood stark and straight,
A few fell at once, shot in the temple or heart, the living and dead lay
    together,
The maim'd and mangled dug in the dirt, the new-comers saw them
    there,
Some half-kill'd attempted to crawl away,
These were despatch'd with bayonets or batter'd with the blunts of
    muskets,
A youth not seventeen years old seiz'd his assassin till two more came
    to release him,
The three were all torn and cover'd with the boy's blood.

At eleven o'clock began the burning of the bodies;
That is the tale of the murder of the four hundred and twelve young
    men.

35

Would you hear of an old-time sea-fight?
Would you learn who won by the light of the moon and stars?
List to the yarn, as my grandmother's father the sailor told it to me.

Our foe was no skulk in his ship I tell you, (said he,)
His was the surly English pluck, and there is no tougher or truer, and
      never was, and never will be;
Along the lower'd eve he came horribly raking us.

We closed with him, the yards entangled, the cannon touch'd,
My captain lash'd fast with his own hands.

We had receiv'd some eighteen pound shots under the water,
On our lower-gun-deck two large pieces had burst at the first fire,
      killing all around and blowing up overhead.

Fighting at sun-down, fighting at dark,
Ten o'clock at night, the full moon well up, our leaks on the gain,
      and five feet of water reported,
The master-at-arms loosing the prisoners confined in the after-hold to
      give them a chance for themselves.

The transit to and from the magazine is now stopt by the sentinels,
They see so many strange faces they do not know whom to trust.

Our frigate takes fire,
The other asks if we demand quarter?
If our colors are struck and the fighting done?

Now I laugh content, for I hear the voice of my little captain,
We have not struck, he composedly cries, *we have just begun our part
      of the fighting.*

Only three guns are in use,
One is directed by the captain himself against the enemy's main-mast,
Two well serv'd with grape* and canister* silence his musketry and
      clear his decks.

The tops alone second the fire of this little battery, especially the
      main-top,
They hold out bravely during the whole of the action.

Not a moment's cease,
The leaks gain fast on the pumps, the fire eats toward the powder-
      magazine.

One of the pumps has been shot away, it is generally thought we are
      sinking.

Serene stands the little captain,
He is not hurried, his voice is neither high nor low,
His eyes give more light to us than our battle-lanterns.

Toward twelve there in the beams of the moon they surrender to us.

36

Stretch'd and still lies the midnight,
Two great hulls motionless on the breast of the darkness,
Our vessel riddled and slowly sinking, preparations to pass to the one
  we have conquer'd,
The captain on the quarter-deck coldly giving his orders through a
  countenance white as a sheet,
Near by the corpse of the child that serv'd in the cabin,
The dead face of an old salt with long white hair and carefully curl'd
  whiskers,
The flames spite of all that can be done flickering aloft and below,
The husky voices of the two or three officers yet fit for duty,
Formless stacks of bodies and bodies by themselves, dabs of flesh upon
  the masts and spars,
Cut of cordage, dangle of rigging, slight shock of the soothe of waves,
Black and impassive guns, litter of powder-parcels, strong scent,
A few large stars overhead, silent and mournful shining,
Delicate sniffs of sea-breeze, smells of sedgy grass and fields by the
  shore, death-messages given in charge to survivors,
The hiss of the surgeon's knife, the gnawing teeth of his saw,
Wheeze, cluck, swash* of falling blood, short wild scream, and long,
  dull, tapering groan,
These so, these irretrievable.

37

You laggards there on guard! look to your arms!
In at the conquer'd doors they crowd! I am possess'd!
Embody all presences outlaw'd or suffering,
See myself in prison shaped like another man,
And feel the dull unintermitted pain.

For me the keepers of convicts shoulder their carbines and keep
  watch,
It is I let out in the morning and barr'd at night.

Not a mutineer walks handcuff'd to jail but I am handcuff'd to him
  and walk by his side,
(I am less the jolly one there, and more the silent one with sweat on
  my twitching lips.)

Not a youngster is taken for larceny but I go up too, and am tried and
  sentenced.

Not a cholera patient lies at the last gasp but I also lie at the last gasp,
My face is ash-color'd, my sinews gnarl, away from me people retreat.

Askers embody themselves in me and I am embodied in them,
I project my hat, sit shame-faced, and beg.

38

Enough! enough! enough!
Somehow I have been stunn'd. Stand back!
Give me a little time beyond my cuff'd head, slumbers, dreams, gaping,
I discover myself on the verge of a usual mistake.

That I could forget the mockers and insults!
That I could forget the trickling tears and the blows of the bludgeons
    and hammers!
That I could look with a separate look on my own crucifixion and
    bloody crowning!

I remember now,
I resume the overstaid fraction,
The grave of rock multiplies what has been confided to it, or to any
    graves,
Corpses rise, gashes heal, fastenings roll from me.

I troop forth replenish'd with supreme power, one of an average un-
    ending procession,
Inland and sea-coast we go, and pass all boundary lines,
Our swift ordinances on their way over the whole earth,
The blossoms we wear in our hats the growth of thousands of years.

Eleves,* I salute you! come forward!
Continue your annotations, continue your questionings.

39

The friendly and flowing savage, who is he?
Is he waiting for civilization, or past it and mastering it?

Is he some Southwesterner rais'd out-doors? is he Kanadian?
Is he from the Mississippi country? Iowa, Oregon, California?
The mountains? prairie-life, bush-life? or sailor from the sea?

Wherever he goes men and women accept and desire him,
They desire he should like them, touch them, speak to them, stay with
    them.

Behavior lawless as snow-flakes, words simple as grass, uncomb'd head,
    laughter, and naivetè,
Slow-stepping feet, common features, common modes and emanations,
They descend in new forms from the tips of his fingers,
They are wafted with the odor of his body or breath, they fly out of
    the glance of his eyes.

40

Flaunt of the sunshine I need not your bask—lie over!
You light surfaces only, I force surfaces and depths also.

Earth! you seem to look for something at my hands,
Say, old top-knot, what do you want?

Man or woman, I might tell how I like you, but cannot,
And might tell what it is in me and what it is in you, but cannot,
And might tell that pining I have, that pulse of my nights and days.

Behold, I do not give lectures or a little charity,
When I give I give myself.

You there, impotent, loose in the knees,
Open your scarf'd* chops till I blow grit within you,
Spread your palms and lift the flaps of your pockets,
I am not to be denied, I compel, I have stores plenty and to spare,
And any thing I have I bestow.

I do not ask who you are, that is not important to me,
You can do nothing and be nothing but what I will infold you.

To cotton-field drudge or cleaner of privies I lean,
On his right cheek I put the family kiss,
And in my soul I swear I never will deny him.

On women fit for conception I start bigger and nimbler babes,
(This day I am jetting* the stuff of far more arrogant republics.)

To any one dying, thither I speed and twist the knob of the door,
Turn the bed-clothes toward the foot of the bed,
Let the physician and the priest go home.

I seize the descending man and raise him with resistless will,
O despairer, here is my neck,
By God, you shall not go down! hang your whole weight upon me.

I dilate you with tremendous breath, I buoy you up,
Every room of the house do I fill with an arm'd force,
Lovers of me, bafflers of graves.

Sleep—I and they keep guard all night,
Not doubt, not decease shall dare to lay finger upon you,
I have embraced you, and henceforth possess you to myself,
And when you rise in the morning you will find what I tell you is so

41

I am he bringing help for the sick as they pant on their backs,
And for strong upright men I bring yet more needed help.

I heard what was said of the universe,
Heard it and heard it of several thousand years;
It is middling well as far as it goes—but is that all?

Magnifying and applying come I,
Outbidding at the start the old cautious hucksters,
Taking myself the exact dimensions of Jehovah,
Lithographing Kronos, Zeus his son, and Hercules his grandson,
Buying drafts of Osiris, Isis, Belus, Brahma, Buddha,
In my portfolio placing Manito loose, Allah on a leaf, the crucifix
    engraved,
With Odin and the hideous-faced Mexitli and every idol and image,
Taking them all for what they are worth and not a cent more,
Admitting they were alive and did the work of their days,
(They bore mites as for unfledg'd birds who have now to rise and fly
    and sing for themselves,)
Accepting the rough deific sketches to fill out better in myself, bestow-
    ing them freely on each man and woman I see,
Discovering as much or more in a framer framing a house,
Putting higher claims for him there with his roll'd-up sleeves driving
    the mallet and chisel,
Not objecting to special revelations, considering a curl of smoke or a
    hair on the back of my hand just as curious as any revelation,
Lads ahold of fire-engines and hook-and-ladder ropes no less to me
    than the gods of the antique wars,
Minding their voices peal through the crash of destruction,
Their brawny limbs passing safe over charr'd laths, their white fore-
    heads whole and unhurt out of the flames;
By the mechanic's wife with her babe at her nipple interceding for
    every person born,
Three scythes at harvest whizzing in a row from three lusty angels
    with shirts bagg'd out at their waists,
The snag-tooth'd hostler with red hair redeeming sins past and to
    come,
Selling all he possesses, traveling on foot to fee lawyers for his brother
    and sit by him while he is tried for forgery;
What was strewn in the amplest strewing the square rod about me,
    and not filling the square rod then,
The bull and the bug never worshipp'd half enough,
Dung and dirt more admirable than was dream'd,
The supernatural of no account, myself waiting my time to be one of
    the supremes,
The day getting ready for me when I shall do as much good as the
    best, and be as prodigious;

By my life-lumps! becoming already a creator,
Putting myself here and now to the ambush'd womb of the shadows.

42

A call in the midst of the crowd,
My own voice, orotund sweeping and final.

Come my children,
Come my boys and girls, my women, household and intimates,
Now the performer launches his nerve, he has pass'd his prelude on the reeds within.

Easily written loose-finger'd chords—I feel the thrum of your climax and close.

My head slues round on my neck,
Music rolls, but not from the organ,
Folks are around me, but they are no household of mine.

Ever the hard unsunk ground,
Ever the eaters and drinkers, ever the upward and downward sun, ever the air and the ceaseless tides,
Ever myself and my neighbors, refreshing, wicked, real,
Ever the old inexplicable query, ever that thorn'd thumb, that breath of itches and thirsts,
Ever the vexer's *hoot! hoot!* till we find where the sly one hides and bring him forth,
Ever love, ever the sobbing liquid of life,
Ever the bandage under the chin, ever the trestles of death.

Here and there with dimes on the eyes walking,
To feed the greed of the belly the brains liberally spooning,
Tickets buying, taking, selling, but in to the feast never once going,
Many sweating, ploughing, thrashing, and then the chaff for payment receiving,
A few idly owning, and they the wheat continually claiming.

This is the city and I am one of the citizens,
Whatever interests the rest interests me, politics, wars, markets, newspapers, schools,
The mayor and councils, banks, tariffs, steamships, factories, stocks, stores, real estate and personal estate,

The little plentiful manikins skipping around in collars and tail'd coats,
I am aware who they are, (they are positively not worms or fleas,)
I acknowledge the duplicates of myself, the weakest and shallowest is deathless with me,
What I do and say the same waits for them,
Every thought that flounders in me the same flounders in them.

I know perfectly well my own egotism,
Know my omnivorous lines and must not write any less,
And would fetch you whoever you are flush with myself.

Not words of routine this song of mine,
But abruptly to question, to leap beyond yet nearer bring;
This printed and bound book—but the printer and the printing-office
    boy?
The well-taken photographs—but your wife or friend close and solid
    in your arms?
The black ship mail'd with iron, her mighty guns in her turrets—
    but the pluck of the captain and engineers?
In the houses the dishes and fare and furniture—but the host and
    hostess, and the look out of their eyes?
The sky up there—yet here or next door, or across the way?
The saints and sages in history—but you yourself?
Sermons, creeds, theology—but the fathomless human brain,
And what is reason? and what is love? and what is life?

43

I do not despise you priests, all time, the world over,
My faith is the greatest of faiths and the least of faiths,
Enclosing worship ancient and modern and all between ancient and
    modern,
Believing I shall come again upon the earth after five thousand years,
Waiting responses from oracles, honoring the gods, saluting the sun,
Making a fetich* of the first rock or stump, powowing with sticks in the
    circle of obis,*
Helping the llama or brahmin as he trims the lamps of the idols,
Dancing yet through the streets in a phallic procession, rapt and
    austere in the woods a gymnosophist,*
Drinking mead from the skull-cup, to Shastas and Vedas admirant,*
    minding the Koran,
Walking the teokallis,* spotted with gore from the stone and knife,
    beating the serpent-skin drum,
Accepting the Gospels, accepting him that was crucified, knowing
    assuredly that he is divine,
To the mass kneeling or the puritan's prayer rising, or sitting patiently
    in a pew,
Ranting and frothing in my insane crisis, or waiting dead-like till my
    spirit arouses me,
Looking forth on pavement and land, or outside of pavement and
    land,
Belonging to the winders of the circuit of circuits.

One of that centripetal and centrifugal gang I turn and talk like a
    man leaving charges before a journey.

Down-hearted doubters, dull and excluded,
Frivolous, sullen, moping, angry, affected, dishearten'd, atheistical,
I know every one of you, I know the sea of torment, doubt, despair
    and unbelief.

How the flukes splash!
How they contort rapid as lightning, with spasms and spouts of blood!

Be at peace bloody flukes of doubters and sullen mopers,
I take my place among you as much as among any,
The past is the push of you, me, all, precisely the same,
And what is yet untried and afterward is for you, me, all precisely the
    same.

I do not know what is untried and afterward,
But I know it will in its turn prove sufficient, and cannot fail.

Each who passes is consider'd, each who stops is consider'd, not a
    single one can it fail.

It cannot fail the young man who died and was buried,
Nor the young woman who died and was put by his side,
Nor the little child that peep'd in at the door, and then drew back
    and was never seen again,
Nor the old man who has lived without purpose, and feels it with
    bitterness worse than gall,
Nor him in the poor house tubercled by rum and the bad disorder,
Nor the numberless slaughter'd and wreck'd, nor the brutish koboo°
    call'd the ordure° of humanity,
Nor the sacs merely floating with open mouths for food to slip in,
Nor any thing in the earth, or down in the oldest graves of the earth,
Nor any thing in the myriads of spheres, nor the myriads of myriads
    that inhabit them,
Nor the present, nor the least wisp that is known.

44

It is time to explain myself—let us stand up.

What is known I strip away,
I launch all men and women forward with me into the Unknown.

The clock indicates the moment—but what does eternity indicate?

We have thus far exhausted trillions of winters and summers,
There are trillions ahead, and trillions ahead of them.

Births have brought us richness and variety,
And other births will bring us richness and variety.

I do not call one greater and one smaller,
That which fills its period and place is equal to any.

Were mankind murderous or jealous upon you, my brother, my sister?
I am sorry for you, they are not murderous or jealous upon me,
All has been gentle with me, I keep no account with lamentation,
(What have I to do with lamentation?)

I am an acme of things accomplish'd, and I an encloser of things to be.

My feet strike an apex* of the apices of the stairs,
On every step bunches of ages, and larger bunches between the steps,
All below duly travel'd, and still I mount and mount.

Rise after rise bow the phantoms behind me,
Afar down I see the huge first Nothing, I know I was even there,
I waited unseen and always, and slept through the lethargic mist,
And took my time, and took no hurt from the fetid carbon.

Long I was hugg'd close—long and long.

Immense have been the preparations for me,
Faithful and friendly the arms that have help'd me.

Cycles ferried my cradle, rowing and rowing like cheerful boatmen,
For room to me stars kept aside in their own rings,
They sent influences to look after what was to hold me.

Before I was born out of my mother generations guided me,
My embryo has never been torpid, nothing could overlay it.

For it the nebula cohered to an orb,
The long slow strata piled to rest it on,
Vast vegetables gave it sustenance,
Monstrous sauroids* transported it in their mouths and deposited it
        with care.

All forces have been steadily employ'd to complete and delight me,
Now on this spot I stand with my robust soul.

45

O span of youth! ever-push'd elasticity.
O manhood, balanced, florid and full.

My lovers suffocate me,
Crowding my lips, thick in the pores of my skin,
Jostling me through streets and public halls, coming naked to me at
        night,

Crying by day *Ahoy!* from the rocks of the river, swinging and chirp-
    ing over my head,
Calling my name from flower-beds, vines, tangled underbrush,
Lighting on every moment of my life,
Bussing my body with soft balsamic busses,
Noiselessly passing handfuls out of their hearts and giving them to be
    mine.

Old age superbly rising! O welcome, ineffable grace of dying days!
Every condition promulges* not only itself, it promulges what grows
    after and out of itself,
And the dark hush promulges as much as any.

I open my scuttle* at night and see the far-sprinkled systems,
And all I see multiplied as high as I can cipher edge but the rim of the
    farther systems.

Wider and wider they spread, expanding, always expanding,
Outward and outward and forever outward.

My sun has his sun and round him obediently wheels,
He joins with his partners a group of superior circuit,
And greater sets follow, making specks of the greatest inside them.

There is no stoppage and never can be stoppage,
If I, you, and the worlds, and all beneath or upon their surfaces, were
    this moment reduced back to a pallid float,* it would not avail
    in the long run,
We should surely bring up again where we now stand,
And surely go as much farther, and then farther and farther.

A few quadrillions of eras, a few octillions of cubic leagues, do not
    hazard the span or make it impatient,
They are but parts, any thing is but a part.

See ever so far, there is limitless space outside of that,
Count ever so much, there is limitless time around that.

My rendezvous is appointed, it is certain,
The Lord will be there and wait till I come on perfect terms,
The great Camerado,* the lover true for whom I pine will be there.

46

I know I have the best of time and space, and was never measured
    and never will be measured.

I tramp a perpetual journey, (come listen all!)
My signs are a rain-proof coat, good shoes, and a staff cut from the
    woods,

No friend of mine takes his ease in my chair,
I have no chair, no church, no philosophy,
I lead no man to a dinner-table, library, exchange,
But each man and each woman of you I lead upon a knoll,
My left hand hooking you round the waist,
My right hand pointing to landscapes of continents and the public
    road.

Not I, not any one else can travel that road for you,
You must travel it for yourself.

It is not far, it is within reach,
Perhaps you have been on it since you were born and did not know,
Perhaps it is everywhere on water and on land.

Shoulder your duds dear son, and I will mine, and let us hasten forth,
Wonderful cities and free nations we shall fetch* as we go.

If you tire, give me both burdens, and rest the chuff* of your hand on
    my hip,
And in due time you shall repay the same service to me,
For after we start we never lie by again.

This day before dawn I ascended a hill and look'd at the crowded
    heaven,
And I said to my spirit *When we become the enfolders of those orbs,
    and the pleasure and knowledge of every thing in them, shall
    we be fill'd and satisfied then?*
And my spirit said *No, we but level that lift to pass and continue
    beyond.*

You are also asking me questions and I hear you,
I answer that I cannot answer, you must find out for yourself.

Sit a while dear son,
Here are biscuits to eat and here is milk to drink,
But as soon as you sleep and renew yourself in sweet clothes, I kiss you
    with a good-by kiss and open the gate for your egress hence.

Long enough have you dream'd contemptible dreams,
Now I wash the gum from your eyes,
You must habit yourself to the dazzle of the light and of every moment
    of your life.

Long have you timidly waded holding a plank by the shore,
Now I will you to be a bold swimmer,
To jump off in the midst of the sea, rise again, nod to me, shout, and
    laughingly dash with your hair.

47

I am the teacher of athletes,
He that by me spreads a wider breast than my own proves the width
　　of my own,
He most honors my style who learns under it to destroy the teacher.

The boy I love, the same becomes a man not through derived power,
　　but in his own right,
Wicked rather than virtuous out of conformity or fear,
Fond of his sweetheart, relishing well his steak,
Unrequited love or a slight cutting him worse than sharp steel cuts,
First-rate to ride, to fight, to hit the bull's eye, to sail a skiff, to sing a
　　song or play on the banjo,
Preferring scars and the beard and faces pitted with small-pox over all
　　latherers,
And those well-tann'd to those that keep out of the sun.

I teach straying from me, yet who can stray from me?
I follow you whoever you are from the present hour,
My words itch at your ears till you understand them.

I do not say these things for a dollar or to fill up the time while I wait
　　for a boat,
(It is you talking just as much as myself, I act as the tongue of you,
Tied in your mouth, in mine it begins to be loosen'd.)

I swear I will never again mention love or death inside a house,
And I swear I will never translate myself at all, only to him or her
　　who privately stays with me in the open air.

If you would understand me go to the heights or water-shore,
The nearest gnat is an explanation, and a drop or motion of waves a
　　key,
The maul, the oar, the hand-saw, second my words.

No shutter'd room or school can commune with me,
But roughs and little children better than they.

The young mechanic is closest to me, he knows me well,
The woodman that takes his axe and jug with him shall take me with
　　him all day,
The farm-boy ploughing in the field feels good at the sound of my
　　voice,
In vessels that sail my words sail, I go with fishermen and seamen
　　and love them.

The soldier camp'd or upon the march is mine,
On the night ere the pending battle many seek me, and I do not fail
　　them,

On that solemn night (it may be their last) those that know me seek
    me.

My face rubs to the hunter's face when he lies down alone in his
    blanket,
The driver thinking of me does not mind the jolt of his wagon,
The young mother and old mother comprehend me,
The girl and the wife rest the needle a moment and forget where they
    are,
They and all would resume what I have told them.

48

I have said that the soul is not more than the body,
And I have said that the body is not more than the soul,
And nothing, not God, is greater to one than one's self is,
And whoever walks a furlong without sympathy walks to his own
    funeral drest in his shroud,
And I or you pocketless of a dime may purchase the pick of the earth,
And to glance with an eye or show a bean in its pod confounds the
    learning of all times,
And there is no trade or employment but the young man following it
    may become a hero,
And there is no object so soft but it makes a hub for the wheel'd uni-
    verse,
And I say to any man or woman, Let your soul stand cool and com-
    posed before a million universes.

And I say to mankind, Be not curious about God,
For I who am curious about each am not curious about God,
(No array of terms can say how much I am at peace about God and
    about death.)

I hear and behold God in every object, yet understand God not in the
    least,
Nor do I understand who there can be more wonderful than myself.

Why should I wish to see God better than this day?
I see something of God each hour of the twenty-four, and each moment
    then,
In the faces of men and women I see God, and in my own face in the
    glass,
I find letters from God dropt in the street, and every one is sign'd by
    God's name,
And I leave them where they are, for I know that wheresoe'er I go
Others will punctually come for ever and ever.

49

And as to you Death, and you bitter hug of mortality, it is idle to try
    to alarm me.

To his work without flinching the accoucheur* comes,
I see the elder-hand pressing receiving supporting,
I recline by the sills of the exquisite flexible doors,
And mark the outlet, and mark the relief and escape.

And as to you Corpse I think you are good manure, but that does **not**
    offend me,
I smell the white roses sweet-scented and growing,
I reach to the leafy lips, I reach to the polish'd breasts of melons.

And as to you Life I reckon you are the leavings of many deaths,
(No doubt I have died myself ten thousand times before.)

I hear you whispering there O stars of heaven,
O suns—O grass of graves—O perpetual transfers and promotions,
If you do not say any thing how can I say any thing?

Of the turbid pool that lies in the autumn forest,
Of the moon that descends the steeps of the soughing twilight,
Toss, sparkles of day and dusk—toss on the black stems that decay **in**
    the muck,
Toss to the moaning gibberish of the dry limbs.

I ascend from the moon, I ascend from the night,
I perceive that the ghastly glimmer is noonday sunbeams reflected,
And debouch* to the steady and central from the offspring great **or**
    small.

50

There is that in me—I do not know what it is—but I know it is in me.

Wrench'd and sweaty—calm and cool then my body becomes,
I sleep—I sleep long.

I do not know it—it is without name—it is a word unsaid,
It is not in any dictionary, utterance, symbol.

Something it swings on more than the earth I swing on,
To it the creation is the friend whose embracing awakes me.

Perhaps I might tell more. Outlines! I plead for my brothers **and**
    sisters.

Do you see O my brothers and sisters?
It is not chaos or death—it is form, union, plan—it is eternal life—**it is**
    Happiness.

51

The past and present wilt*—I have fill'd them, emptied them,
And proceed to fill my next fold of the future.

Listener up there! what have you to confide to me?
Look in my face while I snuff the sidle* of evening,
(Talk honestly, no one else hears you, and I stay only a minute longer.)

Do I contradict myself?
Very well then I contradict myself,
(I am large, I contain multitudes.)

I concentrate toward them that are nigh, I wait on the door-slab.

Who has done his day's work? who will soonest be through with his
    supper?
Who wishes to walk with me?

Will you speak before I am gone? will you prove already too late?

52

The spotted hawk swoops by and accuses me, he complains of my gab
    and my loitering.

I too am not a bit tamed, I too am untranslatable,
I sound my barbaric yawp* over the roofs of the world.

The last scud* of day holds back for me,
It flings my likeness after the rest and true as any on the shadow'd
    wilds,
It coaxes me to the vapor and the dusk.

I depart as air, I shake my white locks at the runaway sun,
I effuse* my flesh in eddies, and drift it in lacy jags.

I bequeath myself to the dirt to grow from the grass I love,
If you want me again look for me under your boot-soles.

You will hardly know who I am or what I mean,
But I shall be good health to you nevertheless,
And filter and fibre your blood.

Failing to fetch me at first keep encouraged,
Missing me one place search another,
I stop somewhere waiting for you.

CHILDREN OF ADAM

TO THE GARDEN THE WORLD

To the garden the world anew ascending,
Potent mates, daughters, sons, preluding,
The love, the life of their bodies, meaning and being,
Curious here behold my resurrection after slumber,
The revolving cycles in their wide sweep having brought me again,
Amorous, mature, all beautiful to me, all wondrous,
My limbs and the quivering fire that ever plays through them, for rea-
      sons, most wondrous,
Existing I peer and penetrate still,
Content with the present, content with the past,
By my side or back of me Eve following,
Or in front, and I following her just the same.

FROM PENT-UP ACHING RIVERS

From pent-up aching rivers,
From that of myself without which I were nothing,
From what I am determin'd to make illustrious, even if I stand sole
      among men,
From my own voice resonant, singing the phallus,
Singing the song of procreation,
Singing the need of superb children and therein superb grown people,
Singing the muscular urge and the blending,
Singing the bedfellow's song, (O resistless yearning!
O for any and each the body correlative attracting!
O for you whoever you are your correlative body! O it, more than all
      else, you delighting!)
From the hungry gnaw that eats me night and day,
From native moments, from bashful pains, singing them,
Seeking something yet unfound though I have diligently sought it
      many a long year,
Singing the true song of the soul fitful at random,
Renascent with grossest Nature or among animals,
Of that, of them and what goes with them my poems informing,
Of the smell of apples and lemons, of the pairing of birds,
Of the wet of woods, of the lapping of waves,
Of the mad pushes of waves upon the land, I them chanting,
The overture lightly sounding, the strain anticipating,
The welcome nearness, the sight of the perfect body,
The swimmer swimming naked in the bath, or motionless on his back
      lying and floating,
The female form approaching, I pensive, love-flesh tremulous aching,
The divine list for myself or you or for any one making,

The face, the limbs, the index from head to foot, and what it arouses,
The mystic deliria, the madness amorous, the utter abandonment,
(Hark close and still what I now whisper to you,
I love you, O you entirely possess me,
O that you and I escape from the rest and go utterly off, free and
 lawless,
Two hawks in the air, two fishes swimming in the sea not more
 lawless than we;)
The furious storm through me careering, I passionately trembling,
The oath of the inseparableness of two together, of the woman that
 loves me and whom I love more than my life, that oath swear-
 ing,
(O I willingly stake all for you,
O let me be lost if it must be so!
O you and I! what is it to us what the rest do or think?
What is all else to us? only that we enjoy each other and exhaust each
 other if it must be so;)
From the master, the pilot I yield the vessel to,
The general commanding me, commanding all, from him permission
 taking,
From time the programme hastening, (I have loiter'd too long as it is,)
From sex, from the warp and from the woof,
From privacy, from frequent repinings alone,
From plenty of persons near and yet the right person not near,
From the soft sliding of hands over me and thrusting of fingers through
 my hair and beard,
From the long sustain'd kiss upon the mouth or bosom,
From the close pressure that makes me or any man drunk, fainting
 with excess,
From what the divine husband knows, from the work of fatherhood,
From exultation, victory and relief from the bedfellow's embrace in the
 night,
From the act-poems of eyes, hands, hips and bosoms,
From the cling of the trembling arm,
From the bending curve and the clinch,*
From side by side the pliant coverlet off-throwing,
From the one so unwilling to have me leave, and me just as unwilling
 to leave,
(Yet a moment O tender waiter, and I return,)
From the hour of shining stars and dropping dews,
From the night a moment I emerging flitting out,
Celebrate you act divine and you children prepared for,
And you stalwart loins.

I SING THE BODY ELECTRIC

1

I sing the body electric,
The armies of those I love engirth me and I engirth them,

They will not let me off till I go with them, respond to them,
And discorrupt them, and charge them full with the charge of the
soul.

Was it doubted that those who corrupt their own bodies conceal them-
selves?
And if those who defile the living are as bad as they who defile the
dead?
And if the body does not do fully as much as the soul?
And if the body were not the soul, what is the soul?

2

The love of the body of man or woman balks account, the body itself
balks account,
That of the male is perfect, and that of the female is perfect.

The expression of the face balks account,
But the expression of a well-made man appears not only in his face,
It is in his limbs and joints also, it is curiously in the joints of his hips
and wrists,
It is in his walk, the carriage of his neck, the flex of his waist and
knees, dress does not hide him,
The strong sweet quality he has strikes through the cotton and broad-
cloth,
To see him pass conveys as much as the best poem, perhaps more,
You linger to see his back, and the back of his neck and shoulder-side.

The sprawl and fulness of babes, the bosoms and heads of women, the
folds of their dress, their style as we pass in the street, the con-
tour of their shape downwards,
The swimmer naked in the swimming-bath, seen as he swims through
the transparent green-shine, or lies with his face up and rolls
silently to and fro in the heave of the water,
The bending forward and backward of rowers in row-boats, the
horseman in his saddle,
Girls, mothers, house-keepers, in all their performances,
The group of laborers seated at noon-time with their open dinner
kettles, and their wives waiting,
The female soothing a child, the farmer's daughter in the garden or
cow-yard,
The young fellow hoeing corn, the sleigh-driver driving his six horses
through the crowd,
The wrestle of wrestlers, two apprentice-boys, quite grown, lusty,
good-natured, native-born, out on the vacant lot at sundown
after work,
The coats and caps thrown down, the embrace of love and resistance,
The upper-hold and under-hold, the hair rumpled over and blinding
the eyes;

The march of firemen in their own costumes, the play of masculine
    muscle through clean-setting trowsers and waist-straps,
The slow return from the fire, the pause when the bell strikes sud-
    denly again, and the listening on the alert,
The natural, perfect, varied attitudes, the bent head, the curv'd neck
    and the counting;
Such-like I love—I loosen myself, pass freely, am at the mother's
    breast with the little child,
Swim with the swimmers, wrestle with wrestlers, march in line with
    the firemen, and pause, listen, count.

3

I knew a man, a common farmer, the father of five sons,
And in them the fathers of sons, and in them the fathers of sons.

This man was of wonderful vigor, calmness, beauty of person,
The shape of his head, the pale yellow and white of his hair and
    beard, the immeasurable meaning of his black eyes, the rich-
    ness and breadth of his manners,
These I used to go and visit him to see, he was wise also,
He was six feet tall, he was over eighty years old, his sons were mas-
    sive, clean, bearded, tan-faced, handsome,
They and his daughters loved him, all who saw him loved him,
They did not love him by allowance, they loved him with personal
    love,
He drank water only, the blood show'd like scarlet through the clear-
    brown skin of his face,
He was a frequent gunner and fisher, he sail'd his boat himself, he had
    a fine one presented to him by a ship-joiner, he had fowling-
    pieces presented to him by men that loved him,
When he went with his five sons and many grand-sons to hunt or fish,
    you would pick him out as the most beautiful and vigorous of
    the gang,
You would wish long and long to be with him, you would wish to sit
    by him in the boat that you and he might touch each other.

4

I have perceiv'd that to be with those I like is enough,
To stop in company with the rest at evening is enough,
To be surrounded by beautiful, curious, breathing, laughing flesh is
    enough,
To pass among them or touch any one, or rest my arm ever so lightly
    round his or her neck for a moment, what is this then?
I do not ask any more delight, I swim in it as in a sea.

There is something in staying close to men and women and looking
    on them, and in the contact and odor of them, that pleases the
    soul well,
All things please the soul, but these please the soul well.

5

This is the female form,
A divine nimbus exhales from it from head to foot,
It attracts with fierce undeniable attraction,
I am drawn by its breath as if I were no more than a helpless vapor,
    all falls aside but myself and it,
Books, art, religion, time, the visible and solid earth, and what was
    expected of heaven or fear'd of hell, are now consumed,
Mad filaments, ungovernable shoots play out of it, the response like-
    wise ungovernable,
Hair, bosom, hips, bend of legs, negligent falling hands all diffused,
    mine too diffused,
Ebb stung by the flow and flow stung by the ebb, love-flesh swelling
    and deliciously aching,
Limitless limpid jets° of love hot and enormous, quivering jelly of
    love, white-blow and delirious juice,
Bridegroom night of love working surely and softly into the prostrate
    dawn,
Undulating into the willing and yielding day,
Lost in the cleave of the clasping and sweet-flesh'd day.

This the nucleus—after the child is born of woman, man is born of
    woman,
This the bath of birth, this the merge of small and large, and the
    outlet again.

Be not ashamed women, your privilege encloses the rest, and is the
    exit of the rest,
You are the gates of the body, and you are the gates of the soul.

The female contains all qualities and tempers them,
She is in her place and moves with perfect balance,
She is all things duly veil'd, she is both passive and active,
She is to conceive daughters as well as sons, and sons as well as
    daughters.

As I see my soul reflected in Nature,
As I see through a mist, One with inexpressible completeness, sanity,
    beauty,
See the bent head and arms folded over the breast, the Female I see.

6

The male is not less the soul nor more, he too is in his place,
He too is all qualities, he is action and power,
The flush of the known universe is in him,
Scorn becomes him well, and appetite and defiance become him well,
The wildest largest passions, bliss that is utmost, sorrow that is utmost
    become him well, pride is for him,

The full-spread pride of man is calming and excellent to the soul,
Knowledge becomes him, he likes it always, he brings every thing to
       the test of himself,
Whatever the survey, whatever the sea and the sail he strikes sound-
       ings at last only here,
(Where else does he strike soundings except here?)

The man's body is sacred and the woman's body is sacred,
No matter who it is, it is sacred—is it the meanest one in the laborers'
       gang?
Is it one of the dull-faced immigrants just landed on the wharf?
Each belongs here or anywhere just as much as the well-off, just as
       much as you,
Each has his or her place in the procession.

(All is a procession,
The universe is a procession with measured and perfect motion.)

Do you know so much yourself that you call the meanest ignorant?
Do you suppose you have a right to a good sight, and he or she has no
       right to a sight?
Do you think matter has cohered together from its diffuse float,° and
       the soil is on the surface, and water runs and vegetation
       sprouts,
For you only, and not for him and her?

7

A man's body at auction,
(For before the war I often go to the slave-mart and watch the sale,)
I help the auctioneer, the sloven does not half know his business.

Gentlemen look on this wonder,
Whatever the bids of the bidders they cannot be high enough for it,
For it the globe lay preparing quintillions of years without one animal
       or plant,
For it the revolving cycles truly and steadily roll'd.

In this head the all-baffling brain,
In it and below it the makings of heroes.

Examine these limbs, red, black, or white, they are cunning in tendon
       and nerve,
They shall be stript that you may see them.

Exquisite senses, life-lit eyes, pluck, volition,
Flakes of breast-muscle, pliant backbone and neck, flesh not flabby,
       good-sized arms and legs,
And wonders within there yet.

Within there runs blood,
The same old blood! the same red-running blood!
There swells and jets a heart, there all passions, desires, reachings,
    aspirations,
(Do you think they are not there because they are not express'd in
    parlors and lecture-rooms?)

This is not only one man, this the father of those who shall be fathers
    in their turns,
In him the start of populous states and rich republics,
Of him countless immortal lives with countless embodiments and en-
    joyments.

How do you know who shall come from the offspring of his offspring
    through the centuries?
(Who might you find you have come from yourself, if you could trace
    back through the centuries?)

8

A woman's body at auction,
She too is not only herself, she is the teeming mother of mothers,
She is the bearer of them that shall grow and be mates to the mothers.

Have you ever loved the body of a woman?
Have you ever loved the body of a man?
Do you not see that these are exactly the same to all in all nations and
    times all over the earth?

If any thing is sacred the human body is sacred,
And the glory and sweet of a man is the token of manhood untainted,
And in man or woman a clean, strong, firm-fibred body, is more
    beautiful than the most beautiful face.

Have you seen the fool that corrupted his own live body? or the fool
    that corrupted her own live body?
For they do not conceal themselves, and cannot conceal themselves.

9

O my body! I dare not desert the likes of you in other men and
    women, nor the likes of the parts of you,
I believe the likes of you are to stand or fall with the likes of the soul,
    (and that they are the soul,)
I believe the likes of you shall stand or fall with my poems, and that
    they are my poems,
Man's, woman's, child's, youth's, wife's, husband's, mother's, father's,
    young man's, young woman's poems,
Head, neck, hair, ears, drop and tympan of the ears,
Eyes, eye-fringes, iris of the eye, eyebrows, and the waking or sleeping
    of the lids,

Mouth, tongue, lips, teeth, roof of the mouth, jaws, and the jaw-
    hinges,
Nose, nostrils of the nose, and the partition,
Cheeks, temples, forehead, chin, throat, back of the neck, neck-slue,
Strong shoulders, manly beard, scapula, hind-shoulders, and the ample
    side-round of the chest,
Upper-arm, armpit, elbow-socket, lower-arm, arm-sinews, arm-bones,
Wrist and wrist-joints, hand, palm, knuckles, thumb, forefinger, finger-
    joints, finger-nails,
Broad breast-front, curling hair of the breast, breast-bone, breast-side,
Ribs, belly, backbone, joints of the backbone,
Hips, hip-sockets, hip-strength, inward and outward round, man-balls,
    man-root,
Strong set of thighs, well carrying the trunk above,
Leg-fibres, knee, knee-pan, upper-leg, under-leg,
Ankles, instep, foot-ball, toes, toe-joints, the heel;
All attitudes, all the shapeliness, all the belongings of my or your
    body or of any one's body, male or female,
The lung-sponges, the stomach-sac, the bowels sweet and clean,
The brain in its folds inside the skull-frame,
Sympathies, heart-valves, palate-valves, sexuality, maternity,
Womanhood and all that is a woman, and the man that comes from
    woman,
The womb, the teats, nipples, breast-milk, tears, laughter, weeping,
    love-looks, love-perturbations and risings,
The voice, articulation, language, whispering, shouting aloud,
Food, drink, pulse, digestion, sweat, sleep, walking, swimming,
Poise on the hips, leaping, reclining, embracing, arm-curving and
    tightening,
The continual changes of the flex of the mouth, and around the eyes,
The skin, the sunburnt shade, freckles, hair,
The curious sympathy one feels when feeling with the hand the naked
    meat of the body,
The circling rivers the breath, and breathing it in and out,
The beauty of the waist, and thence of the hips, and thence downward
    toward the knees,
The thin red jellies within you or within me, the bones and the marrow
    in the bones,
The exquisite realization of health;
O I say these are not the parts and poems of the body only, but of
    the soul,
O I say now these are the soul!

A WOMAN WAITS FOR ME

A woman waits for me, she contains all, nothing is lacking,
Yet all were lacking if sex were lacking, or if the moisture of the right
    man were lacking.

Sex contains all, bodies, souls,
Meanings, proofs, purities, delicacies, results, promulgations,
Songs, commands, health, pride, the maternal mystery, the seminal
      milk,
All hopes, benefactions, bestowals, all the passions, loves, beauties,
      delights of the earth,
All the governments, judges, gods, follow'd persons of the earth,
These are contain'd in sex as parts of itself and justifications of itself.

Without shame the man I like knows and avows the deliciousness of
      his sex,
Without shame the woman I like knows and avows hers.

Now I will dismiss myself from impassive women,
I will go stay with her who waits for me, and with those women that
      are warm-blooded and sufficient for me,
I see that they understand me and do not deny me,
I see that they are worthy of me, I will be the robust husband of those
      women.

They are not one jot less than I am,
They are tann'd in the face by shining suns and blowing winds,
Their flesh has the old divine suppleness and strength,
They know how to swim, row, ride, wrestle, shoot, run, strike, retreat,
      advance, resist, defend themselves,
They are ultimate in their own right—they are calm, clear, well-pos-
      sess'd of themselves.

I draw you close to me, you women,
I cannot let you go, I would do you good,
I am for you, and you are for me, not only for our own sake, but for
      others' sakes,
Envelop'd in you sleep greater heroes and bards,
They refuse to awake at the touch of any man but me.

It is I, you women, I make my way,
I am stern, acrid, large, undissuadable, but I love you,
I do not hurt you any more than is necessary for you,
I pour the stuff to start sons and daughters fit for these States, I press
      with slow rude muscle,
I brace myself effectually, I listen to no entreaties,
I dare not withdraw till I deposit what has so long accumulated within
      me.

Through you I drain the pent-up rivers of myself,
In you I wrap a thousand onward years,
On you I graft the grafts of the best-beloved of me and America,
The drops I distil upon you shall grow fierce and athletic girls, new
      artists, musicians, and singers,

The babes I beget upon you are to beget babes in their turn,
I shall demand perfect men and women out of my love-spendings,
I shall expect them to interpenetrate with others, as I and you inter-
  penetrate now,
I shall count on the fruits of the gushing showers of them, as I count
  on the fruits of the gushing showers I give now,
I shall look for loving crops from the girth, life, death, immortality,
  I plant so lovingly now.

SPONTANEOUS ME

Spontaneous me, Nature,
The loving day, the mounting sun, the friend I am happy with,
The arm of my friend hanging idly over my shoulder,
The hillside whiten'd with blossoms of the mountain ash,
The same late in autumn, the hues of red, yellow, drab, purple, and
  light and dark green,
The rich coverlet of the grass, animals and birds, the private un-
  trimm'd bank, the primitive apples, the pebble-stones,
Beautiful dripping fragments, the negligent list of one after another
  as I happen to call them to me or think of them,
The real poems, (what we call poems being merely pictures,)
The poems of the privacy of the night, and of men like me,
This poem drooping shy and unseen that I always carry, and that all
  men carry,
(Know once for all, avow'd on purpose, wherever are men like me,
  are our lusty lurking masculine poems,)
Love-thoughts, love-juice, love-odor, love-yielding, love-climbers, and
  the climbing sap,
Arms and hands of love, lips of love, phallic thumb of love, breasts
  of love, bellies press'd and glued together with love,
Earth of chaste love, life that is only life after love,
The body of my love, the body of the woman I love, the body of the
  man, the body of the earth,
Soft forenoon airs that blow from the south-west,
The hairy wild-bee that murmurs and hankers up and down, that
  gripes the full-grown lady-flower, curves upon her with amorous
  firm legs, takes his will of her, and holds himself tremulous and
  tight till he is satisfied;
The wet of woods through the early hours,
Two sleepers at night lying close together as they sleep, one with an
  arm slanting down across and below the waist of the other,
The smell of apples, aromas from crush'd sage-plant, mint, birch-bark,
The boy's longings, the glow and pressure as he confides to me what
  he was dreaming,
The dead leaf whirling its spiral whirl and falling still and content to
  the ground,
The no-form'd stings that sights, people, objects, sting me with,

The hubb'd sting of myself, stinging me as much as it ever can any one,
The sensitive, orbic, underlapp'd brothers, that only privileged feelers
 may be intimate where they are,
The curious roamer the hand roaming all over the body, the bashful
 withdrawing of flesh where the fingers soothingly pause and
 edge themselves,
The limpid liquid within the young man,
The vex'd corrosion so pensive and so painful,
The torment, the irritable tide that will not be at rest,
The like of the same I feel, the like of the same in others,
The young man that flushes and flushes, and the young woman that
 flushes and flushes,
The young man that wakes deep at night, the hot hand seeking to re-
 press what would master him,
The mystic amorous night, the strange half-welcome pangs, visions,
 sweats,
The pulse pounding through palms and trembling encircling fingers,
 the young man all color'd, red, ashamed, angry;
The souse upon me of my lover the sea, as I lie willing and naked,
The merriment of the twin babies that crawl over the grass in the
 sun, the mother never turning her vigilant eyes from them,
The walnut-trunk, the walnut-husks, and the ripening or ripen'd long-
 round walnuts,
The continence of vegetables, birds, animals,
The consequent meanness of me should I skulk or find myself in-
 decent, while birds and animals never once skulk or find them-
 selves indecent,
The great chastity of paternity, to match the great chastity of mater-
 nity,
The oath of procreation I have sworn, my Adamic and fresh daughters,
The greed that eats me day and night with hungry gnaw, till I saturate
 what shall produce boys to fill my place when I am through,
The wholesome relief, repose, content,
And this bunch pluck'd at random from myself,
It has done its work—I toss it carelessly to fall where it may.

ONE HOUR TO MADNESS AND JOY

One hour to madness and joy! O furious! O confine me not!
(What is this that frees me so in storms?
What do my shouts amid lightnings and raging winds mean?)

O to drink the mystic deliria deeper than any other man!
O savage and tender achings! (I bequeath them to you, my children,
I tell them to you, for reasons, O bridegroom and bride.)

O to be yielded to you whoever you are, and you to be yielded to me
 in defiance of the world!

O to return to Paradise! O bashful and feminine!
O to draw you to me, to plant on you for the first time the lips of a
     determin'd man.

O the puzzle, the thrice-tied knot, the deep and dark pool, all untied
     and illumin'd!
O to speed where there is space enough and air enough at last!
To be absolv'd from previous ties and conventions, I from mine and
     you from yours!
To find a new unthought-of nonchalance with the best of Nature!
To have the gag remov'd from one's mouth!
To have the feeling to-day or any day I am sufficient as I am.

O something unprov'd! something in a trance!
To escape utterly from others' anchors and holds!
To drive free! to love free! to dash reckless and dangerous!
To court destruction with taunts, with invitations!
To ascend, to leap to the heavens of the love indicated to me!
To rise thither with my inebriate soul!
To be lost if it must be so!
To feed the remainder of life with one hour of fulness and freedom!
With one brief hour of madness and joy.

OUT OF THE ROLLING OCEAN THE CROWD

Out of the rolling ocean the crowd came a drop gently to me,
Whispering *I love you, before long I die,*
I have travel'd a long way merely to look on you to touch you,
For I could not die till I once look'd on you,
For I fear'd I might afterward lose you.

Now we have met, we have look'd, we are safe,
Return in peace to the ocean my love,
I too am part of that ocean my love, we are not so much separated,
Behold the great rondure, the cohesion of all, how perfect!
But as for me, for you, the irresistible sea is to separate us,
As for an hour carrying us diverse, yet cannot carry us diverse forever;
Be not impatient—a little space—know you I salute the air, the ocean
     and the land,
Every day at sundown for your dear sake my love.

AGES AND AGES RETURNING AT INTERVALS

Ages and ages returning at intervals,
Undestroy'd, wandering immortal,
Lusty, phallic, with the potent original loins, perfectly sweet,
I, chanter of Adamic songs,

Through the new garden the West, the great cities calling,
Deliriate, thus prelude what is generated, offering these, offering
    myself,
Bathing myself, bathing my songs in Sex,
Offspring of my loins.

WE TWO, HOW LONG WE WERE FOOL'D

We two, how long we were fool'd,
Now transmuted, we swiftly escape as Nature escapes,
We are Nature, long have we been absent, but now we return,
We become plants, trunks, foliage, roots, bark,
We are bedded in the ground, we are rocks,
We are oaks, we grow in the openings side by side,
We browse, we are two among the wild herds spontaneous as any,
We are two fishes swimming in the sea together,
We are what locust blossoms are, we drop scent around lanes morn-
    ings and evenings,
We are also the coarse smut of beasts, vegetables, minerals,
We are two predatory hawks, we soar above and look down,
We are two resplendent suns, we it is who balance ourselves orbic and
    stellar, we are as two comets,
We prowl fang'd and four-footed in the woods, we spring on prey,
We are two clouds forenoons and afternoons driving overhead,
We are seas mingling, we are two of those cheerful waves rolling over
    each other and interwetting each other,
We are what the atmosphere is, transparent, receptive, pervious, im-
    pervious,
We are snow, rain, cold, darkness, we are each product and influence
    of the globe,
We have circled and circled till we have arrived home again, we two,
We have voided all but freedom and all but our own joy.

O HYMEN! O HYMENEE!

O hymen!* O hymenee! why do you tantalize me thus?
O why sting me for a swift moment only?
Why can you not continue? O why do you now cease?
Is it because if you continued beyond the swift moment you would
    soon certainly kill me?

I AM HE THAT ACHES WITH LOVE

I am he that aches with amorous love;
Does the earth gravitate? does not all matter, aching, attract all
    matter?
So the body of me to all I meet or know.

NATIVE MOMENTS

Native moments—when you come upon me—ah you are here now,
Give me now libidinous joys only,
Give me the drench of my passions, give me life coarse and rank,
To-day I go consort with Nature's darlings, to-night too,
I am for those who believe in loose delights, I share the midnight
    orgies of young men,
I dance with the dancers and drink with the drinkers,
The echoes ring with our indecent calls, I pick out some low person
    for my dearest friend,
He shall be lawless, rude, illiterate, he shall be one condemned by
    others for deeds done,
I will play a part no longer, why should I exile myself from my com-
    panions?
O you shunn'd persons, I at least do not shun you,
I come forthwith in your midst, I will be your poet,
I will be more to you than to any of the rest.

ONCE I PASS'D THROUGH A POPULOUS CITY

Once I pass'd through a populous city imprinting my brain for future
    use with its shows, architecture, customs, traditions,
Yet now of all that city I remember only a woman I casually met
    there who detain'd me for love of me,
Day by day and night by night we were together—all else has long
    been forgotten by me,
I remember I say only that woman who passionately clung to me,
Again we wander, we love, we separate again,
Again she holds me by the hand, I must not go,
I see her close beside me with silent lips sad and tremulous.

I HEARD YOU SOLEMN-SWEET PIPES OF THE ORGAN

I heard you solemn-sweet pipes of the organ as last Sunday morn I
    pass'd the church,
Winds of autumn, as I walk'd the woods at dusk I heard your long-
    stretch'd sighs up above so mournful,
I heard the perfect Italian tenor singing at the opera, I heard the
    soprano in the midst of the quartet singing;
Heart of my love! you too I heard murmuring low through one of the
    wrists around my head,
Heard the pulse of you when all was still ringing little bells last night
    under my ear.

FACING WEST FROM CALIFORNIA'S SHORES

Facing west from California's shores,
Inquiring, tireless, seeking what is yet unfound,
I, a child, very old, over waves, towards the house of maternity, the
    land of migrations, look afar,
Look off the shores of my Western sea, the circle almost circled;
For starting westward from Hindustan, from the vales of Kashmere,
From Asia, from the north, from the God, the sage, and the hero,
From the south, from the flowery peninsulas and the spice islands,
Long having wander'd since, round the earth having wander'd,
Now I face home again, very pleas'd and joyous,
(But where is what I started for so long ago?
And why is it yet unfound?)

AS ADAM EARLY IN THE MORNING

As Adam early in the morning,
Walking forth from the bower refresh'd with sleep,
Behold me where I pass, hear my voice, approach,
Touch me, touch the palm of your hand to my body as I pass,
Be not afraid of my body.

CALAMUS*

IN PATHS UNTRODDEN

In paths untrodden,
In the growth by margins of pond-waters,
Escaped from the life that exhibits itself,
From all the standards hitherto publish'd, from the pleasures, profits,
        conformities,
Which too long I was offering to feed my soul,
Clear to me now standards not yet publish'd, clear to me that my soul,
That the soul of the man I speak for rejoices in comrades,
Here by myself away from the clank of the world,
Tallying and talk'd to here by tongues aromatic,
No longer abash'd, (for in this secluded spot I can respond as I would
        not dare elsewhere,)
Strong upon me the life that does not exhibit itself, yet contains all
        the rest,
Resolv'd to sing no songs to-day but those of manly attachment,
Projecting them along that substantial life,
Bequeathing hence types of athletic love,
Afternoon this delicious Ninth-month in my forty-first year,
I proceed for all who are or have been young men,
To tell the secret of my nights and days,
To celebrate the need of comrades.

SCENTED HERBAGE OF MY BREAST

Scented herbage of my breast,
Leaves from you I glean, I write, to be perused best afterwards,
Tomb-leaves, body-leaves growing up above me above death,
Perennial roots, tall leaves, O the winter shall not freeze you delicate
        leaves,
Every year shall you bloom again, out from where you retired you
        shall emerge again;
O I do not know whether many passing by will discover you or inhale
        your faint odor, but I believe a few will;
O slender leaves! O blossoms of my blood! I permit you to tell in your
        own way of the heart that is under you,
O I do not know what you mean there underneath yourselves, you
        are not happiness,
You are often more bitter than I can bear, you burn and sting me,
Yet you are beautiful to me you faint-tinged roots, you make me think
        of death,
Death is beautiful from you, (what indeed is finally beautiful except
        death and love?)

O I think it is not for life I am chanting here my chant of lovers,
    I think it must be for death,
For how calm, how solemn it grows to ascend to the atmosphere of
    lovers,
Death or life I am then indifferent, my soul declines to prefer,
(I am not sure but the high soul of lovers welcomes death most,)
Indeed O death, I think now these leaves mean precisely the same as
    you mean,
Grow up taller sweet leaves that I may see! grow up out of my breast!
Spring away from the conceal'd heart there!
Do not fold yourself so in your pink-tinged roots timid leaves!
Do not remain down there so ashamed, herbage of my breast!
Come I am determin'd to unbare this broad breast of mine, I have
    long enough stifled and choked;
Emblematic and capricious blades I leave you, now you serve me not,
I will say what I have to say by itself,
I will sound myself and comrades only, I will never again utter a call
    only their call,
I will raise with it immortal reverberations through the States,
I will give an example to lovers to take permanent shape and will
    through the States,
Through me shall the words be said to make death exhilarating.
Give me your tone therefore O death, that I may accord with it,
Give me yourself, for I see that you belong to me now above all, and
    are folded inseparably together, you love and death are,
Nor will I allow you to balk me any more with what I was calling life,
For now it is convey'd to me that you are the purports essential,
That you hide in these shifting forms of life, for reasons, and that they
    are mainly for you,
That you beyond them come forth to remain, the real reality,
That behind the mask of materials you patiently wait, no matter how
    long,
That you will one day perhaps take control of all,
That you will perhaps dissipate this entire show of appearance,
That may-be you are what it is all for, but it does not last so very long,
But you will last very long.

WHOEVER YOU ARE HOLDING ME NOW IN HAND

Whoever you are holding me now in hand,
Without one thing all will be useless,
I give you fair warning before you attempt me further,
I am not what you supposed, but far different.

Who is he that would become my follower?
Who would sign himself a candidate for my affections?

The way is suspicious, the result uncertain, perhaps destructive,
You would have to give up all else, I alone would expect to be your
    sole and exclusive standard,
Your novitiate would even then be long and exhausting,
The whole past theory of your life and all conformity to the lives
    around you would have to be abandon'd,
Therefore release me now before troubling yourself any further, let go
    your hand from my shoulders,
Put me down and depart on your way.

Or else by stealth in some wood for trial,
Or back of a rock in the open air,
(For in any roof'd room of a house I emerge not, nor in company,
And in libraries I lie as one dumb, a gawk, or unborn, or dead,)
But just possibly with you on a high hill, first watching lest any person
    for miles around approach unawares,
Or possibly with you sailing at sea, or on the beach of the sea or some
    quiet island,
Here to put your lips upon mine I permit you,
With the comrade's long-dwelling kiss or the new husband's kiss,
For I am the new husband and I am the comrade.

Or if you will, thrusting me beneath your clothing,
Where I may feel the throbs of your heart or rest upon your hip,
Carry me when you go forth over land or sea;
For thus merely touching you is enough, is best,
And thus touching you would I silently sleep and be carried eternally.

But these leaves conning you con at peril,
For these leaves and me you will not understand,
They will elude you at first and still more afterward, I will certainly
    elude you,
Even while you should think you had unquestionably caught me, be-
    hold!
Already you see I have escaped from you.

For it is not for what I have put into it that I have written this book,
Nor is it by reading it you will acquire it,
Nor do those know me best who admire me and vauntingly praise me,
Nor will the candidates for my love (unless at most a very few) prove
    victorious,
Nor will my poems do good only, they will do just as much evil, per-
    haps more,
For all is useless without that which you may guess at many times and
    not hit, that which I hinted at;
Therefore release me and depart on your way.

FOR YOU O DEMOCRACY

Come, I will make the continent indissoluble,
I will make the most splendid race the sun ever shone upon,
I will make divine magnetic lands,
      With the love of comrades,
        With the life-long love of comrades.

I will plant companionship thick as trees along all the rivers of
    America, and along the shores of the great lakes, and all over
    the prairies,
I will make inseparable cities with their arms about each other's necks,
      By the love of comrades,
        By the manly love of comrades,

For you these from me, O Democracy, to serve you ma femme!*
For you, for you I am trilling these songs.

THESE I SINGING IN SPRING

These I singing in spring collect for lovers,
(For who but I should understand lovers and all their sorrow and joy?
And who but I should be the poet of comrades?)
Collecting I traverse the garden the world, but soon I pass the gates,
Now along the pond-side, now wading in a little, fearing not the wet,
Now by the post-and-rail fences where the old stones thrown there,
    pick'd from the fields, have accumulated,
(Wild-flowers and vines and weeds come up through the stones and
    partly cover them, beyond these I pass,)
Far, far in the forest, or sauntering later in summer, before I think
    where I go,
Solitary, smelling the earthy smell, stopping now and then in the
    silence,
Alone I had thought, yet soon a troop gathers around me,
Some walk by my side and some behind, and some embrace my arms
    or neck,
They the spirits of dear friends dead or alive, thicker they come, a
    great crowd, and I in the middle,
Collecting, dispensing, singing, there I wander with them,
Plucking something for tokens, tossing toward whoever is near me,
Here, lilac, with a branch of pine,
Here, out of my pocket, some moss which I pull'd off a live-oak in
    Florida as it hung trailing down,
Here, some pinks and laurel leaves, and a handful of sage,
And here what I now draw from the water, wading in the pond-side,
(O here I last saw him that tenderly loves me, and returns again never
    to separate from me,

And this, O this shall henceforth be the token of comrades, this cala-
　　mus-root shall,
Interchange it youths with each other! let none render it back!)
And twigs of maple and a bunch of wild orange and chestnut,
And stems of currants and plum-blows, and the aromatic cedar,
These I compass'd around by a thick cloud of spirits,
Wandering, point to or touch as I pass, or throw them loosely from me,
Indicating to each one what he shall have, giving something to each;
But what I drew from the water by the pond-side, that I reserve,
I will give of it, but only to them that love as I myself am capable of
　　loving.

NOT HEAVING FROM MY RIBB'D BREAST ONLY

Not heaving from my ribb'd breast only,
Not in sighs at night in rage dissatisfied with myself,
Not in those long-drawn, ill-supprest sighs,
Not in many an oath and promise broken,
Not in my wilful and savage soul's volition,
Not in the subtle nourishment of the air,
Not in this beating and pounding at my temples and wrists,
Not in the curious systole and diastole within which will one day cease,
Not in many a hungry wish told to the skies only,
Not in cries, laughter, defiances, thrown from me when alone far in the
　　wilds,
Not in husky pantings through clinch'd teeth,
Not in sounded and resounded words, chattering words, echoes, dead
　　words,
Not in the murmurs of my dreams while I sleep,
Nor the other murmurs of these incredible dreams of every day,
Nor in the limbs and senses of my body that take you and dismiss you
　　continually—not there,
Not in any or all of them O adhesiveness!° O pulse of my life!
Need I that you exist and show yourself any more than in these songs.

OF THE TERRIBLE DOUBT OF APPEARANCES

Of the terrible doubt of appearances,
Of the uncertainty after all, that we may be deluded,
That may-be reliance and hope are but speculations after all,
That may-be identity beyond the grave is a beautiful fable only,
May-be the things I perceive, the animals, plants, men, hills, shining
　　and flowing waters,
The skies of day and night, colors, densities, forms, may-be these are
　　(as doubtless they are) only apparitions, and the real some-
　　thing has yet to be known,

(How often they dart out of themselves as if to confound me and
    mock me!
How often I think neither I know, nor any man knows, aught of them,)
May-be seeming to me what they are (as doubtless they indeed but
       seem) as from my present point of view, and might prove (as
       of course they would) nought of what they appear, or nought
       anyhow, from entirely changed points of view;
To me these and the like of these are curiously answer'd by my lovers,
    my dear friends,
When he whom I love travels with me or sits a long while holding
    me by the hand,
When the subtle air, the impalpable, the sense that words and reason
    hold not, surround us and pervade us,
Then I am charged with untold and untellable wisdom, I am silent,
    I require nothing further,
I cannot answer the question of appearances or that of identity be-
    yond the grave,
But I walk or sit indifferent, I am satisfied,
He ahold of my hand has completely satisfied me.

THE BASE OF ALL METAPHYSICS

And now gentlemen,
A word I give to remain in your memories and minds,
As base and finalè too for all metaphysics.

(So to the students the old professor,
At the close of his crowded course.)

Having studied the new and antique, the Greek and Germanic systems,
Kant having studied and stated, Fichte and Schelling and Hegel,
Stated the lore of Plato, and Socrates greater than Plato,
And greater than Socrates sought and stated, Christ divine having
    studied long,
I see reminiscent to-day those Greek and Germanic systems,
See the philosophies all, Christian churches and tenets see,
Yet underneath Socrates clearly see, and underneath Christ the divine
    I see,
The dear love of man for his comrade, the attraction of friend to
    friend,
Of the well-married husband and wife, of children and parents,
Of city for city and land for land.

RECORDERS AGES HENCE

Recorders ages hence,
Come, I will take you down underneath this impassive exterior, I will
    tell you what to say of me,

Publish my name and hang up my picture as that of the tenderest
lover,
The friend the lover's portrait, of whom his friend his lover was
fondest,
Who was not proud of his songs, but of the measureless ocean of love
within him, and freely pour'd it forth,
Who often walk'd lonesome walks thinking of his dear friends, his
lovers,
Who pensive away from one he lov'd often lay sleepless and dissatisfied at night,
Who knew too well the sick, sick dread lest the one he lov'd might
secretly be indifferent to him,
Whose happiest days were far away through fields, in woods, on hills,
he and another wandering hand in hand, they twain apart
from other men,
Who oft as he saunter'd the streets curv'd with his arm the shoulder
of his friend, while the arm of his friend rested upon him also.

WHEN I HEARD AT THE CLOSE OF THE DAY

When I heard at the close of the day how my name had been receiv'd
with plaudits in the capitol, still it was not a happy night for
me that follow'd,
And else when I carous'd, or when my plans were accomplish'd, still I
was not happy,
But the day when I rose at dawn from the bed of perfect health, refresh'd, singing, inhaling the ripe breath of autumn,
When I saw the full moon in the west grow pale and disappear in the
morning light,
When I wander'd alone over the beach, and undressing bathed, laughing with the cool waters, and saw the sun rise,
And when I thought how my dear friend my lover was on his way
coming, O then I was happy,
O then each breath tasted sweeter, and all that day my food nourish'd
me more, and the beautiful day pass'd well,
And the next came with equal joy, and with the next at evening came
my friend,
And that night while all was still I heard the waters roll slowly continually up the shores,
I heard the hissing rustle of the liquid and sands as directed to me
whispering to congratulate me,
For the one I love most lay sleeping by me under the same cover in
the cool night,
In the stillness in the autumn moonbeams his face was inclined toward
me,
And his arm lay lightly around my breast—and that night I was
happy.

ARE YOU THE NEW PERSON DRAWN TOWARD ME?

Are you the new person drawn toward me?
To begin with take warning, I am surely far different from what you
  suppose;
Do you suppose you will find in me your ideal?
Do you think it is so easy to have me become your lover?
Do you think the friendship of me would be unalloy'd satisfaction?
Do you think I am trusty and faithful?
Do you see no further than this façade, this smooth and tolerant
  manner of me?
Do you suppose yourself advancing on real ground toward a real
  heroic man?
Have you no thought O dreamer that it may be all maya,* illusion?

ROOTS AND LEAVES THEMSELVES ALONE

Roots and leaves themselves alone are these,
Scents brought to men and women from the wild woods and pond-
  side,
Breast-sorrel and pinks of love, fingers that wind around tighter than
  vines,
Gushes from the throats of birds hid in the foliage of trees as the sun
  is risen,
Breezes of land and love set from living shores to you on the living
  sea, to you O sailors!
Frost-mellow'd berries and Third-month twigs offer'd fresh to young
  persons wandering out in the fields when the winter breaks up,
Love-buds put before you and within you whoever you are,
Buds to be unfolded on the old terms,
If you bring the warmth of the sun to them they will open and bring
  form, color, perfume, to you,
If you become the aliment* and the wet they will become flowers,
  fruits, tall branches and trees.

NOT HEAT FLAMES UP AND CONSUMES

Not heat flames up and consumes,
Not sea-waves hurry in and out,
Not the air delicious and dry, the air of ripe summer, bears lightly
  along white down-balls of myriads of seeds,
Wafted, sailing gracefully, to drop where they may;
Not these, O none of these more than the flames of me, consuming,
  burning for his love whom I love,
O none more than I hurrying in and out;

Does the tide hurry, seeking something, and never give up? O I the
      same,
O nor down-balls nor perfumes, nor the high rain-emitting clouds, are
      borne through the open air,
Any more than my soul is borne through the open air,
Wafted in all directions O love, for friendship, for you.

TRICKLE DROPS

Trickle drops! my blue veins leaving!
O drops of me! trickle, slow drops,
Candid from me falling, drip, bleeding drops,
From wounds made to free you whence you were prison'd,
From my face, from my forehead and lips,
From my breast, from within where I was conceal'd, press forth red
      drops, confession drops,
Stain every page, stain every song I sing, every word I say, bloody
      drops,
Let them know your scarlet heat, let them glisten,
Saturate them with yourself all ashamed and wet,
Glow upon all I have written or shall write, bleeding drops,
Let it all be seen in your light, blushing drops.

CITY OF ORGIES

City of orgies, walks and joys,
City whom that I have lived and sung in your midst will one day
      make you illustrious,
Not the pageants of you, not your shifting tableaus, your spectacles,
      repay me,
Not the interminable rows of your houses, nor the ships at the
      wharves,
Nor the processions in the streets, nor the bright windows with goods
      in them,
Nor to converse with learn'd persons, or bear my share in the soiree
      or feast;
Not those, but as I pass O Manhattan, your frequent and swift flash of
      eyes offering me love,
Offering response to my own—these repay me,
Lovers, continual lovers, only repay me.

BEHOLD THIS SWARTHY FACE

Behold this swarthy face, these gray eyes,
This beard, the white wool unclipt upon my neck,
My brown hands and the silent manner of me without charm;

Yet comes one a Manhattanese and ever at parting kisses me lightly
      on the lips with robust love,
And I on the crossing of the street or on the ship's deck give a kiss in
      return,
We observe that salute of American comrades land and sea,
We are those two natural and nonchalant persons.

I SAW IN LOUISIANA A LIVE-OAK GROWING

I saw in Louisiana a live-oak growing,
All alone stood it and the moss hung down from the branches,
Without any companion it grew there uttering joyous leaves of dark
      green,
And its look, rude, unbending, lusty, made me think of myself,
But I wonder'd how it could utter joyous leaves standing alone there
      without its friend near, for I knew I could not,
And I broke off a twig with a certain number of leaves upon it, and
      twined around it a little moss,
And brought it away, and I have placed it in sight in my room,
It is not needed to remind me as of my own dear friends,
(For I believe lately I think of little else than of them,)
Yet it remains to me a curious token, it makes me think of manly love;
For all that, and though the live-oak glistens there in Louisiana soli-
      tary in a wide flat space,
Uttering joyous leaves all its life without a friend a lover near,
I know very well I could not.

TO A STRANGER

Passing stranger! you do not know how longingly I look upon you,
You must be he I was seeking, or she I was seeking, (it comes to me
      as of a dream,)
I have somewhere surely lived a life of joy with you,
All is recall'd as we flit by each other, fluid, affectionate, chaste,
      matured,
You grew up with me, were a boy with me or a girl with me,
I ate with you and slept with you, your body has become not yours
      only nor left my body mine only,
You give me the pleasure of your eyes, face, flesh, as we pass, you take
      of my beard, breast, hands, in return,
I am not to speak to you, I am to think of you when I sit alone or
      wake at night alone,
I am to wait, I do not doubt I am to meet you again,
I am to see to it that I do not lose you.

THIS MOMENT YEARNING AND THOUGHTFUL

This moment yearning and thoughtful sitting alone,
It seems to me there are other men in other lands yearning and
thoughtful,
It seems to me I can look over and behold them in Germany, Italy,
France, Spain,
Or far, far away, in China, or in Russia or Japan, talking other dialects,
And it seems to me if I could know those men I should become
attached to them as I do to men in my own lands,
O I know we should be brethren and lovers,
I know I should be happy with them.

I HEAR IT WAS CHARGED AGAINST ME

I hear it was charged against me that I sought to destroy institutions,
But really I am neither for nor against institutions,
(What indeed have I in common with them? or what with the de-
struction of them?)
Only I will establish in the Mannahatta° and in every city of these
States inland and seaboard,
And in the fields and woods, and above every keel little or large that
dents the water,
Without edifices or rules or trustees or any argument,
The institution of the dear love of comrades.

THE PRAIRIE-GRASS DIVIDING

The prairie-grass dividing, its special odor breathing,
I demand of it the spiritual corresponding,
Demand the most copious and close companionship of men,
Demand the blades to rise of words, acts, beings,
Those of the open atmosphere, coarse, sunlit, fresh, nutritious,
Those that go their own gait, erect, stepping with freedom and com-
mand, leading not following,
Those with a never-quell'd audacity, those with sweet and lusty flesh
clear of taint,
Those that look carelessly in the faces of Presidents and governors, as
to say *Who are you?*
Those of earth-born passion, simple, never constrain'd, never obedient,
Those of inland America.

WHEN I PERUSE THE CONQUER'D FAME

When I peruse the conquer'd fame of heroes and the victories of
mighty generals, I do not envy the generals,

Nor the President in his Presidency, nor the rich in his great house,
But when I hear of the brotherhood of lovers, how it was with them,
How together through life, through dangers, odium, unchanging, long
    and long,
Through youth and through middle and old age, how unfaltering, how
    affectionate and faithful they were,
Then I am pensive—I hastily walk away fill'd with the bitterest envy.

WE TWO BOYS TOGETHER CLINGING

We two boys together clinging,
One the other never leaving,
Up and down the roads going, North and South excursions making,
Power enjoying, elbows stretching, fingers clutching,
Arm'd and fearless, eating, drinking, sleeping, loving,
No law less than ourselves owning, sailing, soldiering, thieving, threat-
    ening,
Misers, menials, priests alarming, air breathing, water drinking, on the
    turf or the sea-beach dancing,
Cities wrenching, ease scorning, statutes mocking, feebleness chasing,
Fulfilling our foray.

A PROMISE TO CALIFORNIA

A promise to California,
Or inland to the great pastoral Plains, and on to Puget sound and
    Oregon;
Sojourning east a while longer, soon I travel toward you, to remain, to
    teach robust American love,
For I know very well that I and robust love belong among you, inland,
    and along the Western sea;
For these States tend inland and toward the Western sea, and I will
    also.

HERE THE FRAILEST LEAVES OF ME

Here the frailest leaves of me and yet my strongest lasting,
Here I shade and hide my thoughts, I myself do not expose them,
And yet they expose me more than all my other poems.

NO LABOR-SAVING MACHINE

No labor-saving machine,
Nor discovery have I made,
Nor will I be able to leave behind me any wealthy bequest to found a
    hospital or library,

Nor reminiscence of any deed of courage for America,
Nor literary success nor intellect, nor book for the book-shelf,
But a few carols vibrating through the air I leave,
For comrades and lovers.

A GLIMPSE

A glimpse through an interstice* caught,
Of a crowd of workmen and drivers in a bar-room around the stove
    late of a winter night, and I unremark'd seated in a corner,
Of a youth who loves me and whom I love, silently approaching and
    seating himself near, that he may hold me by the hand,
A long while amid the noises coming and going, of drinking and oath
    and smutty jest,
There we two, content, happy in being together, speaking little, per-
    haps not a word.

A LEAF FOR HAND IN HAND

A leaf for hand in hand;
You natural persons old and young!
You on the Mississippi and on all the branches and bayous of the
    Mississippi!
You friendly boatmen and mechanics! you roughs!
You twain! and all processions moving along the streets!
I wish to infuse myself among you till I see it common for you to walk
    hand in hand.

EARTH, MY LIKENESS

Earth, my likeness,
Though you look so impassive, ample and spheric there,
I now suspect that is not all;
I now suspect there is something fierce in you eligible to burst forth,
For an athlete is enamour'd of me, and I of him,
But toward him there is something fierce and terrible in me eligible to
    burst forth,
I dare not tell it in words, not even in these songs.

I DREAM'D IN A DREAM

I dream'd in a dream I saw a city invincible to the attacks of the whole
    of the rest of the earth,
I dream'd that was the new city of Friends,

Nothing was greater there than the quality of robust love, it led the
  rest,
It was seen every hour in the actions of the men of that city,
And in all their looks and words.

WHAT THINK YOU I TAKE MY PEN IN HAND?

What think you I take my pen in hand to record?
The battle-ship, perfect-model'd, majestic, that I saw pass the offing
  to-day under full sail?
The splendors of the past day? or the splendor of the night that en-
  velops me?
Of the vaunted glory and growth of the great city spread around me?
  —no;
But merely of two simple men I saw to-day on the pier in the midst
  of the crowd, parting the parting of dear friends,
The one to remain hung on the other's neck and passionately kiss'd
  him,
While the one to depart tightly prest the one to remain in his arms.

TO THE EAST AND TO THE WEST

To the East and to the West,
To the man of the Seaside State and of Pennsylvania,
To the Kanadian of the north, to the Southerner I love,
These with perfect trust to depict you as myself, the germs are in all
  men,
I believe the main purport of these States is to found a superb friend-
  ship, exaltè, previously unknown,
Because I perceive it waits, and has been always waiting, latent in all
  men.

SOMETIMES WITH ONE I LOVE

Sometimes with one I love I fill myself with rage for fear I effuse*
  unreturn'd love,
But now I think there is no unreturn'd love, the pay is certain one
  way or another,
(I loved a certain person ardently and my love was not return'd,
Yet out of that I have written these songs.)

TO A WESTERN BOY

Many things to absorb I teach to help you become eleve* of mine;
Yet if blood like mine circle not in your veins,

If you be not silently selected by lovers and do not silently select lovers,
Of what use is it that you seek to become eleve of mine?

FAST-ANCHOR'D ETERNAL O LOVE!

Fast-anchor'd eternal O love! O woman I love!
O bride! O wife! more resistless than I can tell, the thought of you!
Then separate, as disembodied or another born,
Ethereal, the last athletic reality, my consolation,
I ascend, I float in the regions of your love O man,
O sharer of my roving life.

AMONG THE MULTITUDE

Among the men and women the multitude,
I perceive one picking me out by secret and divine signs,
Acknowledging none else, not parent, wife, husband, brother, child,
    any nearer than I am,
Some are baffled, but that one is not—that one knows me.

Ah lover and perfect equal,
I meant that you should discover me so by faint indirections,
And I when I meet you mean to discover you by the like in you.

O YOU WHOM I OFTEN AND SILENTLY COME

O you whom I often and silently come where you are that I may be
    with you,
As I walk by your side or sit near, or remain in the same room with
    you,
Little you know the subtle electric fire that for your sake is playing
    within me.

THAT SHADOW MY LIKENESS

That shadow my likeness that goes to and fro seeking a livelihood,
    chattering, chaffering,
How often I find myself standing and looking at it where it flits,
How often I question and doubt whether that is really me;
But among my lovers and caroling these songs,
O I never doubt whether that is really me.

FULL OF LIFE NOW

Full of life now, compact, visible,
I, forty years old the eighty-third year of the States,
To one a century hence or any number of centuries hence,
To you yet unborn these, seeking you.

When you read these I that was visible am become invisible,
Now it is you, compact, visible, realizing my poems, seeking me,
Fancying how happy you were if I could be with you and become
      your comrade;
Be it as if I were with you. (Be not too certain but I am now with
      you.)

SALUT AU MONDE!

1

O take my hand Walt Whitman!
Such gliding wonders! such sights and sounds!
Such join'd unended links, each hook'd to the next,
Each answering all, each sharing the earth with all.

What widens within you Walt Whitman?
What waves and soils exuding?
What climes? what persons and cities are here?
Who are the infants, some playing, some slumbering?
Who are the girls? who are the married women?
Who are the groups of old men going slowly with their arms about
    each other's necks?
What rivers are these? what forests and fruits are these?
What are the mountains call'd that rise so high in the mists?
What myriads of dwellings are they fill'd with dwellers?

2

Within me latitude widens, longitude lengthens,
Asia, Africa, Europe, are to the east—America is provided for in the
    west,
Banding the bulge of the earth winds the hot equator,
Curiously north and south turn the axis-ends,
Within me is the longest day, the sun wheels in slanting rings, it does
    not set for months,
Stretch'd in due time within me the midnight sun just rises above the
    horizon and sinks again,
Within me zones, seas, cataracts, forests, volcanoes, groups,
Malaysia, Polynesia, and the great West Indian islands.

3

What do you hear Walt Whitman?

I hear the workman singing and the farmer's wife singing,
I hear in the distance the sounds of children and of animals early in
    the day,
I hear emulous shouts of Australians pursuing the wild horse,
I hear the Spanish dance with castanets in the chestnut shade, to the
    rebeck and guitar,
I hear continual echoes from the Thames,
I hear fierce French liberty songs,
I hear of the Italian boat-sculler the musical recitative of old poems,
I hear the locusts in Syria as they strike the grain and grass with the
    showers of their terrible clouds,

I hear the Coptic refrain toward sundown, pensively falling on the
    breast of the black venerable vast mother the Nile,
I hear the chirp of the Mexican muleteer, and the bells of the mule,
I hear the Arab muezzin calling from the top of the mosque,
I hear the Christian priests at the altars of their churches, I hear the
    responsive base and soprano,
I hear the cry of the Cossack, and the sailor's voice putting to sea at
    Okotsk,
I hear the wheeze of the slave-coffle as the slaves march on, as the
    husky gangs pass on by twos and threes, fasten'd together with
    wrist-chains and ankle-chains,
I hear the Hebrew reading his records and psalms,
I hear the rhythmic myths of the Greeks, and the strong legends of the
    Romans,
I hear the tale of the divine life and bloody death of the beautiful God
    the Christ,
I hear the Hindoo teaching his favorite pupil the loves, wars, adages,
    transmitted safely to this day from poets who wrote three
    thousand years ago.

4

What do you see Walt Whitman?
Who are they you salute, and that one after another salute you?

I see a great round wonder rolling through space,
I see diminute° farms, hamlets, ruins, graveyards, jails, factories,
    palaces, hovels, huts of barbarians, tents of nomads upon the
    surface,
I see the shaded part on one side where the sleepers are sleeping, and
    the sunlit part on the other side,
I see the curious rapid change of the light and shade,
I see distant lands, as real and near to the inhabitants of them as my
    land is to me.

I see plenteous waters,
I see mountain peaks, I see the sierras of Andes where they range,
I see plainly the Himalayas, Chian Shahs, Altays, Ghauts,
I see the giant pinnacles of Elbruz, Kazbek, Bazardjusi,
I see the Styrian Alps, and the Karnac Alps,
I see the Pyrenees, Balks, Carpathians, and to the north the Dofra-
    fields, and off at sea mount Hecla,
I see Vesuvius and Etna, the mountains of the Moon, and the Red
    mountains of Madagascar,
I see the Lybian, Arabian, and Asiatic deserts,
I see huge dreadful Arctic and Antarctic icebergs,
I see the superior oceans and the interior ones, the Atlantic and
    Pacific, the sea of Mexico, the Brazilian sea, and the sea of
    Peru,
The waters of Hindustan, the China sea, and the gulf of Guinea,

The Japan waters, the beautiful bay of Nagasaki land-lock'd in its
 mountains,
The spread of the Baltic, Caspian, Bothnia, the British shores, and the
 bay of Biscay,
The clear-sunn'd Mediterranean, and from one to another of its
 islands,
The White sea, and the sea around Greenland.

I behold the mariners of the world,
Some are in storms, some in the night with the watch on the lookout,
Some drifting helplessly, some with contagious diseases.

I behold the sail and steamships of the world, some in clusters in port,
 some on their voyages,
Some double the cape of Storms, some cape Verde, others capes
 Guardafui, Bon, or Bajadore,
Others Dondra head, others pass the straits of Sunda, others cape
 Lopatka, others Behring's straits,

Others cape Horn, others sail the gulf of Mexico or along Cuba or
 Hayti, others Hudson's bay or Baffin's bay,
Others pass the straits of Dover, others enter the Wash, others the
 firth of Solway, others round cape Clear, others the Land's End,
Others traverse the Zuyder Zee or the Scheld,
Others as comers and goers at Gibraltar or the Dardanelles,
Others sternly push their way through the northern winter-packs,
Others descend or ascend the Obi or the Lena,
Others the Niger or the Congo, others the Indus, the Burampooter
 and Cambodia,
Others wait steam'd up ready to start in the ports of Australia,
Wait at Liverpool, Glasgow, Dublin, Marseilles, Lisbon, Naples,
 Hamburg, Bremen, Bordeaux, the Hague, Copenhagen,
Wait at Valparaiso, Rio Janeiro, Panama.

5

I see the tracks of the railroads of the earth,
I see them in Great Britain, I see them in Europe,
I see them in Asia and in Africa.

I see the electric telegraphs of the earth,
I see the filaments of the news of the wars, deaths, losses, gains, passions, of my race.

I see the long river-stripes of the earth,
I see the Amazon and the Paraguay,
I see the four great rivers of China, the Amour, the Yellow River, the
 Yiang-tse, and the Pearl,
I see where the Seine flows, and where the Danube, the Loire, the
 Rhone, and the Guadalquiver flow,

I see the windings of the Volga, the Dnieper, the Oder,
I see the Tuscan going down the Arno, and the Venetian along the Po,
I see the Greek seaman sailing out of Egina bay.

6

I see the site of the old empire of Assyria, and that of Persia, and that of India,
I see the falling of the Ganges over the high rim of Saukara.

I see the place of the idea of the Deity incarnated by avatars in human forms,
I see the spots of the successions of priests on the earth, oracles, sacrificers, brahmins, sabians, llamas, monks, muftis, exhorters,
I see where druids walk'd the groves of Mona, I see the mistletoe and vervain,
I see the temples of the deaths of the bodies of Gods, I see the old signifiers.

I see Christ eating the bread of his last supper in the midst of youths and old persons,
I see where the strong divine young man the Hercules toil'd faithfully and long and then died,
I see the place of the innocent rich life, and hapless fate of the beautiful nocturnal son, the full-limb'd Bacchus,
I see Kneph, blooming, drest in blue, with the crown of feathers on his head,
I see Hermes, unsuspected, dying, well-belov'd, saying to the people *Do not weep for me,*
This is not my true country, I have lived banish'd from my true country, I now go back there,
I return to the celestial sphere where every one goes in his turn.

7

I see the battle-fields of the earth, grass grows upon them and blossoms and corn,
I see the tracks of ancient and modern expeditions.

I see the nameless masonries, venerable messages of the unknown events, heroes, records of the earth.

I see the places of the sagas,
I see pine-trees and fir-trees torn by northern blasts,
I see granite bowlders and cliffs, I see green meadows and lakes,
I see the burial-cairns of Scandinavian warriors,
I see them raised high with stones by the marge of restless oceans, that the dead men's spirits when they wearied of their quiet graves might rise up through the mounds and gaze on the tossing billows, and be refresh'd by storms, immensity, liberty, action.

I see the steppes of Asia,
I see the tumuli of Mongolia, I see the tents of Kalmucks and Baskirs,
I see the nomadic tribes with herds of oxen and cows,
I see the table-lands notch'd with ravines, I see the jungles and deserts,
I see the camel, the wild steed, the bustard,° the fat-tail'd sheep, the
      antelope, and the burrowing wolf.

I see the highlands of Abyssinia,
I see flocks of goats feeding, and see the fig-tree, tamarind, date,
And see fields of teff-wheat and places of verdure and gold.

I see the Brazilian vaquero,
I see the Bolivian ascending mount Sorata,
I see the Wacho crossing the plains, I see the incomparable rider of
      horses with his lasso on his arm,
I see over the pampas the pursuit of wild cattle for their hides.

8

I see the regions of snow and ice,
I see the sharp-eyed Samoiede and the Finn,
I see the seal-seeker in his boat poising his lance,
I see the Siberian on his slight-built sledge drawn by dogs,
I see the porpoise-hunters, I see the whale-crews of the south Pacific
      and the north Atlantic,
I see the cliffs, glaciers, torrents, valleys, of Switzerland—I mark the
      long winters and the isolation.

9

I see the cities of the earth and make myself at random a part of them,
I am a real Parisian,
I am a habitan° of Vienna, St. Petersburg, Berlin, Constantinople,
I am of Adelaide, Sidney, Melbourne,
I am of London, Manchester, Bristol, Edinburgh, Limerick,
I am of Madrid, Cadiz, Barcelona, Oporto, Lyons, Brussels, Berne,
      Frankfort, Stuttgart, Turin, Florence,
I belong in Moscow, Cracow, Warsaw, or northward in Christiania or
      Stockholm, or in Siberian Irkutsk, or in some street in Iceland,
I descend upon all those cities, and rise from them again.

10

I see vapors exhaling from unexplored countries,
I see the savage types, the bow and arrow, the poison'd splint, the
      fetich,° and the obi.°

I see African and Asiatic towns,
I see Algiers, Tripoli, Derne, Mogadore, Timbuctoo, Monrovia,
I see the swarms of Pekin, Canton, Benares, Delhi, Calcutta, Tokio,
I see the Kruman in his hut, and the Dahoman and Ashantee-man in
      their huts,

I see the Turk smoking opium in Aleppo,
I see the picturesque crowds at the fairs of Khiva and those of Herat,
I see Teheran, I see Muscat and Medina and the intervening sands,
    I see the caravans toiling onward,
I see Egypt and the Egyptians, I see the pyramids and obelisks,
I look on chisel'd histories, records of conquering kings, dynasties,
    cut in slabs of sand-stone, or on granite-blocks,
I see at Memphis mummy-pits containing mummies embalm'd, swathed
    in linen cloth, lying there many centuries,
I look on the fall'n Theban, the large-ball'd eyes, the side-drooping
    neck, the hands folded across the breast.

I see all the menials of the earth, laboring,
I see all the prisoners in the prisons,
I see the defective human bodies of the earth,
The blind, the deaf and dumb, idiots, hunchbacks, lunatics,
The pirates, thieves, betrayers, murderers, slave-makers of the earth,
The helpless infants, and the helpless old men and women.

I see male and female everywhere,
I see the serene brotherhood of philosophs,
I see the constructiveness of my race,
I see the results of the perseverance and industry of my race,
I see ranks, colors, barbarisms, civilizations, I go among them, I mix
    indiscriminately,
And I salute all the inhabitants of the earth.

11

You whoever you are!
You daughter or son of England!
You of the mighty Slavic tribes and empires! you Russ in Russia!
You dim-descended, black, divine-soul'd African, large, fine-headed,
    nobly-form'd, superbly destin'd, on equal terms with me!
You Norwegian! Swede! Dane! Icelander! you Prussian!
You Spaniard of Spain! you Portuguese!
You Frenchwoman and Frenchman of France!
You Belge! you liberty-lover of the Netherlands! (you stock whence I
    myself have descended;)
You sturdy Austrian! you Lombard! Hun! Bohemian! farmer of Styria!
You neighbor of the Danube!
You working-man of the Rhine, the Elbe, or the Weser! you working-
    woman too!
You Sardinian! you Bavarian! Swabian! Saxon! Wallachian! Bulga-
    rian!
You Roman! Neapolitan! you Greek!
You lithe matador in the arena at Seville!
You mountaineer living lawlessly on the Taurus or Caucasus!
You Bokh horse-herd watching your mares and stallions feeding!

You beautiful-bodied Persian at full speed in the saddle shooting
    arrows to the mark!
You Chinaman and Chinawoman of China! you Tartar of Tartary!
You women of the earth subordinated at your tasks!
You Jew journeying in your old age through every risk to stand once
    on Syrian ground!
You other Jews waiting in all lands for your Messiah!
You thoughtful Armenian pondering by some stream of the Eu-
    phrates! you peering amid the ruins of Nineveh! you ascending
    mount Ararat!
You foot-worn pilgrim welcoming the far-away sparkle of the minarets
    of Mecca!
You sheiks along the stretch from Suez to Bab-el-mandeb ruling your
    families and tribes!
You olive-grower tending your fruit on fields of Nazareth, Damascus,
    or lake Tiberias!
You Thibet trader on the wide inland or bargaining in the shops of
    Lassa!
You Japanese man or woman! you liver in Madagascar, Ceylon, Su-
    matra, Borneo!
All you continentals of Asia, Africa, Europe, Australia, indifferent of
    place!
All you on the numberless islands of the archipelagoes of the sea!
And you of centuries hence when you listen to me!
And you each and everywhere whom I specify not, but include just
    the same!
Health to you! good will to you all, from me and America sent!

Each of us inevitable,
Each of us limitless—each of us with his or her right upon the earth,
Each of us allow'd the eternal purports of the earth,
Each of us here as divinely as any is here.

12

You Hottentot with clicking palate! you woolly-hair'd hordes!
You own'd persons dropping sweat-drops or blood-drops!
You human forms with the fathomless ever-impressive countenances of
    brutes!
You poor koboo° whom the meanest of the rest look down upon for all
    your glimmering language and spirituality!
You dwarf'd Kamtschatkan, Greenlander, Lapp!
You Austral negro, naked, red, sooty, with protrusive lip, groveling,
    seeking your food!
You Caffre, Berber, Soudanese!
You haggard, uncouth, untutor'd Bedowee!
You plague-swarms in Madras, Nankin, Kaubul, Cairo!
You benighted roamer of Amazonia! you Patagonian! you Feejee-man!
I do not prefer others so very much before you either,

I do not say one word against you, away back there where you stand,
(You will come forward in due time to my side.)

13

My spirit has pass'd in compassion and determination around the
whole earth,
I have look'd for equals and lovers and found them ready for me in
all lands,
I think some divine rapport has equalized me with them.

You vapors, I think I have risen with you, moved away to distant con-
tinents, and fallen down there, for reasons,
I think I have blown with you you winds;
You waters I have finger'd every shore with you,
I have run through what any river or strait of the globe has run
through.
I have taken my stand on the bases of peninsulas and on the high
embedded rocks, to cry thence:

Salut au monde!
What cities the light or warmth penetrates I penetrate those cities
myself,
All islands to which birds wing their way I wing my way myself.

Toward you all, in America's name,
I raise high the perpendicular hand, I make the signal,
To remain after me in sight forever,
For all the haunts and homes of men.

SONG OF THE OPEN ROAD

1

Afoot and light-hearted I take to the open road,
Healthy, free, the world before me,
The long brown path before me leading wherever I choose.

Henceforth I ask not good-fortune, I myself am good-fortune,
Henceforth I whimper no more, postpone no more, need nothing,
Done with indoor complaints, libraries, querulous criticisms,
Strong and content I travel the open road.

The earth, that is sufficient,
I do not want the constellations any nearer,
I know they are very well where they are,
I know they suffice for those who belong to them.

(Still here I carry my old delicious burdens,
I carry them, men and women, I carry them with me wherever I go,
I swear it is impossible for me to get rid of them,
I am fill'd with them, and I will fill them in return.)

2

You road I enter upon and look around, I believe you are not all that
    is here,
I believe that much unseen is also here.

Here the profound lesson of reception, nor preference nor denial,
The black with his woolly head, the felon, the diseas'd, the illiterate
    person, are not denied;
The birth, the hasting after the physician, the beggar's tramp, the
    drunkard's stagger, the laughing party of mechanics,
The escaped youth, the rich persons' carriage, the fop, the eloping
    couple,
The early market-man, the hearse, the moving of furniture into the
    town, the return back from the town,
They pass, I also pass, any thing passes, none can be interdicted,
None but are accepted, none but shall be dear to me.

3

You air that serves me with breath to speak!
You objects that call from diffusion my meanings and give them shape!
You light that wraps me and all things in delicate equable showers!
You paths worn in the irregular hollows by the roadsides!
I believe you are latent with unseen existences, you are so dear to me.

You flagg'd walks of the cities! you strong curbs at the edges!
You ferries! you planks and posts of wharves! you timber-lined sides!
    you distant ships!
You rows of houses! you window-pierc'd façades! you roofs!
You porches and entrances! you copings and iron guards!
You windows whose transparent shells might expose so much!
You doors and ascending steps! you arches!
You gray stones of interminable pavements! you trodden crossings!
From all that has touch'd you I believe you have imparted to your-
    selves, and now would impart the same secretly to me,
From the living and the dead you have peopled your impassive sur-
    faces, and the spirits thereof would be evident and amicable
    with me.

4

The earth expanding right hand and left hand,
The picture alive, every part in its best light,
The music falling in where it is wanted, and stopping where it is not
    wanted,
The cheerful voice of the public road, the gay fresh sentiment of the
    road.

O highway I travel, do you say to me *Do not leave me?*
Do you say *Venture not—if you leave me you are lost?*
Do you say *I am already prepared, I am well-beaten and undenied,*
    adhere to me?

O public road, I say back I am not afraid to leave you, yet I love you,
You express me better than I can express myself,
You shall be more to me than my poem.

I think heroic deeds were all conceiv'd in the open air, and all free
    poems also,
I think I could stop here myself and do miracles,
I think whatever I shall meet on the road I shall like, and whoever
    beholds me shall like me,
I think whoever I see must be happy.

5

From this hour I ordain myself loos'd of limits and imaginary lines,
Going where I list, my own master total and absolute,
Listening to others, considering well what they say,
Pausing, searching, receiving, contemplating,
Gently, but with undeniable will, divesting myself of the holds that
    would hold me.

I inhale great draughts of space,
The east and the west are mine, and the north and the south are mine.

I am larger, better than I thought,
I did not know I held so much goodness.

All seems beautiful to me,
I can repeat over to men and women You have done such good to me
      I would do the same to you,
I will recruit for myself and you as I go,
I will scatter myself among men and women as I go,
I will toss a new gladness and roughness among them,
Whoever denies me it shall not trouble me,
Whoever accepts me he or she shall be blessed and shall bless me.

6

Now if a thousand perfect men were to appear it would not amaze me,
Now if a thousand beautiful forms of women appear'd it would not
      astonish me.

Now I see the secret of the making of the best persons,
It is to grow in the open air and to eat and sleep with the earth.

Here a great personal deed has room,
(Such a deed seizes upon the hearts of the whole race of men,
Its effusion of strength and will overwhelms law and mocks all
      authority and all argument against it.)

Here is the test of wisdom,
Wisdom is not finally tested in schools,
Wisdom cannot be pass'd from one having it to another not having it,
Wisdom is of the soul, is not susceptible of proof, is its own proof,
Applies to all stages and objects and qualities and is content,
Is the certainty of the reality and immortality of things, and the
      excellence of things;
Something there is in the float* of the sight of things that provokes it
      out of the soul.

Now I re-examine philosophies and religions,
They may prove well in lecture-rooms, yet not prove at all under the
      spacious clouds and along the landscape and flowing currents.

Here is realization,
Here is a man tallied—he realizes here what he has in him,
The past, the future, majesty, love—if they are vacant of you, you are
      vacant of them.

Only the kernel of every object nourishes;
Where is he who tears off the husks for you and me?
Where is he that undoes stratagems and envelopes for you and me?

Here is adhesiveness,* it is not previously fashion'd, it is apropos;
Do you know what it is as you pass to be loved by strangers?
Do you know the talk of those turning eye-balls?

7

Here is the efflux of the soul,
The efflux of the soul comes from within through embower'd gates,
    ever provoking questions,
These yearnings why are they? these thoughts in the darkness why
    are they?
Why are there men and women that while they are nigh me the sun-
    light expands my blood?
Why when they leave me do my pennants of joy sink flat and lank?
Why are there trees I never walk under but large and melodious
    thoughts descend upon me?
(I think they hang there winter and summer on those trees and
    always drop fruit as I pass;)
What is it I interchange so suddenly with strangers?
What with some driver as I ride on the seat by his side?
What with some fisherman drawing his seine by the shore as I walk
    by and pause?
What gives me to be free to a woman's and man's good-will? what
    gives them to be free to mine?

8

The efflux of the soul is happiness, here is happiness,
I think it pervades the open air, waiting at all times,
Now it flows unto us, we are rightly charged.

Here rises the fluid and attaching character,
The fluid and attaching character is the freshness and sweetness of
    man and woman,
(The herbs of the morning sprout no fresher and sweeter every day
    out of the roots of themselves, than it sprouts fresh and sweet
    continually out of itself.)

Toward the fluid and attaching character exudes the sweat of the love
    of young and old,
From it falls distill'd the charm that mocks beauty and attainments,
Toward it heaves the shuddering longing ache of contact.

9

Allons!* whoever you are come travel with me!
Traveling with me you find what never tires.

The earth never tires,
The earth is rude, silent, incomprehensible at first, Nature is rude and
    incomprehensible at first,
Be not discouraged, keep on, there are divine things well envelop'd,
I swear to you there are divine things more beautiful than words can
    tell.

Allons! we must not stop here,
However sweet these laid-up stores, however convenient this dwelling
    we cannot remain here,
However shelter'd this port and however calm these waters we must
    not anchor here,
However welcome the hospitality that surrounds us we are permitted
    to receive it but a little while.

10

Allons! the inducements shall be greater,
We will sail pathless and wild seas,
We will go where winds blow, waves dash, and the Yankee clipper
    speeds by under full sail.

Allons! with power, liberty, the earth, the elements,
Health, defiance, gayety, self-esteem, curiosity;
Allons! from all formules!*
From your formules, O bat-eyed and materialistic priests.

The stale cadaver blocks up the passage—the burial waits no longer.

Allons! yet take warning!
He traveling with me needs the best blood, thews,* endurance,
None may come to the trial till he or she bring courage and health,
Come not here if you have already spent the best of yourself,
Only those may come who come in sweet and determin'd bodies,
No diseas'd person, no rum-drinker or venereal taint is permitted here.

(I and mine do not convince by arguments, similes, rhymes,
We convince by our presence.)

11

Listen! I will be honest with you,
I do not offer the old smooth prizes, but offer rough new prizes,
These are the days that must happen to you:
You shall not heap up what is call'd riches,
You shall scatter with lavish hand all that you earn or achieve,
You but arrive at the city to which you were destin'd, you hardly
    settle yourself to satisfaction, before you are call'd by an irre-
    sistible call to depart,
You shall be treated to the ironical smiles and mockings of those who
    remain behind you,
What beckonings of love you receive you shall only answer with pas-
    sionate kisses of parting,
You shall not allow the hold of those who spread their reach'd hands
    toward you.

12

Allons! after the great Companions, and to belong to them!

They too are on the road—they are the swift and majestic men—they
  are the greatest women,
Enjoyers of calms of seas and storms of seas,
Sailors of many a ship, walkers of many a mile of land,
Habituès of many distant countries, habituès of far-distant dwellings,
Trusters of men and women, observers of cities, solitary toilers,
Pausers and contemplators of tufts, blossoms, shells of the shore,
Dancers at wedding-dances, kissers of brides, tender helpers of chil-
  dren, bearers of children,
Soldiers of revolts, standers by gaping graves, lowerers-down of coffins,
Journeyers over consecutive seasons, over the years, the curious years
  each emerging from that which preceded it,
Journeyers as with companions, namely their own diverse phases,
Forth-steppers from the latent unrealized baby-days,
Journeyers gayly with their own youth, journeyers with their bearded
  and well-grain'd manhood,
Journeyers with their womanhood, ample, unsurpass'd, content,
Journeyers with their own sublime old age of manhood or womanhood,
Old age, calm, expanded, broad with the haughty breadth of the uni-
  verse,
Old age, flowing free with the delicious near-by freedom of death.

13
Allons! to that which is endless as it was beginningless,
To undergo much, tramps of days, rests of nights,
To merge all in the travel they tend to, and the days and nights they
  tend to,
Again to merge them in the start of superior journeys,
To see nothing anywhere but what you may reach it and pass it,
To conceive no time, however distant, but what you may reach it and
  pass it,
To look up or down no road but it stretches and waits for you, however
  long but it stretches and waits for you,
To see no being, not God's or any, but you also go thither,
To see no possession but you may possess it, enjoying all without
  labor or purchase, abstracting the feast yet not abstracting one
  particle of it,
To take the best of the farmer's farm and the rich man's elegant villa,
  and the chaste blessings of the well-married couple, and the
  fruits of orchards and flowers of gardens,
To take to your use out of the compact cities as you pass through,
To carry buildings and streets with you afterward wherever you go,
To gather the minds of men out of their brains as you encounter them,
  to gather the love out of their hearts,
To take your lovers on the road with you, for all that you leave them
  behind you,
To know the universe itself as a road, as many roads, as roads for
  traveling souls.

All parts away for the progress of souls,
All religion, all solid things, arts, governments—all that was or is
    apparent upon this globe or any globe, falls into niches and
    corners before the procession of souls along the grand roads of
    the universe.

Of the progress of the souls of men and women along the grand roads
    of the universe, all other progress is the needed emblem and
    sustenance.

Forever alive, forever forward,
Stately, solemn, sad, withdrawn, baffled, mad, turbulent, feeble, dis-
    satisfied,
Desperate, proud, fond, sick, accepted by men, rejected by men,
They go! they go! I know that they go, but I know not where they go,
But I know that they go toward the best—toward something great.

Whoever you are, come forth! or man or woman come forth!
You must not stay sleeping and dallying there in the house, though
    you built it, or though it has been built for you.

Out of the dark confinement! out from behind the screen!
It is useless to protest. I know all and expose it.

Behold through you as bad as the rest,
Through the laughter, dancing, dining, supping, of people,
Inside of dresses and ornaments, inside of those wash'd and trimm'd
    faces,
Behold a secret silent loathing and despair.

No husband, no wife, no friend, trusted to hear the confession,
Another self, a duplicate of every one, skulking and hiding it goes,
Formless and wordless through the streets of the cities, polite and
    bland in the parlors,
In the cars of railroads, in steamboats, in the public assembly,
Home to the houses of men and women, at the table, in the bedroom,
    everywhere,
Smartly attired, countenance smiling, form upright, death under the
    breast-bones, hell under the skull-bones,
Under the broadcloth and gloves, under the ribbons and artificial
    flowers,
Keeping fair with the customs, speaking not a syllable of itself,
Speaking of any thing else but never of itself.

14

Allons! through struggles and wars!
The goal that was named cannot be countermanded.

Have the past struggles succeeded?
What has succeeded? yourself? your nation? Nature?
Now understand me well—it is provided in the essence of things that
    from any fruition of success, no matter what, shall come forth
    something to make a greater struggle necessary.

My call is the call of battle, I nourish active rebellion,
He going with me must go well arm'd,
He going with me goes often with spare diet, poverty, angry enemies,
    desertions.

15

Allons! the road is before us!
It is safe—I have tried it—my own feet have tried it well—be not
    detain'd!
Let the paper remain on the desk unwritten, and the book on the shelf
    unopen'd!
Let the tools remain in the workshop! let the money remain unearn'd!
Let the school stand! mind not the cry of the teacher!
Let the preacher preach in his pulpit! let the lawyer plead in the
    court, and the judge expound the law.

Camerado,* I give you my hand!
I give you my love more precious than money,
I give you myself before preaching or law;
Will you give me yourself? will you come travel with me?
Shall we stick by each other as long as we live?

CROSSING BROOKLYN FERRY

1

Flood-tide below me! I see you face to face!
Clouds of the west—sun there half an hour high—I see you also face
    to face.

Crowds of men and women attired in the usual costumes, how curious
    you are to me!
On the ferry-boats the hundreds and hundreds that cross, returning
    home, are more curious to me than you suppose,
And you that shall cross from shore to shore years hence are more to
    me, and more in my meditations, than you might suppose.

2

The impalpable sustenance of me from all things at all hours of the
    day,
The simple, compact, well-join'd scheme, myself disintegrated, every
    one disintegrated yet part of the scheme,
The similitudes* of the past and those of the future,
The glories strung like beads on my smallest sights and hearings, on
    the walk in the street and the passage over the river,
The current rushing so swiftly and swimming with me far away,
The others that are to follow me, the ties between me and them,
The certainty of others, the life, love, sight, hearing of others.

Others will enter the gates of the ferry and cross from shore to shore,
Others will watch the run of the flood-tide,
Others will see the shipping of Manhattan north and west, and the
    heights of Brooklyn to the south and east,
Others will see the islands large and small;
Fifty years hence, others will see them as they cross, the sun half an
    hour high,
A hundred years hence, or ever so many hundred years hence, others
    will see them,
Will enjoy the sunset, the pouring-in of the flood-tide, the falling-back
    to the sea of the ebb-tide.

3

It avails not, time nor place—distance avails not,
I am with you, you men and women of a generation, or ever so many
    generations hence,
Just as you feel when you look on the river and sky, so I felt,
Just as any of you is one of a living crowd, I was one of a crowd,
Just as you are refresh'd by the gladness of the river and the bright
    flow, I was refresh'd,

Just as you stand and lean on the rail, yet hurry with the swift
current, I stood yet was hurried,
Just as you look on the numberless masts of ships and the thick-
stemm'd pipes of steamboats, I look'd.

I too many and many a time cross'd the river of old,
Watched the Twelfth-month sea-gulls, saw them high in the air float-
ing with motionless wings, oscillating their bodies,
Saw how the glistening yellow lit up parts of their bodies and left the
rest in strong shadow,
Saw the slow-wheeling circles and the gradual edging toward the
south,
Saw the reflection of the summer sky in the water,
Had my eyes dazzled by the shimmering track of beams,
Look'd at the fine centrifugal spokes of light round the shape of my
head in the sunlit water,
Look'd on the haze on the hills southward and south-westward,
Look'd on the vapor as it flew in fleeces tinged with violet,
Look'd toward the lower bay to notice the vessels arriving,
Saw their approach, saw aboard those that were near me,
Saw the white sails of schooners and sloops, saw the ships at anchor,
The sailors at work in the rigging or out astride the spars,
The round masts, the swinging motion of the hulls, the slender ser-
pentine pennants,
The large and small steamers in motion, the pilots in their pilot-
houses,
The white wake left by the passage, the quick tremulous whirl of the
wheels,
The flags of all nations, the falling of them at sunset,
The scallop-edged waves in the twilight, the ladled cups, the frolic-
some crests and glistening,
The stretch afar growing dimmer and dimmer, the gray walls of the
granite storehouses by the docks,
On the river the shadowy group, the big steam-tug closely flank'd on
each side by the barges, the hay-boat, the belated lighter,
On the neighboring shore the fires from the foundry chimneys burning
high and glaringly into the night,
Casting their flicker of black contrasted with wild red and yellow
light over the tops of houses, and down into the clefts of
streets.

4

These and all else were to me the same as they are to you,
I loved well those cities, loved well the stately and rapid river,
The men and women I saw were all near to me,
Others the same—others who look back on me because I look'd for-
ward to them,
(The time will come, though I stop here to-day and to-night.)

5

What is it then between us?
What is the count of the scores or hundreds of years between us?

Whatever it is, it avails not—distance avails not, and place avails not,
I too lived, Brooklyn of ample hills was mine,
I too walk'd the streets of Manhattan island, and bathed in the waters
    around it,
I too felt the curious abrupt questionings stir within me,
In the day among crowds of people sometimes they came upon me,
In my walks home late at night or as I lay in my bed they came upon
    me,
I too had been struck from the float° forever held in solution,
I too had receiv'd identity by my body,
That I was I knew was of my body, and what I should be I knew I
    should be of my body.

6

It is not upon you alone the dark patches fall,
The dark threw its patches down upon me also,
The best I had done seem'd to me blank and suspicious,
My great thoughts as I supposed them, were they not in reality
    meagre?
Nor is it you alone who know what it is to be evil,
I am he who knew what it was to be evil,
I too knitted the old knot of contrariety,°
Blabb'd,° blush'd, resented, lied, stole, grudg'd,
Had guile, anger, lust, hot wishes I dared not speak,
Was wayward, vain, greedy, shallow, sly, cowardly, malignant,
The wolf, the snake, the hog, not wanting in me,
The cheating look, the frivolous word, the adulterous wish, not want-
    ing,
Refusals, hates, postponements, meanness, laziness, none of these
    wanting,
Was one with the rest, the days and haps° of the rest,
Was call'd by my nighest name by clear loud voices of young men as
    they saw me approaching or passing,
Felt their arms on my neck as I stood, or the negligent leaning of
    their flesh against me as I sat,
Saw many I loved in the street or ferry-boat or public assembly, yet
    never told them a word,
Lived the same life with the rest, the same old laughing, gnawing,
    sleeping,
Play'd the part that still looks back on the actor or actress,
The same old role, the role that is what we make it, as great as we
    like,
Or as small as we like, or both great and small.

7

Closer yet I approach you,
What thought you have of me now, I had as much of you—I laid in
my stores in advance,
I consider'd long and seriously of you before you were born.

Who was to know what should come home to me?
Who knows but I am enjoying this?
Who knows, for all the distance, but I am as good as looking at you
now, for all you cannot see me?

8

Ah, what can ever be more stately and admirable to me than mast-
hemm'd Manhattan?
River and sunset and scallop-edg'd waves of flood-tide?
The sea-gulls oscillating their bodies, the hay-boat in the twilight, and
the belated lighter?
What gods can exceed these that clasp me by the hand, and with
voices I love call me promptly and loudly by my nighest name
as I approach?
What is more subtle than this which ties me to the woman or man
that looks in my face?
Which fuses me into you now, and pours my meaning into you?

We understand then do we not?
What I promis'd without mentioning it, have you not accepted?
What the study could not teach—what the preaching could not
accomplish is accomplish'd, is it not?

9

Flow on, river! flow with the flood-tide, and ebb with the ebb-tide!
Frolic on, crested and scallop-edg'd waves!
Gorgeous clouds of the sunset! drench with your splendor me, or the
men and women generations after me!
Cross from shore to shore, countless crowds of passengers!
Stand up, tall masts of Mannahatta! stand up, beautiful hills of
Brooklyn!
Throb, baffled and curious brain! throw out questions and answers!
Suspend here and everywhere, eternal float of solution!
Gaze, loving and thirsting eyes, in the house or street or public as-
sembly!
Sound out, voices of young men! loudly and musically call me by my
nighest name!
Live, old life! play the part that looks back on the actor or actress!
Play the old role, the role that is great or small according as one
makes it!
Consider, you who peruse me, whether I may not in unknown ways
be looking upon you;

Be firm, rail over the river, to support those who lean idly, yet haste
    with the hasting current;
Fly on, sea-birds! fly sideways, or wheel in large circles high in the air;
Receive the summer sky, you water, and faithfully hold it till all down-
    cast eyes have time to take it from you!
Diverge, fine spokes of light, from the shape of my head, or any one's
    head, in the sunlit water!
Come on, ships from the lower bay! pass up or down, white-sail'd
    schooners, sloops, lighters!
Flaunt away, flags of all nations! be duly lower'd at sunset!
Burn high your fires, foundry chimneys! cast black shadows at night-
    fall! cast red and yellow light over the tops of the houses!
Appearances, now or henceforth, indicate what you are,
You necessary film, continue to envelop the soul,
About my body for me, and your body for you, be hung our divinest
    aromas,
Thrive, cities—bring your freight, bring your shows, ample and suffi-
    cient rivers,
Expand, being than which none else is perhaps more spiritual,
Keep your places, objects than which none else is more lasting.

You have waited, you always wait, you dumb, beautiful ministers,
We receive you with free sense at last, and are insatiate henceforward,
Not you any more shall be able to foil us, or withhold yourselves
    from us,
We use you, and do not cast you aside—we plant you permanently
    within us,
We fathom you not—we love you—there is perfection in you also,
You furnish your parts toward eternity,
Great or small, you furnish your parts toward the soul.

SONG OF THE ANSWERER

1

Now list to my morning's romanza,* I tell the signs of the Answerer,
To the cities and farms I sing as they spread in the sunshine before me.

A young man comes to me bearing a message from his brother,
How shall the young man know the whether and when of his brother?
Tell him to send me the signs.

And I stand before the young man face to face, and take his right
      hand in my left hand and his left hand in my right hand,
And I answer for his brother and for men, and I answer for him that
      answers for all, and send these signs.

Him all wait for, him all yield up to, his word is decisive and final,
Him they accept, in him lave, in him perceive themselves as amid
      light,
Him they immerse and he immerses them.

Beautiful women, the haughtiest nations, laws, the landscape, people,
      animals,
The profound earth and its attributes and the unquiet ocean, (so tell I
      my morning's romanza,)
All enjoyments and properties and money, and whatever money will
      buy,
The best farms, others toiling and planting and he unavoidably reaps,
The noblest and costliest cities, others grading and building and he
      domiciles there,
Nothing for any one but what is for him, near and far are for him, the
      ships in the offing,
The perpetual shows and marches on land are for him if they are for
      anybody.
He puts things in their attitudes,
He puts to-day out of himself with plasticity and love,
He places his own times, reminiscences, parents, brothers and sisters,
      associations, employment, politics, so that the rest never shame
      them afterward, nor assume to command them.

He is the Answerer,
What can be answer'd he answers, and what cannot be answer'd he
      shows how it cannot be answer'd.

A man is a summons and challenge,
(It is vain to skulk—do you hear that mocking and laughter? do you
      hear the ironical echoes?)

Books, friendships, philosophers, priests, action, pleasure, pride, beat
     up and down seeking to give satisfaction,
He indicates the satisfaction, and indicates them that beat up and
     down also.

Whichever the sex, whatever the season or place, he may go freshly
     and gently and safely by day or by night,
He has the pass-key of hearts, to him the response of the prying of
     hands on the knobs.

His welcome is universal, the flow of beauty is not more welcome or
     universal than he is,
The person he favors by day or sleeps with at night is blessed.

Every existence has its idiom, every thing has an idiom and tongue,
He resolves all tongues into his own and bestows it upon men, and
     any man translates, and any man translates himself also,
One part does not counteract another part, he is the joiner, he sees
     how they join.

He says indifferently and alike *How are you friend?* to the President
     at his levee,
And he says *Good-day my brother*, to Cudge that hoes in the sugar-
     field,
And both understand him and know that his speech is right.

He walks with perfect ease in the capitol,
He walks among the Congress, and one Representative says to an-
     other, *Here is our equal appearing and new.*

Then the mechanics take him for a mechanic,
And the soldiers suppose him to be a soldier, and the sailors that he
     has follow'd the sea,
And the authors take him for an author, and the artists for an artist,
And the laborers perceive he could labor with them and love them,
No matter what the work is, that he is the one to follow it or has
     follow'd it,
No matter what the nation, that he might find his brothers and sisters
     there.

The English believe he comes of their English stock,
A Jew to the Jew he seems, a Russ to the Russ, usual and near, re-
     moved from none.

Whoever he looks at in the traveler's coffee-house claims him,
The Italian or Frenchman is sure, the German is sure, the Spaniard is
     sure, and the island Cuban is sure,

The engineer, the deck-hand on the great lakes, or on the Mississippi
or St. Lawrence or Sacramento, or Hudson or Paumanok sound,
claims him.

The gentleman of perfect blood acknowledges his perfect blood,
The insulter, the prostitute, the angry person, the beggar, see themselves in the ways of him, he strangely transmutes them,
They are not vile any more, they hardly know themselves they are so
grown.

2

The indications and tally of time,
Perfect sanity shows the master among philosophs,
Time, always without break, indicates itself in parts,
What always indicates the poet is the crowd of the pleasant company
of singers, and their words,
The words of the singers are the hours or minutes of the light or dark,
but the words of the maker of poems are the general light and
dark,
The maker of poems settles justice, reality, immortality,
His insight and power encircle things and the human race,
He is the glory and extract thus far of things and of the human race.

The singers do not beget, only the Poet begets,
The singers are welcom'd, understood, appear often enough, but rare
has the day been, likewise the spot, of the birth of the maker of
poems, the Answerer,
(Not every century nor every five centuries has contain'd such a day,
for all its names.)

The singers of successive hours of centuries may have ostensible
names, but the name of each of them is one of the singers,
The name of each is, eye-singer, ear-singer, head-singer, sweet-singer,
night-singer, parlor-singer, love-singer, weird-singer, or something else.

All this time and at all times wait the words of true poems,
The words of true poems do not merely please,
The true poets are not followers of beauty but the august masters of
beauty;
The greatness of sons is the exuding of the greatness of mothers and
fathers,
The words of true poems are the tuft* and final applause of science.

Divine instinct, breadth of vision, the law of reason, health, rudeness
of body, withdrawnness,
Gayety, sun-tan, air-sweetness, such are some of the words of poems.

The sailor and traveler underlie the maker of poems, the Answerer,
The builder, geometer, chemist, anatomist, phrenologist, artist, all
    these underlie the maker of poems, the Answerer.

The words of the true poems give you more than poems,
They give you to form for yourself poems, religions, politics, war,
    peace, behavior, histories, essays, daily life, and every thing
    else,
They balance ranks, colors, races, creeds, and the sexes,
They do not seek beauty, they are sought,
Forever touching them or close upon them follows beauty, longing,
    fain, love-sick.

They prepare for death, yet they are not the finish, but rather the
    outset,
They bring none to his or her terminus or to be content and full,
Whom they take they take into space to behold the birth of stars, to
    learn one of the meanings,
To launch off with absolute faith, to sweep through the ceaseless rings
    and never be quiet again.

OUR OLD FEUILLAGE

Always our old feuillage!*
Always Florida's green peninsula—always the priceless delta of Loui-
siana—always the cotton-fields of Alabama and Texas,
Always California's golden hills and hollows, and the silver mountains
of New Mexico—always soft-breath'd Cuba,
Always the vast slope drain'd by the Southern sea, inseparable with
the slopes drain'd by the Eastern and Western seas,
The area the eighty-third year of these States, the three and a half
millions of square miles,
The eighteen thousand miles of sea-coast and bay-coast on the main,
the thirty thousand miles of river navigation,
The seven millions of distinct families and the same number of dwellings—always these, and more, branching forth into numberless
branches,
Always the free range and diversity—always the continent of Democracy;
Always the prairies, pastures, forests, vast cities, travelers, Kanada, the
snows;
Always these compact lands tied at the hips with the belt stringing
the huge oval lakes;
Always the West with strong native persons, the increasing density
there, the habitans,* friendly, threatening, ironical, scorning in-
vaders;
All sights, South, North, East—all deeds promiscuously done at all
times,
All characters, movements, growths, a few noticed, myriads unnoticed,
Through Mannahatta's streets I walking, these things gathering,
On interior rivers by night in the glare of pine knots, steamboats
wooding up,
Sunlight by day on the valley of the Susquehanna, and on the valleys
of the Potomac and Rappahannock, and the valleys of the
Roanoke and Delaware,
In their northerly wilds beasts of prey haunting the Adirondacks the
hills, or lapping the Saginaw waters to drink,
In a lonesome inlet a sheldrake lost from the flock, sitting on the water
rocking silently,
In farmers' barns oxen in the stable, their harvest labor done, they rest
standing, they are too tired,
Afar on arctic ice the she-walrus lying drowsily while her cubs play
around,
The hawk sailing where men have not yet sail'd, the farthest polar sea,
ripply, crystalline, open, beyond the floes,
White drift spooning ahead where the ship in the tempest dashes,
On solid land what is done in cities as the bells strike midnight together,

In primitive woods the sounds there also sounding, the howl of the
wolf, the scream of the panther, and the hoarse bellow of the
elk,

In winter beneath the hard blue ice of Moosehead lake, in summer
visible through the clear waters, the great trout swimming,

In lower latitudes in warmer air in the Carolinas the large black buzzard floating slowly high beyond the tree tops,

Below, the red cedar festoon'd with tylandria, the pines and cypresses
growing out of the white sand that spreads far and flat,

Rude boats descending the big Pedee, climbing plants, parasites with
color'd flowers and berries enveloping huge trees,

The waving drapery on the live-oak trailing long and low, noiselessly
waved by the wind,

The camp of Georgia wagoners just after dark, the supper-fires and
the cooking and eating by whites and negroes,

Thirty or forty great wagons, the mules, cattle, horses, feeding from
troughs,

The shadows, gleams, up under the leaves of the old sycamore-trees,
the flames with the black smoke from the pitch-pine curling
and rising;

Southern fishermen fishing, the sounds and inlets of North Carolina's
coast, the shad-fishery and the herring-fishery, the large sweep-
seines, the windlasses on shore work'd by horses, the clearing,
curing, and packing-houses;

Deep in the forest in piney woods turpentine dropping from the
incisions in the trees, there are the turpentine works,

There are the negroes at work in good health, the ground in all directions is cover'd with pine straw;

In Tennessee and Kentucky slaves busy in the coalings, at the forge,
by the furnace-blaze, or at the corn-shucking,

In Virginia, the planter's son returning after a long absence, joyfully
welcom'd and kiss'd by the aged mulatto nurse,

On rivers boatmen safely moor'd at nightfall in their boats under
shelter of high banks,

Some of the younger men dance to the sound of the banjo or fiddle,
others sit on the gunwale smoking and talking;

Late in the afternoon the mocking-bird, the American mimic, singing
in the Great Dismal Swamp,

There are the greenish waters, the resinous odor, the plenteous moss,
the cypress-tree, and the juniper-tree;

Northward, young men of Mannahatta,* the target company from an
excursion returning home at evening, the musket-muzzles all
bear bunches of flowers presented by women;

Children at play, or on his father's lap a young boy fallen asleep,
(how his lips move! how he smiles in his sleep!)

The scout riding on horseback over the plains west of the Mississippi,
he ascends a knoll and sweeps his eyes around;

California life, the miner, bearded, dress'd in his rude costume, the
 stanch California friendship, the sweet air, the graves one in
 passing meets solitary just aside the horse-path;
Down in Texas the cotton-field, the negro-cabins, drivers driving mules
 or oxen before rude carts, cotton bales piled on banks and
 wharves;
Encircling all, vast-darting up and wide, the American Soul, with
 equal hemispheres, one Love, one Dilation or Pride;
In arriere° the peace-talk with the Iroquois the aborigines, the calumet,
 the pipe of good-will, arbitration, and indorsement,
The sachem blowing the smoke first toward the sun and then toward
 the earth,
The drama of the scalp-dance enacted with painted faces and guttural
 exclamations,
The setting out of the war-party, the long and stealthy march,
The single file, the swinging hatchets, the surprise and slaughter of
 enemies;
All the acts, scenes, ways, persons, attitudes of these States, reminis-
 cences, institutions,
All these States compact, every square mile of these States without
 excepting a particle;
Me pleas'd, rambling in lanes and country fields, Paumanok's° fields,
Observing the spiral flight of two little yellow butterflies shuffling
 between each other, ascending high in the air,
The darting swallow, the destroyer of insects, the fall traveler south-
 ward but returning northward early in the spring,
The country boy at the close of the day driving the herd of cows and
 shouting to them as they loiter to browse by the roadside,
The city wharf, Boston, Philadelphia, Baltimore, Charleston, New
 Orleans, San Francisco,
The departing ships when the sailors heave at the capstan;
Evening—me in my room—the setting sun,
The setting summer sun shining in my open window, showing the
 swarm of flies, suspended, balancing in the air in the centre of
 the room, darting athwart, up and down, casting swift shadows
 in specks on the opposite wall where the shine is;
The athletic American matron speaking in public to crowds of
 listeners,
Males, females, immigrants, combinations, the copiousness, the in-
 dividuality of the States, each for itself—the money-makers,
Factories, machinery, the mechanical forces, the windlass, lever, pulley,
 all certainties,
The certainty of space, increase, freedom, futurity,
In space the sporades,° the scatter'd islands, the stars—on the firm
 earth, the lands, my lands,
O lands! all so dear to me—what you are, (whatever it is,) I putting it
 at random in these songs, become a part of that, whatever it is,
Southward there, I screaming, with wings slow flapping, with the
 myriads of gulls wintering along the coasts of Florida,

Otherways there atwixt the banks of the Arkansas, the Rio Grande,
the Nueces, the Brazos, the Tombigbee, the Red River, the
Saskatchawan or the Osage, I with the spring waters laughing
and skipping and running,

Northward, on the sands, on some shallow bay of Paumanok, I with
parties of snowy herons wading in the wet to seek worms and
aquatic plants,

Retreating, triumphantly twittering, the king-bird, from piercing the
crow with its bill, for amusement—and I triumphantly twittering,

The migrating flock of wild geese alighting in autumn to refresh
themselves, the body of the flock feed, the sentinels outside
move around with erect heads watching, and are from time to
time reliev'd by other sentinels—and I feeding and taking turns
with the rest,

In Kanadian forests the moose, large as an ox, corner'd by hunters,
rising desperately on his hind-feet, and plunging with his
forefeet, the hoofs as sharp as knives—and I, plunging at the
hunters, corner'd and desperate,

In the Mannahatta,* streets, piers, shipping, store-houses, and the
countless workmen working in the shops,

And I too of the Mannahatta, singing thereof—and no less in myself
than the whole of the Mannahatta in itself,

Singing the song of These, my ever-united lands—my body no more
inevitably united, part to part, and made out of a thousand
diverse contributions one identity, any more than my lands are
inevitably united and made ONE IDENTITY;

Nativities, climates, the grass of the great pastoral Plains,

Cities, labors, death, animals, products, war, good and evil—these me,

These affording, in all their particulars, the old feuillage to me and to
America, how can I do less than pass the clew of the union of
them, to afford the like to you?

Whoever you are! how can I but offer you divine leaves, that you also
be eligible as I am?

How can I but as here chanting, invite you for yourself to collect bouquets of the incomparable feuillage of these States?

A SONG OF JOYS

O to make the most jubilant song!
Full of music—full of manhood, womanhood, infancy!
Full of common employments—full of grain and trees.

O for the voices of animals—O for the swiftness and balance of fishes!
O for the dropping of raindrops in a song!
O for the sunshine and motion of waves in a song!

O the joy of my spirit—it is uncaged—it darts like lightning!
It is not enough to have this globe or a certain time,
I will have thousands of globes and all time.

O the engineer's joys! to go with a locomotive!
To hear the hiss of steam, the merry shriek, the steam-whistle, the
      laughing locomotive!
To push with resistless way and speed off in the distance.

O the gleesome saunter over fields and hillsides!
The leaves and flowers of the commonest weeds, the moist fresh still-
      ness of the woods,
The exquisite smell of the earth at daybreak, and all through the fore-
      noon.

O the horseman's and horsewoman's joys!
The saddle, the gallop, the pressure upon the seat, the cool gurgling
      by the ears and hair.

O the fireman's joys!
I hear the alarm at dead of night,
I hear bells, shouts! I pass the crowd, I run!
The sight of the flames maddens me with pleasure.

O the joy of the strong-brawn'd fighter, towering in the arena in perfect
      condition, conscious of power, thirsting to meet his opponent.

O the joy of that vast elemental sympathy which only the human soul
      is capable of generating and emitting in steady and limitless
      floods.

O the mother's joys!
The watching, the endurance, the precious love, the anguish, the
      patiently yielded life.

O the joy of increase, growth, recuperation,
The joy of soothing and pacifying, the joy of concord and harmony.

O to go back to the place where I was born,
To hear the birds sing once more,
To ramble about the house and barn and over the fields once more,
And through the orchard and along the old lanes once more.

O to have been brought up on bays, lagoons, creeks, or along the
     coast,
To continue and be employ'd there all my life,
The briny and damp smell, the shore, the salt weeds exposed at low
     water,
The work of fishermen, the work of the eel-fisher and clam-fisher;
I come with my clam-rake and spade, I come with my eel-spear,
Is the tide out? I join the group of clam-diggers on the flats,
I laugh and work with them, I joke at my work like a mettlesome
     young man;
In winter I take my eel-basket and eel-spear and travel out on foot on
     the ice—I have a small axe to cut holes in the ice,
Behold me well-clothed going gayly or returning in the afternoon,
     my brood of tough boys accompanying me,
My brood of grown and part-grown boys, who love to be with no one
     else so well as they love to be with me,
By day to work with me, and by night to sleep with me.

Another time in warm weather out in a boat, to lift the lobster-pots
     where they are sunk with heavy stones, (I know the buoys,)
O the sweetness of the Fifth-month morning upon the water as I row
     just before sunrise toward the buoys,
I pull the wicker pots up slantingly, the dark green lobsters are des-
     perate with their claws as I take them out, I insert wooden
     pegs in the joints of their pincers,
I go to all the places one after another, and then row back to the
     shore,
There in a huge kettle of boiling water the lobsters shall be boil'd till
     their color becomes scarlet.

Another time mackerel-taking,
Voracious, mad for the hook, near the surface, they seem to fill the
     water for miles;
Another time fishing for rock-fish in Chesapeake Bay, I one of the
     brown-faced crew;
Another time trailing for blue-fish off Paumanok,* I stand with braced
     body,
My left foot is on the gunwale, my right arm throws far out the coils
     of slender rope,
In sight around me the quick veering and darting of fifty skiffs, my
     companions.

O boating on the rivers,
The voyage down the St. Lawrence, the superb scenery, the steamers,

The ships sailing, the Thousand Islands, the occasional timber-raft
and the raftsmen with long-reaching sweep-oars,
The little huts on the rafts, and the stream of smoke when they cook
supper at evening.

(O something pernicious and dread!
Something far away from a puny and pious life!
Something unproved! something in a trance!
Something escaped from the anchorage and driving free.)

O to work in mines, or forging iron,
Foundry casting, the foundry itself, the rude high roof, the ample and
shadow'd space,
The furnace, the hot liquid pour'd out and running.

O to resume the joys of the soldier!
To feel the presence of a brave commanding officer—to feel his sym-
pathy!
To behold his calmness—to be warm'd in the rays of his smile!
To go to battle—to hear the bugles play and the drums beat!
To hear the crash of artillery—to see the glittering of the bayonets and
musket-barrels in the sun!
To see men fall and die and not complain!
To taste the savage taste of blood—to be so devilish!
To gloat so over the wounds and deaths of the enemy.

O the whaleman's joys! O I cruise my old cruise again!
I feel the ship's motion under me, I feel the Atlantic breezes fanning
me,
I hear the cry again sent down from the mast-head, *There—she blows!*
Again I spring up the rigging to look with the rest—we descend, wild
with excitement,
I leap in the lower'd boat, we row toward our prey where he lies,
We approach stealthy and silent, I see the mountainous mass, lethar-
gic, basking,
I see the harpooner standing up, I see the weapon dart from his vigor-
ous arm;
O swift again far out in the ocean, the wounded whale, settling, run-
ning to windward, tows me,
Again I see him rise to breathe, we row close again,
I see a lance driven through his side, press'd deep, turn'd in the
wound,
Again we back off, I see him settle again, the life is leaving him fast,
As he rises he spouts blood, I see him swim in circles narrower and
narrower, swiftly cutting the water—I see him die,
He gives one convulsive leap in the centre of the circle, and then falls
flat and still in the bloody foam.

O the old manhood of me, my noblest joy of all!
My children and grand-children, my white hair and beard,
My largeness, calmness, majesty, out of the long stretch of my life.

O ripen'd joy of womanhood! O happiness at last!
I am more than eighty years of age, I am the most venerable mother,
How clear is my mind—how all people draw nigh to me!
What attractions are these beyond any before? what bloom more than
    the bloom of youth?
What beauty is this that descends upon me and rises out of me?

O the orator's joys.
To inflate the chest, to roll the thunder of the voice out from the ribs
    and throat,
To make the people rage, weep, hate, desire, with yourself,
To lead America—to quell America with a great tongue.

O the joy of my soul leaning pois'd on itself, receiving identity
    through materials and loving them, observing characters and
    absorbing them,
My soul vibrated back to me from them, from sight, hearing, touch,
    reason, articulation, comparison, memory, and the like,
The real life of my senses and flesh transcending my senses and flesh,
My body done with materials, my sight done with my material eyes,
Proved to me this day beyond cavil that it is not my material eyes
    which finally see,
Nor my material body which finally loves, walks, laughs, shouts, em-
    braces, procreates.

O the farmer's joys!
Ohioan's, Illinoisian's, Wisconsinese', Kanadian's, Iowan's, Kansian's,
    Missourian's, Oregonese' joys!
To rise at peep of day and pass forth nimbly to work,
To plough land in the fall for winter-sown crops,
To plough land in the spring for maize,
To train orchards, to graft the trees, to gather apples in the fall.

O to bathe in the swimming-bath, or in a good place along shore,
To splash the water! to walk ankle-deep, or race naked along the shore.

O to realize space!
The plenteousness of all, that there are no bounds,
To emerge and be of the sky, of the sun and moon and flying clouds,
    as one with them.

O the joy of a manly self-hood!
To be servile to none, to defer to none, not to any tyrant known or un-
    known,
To walk with erect carriage, a step springy and elastic,

To look with calm gaze or with a flashing eye,
To speak with a full and sonorous voice out of a broad chest,
To confront with your personality all the other personalities of the
    earth.

Know'st thou the excellent joys of youth?
Joys of the dear companions and of the merry word and laughing face?
Joy of the glad light-beaming day, joy of the wide-breath'd games?
Joy of sweet music, joy of the lighted ball-room and the dancers?
Joy of the plenteous dinner, strong carouse and drinking?

Yet O my soul supreme!
Know'st thou the joys of pensive thought?
Joys of the free and lonesome heart, the tender, gloomy heart?
Joys of the solitary walk, the spirit bow'd yet proud, the suffering and
    the struggle?
The agonistic throes, the ecstasies, joys of the solemn musings day or
    night?
Joys of the thought of Death, the great spheres Time and Space?
Prophetic joys of better, loftier love's ideals, the divine wife, the
    sweet, eternal, perfect comrade?
Joys all thine own undying one, joys worthy thee O soul.

O while I live to be the ruler of life, not a slave,
To meet life as a powerful conqueror,
No fumes, no ennui, no more complaints or scornful criticisms,
To these proud laws of the air, the water and the ground, proving my
    interior soul impregnable,
And nothing exterior shall ever take command of me.

For not life's joys alone I sing, repeating—the joy of death!
The beautiful touch of Death, soothing and benumbing a few mo-
    ments, for reasons,
Myself discharging my excrementitious body to be burn'd, or render'd
    to powder, or buried,
My real body doubtless left to me for other spheres,
My voided body nothing more to me, returning to the purifications,
    further offices, eternal uses of the earth.

O to attract by more than attraction!
How it is I know not—yet behold! the something which obeys none of
    the rest,

It is offensive, never defensive—yet how magnetic it draws.

O to struggle against great odds, to meet enemies undaunted!
To be entirely alone with them, to find how much one can stand!
To look strife, torture, prison, popular odium, face to face!
To mount the scaffold, to advance to the muzzles of guns with perfect
    nonchalance!
To be indeed a God!

O to sail to sea in a ship!
To leave this steady unendurable land,
To leave the tiresome sameness of the streets, the sidewalks and the
    houses,
To leave you O you solid motionless land, and entering a ship,
To sail and sail and sail!

O to have life henceforth a poem of new joys!
To dance, clap hands, exult, shout, skip, leap, roll on, float on!
To be a sailor of the world bound for all ports,
A ship itself, (see indeed these sails I spread to the sun and air,)
A swift and swelling ship full of rich words, full of joys.

SONG OF THE BROAD-AXE

1

Weapon shapely, naked, wan,
Head from the mother's bowels drawn,
Wooded flesh and metal bone, limb only one and lip only one,
Gray-blue leaf by red-heat grown, helve produced from a little seed
     sown,
Resting the grass amid and upon,
To be lean'd and to lean on.

Strong shapes and attributes of strong shapes, masculine trades, sights
     and sounds,
Long varied train of an emblem, dabs of music,
Fingers of the organist skipping staccato over the keys of the great
     organ.

2

Welcome are all earth's lands, each for its kind,
Welcome are lands of pine and oak,
Welcome are lands of the lemon and fig,
Welcome are lands of gold,
Welcome are lands of wheat and maize, welcome those of the grape,
Welcome are lands of sugar and rice,
Welcome the cotton-lands, welcome those of the white potato and
     sweet potato,
Welcome are mountains, flats, sands, forests, prairies,
Welcome the rich borders of rivers, table-lands, openings,
Welcome the measureless grazing-lands, welcome the teeming soil of
     orchards, flax, honey, hemp;
Welcome just as much the other more hard-faced lands,
Lands rich as lands of gold or wheat and fruit lands,
Lands of mines, lands of the manly and rugged ores,
Lands of coal, copper, lead, tin, zinc,
Lands of iron—lands of the make of the axe.

3

The log at the wood-pile, the axe supported by it,
The sylvan hut, the vine over the doorway, the space clear'd for a
     garden,
The irregular tapping of rain down on the leaves after the storm is
     lull'd,
The wailing and moaning at intervals, the thought of the sea,
The thought of ships struck in the storm and put on their beam ends,
     and the cutting away of masts,
The sentiment of the huge timbers of old-fashion'd houses and barns,

The remember'd print or narrative, the voyage at a venture of men, families, goods,

The disembarkation, the founding of a new city,

The voyage of those who sought a New England and found it, the outset anywhere,

The settlements of the Arkansas, Colorado, Ottawa, Willamette,

The slow progress, the scant fare, the axe, rifle, saddle-bags;

The beauty of all adventurous and daring persons,

The beauty of wood-boys and wood-men with their clear untrimm'd faces,

The beauty of independence, departure, actions that rely on themselves,

The American contempt for statutes and ceremonies, the boundless impatience of restraint,

The loose drift of character, the inkling through random types, the solidification;

The butcher in the slaughter-house, the hands aboard schooners and sloops, the raftsman, the pioneer,

Lumbermen in their winter camp, daybreak in the woods, stripes of snow on the limbs of trees, the occasional snapping,

The glad clear sound of one's own voice, the merry song, the natural life of the woods, the strong day's work,

The blazing fire at night, the sweet taste of supper, the talk, the bed of hemlock-boughs and the bear-skin;

The house-builder at work in cities or anywhere,

The preparatory jointing, squaring, sawing, mortising,

The hoist-up of beams, the push of them in their places, laying them regular,

Setting the studs by their tenons* in the mortises* according as they were prepared,

The blows of mallets and hammers, the attitudes of the men, their curv'd limbs,

Bending, standing, astride the beams, driving in pins, holding on by posts and braces,

The hook'd arm over the plate, the other arm wielding the axe,

The floor-men forcing the planks close to be nail'd,

Their postures bringing their weapons downward on the bearers,

The echoes resounding through the vacant building;

The huge storehouse carried up in the city well under way,

The six framing-men, two in the middle and two at each end, carefully bearing on their shoulders a heavy stick for a cross-beam,

The crowded line of masons with trowels in their right hands rapidly laying the long side-wall, two hundred feet from front to rear,

The flexible rise and fall of backs, the continual click of the trowels striking the bricks,

The bricks one after another each laid so workmanlike in its place, and set with a knock of the trowel-handle,

The piles of materials, the mortar on the mortar-boards, and the steady replenishing by the hod-men;

Spar-makers in the spar-yard, the swarming row of well-grown apprentices,

The swing of their axes on the square-hew'd log shaping it toward the shape of a mast,

The brisk short crackle of the steel driven slantingly into the pine,

The butter-color'd chips flying off in great flakes and slivers,

The limber motion of brawny young arms and hips in easy costumes,

The constructor of wharves, bridges, piers, bulk-heads, floats, stays against the sea;

The city fireman, the fire that suddenly bursts forth in the close-pack'd square,

The arriving engines, the hoarse shouts, the nimble stepping and daring,

The strong command through the fire-trumpets, the falling in line, the rise and fall of the arms forcing the water,

The slender, spasmic, blue-white jets, the bringing to bear of the hooks and ladders and their execution,

The crash and cut away of connecting wood-work, or through floors if the fire smoulders under them,

The crowd with their lit faces watching, the glare and dense shadows;

The forger at his forge-furnace and the user of iron after him,

The maker of the axe large and small, and the welder and temperer,

The chooser breathing his breath on the cold steel and trying the edge with his thumb,

The one who clean-shapes the handle and sets it firmly in the socket;

The shadowy processions of the portraits of the past users also,

The primal patient mechanics, the architects and engineers,

The far-off Assyrian edifice and Mizra edifice,

The Roman lictors* preceding the consuls,

The antique European warrior with his axe in combat,

The uplifted arm, the clatter of blows on the helmeted head,

The death-howl, the limpsy* tumbling body, the rush of friend and foe thither,

The siege of revolted lieges determin'd for liberty,

The summons to surrender, the battering at castle gates, the truce and parley,

The sack of an old city in its time,

The bursting in of mercenaries and bigots tumultuously and disorderly,

Roar, flames, blood, drunkenness, madness,

Goods freely rifled from houses and temples, screams of women in the gripe of brigands,

Craft and thievery of camp-followers, men running, old persons despairing,

The hell of war, the cruelties of creeds,

The list of all executive deeds and words just or unjust,

The power of personality just or unjust.

4

Muscle and pluck forever!
What invigorates life invigorates death,
And the dead advance as much as the living advance,
And the future is no more uncertain than the present,
For the roughness of the earth and of man encloses as much as the
    delicatesse* of the earth and of man,
And nothing endures but personal qualities.

What do you think endures?
Do you think a great city endures?
Or a teeming manufacturing state? or a prepared constitution? or the
    best built steamships?
Or hotels of granite and iron? or any chef-d'œuvres* of engineering,
    forts, armaments?

Away! these are not to be cherish'd for themselves,
They fill their hour, the dancers dance, the musicians play for them,
The show passes, all does well enough of course,
All does very well till one flash of defiance.

A great city is that which has the greatest men and women,
If it be a few ragged huts it is still the greatest city in the whole world.

5

The place where a great city stands is not the place of stretch'd
    wharves, docks, manufactures, deposits of produce merely,
Nor the place of ceaseless salutes of new-comers or the anchor-lifters
    of the departing,
Nor the place of the tallest and costliest buildings or shops selling
    goods from the rest of the earth,
Nor the place of the best libraries and schools, nor the place where
    money is plentiest,
Nor the place of the most numerous population.

Where the city stands with the brawniest breed of orators and bards,
Where the city stands that is belov'd by these, and loves them in return
    and understands them,
Where no monuments exist to heroes but in the common words and
    deeds,
Where thrift is in its place, and prudence is in its place,
Where the men and women think lightly of the laws,
Where the slave ceases, and the master of slaves ceases,
Where the populace rise at once against the never-ending audacity of
    elected persons,
Where fierce men and women pour forth as the sea to the whistle of
    death pours its sweeping and unript* waves,
Where outside authority enters always after the precedence of inside
    authority,

Where the citizen is always the head and ideal, and President, Mayor,
Governor and what not, are agents for pay,
Where children are taught to be laws to themselves, and to depend on
themselves,
Where equanimity is illustrated in affairs,
Where speculations on the soul are encouraged,
Where women walk in public processions in the streets the same as
the men,
Where they enter the public assembly and take places the same as the
men;
Where the city of the faithfulest friends stands,
Where the city of the cleanliness of the sexes stands,
Where the city of the healthiest fathers stands,
Where the city of the best-bodied mothers stands,
There the great city stands.

6

How beggarly appear arguments before a defiant deed!
How the floridness of the materials of cities shrivels before a man's
or woman's look!

All waits or goes by default till a strong being appears;
A strong being is the proof of the race and of the ability of the uni-
verse,
When he or she appears materials are overaw'd,
The dispute on the soul stops,
The old customs and phrases are confronted, turn'd back, or laid away.

What is your money-making now? what can it do now?
What is your respectability now?
What are your theology, tuition, society, traditions, statute-books, now?
Where are your jibes of being now?
Where are your cavils about the soul now?

7

A sterile landscape covers the ore, there is as good as the best for all
the forbidding appearance,
There is the mine, there are the miners,
The forge-furnace is there, the melt is accomplish'd, the hammers-
men are at hand with their tongs and hammers,
What always served and always serves is at hand.

Than this nothing has better served, it has served all,
Served the fluent-tongued and subtle-sensed Greek, and long ere the
Greek,
Served in building the buildings that last longer than any,
Served the Hebrew, the Persian, the most ancient Hindustanee,
Served the mound-raiser on the Mississippi, served those whose relics
remain in Central America,
Served Albic temples in woods or on plains, with unhewn pillars and
the druids,

Served the artificial clefts, vast, high, silent, on the snow-cover'd hills
    of Scandinavia,
Served those who time out of mind made on the granite walls rough
    sketches of the sun, moon, stars, ships, ocean waves,
Served the paths of the irruptions* of the Goths, served the pastoral
    tribes and nomads,
Served the long distant Kelt, served the hardy pirates of the Baltic,
Served before any of those the venerable and harmless men of Ethiopia,
Served the making of helms for the galleys of pleasure and the making
    of those for war,
Served all great works on land and all great works on the sea,
For the mediæval ages and before the mediæval ages,
Served not the living only then as now, but served the dead.

8

I see the European headsman,
He stands mask'd, clothed in red, with huge legs and strong naked
    arms,
And leans on a ponderous axe.

(Whom have you slaughter'd lately European headsman?
Whose is that blood upon you so wet and sticky?)

I see the clear sunsets of the martyrs,
I see from the scaffolds the descending ghosts,
Ghosts of dead lords, uncrown'd ladies, impeach'd ministers, rejected
    kings,
Rivals, traitors, poisoners, disgraced chieftains and the rest.

I see those who in any land have died for the good cause,
The seed is spare, nevertheless the crop shall never run out,
(Mind you O foreign kings, O priests, the crop shall never run out.)

I see the blood wash'd entirely away from the axe,
Both blade and helve are clean,
They spirt* no more the blood of European nobles, they clasp no more
    the necks of queens.

I see the headsman withdraw and become useless,
I see the scaffold untrodden and mouldy, I see no longer any axe
    upon it,
I see the mighty and friendly emblem of the power of my own race,
    the newest, largest race.

9

(America! I do not vaunt my love for you,
I have what I have.)

The axe leaps!
The solid forest gives fluid utterances,
They tumble forth, they rise and form,

Hut, tent, landing, survey,
Flail, plough, pick, crowbar, spade,
Shingle, rail, prop, wainscot, jamb, lath, panel, gable,
Citadel, ceiling, saloon, academy, organ, exhibition-house, library,
Cornice, trellis, pilaster, balcony, window, turret, porch,
Hoe, rake, pitchfork, pencil, wagon, staff, saw, jack-plane, mallet,
    wedge, rounce,
Chair, tub, hoop, table, wicket, vane, sash, floor,
Work-box, chest, string'd instrument, boat, frame, and what not,
Capitols of States, and capitols of the nation of States,
Long stately rows in avenues, hospitals for orphans or for the poor or
    sick,
Manhattan steamboats and clippers taking the measure of all seas.

The shapes arise!
Shapes of the using of axes anyhow, and the users and all that neigh-
    bors them,
Cutters down of wood and haulers of it to the Penobscot or Kennebec,
Dwellers in cabins among the California mountains or by the little
    lakes, or on the Columbia,
Dwellers south on the banks of the Gila or Rio Grande, friendly gather-
    ings, the characters and fun,
Dwellers along the St. Lawrence, or north in Kanada, or down by the
    Yellowstone, dwellers on coasts and off coasts,
Seal-fishers, whalers, arctic seamen breaking passages through the ice.

The shapes arise!
Shapes of factories, arsenals, foundries, markets,
Shapes of the two-threaded tracks of railroads,
Shapes of the sleepers of bridges, vast frameworks, girders, arches,
Shapes of the fleets of barges, tows, lake and canal craft, river craft,
Ship-yards and dry-docks along the Eastern and Western seas, and in
    many a bay and by-place,
The live-oak kelsons,* the pine planks, the spars, the hackmatack*-
    roots for knees,*
The ships themselves on their ways, the tiers of scaffolds, the workmen
    busy outside and inside,
The tools lying around, the great auger and little auger, the adze, bolt,
    line, square, gouge, and bead-plane.

10

The shapes arise!
The shape measur'd, saw'd, jack'd, join'd, stain'd,
The coffin-shape for the dead to lie within in his shroud,
The shape got out in posts, in the bedstead posts, in the posts of the
    bride's bed,
The shape of the little trough, the shape of the rockers beneath, the
    shape of the babe's cradle,
The shape of the floor-planks, the floor-planks for dancer's feet,

The shape of the planks of the family home, the home of the friendly
    parents and children,
The shape of the roof of the home of the happy young man and
    woman, the roof over the well-married young man and woman,
The roof over the supper joyously cook'd by the chaste wife, and joy-
    ously eaten by the chaste husband, content after his day's work.

The shapes arise!
The shape of the prisoner's place in the court-room, and of him or her
    seated in the place.
The shape of the liquor-bar lean'd against by the young rum-drinker
    and the old rum-drinker,
The shape of the shamed and angry stairs trod by sneaking footsteps,
The shape of the sly settee, and the adulterous unwholesome couple,
The shape of the gambling-board with its devilish winnings and losings,
The shape of the step-ladder for the convicted and sentenced mur-
    derer, the murderer with haggard face and pinion'd arms,
The sheriff at hand with his deputies, the silent and white-lipp'd
    crowd, the dangling of the rope.

The shapes arise!
Shapes of doors giving many exits and entrances,
The door passing the dissever'd° friend flush'd and in haste,
The door that admits good news and bad news,
The door whence the son left home confident and puff'd up,
The door he enter'd again from a long and scandalous absence,
    diseas'd, broken down, without innocence, without means.

11

Her shape arises,
She less guarded than ever, yet more guarded than ever,
The gross and soil'd she moves among do not make her gross and
    soil'd,
She knows the thoughts as she passes, nothing is conceal'd from her,
She is none the less considerate or friendly therefor,
She is the best belov'd, it is without exception, she has no reason to
    fear and she does not fear,
Oaths, quarrels, hiccupp'd songs, smutty expressions are idle to her as
    she passes,
She is silent, she is possess'd of herself, they do not offend her,
She receives them as the laws of Nature receive them, she is strong,
She too is a law of Nature—there is no law stronger than she is.

12

The main shapes arise!
Shapes of Democracy total, result of centuries,
Shapes ever projecting other shapes,
Shapes of turbulent manly cities,
Shapes of the friends and home-givers of the whole earth,
Shapes bracing the earth and braced with the whole earth.

SONG OF THE EXPOSITION

1

(Ah little recks* the laborer,
How near his work is holding him to God,
The loving Laborer through space and time.)

After all not to create only, or found only,
But to bring perhaps from afar what is already founded,
To give it our own identity, average, limitless, free,
To fill the gross the torpid bulk with vital religious fire,
Not to repel or destroy so much as accept, fuse, rehabilitate,
To obey as well as command, to follow more than to lead,
These also are the lessons of our New World;
While how little the New after all, how much the Old, Old World!

Long and long has the grass been growing,
Long and long has the rain been falling,
Long has the globe been rolling round.

2

Come Muse migrate from Greece and Ionia,
Cross out please those immensely overpaid accounts,
That matter of Troy and Achilles' wrath, and Aeneas', Odysseus' wan-
       derings,
Placard "Removed" and "To Let" on the rocks of your snowy Par-
       nassus,
Repeat at Jerusalem, place the notice high on Jaffa's gate and on
       Mount Moriah,
The same on the walls of your German, French and Spanish castles,
       and Italian collections,
For know a better, fresher, busier sphere, a wide, untried domain
       awaits, demands you.

3

Responsive to our summons,
Or rather to her long-nurs'd inclination,
Join'd with an irresistible, natural gravitation,
She comes! I hear the rustling of her gown,
I scent* the odor of her breath's delicious fragrance,
I mark her step divine, her curious eyes a-turning, rolling,
Upon this very scene.

The dame of dames! can I believe then,
Those ancient temples, sculptures classic, could none of them retain
       her?

Nor shades of Virgil and Dante, nor myriad memories, poems, old
associations, magnetize and hold on to her?
But that she's left them all—and here?

Yes, if you will allow me to say so,
I, my friends, if you do not, can plainly see her,
The same undying soul of earth's, activity's, beauty's, heroism's ex-
pression,
Out from her evolutions hither come, ended the strata of her former
themes,
Hidden and cover'd by to-day's, foundation of to-day's,
Ended, deceas'd through time, her voice by Castaly's fountain,
Silent the broken-lipp'd Sphynx in Egypt, silent all those century-
baffling tombs,
Ended for aye the epics of Asia's, Europe's helmeted warriors, ended
the primitive call of the muses,
Calliope's call forever closed, Clio, Melpomene, Thalia dead,
Ended the stately rhythmus of Una and Oriana, ended the quest of
the Holy Graal,
Jerusalem a handful of ashes blown by the wind, extinct,
The Crusaders' streams of shadowy midnight troops sped with the
sunrise,
Amadis, Tancred, utterly gone, Charlemagne, Roland, Oliver gone,
Palmerin, ogre, departed, vanish'd the turrets that Usk from its
waters reflected,
Arthur vanish'd with all his knights, Merlin and Lancelot and Gala-
had, all gone, dissolv'd utterly like an exhalation;
Pass'd! pass'd! for us, forever pass'd, that once so mighty world, now
void, inanimate, phantom world,
Embroider'd, dazzling, foreign world, with all its gorgeous legends,
myths,
Its kings and castles proud, its priests and warlike lords and courtly
dames,
Pass'd to its charnel vault, coffin'd with crown and armor on,
Blazon'd with Shakspere's purple page,
And dirged by Tennyson's sweet sad rhyme.

I say I see, my friends, if you do not, the illustrious emigré, (having
it is true in her day, although the same, changed, journey'd
considerable,)
Making directly for this rendezvous, vigorously clearing a path for
herself, striding through the confusion,
By thud of machinery and shrill steam-whistle undismay'd,
Bluff'd not a bit by drain-pipe, gasometers, artificial fertilizers,
Smiling and pleas'd with palpable intent to stay,
She's here, install'd amid the kitchen ware!

4

But hold—don't I forget my manners?
To introduce the stranger, (what else indeed do I live to chant for?)
    to thee Columbia;
In liberty's name welcome immortal! clasp hands,
And ever henceforth sisters dear be both.

Fear not O Muse! truly new ways and days receive, surround you,
I candidly confess a queer, queer race, of novel fashion,
And yet the same old human race, the same within, without,
Faces and hearts the same, feelings the same, yearnings the same,
The same old love, beauty and use the same.

5

We do not blame thee elder World, nor really separate ourselves
    from thee,
(Would the son separate himself from the father?)
Looking back on thee, seeing thee to thy duties, grandeurs, through
    past ages bending, building,
We build to ours to-day.

Mightier than Egypt's tombs,
Fairer than Grecia's, Roma's temples,
Prouder than Milan's statued, spired cathedral,
More picturesque than Rhenish castle-keeps,
We plan even now to raise, beyond them all,
Thy great cathedral sacred industry, no tomb,
A keep for life for practical invention.

As in a waking vision,
E'en while I chant I see it rise, I scan and prophesy outside and in,
Its manifold ensemble.

Around a palace, loftier, fairer, ampler than any yet,
Earth's modern wonder, history's seven outstripping,
High rising tier on tier with glass and iron façades,
Gladdening the sun and sky, enhued in cheerfulest hues,
Bronze, lilac, robin's-egg, marine and crimson,
Over whose golden roof shall flaunt, beneath thy banner Freedom,
The banners of the States and flags of every land,
A brood of lofty, fair, but lesser palaces shall cluster.

Somewhere within their walls shall all that forwards perfect human
    life be started,
Tried, taught, advanced, visibly exhibited.

Not only all the world of works, trade, products,
But all the workmen of the world here to be represented.

Here shall you trace in flowing operation,
In every state of practical, busy movement, the rills of civilization,
Materials here under your eye shall change their shape as if by magic,
The cotton shall be pick'd almost in the very field,
Shall be dried, clean'd, ginn'd, baled, spun into thread and cloth
    before you,
You shall see hands at work at all the old processes and all the new
    ones,
You shall see the various grains and how flour is made and then
    bread baked by the bakers,
You shall see the crude ores of California and Nevada passing on
    and on till they become bullion,
You shall watch how the printer sets type, and learn what a composing-
    stick is,
You shall mark in amazement the Hoe press whirling its cylinders,
    shedding the printed leaves steady and fast,
The photograph, model, watch, pin, nail, shall be created before you.

In large calm halls, a stately museum shall teach you the infinite
    lessons of minerals,
In another, woods, plants, vegetation shall be illustrated—in another
    animals, animal life and development.

One stately house shall be the music house,
Others for other arts—learning, the sciences, shall all be here,
None shall be slighted, none but shall here be honor'd, help'd,
    exampled.

6

(This, this and these, America, shall be *your* pyramids and obelisks,
Your Alexandrian Pharos, gardens of Babylon,
Your temple at Olympia.)

The male and female many laboring not,
Shall ever here confront the laboring many,
With precious benefits to both, glory to all,
To thee America, and thee eternal Muse.

And here shall ye inhabit powerful Matrons!
In your vast state vaster than all the old,
Echoed through long, long centuries to come,
To sound of different, prouder songs, with stronger themes,
Practical, peaceful life, the people's life, the People themselves,
Lifted, illumin'd, bathed in peace—elate,* secure in peace.

7

Away with themes of war! away with war itself!
Hence from my shuddering sight to never more return that show of
    blacken'd, mutilated corpses!

That hell unpent and raid of blood, fit for wild tigers or for lop-
    tongued wolves, not reasoning men,
And in its stead speed industry's campaigns,
With thy undaunted armies, engineering,
Thy pennants labor, loosen'd to the breeze,
Thy bugles sounding loud and clear.

Away with old romance!
Away with old novels, plots and plays of foreign courts,
Away with love-verses sugar'd in rhyme, the intrigues, amours of
    idlers,
Fitted for only banquets of the night where dancers to late music
    slide,
The unhealthy pleasures, extravagant dissipations of the few,
With perfumes, heat and wine, beneath the dazzling chandeliers.

To you ye reverent sane sisters,
I raise a voice for far superber themes for poets and for art,
To exalt the present and the real,
To teach the average man the glory of his daily walk and trade,
To sing in songs how exercise and chemical life are never to be
    baffled,
To manual work for each and all, to plough, hoe, dig,
To plant and tend the tree, the berry, vegetables, flowers,
For every man to see to it that he really do something, for every
    woman too;
To use the hammer and the saw, (rip, or cross-cut,)
To cultivate a turn for carpentering, plastering, painting,
To work as tailor, tailoress, nurse, hostler, porter,
To invent a little, something ingenious, to aid the washing, cooking,
    cleaning,
And hold it no disgrace to take a hand at them themselves.

I say I bring thee Muse to-day and here,
All occupations, duties broad and close,
Toil, healthy toil and sweat, endless, without cessation,
The old, old practical burdens, interests, joys,
The family, parentage, childhood, husband and wife,
The house-comforts, the house itself and all its belongings,
Food and its preservation, chemisty applied to it,
Whatever forms the average, strong, complete, sweet-blooded man or
    woman, the perfect longeve° personality,
And helps its present life to health and happiness, and shapes its soul,
For the eternal real life to come.

With latest connections, works, the inter-transportation of the world,
Steam-power, the great express lines, gas, petroleum,
These triumphs of our time, the Atlantic's delicate cable,

The Pacific railroad, the Suez canal, the Mont Cenis and Gothard
and Hoosac tunnels, the Brooklyn bridge,
This earth all spann'd with iron rails, with lines of steamships threading every sea,
Our own rondure, the current globe I bring.

8

And thou America,
Thy offspring towering e'er so high, yet higher Thee above all tower-
ing,
With Victory on thy left, and at thy right hand Law;
Thou Union holding all, fusing, absorbing, tolerating all,
Thee, ever thee, I sing.

Thou, also thou, a World,
With all thy wide geographies, manifold, different, distant,
Rounded by thee in one—one common orbic language,
One common indivisible destiny for All.

And by the spells which ye vouchsafe to those your ministers in
earnest,
I here personify and call my themes, to make them pass before ye.

Behold, America! (and thou, ineffable guest and sister!)
For thee come trooping up thy waters and thy lands;
Behold! thy fields and farms, thy far-off woods and mountains,
As in procession coming.

Behold, the sea itself,
And on its limitless, heaving breast, the ships;
See, where their white sails, bellying in the wind, speckle the green
and blue,
See, the steamers coming and going, steaming in or out of port,
See, dusky and undulating, the long pennants of smoke.

Behold, in Oregon, far in the north and west,
Or in Maine, far in the north and east, thy cheerful axemen,
Wielding all day their axes.

Behold, on the lakes, thy pilots at their wheels, thy oarsmen,
How the ash writhes under those muscular arms!

There by the furnace, and there by the anvil,
Behold thy sturdy blacksmiths swinging their sledges,
Overhand so steady, overhand they turn and fall with joyous clank,
Like a tumult of laughter.

Mark the spirit of invention everywhere, thy rapid patents,
The continual workshops, foundries, risen or rising,
See, from their chimneys how the tall flame-fires stream.

Mark, thy interminable farms, North, South,
Thy wealthy daughter-states, Eastern and Western,
The varied products of Ohio, Pennsylvania, Missouri, Georgia, Texas,
    and the rest,
Thy limitless crops, grass, wheat, sugar, oil, corn, rice, hemp, hops,
Thy barns all fill'd, the endless freight-train and the bulging storehouse,
The grapes that ripen on thy vines, the apples in thy orchards,
Thy incalculable lumber, beef, pork, potatoes, thy coal, thy gold and
    silver,
The inexhaustible iron in thy mines.

All thine, O sacred Union!
Ships, farms, shops, barns, factories, mines,
City and State, North, South, item and aggregate,
We dedicate, dread Mother, all to thee!

Protectress absolute, thou! bulwark of all!
For well we know that while thou givest each and all, (generous as
    God,)
Without thee neither all nor each, nor land, home,
Nor ship, nor mine, nor any here this day secure,
Nor aught, nor any day secure.

9

And thou, the Emblem waving over all!
Delicate beauty, a word to thee, (it may be salutary,)
Remember thou hast not always been as here to-day so comfortably
    ensovereign'd,
In other scenes than these have I observ'd thee flag,
Not quite so trim and whole and freshly blooming in folds of stainless
    silk,
But I have seen thee bunting, to tatters torn upon thy splinter'd staff,
Or clutch'd to some young color-bearer's breast with desperate hands,
Savagely struggled for, for life or death, fought over long,
'Mid cannons' thunder-crash and many a curse and groan and yell,
    and rifle-volleys cracking sharp,
And moving masses as wild demons surging, and lives as nothing
    risk'd,
For thy mere remnant grimed with dirt and smoke and sopp'd in
    blood,
For sake of that, my beauty, and that thou might'st dally as now
    secure up there,
Many a good man have I seen go under.

Now here and these and hence in peace, all thine, O flag!
And here and hence for thee, O universal Muse! and thou for them!
And here and hence O Union, all the work and workmen thine!
None separate from thee—henceforth One only, we and thou,

(For the blood of the children, what is it, only the blood maternal?
And lives and works, what are they all at last, except the roads to
faith and death?)

While we rehearse our measureless wealth, it is for thee, dear Mother,
We own it all and several to-day indissoluble in thee;
Think not our chant, our show, merely for products gross or lucre—it
is for thee, the soul in thee, electric, spiritual!
Our farms, inventions, crops, we own in thee! cities and States in
thee!
Our freedom all in thee! our very lives in thee!

SONG OF THE REDWOOD-TREE

1

A California song,
A prophecy and indirection, a thought impalpable to breathe as air,
A chorus of dryads, fading, departing, or hamadryads departing,
A murmuring, fateful, giant voice, out of the earth and sky,
Voice of a mighty dying tree in the redwood forest dense.

Farewell my brethren,
Farewell O earth and sky, farewell ye neighboring waters,
My time has ended, my term has come.

Along the northern coast,
Just back from the rock-bound shore and the caves,
In the saline air from the sea in the Mendocino country,
With the surge for base and accompaniment low and hoarse,
With crackling blows of axes sounding musically driven by strong
      arms,
Riven deep by the sharp tongues of the axes, there in the redwood
      forest dense,
I heard the mighty tree its death-chant chanting.

The choppers heard not, the camp shanties echoed not,
The quick-ear'd teamsters and chain and jack-screw men heard not,
As the wood-spirits came from their haunts of a thousand years to
      join the refrain,
But in my soul I plainly heard.

Murmuring out of its myriad leaves,
Down from its lofty top rising two hundred feet high,
Out of its stalwart trunk and limbs, out of its foot-thick bark,
That chant of the seasons and time, chant not of the past only but
      the future.

You untold life of me,
And all you venerable and innocent joys,
Perennial hardy life of me with joys 'mid rain and many a summer
      sun,
And the white snows and night and the wild winds;
O the great patient rugged joys, my soul's strong joys unreck'd by
      man,
(For know I bear the soul befitting me, I too have consciousness,
      identity,
And all the rocks and mountains have, and all the earth,)
Joys of the life befitting me and brothers mine,
Our time, our term has come.

Nor yield we mournfully majestic brothers,
We who have grandly fill'd our time;
With Nature's calm content, with tacit huge delight,
We welcome what we wrought for through the past,
And leave the field for them.
For them predicted long,
For a superber race, they too to grandly fill their time,
For them we abdicate, in them ourselves ye forest kings!
In them these skies and airs, these mountain peaks, Shasta, Nevadas,
These huge precipitous cliffs, this amplitude, these valleys, far Yo-
semite,
To be in them absorb'd, assimilated.

Then to a loftier strain,
Still prouder, more ecstatic rose the chant,
As if the heirs, the deities of the West,
Joining with master-tongue bore part.

Not wan from Asia's fetiches,°
Nor red from Europe's old dynastic slaughter-house,
(Area of murder-plots of thrones, with scent left yet of wars and
scaffolds everywhere,)
But come from Nature's long and harmless throes, peacefully builded
thence,
These virgin lands, lands of the Western shore,
To the new culminating man, to you, the empire new,
You promis'd long, we pledge, we dedicate.

You occult deep volitions,
You average spiritual manhood, purpose of all, pois'd on yourself,
giving not taking law,
You womanhood divine, mistress and source of all, whence life and
love and aught that comes from life and love,
You unseen moral essence of all the vast materials of America, (age
upon age working in death the same as life,)
You that, sometimes known, oftener unknown, really shape and mould
the New World, adjusting it to Time and Space,
You hidden national will lying in your abysms, conceal'd but ever
alert,
You past and present purposes tenaciously pursued, may-be uncon-
scious of yourselves,
Unswerv'd by all the passing errors, perturbations° *of the surface;*
You vital, universal, deathless germs, beneath all creeds, arts, statutes,
literatures,
Here build your homes for good, establish here, these areas entire,
lands of the Western shore,
We pledge, we dedicate to you.

For man of you, your characteristic race,
Here may he hardy, sweet, gigantic grow, here tower proportionate
to Nature,
Here climb the vast pure spaces unconfined, uncheck'd, by wall or
roof,
Here laugh with storm or sun, here joy, here patiently inure,*
Here heed himself, unfold himself, (not others' formulas heed,) here
fill his time,
To duly fall, to aid, unreck'd at last,
To disappear, to serve.

Thus on the northern coast,
In the echo of teamsters' calls and the clinking chains, and the music
of choppers' axes,
The falling trunk and limbs, the crash, the muffled shriek, the groan,
Such words combined from the redwood-tree, as of voices ecstatic,
ancient and rustling,
The century-lasting, unseen dryads, singing, withdrawing,
All their recesses of forests and mountains leaving,
From the Cascade range to the Wasatch, or Idaho far, or Utah,
To the deities of the modern henceforth yielding,
The chorus and indications, the vistas of coming humanity, the settle-
ments, features all,
In the Mendocino woods I caught.

2

The flashing and golden pageant of California,
The sudden and gorgeous drama, the sunny and ample lands,
The long and varied stretch from Puget sound to Colorado south,
Lands bathed in sweeter, rarer, healthier air, valley and mountain
cliffs,
The fields of Nature long prepared and fallow, the silent, cyclic
chemistry,
The slow and steady ages plodding, the unoccupied surface ripening,
the rich ores forming beneath;
At last the New arriving, assuming, taking possession,
A swarming and busy race settling and organizing everywhere,
Ships coming in from the whole round world, and going out to the
whole world,
To India and China and Australia and the thousand island paradises
of the Pacific,
Populous cities, the latest inventions, the steamers on the rivers, the
railroads, with many a thrifty farm, with machinery,
And wool and wheat and the grape, and diggings of yellow gold.

3

But more in you than these, lands of the Western shore,
(These but the means, the implements, the standing-ground,)

I see in you, certain to come, the promise of thousands of years, till
    now deferr'd,
Promis'd to be fulfill'd, our common kind, the race.

The new society at last, proportionate to Nature,
In man of you, more than your mountain peaks or stalwart trees
    imperial,
In woman more, far more, than all your gold or vines, or even vital
    air.

Fresh come, to a new world indeed, yet long prepared,
I see the genius of the modern, child of the real and ideal,
Clearing the ground for broad humanity, the true America, heir of
    the past so grand,
To build a grander future.

A SONG FOR OCCUPATIONS

1

A song for occupations!
In the labor of engines and trades and the labor of fields I find the
developments,
And find the eternal meanings.

Workmen and Workwomen!
Were all educations practical and ornamental well display'd out of
me, what would it amount to?
Were I as the head teacher, charitable proprietor, wise statesman,
what would it amount to?
Were I to you as the boss employing and paying you, would that
satisfy you?

The learn'd, virtuous, benevolent, and the usual terms,
A man like me and never the usual terms.

Neither a servant nor a master I,
I take no sooner a large price than a small price, I will have my own
whoever enjoys me,
I will be even* with you and you shall be even with me.

If you stand at work in a shop I stand as nigh as the nighest in the
same shop,
If you bestow gifts on your brother or dearest friend I demand as
good as your brother or dearest friend,
If your lover, husband, wife, is welcome by day or night, I must be
personally as welcome,
If you become degraded, criminal, ill, then I become so for your sake,
If you remember your foolish and outlaw'd deeds, do you think I
cannot remember my own foolish and outlaw'd deeds?
If you carouse at the table I carouse at the opposite side of the table,
If you meet some stranger in the streets and love him or her, why I
often meet strangers in the street and love them.

Why what have you thought of yourself?
Is it you then that thought yourself less?
Is it you that thought the President greater than you?
Or the rich better off than you? or the educated wiser than you?

(Because you are greasy or pimpled, or were once drunk, or a thief,
Or that you are diseas'd, or rheumatic, or a prostitute,
Or from frivolity or impotence, or that you are no scholar and never
saw your name in print,
Do you give in that you are any less immortal?)

2

Souls of men and women! it is not you I call unseen, unheard,
        untouchable and untouching,
It is not you I go argue pro and con about, and to settle whether you
        are alive or no,
I own publicly who you are, if nobody else owns.

Grown, half-grown and babe, of this country and every country,
        in-doors and out-doors, one just as much as the other, I see,
And all else behind or through them.

The wife, and she is not one jot less than the husband,
The daughter, and she is just as good as the son,
The mother, and she is every bit as much as the father.

Offspring of ignorant and poor, boys apprenticed to trades,
Young fellows working on farms and old fellows working on farms,
Sailor-men, merchant-men, coasters, immigrants,
All these I see, but nigher and farther the same I see,
None shall escape me and none shall wish to escape me.

I bring what you much need yet always have,
Not money, amours, dress, eating, erudition, but as good,
I send no agent or medium, offer no representative of value, but offer
        the value itself.

There is something that comes to one now and perpetually,
It is not what is printed, preach'd, discussed, it eludes discussion and
        print,
It is not to be put in a book, it is not in this book,
It is for you whoever your are, it is no farther from you than your
        hearing and sight are from you,
It is hinted by nearest, commonest, readiest, it is ever provoked by
        them.

You may read in many languages, yet read nothing about it,
You may read the President's message and read nothing about it there,
Nothing in the reports from the State department or Treasury depart-
        ment, or in the daily papers or weekly papers,
Or in the census or revenue returns, prices current, or any accounts of
        stock.

3

The sun and stars that float in the open air,
The apple-shaped earth and we upon it, surely the drift of them is
        something grand,
I do not know what it is except that it is grand, and that it is happiness,
And that the enclosing purport of us here is not a speculation or bon-
        mot* or reconnoissance,*

And that it is not something which by luck may turn out well for us,
and without luck must be a failure for us,
And not something which may yet be retracted in a certain contingency.

The light and shade, the curious sense of body and identity, the greed
that with perfect complaisance* devours all things,
The endless pride and outstretching of man, unspeakable joys and
sorrows,
The wonder every one sees in every one else he sees, and the wonders
that fill each minute of time forever,
What have you reckon'd them for, camerado?*
Have you reckon'd them for your trade or farm-work? or for the profits
of your store?
Or to achieve yourself a position? or to fill a gentleman's leisure, or a
lady's leisure?

Have you reckon'd that the landscape took substance and form that it
might be painted in a picture?
Or men and women that they might be written of, and songs sung?
Or the attraction of gravity, and the great laws and harmonious com-
binations and the fluids of the air, as subjects for the savans?*
Or the brown land and the blue sea for maps and charts?
Or the stars to be put in constellations and named fancy names?
Or that the growth of seeds is for agricultural tables, or agriculture
itself?

Old institutions, these arts, libraries, legends, collections, and the
practice handed along in manufactures, will we rate them so
high?
Will we rate our cash and business high? I have no objection,
I rate them as high as the highest—then a child born of a woman and
man I rate beyond all rate.

We thought our Union grand, and our Constitution grand,
I do not say they are not grand and good, for they are,
I am this day just as much in love with them as you,
Then I am in love with You, and with all my fellows upon the earth.

We consider bibles and religions divine—I do not say they are not
divine,
I say they have all grown out of you, and may grow out of you still,
It is not they who give the life, it is you who give the life,
Leaves are not more shed from the trees, or trees from the earth, than
they are shed out of you.

4

The sum of all known reverence I add up in you whoever you are,
The President is there in the White House for you, it is not you who
are here for him,

The Secretaries act in their bureaus for you, not you here for them,
The Congress convenes every Twelfth-month for you,
Laws, courts, the forming of States, the charters of cities, the going
and coming of commerce and mails, are all for you.

List close my scholars dear,
Doctrines, politics and civilization exurge° from you,
Sculpture and monuments and any thing inscribed anywhere are
tallied in you,
The gist of histories and statistics as far back as the records reach is
in you this hour, and myths and tales the same,
If you were not breathing and walking here, where would they all be?
The most renown'd poems would be ashes, orations and plays would
be vacuums.

All architecture is what you do to it when you look upon it,
(Did you think it was in the white or gray stone? or the lines of the
arches and cornices?)

All music is what awakes from you when you are reminded by the
instruments,
It is not the violins and the cornets, it is not the oboe nor the beating
drums, nor the score of the baritone singer singing his sweet
romanza,° nor that of the men's chorus, nor that of the women's
chorus,
It is nearer and farther than they.

5

Will the whole come back then?
Can each see signs of the best by a look in the looking-glass? is there
nothing greater or more?
Does all sit there with you, with the mystic unseen soul?

Strange and hard that paradox true I give,
Objects gross and the unseen soul are one.

House-building, measuring, sawing the boards,
Blacksmithing, glass-blowing, nail-making, coopering, tin-roofing,
shingle-dressing,
Ship-joining, dock-building, fish-curing, flagging of sidewalks by
flaggers,
The pump, the pile-driver, the great derrick, the coal-kiln and brick-
kiln,
Coal-mines and all that is down there, the lamps in the darkness,
echoes, songs, what meditations, what vast native thoughts
looking through smutch'd faces,
Iron-works, forge-fires in the mountains or by river-banks, men around
feeling the melt with huge crowbars, lumps of ore, the due
combining of ore, limestone, coal,

The blast-furnace and the puddling-furnace, the loup-lump* at the
bottom of the melt at last, the rolling-mill, the stumpy bars of
pig-iron, the strong, clean-shaped T-rail for railroads,
Oil-works, silk-works, white-lead-works, the sugar-house, steam-saws,
the great mills and factories,
Stone-cutting, shapely trimmings for façades or window or door-lintels,
the mallet, the tooth-chisel, the jib to protect the thumb,
The calking-iron, the kettle of boiling vault-cement, and the fire
under the kettle,
The cotton-bale, the stevedore's hook, the saw and buck of the
sawyer, the mould of the moulder, the working-knife of the
butcher, the ice-saw, and all the work with ice,
The work and tools of the rigger, grappler, sail-maker, block-maker,
Goods of gutta-percha, papier-maché, colors, brushes, brush-making,
glazier's implements,
The veneer and glue-pot, the confectioner's ornaments, the decanter
and glasses, the shears and flat-iron,
The awl and knee-strap, the pint measure and quart measure, the
counter and stool, the writing-pen of quill or metal, the making
of all sorts of edged tools,
The brewery, brewing, the malt, the vats, everything that is done by

brewers, wine-makers, vinegar-makers,
Leather-dressing, coach-making, boiler-making, rope-twisting, distill-
ing, sign-painting, lime-burning, cotton-picking, electroplating,
electrotyping, stereotyping,
Stave-machines, planing-machines, reaping-machines, ploughing-
machines, thrashing-machines, steam wagons,
The cart of the carman, the omnibus, the ponderous dray,
Pyrotechny, letting off color'd fireworks at night, fancy figures and
jets,
Beef on the butcher's stall, the slaughter-house of the butcher, the
butcher in his killing-clothes,
The pens of live pork, the killing-hammer, the hog-hook, the scalder's
tub, gutting, the cutter's cleaver, the packer's maul, and the
plenteous winterwork of pork-packing,
Flour-works, grinding of wheat, rye, maize, rice, the barrels and the
half and quarter barrels, the loaded barges, the high piles on
wharves and levees,
The men and the work of the men on ferries, railroad, coasters, fish-
boats, canals;
The hourly routine of your own or any man's life, the shop, yard,
store, or factory,
These shows all near you by day and night—workman! whoever you
are, your daily life!
In that and them the heft of the heaviest—in that and them far more
than you estimated, (and far less also,)
In them realities for you and me, in them poems for you and me,

In them, not yourself—you and your soul enclose all things, regardless
    of estimation,
In them the development good—in them all themes, hints, possibilities.

I do not affirm that what you see beyond is futile, I do not advise you
    to stop,
I do not say leadings you thought great are not great,
But I say that none lead to greater than these lead to.

6

Will you seek afar off? you surely come back at last,
In things best known to you finding the best, or as good as the best,
In folks nearest to you finding the sweetest, strongest, lovingest,
Happiness, knowledge, not in another place but this place, not for
    another hour but this hour,
Man in the first you see or touch, always in friend, brother, nighest
    neighbor—woman in mother, sister, wife,
The popular tastes and employments taking precedence in poems or
    anywhere,
You workwomen and workmen of these States having your own divine
    and strong life,
And all else giving place to men and women like you.

When the psalm sings instead of the singer,
When the script preaches instead of the preacher,
When the pulpit descends and goes instead of the carver that carved
    the supporting desk,
When I can touch the body of books by night or by day, and when
    they touch my body back again,
When a university course convinces like a slumbering woman and
    child convince,
When the minted gold in the vault smiles like the night-watchman's
    daughter,
When warrantee deeds loafe in chairs opposite and are my friendly
    companions,
I intend to reach them my hand, and make as much of them as I do of
    men and women like you.

A SONG OF THE ROLLING EARTH

1

A song of the rolling earth, and of words according,
Were you thinking that those were the words, those upright lines?
    those curves, angles, dots?
No, those are not the words, the substantial words are in the ground
    and sea,
They are in the air, they are in you.

Were you thinking that those were the words, those delicious sounds
    out of your friends' mouths?
No, the real words are more delicious than they.

Human bodies are words, myriads of words,
(In the best poems re-appears the body, man's or woman's, well-
    shaped, natural, gay,
Every part able, active, receptive, without shame or the need of
    shame.)

Air, soil, water, fire—those are words,
I myself am a word with them—my qualities interpenetrate with
    theirs—my name is nothing to them,
Though it were told in the three thousand languages, what would
    air, soil, water, fire, know of my name?

A healthy presence, a friendly or commanding gesture, are words, say-
    ings, meanings,
The charms that go with the mere looks of some men and women, are
    sayings and meanings also.

The workmanship of souls is by those inaudible words of the earth,
The masters know the earth's words and use them more than audible
    words.

Amelioration is one of the earth's words,
The earth neither lags nor hastens,
It has all attributes, growths, effects, latent in itself from the jump,
It is not half beautiful only, defects and excrescences show just as
    much as perfections show.

The earth does not withhold, it is generous enough,
The truths of the earth continually wait, they are not so conceal'd
    either,
They are calm, subtle, untransmissible by print,
They are imbued through all things conveying themselves willingly,
Conveying a sentiment and invitation, I utter and utter,

I speak not, yet if you hear me not of what avail am I to you?
To bear, to better, lacking these of what avail am I?

(Accouche! accouchez!*
Will you rot your own fruit in yourself there?
Will you squat and stifle there?)

The earth does not argue,
Is not pathetic, has no arrangements,
Does not scream, haste, persuade, threaten, promise,
Makes no discriminations, has no conceivable failures,
Closes nothing, refuses nothing, shuts none out,
Of all the powers, objects, states, it notifies, shuts none out.

The earth does not exhibit itself nor refuse to exhibit itself, possesses
    still underneath,
Underneath the ostensible sounds, the august chorus of heroes, the
    wail of slaves,
Persuasions of lovers, curses, gasps of the dying, laughter of young
    people, accents of bargainers,
Underneath these possessing words that never fail.

To her children the words of the eloquent dumb great mother never
    fail,
The true words do not fail, for motion does not fail and reflection does
    not fail,
Also the day and night do not fail, and the voyage we pursue does not
    fail.

Of the interminable sisters,
Of the ceaseless cotillions of sisters,
Of the centripetal and centrifugal sisters, the elder and younger sisters,
The beautiful sister we know dances on with the rest.

With her ample back towards every beholder,
With the fascinations of youth and the equal fascinations of age,
Sits she whom I too love like the rest, sits undisturb'd,
Holding up in her hand what has the character of a mirror, while her
    eyes glance back from it,
Glace as she sits, inviting none, denying none,
Holding a mirror day and night tirelessly before her own face.

Seen at hand or seen at a distance,
Duly the twenty-four appear in public every day,
Duly approach and pass with their companions or a companion,
Looking from no countenances of their own, but from the counte-
    nances of those who are with them,
From the countenances of children or women or the manly counte-
    nance,

From the open countenances of animals or from inanimate things,
From the landscape or waters or from the exquisite apparition of the
sky,
From our countenances, mine and yours, faithfully returning them,
Every day in public appearing without fail, but never twice with the
same companions.

Embracing man, embracing all, proceed the three hundred and sixty-
five resistlessly round the sun;
Embracing all, soothing, supporting, follow close three hundred and
sixty-five offsets of the first, sure and necessary as they.

Tumbling on steadily, nothing dreading,
Sunshine, storm, cold heat, forever withstanding, passing, carrying,
The soul's realization and determination still inheriting,
The fluid vacuum around and ahead still entering and dividing,
No balk retarding, no anchor anchoring, or no rock striking,
Swift, glad, content, unbereav'd, nothing losing,
Of all able and ready at any time to give strict account,
The divine ship sails the divine sea.

2

Whoever you are! motion and reflection are especially for you,
The divine ship sails the divine sea for you.

Whoever you are! you are he or she for whom the earth is solid and
liquid,
You are he or she for whom the sun and moon hang in the sky,
For none more than you are the present and the past,
For none more than you is immortality.

Each man to himself and each woman to herself, is the word of the
past and present, and the true word of immortality;
No one can acquire for another—not one,
Not one can grow for another—not one.

The song is to the singer, and comes back most to him,
The teaching is to the teacher, and comes back most to him,
The murder is to the murderer, and comes back most to him,
The theft is to the thief, and comes back most to him,
The love is to the lover, and comes back most to him,
The gift is to the giver, and comes back most to him—it cannot fail,
The oration is to the orator, the acting is to the actor and actress not
to the audience,
And no man understands any greatness or goodness but his own, or
the indication of his own.

3

I swear the earth shall surely be complete to him or her who shall be
complete,
The earth remains jagged and broken only to him or her who remains
jagged and broken.

I swear there is no greatness or power that does not emulate those of
the earth,
There can be no theory of any account unless it corroborate the theory
of the earth,
No politics, song, religion, behavior, or what not, is of account, unless
it compare with the amplitude of the earth,
Unless it face the exactness, vitality, impartiality, rectitude of the earth.

I swear I begin to see love with sweeter spasms than that which
responds love,
It is that which contains itself, which never invites and never refuses.

I swear I begin to see little or nothing in audible words,
All merges toward the presentation of the unspoken meanings of the
earth,
Toward him who sings the songs of the body and of the truths of
the earth,
Toward him who makes the dictionaries of words that print cannot
touch.

I swear I see what is better than to tell the best,
It is always to leave the best untold.

When I undertake to tell the best I find I cannot,
My tongue is ineffectual on its pivots,
My breath will not be obedient to its organs,
I become a dumb man.

The best of the earth cannot be told anyhow, all or any is best,
It is not what you anticipated, it is cheaper, easier, nearer,
Things are not dismiss'd from the places they held before,
The earth is just as positive and direct as it was before,
Facts, religions, improvements, politics, trades, are as real as before,
But the soul is also real, it too is positive and direct,
No reasoning, no proof has establish'd it,
Undeniable growth has establish'd it.

4

These to echo the tones of souls and the phrases of souls,
(If they did not echo the phrases of souls what were they then?
If they had not reference to you in especial what were they then?)

I swear I will never henceforth have to do with the faith that tells the
best,
I will have to do only with that faith that leaves the best untold.

Say on, sayers! sing on, singers!
Delve! mould! pile the words of the earth!
Work on, age after age, nothing is to be lost,
It may have to wait long, but it will certainly come in use,
When the materials are all prepared and ready, the architects shall
appear.

I swear to you the architects shall appear without fail,
I swear to you they will understand you and justify you,
The greatest among them shall be he who best knows you, and
encloses all and is faithful to all,
He and the rest shall not forget you, they shall perceive that you are
not an iota less than they,
You shall be fully glorified in them.

YOUTH, DAY, OLD AGE AND NIGHT

Youth, large, lusty, loving—youth full of grace, force, fascination,
Do you know that Old Age may come after you with equal grace,
force, fascination?

Day full-blown and splendid—day of the immense sun, action, ambition, laughter,
The Night follows close with millions of suns, and sleep and restoring
darkness.

BIRDS OF PASSAGE

1

Come said the Muse,
Sing me a song no poet yet has chanted,
Sing me the universal.

In this broad earth of ours,
Amid the measureless grossness and the slag,
Enclosed and safe within its central heart,
Nestles the seed perfection.

By every life a share or more or less,
None born but it is born, conceal'd or unconceal'd the seed is waiting.

2

Lo! keen-eyed towering science,
As from tall peaks the modern overlooking,
Successive absolute fiats issuing.

Yet again, lo! the soul, above all science,
For it has history gather'd like husks around the globe,
For it the entire star-myriads roll through the sky.

In spiral routes by long detours,
(As a much-tacking ship upon the sea,)
For it the partial to the permanent flowing,
For it the real to the ideal tends.

For it the mystic evolution,
Not the right only justified, what we call evil also justified.

Forth from their masks, no matter what,
From the huge festering trunk, from craft and guile and tears,
Health to emerge and joy, joy universal.

Out of the bulk, the morbid and the shallow,
Out of the bad majority, the varied countless frauds of men and states,
Electric, antiseptic yet, cleaving, suffusing all,
Only the good is universal.

3

Over the mountain-growths disease and sorrow,
An uncaught bird is ever hovering, hovering,
High in the purer, happier air.

From imperfection's murkiest cloud,
Darts always forth one ray of perfect light,
One flash of heaven's glory.

To fashion's, custom's discord,
To the mad Babel-din, the deafening orgies,
Soothing each lull a strain is heard, just heard,
From some far shore the final chorus sounding.

O the blest eyes, the happy hearts,
That see, that know the guiding thread so fine,
Along the mighty labyrinth.

4

And thou America,
For the scheme's culmination, its thought and its reality,
For these (not for thyself) thou hast arrived.

Thou too surroundest all,
Embracing carrying welcoming all, thou too by pathways broad and
    new,
To the ideal tendest.

The measur'd faiths of other lands, the grandeurs of the past,
Are not for thee, but grandeurs of thine own,
Deific faiths and amplitudes, absorbing, comprehending all,
All eligible to all.

All, all for immortality,
Love like the light silently wrapping all,
Nature's amelioration blessing all,
The blossoms, fruits of ages, orchards divine and certain,
Forms, objects, growths, humanities, to spiritual images ripening.

Give me O God to sing that thought,
Give me, give him or her I love this quenchless faith,
In Thy ensemble, whatever else withheld withhold not from us,
Belief in plan of Thee enclosed in Time and Space,
Health, peace, salvation universal.

Is it a dream?
Nay but the lack of it the dream,
And failing it life's lore and wealth a dream,
And all the world a dream.

PIONEERS! O PIONEERS!

Come my tan-faced children,
Follow well in order, get your weapons ready,
Have you your pistols? have you your sharp-edged axes?
    Pioneers! O pioneers!

For we cannot tarry here,
We must march my darlings, we must bear the brunt of danger,
We the youthful sinewy races, all the rest on us depend,
    Pioneers! O pioneers!

O you youths, Western youths,
So impatient, full of action, full of manly pride and friendship,
Plain I see you Western youths, see you tramping with the foremost,
    Pioneers! O pioneers!

Have the elder races halted?
Do they droop and end their lesson, wearied over there beyond the
    seas?
We take up the task eternal, and the burden and the lesson,
    Pioneers! O pioneers!

All the past we leave behind,
We debouch° upon a newer mightier world, varied world,
Fresh and strong the world we seize, world of labor and the march,
    Pioneers! O pioneers!

We detachments steady throwing,
Down the edges, through the passes, up the mountains steep,
Conquering, holding, daring, venturing as we go the unknown ways,
    Pioneers! O pioneers!

We primeval forests felling,
We the rivers stemming, vexing we and piercing deep the mines within,
We the surface broad surveying, we the virgin soil upheaving,
    Pioneers! O pioneers!

Colorado men are we,
From the peaks gigantic, from the great sierras and the high plateaus,
From the mine and from the gully, from the hunting trail we come,
    Pioneers! O pioneers!

From Nebraska, from Arkansas,
Central inland race are we, from Missouri, with the continental blood
    intervein'd,
All the hands of comrades clasping, all the Southern, all the Northern,
    Pioneers! O pioneers!

O resistless restless race!
O beloved race in all! O my breast aches with tender love for all!
O I mourn and yet exult, I am rapt with love for all,
        Pioneers! O pioneers!

Raise the mighty mother mistress,
Waving high the delicate mistress, over all the starry mistress, (bend
    your heads all,)
Raise the fang'd and warlike mistress, stern, impassive, weapon'd
    mistress,
        Pioneers! O pioneers!

See my children, resolute children,
By those swarms upon our rear we must never yield or falter,
Ages back in ghostly millions frowning there behind us urging,
        Pioneers! O pioneers!

On and on the compact ranks,
With accessions ever waiting, with the places of the dead quickly fill'd,
Through the battle, through defeat, moving yet and never stopping,
        Pioneers! O pioneers!

O to die advancing on!
Are there some of us to droop and die? has the hour come?
Then upon the march we fittest die, soon and sure the gap is fill'd,
        Pioneers! O pioneers!

All the pulses of the world,
Falling in they beat for us, with the Western movement beat,
Holding single or together, steady moving to the front, all for us,
        Pioneers! O pioneers!

Life's involv'd and varied pageants,
All the forms and shows, all the workmen at their work,
All the seamen and the landsmen, all the masters with their slaves,
        Pioneers! O pioneers!

All the hapless silent lovers,
All the prisoners in the prisons, all the righteous and the wicked,
All the joyous, all the sorrowing, all the living, all the dying,
        Pioneers! O pioneers!

I too with my soul and body,
We, a curious trio, picking, wandering on our way,
Through these shores amid the shadows, with the apparitions pressing,
        Pioneers! O pioneers!

Lo, the darting bowling orb!
Lo, the brother orbs around, all the clustering suns and planets,
All the dazzling days, all the mystic nights with dreams,
            Pioneers! O pioneers!

These are of us, they are with us,
All for primal needed work, while the followers there in embryo wait
    behind,
We to-day's procession heading, we the route for travel clearing,
            Pioneers! O pioneers!

O you daughters of the West!
O you young and elder daughters! O you mothers and you wives!
Never must you be divided, in our ranks you move united,
            Pioneers! O pioneers!

Minstrels latent on the prairies!
(Shrouded bards of other lands, you may rest, you have done your
    work,)
Soon I hear you coming warbling, soon you rise and tramp amid us,
            Pioneers! O pioneers!

Not for delectations sweet,
Not the cushion and the slipper, not the peaceful and the studious,
Not the riches safe and palling, not for us the tame enjoyment,
            Pioneers! O pioneers!

Do the feasters gluttonous feast?
Do the corpulent sleepers sleep? have they lock'd and bolted doors?
Still be ours the diet hard, and the blanket on the ground,
            Pioneers! O pioneers!

Has the night descended?
Was the road of late so toilsome? did we stop discouraged nodding on
    our way?
Yet a passing hour I yield you in your tracks to pause oblivious,
            Pioneers! O pioneers!

Till with sound of trumpet,
Far, far off the daybreak call—hark! how loud and clear I hear it wind,
Swift! to the head of the army!—swift! spring to your places,
            Pioneers! O pioneers!

TO YOU

Whoever you are, I fear you are walking the walks of dreams,
I fear these supposed realities are to melt from under your feet and
    hands,
Even now your features, joys, speech, house, trade, manners, troubles,
    follies, costume, crimes, dissipate away from you,

Your true soul and body appear before me,
They stand forth out of affairs, out of commerce, shops, work, farms
    clothes, the house, buying, selling, eating, drinking, suffering,
    dying.

Whoever you are, now I place my hand upon you, that you be my
    poem,
I whisper with my lips close to your ear,
I have loved many women and men, but I love none better than you.

O I have been dilatory and dumb,
I should have made my way straight to you long ago,
I should have blabb'd* nothing but you, I should have chanted nothing
    but you.

I will leave all and come and make the hymns of you,
None has understood you, but I understand you,
None has done justice to you, you have not done justice to yourself,
None but has found you imperfect, I only find no imperfection in you,
None but would subordinate you, I only am he who will never consent
    to subordinate you,
I only am he who places over you no master, owner, better, God,
    beyond what waits intrinsically in yourself.

Painters have painted their swarming groups and the centre-figure of
    all,
From the head of the centre-figure spreading a nimbus of gold-color'd
    light,
But I paint myriads of heads, but paint no head without its nimbus of
    gold-color'd light,
From my hand from the brain of every man and woman it streams,
    effulgently* flowing forever.

O I could sing such grandeurs and glories about you!
You have not known what you are, you have slumber'd upon yourself
    all your life,
Your eyelids have been the same as closed most of the time,
What you have done returns already in mockeries,
(Your thrift, knowledge, prayers, if they do not return in mockeries,
    what is their return?)

The mockeries are not you,
Underneath them and within them I see you lurk,
I pursue you where none else has pursued you,
Silence, the desk, the flippant expression, the night, the accustom'd
    routine, if these conceal you from others or from yourself, they
    do not conceal you from me,
The shaved face, the unsteady eye, the impure complexion, if these
    balk others they do not balk me,

The pert apparel, the deform'd attitude, drunkenness, greed, premature
death, all these I part aside.

There is no endowment in man or woman that is not tallied in you,
There is no virtue, no beauty in man or woman, but as good is in you,
No pluck, no endurance in others, but as good is in you,
No pleasure waiting for others, but an equal pleasure waits for you.

As for me, I give nothing to any one except I give the like carefully to
you,
I sing the songs of the glory of none, not God, sooner than I sing the
songs of the glory of you.

Whoever you are! claim your own at any hazard!
These shows of the East and West are tame compared to you,
These immense meadows, these interminable rivers, you are immense
and interminable as they,
These furies, elements, storms, motions of Nature, throes of apparent
dissolution, you are he or she who is master or mistress over
them,
Master or mistress in your own right over Nature, elements, pain,
passion, dissolution.

The hopples* fall from your ankles, you find an unfailing sufficiency,
Old or young, male or female, rude, low, rejected by the rest, whatever you are promulges* itself,
Through birth, life, death, burial, the means are provided, nothing is
scanted,
Through angers, losses, ambition, ignorance, ennui, what you are picks
its way.

FRANCE

The 18th Year of these States

A great year and place,
A harsh discordant natal scream out-sounding, to touch the mother's
heart closer than any yet.

I walk'd the shores of my Eastern sea,
Heard over the waves the little voice,
Saw the divine infant where she woke mournfully wailing, amid the
roar of cannon, curses, shouts, crash of falling buildings,
Was not so sick from the blood in the gutters running, nor from the
single corpses, nor those in heaps, nor those borne away in the
tumbrils,
Was not so desperate at the battues* of death—was not so shock'd at
the repeated fusillades of the guns.

Pale, silent, stern, what could I say to that long-accrued retribution?

Could I wish humanity different?
Could I wish the people made of wood and stone?
Or that there be no justice in destiny or time?

O Liberty! O mate for me!
Here too the blaze, the grape-shot and the axe, in reserve, to fetch
      them out in case of need,
Here too, though long represt, can never be destroy'd,
Here too could rise at last murdering and ecstatic,
Here too demanding full arrears of vengeance.

Hence I sign this salute over the sea,
And I do not deny that terrible red birth and baptism,
But remember the little voice that I heard wailing, and wait with per-
      fect trust, no matter how long,
And from to-day sad and cogent I maintain the bequeath'd cause, as
      for all lands,
And I send these words to Paris with my love,
And I guess some chansonniers* there will understand them,
For I guess there is latent music yet in France, floods of it,
O I hear already the bustle of instruments, they will soon be drowning
      all that would interrupt them,
O I think the east wind brings a triumphal and free march,
It reaches hither, it swells me to joyful madness,
I will run transpose it in words, to justify it,
I will yet sing a song for you ma femme.*

MYSELF AND MINE

Myself and mine gymnastic ever,
To stand the cold or heat, to make good aim with a gun, to sail a boat,
      to manage horses, to beget superb children,
To speak readily and clearly, to feel at home among common people,
And to hold our own in terrible positions on land and sea.

Not for an embroiderer,
(There will always be plenty of embroiderers, I welcome them also,)
But for the fibre of things and for inherent men and women.

Not to chisel ornaments,
But to chisel with free stroke the heads and limbs of plenteous
      supreme Gods, that the States may realize them walking and
      talking.

Let me have my own way,
Let others promulge* the laws, I will make no account of the laws,
Let others praise eminent men and hold up peace, I hold up agitation
      and conflict,

I praise no eminent man, I rebuke to his face the one that was thought
most worthy.

(Who are you? and what are you secretly guilty of all your life?
Will you turn aside all your life? will you grub and chatter all your life?
And who are you, blabbling° by rote, years, pages, languages, remi-
niscences,
Unwitting to-day that you do not know how to speak properly a single
word?)

Let others finish specimens, I never finish specimens,
I start them by exhaustless laws as Nature does, fresh and modern
continually.

I give nothing as duties,
Where others give as duties I give as living impulses,
(Shall I give the heart's action as a duty?)

Let others dispose of questions, I dispose of nothing, I arouse un-
answerable questions,
Who are they I see and touch, and what about them?
What about these likes of myself that draw me so close by tender
directions and indirections?

I call to the world to distrust the accounts of my friends, but listen to
my enemies, as I myself do,
I charge you forever reject those who would expound me, for I cannot
expound myself,

I charge that there be no theory or school founded out of me,
I charge you to leave all free, as I have left all free.

After me, vista!
O I see life is not short, but immeasurably long,
I henceforth tread the world chaste, temperate, an early riser, a steady
grower,
Every hour the semen of centuries, and still of centuries.

I must follow up these continual lessons of the air, water, earth,
I perceive I have no time to lose.

YEAR OF METEORS
(1859-60)

Year of meteors! brooding year!
I would bind in words retrospective some of your deeds and signs,
I would sing your contest for the 19th Presidentiad,°
I would sing how an old man, tall, with white hair, mounted the
scaffold in Virginia,
(I was at hand, silent I stood with teeth shut close, I watch'd,

I stood very near you old man when cool and indifferent, but trembling
    with age and your unheal'd wounds, you mounted the scaffold;)
I would sing in my copious song your census returns of the States,
The tables of population and products, I would sing of your ships and
    their cargoes,
The proud black ships of Manhattan arriving, some fill'd with immi-
    grants, some from the isthmus with cargoes of gold,
Songs thereof would I sing, to all that hitherward comes would I wel-
    come give,
And you would I sing, fair stripling! welcome to you from me, young
    prince of England!
(Remember you surging Manhattan's crowds as you pass'd with your
    cortege of nobles?
There in the crowds stood I, and singled you out with attachment;)
Not forget I to sing of the wonder, the ship as she swam up my bay,
Well-shaped and stately the Great Eastern swam up my bay, she was
    600 feet long,
Her moving swiftly surrounded by myriads of small craft I forget not
    to sing;
Nor the comet that came unannounced out of the north flaring in
    heaven,
Nor the strange huge meteor-procession dazzling and clear shooting
    over our heads,
(A moment, a moment long it sail'd its balls of unearthly light over
    our heads,
Then departed, dropt in the night, and was gone;)
Of such, and fitful as they, I sing—with gleams from them would I
    gleam and patch these chants,
Your chants, O year all mottled with evil and good—year of fore-
    bodings!
Year of comets and meteors transient and strange—lo! even here one
    equally transient and strange!
As I flit through you hastily, soon to fall and be gone, what is this
    chant,
What am I myself but one of your meteors?

WITH ANTECEDENTS

1

With antecedents,
With my fathers and mothers and the accumulations of past ages,
With all which, had it not been, I would not now be here, as I am,
With Egypt, India, Phenicia, Greece and Rome,
With the Kelt, the Scandinavian, the Alb and the Saxon,
With antique maritime ventures, laws, artisanship, wars and journeys,
With the poet, the skald, the saga, the myth, and the oracle,
With the sale of slaves, with enthusiasts, with the troubadour, the
    crusader, and the monk,

With those old continents whence we have come to this new continent,
With the fading kingdoms and kings over there,
With the fading religions and priests,
With the small shores we look back to from our own large and present
     shores,
With countless years drawing themselves onward and arrived at these
     years,
You and me arrived—America arrived and making this year,
This year! sending itself ahead countless years to come.

2

O but it is not the years—it is I, it is You,
We touch all laws and tally all antecedents,
We are the skald, the oracle, the monk and the knight, we easily
     include them and more,
We stand amid time beginningless and endless, we stand amid evil
     and good,
All swings around us, there is as much darkness as light,
The very sun swings itself and its system of planets around us,
Its sun, and its again, all swing around us.

As for me, (torn, stormy, amid these vehement days,)
I have the idea of all, and am all and believe in all,
I believe materialism is true and spiritualism is true, I reject no part

(Have I forgotten any part? any thing in the past?
Come to me whoever and whatever, till I give you recognition.)

I respect Assyria, China, Teutonia, and the Hebrews,
I adopt each theory, myth, god, and demi-god,
I see that the old accounts, bibles, genealogies, are true, without
     exception,
I assert that all past days were what they must have been,
And that they could no-how have been better than they were,
And that to-day is what it must be, and that America is,
And that to-day and America could no-how be better than they are.

3

In the name of these States and in your and my name, the Past,
And in the name of these States and in your and my name, the Present
     time.

I know that the past was great and the future will be great,
And I know that both curiously conjoint* in the present time,
(For the sake of him I typify, for the common average man's sake, your
     sake if you are he,)
And that where I am or you are this present day, there is the centre of
     all days, all races,
And there is the meaning to us of all that has ever come of races and
     days, or ever will come.

A BROADWAY PAGEANT

1

Over the Western sea hither from Niphon* come,
Courteous, the swart-cheek'd two-sworded envoys,
Leaning back in their open barouches, bare-headed, impassive,
Ride to-day through Manhattan.

Libertad! I do not know whether others behold what I behold,
In the procession along with the nobles of Niphon, the errand-bearers,
Bringing up the rear, hovering above, around, or in the ranks marching,
But I will sing you a song of what I behold Libertad.*

When million-footed Manhattan unpent descends to her pavements,
When the thunder-cracking guns arouse me with the proud roar I love,
When the round-mouth'd guns out of the smoke and smell I love spit
    their salutes,
When the fire-flashing guns have fully alerted me, and heaven-clouds
    canopy my city with a delicate thin haze,
When gorgeous the countless straight stems, the forests at the wharves,
    thicken with colors,
When every ship richly drest carries her flag at the peak,
When pennants trail and street-festoons hang from the windows,
When Broadway is entirely given up to foot-passengers and foot-
    standers, when the mass is densest,
When the façades of the houses are alive with people, when eyes gaze
    riveted tens of thousands at a time,
When the guests from the islands advance, when the pageant moves
    forward visible,
When the summons is made, when the answer that waited thousands
    of years answers,
I too arising, answering, descend to the pavements, merge with the
    crowd, and gaze with them.

2

Superb-faced Manhattan!
Comrade Americanos! to us, then at last the Orient comes.

To us, my city,
Where our tall-topt marble and iron beauties range on opposite sides,
    to walk in the space between,
To-day our Antipodes comes.

The Originatress comes,
The nest of languages, the bequeather of poems, the race of eld,*
Florid with blood, pensive, rapt with musings, hot with passion,
Sultry with perfume, with ample and flowing garments,

With sunburnt visage, with intense soul and glittering eyes,
The race of Brahma comes.

See my cantabile!° these and more are flashing to us from the procession,
As it moves changing, a kaleidoscope divine it moves changing before
us.

For not the envoys nor the tann'd Japanese from his island only,
Lithe and silent the Hindoo appears, the Asiatic continent itself
appears, the past, the dead,
The murky night-morning of wonder and fable inscrutable,
The envelop'd mysteries, the old and unknown hive-bees,
The north, the sweltering south, eastern Assyria, the Hebrews, the
ancient of ancients,
Vast desolated cities, the gliding present, all of these and more are in
the pageant-procession.

Geography, the world, is in it,
The Great Sea, the brood of islands, Polynesia, the coast beyond,
The coast you henceforth are facing—you, Libertad! from your West-
ern golden shores,
The countries there with their populations, the millions en-masse° are
curiously here,
The swarming market-places, the temples with idols ranged along the
sides or at the end, bonze,° brahmin, and llama,
Mandarin, farmer, merchant, mechanic, and fisherman,
The singing-girl and the dancing-girl, the ecstatic persons, the secluded
emperors,
Confucius himself, the great poets and heroes, the warriors, the castes,
all,
Trooping up, crowding from all directions, from the Altay mountains,
From Thibet, from the four winding and far-flowing rivers of China,
From the southern peninsulas and the demi-continental islands, from
Malaysia,
These and whatever belongs to them palpable show forth to me, and
are seiz'd by me,
And I am seiz'd by them, and friendlily° held by them,
Till as here them all I chant, Libertad! for themselves and for you.

For I too raising my voice join the ranks of this pageant,
I am the chanter, I chant aloud over the pageant,
I chant the world on my Western sea,
I chant copious the islands beyond, thick as stars in the sky,
I chant the new empire grander than any before, as in a vision it comes
to me,
I chant America the mistress, I chant a greater supremacy,
I chant projected a thousand blooming cities yet in time on those
groups of sea-islands,

My sail-ships and steam-ships threading the archipelagoes,
My stars and stripes fluttering in the wind,
Commerce opening, the sleep of ages having done its work, races
    reborn, refresh'd,
Lives, works resumed—the object I know not—but the old, the Asiatic
    renew'd as it must be,
Commencing from this day surrounded by the world.

3

And you Libertad of the world!
You shall sit in the middle well-pois'd thousands and thousands of
    years,
As to-day from one side the nobles of Asia come to you,
As to-morrow from the other side the queen of England sends her
    eldest son to you.

The sign is reversing, the orb is enclosed,
The ring is circled, the journey is done,
The box-lid is but perceptibly open'd, nevertheless the perfume pours
    copiously out of the whole box.

Young Libertad! with the venerable Asia, the all-mother,
Be considerate with her now and ever hot Libertad, for you are all,
Bend your proud neck to the long-off mother now sending messages
    over the archipelagoes to you,
Bend your proud neck low for once, young Libertad.

Were the children straying westward so long? so wide the tramping?
Were the precedent dim ages debouching westward from Paradise so
    long?
Were the centuries steadily footing it that way, all the while unknown,
    for you, for reasons?

They are justified, they are accomplish'd, they shall now be turn'd the
    other way also, to travel toward you thence,
They shall now also march obediently eastward for your sake Libertad.

SEA-DRIFT

OUT OF THE CRADLE ENDLESSLY ROCKING

Out of the cradle endlessly rocking,
Out of the mocking-bird's throat, the musical shuttle,
Out of the Ninth-month midnight,
Over the sterile sands and the fields beyond, where the child leaving
    his bed wander'd alone, bareheaded, barefoot,
Down from the shower'd halo,
Up from the mystic play of shadows twining and twisting as if they
    were alive,
Out from the patches of briers and blackberries,
From the memories of the bird that chanted to me,
From your memories sad brother, from the fitful risings and fallings I
    heard,
From under that yellow half-moon late-risen and swollen as if with
    tears,
From those beginning notes of yearning and love there in the mist,
From the thousand responses of my heart never to cease,
From the myriad thence-arous'd words,
From the word stronger and more delicious than any,
From such as now they start the scene revisiting,
As a flock, twittering, rising, or overhead passing,
Borne hither, ere all eludes me, hurriedly,
A man, yet by these tears a little boy again,
Throwing myself on the sand, confronting the waves,
I, chanter of pains and joys, uniter of here and hereafter,
Taking all hints to use them, but swiftly leaping beyond them,
A reminiscence sing.

Once Paumanok,*
When the lilac-scent was in the air and Fifth-month grass was grow-
    ing,
Up this seashore in some briers,
Two feather'd guests from Alabama, two together,
And their nest, and four light-green eggs spotted with brown,
And every day the he-bird to and fro near at hand,
And every day the she-bird crouch'd on her nest, silent, with bright
    eyes,
And every day I, a curious boy, never too close, never disturbing
    them,
Cautiously peering, absorbing, translating.

Shine! shine! shine!
Pour down your warmth, great sun!
While we bask, we two together.

Two together!
Winds blow south, or winds blow north,
Day come white, or night come black,
Home, or rivers and mountains from home,
Singing all time, minding no time,
While we two keep together.

Till of a sudden,
May-be kill'd, unknown to her mate,
One forenoon the she-bird crouch'd not on the nest,
Nor return'd that afternoon, nor the next,
Nor ever appear'd again.

And thenceforward all summer in the sound of the sea,
And at night under the full of the moon in calmer weather,
Over the hoarse surging of the sea,
Or flitting from brier to brier by day,
I saw, I heard at intervals the remaining one, the he-bird,
The solitary guest from Alabama.

Blow! blow! blow!
Blow up sea-winds along Paumanok's shore;
I wait and I wait till you blow my mate to me.

Yes, when the stars glisten'd,
All night long on the prong of a moss-scallop'd stake,
Down almost amid the slapping waves,
Sat the lone singer wonderful causing tears.

He call'd on his mate,
He pour'd forth the meanings which I of all men know.

Yes my brother I know,
The rest might not, but I have treasur'd every note,
For more than once dimly down to the beach gliding,
Silent, avoiding the moonbeams, blending myself with the shadows,
Recalling now the obscure shapes, the echoes, the sounds and sights
    after their sorts,
The white arms out in the breakers tirelessly tossing,
I, with bare feet, a child, the wind wafting my hair,
Listen'd long and long.

Listen'd to keep, to sing, now translating the notes,
Following you my brother.

Soothe! soothe! soothe!
Close on its wave soothes the wave behind,
And again another behind embracing and lapping, every one close,
But my love soothes not me, not me.

Low hangs the moon, it rose late,
It is lagging*—O I think it is heavy with love, with love.

O madly the sea pushes upon the land,
With love, with love.

O night! do I not see my love fluttering out among the breakers?
What is that little black thing I see there in the white?

Loud! loud! loud!
Loud I call to you, my love!
High and clear I shoot my voice over the waves,
Surely you must know who is here, is here,
You must know who I am, my love.

Low-hanging moon!
What is that dusky spot in your brown yellow?
O it is the shape, the shape of my mate!
O moon do not keep her from me any longer.

Land! land! O land!
Whichever way I turn, O I think you could give me my mate back
*   again if you only would,*
For I am almost sure I see her dimly whichever way I look.

O rising stars!
Perhaps the one I want so much will rise, will rise with some of you.

O throat! O trembling throat!
Sound clearer through the atmosphere!
Pierce the woods, the earth,
Somewhere listening to catch you must be the one I want.

Shake out carols!
Solitary here, the night's carols!
Carols of lonesome love! death's carols!
Carols under that lagging, yellow, waning moon!
O under that moon where she droops almost down into the sea!
O reckless despairing carols.

But soft! sink low!
Soft! let me just murmur,
And do you wait a moment you husky-nois'd sea,
For somewhere I believe I heard my mate responding to me,
So faint, I must be still, be still to listen,
But not altogether still, for then she might not come immediately to me.

Hither my love!
Here I am! here!

With this just-sustain'd note I announce myself to you,
This gentle call is for you my love, for you.

Do not be decoy'd elsewhere,
That is the whistle of the wind, it is not my voice,
That is the fluttering, the fluttering of the spray,
Those are the shadows of leaves.

O darkness! O in vain!
O I am very sick and sorrowful.

O brown halo in the sky near the moon, drooping upon the sea!
O troubled reflection in the sea!
O throat! O throbbing heart!
And I singing uselessly, uselessly all the night.

O past! O happy life! O songs of joy!
In the air, in the woods, over fields,
Loved! loved! loved! loved! loved!
But my mate no more, no more with me!
We two together no more.

The aria sinking,
All else continuing, the stars shining,
The winds blowing, the notes of the bird continuous echoing,
With angry moans the fierce old mother incessantly moaning,
On the sands of Paumanok's shore gray and rustling,
The yellow half-moon enlarged, sagging down, drooping, the face of
        the sea almost touching,
The boy ecstatic, with his bare feet the waves, with his hair the
        atmosphere dallying,
The love in the heart long pent, now loose, now at last tumultuously
        bursting,
The aria's meaning, the ears, the soul, swiftly depositing,
The strange tears down the cheeks coursing,
The colloquy there, the trio, each uttering,
The undertone, the savage old mother incessantly crying,
To the boy's soul's questions sullenly timing, some drown'd secret
        hissing,
To the outsetting bard.

Demon or bird! (said the boy's soul,)
Is it indeed toward your mate you sing? or is it really to me?
For I, that was a child, my tongue's use sleeping, now I have heard
        you,
Now in a moment I know what I am for, I awake,
And already a thousand singers, a thousand songs, clearer, louder and
        more sorrowful than yours,
A thousand warbling echoes have started to life within me, never to
        die.

O you singer solitary, singing by yourself, projecting me,
O solitary me listening, never more shall I cease perpetuating you,
Never more shall I escape, never more the reverberations,
Never more the cries of unsatisfied love be absent from me,
Never again leave me to be the peaceful child I was before what
       there in the night,
By the sea under the yellow and sagging moon,
The messenger there arous'd, the fire, the sweet hell within,
The unknown want, the destiny of me.

O give me the clew! (it lurks in the night here somewhere,)
O if I am to have so much, let me have more!

A word then, (for I will conquer it,)
The word final, superior to all,
Subtle, sent up—what is it?—I listen;
Are you whispering it, and have been all the time, you sea-waves?
Is that it from your liquid rims and wet sands?

Whereto answering, the sea,
Delaying not, hurrying not,
Whisper'd me through the night, and very plainly before daybreak,
Lisp'd to me the low and delicious word death,
And again death, death, death, death,
Hissing melodious, neither like the bird nor like my arous'd child's
      heart,
But edging near as privately for me rustling at my feet,
Creeping thence steadily up to my ears and laving me softly all over,
Death, death, death, death, death.

Which I do not forget,
But fuse the song of my dusky demon and brother,
That he sang to me in the moonlight on Paumanok's gray beach,
With the thousand responsive songs at random,
My own songs awaked from that hour,
And with them the key, the word up from the waves,
The word of the sweetest song and all songs,
That strong and delicious word which, creeping to my feet,
(Or like some old crone rocking the cradle, swathed in sweet garments,
      bending aside,)
The sea whisper'd me.

AS I EBB'D WITH THE OCEAN OF LIFE

1

As I ebb'd with the ocean of life,
As I wended the shores I know,
As I walk'd where the ripples continually wash you Paumanok,*

Where they rustle up hoarse and sibilant,
Where the fierce old mother endlessly cries for her castaways,
I musing late in the autumn day, gazing off southward,
Held by this electric self out of the pride of which I utter poems,
Was seiz'd by the spirit that trails in the lines underfoot,
The rim, the sediment that stands for all the water and all the land of
    the globe.

Fascinated, my eyes reverting from the south, dropt, to follow those
    slender windrows,
Chaff, straw, splinters of wood, weeds, and the sea-gluten,
Scum, scales from shining rocks, leaves of salt-lettuce, left by the tide,
Miles walking, the sound of breaking waves the other side of me,
Paumanok there and then as I thought the old thought of likenesses,
These you presented to me you fish-shaped island,
As I wended the shores I know,
As I walk'd with that electric self seeking types.

2

As I wend to the shores I know not,
As I list to the dirge, the voices of men and women wreck'd,
As I inhale the impalpable breezes that set in upon me,
As the ocean so mysterious rolls toward me closer and closer,
I too but signify at the utmost a little wash'd-up drift,
A few sands and dead leaves to gather,
Gather, and merge myself as part of the sands and drift.

O baffled, balk'd, bent to the very earth,
Oppress'd with myself that I have dared to open my mouth,
Aware now that amid all that blab* whose echoes recoil upon me I
    have not once had the least idea who or what I am,
But that before all my arrogant poems the real Me stands yet
    untouch'd, untold, altogether unreach'd,
Withdrawn far, mocking me with mock-congratulatory signs and bows,
With peals of distant ironical laughter at every word I have written,
Pointing in silence to these songs, and then to the sand beneath.

I perceive I have not really understood any thing, not a single object,
    and that no man ever can,
Nature here in sight of the sea taking advantage of me to dart upon
    me and sting me,
Because I have dared to open my mouth to sing at all.

3

You oceans both, I close with you,
We murmur alike reproachfully rolling sands and drift, knowing not
    why,
These little shreds indeed standing for you and me and all.

You friable shore with trails of debris,
You fish-shaped island, I take what is underfoot,
What is yours is mine my father.

I too Paumanok,
I too have bubbled up, floated the measureless float,* and been wash'd
    on your shores,
I too am but a trail of drift and debris,
I too leave little wrecks upon you, you fish-shaped island.

I throw myself upon your breast my father,
I cling to you so that you cannot unloose me,
I hold you so firm till you answer me something.

Kiss me my father,
Touch me with your lips as I touch those I love,
Breathe to me while I hold you close the secret of the murmuring I
    envy.

4

Ebb, ocean of life, (the flow will return,)
Cease not your moaning you fierce old mother,
Endlessly cry for your castaways, but fear not, deny not me,
Rustle not up so hoarse and angry against my feet as I touch you or
    gather from you.

I mean tenderly by you and all,
I gather for myself and for this phantom looking down where we lead,
    and following me and mine.

Me and mine, loose windrows, little corpses,
Froth, snowy white, and bubbles,
(See, from my dead lips the ooze exuding at last,
See, the prismatic colors glistening and rolling,)
Tufts of straw, sands, fragments,
Buoy'd hither from many moods, one contradicting another,
From the storm, the long calm, the darkness, the swell,
Musing, pondering, a breath, a briny tear, a dab of liquid or soil,
Up just as much out of fathomless workings fermented and thrown,
A limp blossom or two, torn, just as much over waves floating, drifted
    at random,
Just as much for us that sobbing dirge of Nature,
Just as much whence we come that blare of the cloud-trumpets,
We, capricious, brought hither we know not whence, spread out before
    you,
You up there walking or sitting,
Whoever you are, we too lie in drifts at your feet.

TEARS

Tears! tears! tears!
In the night, in solitude, tears,
On the white shore dripping, dripping, suck'd in by the sand,
Tears, not a star shining, all dark and desolate,
Moist tears from the eyes of a muffled head;
O who is that ghost? that form in the dark, with tears?
What shapeless lump is that, bent, crouch'd there on the sand?
Streaming tears, sobbing tears, throes, choked with wild cries;
O storm, embodied, rising, careering with swift steps along the beach!
O wild and dismal night storm, with wind—O belching and desperate!
O shade so sedate and decorous by day, with calm countenance and
      regulated pace,
But away at night as you fly, none looking—O then the unloosen'd
      ocean,
Of tears! tears! tears!

TO THE MAN-OF-WAR-BIRD

Thou who hast slept all night upon the storm,
Waking renew'd on thy prodigious pinions,
(Burst the wild storm? above it thou ascended'st,
And rested on the sky, thy slave that cradled thee,)
Now a blue point, far, far in heaven floating,
As to the light emerging here on deck I watch thee,
(Myself a speck, a point on the world's floating vast.)
Far, far at sea,
After the night's fierce drifts have strewn the shore with wrecks,
With re-appearing day as now so happy and serene,
The rosy and elastic dawn, the flashing sun,
The limpid spread of air cerulean,
Thou also re-appearest.

Thou born to match the gale, (thou art all wings,)
To cope with heaven and earth and sea and hurricane,
Thou ship of air that never furl'st thy sails,
Days, even weeks untired and onward, through spaces, realms gyrating,
At dusk that look'st on Senegal, at morn America,
That sport'st amid the lightning-flash and thunder-cloud,
In them, in thy experiences, had'st thou my soul,
What joys! what joys were thine!

ABOARD AT A SHIP'S HELM

Aboard at a ship's helm,
A young steersman steering with care.

Through fog on a sea-coast dolefully ringing,
An ocean-bell—O a warning bell, rock'd by the waves.

O you give good notice indeed, you bell by the sea-reefs ringing,
Ringing, ringing, to warn the ship from its wreck-place.

For as on the alert O steersman, you mind the loud admonition,
The bows turn, the freighted ship tacking speeds away under her gray
      sails,
The beautiful and noble ship with all her precious wealth speeds away
      gayly and safe.

But O the ship, the immortal ship! O ship aboard the ship!
Ship of the body, ship of the soul, voyaging, voyaging, voyaging.

ON THE BEACH AT NIGHT

On the beach at night,
Stands a child with her father,
Watching the east, the autumn sky.

Up through the darkness,
While ravening clouds, the burial clouds, in black masses spreading,
Lower sullen and fast athwart and down the sky,
Amid a transparent clear belt of ether yet left in the east,
Ascends large and calm the lord-star Jupiter,
And nigh at hand, only a very little above,
Swim the delicate sisters the Pleiades.

From the beach the child holding the hand of her father,
Those buried clouds that lower victorious soon to devour all,
Watching, silently weeps.

Weep not, child,
Weep not, my darling,
With these kisses let me remove your tears,
The ravening clouds shall not long be victorious,
They shall not long possess the sky, they devour the stars only in
      apparition,
Jupiter shall emerge, be patient, watch again another night, the
      Pleiades shall emerge,
They are immortal, all those stars both silvery and golden shall shine
      out again,
The great stars and the little ones shall shine out again, they endure,
The vast immortal suns and the long-enduring pensive moons shall
      again shine.

Then dearest child mournest thou only for Jupiter?
Considerest thou alone the burial of the stars?

Something there is,
(With my lips soothing thee, adding I whisper,
I give thee the first suggestion, the problem and indirection,)
Something there is more immortal even than the stars,
(Many the burials, many the days and nights, passing away,)
Something that shall endure longer even than lustrous Jupiter,
Longer than sun or any revolving satellite,
Or the radiant sisters the Pleiades.

THE WORLD BELOW THE BRINE

The world below the brine,
Forests at the bottom of the sea, the branches and leaves,
Sea-lettuce, vast lichens, strange flowers and seeds, the thick tangle,
    openings, and pink turf,
Different colors, pale gray and green, purple, white, and gold, the play
    of light through the water,
Dumb swimmers there among the rocks, coral, gluten, grass. rushes,
    and the aliment° of the swimmers,
Sluggish existences grazing there suspended, or slowly crawling close
    to the bottom,
The sperm-whale at the surface blowing air and spray, or disporting
    with his flukes,
The leaden-eyed shark, the walrus, the turtle, the hairy sea-leopard,
    and the sting-ray,
Passions there, wars, pursuits, tribes, sight in those ocean-depths,
    breathing that thick-breathing air, as so many do,
The change thence to the sight here, and to the subtle air breathed by
    beings like us who walk this sphere,
The change onward from ours to that of beings who walk other spheres.

ON THE BEACH AT NIGHT ALONE

On the beach at night alone,
As the old mother sways her to and fro singing her husky song,
As I watch the bright stars shining, I think a thought of the clef of the
    universes and of the future.

A vast similitude° interlocks all,
All spheres, grown, ungrown, small, large, suns, moons, planets,
All distances of place however wide,
All distances of time, all inanimate forms,
All souls, all living bodies though they be ever so different, or in dif-
    ferent worlds,
All gaseous, watery, vegetable, mineral processes, the fishes, the brutes,
All nations, colors, barbarisms, civilizations, languages,
All identities that have existed or may exist on this globe, or any globe,

All lives and deaths, all of the past, present, future,
This vast similitude spans them, and always has spann'd,
And shall forever span them and compactly hold and enclose them.

SONG FOR ALL SEAS, ALL SHIPS

1

To-day a rude brief recitative,
Of ships sailing the seas, each with its special flag or ship-signal,
Of unnamed heroes in the ships—of waves spreading and spreading
  far as the eye can reach,
Of dashing spray, and the winds piping and blowing,
And out of these a chant for the sailors of all nations,
Fitful, like a surge.

Of sea-captains young or old, and the mates, and of all intrepid sailors,
Of the few, very choice, taciturn, whom fate can never surprise nor
      death dismay,
Pick'd sparingly without noise by thee old ocean, chosen by thee,
Thou sea that pickest and cullest the race in time, and unitest nations,
Suckled by thee, old husky nurse, embodying thee,
Indomitable, untamed as thee.

(Ever the heroes on water or on land, by ones or twos appearing,
Ever the stock preserv'd and never lost, though rare, enough for seed
      preserv'd.)

2

Flaunt out O sea your separate flags of nations!
Flaunt out visible as ever the various ship-signals!
But do you reserve especially for yourself and for the soul of man one
      flag above all the rest,
A spiritual woven signal for all nations, emblem of man elate* above
      death,
Token of all brave captains and all intrepid sailors and mates,
And all that went down doing their duty,
Reminiscent of them, twined from all intrepid captains young or old,
A pennant universal, subtly waving all time, o'er all brave sailors,
All seas, all ships.

PATROLING BARNEGAT*

Wild, wild the storm, and the sea high running,
Steady the roar of the gale, with incessant undertone muttering,
Shouts of demoniac laughter fitfully piercing and pealing,
Waves, air, midnight, their savagest trinity lashing,
Out in the shadows there milk-white combs careering,

On beachy slush and sand spirts* of snow fierce slanting,
Where through the murk the easterly death-wind breasting,
Through cutting swirl and spray watchful and firm advancing,
(That in the distance! is that a wreck? is the red signal flaring?)
Slush and sand of the beach tireless till daylight wending,
Steadily, slowly, through hoarse roar never remitting,
Along the midnight edge by those milk-white combs careering,
A group of dim, weird forms, struggling, the night confronting,
That savage trinity warily watching.

AFTER THE SEA-SHIP

After the sea-ship, after the whistling winds,
After the white-gray sails taut to their spars and ropes,
Below, a myriad myriad waves hastening, lifting up their necks,
Tending in ceaseless flow toward the track of the ship,
Waves of the ocean bubbling and gurgling, blithely prying,
Waves, undulating waves, liquid, uneven, emulous* waves,
Toward that whirling current, laughing and buoyant, with curves,
Where the great vessel sailing and tacking displaced the surface,
Larger and smaller waves in the spread of the ocean yearnfully flowing,
The wake of the sea-ship after she passes, flashing and frolicsome under
        the sun,
A motley procession with many a fleck of foam and many fragments,
Following the stately and rapid ship, in the wake following.

BY THE ROADSIDE

A BOSTON BALLAD
(1854)

To get betimes in Boston town I rose this morning early,
Here's a good place at the corner, I must stand and see the show.

Clear the way there Jonathan!
Way for the President's marshal—way for the government cannon!
Way for the Federal foot and dragoons, (and the apparitions copiously
       tumbling.)

I love to look on the Stars and Stripes, I hope the fifes will play
       Yankee Doodle.

How bright shine the cutlasses of the foremost troops!
Every man holds his revolver, marching stiff through Boston town.

A fog follows, antiques of the same come limping,
Some appear wooden-legged, and some appear bandaged and blood-
       less.

Why this is indeed a show—it has called the dead out of the earth!
The old graveyards of the hills have hurried to see!
Phantoms! phantoms countless by flank and rear!
Cock'd hats of mothy mould—crutches made of mist!
Arms in slings—old men leaning on young men's shoulders.

What troubles you Yankee phantoms? what is all this chattering of
       bare gums?
Does the ague convulse your limbs? do you mistake your crutches for
       firelocks and level them?

If you blind your eyes with tears you will not see the President's
       marshal,
If you groan such groans you might balk the government cannon.

For shame old maniacs—bring down those toss'd arms, and let your
       white hair be,
Here gape your great-grandsons, their wives gaze at them from the
       windows,
See how well dress'd, see how orderly they conduct themselves.

Worse and worse—can't you stand it? are you retreating?
Is this hour with the living too dead for you?

Retreat then—pell-mell!
To your graves—back—back to the hills old limpers!
I do not think you belong here anyhow.

But there is one thing that belongs here—shall I tell you what it is,
    gentlemen of Boston?

I will whisper it to the Mayor, he shall send a committee to England,
They shall get a grant from the Parliament, go with a cart to the royal
    vault,
Dig out King George's coffin, unwrap him quick from the grave-
    clothes, box up his bones for a journey,
Find a swift Yankee clipper—here is freight for you, black-bellied
    clipper,
Up with your anchor—shake out your sails—steer straight toward
    Boston bay.

Now call for the President's marshal again, bring out the government
    cannon,
Fetch home the roarers from Congress, make another procession, guard
    it with foot and dragoons.

This centre-piece for them;
Look, all orderly citizens—look from the windows, women!

The committee open the box, set up the regal ribs, glue those that will
    not stay,
Clap the skull on top of the ribs, and clap a crown on top of the skull.

You have got your revenge, old buster—the crown is come to its own,
    and more than its own.
Stick your hands in your pockets, Jonathan—you are a made man from
    this day,
You are mighty cute—and here is one of your bargains.

EUROPE

The 72d and 73d Years of These States

Suddenly out of its stale and drowsy lair, the lair of slaves,
Like lightning it le'pt forth half startled at itself,
Its feet upon the ashes and the rags, its hand tight to the throats of
    kings.

O hope and faith!
O aching close of exiled patriots' lives!
O many a sicken'd heart!
Turn back unto this day and make yourselves afresh.

And you, paid to defile the People—you liars, mark!
Not for numberless agonies, murders, lusts,
For court thieving in its manifold mean forms, worming from his
    simplicity the poor man's wages,
For many a promise sworn by royal lips and broken and laugh'd at in
    the breaking,
Then in their power not for all these did the blows strike revenge, or
    the heads of the nobles fall;
The People scorn'd the ferocity of kings.

But the sweetness of mercy brew'd bitter destruction, and the frighten'd
    monarchs come back,
Each comes in state with his train, hangman, priest, tax-gatherer,
Soldier, lawyer, lord, jailer, and sycophant.

Yet behind all lowering stealing, lo, a shape,
Vague as the night, draped interminably, head, front and form, in
    scarlet folds,
Whose face and eyes none may see,
Out of its robes only this, the red robes lifted by the arm,
One finger crook'd pointed high over the top, like the head of a snake
    appears.

Meanwhile corpses lie in new-made graves, bloody corpses of young
    men,
The rope of the gibbet hangs heavily, the bullets of princes are flying,
    the creatures of power laugh aloud,
And all these things bear fruits, and they are good.

Those corpses of young men,
Those martyrs that hang from the gibbets, those hearts pierc'd by the
    gray lead,
Cold and motionless as they seem live elsewhere with unslaughter'd
    vitality.

They live in other young men O kings!
They live in brothers again ready to defy you,
They were purified by death, they were taught and exalted.

Not a grave of the murder'd for freedom but grows seed for freedom,
    in its turn to bear seed,
Which the winds carry afar and re-sow, and the rains and the snows
    nourish.

Not a disembodied spirit can the weapons of tyrants let loose,
But it stalks invisibly over the earth, whispering, counseling, caution-
    ing.

Liberty, let others despair of you—I never despair of you.

Is the house shut? is the master away?
Nevertheless, be ready, be not weary of watching,
He will soon return, his messengers come anon.

A HAND-MIRROR

Hold it up sternly—see this it sends back, (who is it? is it you?)
Outside fair costume, within ashes and filth,
No more a flashing eye, no more a sonorous voice or springy step,
Now some slave's eye, voice, hands, step,
A drunkard's breath, unwholesome eater's face, venerealee's flesh,
Lungs rotting away piecemeal, stomach sour and cankerous,
Joints rheumatic, bowels clogged with abomination,
Blood circulating dark and poisonous streams,
Words babble, hearing and touch callous,
No brain, no heart left, no magnetism of sex;
Such from one look in this looking-glass ere you go hence,
Such a result so soon—and from such a beginning!

GODS

Lover divine and perfect Comrade,
Waiting content, invisible yet, but certain,
Be thou my God.

Thou, thou, the Ideal Man,
Fair, able, beautiful, content, and loving,
Complete in body and dilate in spirit,
Be thou my God.

O Death, (for Life has served its turn,)
Opener and usher to the heavenly mansion,
Be thou my God.

Aught, aught of mightiest, best I see, conceive, or know,
(To break the stagnant tie—thee, thee to free, O soul,)
Be thou my God.

All great ideas, the races' aspirations,
All heroisms, deeds of rapt enthusiasts,
Be ye my Gods.

Or Time and Space,
Or shape of Earth divine and wondrous,
Or some fair shape I viewing, worship,
Or lustrous orb of sun or star by night,
Be ye my Gods.

GERMS

Forms, qualities, lives, humanity, language, thoughts,
The ones known, and the ones unknown, the ones on the stars,
The stars themselves, some shaped, others unshaped,
Wonders as of those countries, the soil, trees, cities, inhabitants, what-
 ever they may be,
Splendid suns, the moons and rings, the countless combinations and
 effects,
Such-like, and as good as such-like, visible here or anywhere, stand
 provided for in a handful of space, which I extend my arm and
 half enclose with my hand,
That containing the start of each and all, the virtue, the germs of all.

THOUGHTS

Of ownership—as if one fit to own things could not at pleasure enter
 upon all, and incorporate them into himself or herself;
Of vista—suppose some sight in arriere* through the formative chaos,
 presuming the growth, fulness, life, now attain'd on the journey,
(But I see the road continued, and the journey ever continued;)
Of what was once lacking on earth, and in due time has become supplied—and of what will yet be supplied,
Because all I see and know I believe to have its main purport in what
 will yet be supplied.

WHEN I HEARD THE LEARN'D ASTRONOMER

When I heard the learn'd astronomer,
When the proofs, the figures, were ranged in columns before me,
When I was shown the charts and diagrams, to add, divide, and meas-
 ure them,
When I sitting heard the astronomer where he lectured with much
 applause in the lecture-room,
How soon unaccountable I became tired and sick,
Till rising and gliding out I wander'd off by myself,
In the mystical moist night air, and from time to time,
Look'd up in perfect silence at the stars.

PERFECTIONS

Only themselves understand themselves and the like of themselves,
As souls only understand souls.

O ME! O LIFE!

O me! O life! of the questions of these recurring,
Of the endless trains of the faithless, of cities fill'd with the foolish,
Of myself forever reproaching myself, (for who more foolish than I,
    and who more faithless?)
Of eyes that vainly crave the light, of the objects mean, of the struggle
    ever renew'd,
Of the poor results of all, of the plodding and sordid crowds I see
    around me,
Of the empty and useless years of the rest, with the rest me inter-
    twined,
The question, O me! so sad, recurring—What good amid these, O me,
    O life?

Answer

That you are here—that life exists and identity,
That the powerful play goes on, and you may contribute a verse.

TO A PRESIDENT

All you are doing and saying is to America dangled mirages,
You have not learn'd of Nature—of the politics of Nature you have
    not learn'd the great amplitude, rectitude, impartiality,
You have not seen that only such as they are for these States,
And that what is less than they must sooner or later lift off from these
    States.

I SIT AND LOOK OUT

I sit and look out upon all the sorrows of the world, and upon all
    oppression and shame,
I hear secret convulsive sobs from young men at anguish with them-
    selves, remorseful after deeds done,
I see in low life the mother misused by her children, dying, neglected,
    gaunt, desperate,
I see the wife misused by her husband, I see the treacherous seducer
    of young women,
I mark the ranklings of jealousy and unrequited love attempted to be
    hid, I see these sights on the earth,
I see the workings of battle, pestilence, tyranny, I see martyrs and
    prisoners,
I observe a famine at sea, I observe the sailors casting lots who shall be
    kill'd to preserve the lives of the rest,
I observe the slights and degradations cast by arrogant persons upon
    laborers, the poor, and upon negroes, and the like;
All these—all the meanness and agony without end I sitting look out
    upon,
See, hear, and am silent.

TO RICH GIVERS

What you give me I cheerfully accept,
A little sustenance, a hut and garden, a little money, as I rendezvous
    with my poems,
A traveler's lodging and breakfast as I journey through the States,—
    why should I be ashamed to own such gifts? why to advertise
    for them?
For I myself am not one who bestows nothing upon man and woman,
For I bestow upon any man or woman the entrance to all the gifts of
    the universe.

THE DALLIANCE OF THE EAGLES

Skirting the river road, (my forenoon walk, my rest,)
Skyward in air a sudden muffled sound, the dalliance of the eagles,
The rushing amorous contact high in space together,
The clinching interlocking claws, a living, fierce, gyrating wheel,
Four beating wings, two beaks, a swirling mass tight grappling,
In tumbling turning clustering loops, straight downward falling,
Till o'er the river pois'd, the twain yet one, a moment's lull,
A motionless still balance in the air, then parting, talons loosing,
Upward again on slow-firm pinions slanting, their separate diverse
    flight,
She hers, he his, pursuing.

ROAMING IN THOUGHT
(After reading Hegel)

Roaming in thought over the Universe, I saw the little that is Good
    steadily hastening towards immortality,
And the vast all that is call'd Evil I saw hastening to merge itself and
    become lost and dead.

A FARM PICTURE

Through the ample open door of the peaceful country barn,
A sunlit pasture field with cattle and horses feeding,
And haze and vista, and the far horizon fading away.

A CHILD'S AMAZE

Silent and amazed even when a little boy,
I remember I heard the preacher every Sunday put God in his state-
    ments,
As contending against some being or influence.

THE RUNNER

On a flat road runs the well-train'd runner,
He is lean and sinewy with muscular legs,
He is thinly clothed, he leans forward as he runs,
With lightly closed fists and arms partially rais'd.

BEAUTIFUL WOMEN

Women sit or move to and fro, some old, some young,
The young are beautiful—but the old are more beautiful than the
  young.

MOTHER AND BABE

I see the sleeping babe nestling the breast of its mother,
The sleeping mother and babe—hush'd, I study them long and long.

THOUGHT

Of obedience, faith, adhesiveness;*
As I stand aloof and look there is to me something profoundly affecting in large masses of men following the lead of those who do
  not believe in men.

VISOR'D

A mask, a perpetual natural disguiser of herself,
Concealing her face, concealing her form,
Changes and transformations every hour, every moment,
Falling upon her even when she sleeps.

THOUGHT

Of Justice—as if Justice could be any thing but the same ample law,
  expounded by natural judges and saviors,
As if it might be this thing or that thing, according to decisions.

GLIDING O'ER ALL

Gliding o'er all, through all,
Through Nature, Time, and Space,
As a ship on the waters advancing,
The voyage of the soul—not life alone,
Death, many deaths I'll sing.

HAST NEVER COME TO THEE AN HOUR

Hast never come to thee an hour,
A sudden gleam divine, precipitating, bursting all these bubbles,
fashions, wealth?
These eager business aims—books, politics, art, amours,
To utter nothingness?

THOUGHT

Of Equality—as if it harm'd me, giving others the same chances and
rights as myself—as if it were not indispensable to my own
rights that others possess the same.

TO OLD AGE

I see in you the estuary that enlarges and spreads itself grandly as it
pours in the great sea.

LOCATIONS AND TIMES

Locations and times—what is it in me that meets them all, whenever
and wherever, and makes me at home?
Forms, color, densities, odors—what is it in me that corresponds with
them?

OFFERINGS

A thousand perfect men and women appear,
Around each gathers a cluster of friends, and gay children and youths,
with offerings.

TO THE STATES
To Identify the 16th, 17th, or 18th Presidentiad

Why reclining, interrogating? why myself and all drowsing?
What deepening twilight—scum floating atop of the waters,
Who are they as bats and night-dogs askant* in the capitol?
What a filthy Presidentiad!* (O South, your torrid suns! O North,
your arctic freezings!)
Are those really Congressmen? are those the great Judges? is that the
President?
Then I will sleep awhile yet, for I see that these States sleep, for
reasons;
(With gathering murk, with muttering thunder and lambent* shoots
we all duly awake,
South, North, East, West, inland and seaboard, we will surely awake.)

DRUM-TAPS

FIRST O SONGS FOR A PRELUDE

First O songs for a prelude,
Lightly strike on the stretch'd tympanum pride and joy in my city,
How she led the rest to arms, how she gave the cue,
How at once with lithe limbs unwaiting a moment she sprang,
(O superb! O Manhattan, my own, my peerless!
O strongest you in the hour of danger, in crisis! O truer than steel!)
How you sprang—how you threw off the costumes of peace with
      indifferent hand,
How your soft opera-music changed, and the drum and fife were heard
      in their stead,
How you led to the war, (that shall serve for our prelude, songs of
      soldiers,)
How Manhattan drum-taps led.

Forty years had I in my city seen soldiers parading,
Forty years as a pageant, till unawares the lady of this teeming and
      turbulent city,
Sleepless amid her ships, her houses, her incalculable wealth,
With her million children around her, suddenly,
At dead of night, at news from the south,
Incens'd struck with clinch'd hand the pavement.

A shock electric, the night sustain'd it,
Till with ominous hum our hive at daybreak pour'd out its myriads.

From the houses then and the workshops, and through all the door-
      ways,
Leapt they tumultuous, and lo! Manhattan arming.

To the drum-taps prompt,
The young men falling in and arming,
The mechanics arming, (the trowel, the jack-plane, the blacksmith's
      hammer, tost aside with precipitation,)
The lawyer leaving his office and arming, the judge leaving the court,
The driver deserting his wagon in the street, jumping down, throwing
      the reins abruptly down on the horses' backs,
The salesman leaving the store, the boss, book-keeper, porter, all leav-
      ing;
Squads gather everywhere by common consent and arm,
The new recruits, even boys, the old men show them how to wear
      their accoutrements, they buckle the straps carefully,
Outdoors arming, indoors arming, the flash of the musket-barrels,

The white tents cluster in camps, the arm'd sentries around, the sunrise
    cannon and again at sunset,
Arm'd regiments arrive every day, pass through the city, and embark
    from the wharves,
(How good they look as they tramp down to the river, sweaty, with
    their guns on their shoulders!
How I love them! how I could hug them, with their brown faces and
    their clothes and knapsacks cover'd with dust!)
The blood of the city up—arm'd! arm'd! the cry everywhere,
The flags flung out from the steeples of churches and from all the
    public buildings and stores,
The tearful parting, the mother kisses her son, the son kisses his
    mother,
(Loth is the mother to part, yet not a word does she speak to detain
    him,)
The tumultuous escort, the ranks of policemen preceding, clearing the
    way,
The unpent enthusiasm, the wild cheers of the crowd for their favorites,
The artillery, the silent cannons bright as gold, drawn along, rumble
    lightly over the stones,
(Silent cannons, soon to cease your silence,
Soon unlimber'd to begin the red business;)
All the mutter of preparation, all the determin'd arming,
The hospital service, the lint, bandages and medicines,
The women volunteering for nurses, the work begun for in earnest, no
    mere parade now;
War! an arm'd race is advancing! the welcome for battle, no turning
    away;
War! be it weeks, months, or years, an arm'd race is advancing to wel-
    come it.

Mannahatta* a-march—and it's O to sing it well!
It's O for a manly life in the camp.

And the sturdy artillery,
The guns bright as gold, the work for giants, to serve well the guns,
Unlimber them! (no more as the past forty years for salute for cour-
    tesies merely,
Put in something now besides powder and wadding.)

And you lady of ships, you Mannahatta,
Old matron of this proud, friendly, turbulent city,
Often in peace and wealth you were pensive or covertly frown'd amid
    all your children,
But now you smile with joy exulting old Mannahatta.

EIGHTEEN SIXTY-ONE

Arm'd year—year of the struggle,
No dainty rhymes or sentimental love verses for you terrible year,
Not you as some pale poetling seated at a desk lisping cadenzas piano,
But as a strong man erect, clothed in blue clothes, advancing, carrying
    a rifle on your shoulder,
With well-gristled body and sunburnt face and hands, with a knife in
    the belt at your side,
As I heard you shouting loud, your sonorous voice ringing across the
    continent,
Your masculine voice O year, as rising amid the great cities,
Amid the men of Manhattan I saw you as one of the workmen, the
    dwellers in Manhattan,
Or with large steps crossing the prairies out of Illinois and Indiana,
Rapidly crossing the West with springy gait and descending the Alle-
    ghanies,
Or down from the great lakes or in Pennsylvania, or on deck along the
    Ohio river,
Or southward along the Tennessee or Cumberland rivers, or at Chat-
    tanooga on the mountain top,
Saw I your gait and saw I your sinewy limbs clothed in blue, bearing
    weapons, robust year,
Heard your determin'd voice launch'd forth again and again,
Year that suddenly sang by the mouths of the round-lipp'd cannon,
I repeat you, hurrying, crashing, sad, distracted year.

BEAT! BEAT! DRUMS!

Beat! beat! drums!—blow! bugles! blow!
Through the windows—through doors—burst like a ruthless force,
Into the solemn church, and scatter the congregation,
Into the school where the scholar is studying;
Leave not the bridegroom quiet—no happiness must he have now
    with his bride,
Nor the peaceful farmer any peace, ploughing his field or gathering
    his grain,
So fierce you whirr and pound you drums—so shrill you bugles blow.

Beat! beat! drums!—blow! bugles! blow!
Over the traffic of cities—over the rumble of wheels in the streets;
Are beds prepared for sleepers at night in the houses? no sleepers must
    sleep in those beds,
No bargainers' bargains by day—no brokers or speculators—would
    they continue?
Would the talkers be talking? would the singer attempt to sing?

Would the lawyer rise in the court to state his case before the judge?
Then rattle quicker, heavier drums—you bugles wilder blow.

Beat! beat! drums!—blow! bugles! blow!
Make no parley—stop for no expostulation,
Mind not the timid—mind not the weeper or prayer,
Mind not the old man beseeching the young man,
Let not the child's voice be heard, nor the mother's entreaties,
Make even the trestles to shake the dead where they lie awaiting the
    hearses,
So strong you thump O terrible drums—so loud you bugles blow.

FROM PAUMANOK STARTING I FLY LIKE A BIRD

From Paumanok* starting I fly like a bird,
Around and around to soar to sing the idea of all,
To the north betaking myself to sing there arctic songs,
To Kanada till I absorb Kanada in myself, to Michigan then,
To Wisconsin, Iowa, Minnesota, to sing their songs, (they are inimi-
    table;)
Then to Ohio and Indiana to sing theirs, to Missouri and Kansas and
    Arkansas to sing theirs,
To Tennessee and Kentucky, to the Carolinas and Georgia to sing
    theirs,
To Texas and so along up toward California, to roam accepted every-
    where;
To sing first, (to the tap of the war-drum if need be,)
The idea of all, of the Western world one and inseparable,
And then the song of each member of these States.

SONG OF THE BANNER AT DAYBREAK

Poet

O a new song, a free song,
Flapping, flapping, flapping, flapping, by sounds, by voices clearer,
By the wind's voice and that of the drum,
By the banner's voice and child's voice and sea's voice and father's
    voice,
Low on the ground and high in the air,
On the ground where father and child stand,
In the upward air where their eyes turn,
Where the banner at daybreak is flapping.

Words! book-words! what are you?
Words no more, for hearken and see,
My song is there in the open air, and I must sing,
With the banner and pennant a-flapping.

I'll weave the chord and twine in,
Man's desire and babe's desire, I'll twine them in, I'll put in life,
I'll put the bayonet's flashing point, I'll let bullets and slugs whizz,
(As one carrying a symbol and menace far into the future,
Crying with trumpet voice, *Arouse and beware! Beware and arouse!*)
I'll pour the verse with streams of blood, full of volition, full of joy,
Then loosen, launch forth, to go and compete,
With the banner and pennant a-flapping.

Pennant

Come up here, bard, bard,
Come up here, soul, soul,
Come up here, dear little child,
To fly in the clouds and winds with me, and play with the measure-
     less light.

Child

Father what is that in the sky beckoning to me with long finger?
And what does it say to me all the while?

Father

Nothing my babe you see in the sky,
And nothing at all to you it says—but look you my babe,
Look at these dazzling things in the houses, and see you the money-
     shops opening,
And see you the vehicles preparing to crawl along the streets with
     goods;
These, ah these, how valued and toil'd for these!
How envied by all the earth!

Poet

Fresh and rosy red the sun is mounting high,
On floats the sea in distant blue careering through its channels,
On floats the wind over the breast of the sea setting in toward land,
The great steady wind from west or west-by-south,
Floating so buoyant with milk-white foam on the waters.

But I am not the sea nor the red sun,
I am not the wind with girlish laughter,
Not the immense wind which strengthens, not the wind which lashes,
Not the spirit that ever lashes its own body to terror and death,
But I am that which unseen comes and sings, sings, sings,
Which babbles in brooks and scoots* in showers on the land,
Which the birds know in the woods mornings and evenings,
And the shore-sands know and the hissing wave, and that banner and
     pennant,
Aloft there flapping and flapping.

Child

O father it is alive—it is full of people—it has children,
O now it seems to me it is talking to its children,
I hear it—it talks to me—O it is wonderful!
O it stretches—it spreads and runs so fast—O my father,
It is so broad it covers the whole sky.

Father

Cease, cease, my foolish babe,
What you are saying is sorrowful to me, much it displeases me;
Behold with the rest again I say, behold not banners and pennants
      aloft,
But the well-prepared pavements behold, and mark the solid-wall'd
      houses.

Banner and Pennant

Speak to the child O bard out of Manhattan,
To our children all, or north or south of Manhattan,
Point this day, leaving all the rest, to us over all—and yet we know not
      why,
For what are we, mere strips of cloth profiting nothing,
Only flapping in the wind?

Poet

I hear and see not strips of cloth alone,
I hear the tramp of armies, I hear the challenging sentry,
I hear the jubilant shouts of millions of men, I hear Liberty!
I hear the drums beat and the trumpets blowing,
I myself move abroad swift-rising flying then,
I use the wings of the land-bird and use the wings of the sea-bird, and
      look down as from a height,
I do not deny the precious results of peace, I see populous cities with
      wealth incalculable,
I see numberless farms, I see the farmers working in their fields or
      barns,
I see mechanics working, I see buildings everywhere founded, going
      up, or finish'd,
I see trains of cars swiftly speeding along railroad tracks drawn by the
      locomotives,
I see the stores, depots, of Boston, Baltimore, Charleston, New
      Orleans,
I see far in the West the immense area of grain, I dwell awhile hover-
      ing,
I pass to the lumber forests of the North, and again to the Southern
      plantation, and again to California;
Sweeping the whole I see the countless profit, the busy gatherings,
      earn'd wages,

See the Identity formed out of thirty-eight spacious and haughty
States, (and many more to come,)
See forts on the shores of harbors, see ships sailing in and out;
Then over all, (aye! aye!) my little and lengthen'd pennant shaped
like a sword,
Runs swiftly up indicating war and defiance—and now the halyards
have rais'd it,
Side of my banner broad and blue, side of my starry banner,
Discarding peace over all the sea and land.

Banner and Pennant

Yet louder, higher, stronger, bard! yet farther, wider cleave!
No longer let our children deem us riches and peace alone,
We may be terror and carnage, and are so now,
Not now are we any one of these spacious and haughty States, (nor
any five, nor ten,)
Nor market nor depot we, nor money-bank in the city,
But these and all, and the brown and spreading land, and the mines
below, are ours,
And the shores of the sea are ours, and the rivers great and small,
And the fields they moisten, and the crops and the fruits are ours,
Bays and channels and ships sailing in and out are ours—while we
over all,
Over the area spread below, the three or four millions of square miles,
the capitals,
The forty millions of people,—O bard! in life and death supreme,
We, even we, henceforth flaunt out masterful, high up above,
Not for the present alone, for a thousand years chanting through you,
This song to the soul of one poor little child.

Child

O my father I like not the houses,
They will never to me be anything, nor do I like money,
But to mount up there I would like, O father dear, that banner I like,
That pennant I would be and must be.

Father

Child of mine you fill me with anguish,
To be that pennant would be too fearful,
Little you know what it is this day, and after this day forever,
It is to gain nothing, but risk and defy everything,
Forward to stand in front of wars—and O, such wars!—what have you
to do with them?
With passions of demons, slaughter, premature death?

Banner

Demons and death then I sing,
Put in all, aye all will I, sword-shaped pennant for war,

And a pleasure new and ecstatic, and the prattled yearning of chil-
dren,
Blent with the sounds of the peaceful land and the liquid wash of the
sea,
And the black ships fighting on the sea envelop'd in smoke,
And the icy cool of the far, far north, with rustling cedars and pines,
And the whirr of drums and the sound of soldiers marching, and the
hot sun shining south,
And the beach-waves combing over the beach on my Eastern shore,
and my Western shore the same,
And all between those shores, and my ever running Mississippi with
bends and chutes,
And my Illinois fields, and my Kansas fields, and my fields of Missouri,
The Continent, devoting the whole identity without reserving an atom,
Pour in! whelm that which asks, which sings, with all and the yield
of all,
Fusing and holding, claiming, devouring the whole,
No more with tender lip, nor musical labial sound,
But out of the night emerging for good, our voice persuasive no more,
Croaking like crows here in the wind.

Poet

My limbs, my veins dilate, my theme is clear at last,
Banner so broad advancing out of the night, I sing you haughty and
resolute,
I burst through where I waited long, too long, deafen'd and blinded,
My hearing and tongue are come to me, (a little child taught me,)
I hear from above O pennant of war your ironical call and demand,
Insensate! insensate (yet I at any rate chant you,) O banner!
Not houses of peace indeed are you, nor any nor all their prosperity,
(if need be, you shall again have every one of those houses to
destroy them,
You thought not to destroy those valuable houses, standing fast, full of
comfort, built with money,
May they stand fast, then? not an hour except you above them and all
stand fast;)
O banner, not money so precious are you, not farm produce you, nor
the material good nutriment,
Nor excellent stores, nor landed on wharves from the ships,
Not the superb ships with sail-power or steam-power, fetching and
carrying cargoes,
Nor machinery, vehicles, trade, nor revenues—but you as henceforth I
see you,
Running up out of the night, bringing your cluster of stars, (ever-
enlarging stars,)
Divider of daybreak you, cutting the air, touch'd by the sun, measur-
ing the sky,
(Passionately seen and yearn'd for by one poor little child,

While others remain busy or smartly talking, forever teaching thrift,
    thrift;)
O you up there! O pennant! where you undulate like a snake hissing
    so curious,
Out of reach, an idea only, yet furiously fought for, risking bloody
    death, loved by me,
So loved—O you banner leading the day with stars brought from the
    night!
Valueless, object of eyes, over all and demanding all—(absolute owner
    of all)—O banner and pennant!
I too leave the rest—great as it is, it is nothing—houses, machines are
    nothing—I see them not,
I see but you, O warlike pennant! O banner so broad, with stripes, I
    sing you only,
Flapping up there in the wind.

RISE O DAYS FROM YOUR FATHOMLESS DEEPS

1

Rise O days from your fathomless deeps, till you loftier, fiercer sweep,
Long for my soul hungering gymnastic I devour'd what the earth gave
    me,
Long I roam'd the woods of the north, long I watch'd Niagara pouring,
I travel'd the prairies over and slept on their breast, I cross'd the
    Nevadas, I cross'd the plateaus,
I ascended the towering rocks along the Pacific, I sail'd out to sea,
I sail'd through the storm, I was refresh'd by the storm,
I watch'd with joy the threatening maws of the waves,
I mark'd the white combs where they career'd so high, curling over,
I heard the wind piping, I saw the black clouds,
Saw from below what arose and mounted, (O superb! O wild as my
    heart, and powerful!)
Heard the continuous thunder as it bellow'd after the lightning,
Noted the slender and jagged threads of lightning as sudden and fast
    amid the din they chased each other across the sky;
These, and such as these, I, elate° saw—saw with wonder, yet pensive
    and masterful,
All the menacing might of the globe uprisen around me,
Yet there with my soul I fed, I fed content, supercilious.

2

'Twas well, O soul—'twas a good preparation you gave me,
Now we advance our latent and ampler hunger to fill,
Now we go forth to receive what the earth and the sea never gave us,
Not through the mighty woods we go, but through the mightier cities,
Something for us is pouring now more than Niagara pouring,
Torrents of men, (sources and rills of the Northwest are you indeed
    inexhaustible?)

What, to pavements and homesteads here, what were those storms of
    the mountains and sea?
What, to passions I witness around me to-day? was the sea risen?
Was the wind piping the pipe of death under the black clouds?
Lo! from deeps more unfathomable, something more deadly and sav-
    age,
Manhattan rising, advancing with menacing front—Cincinnati, Chi-
    cago, unchain'd;
What was that swell I saw on the ocean? behold what comes here,
How it climbs with daring feet and hands—how it dashes!
How the true thunder bellows after the lightning—how bright the
    flashes of lightning!
How Democracy with desperate vengeful port strides on, shown
    through the dark by those flashes of lightning!
(Yet a mournful wail and low sob I fancied I heard through the dark,
In a lull of the deafening confusion.)

3

Thunder on! stride on, Democracy! strike with vengeful stroke!
And do you rise higher than ever yet O days, O cities!
Crash heavier, heavier yet O storms! you have done me good,
My soul prepared in the mountains absorbs your immortal strong
    nutriment,
Long had I walk'd my cities, my country roads through farms, only
    half satisfied,
One doubt nauseous undulating like a snake, crawl'd on the ground
    before me
Continually preceding my steps, turning upon me oft, ironically hissing
    low;
The cities I loved so well I abandon'd and left, I sped to the certainties
    suitable to me,
Hungering, hungering, hungering, for primal energies and Nature's
    dauntlessness,
I refresh'd myself with it only, I could relish it only,
I waited the bursting forth of the pent fire—on the water and air I
    waited long;
But now I no longer wait, I am fully satisfied, I am glutted,
I have witness'd the true lightning, I have witness'd my cities electric,
I have lived to behold man burst forth and warlike America rise,
Hence I will seek no more the food of the northern solitary wilds,
No more the mountains roam or sail the stormy sea.

VIRGINIA—THE WEST

The noble sire fallen on evil days,
I saw with hand uplifted, menacing, brandishing,
(Memories of old in abeyance, love and faith in abeyance,)
The insane knife toward the Mother of All.

The noble son on sinewy feet advancing,
I saw, out of the land of prairies, land of Ohio's waters and of Indiana,
To the rescue the stalwart giant hurry his plenteous offspring,
Drest in blue, bearing their trusty rifles on their shoulders.

Then the Mother of All with calm voice speaking,
As to you Rebellious, (I seemed to hear her say,) why strive against
    me, and why seek my life?
When you yourself forever provide to defend me?
For you provided me Washington—and now these also.

CITY OF SHIPS

City of Ships!
(O the black ships! O the fierce ships!
O the beautiful sharp-bow'd steam-ships and sail-ships!)
City of the world! (for all races are here,
All the lands of the earth make contributions here;)
City of the sea! city of hurried and glittering tides!
City whose gleeful tides continually rush or recede, whirling in and
    out with eddies and foam!
City of wharves and stores—city of tall façades of marble and iron!
Proud and passionate city—mettlesome, mad, extravagant city!
Spring up O city—not for peace alone, but be indeed yourself, warlike!
Fear not—submit to no models but your own O city!
Behold me—incarnate me as I have incarnated you!
I have rejected nothing you offer'd me—whom you adopted I have
    adopted,
Good or bad I never question you—I love all—I do not condemn any-
    thing,
I chant and celebrate all that is yours—yet peace no more,
In peace I chanted peace, but now the drum of war is mine,
War, red war is my song through your streets, O city!

THE CENTENARIAN'S STORY

Volunteer of 1861-2 (at Washington Park, Brooklyn, assisting the
Centenarian)
Give me your hand old Revolutionary,
The hill-top is nigh, but a few steps, (make room gentlemen,)
Up the path you have follow'd me well, spite of your hundred and
    extra years,
You can walk old man, though your eyes are almost done,
Your faculties serve you, and presently I must have them serve me.

Rest, while I tell what the crowd around us means,
On the plain below recruits are drilling and exercising,

There is the camp, one regiment departs to-morrow,
Do you hear the officers giving their orders?
Do you hear the clank of the muskets?

Why what comes over you now old man?
Why do you tremble and clutch my hand so convulsively?
The troops are but drilling, they are yet surrounded with smiles,
Around them at hand the well-drest friends and the women,
While splendid and warm the afternoon sun shines down,
Green the midsummer verdure and fresh blows the dallying breeze,
O'er proud and peaceful cities and arm of the sea between.

But drill and parade are over, they march back to quarters,
Only hear that approval of hands! hear what a clapping!

As wending the crowds now part and disperse—but we old man,
Not for nothing have I brought you hither—we must remain,
You to speak in your turn, and I to listen and tell.

The Centenarian

When I clutch'd your hand it was not with terror,
But suddenly pouring about me here on every side,
And below there where the boys were drilling, and up the slopes they
    ran,
And where tents are pitch'd, and wherever you see south and south-
    east and south-west,
Over hills, across lowlands and in the skirts of woods,
And along the shores in mire (now fill'd over) came again and sud-
    denly raged,
As eighty-five years a-gone no mere parade receiv'd with applause of
    friends,
But a battle which I took part in myself—aye, long ago as it is, I took
    part in it,
Walking then this hilltop, this same ground.

Aye, this is the ground,
My blind eyes even as I speak behold it re-peopled from graves,
The years recede, pavements and stately houses disappear,
Rude forts appear again, the old hoop'd guns are mounted,
I see the lines of rais'd earth stretching from river to bay,
I mark the vista of waters, I mark the uplands and slopes;
Here we lay encamp'd, it was this time in summer also.

As I talk I remember all, I remember the Declaration,
It was read here, the whole army paraded, it was read to us here,
By his staff surrounded the General stood in the middle, he held up
    his unsheath'd sword,
It glitter'd in the sun in full sight of the army.

'Twas a bold act then—the English war-ships had just arrived,
We could watch down the lower bay where they lay at anchor,
And the transports swarming with soldiers.

A few days more and they landed, and then the battle.

Twenty thousand were brought against us,
A veteran force furnish'd with good artillery.

I tell not now the whole of the battle,
But one brigade early in the forenoon order'd forward to engage the
    red-coats,
Of that brigade I tell, and how steadily it march'd,
And how long and well it stood confronting death.

Who do you think that was marching steadily sternly confronting
    death?
It was the brigade of the youngest men, two thousand strong,
Rais'd in Virginia and Maryland, and most of them known personally
    to the General.

Jauntily forward they went with quick step toward Gowanus' waters,
Till of a sudden unlook'd for by defiles through the woods, gain'd at
    night,
The British advancing, rounding in from the east, fiercely playing
    their guns,
That brigade of the youngest was cut off and at the enemy's mercy.

The General watch'd them from this hill,
They made repeated desperate attempts to burst their environment,
Then drew close together, very compact, their flag flying in the
    middle,
But O from the hills how the cannon were thinning and thinning them!

It sickens me yet, that slaughter!
I saw the moisture gather in drops on the face of the General.
I saw how he wrung his hands in anguish.

Meanwhile the British manœuvr'd to draw us out for a pitch'd battle,
But we dared not trust the chances of a pitch'd battle.

We fought the fight in detachments,
Sallying forth we fought at several points, but in each the luck was
    against us,
Our foe advancing, steadily getting the best of it, push'd us back to
    the works on this hill,
Till we turn'd menacing here, and then he left us.

That was the going out of the brigade of the youngest men, two thou-
    sand strong,
Few return'd, nearly all remain in Brooklyn.

That and here my General's first battle,
No women looking on nor sunshine to bask in, it did not conclude
    with applause,
Nobody clapp'd hands here then.

But in darkness in mist on the ground under a chill rain,
Wearied that night we lay foil'd and sullen,
While scornfully laugh'd many an arrogant lord off against us en-
    camp'd,
Quite within hearing, feasting, clinking wineglasses together over their
    victory.

So dull and damp and another day,
But the night of that, mist lifting, rain ceasing,
Silent as a ghost while they thought they were sure of him, my General
    retreated.

I saw him at the river-side,
Down by the ferry lit by torches, hastening the embarcation;
My general waited till the soldiers and wounded were all passed over,
And then, (it was just ere sunrise,) these eyes rested on him for the
    last time.
Every one else seem'd fill'd with gloom,
Many no doubt thought of capitulation.

But when my General pass'd me,
As he stood in his boat and look'd toward the coming sun,
I saw something different from capitulation.

Terminus

Enough, the Centenarian's story ends,
The two, the past and present, have interchanged,
I myself as connector, a chansonnier* of a great future, am now speak-
    ing.

And is this the ground Washington trod?
And these waters I listlessly daily cross, are these the waters he cross'd,
As resolute in defeat as other generals in their proudest triumphs?

I must copy the story, and send it eastward and westward,
I must preserve that look as it beam'd on you rivers of Brooklyn.

See—as the annual round returns the phantoms return,
It is the 27th of August and the British have landed,

The battle begins and goes against us, behold through the smoke
    Washington's face,
The brigade of Virginia and Maryland have march'd forth to intercept
    the enemy,
They are cut off, murderous artillery from the hills plays upon them,
Rank after rank falls, while over them silently droops the flag,
Baptized that day in many a young man's bloody wounds,
In death, defeat, and sisters', mothers' tears.

Ah, hills and slopes of Brooklyn! I perceive you are more valuable than
    your owners supposed;
In the midst of you stands an encampment very old,
Stands forever the camp of that dead brigade.

CAVALRY CROSSING A FORD

A line in long array where they wind betwixt green islands,
They take a serpentine course, their arms flash in the sun—hark to the
    musical clank,
Behold the silvery river, in it the splashing horses loitering stop to
    drink,
Behold the brown-faced men, each group, each person a picture, the
    negligent rest on the saddles,
Some emerge on the opposite bank, others are just entering the ford—
    while,
Scarlet and blue and snowy white,
The guidon flags flutter gayly in the wind.

BIVOUAC ON A MOUNTAIN SIDE

I see before me now a traveling army halting,
Below a fertile valley spread, with barns and the orchards of summer,
Behind, the terraced sides of a mountain, abrupt, in places rising high,
Broken, with rocks, with clinging cedars, with tall shapes dingily seen,
The numerous camp-fires scatter'd near and far, some away up on the
    mountain,
The shadowy forms of men and horses, looming, large-sized, flickering,
And over all the sky—the sky! far, far out of reach, studded, breaking
    out, the eternal stars.

AN ARMY CORPS ON THE MARCH

With its cloud of skirmishers in advance,
With now the sound of a single shot snapping like a whip, and now an
    irregular volley,
The swarming ranks press on and on, the dense brigades press on,

Glittering dimly, toiling under the sun—the dust-cover'd men,
In columns rise and fall to the undulations of the ground,
With artillery interspers'd—the wheels rumble, the horses sweat,
As the army corps advances.

BY THE BIVOUAC'S FITFUL FLAME

By the bivouac's fitful flame,
A procession winding around me, solemn and sweet and slow—but
    first I note,
The tents of the sleeping army, the fields' and woods' dim outline,
The darkness lit by spots of kindled fire, the silence,
Like a phantom far or near an occasional figure moving,
The shrubs and trees, (as I lift my eyes they seem to be stealthily
    watching me,)
While wind in procession thoughts, O tender and wondrous thoughts,
Of life and death, of home and the past and loved, and of those that
    are far away;
A solemn and slow procession there as I sit on the ground,
By the bivouac's fitful flame.

COME UP FROM THE FIELDS FATHER

Come up from the fields father, here's a letter from our Pete,
And come to the front door mother, here's a letter from thy dear son.

Lo, 'tis autumn,
Lo, where the trees, deeper green, yellower and redder,
Cool and sweeten Ohio's villages with leaves fluttering in the mod-
    erate wind,
Where apples ripe in the orchards hang and grapes on the trellis'd
    vines,
(Smell you the smell of the grapes on the vines?
Smell you the buckwheat where the bees were lately buzzing?)
Above all, lo, the sky so calm, so transparent after the rain, and with
    wondrous clouds,
Below too, all calm, all vital and beautiful, and the farm prospers well.

Down in the fields all prospers well,
But now from the fields come father, come at the daughter's call,
And come to the entry mother, to the front door come right away.

Fast as she can she hurries, something ominous, her steps trembling,
She does not tarry to smooth her hair nor adjust her cap.

Open the envelope quickly,
O this is not our son's writing, yet his name is sign'd,

O a strange hand writes for our dear son, O stricken mother's soul!
All swims before her eyes, flashes with black, she catches the main
    words only,
Sentences broken, *gunshot wound in the breast, cavalry skirmish,
    taken to hospital,*
At present low, but will soon be better.

Ah now the single figure to me,
Amid all teeming and wealthy Ohio with all its cities and farms,
Sickly white in the face and dull in the head, very faint,
By the jamb of a door leans.

Grieve not so, dear mother, (the just-grown daughter speaks through
    her sobs,
The little sisters huddle around speechless and dismay'd,)
See, dearest mother, the letter says Pete will soon be better.

Alas poor boy, he will never be better, (nor may-be needs to be better,
    that brave and simple soul,)
While they stand at home at the door he is dead already,
The only son is dead.

But the mother needs to be better,
She with thin form presently drest in black,
By day her meals untouch'd, then at night fitfully sleeping, often
    waking,
In the midnight waking, weeping, longing with one deep longing,
O that she might withdraw unnoticed, silent from life escape and
    withdraw,
To follow, to seek, to be with her dear dead son.

VIGIL STRANGE I KEPT ON THE FIELD ONE NIGHT

Vigil strange I kept on the field one night;
When you my son and my comrade dropt at my side that day,
One look I but gave which your dear eyes return'd with a look I shall
    never forget,
One touch of your hand to mine O boy, reach'd up as you lay on the
    ground,
Then onward I sped in the battle, the even-contested battle,
Till late in the night reliev'd to the place at last again I made my way,
Found you in death so cold dear comrade, found your body son of
    responding kisses, (never again on earth responding,)
Bared your face in the starlight, curious the scene, cool blew the
    moderate night-wind,
Long there and then in vigil I stood, dimly around me the battlefield
    spreading,
Vigil wondrous and vigil sweet there in the fragrant silent night,

But not a tear fell, not even a long-drawn sigh, long, long I gazed,
Then on the earth partially reclining sat by your side leaning my chin
in my hands,
Passing sweet hours, immortal and mystic hours with you dearest
comrade—not a tear, not a word,
Vigil of silence, love and death, vigil for you my son and my soldier,
As onward silently stars aloft, eastward new ones upward stole,
Vigil final for you brave boy, (I could not save you, swift was your
death,
I faithfully loved you and cared for you living, I think we shall surely
meet again,)
Till at latest lingering of the night, indeed just as the dawn appear'd,
My comrade I wrapt in his blanket, envelop'd well his form,
Folded the blanket well, tucking it carefully over head and carefully
under feet,
And there and then and bathed by the rising sun, my son in his grave,
in his rude-dug grave I deposited,
Ending my vigil strange with that, vigil of night and battle-field dim,
Vigil for boy of responding kisses, (never again on earth responding,)
Vigil for comrade swiftly slain, vigil I never forget, how as day
brighten'd,
I rose from the chill ground and folded my soldier well in his blanket,
And buried him where he fell.

A MARCH IN THE RANKS HARD-PREST, AND THE ROAD UNKNOWN

A march in the ranks hard-prest, and the road unknown,
A route through a heavy wood with muffled steps in the darkness,
Our army foil'd with loss severe, and the sullen remnant retreating,
Till after midnight glimmer upon us the lights of a dim-lighted build-
ing,
We come to an open space in the woods, and halt by the dim-lighted
building,
'Tis a large old church at the crossing roads, now an impromptu
hospital,
Entering but for a minute I see a sight beyond all the pictures and
poems ever made,
Shadows of deepest, deepest black, just lit by moving candles and
lamps,
And by one great pitchy torch stationary with wild red flame and
clouds of smoke,
By these, crowds, groups of forms vaguely I see on the floor, some in
the pews laid down,
At my feet more distinctly a soldier, a mere lad, in danger of bleeding
to death, (he is shot in the abdomen,)
I stanch the blood temporarily, (the youngster's face is white as a
lily,)

Then before I depart I sweep my eyes o'er the scene fain to absorb it
    all,
Faces, varieties, postures beyond description, most in obscurity, some
    of them dead,
Surgeons operating, attendants holding lights, the smell of ether, the
    odor of blood,
The crowd, O the crowd of the bloody forms, the yard outside also
    fill'd,
Some on the bare ground, some on planks or stretchers, some in the
    death-spasm sweating,
An occasional scream or cry, the doctor's shouted orders or calls,
The glisten of the little steel instruments catching the glint of the
    torches,
These I resume as I chant, I see again the forms, I smell the odor,
Then hear outside the orders given, *Fall in, my men, fall in;*
But first I bend to the dying lad, his eyes open, a half-smile gives he
    me,
Then the eyes close, calmly close, and I speed forth to the darkness,
Resuming, marching, ever in darkness marching, on in the ranks,
The unknown road still marching.

A SIGHT IN CAMP IN THE DAYBREAK GRAY AND DIM

A sight in camp in the daybreak gray and dim,
As from my tent I emerge so early sleepless,
As slow I walk in the cool fresh air the path near by the hospital tent,
Three forms I see on stretchers lying, brought out there untended
    lying,
Over each the blanket spread, ample brownish woolen blanket,
Gray and heavy blanket, folding, covering all.

Curious I halt and silent stand,
Then with light fingers I from the face of the nearest the first just lift
    the blanket;
Who are you elderly man so gaunt and grim, with well-gray'd hair,
    and flesh all sunken about the eyes?
Who are you my dear comrade?

Then to the second I step—and who are you my child and darling?
Who are you sweet boy with cheeks yet blooming?

Then to the third—a face nor child nor old, very calm, as of beautiful
    yellow-white ivory;
Young man I think I know you—I think this face is the face of the
    Christ himself,
Dead and divine and brother of all, and here again he lies.

AS TOILSOME I WANDER'D VIRGINIA'S WOODS

As toilsome I wander'd Virginia's woods,
To the music of rustling leaves kick'd by my feet, (for 'twas autumn,)
I mark'd at the foot of a tree the grave of a soldier;
Mortally wounded he and buried on the retreat, (easily all could I
     understand,)
The halt of a mid-day hour, when up! no time to lose—yet this sign
     left,
On a tablet scrawl'd and nail'd on the tree by the grave,
Bold, cautious, true, and my loving comrade.

Long, long I muse, then on my way go wandering,
Many a changeful season to follow, and many a scene of life,
Yet at times through changeful season and scene, abrupt, alone, or in
     the crowded street,
Comes before me the unknown soldier's grave, comes the inscription
     rude in Virginia's woods,
Bold, cautious, true, and my loving comrade.

NOT THE PILOT

Not the pilot has charged himself to bring his ship into port, though
     beaten back and many times baffled;
Not the pathfinder penetrating inland weary and long,
By deserts parch'd, snows chill'd, rivers wet, perseveres till he reaches
     his destination,
More than I have charged myself, heeded or unheeded, to compose a
     march for these States,
For a battle-call, rousing to arms if need be, years, centuries hence.

YEAR THAT TREMBLED AND REEL'D BENEATH ME

Year that trembled and reel'd beneath me!
Your summer wind was warm enough, yet the air I breathed froze me,
A thick gloom fell through the sunshine and darken'd me,
Must I change my triumphant songs? said I to myself,
Must I indeed learn to chant the cold dirges of the baffled?
And sullen hymns of defeat?

THE WOUND-DRESSER

1

An old man bending I come among new faces,
Years looking backward resuming in answer to children,

Come tell us old man, as from young men and maidens that love me,
(Arous'd and angry, I'd thought to beat the alarum, and urge relentless
    war,
But soon my fingers fail'd me, my face droop'd and I resign'd myself
To sit by the wounded and soothe them, or silently watch the dead;)
Years hence of these scenes, of these furious passions, these chances,
Of unsurpass'd heroes, (was one side so brave? the other was equally
    brave;)
Now be witness again, paint the mightiest armies of earth,
Of those armies so rapid so wondrous what saw you to tell us?
What stays with you latest and deepest? of curious panics,
Of hard-fought engagements or sieges tremendous what deepest
    remains?

2

O maidens and young men I love and that love me,
What you ask of my days those the strangest and sudden your talking
    recalls,
Soldier alert I arrive after a long march cover'd with sweat and dust,
In the nick of time I come, plunge in the fight, loudly shout in the
    rush of successful charge,
Enter the captur'd works—yet lo, like a swift-running river they fade,
Pass and are gone they fade—I dwell not on soldiers' perils or soldiers'
    joys,
(Both I remember well—many of the hardships, few the joys, yet I
    was content.)

But in silence, in dreams' projections,
While the world of gain and appearance and mirth goes on,
So soon what is over forgotten, and waves wash the imprints off the
    sand,
With hinged knees returning I enter the doors, (while for you up there,
Whoever you are, follow without noise and be of strong heart.)

Bearing the bandages, water and sponge,
Straight and swift to my wounded I go,
Where they lie on the ground after the battle brought in,
Where their priceless blood reddens the grass the ground,
Or to the rows of the hospital tent, or under the roof'd hospital,
To the long rows of cots up and down each side I return,
To each and all one after another I draw near, not one do I miss,
An attendant follows holding a tray, he carries a refuse pail,
Soon to be fill'd with clotted rags and blood, emptied, and fill'd again.

I onward go, I stop,
With hinged knees and steady hand to dress wounds,
I am firm with each, the pangs are sharp yet unavoidable,
One turns to me his appealing eyes—poor boy! I never knew you,
Yet I think I could not refuse this moment to die for you, if that would
    save you.

3

On, on I go, (open doors of time! open hospital doors!)
The crush'd head I dress, (poor crazed hand tear not the bandage
    away,)
The neck of the cavalry-man with the bullet through and through I
    examine,
Hard the breathing rattles, quite glazed already the eye, yet life
    struggles hard,
(Come sweet death! be persuaded O beautiful death!
In mercy come quickly.)

From the stump of the arm, the amputated hand,
I undo the clotted lint, remove the slough, wash off the matter and
    blood,
Back on his pillow the soldier bends with curv'd neck and side falling
    head,
His eyes are closed, his face is pale, he dares not look on the bloody
    stump,
And has not yet look'd on it.

I dress a wound in the side, deep, deep,
But a day or two more, for see the frame all wasted and sinking,
And the yellow-blue countenance see.

I dress the perforated shoulder, the foot with the bullet-wound,
Cleanse the one with a gnawing and putrid gangrene, so sickening, so
    offensive,
While the attendant stands behind aside me holding the tray and pail.

I am faithful, I do not give out,
The fractur'd thigh, the knee, the wound in the abdomen,
These and more I dress with impassive hand, (yet deep in my breast
    a fire, a burning flame.)

4

Thus in silence in dreams' projections,
Returning, resuming, I thread my way through the hospitals,
The hurt and wounded I pacify with soothing hand,
I sit by the restless all the dark night, some are so young,
Some suffer so much, I recall the experience sweet and sad,
(Many a soldier's loving arms about this neck have cross'd and rested,
Many a soldier's kiss dwells on these bearded lips.)

LONG, TOO LONG AMERICA

Long, too long America,
Traveling roads all even and peaceful you learn'd from joys and
    prosperity only,

But now, ah now, to learn from crises of anguish, advancing, grappling
      with direst fate and recoiling not,
And now to conceive and show to the world what your children
      enmasse really are,
(For who except myself has yet conceiv'd what your children enmasse
      really are?)

GIVE ME THE SPLENDID SILENT SUN

1

Give me the splendid silent sun with all his beams full-dazzling,
Give me juicy autumnal fruit ripe and red from the orchard,
Give me a field where the unmow'd grass grows,
Give me an arbor, give me the trellis'd grape,
Give me fresh corn and wheat, give me serene-moving animals teaching
      content,
Give me nights perfectly quiet as on high plateaus west of the Mis-
      sissippi, and I looking up at the stars,
Give me odorous at sunrise a garden of beautiful flowers where I can
      walk undisturb'd,
Give me for marriage a sweet-breath'd woman of whom I should never
      tire,
Give me a perfect child, give me away aside from the noise of the
      world a rural domestic life,
Give me to warble spontaneous songs recluse by myself, for my own
      ears only,
Give me solitude, give me Nature, give me again O Nature your
      primal sanities!

These demanding to have them, (tired with ceaseless excitement, and
      rack'd by the war-strife,)
These to procure incessantly asking, rising in cries from my heart,
While yet incessantly asking still I adhere to my city,
Day upon day and year upon year O city, walking your streets,
Where you hold me enchain'd a certain time refusing to give me up,
Yet giving to make me glutted, enrich'd of soul, you give me forever
      faces;
(O I see what I sought to escape, confronting, reversing my cries,
I see my own soul trampling down what it ask'd for.)

2

Keep your splendid silent sun,
Keep your woods O Nature, and the quiet places by the woods,
Keep your fields of clover and timothy, and your corn-fields and
      orchards,
Keep the blossoming buckwheat fields where the Ninth-month bees
      hum;

Give me faces and streets—give me these phantoms incessant and
    endless along the trottoirs!°
Give me interminable eyes—give me women—give me comrades and
    lovers by the thousand!
Let me see new ones every day—let me hold new ones by the hand
    every day!
Give me such shows—give me the streets of Manhattan!
Give me Broadway, with the soldiers marching—give me the sound
    of the trumpets and drums!
(The soldiers in companies or regiments—some starting away, flush'd
    and reckless,
Some, their time up, returning with thinn'd ranks, young, yet very old,
    worn, marching, noticing nothing;)
Give me the shores and wharves heavy-fringed with black ships!
O such for me! O an intense life, full to repletion and varied!
The life of the theatre, bar-room, huge hotel, for me!
The saloon of the steamer! the crowded excursion for me! the torch-
    light procession!
The dense brigade bound for the war, with high piled military wagons
    following;
People, endless, streaming, with strong voices, passions, pageants,
Manhattan streets with their powerful throbs, with beating drums as
    now,
The endless and noisy chorus, the rustle and clank of muskets, (even
    the sight of the wounded,)
Manhattan crowds, with their turbulent musical chorus!
Manhattan faces and eyes forever for me.

DIRGE FOR TWO VETERANS

    The last sunbeam
Lightly falls from the finish'd Sabbath,
On the pavement here, and there beyond it is looking,
    Down a new-made double grave.

    Lo, the moon ascending,
Up from the east the silvery round moon,
Beautiful over the house-tops, ghastly, phantom moon,
    Immense and silent moon.

    I see a sad procession,
And I hear the sound of coming full-key'd bugles,
All the channels of the city streets they're flooding,
    As with voices and with tears.

    I hear the great drums pounding,
And the small drums steady whirring,
And every blow of the great convulsive drums,
    Strikes me through and through.

For the son is brought with the father,
(In the foremost ranks of the fierce assault they fell,
Two veterans son and father dropt together,
    And the double grave awaits them.)

Now nearer blow the bugles,
And the drums strike more convulsive,
And the daylight o'er the pavement quite has faded,
    And the strong dead-march enwraps me.

In the eastern sky up-buoying,
The sorrowful vast phantom moves illumin'd,
('Tis some mother's large transparent face,
    In heaven brighter growing.)

O strong dead-march you please me!
O moon immense with your silvery face you soothe me!
O my soldiers twain! O my veterans passing to burial!
    What I have I also give you.

The moon gives you light,
And the bugles and the drums give you music,
And my heart, O my soldiers, my veterans,
    My heart gives you love.

OVER THE CARNAGE ROSE PROPHETIC A VOICE

Over the carnage rose prophetic a voice,
Be not dishearten'd, affection shall solve the problems of freedom yet,
Those who love each other shall become invincible,
They shall yet make Columbia victorious.

Sons of the Mother of All, you shall yet be victorious,
You shall yet laugh to scorn the attacks of all the remainder of the
    earth.

No danger shall balk Columbia's lovers,
If need be a thousand shall sternly immolate themselves for one.

One from Massachusetts shall be a Missourian's comrade,
From Maine and from hot Carolina, and another an Oregonese, shall
    be friends triune,
More precious to each other than all the riches of the earth.

To Michigan, Florida perfumes shall tenderly come,
Not the perfumes of flowers, but sweeter, and wafted beyond death.

It shall be customary in the houses and streets to see manly affection,
The most dauntless and rude shall touch face to face lightly,
The dependence of Liberty shall be lovers,
The continuance of Equality shall be comrades.

These shall tie you and band you stronger than hoops of iron,
I, ecstatic, O partners! O lands! with the love of lovers tie you.

(Were you looking to be held together by lawyers?
Or by an agreement on a paper? or by arms?
Nay, nor the world, nor any living thing, will so cohere.)

I SAW OLD GENERAL AT BAY

I saw old General at bay,
(Old as he was, his gray eyes yet shone out in battle like stars,)
His small force was now completely hemm'd in, his works,
He call'd for volunteers to run the enemy's lines, a desperate emergency,
I saw a hundred and more step forth from the ranks, but two or three were selected,
I saw them receive their orders aside, they listen'd with care, the adjutant was very grave,
I saw them depart with cheerfulness, freely risking their lives.

THE ARTILLERYMAN'S VISION

While my wife at my side lies slumbering, and the wars are over long,
And my head on the pillow rests at home, and the vacant midnight passes,
And through the stillness, through the dark, I hear, just hear, the breath of my infant,
There in the room as I wake from sleep this vision presses upon me;
The engagement opens there and then in fantasy unreal,
The skirmishers begin, they crawl cautiously ahead, I hear the irregular snap! snap!
I hear the sounds of the different missiles, the short *t-h-t! t-h-t!* of the rifle-balls,
I see the shells exploding leaving small white clouds, I hear the great shells shrieking as they pass,
The grape° like the hum and whirr of wind through the trees, (tumultuous now the contest rages,)
All the scenes at the batteries rise in detail before me again,
The crashing and smoking, the pride of the men in their pieces,
The chief-gunner ranges and sights his piece and selects a fuse of the right time,
After firing I see him lean aside and look eagerly off to note the effect;

Elsewhere I hear the cry of a regiment charging, (the young colonel
    leads himself this time with brandish'd sword,)
I see the gaps cut by the enemy's volleys, (quickly fill'd up, no delay,)
I breathe the suffocating smoke, then the flat clouds hover low con-
    cealing all;
Now a strange lull for a few seconds, not a shot fired on either side,
Then resumed the chaos louder than ever, with eager calls and orders
    of officers,
While from some distant part of the field the wind wafts to my ears a
    shout of applause, (some special success,)
And ever the sound of the cannon far or near, (rousing even in dreams
    a devilish exultation and all the old mad joy in the depths of
    my soul,)
And ever the hastening of infantry shifting positions, batteries, cavalry,
    moving hither and thither,
(The falling, dying, I heed not, the wounded dripping and red I heed
    not, some to the rear are hobbling,)
Grime, heat, rush, aides-de-camp galloping by or on a full run,
With the patter of small arms, the warning *s-s-t* of the rifles, (these in
    my vision I hear or see,)
And bombs bursting in air, and at night the vari-color'd rockets.

ETHIOPIA SALUTING THE COLORS

Who are you dusky woman, so ancient hardly human,
With your wooly-white and turban'd head, and bare bony feet?
Why rising by the roadside here, do you the colors greet?

('Tis while our army lines Carolina's sands and pines,
Forth from thy hovel door thou Ethiopia com'st to me,
As under doughty Sherman I march toward the sea.)

Me master years a hundred since from my parents sunder'd,
A little child, they caught me as the savage beast is caught,
Then hither me across the sea the cruel slaver brought.

No further does she say, but lingering all the day,
Her high-borne turban'd head she wags, and rolls her darkling eye,
And courtesies to the regiments, the guidons moving by.

What is it fateful woman, so blear, hardly human?
Why wag your head with turban bound, yellow, red and green?
Are the things so strange and marvelous you see or have seen?

NOT YOUTH PERTAINS TO ME

Not youth pertains to me,
Nor delicatesse,* I cannot beguile the time with talk,

Awkward in the parlor, neither a dancer nor elegant,
In the learn'd coterie sitting constrain'd and still, for learning inures
    not to me,
Beauty, knowledge, inure* not to me—yet there are two or three
    things inure to me,
I have nourish'd the wounded and sooth'd many a dying soldier,
And at intervals waiting or in the midst of camp,
Composed these songs.

RACE OF VETERANS

Race of veterans—race of victors!
Race of the soil, ready for conflict—race of the conquering march!
(No more credulity's race, abiding-temper'd race,)
Race henceforth owning no law but the law of itself,
Race of passion and the storm.

WORLD TAKE GOOD NOTICE

World take good notice, silver stars fading,
Milky hue ript, weft of white detaching,
Coals thirty-eight, baleful and burning,
Scarlet, significant, hands off warning,
Now and henceforth flaunt from these shores.

O TAN-FACED PRAIRIE-BOY

O tan-faced prairie-boy,
Before you came to camp came many a welcome gift,
Praises and presents came and nourishing food, till at last among the
    recruits,
You came, taciturn, with nothing to give—we but look'd on each other,
When lo! more than all the gifts of the world you gave me.

LOOK DOWN FAIR MOON

Look down fair moon and bathe this scene,
Pour softly down night's nimbus floods on faces ghastly, swollen,
    purple,
On the dead on their backs with arms toss'd wide,
Pour down your unstinted nimbus sacred moon.

RECONCILIATION

Word over all, beautiful as the sky,
Beautiful that war and all its deeds of carnage must in time be utterly
    lost,

That the hands of the sisters Death and Night incessantly softly wash
      again, and ever again, this soil'd world;
For my enemy is dead, a man divine as myself is dead,
I look where he lies white-faced and still in the coffin—I draw near,
Bend down and touch lightly with my lips the white face in the coffin.

HOW SOLEMN AS ONE BY ONE
(Washington City, 1865)

How solemn as one by one,
As the ranks returning worn and sweaty, as the men file by where I
      stand,
As the faces the masks appear, as I glance at the faces studying the
      masks,
(As I glance upward out of this page studying you, dear friend, who-
      ever you are,)
How solemn the thought of my whispering soul to each in the ranks,
      and to you!
I see behind each mask that wonder a kindred soul,
O the bullet could never kill what you really are, dear friend,
Nor the bayonet stab what you really are;
The soul! yourself I see, great as any, good as the best,
Waiting secure and content, which the bullet could never kill,
Nor the bayonet stab O friend.

AS I LAY WITH MY HEAD IN YOUR LAP CAMERADO

As I lay with my head in your lap camerado,*
The confession I made I resume, what I said to you and the open air
      I resume,
I know I am restless and make others so,
I know my words are weapons full of danger, full of death,
For I confront peace, security, and all the settled laws, to unsettle
      them,
I am more resolute because all have denied me than I could ever have
      been had all accepted me,
I heed not and have never heeded either experience, cautions, majori-
      ties, nor ridicule,
And the threat of what is call'd hell is little or nothing to me,
And the lure of what is call'd heaven is little or nothing to me;
Dear camerado! I confess I have urged you onward with me, and still
      urge you, without the least idea what is our destination,
Or whether we shall be victorious, or utterly quell'd and defeated.

DELICATE CLUSTER

Delicate cluster! flag of teeming life!
Covering all my lands—all my seashores lining!

Flag of death! (how I watch'd you through the smoke of battle press-
      ing!
How I heard you flap and rustle, cloth defiant!)
Flag cerulean—sunny flag, with the orbs of night dappled!
Ah my silvery beauty—ah my woolly white and crimson!
Ah to sing the song of you, my matron mighty!
My sacred one, my mother!

TO A CERTAIN CIVILIAN

Did you ask dulcet rhymes from me?
Did you seek the civilian's peaceful and languishing rhymes?
Did you find what I sang erewhile so hard to follow?
Why I was not singing erewhile for you to follow, to understand—nor
      am I now;
(I have been born of the same as the war was born,
The drum-corps' rattle is ever to me sweet music, I love well the
      martial dirge,
With slow wail and convulsive throb leading the officer's funeral;)
What to such as you anyhow such a poet as I? therefore leave my
      works,
And go lull yourself with what you can understand, and with piano-
      tunes,
For I lull nobody, and you will never understand me.

LO, VICTRESS ON THE PEAKS

Lo, Victress on the peaks,
Where thou with mighty brow regarding the world,
(The world O Libertad,* that vainly conspired against thee,)
Out of its countless beleaguering toils, after thwarting them all,
Dominant, with the dazzling sun around thee,
Flauntest now unharm'd in immortal soundness and bloom—lo, in
      these hours supreme,
No poem proud, I chanting bring to thee, nor mastery's rapturous
      verse,
But a cluster containing night's darkness and blood-dripping wounds,
And psalms of the dead.

SPIRIT WHOSE WORK IS DONE
(Washington City, 1865)

Spirit whose work is done—spirit of dreadful hours!
Ere departing fade from my eyes your forests of bayonets;
Spirit of gloomiest fears and doubts, (yet onward ever unfaltering
      pressing,)

Spirit of many a solemn day and many a savage scene—electric spirit,
That with muttering voice through the war now closed, like a tireless
  phantom flitted,
Rousing the land with breath of flame, while you beat and beat the
  drum,
Now as the sound of the drum, hollow and harsh to the last, reverber-
  ates round me,
As your ranks, your immortal ranks, return, return from the battles,
As the muskets of the young men yet lean over their shoulders,
As I look on the bayonets bristling over their shoulders,
As those slanted bayonets, whole forests of them appearing in the
  distance, approach and pass on, returning homeward,
Moving with steady motion, swaying to and fro to the right and left,
Evenly, lightly rising and falling while the steps keep time;
Spirit of hours I knew, all hectic red one day, but pale as death next
  day,
Touch my mouth ere you depart, press my lips close,
Leave me your pulses of rage—bequeath them to me—fill me with
  currents convulsive,
Let them scorch and blister out of my chants when you are gone,
Let them identify you to the future in these songs.

ADIEU TO A SOLDIER

Adieu O soldier,
You of the rude campaigning, (which we shared,)
The rapid march, the life of the camp,
The hot contention of opposing fronts, the long manœuvre,
Red battles with their slaughter, the stimulus, the strong terrific game,
Spell of all brave and manly hearts, the trains of time through you
  and like of you all fill'd,
With war and war's expression.

Adieu dear comrade,
Your mission is fulfill'd—but I, more warlike,
Myself and this contentious soul of mine,
Still on our own campaigning bound,
Through untried roads with ambushes opponents lined,
Through many a sharp defeat and many a crisis, often baffled,
Here marching, ever marching on, a war fight out—aye here,
To fiercer, weightier battles give expression.

TURN O LIBERTAD

Turn O Libertad,* for the war is over,
From it and all henceforth expanding, doubting no more, resolute
  sweeping the world,

Turn from lands retrospective recording proofs of the past,
From the singers that sing the trailing glories of the past,
From the chants of the feudal world, the triumphs of kings, slavery,
    caste,
Turn to the world, the triumphs reserv'd and to come—give up that
    backward world,
Leave to the singers of hitherto, give them the trailing past,
But what remains remains for singers for you—wars to come are for
    you,
(Lo, how the wars of the past have duly inured* to you, and the wars
    of the present also inure;)
Then turn, and be not alarm'd O Libertad—turn your undying face,
To where the future, greater than all the past,
Is swiftly, surely preparing for you.

TO THE LEAVEN'D SOIL THEY TROD

To the leaven'd soil they trod calling I sing for the last,
(Forth from my tent emerging for good, loosing, untying the tent-
    ropes,)
In the freshness the forenoon air, in the far-stretching circuits and
    vistas again to peace restored,
To the fiery fields emanative and the endless vistas beyond, to the
    South and the North,
To the leaven'd soil of the general Western world to attest my songs,
To the Alleghanian hills and the tireless Mississippi,
To the rocks I calling sing, and all the trees in the woods,
To the plains of the poems of heroes, to the prairies spreading wide,
To the far-off sea and the unseen winds, and the sane impalpable air;
And responding they answer all, (but not in words,)
The average earth, the witness of war and peace, acknowledges mutely,
The prairie draws me close, as the father to bosom broad the son,
The Northern ice and rain that began me nourish me to the end,
But the hot sun of the South is to fully ripen my songs.

MEMORIES OF PRESIDENT LINCOLN

WHEN LILACS LAST IN THE DOORYARD BLOOM'D

1

When lilacs last in the dooryard bloom'd,
And the great star early droop'd in the western sky in the night,
I mourn'd, and yet shall mourn with ever-returning spring.

Ever-returning spring, trinity sure to me you bring,
Lilac blooming perennial and drooping star in the west,
And thought of him I love.

2

O powerful western fallen star!
O shades of night—O moody, tearful night!
O great star disappear'd—O the black murk that hides the star!
O cruel hands that hold me powerless—O helpless soul of me!
O harsh surrounding cloud that will not free my soul.

3

In the dooryard fronting an old farm-house near the white-wash'd
    palings,
Stands the lilac-bush tall-growing with heart-shaped leaves of rich
    green,
With many a pointed blossom rising delicate, with the perfume strong
    I love,
With every leaf a miracle—and from this bush in the dooryard,
With delicate-color'd blossoms and heart-shaped leaves of rich green,
A sprig with its flower I break.

4

In the swamp in secluded recesses,
A shy and hidden bird is warbling a song.

Solitary the thrush,
The hermit withdrawn to himself, avoiding the settlements,
Sings by himself a song.

Song of the bleeding throat,
Death's outlet song of life, (for well dear brother I know,
If thou wast not granted to sing thou would'st surely die.)

5

Over the breast of the spring, the land, amid cities,
Amid lanes and through old woods, where lately the violets peep'd
    from the ground, spotting the gray debris,

Amid the grass in the fields each side of the lanes, passing the endless
    grass,
Passing the yellow-spear'd wheat, every grain from its shroud in the
    dark-brown fields uprisen,
Passing the apple-tree blows of white and pink in the orchards,
Carrying a corpse to where it shall rest in the grave,
Night and day journeys a coffin.

6

Coffin that passes through lanes and streets,
Through day and night with the great cloud darkening the land,
With the pomp of the inloop'd flags with the cities draped in black,
With the show of the States themselves as of crape-veil'd women
    standing,
With processions long and winding and the flambeaus of the night,
With the countless torches lit, with the silent sea of faces and the
    unbared heads,
With the waiting depot, the arriving coffin, and the sombre faces,
With dirges through the night, with the thousand voices rising strong
    and solemn,
With all the mournful voices of the dirges pour'd around the coffin,
The dim-lit churches and the shuddering organs—where amid these
    you journey,
With the tolling tolling bells' perpetual clang,
Here, coffin that slowly passes,
I give you my sprig of lilac.

7

(Nor for you, for one alone,
Blossoms and branches green to coffins all I bring,
For fresh as the morning, thus would I chant a song for you O sane
    and sacred death.

All over bouquets of roses,
O death, I cover you over with roses and early lilies,
But mostly and now the lilac that blooms the first,
Copious I break, I break the sprigs from the bushes,
With loaded arms I come, pouring for you,
For you and the coffins all of you O death.)

8

O western orb sailing the heaven,
Now I know what you must have meant as a month since I walk'd,
As I walk'd in silence the transparent shadowy night,
As I saw you had something to tell as you bent to me night after night,
As you droop'd from the sky low down as if to my side, (while the
    other stars all look'd on,)
As we wander'd together the solemn night, (for something I know not
    what kept me from sleep,)

As the night advanced, and I saw on the rim of the west how full you
    were of woe,
As I stood on the rising ground in the breeze in the cool transparent
    night,
As I watch'd where you pass'd and was lost in the netherward black
    of the night,
As my soul in its trouble dissatisfied sank, as where you sad orb,
Concluded, dropt in the night, and was gone.

9

Sing on there in the swamp,
O singer bashful and tender, I hear your notes, I hear your call,
I hear, I come presently, I understand you,
But a moment I linger, for the lustrous star has detain'd me,
The star my departing comrade holds and detains me.

10

O how shall I warble myself for the dead one there I loved?
And how shall I deck my song for the large sweet soul that has gone?
And what shall my perfume be for the grave of him I love?

Sea-winds blown from east and west,
Blown from the Eastern sea and blown from the Western sea, till
    there on the prairies meeting,
These and with these and the breath of my chant,
I'll perfume the grave of him I love.

11

O what shall I hang on the chamber walls?
And what shall the pictures be that I hang on the walls,
To adorn the burial-house of him I love?

Pictures of growing spring and farms and homes,
With the Fourth-month eve at sundown, and the gray smoke lucid and
    bright,
With floods of the yellow gold of the gorgeous, indolent, sinking sun,
    burning, expanding the air,
With the fresh sweet herbage under foot, and the pale green leaves of
    the trees prolific,
In the distance the flowing glaze, the breast of the river, with a wind-
    dapple here and there,
With ranging hills on the banks, with many a line against the sky, and
    shadows,
And the city at hand with dwellings so dense, and stacks of chimneys,
And all the scenes of life and the workshops, and the workmen home-
    ward returning.

12

Lo, body and soul—this land,
My own Manhattan with spires, and the sparkling and hurrying tides,
    and the ships,
The varied and ample land, the South and the North in the light,
    Ohio's shores and flashing Missouri,
And ever the far-spreading prairies cover'd with grass and corn.

Lo, the most excellent sun so calm and haughty,
The violet and purple morn with just-felt breezes,
The gentle soft-born measureless light,
The miracle spreading bathing all, the fulfill'd noon,
The coming eve delicious, the welcome night and the stars,
Over my cities shining all, enveloping man and land.

13

Sing on, sing on you gray-brown bird,
Sing from the swamps, the recesses, pour your chant from the bushes,
Limitless out of the dusk, out of the cedars and pines.

Sing on dearest brother, warble your reedy song,
Loud human song, with voice of uttermost woe.

O liquid and free and tender!
O wild and loose to my soul—O wondrous singer,
You only I hear—yet the star holds me, (but will soon depart,)
Yet the lilac with mastering odor holds me.

14

Now while I sat in the day and look'd forth,
In the close of the day with its light and the fields of spring, and the
    farmers preparing their crops,
In the large unconscious scenery of my land with its lakes and forests,
In the heavenly aerial beauty, (after the perturb'd winds and the
    storms,)
Under the arching heavens of the afternoon swift passing, and the
    voices of children and women,
The many-moving sea-tides, and I saw the ships how they sail'd,
And the summer approaching with richness, and the fields all busy
    with labor,
And the infinite separate houses, how they all went on, each with its
    meals and minutia of daily usages,
And the streets how their throbbings throbb'd, and the cities pent—
    lo, then and there,
Falling upon them all and among them all, enveloping me with the
    rest,
Appear'd the cloud, appear'd the long black trail,
And I knew death, its thought, and the sacred knowledge of death.

Then with the knowledge of death as walking one side of me,
And the thought of death close-walking the other side of me,
And I in the middle as with companions, and as holding the hands of
    companions,
I fled forth to the hiding receiving night that talks not,
Down to the shores of the water, the path by the swamp in the dim-
    ness,
To the solemn shadowy cedars and ghostly pines so still.

And the singer so shy to the rest receiv'd me,
The gray-brown bird I know receiv'd us comrades three,
And he sang the carol of death, and a verse for him I love.

From deep secluded recesses,
From the fragrant cedars and the ghostly pines so still,
Came the carol of the bird.

And the charm of the carol rapt me,
As I held as if by their hands my comrades in the night,
And the voice of my spirit tallied the song of the bird.

Come lovely and soothing death,
Undulate round the world, serenely arriving, arriving,
In the day, in the night, to all, to each,
Sooner or later delicate death.

Prais'd be the fathomless universe,
For life and joy, and for objects and knowledge curious,
And for love, sweet love—but praise! praise! praise!
For the sure-enwinding arms of cool-enfolding death.

Dark mother always gliding near with soft feet,
Have none chanted for thee a chant of fullest welcome?
Then I chant it for thee, I glorify thee above all,
I bring thee a song that when thou must indeed come, come unfalter-
    ingly.

Approach strong deliveress,
When it is so, when thou hast taken them I joyously sing the dead,
Lost in the loving floating ocean of thee,
Laved in the flood of thy bliss O death.

From me to thee glad serenades,
Dances for thee I propose saluting thee, adornments and feastings for
    thee,
And the sights of the open landscape and the high-spread sky are fit-
    ting,
And life and the fields, and the huge and thoughtful night.

The night in silence under many a star,
The ocean shore and the husky whispering wave whose voice I know,
And the soul turning to thee O vast and well-veil'd death,
And the body gratefully nestling close to thee.

Over the tree-tops I float thee a song,
Over the rising and sinking waves, over the myriad fields and the
*   prairies wide,*
Over the dense-pack'd cities all and the teeming wharves and ways,
I float this carol with joy, with joy to thee O death.

15

To the tally of my soul,
Loud and strong kept up the gray-brown bird,
With pure deliberate notes spreading filling the night.

Loud in the pines and cedars dim,
Clear in the freshness moist and the swamp-perfume,
And I with my comrades there in the night.

While my sight that was bound in my eyes unclosed,
As to long panoramas of visions.

And I saw askant* the armies,
I saw as in noiseless dreams hundreds of battle-flags,
Borne through the smoke of the battles and pierc'd with missiles I saw
    them,
And carried hither and yon through the smoke, and torn and bloody,
And at last but a few shreds left on the staffs, (and all in silence,)
And the staffs all splinter'd and broken.

I saw battle-corpses, myriads of them,
And the white skeletons of young men, I saw them,
I saw the debris and debris of all the slain soldiers of the war,
But I saw they were not as was thought,
They themselves were fully at rest, they suffer'd not,
The living remain'd and suffer'd, the mother suffer'd,
And the wife and the child and the musing comrade suffer'd,
And the armies that remain'd suffer'd.

16

Passing the visions, passing the night,
Passing, unloosing the hold of my comrade's hands,
Passing the song of the hermit bird and the tallying song of my soul,
Victorious song, death's outlet song, yet varying ever-altering song,
As low and wailing, yet clear the notes, rising and falling, flooding
    the night,
Sadly sinking and fainting, as warning and warning, and yet again
    bursting with joy,

Covering the earth and filling the spread of the heaven,
As that powerful psalm in the night I heard from recesses,
Passing, I leave thee lilac with heart-shaped leaves,
I leave thee there in the door-yard, blooming, returning with spring.

I cease from my song for thee,
From my gaze on thee in the west, fronting the west, communing with
  thee,
O comrade lustrous with silver face in the night.

Yet each to keep and all, retrievements out of the night,
The song, the wondrous chant of the gray-brown bird,
And the tallying chant, the echo arous'd in my soul,
With the lustrous and drooping star with the countenance full of woe,
With the holders holding my hand nearing the call of the bird,
Comrades mine and I in the midst, and their memory ever to keep, for
  the dead I loved so well,
For the sweetest, wisest soul of all my days and lands—and this for
  his dear sake,
Lilac and star and bird twined with the chant of my soul,
There in the fragrant pines and the cedars dusk and dim.

O CAPTAIN! MY CAPTAIN!

O Captain! my Captain! our fearful trip is done,
The ship has weather'd every rack, the prize we sought is won,
The port is near, the bells I hear, the people all exulting,
While follow eyes the steady keel, the vessel grim and daring;
   But O heart! heart! heart!
    O the bleeding drops of red,
     Where on the deck my Captain lies,
     Fallen cold and dead.

O Captain! my Captain! rise up and hear the bells;
Rise up—for you the flag is flung—for you the bugle trills,
For you bouquets and ribbon'd wreaths—for you the shores a-crowd-
  ing,
For you they call, the swaying mass, their eager faces turning;
    Here Captain! dear father!
    This arm beneath your head!
     It is some dream that on the deck,
     You've fallen cold and dead.

My Captain does not answer, his lips are pale and still,
My father does not feel my arm, he has no pulse nor will,
The ship is anchor'd safe and sound, its voyage closed and done,
From fearful trip the victor ship comes in with object won:

Exult O shores, and ring O bells!
But I with mournful tread,
Walk the deck my Captain lies,
Fallen cold and dead.

HUSH'D BE THE CAMPS TO-DAY
(May 4, 1865)

Hush'd be the camps to-day,
And soldiers let us drape our war-worn weapons,
And each with musing soul retire to celebrate,
Our dear commander's death.

No more for him life's stormy conflicts,
Nor victory, nor defeat—no more time's dark events,
Charging like ceaseless clouds across the sky.

But sing poet in our name,
Sing of the love we bore him—because you,—dweller in camps, know
it truly.

As they invault the coffin there,
Sing—as they close the doors of earth upon him—one verse,
For the heavy hearts of soldiers.

THIS DUST WAS ONCE THE MAN

This dust was once the man,
Gentle, plain, just and resolute, under whose cautious hand,
Against the foulest crime in history known in any land or age,
Was saved the Union of these States.

BY BLUE ONTARIO'S SHORE

1

By blue Ontario's shore,
As I mused of these warlike days and of peace return'd, and the dead
  that return no more,
A Phantom gigantic superb, with stern visage accosted me,
Chant me the poem, it said, *that comes from the soul of America,*
  chant me the carol of victory,
And strike up the marches of Libertad,* *marches more powerful yet,*
And sing me before you go the song of the throes of Democracy.

(Democracy, the destin'd conqueror, yet treacherous lip-smiles everywhere,
And death and infidelity at every step.)

2

A Nation announcing itself,
I myself make the only growth by which I can be appreciated,
I reject none, accept all, then reproduce all in my own forms.

A breed whose proof is in time and deeds,
What we are we are, nativity is answer enough to objections,
We wield ourselves as a weapon is wielded,
We are powerful and tremendous in ourselves,
We are executive in ourselves, we are sufficient in the variety of our-
  selves,
We are the most beautiful to ourselves and in ourselves,
We stand self-pois'd in the middle, branching thence over the world,
From Missouri, Nebraska, or Kansas, laughing attack to scorn.

Nothing is sinful to us outside of ourselves,
Whatever appears, whatever does not appear, we are beautiful or sinful in ourselves only.

(O Mother—O Sisters dear!
If we are lost, no victor else has destroy'd us,
It is by ourselves we go down to eternal night.)

3

Have you thought there could be but a single supreme?
There can be any number of supremes—one does not countervail
  another any more than one eyesight countervails another, or
  one life countervails another.

All is eligible to all,
All is for individuals, all is for you,
No condition is prohibited, not God's or any.

All comes by the body, only health puts you rapport° with the universe.

Produce great Persons, the rest follows.

4

Piety and conformity to them that like,
Peace, obesity, allegiance, to them that like,
I am he who tauntingly compels men, women, nations,
Crying, Leap from your seats and contend for your lives!

I am he who walks the States with a barb'd tongue, questioning every
one I meet,
Who are you that wanted only to be told what you knew before?
Who are you that wanted only a book to join you in your nonsense?

(With pangs and cries as thine own O bearer of many children,
These clamors wild to a race of pride I give.)

O lands, would you be freer than all that has ever been before?
If you would be freer than all that has been before, come listen to me.

Fear grace, elegance, civilization, delicatesse,°
Fear the mellow sweet, the sucking of honey-juice,
Beware the advancing mortal ripening of Nature,
Beware what precedes the decay of the ruggedness of states and men.

5

Ages, precedents, have long been accumulating undirected materials,
America brings builders, and brings its own styles.

The immortal poets of Asia and Europe have done their work and
pass'd to other spheres,
A work remains, the work of surpassing all they have done.

America, curious toward foreign characters, stands by its own at all
hazards,
Stands removed, spacious, composite, sound, initiates the true use of
precedents,
Does not repel them or the past or what they have produced under
their forms,
Takes the lesson with calmness, perceives the corpse slowly borne
from the house,
Perceives that it waits a little while in the door, that it was fittest for
its days,
That its life has descended to the stalwart and well-shaped heir who
approaches,
And that he shall be fittest for his days.

Any period one nation must lead,
One land must be the promise and reliance of the future.

These States are the amplest poem,
Here is not merely a nation but a teeming Nation of nations,
Here the doings of men correspond with the broadcast doings of the
    day and night,
Here is what moves in magnificent masses careless of particulars,
Here are the roughs, beards, friendliness, combativeness, the soul loves,
Here the flowing trains, here the crowds, equality, diversity, the soul
    loves.

6

Land of lands and bards to corroborate!
Of them standing among them, one lifts to the light a west-bred face,
To him the hereditary countenance bequeath'd both mother's and
    father's,
His first parts substances, earth, water, animals, trees,
Built of the common stock, having room for far and near,
Used to dispense with other lands, incarnating this land,
Attracting its body and soul to himself, hanging on its neck with
    incomparable love,
Plunging his seminal muscle into its merits and demerits,
Making its cities, beginnings, events, diversities, wars, vocal in him,
Making its rivers, lakes, bays, embouchure* in him,
Mississippi with yearly freshets and changing chutes, Columbia,
    Niagara, Hudson, spending themselves lovingly in him,
If the Atlantic coast stretch or the Pacific coast stretch, he stretching
    with them North or South,
Spanning between them East and West, and touching whatever is
    between them,
Growths growing from him to offset the growths of pine, cedar, hem-
    lock, live-oak, locust, chestnut, hickory, cottonwood, orange,
    magnolia,
Tangles as tangled in him as any canebrake or swamp,
He likening sides and peaks of mountains, forests coated with northern
    transparent ice,
Off him pasturage sweet and natural as savanna, upland, prairie,
Through him flights, whirls, screams, answering those of the fish-
    hawk, mocking-bird, night-heron, and eagle,
His spirit surrounding his country's spirit, unclosed to good and evil,
Surrounding the essences of real things, old times and present times,
Surrounding just found shores, islands, tribes of red aborigines,
Weather-beaten vessels, landings, settlements, embryo stature and
    muscle,
The haughty defiance of the Year One, war, peace, the formation of
    the Constitution,
The separate States, the simple elastic scheme, the immigrants,

The Union always swarming with blatherers* and always sure and
  impregnable,
The unsurvey'd interior, log-houses, clearings, wild animals, hunters,
  trappers,
Surrounding the multiform agriculture, mines, temperature, the gestation of new States,
Congress convening every Twelfth-month, the members duly coming
  up from the uttermost parts,
Surrounding the noble character of mechanics and farmers, especially
  the young men,
Responding their manners, speech, dress, friendship, the gait they
  have of persons who never knew how it felt to stand in the
  presence of superiors,
The freshness and candor of their physiognomy, the copiousness and
  decision of their phrenology,
The picturesque looseness of their carriage, their fierceness when
  wrong'd,
The fluency of their speech, their delight in music, their curiosity,
  good temper and open-handedness, the whole composite make,
The prevailing ardor and enterprise, the large amativeness,*
The perfect equality of the female with the male, the fluid movement
  of the population,
The superior marine, free commerce, fisheries, whaling, gold-digging,
Wharf-hemm'd cities, railroad and steamboat lines intersecting all
  points,
Factories, mercantile life, labor-saving machinery, the Northeast,
  Northwest, Southwest,
Manhattan firemen, the Yankee swap, southern plantation life,
Slavery—the murderous, treacherous conspiracy to raise it upon the
  ruins of all the rest,
On and on to the grapple with it—Assassin! then your life or ours be
  the stake, and respite no more.

7

(Lo, high toward heaven, this day,
Libertad, from the conqueress' field return'd,
I mark the new aureola around your head,
No more of soft astral, but dazzling and fierce,
With war's flames and the lambent* lightnings playing,
And your port immovable where you stand,
With still the inextinguishable glance and the clinch'd and lifted fist,
And your foot on the neck of the menacing one, the scorner utterly
  crush'd beneath you,
The menacing arrogant one that strode and advanced with his sense-
  less scorn, bearing the murderous knife,
The wide-swelling one, the braggart that would yesterday do so much,
To-day a carrion dead and damn'd, the despised of all the earth,
An offal rank, to the dunghill maggots spurn'd.)

8

Others take the finish, but the Republic is ever constructive and ever
    keeps vista,
Others adorn the past, but you O days of the present, I adorn you,
O days of the future I believe in you—I isolate myself for your sake,
O America because you build for mankind I build for you.
O well-beloved stone-cutters, I lead them who plan with decision and
    science,
Lead the present with friendly hand toward the future.

(Bravas to all impulses sending sane children to the next age!
But damn that which spends itself with no thought of the stain, pains,
    dismay, feebleness, it is bequeathing.)

9

I listened to the Phantom by Ontario's shore,
I heard the voice arising demanding bards,
By them all native and grand, by them alone can these States be
    fused into the compact organism of a Nation.

To hold men together by paper and seal or by compulsion is no
    account,
That only holds men together which aggregates all in a living principle,
    as the hold of the limbs of the body or the fibres of plants.

Of all races and eras these States with veins full of poetical stuff most
    need poets, and are to have the greatest, and use them the
    greatest,
Their Presidents shall not be their common referee so much as their
    poets shall.

(Soul of love and tongue of fire!
Eye to pierce the deepest deeps and sweep the world!
Ah Mother, prolific and full in all besides, yet how long barren,
    barren?)

10

Of these States the poet is the equable man,
Not in him but off from him things are grotesque, eccentric, fail of
    their full returns,
Nothing out of its place is good, nothing in its place is bad,
He bestows on every object or quality its fit proportion, neither more
    nor less,
He is the arbiter of the diverse, he is the key,
He is the equalizer of his age and land,
He supplies what wants supplying, he checks what wants checking,

In peace out of him speaks the spirit of peace, large, rich, thrifty,
        building populous towns, encouraging agriculture, arts, com-
        merce, lighting the study of man, the soul, health, immortality, '
        government,
In war he is the best backer of the war, he fetches artillery as good as
        the engineer's, he can make every word he speaks draw blood,
The years straying toward infidelity he withholds by his steady faith,
He is no arguer, he is judgment, (Nature accepts him absolutely,)
He judges not as the judge judges but as the sun falling round a help-
        less thing,
As he sees the farthest he has the most faith,
His thoughts are the hymns of the praise of things,
In the dispute on God and eternity he is silent,
He sees eternity less like a play with a prologue and denouement,
He sees eternity in men and women, he does not see men and women
        as dreams or dots.

For the great Idea, the idea of perfect and free individuals,
For that, the bard walks in advance, leader of leaders,
The attitude of him cheers up slaves and horrifies foreign despots.

Without extinction is Liberty, without retrograde is Equality,
They live in the feelings of young men and the best women,
(Not for nothing have the indomitable heads of the earth been always
        ready to fall for Liberty.)

11

For the great Idea,
That, O my brethren, that is the mission of poets.

Songs of stern defiance ever ready,
Songs of the rapid arming and the march,
The flag of peace quick-folded, and instead the flag we know,
Warlike flag of the great Idea.

(Angry cloth I saw there leaping!
I stand again in leaden rain your flapping folds saluting,
I sing you over all, flying beckoning through the fight—O the hard-
        contested fight!
The cannons ope their rosy-flashing muzzles—the hurtled balls scream,
The battle-front forms amid the smoke—the volleys pour incessant
        from the line,
Hark, the ringing word *Charge!*—now the tussle and the furious mad-
        dening yells,
Now the corpses tumble curl'd upon the ground,
Cold, cold in death, for precious life of you,
Angry cloth I saw there leaping.)

12

Are you he who would assume a place to teach or be a poet here in
the States?
The place is august, the terms obdurate.

Who would assume to teach here may well prepare himself body and
mind,
He may well survey, ponder, arm, fortify, harden, make lithe himself,
He shall surely be question'd beforehand by me with many and stern
questions.

Who are you indeed who would talk or sing to America?
Have you studied out the land, its idioms and men?
Have you learn'd the physiology, phrenology, politics, geography,
pride, freedom, friendship of the land? its substratums and
objects?
Have you consider'd the organic compact of the first day of the first
year of Independence, sign'd by the Commissioners, ratified by
the States, and read by Washington at the head of the army?
Have you possess'd yourself of the Federal Constitution?
Do you see who have left all feudal processes and poems behind them,
and assumed the poems and processes of Democracy?
Are you faithful to things? do you teach what the land and sea, the
bodies of men, womanhood, amativeness,° heroic angers, teach?
Have you sped through fleeting customs, popularities?
Can you hold your hand against all seductions, follies, whirls, fierce
contentions? are you very strong? are you really of the whole
People?
Are you not of some coterie? some school or mere religion?
Are you done with reviews and criticisms of life? animating now to
life itself?
Have you vivified yourself from the maternity of these States?
Have you too the old ever-fresh forbearance and impartiality?
Do you hold the like love for those hardening to maturity? for the
last-born? little and big? and for the errant?

What is this you bring my America?
Is it uniform with my country?
Is it not something that has been better told or done before?
Have you not imported this or the spirit of it in some ship?
Is it not a mere tale? a rhyme? a prettiness?—is the good old cause
in it?
Has it not dangled long at the heels of the poets, politicians, literats,°
of enemies' lands?
Does it not assume that what is notoriously gone is still here?
Does it answer universal needs? will it improve manners?
Does it sound with trumpet-voice the proud victory of the Union in
that secession war?

Can your performance face the open fields and the seaside?
Will it absorb into me as I absorb food, air, to appear again in my
strength, gait, face?
Have real employments contributed to it? original makers, not mere
amanuenses?
Does it meet modern discoveries, calibres, facts, face to face?
What does it mean to American persons, progresses, cities? Chicago,
Kanada, Arkansas?
Does it see behind the apparent custodians the real custodians stand-
ing, menacing, silent, the mechanics, Manhattanese, Western
men, Southerners, significant alike in their apathy, and in the
promptness of their love?
Does it see what finally befalls, and has always finally befallen, each
temporizer, patcher, outsider, partialist, alarmist, infidel, who
has ever ask'd any thing of America?
What mocking and scornful negligence?
The track strew'd with the dust of skeletons,
By the roadside others disdainfully toss'd.

13

Rhymes and rhymers pass away, poems distill'd from poems pass
away,
The swarms of reflectors and the polite pass, and leave ashes,
Admirers, importers, obedient persons, make but the soil of literature,
America justifies itself, give it time, no disguise can deceive it or con-
ceal from it, it is impassive enough,
Only toward the likes of itself will it advance to meet them,
If its poets appear it will in due time advance to meet them, there is
no fear of mistake,
(The proof of a poet shall be sternly deferr'd till his country absorbs
him as affectionately as he has absorb'd it.)

He masters whose spirit masters, he tastes sweetest who results
sweetest in the long run,
The blood of the brawn beloved of time is unconstraint;
In the need of songs, philosophy, an appropriate native grand-opera,
shipcraft, any craft,
He or she is greatest who contributes the greatest original practical
example.

Already a nonchalant breed, silently emerging, appears on the streets,
People's lips salute only doers, lovers, satisfiers, positive knowers,
There will shortly be no more priests, I say their work is done,
Death is without emergencies here, but life is perpetual emergencies
here,
Are your body, days, manners, superb? after death you shall be superb,
Justice, health, self-esteem, clear the way with irresistible power;
How dare you place any thing before a man?

14

Fall behind me States!
A man before all—myself, typical, before all.

Give me the pay I have served for,
Give to sing the songs of the great Idea, take all the rest,
I have loved the earth, sun, animals, I have despised riches,
I have given alms to every one that ask'd, stood up for the stupid and
     crazy, devoted my income and labor to others,
Hated tyrants, argued not concerning God, had patience and indul-
     gence toward the people, taken off my hat to nothing known
     or unknown,
Gone freely with powerful uneducated persons and with the young,
     and with the mothers of families,
Read these leaves to myself in the open air, tried them by trees, stars,
     rivers,
Dismiss'd whatever insulted my own soul or defiled my body,
Claim'd nothing to myself which I have not carefully claim'd for
     others on the same terms,
Sped to the camps, and comrades found and accepted from every
     State,
(Upon this breast has many a dying soldier lean'd to breathe his last,
This arm, this hand, this voice, have nourish'd, rais'd, restored,
To life recalling many a prostrate form;)
I am willing to wait to be understood by the growth of the taste of
     myself,
Rejecting none, permitting all.

(Say O Mother, have I not to your thought been faithful?
Have I not through life kept you and yours before me?)

15

I swear I begin to see the meaning of these things,
It is not the earth, it is not America who is so great,
It is I who am great or to be great, it is You up there, or any one,
It is to walk rapidly through civilizations, governments, theories,
Through poems, pageants, shows, to form individuals.

Underneath all, individuals,
I swear nothing is good to me now that ignores individuals,
The American compact is altogether with individuals,
The only government is that which makes minute of individuals,
The whole theory of the universe is directed unerringly to one single
     individual—namely to You.

(Mother! with subtle sense severe, with the naked sword in your hand,
I saw you at last refuse to treat but directly with individuals.)

16

Underneath all, Nativity,
I swear I will stand by my own nativity, pious or impious so be it;
I swear I am charm'd with nothing except nativity,
Men, women, cities, nations, are only beautiful from nativity.

Underneath all is the Expression of love for men and women,
(I swear I have seen enough of mean and impotent modes of expressing love for men and women,
After this day I take my own modes of expressing love for men and
women.)

I swear I will have each quality of my race in myself,
(Talk as you like, he only suits these States whose manners favor the
audacity and sublime turbulence of the States.)

Underneath the lessons of things, spirits, Nature, governments, owner-
ships, I swear I perceive other lessons,
Underneath all to me is myself, to you yourself, (the same monotonous old song.)

17

O I see flashing that this America is only you and me,
Its power, weapons, testimony, are you and me,
Its crimes, lies, thefts, defections, are you and me,
Its Congress is you and me, the officers, capitols, armies, ships, are
you and me,
Its endless gestations of new States are you and me,
The war, (that war so bloody and grim, the war I will henceforth
forget), was you and me,
Natural and artificial are you and me,
Freedom, language, poems, employments, are you and me,
Past, present, future, are you and me.

I dare not shirk any part of myself,
Not any part of America good or bad,
Not to build for that which builds for mankind,
Not to balance ranks, complexions, creeds, and the sexes,
Not to justify science nor the march of equality,
Nor to feed the arrogant blood of the brawn belov'd of time.

I am for those that have never been master'd,
For men and women whose tempers have never been master'd,
For those whom laws, theories, conventions, can never master.

I am for those who walk abreast with the whole earth,
Who inaugurate one to inaugurate all.

I will not be outfaced by irrational things,
I will penetrate what it is in them that is sarcastic upon me,
I will make cities and civilizations defer to me,
This is what I have learnt from America—it is the amount, and it I
      teach again.

(Democracy, while weapons were everywhere aim'd at your breast,
I saw you serenely give birth to immortal children, saw in dreams your
      dilating form,
Saw you with spreading mantle covering the world.)

18

I will confront these shows of the day and night,
I will know if I am to be less than they,
I will see if I am not as majestic as they,
I will see if I am not as subtle and real as they,
I will see if I am to be less generous than they,
I will see if I have no meaning, while the houses and ships have
      meaning,
I will see if the fishes and birds are to be enough for themselves, and
      I am not to be enough for myself.

I match my spirit against yours you orbs, growths, mountains, brutes,
Copious as you are I absorb you all in myself, and become the master
      myself,
America isolated yet embodying all, what is it finally except myself?
These States, what are they except myself?

I know now why the earth is gross, tantalizing, wicked, it is for my
      sake,
I take you specially to be mine, you terrible, rude forms.

(Mother, bend down, bend close to me your face,
I know not what these plots and wars and deferments are for,
I know not fruition's success, but I know that through war and crime
      your work goes on, and must yet go on.)

19

Thus by blue Ontario's shore,
While the winds fann'd me and the waves came trooping toward me,
I thrill'd with the power's pulsations, and the charm of my theme was
      upon me,
Till the tissues that held me parted their ties upon me.

And I saw the free souls of poets,
The loftiest bards of past ages strode before me,
Strange large men, long unwaked, undisclosed, were disclosed to me.

20

O my rapt verse, my call, mock me not!
Not for the bards of the past, not to invoke them have I launch'd you
    forth,
Not to call even those lofty bards here by Ontario's shores,
Have I sung so capricious and loud my savage song.

Bards for my own land only I invoke,
(For the war, the war is over, the field is clear'd,)
Till they strike up marches henceforth triumphant and onward,
To cheer O Mother your boundless expectant soul.

Bards of the great Idea! bards of the peaceful inventions! (for the
    war, the war is over!)
Yet bards of latent armies, a million soldiers waiting ever-ready,
Bards with songs as from burning coals or the lightning's fork'd stripes!
Ample Ohio's, Kanada's bards—bards of California! inland bards—
    bards of the war!
You by my charm I invoke.

REVERSALS

Let that which stood in front go behind,
Let that which was behind advance to the front,
Let bigots, fools, unclean persons, offer new propositions,
Let the old propositions be postponed,
Let a man seek pleasure everywhere except in himself,
Let a woman seek happiness everywhere except in herself.

AUTUMN RIVULETS

AS CONSEQUENT, ETC.

As consequent from store of summer rains,
Or wayward rivulets in autumn flowing,
Or many a herb-lined brook's reticulations,
Or subterranean sea-rills making for the sea,
Songs of continued years I sing.

Life's ever-modern rapids first, (soon, soon to blend,
With the old streams of death.)

Some threading Ohio's farm-fields or the woods,
Some down Colorado's cañons from sources of perpetual snow,
Some half-hid in Oregon, or away southward in Texas,
Some in the north finding their way to Erie, Niagara, Ottawa,
Some to Atlantica's bays, and so to the great salt brine.

In you whoe'er you are my book perusing,
In I myself, in all the world, these currents flowing,
All, all toward the mystic ocean tending.

Currents for starting a continent new,
Overtures sent to the solid out of the liquid,
Fusion of ocean and land, tender and pensive waves,
(Not safe and peaceful only, waves rous'd and ominous too,
Out of the depths the storm's abysmic waves, who knows whence?
Raging over the vast, with many a broken spar and tatter'd sail.)

Or from the sea of Time, collecting vasting* all, I bring,
A windrow-drift of weeds and shells.

O little shells, so curious-convolute, so limpid-cold and voiceless,
Will you not little shells to the tympans of temples held,
Murmurs and echoes still call up, eternity's music faint and far,
Wafted inland, sent from Atlantica's rim, strains for the soul of the
    prairies,
Whisper'd reverberations, chords for the ear of the West joyously
    sounding,
Your tidings old, yet ever new and untranslatable,
Infinitesimals out of my life, and many a life,
(For not my life and years alone I give—all, all I give,)
These waifs from the deep, cast high and dry,
Wash'd on America's shores?

THE RETURN OF THE HEROES

1

For the lands and for these passionate days and for myself,
Now I awhile retire to thee O soil of autumn fields,
Reclining on thy breast, giving myself to thee,
Answering the pulses of thy sane and equable heart,
Tuning a verse for thee.

O earth that hast no voice, confide to me a voice,
O harvest of my lands—O boundless summer growths,
O lavish brown parturient earth—O infinite teeming womb,
A song to narrate thee.

2

Ever upon this stage,
Is acted God's calm annual drama,
Gorgeous processions, songs of birds,
Sunrise that fullest feeds and freshens most the soul,
The heaving sea, the waves upon the shore, the musical, strong waves,
The woods, the stalwart trees, the slender, tapering trees,
The liliput countless armies of the grass,
The heat, the showers, the measureless pasturages,
The scenery of the snows, the winds' free orchestra,
The stretching light-hung roof of clouds, the clear cerulean and the
    silvery fringes,
The high dilating stars, the placid beckoning stars,
The moving flocks and herbs, the plains and emerald meadows,
The shows of all the varied lands and all the growths and products.

3

Fecund America—to-day,
Thou art all over set in births and joys!
Thou groan'st with riches, thy wealth clothes thee as a swathing-
    garment,
Thou laughest loud with ache of great possessions,
A myriad-twining life like interlacing vines binds all thy vast demesne,°
As some huge ship freighted to water's edge thou ridest into port,
As rain falls from the heaven and vapors rise from earth, so have the
    precious values fallen upon thee and risen out of thee;
Thou envy of the globe! thou miracle!
Thou, bathed, choked, swimming in plenty,
Thou lucky Mistress of the tranquil barns,
Thou Prairie Dame that sittest in the middle and lookest out upon
    thy world, and lookest East and lookest West,
Dispensatress, that by a word givest a thousand miles, a million farms,
    and missest nothing,
Thou all-acceptress—thou hospitable, (thou only art hospitable as God
    is hospitable.)

4

When late I sang sad was my voice,
Sad were the shows around me with deafening noises of hatred and
    smoke of war;
In the midst of the conflict, the heroes, I stood,
Or pass'd with slow step through the wounded and dying.

But now I sing not war,
Nor the measur'd march of soldiers, nor the tents of camps,
Nor the regiments hastily coming up deploying in line of battle;
No more the sad, unnatural shows of war.

Ask'd room those flush'd immortal ranks, the first forth-stepping
    armies?
Ask room alas the ghastly ranks, the armies dread that follow'd.

(Pass, pass, ye proud brigades, with your tramping sinewy legs,
With your shoulders young and strong, with your knapsacks and your
    muskets;
How elate* I stood and watch'd you, where starting off you march'd.

Pass—then rattle drums again,
For an army heaves in sight, O another gathering army,
Swarming, trailing on the rear, O you dread accruing army,
O you regiments so piteous, with your mortal diarrhœa, with your fever,
O my land's maim'd darlings, with the plenteous bloody bandage and
    the crutch,
Lo, your pallid army follows.)

5

But on these days of brightness,
On the far-stretching beauteous landscape, the roads and lanes, the
    high-piled farm-wagons, and the fruits and barns,
Should the dead intrude?

Ah the dead to me mar not, they fit well in Nature,
They fit very well in the landscape under the trees and grass,
And along the edge of the sky in the horizon's far margin.

Nor do I forget you Departed,
Nor in winter or summer my lost ones,
But most in the open air as now when my soul is rapt and at peace,
    like pleasing phantoms,
Your memories rising glide silently by me.

6

I saw the day the return of the heroes,
(Yet the heroes never surpass'd shall never return,
Them that day I saw not.)

I saw the interminable corps, I saw the procession of armies,
I saw them approaching, defiling by with divisions,
Streaming northward, their work done, camping awhile in clusters of
    mighty camps.

No holiday soldiers—youthful, yet veterans,
Worn, swart, handsome, strong, of the stock of homestead and work-
    shop,
Harden'd of many a long campaign and sweaty march,
Inured on many a hard-fought bloody field.

A pause—the armies wait,
A million flush'd embattled conquerors wait,
The world too waits, then soft as breaking night and sure as dawn,
They melt, they disappear.

Exult O lands! victorious lands!
Not there your victory on those red shuddering fields,
But here and hence your victory.

Melt, melt away ye armies—disperse ye blue-clad soldiers,
Resolve ye back again, give up for good your deadly arms,
Other the arms the fields henceforth for you, or South or North,
With saner wars, sweet wars, life-giving wars.

7

Loud O my throat, and clear O soul!
The season of thanks and the voice of full-yielding,
The chant of joy and power for boundless fertility.

All till'd and untill'd fields expand before me,
I see the true arenas of my race, or first or last,
Man's innocent and strong arenas.

I see the heroes at other toils,
I see well-wedded in their hands the better weapons.

I see where the Mother of All,
With full-spanning eye gazes forth, dwells long,
And counts the varied gathering of the products.

Busy the far, the sunlit panorama,
Prairie, orchard, and yellow grain of the North,
Cotton and rice of the South and Louisianian cane,
Open unseeded fallows, rich fields of clover and timothy,
Kine and horses feeding, and droves of sheep and swine,
And many a stately river flowing and many a jocund brook,
And healthy uplands with herby-perfumed breezes,
And the good green grass, that delicate miracle the ever-recurring grass.

8

Toil on heroes! harvest the products!
Not alone on those warlike fields the Mother of All,
With dilated form and lambent eyes* watch'd you.

Toil on heroes! toil well! handle the weapons well!
The Mother of All, yet here as ever she watches you.

Well-pleased America thou beholdest,
Over the fields of the West those crawling monsters,
The human-divine inventions, the labor-saving implements;
Beholdest moving in every direction imbued as with life the revolving
    hay-rakes,
The steam-power reaping-machines and the horse-power machines,
The engines, thrashers of grain and cleaners of grain, well separating
    the straw, the nimble work of the patent pitchfork,
Beholdest the newer saw-mill, the southern cotton-gin, and the rice-
    cleanser.

Beneath thy look O Maternal,
With these and else and with their own strong hands the heroes
    harvest.

All gather and all harvest,
Yet but for thee O Powerful, not a scythe might swing as now in
    security,
Not a maize-stalk dangle as now its silken tassels in peace.

Under thee only they harvest, even but a wisp of hay under thy great
    face only,
Harvest the wheat of Ohio, Illinois, Wisconsin, every barbed spear
    under thee,
Harvest the maize of Missouri, Kentucky, Tennessee, each ear in its
    light-green sheath,
Gather the hay to its myriad mows in the odorous tranquil barns,
Oats to their bins, the white potato, the buckwheat of Michigan, to
    theirs;
Gather the cotton in Mississippi or Alabama, dig and hoard the golden
    the sweet potato of Georgia and the Carolinas,
Clip the wool of California or Pennsylvania,
Cut the flax in the Middle States, or hemp or tobacco in the Borders,
Pick the pea and the bean, or pull apples from the trees or bunches of
    grapes from the vines,
Or aught that ripens in all these States or North or South,
Under the beaming sun and under thee.

THERE WAS A CHILD WENT FORTH

There was a child went forth every day,
And the first object he look'd upon, that object he became,
And that object became part of him for the day or a certain part of
the day,
Or for many years or stretching cycles of years.

The early lilacs became part of this child,
And grass and white and red morning-glories, and white and red
clover, and the song of the phœbe-bird,
And the Third-month lambs and the sow's pink-faint litter, and the
mare's foal and the cow's calf,
And the noisy brood of the barnyard or by the mire of the pond-side,
And the fish suspending themselves so curiously below there, and the
beautiful curious liquid,
And the water-plants with their graceful flat heads, all became part of
him.

The field-sprouts of Fourth-month and Fifth-month became part of
him,
Winter-grain sprouts and those of the light-yellow corn, and the escu-
lent roots of the garden,
And the apple-trees cover'd with blossoms and the fruit afterward,
and wood-berries, and the commonest weeds by the road,
And the old drunkard staggering home from the outhouse of the
tavern whence he had lately risen,
And the schoolmistress that pass'd on her way to the school,
And the friendly boys that pass'd, and the quarrelsome boys,
And the tidy and fresh-cheek'd girls, and the barefoot negro boy and
girl,
And all the changes of city and country wherever he went.

His own parents, he that had father'd him and she that had conceiv'd
him in her womb and birth'd him,
They gave this child more of themselves than that,
They gave him afterward every day, they became part of him.

The mother at home quietly placing the dishes on the supper-table,
The mother with mild words, clean her cap and gown, a wholesome
odor falling off her person and clothes as she walks by,
The father, strong, self-sufficient, manly, mean, anger'd, unjust,
The blow, the quick loud word, the tight bargain, the crafty lure,
The family usages, the language, the company, the furniture, the
yearning and swelling heart,
Affection that will not be gainsay'd, the sense of what is real, the
thought if after all it should prove unreal,

The doubts of day-time and the doubts of night-time, the curious
    whether and how,
Whether that which appears so is so, or is it all flashes and specks?
Men and women crowding fast in the streets, if they are not flashes
    and specks what are they?
The streets themselves and the façades of houses, and goods in the
    windows,
Vehicles, teams, the heavy-plank'd wharves, the huge crossing at the
    ferries,
The village on the highland seen from afar at sunset, the river be-
    tween,
Shadows, aureola and mist, the light falling on roofs and gables of
    white or brown two miles off,
The schooner near by sleepily dropping down the tide, the little boat
    slack-tow'd astern,
The hurrying tumbling waves, quick-broken crests, slapping,
The strata of color'd clouds, the long bar of maroon-tint away solitary
    by itself, the spread of purity it lies motionless in,
The horizon's edge, the flying sea-crow, the fragrance of salt marsh
    and shore mud,
These became part of that child who went forth every day, and who
    now goes, and will always go forth every day.

OLD IRELAND

Far hence amid an isle of wondrous beauty,
Crouching over a grave an ancient sorrowful mother,
Once a queen, now lean and tatter'd seated on the ground,
Her old white hair drooping dishevel'd round her shoulders,
At her feet fallen an unused royal harp,
Long silent, she too long silent, mourning her shrouded hope and heir,
Of all the earth her heart most full of sorrow because most full of love.

Yet a word ancient mother,
You need crouch there no longer on the cold ground with forehead
    between your knees,
O you need not sit there veil'd in your old white hair so dishevel'd,
For know you the one you mourn is not in that grave,
It was an illusion, the son you love was not really dead,
The Lord is not dead, he is risen again young and strong in another
    country,
Even while you wept there by your fallen harp by the grave,
What you wept for was translated, pass'd from the grave,
The winds favor'd and the sea sail'd it,
And now with rosy and new blood,
Moves to-day in a new country.

THE CITY DEAD-HOUSE

By the city dead-house by the gate,
As idly sauntering wending my way from the clangor,
I curious pause, for lo, an outcast form, a poor dead prostitute brought,
Her corpse they deposit unclaim'd, it lies on the damp brick pavement,
The divine woman, her body, I see the body, I look on it alone,
That house once full of passion and beauty, all else I notice not,
Nor stillness so cold, nor running water from faucet, nor odors mor-
    bific* impress me,
But the house alone—that wondrous house—that delicate fair house—
    that ruin!
That immortal house more than all the rows of dwellings ever built!
Or white-domed capitol with majestic figure surmounted, or all the
    old high-spired cathedrals,
That little house alone more than them all—poor, desperate house!
Fair, fearful wreck—tenement of a soul—itself a soul,
Unclaim'd, avoided house—take one breath from my tremulous lips,
Take one tear dropt aside as I go for thought of you,
Dead house of love—house of madness and sin, crumbled, crush'd.
House of life, erewhile talking and laughing—but ah, poor house, dead
    even then,
Months, years, an echoing garnish'd house—but dead, dead, dead.

THIS COMPOST

1

Something startles me where I thought I was safest,
I withdraw from the still woods I loved,
I will not go now on the pastures to walk,
I will not strip the clothes from my body to meet my lover the sea,
I will not touch my flesh to the earth as to other flesh to renew me.

O how can it be that the ground itself does not sicken?
How can you be alive you growths of spring?
How can you furnish health you blood of herbs, roots, orchards, grain?
Are they not continually putting distemper'd corpses within you?
Is not every continent work'd over and over with sour dead?

Where have you disposed of their carcasses?
Those drunkards and gluttons of so many generations?
Where have you drawn off all the foul liquid and meat?
I do not see any of it upon you to-day, or perhaps I am deceiv'd,
I will run a furrow with my plough, I will press my spade through
    the sod and turn it up underneath,
I am sure I shall expose some of the foul meat.

2

Behold this compost! behold it well!
Perhaps every mite has once form'd part of a sick person—yet behold!
The grass of spring covers the prairies,
The bean bursts noiselessly through the mould in the garden,
The delicate spear of the onion pierces upward,
The apple-buds cluster together on the apple-branches,
The resurrection of the wheat appears with pale visage out of its
    graves,
The tinge awakes over the willow-tree and the mulberry-tree,
The he-birds carol mornings and evenings while the she-birds sit on
    their nests,
The young of the poultry break through the hatch'd eggs,
The new-born of animals appear, the calf is dropt from the cow, the
    colt from the mare,
Out of its little hill faithfully rise the potato's dark green leaves,
Out of its hill rises the yellow maize-stalk, the lilacs bloom in the
    dooryards,
The summer growth is innocent and disdainful above all those strata
    of sour dead.

What chemistry!
That the winds are really not infectious,
That this is no cheat, this transparent green-wash of the sea which is
    so amorous after me,
That it is safe to allow it to lick my naked body all over with its
    tongues,
That it will not endanger me with the fevers that have deposited
    themselves in it,
That all is clean forever and forever,
That the cool drink from the well tastes so good,
That blackberries are so flavorous and juicy,
That the fruits of the apple-orchard and the orange-orchard, that
    melons, grapes, peaches, plums, will none of them poison me,
That when I recline on the grass I do not catch any disease,
Though probably every spear of grass rises out of what was once a
    catching disease.

Now I am terrified at the Earth, it is that calm and patient,
It grows such sweet things out of such corruptions,
It turns harmless and stainless on its axis, with such endless successions
    of diseas'd corpses,
It distills such exquisite winds out of such infused fetor,
It renews with such unwitting looks its prodigal, annual, sumptuous
    crops,
It gives such divine materials to men, and accepts such leavings from
    them at last.

TO A FOIL'D EUROPEAN REVOLUTIONAIRE

Courage yet, my brother or my sister!
Keep on—Liberty is to be subserv'd whatever occurs;
That is nothing that is quell'd by one or two failures, or any number
of failures,
Or by the indifference or ingratitude of the people, or by any unfaith-
fulness,
Or the show of the tushes of power, soldiers, cannon, penal statutes.

What we believe in waits latent forever through all the continents,
Invites no one, promises nothing, sits in calmness and light, is positive
and composed, knows no discouragement,
Waiting patiently, waiting its time.

(Not songs of loyalty alone are these,
But songs of insurrection also,
For I am the sworn poet of every dauntless rebel the world over,
And he going with me leaves peace and routine behind him,
And stakes his life to be lost at any moment.)

The battle rages with many a loud alarm and frequent advance and
retreat,
The infidel triumphs, or supposes he triumphs,
The prison, scaffold, garrote, handcuffs, iron necklace and lead-balls
do their work,
The named and unnamed heroes pass to other spheres,
The great speakers and writers are exiled, they lie sick in distant lands,
The cause is asleep, the strongest throats are choked with their own
blood,
The young men droop their eyelashes toward the ground when they
meet;
But for all this Liberty has not gone out of the place, nor the infidel
enter'd into full possession.

When Liberty goes out of a place it is not the first to go, nor the
second or third to go,
It waits for all the rest to go, it is the last.

When there are no more memories of heroes and martyrs,
And when all life and all the souls of men and women are discharged
from any part of the earth,
Then only shall liberty or the idea of liberty be discharged from that
part of the earth,
And the infidel come into full possession.

Then courage European revolter, revoltress!
For till all ceases neither must you cease.

I do not know what you are for, (I do not know what I am for myself,
    nor what any thing is for,)
But I will search carefully for it even in being foil'd,
In defeat, poverty, misconception, imprisonment—for they too are
    great.

Did we think victory great?
So it is—but now it seems to me, when it cannot be help'd, that defeat
    is great,
And that death and dismay are great.

UNNAMED LANDS

Nations ten thousand years before these States, and many times ten
    thousand years before these States,
Garner'd clusters of ages that men and women like us grew up and
    travel'd their course and pass'd on,
What vast-built cities, what orderly republics, what pastoral tribes and
    nomads,
What histories, rulers, heroes, perhaps transcending all others,
What laws, customs, wealth, arts, traditions,
What sort of marriage, what costumes, what physiology and phre-
    nology,
What of liberty and slavery among them, what they thought of death
    and the soul,
Who were witty and wise, who beautiful and poetic, who brutish and
    undevelop'd,
Not a mark, not a record remains—and yet all remains.

O I know that those men and women were not for nothing, any more
    than we are for nothing,
I know that they belong to the scheme of the world every bit as much
    as we now belong to it.

Afar they stand, yet near to me they stand,
Some with oval countenances learn'd and calm,
Some naked and savage, some like huge collections of insects,
Some in tents, herdsmen, patriarchs, tribes, horsemen,
Some prowling through woods, some living peaceably on farms, labor-
    ing, reaping, filling barns,
Some traversing paved avenues, amid temples, palaces, factories,
    libraries, shows, courts, theatres, wonderful monuments.

Are those billions of men really gone?
Are those women of the old experience of the earth gone?
Do their lives, cities, arts, rest only with us?
Did they achieve nothing for good for themselves?

I believe of all those men and women that fill'd the unnamed lands,
      every one exists this hour here or elsewhere, invisible to us,
In exact proportion to what he or she grew from in life, and out of
      what he or she did, felt, became, loved, sinn'd, in life.

I believe that was not the end of those nations or any person of them,
      any more than this shall be the end of my nation, or of me;
Of their languages, governments, marriage, literature, products, games,
      wars, manners, crimes, prisons, slaves, heroes, poets,
I suspect their results curiously await in the yet unseen world,
      counterparts of what accrued to them in the seen world,
I suspect I shall meet them there,
I suspect I shall there find each old particular of those unnamed lands.

SONG OF PRUDENCE

Manhattan's streets I saunter'd, pondering
On Time, Space, Reality—on such as these, and abreast with them
      Prudence.

The last explanation always remains to be made about prudence,
Little and large alike drop quietly aside from the prudence that suits
      immortality.

The soul is of itself,
All verges to it, all has reference to what ensues,
All that a person does, says, thinks, is of consequence,
Not a move can a man or woman make, that affects him or her in a
      day, month, any part of the direct lifetime, or the hour of death,
But the same affects him or her onward afterward through the indirect
      lifetime.
The indirect is just as much as the direct,
The spirit receives from the body just as much as it gives to the body,
      if not more.

Not one word or deed, not venereal sore, discoloration, privacy of the
      onanist,
Putridity of gluttons or rum-drinkers, peculation, cunning, betrayal,
      murder, seduction, prostitution,
But has results beyond death as really as before death.

Charity and personal force are the only investments worth any thing.

No specification is necessary, all that a male or female does, that is
      vigorous, benevolent, clean, is so much profit to him or her,
In the unshakable order of the universe and through the whole scope
      of it forever.

Who has been wise receives interest,
Savage, felon, President, judge, farmer, sailor, mechanic, literat,°
    young, old, it is the same,
The interest will come round—all will come round.

Singly, wholly, to affect now, affected their time, will forever affect,
    all of the past and all of the present and all of the future,
All the brave actions of war and peace,
All help given to relatives, strangers, the poor, old, sorrowful, young
    children, widows, the sick, and to shunn'd persons,
All self-denial that stood steady and aloof on wrecks, and saw others
    fill the seats of the boats,
All offering of substance or life for the good old cause, or for a friend's
    sake, or opinion's sake,
All pains of enthusiasts scoff'd at by their neighbors,
All the limitless sweet love and precious suffering of mothers,
All honest men baffled in strifes recorded or unrecorded,
All the grandeur and good of ancient nations whose fragments we
    inherit,
All the good of the dozens of ancient nations unknown to us by name,
    date, location,
All that was ever manfully begun, whether it succeeded or no,
All suggestions of the divine mind of man or the divinity of his mouth,
    or the shaping of his great hands,
All that is well thought or said this day on any part of the globe, or on
    any of the wandering stars, or on any of the fix'd stars, by those
    there as we are here,
All that is henceforth to be thought or done by you whoever you are,
    or by any one,
These inure,° have inured, shall inure, to the identities from which
    they sprang, or shall spring.

Did you guess any thing lived only its moment?
The world does not so exist, no parts palpable or impalpable so exist,
No consummation exists without being from some long previous con-
    summation, and that from some other,
Without the farthest conceivable one coming a bit nearer the beginning
    than any.

Whatever satisfies souls is true;
Prudence entirely satisfies the craving and glut of souls,
Itself only finally satisfies the soul,
The soul has that measureless pride which revolts from every lesson
    but its own.

Now I breathe the word of the prudence that walks abreast with time,
    space, reality,
That answers the pride which refuses every lesson but its own.

What is prudence is indivisible,
Declines to separate one part of life from every part,
Divides not the righteous from the unrighteous or the living from the
    dead,
Matches every thought or act by its correlative,
Knows no possible forgiveness or deputed atonement,
Knows that the young man who composedly peril'd his life and lost it
    has done exceedingly well for himself without doubt,
That he who never peril'd his life, but retains it to old age in riches
    and ease, has probably achiev'd nothing for himself worth
    mentioning,
Knows that only that person has really learn'd who has learn'd to
    prefer results,
Who favors body and soul the same,
Who perceives the indirect assuredly following the direct,
Who in his spirit in any emergency whatever neither hurries nor
    avoids death.

THE SINGER IN THE PRISON

1
O sight of pity, shame and dole!
O fearful thought—a convict soul.

Rang the refrain along the hall, the prison,
Rose to the roof, the vaults of heaven above,
Pouring in floods of melody in tones so pensive sweet and strong the
    like whereof was never heard,
Reaching the far-off sentry and the armed guards, who ceas'd their
    pacing,
Making the hearer's pulses stop for ecstasy and awe.

2
The sun was low in the west one winter day,
When down a narrow aisle amid the thieves and outlaws of the land,
(There by the hundreds seated, sear-faced murderers, wily counter-
    feiters,
Gather'd to Sunday church in prison walls, the keepers round,
Plenteous, well-armed, watching with vigilant eyes,)
Calmly a lady walk'd holding a little innocent child by either hand,
Whom seating on their stools beside her on the platform,
She, first preluding with the instrument a low and musical prelude,
In voice surpassing all, sang forth a quaint old hymn.

    A soul confined by bars and bands,
    Cries, help! O help! and wrings her hands
    Blinded her eyes, bleeding her breast,
    Nor pardon finds, nor balm of rest.

Ceaseless she paces to and fro,
O heart-sick days! O nights of woe!
Nor hand of friend, nor loving face,
Nor favor comes, nor word of grace.

It was not I that sinn'd the sin,
The ruthless body dragged me in;
Though long I strove courageously,
The body was too much for me.

Dear prison'd soul bear up a space,
For soon or late the certain grace;
To set thee free and bear thee home,
The heavenly pardoner death shall come.

Convict no more, nor shame, nor dole!
Depart—a God-enfranchis'd soul!

3

The singer ceas'd,
One glance swept from her clear calm eyes o'er all those upturn'd
    faces,
Strange sea of prison faces, a thousand varied, crafty, brutal, seam'd
    and beauteous faces,
Then rising, passing back along the narrow aisle between them,
While her gown touch'd them rustling in the silence,
She vanish'd with her children in the dusk.

While upon all, convicts and armed keepers ere they stirr'd,
(Convict forgetting prison, keeper his loaded pistol,)
A hush and pause fell down a wondrous minute,
With deep half-stifled sobs and sound of bad men bow'd and moved
    to weeping,
And youth's convulsive breathings, memories of home,
The mother's voice in lullaby, the sister's care, the happy childhood,
The long-pent spirit rous'd to reminiscence;
A wondrous minute then—but after in the solitary night, to many,
    many there,
Years after, even in the hour of death, the sad refrain, the tune, the
    voice, the words,
Resumed, the large calm lady walks the narrow aisle,
The wailing melody again, the singer in the prison sings,

O sight of pity, shame and dole!
O fearful thought—a convict soul.

WARBLE FOR LILAC-TIME

Warble me now for joy of lilac-time, (returning in reminiscence,)
Sort me O tongue and lips for Nature's sake, souvenirs of earliest
    summer,
Gather the welcome signs, (as children with pebbles or stringing
    shells,)
Put in April and May, the hylas croaking in the ponds, the elastic air,
Bees, butterflies, the sparrow with its simple notes,
Blue-bird and darting swallow, nor forget the high-hole flashing his
    golden wings,
The tranquil sunny haze, the clinging smoke, the vapor,
Shimmer of waters with fish in them, the cerulean above,
All that is jocund and sparkling, the brooks running,
The maple woods, the crisp February days and the sugar-making,
The robin where he hops, bright-eyed, brown-breasted,
With musical clear call at sunrise, and again at sunset,
Or flitting among the trees of the apple-orchard, building the nest of
    his mate,
The melted snow of March, the willow sending forth its yellow-green
    sprouts,
For spring-time is here! the summer is here! and what is this in it and
    from it?
Thou, soul, unloosen'd—the restlessness after I know not what;
Come, let us lag* here no longer, let us be up and away!
O if one could but fly like a bird!
O to escape, to sail forth as in a ship!
To glide with thee O soul, o'er all, in all, as a ship o'er the waters;
Gathering these hints, the preludes, the blue sky, the grass, the morn-
    ing drops of dew,
The lilac-scent, the bushes with dark green heart-shaped leaves,
Wood-violets, the little delicate pale blossoms called innocence,
Samples and sorts not for themselves alone, but for their atmosphere,
To grace the bush I love—to sing with the birds,
A warble for joy of lilac-time, returning in reminiscence.

OUTLINES FOR A TOMB
(G.P., Buried 1870)

1

What may we chant, O thou within this tomb?
What tablets, outlines, hang for thee, O millionaire?
The life thou lived'st we know not,
But that thou walk'dst thy years in barter, 'mid the haunts of brokers,
Nor heroism thine, nor war, nor glory.

2

Silent, my soul,
With drooping lids, as waiting, ponder'd,
Turning from all the samples, monuments of heroes.

While through the interior vistas,
Noiseless uprose, phantasmic, (as by night Auroras of the north,)
Lambent* tableaus, prophetic, bodiless scenes,
Spiritual projections.

In one, among the city streets a laborer's home appear'd,
After his day's work done, cleanly, sweet-air'd, the gaslight burning,
The carpet swept and a fire in the cheerful stove.

In one, the sacred parturition scene,
A happy painless mother birth'd a perfect child.

In one, at a bounteous morning meal,
Sat peaceful parents with contented sons.

In one, by twos and threes, young people,
Hundreds concentring, walk'd the paths and streets and roads,
Toward a tall-domed school.

In one a trio beautiful,
Grandmother, loving daughter, loving daughter's daughter, sat,
Chatting and sewing.

In one, along a suite of noble rooms,
'Mid plenteous books and journals, paintings on the walls, fine statu-
        ettes,
Were groups of friendly journeymen, mechanics young and old,
Reading, conversing.

All, all the shows of laboring life,
City and country, women's, men's and children's,
Their wants provided for, hued in the sun and tinged for once with
        joy,
Marriage, the street, the factory, farm, the house-room, lodging-room,
Labor and toil, the bath, gymnasium, playground, library, college,
The student, boy or girl, led forward to be taught,
The sick cared for, the shoeless shod, the orphan father'd and mother'd,
The hungry fed, the houseless housed;
(The intentions perfect and divine,
The workings, details, haply* human.)

3

O thou within this tomb,
From thee such scenes, thou stintless, lavish giver,
Tallying the gifts of earth, large as the earth,
Thy name an earth, with mountains, fields and tides.

Nor by your streams alone, you rivers,
By you, your banks Connecticut,
By you and all your teeming life old Thames,
By you Potomac laving the ground Washington trod, by you Patapsco,
You Hudson, you endless Mississippi—nor you alone,
But to the high seas launch, my thought, his memory.

OUT FROM BEHIND THIS MASK
(To Confront a Portrait)

1

Out from behind this bending rough-cut mask,
These lights and shades, this drama of the whole,
This common curtain of the face contain'd in me for me, in you for
    you, in each for each,
(Tragedies, sorrows, laughter, tears—O heaven!
The passionate teeming plays this curtain hid!)
This glaze of God's serenest purest sky,
This film of Satan's seething pit,
This heart's geography's map, this limitless small continent, this
    soundless sea;
Out from the convolutions of this globe,
This subtler astronomic orb than sun or moon, than Jupiter, Venus,
    Mars,
This condensation of the universe, (nay here the only universe,
Here the idea, all in this mystic handful wrapt;)
These burin'd° eyes, flashing to you to pass to future time,
To launch and spin through space revolving sideling, from these to
    emanate,
To you whoe'er you are—a look.

2

A traveler of thoughts and years, of peace and war,
Of youth long sped and middle age declining,
(As the first volume of a tale perused and laid away, and this the
    second,
Songs, ventures, speculations, presently to close,)
Lingering a moment here and now, to you I opposite turn,
As on the road or at some crevice door by chance, or open'd window,
Pausing, inclining, baring my head, you specially I greet,
To draw and clinch° your soul for once inseparably with mine,
Then travel travel on.

VOCALISM

1

Vocalism, measure, concentration, determination, and the divine power
    to speak words;
Are you full-lung'd and limber-lipp'd from long trial? from vigorous
    practice? from physique?
Do you move in these broad lands as broad as they?
Come duly to the divine power to speak words?
For only at last after many years, after chastity, friendship, procrea-
    tion, prudence, and nakedness,
After treading ground and breasting river and lake,
After a loosen'd throat, after absorbing eras, temperaments, races,
    after knowledge, freedom, crimes,
After complete faith, after clarifyings, elevations, and removing
    obstructions,
After these and more, it is just possible there comes to a man, a
    woman, the divine power to speak words;
Then toward that man or that woman swiftly hasten all—none refuse,
    all attend,
Armies, ships, antiquities, libraries, paintings, machines, cities, hate,
    despair, amity, pain, theft, murder, aspiration, form in close
    ranks,
They debouch* as they are wanted to march obediently through the
    mouth of that man or that woman.

2

O what is it in me that makes me tremble so at voices?
Surely whoever speaks to me in the right voice, him or her I shall
    follow,
As the water follows the moon, silently, with fluid steps, anywhere
    around the globe.

All waits for the right voices;
Where is the practis'd and perfect organ? where is the develop'd soul?
For I see every word utter'd thence has deeper, sweeter, new sounds,
    impossible on less terms.

I see brains and lips closed, tympans and temples unstruck,
Until that comes which has the quality to strike and to unclose,
Until that comes which has the quality to bring forth what lies
    slumbering forever ready in all words.

TO HIM THAT WAS CRUCIFIED

My spirit to yours dear brother,
Do not mind because many sounding your name do not understand
    you,

I do not sound your name, but I understand you,
I specify you with joy O my comrade to salute you, and to salute those
      who are with you, before and since, and those to come also,
That we all labor together transmitting the same charge and succession,
We few equals indifferent of lands, indifferent of times,
We, enclosers of all continents, all castes, allowers of all theologies,
Compassionaters, perceivers, rapport° of men.
We walk silent among disputes and assertions, but reject not the
      disputers nor any thing that is asserted,
We hear the bawling and din, we are reach'd at by divisions, jealousies,
      recriminations on every side,
They close peremptorily upon us to surround us, my comrade,
Yet we walk unheld, free, the whole earth over, journeying up and
      down till we make our ineffaceable mark upon time and the
      diverse eras,
Till we saturate time and eras, that the men and women of races, ages
      to come, may prove brethren and lovers as we are.

YOU FELONS ON TRIAL IN COURTS

You felons on trial in courts,
You convicts in prison-cells, you sentenced assassins chain'd and
      handcuff'd with iron,
Who am I too that I am not on trial or in prison?
Me ruthless and devilish as any, that my wrists are not chain'd with
      iron, or my ankles with iron?

You prostitutes flaunting over the trottoirs° or obscene in your rooms,
Who am I that I should call you more obscene than myself?

O culpable! I acknowledge—I exposé!
(O admirers, praise me not—compliment not me—you make me wince,
I see what you do not—I know what you do not.)

Inside these breast-bones I lie smutch'd and choked,
Beneath this face that appears so impassive hell's tides continually run.
Lusts and wickedness are acceptable to me,
I walk with delinquents with passionate love,
I feel I am of them—I belong to those convicts and prostitutes myself,
And henceforth I will not deny them—for how can I deny myself?

LAWS FOR CREATIONS

Laws for creations,
For strong artists and leaders, for fresh broods of teachers and perfect
      literats° for America,
For noble savans° and coming musicians.

All must have reference to the ensemble of the world, and the compact
    truth of the world,
There shall be no subject too pronounced—all works shall illustrate
    the divine law of indirections.

What do you suppose creation is?
What do you suppose will satisfy the soul, except to walk free and
    own no superior?
What do you suppose I would intimate to you in a hundred ways, but
    that man or woman is as good as God?
And that there is no God any more divine than Yourself?
And that that is what the oldest and newest myths finally mean?
And that you or any one must approach creations through such laws?

TO A COMMON PROSTITUTE

Be composed—be at ease with me—I am Walt Whitman, liberal and
    lusty as Nature,
Not till the sun excludes you do I exclude you,
Not till the waters refuse to glisten for you and the leaves to rustle
    for you, do my words refuse to glisten and rustle for you.

My girl I appoint with you an appointment, and I charge you that
    you make preparation to be worthy to meet me,
And I charge you that you be patient and perfect till I come.

Till then I salute you with a significant look that you do not forget me.

I WAS LOOKING A LONG WHILE

I was looking a long while for Intentions,
For a clew to the history of the past for myself, and for these chants—
    and now I have found it,
It is not in those paged fables in the libraries, (them I neither accept
    nor reject,)
It is no more in the legends than in all else,
It is in the present—it is this earth to-day,
It is in Democracy—(the purport and aim of all the past,)
It is the life of one man or one woman to-day—the average man of
    to-day,
It is in languages, social customs, literatures, arts,
It is in the broad show of artificial things, ships, machinery, politics,
    creeds, modern improvements, and the interchange of nations,
All for the modern—all for the average man of to-day.

THOUGHT

Of persons arrived at high positions, ceremonies, wealth, scholarships,
        and the like;
(To me all that those persons have arrived at sinks away from them,
        except as it results to their bodies and souls,
So that often to me they appear gaunt and naked,
And often to me each one mocks the others, and mocks himself or
        herself,
And of each one the core of life, namely happiness, is full of the
        rotten excrement of maggots,
And often to me those men and women pass unwittingly the true
        realities of life, and go toward false realities,
And often to me they are alive after what custom has served them,
        but nothing more,
And often to me they are sad, hasty, unwaked somnambules° walking
        the dusk.)

MIRACLES

Why, who makes much of a miracle?
As to me I know of nothing else but miracles,
Whether I walk the streets of Manhattan,
Or dart my sight over the roofs of houses toward the sky,
Or wade with naked feet along the beach just in the edge of the water,
Or stand under trees in the woods,
Or talk by day with any one I love, or sleep in the bed at night with
        any one I love,
Or sit at table at dinner with the rest,
Or look at strangers opposite me riding in the car,
Or watch honey-bees busy around the hive of a summer forenoon,
Or animals feeding in the fields,
Or birds, or the wonderfulness of insects in the air,
Or the wonderfulness of the sundown, or of stars shining so quiet and
        bright,
Or the exquisite delicate thin curve of the new moon in spring;
These with the rest, one and all, are to me miracles,
The whole referring, yet each distinct and in its place.

To me every hour of the light and dark is a miracle,
Every cubic inch of space is a miracle,
Every square yard of the surface of the earth is spread with the same,
Every foot of the interior swarms with the same.

To me the sea is a continual miracle,
The fishes that swim—the rocks—the motion of the waves—the ships
        with men in them,
What stranger miracles are there?

SPARKLES FROM THE WHEEL

Where the city's ceaseless crowd moves on the livelong day,
Withdrawn I join a group of children watching, I pause aside with
    them.

By the curb toward the edge of the flagging,
A knife-grinder works at his wheel sharpening a great knife,
Bending over he carefully holds it to the stone, by foot and knee,
With measur'd tread he turns rapidly, as he presses with light but firm
    hand,
Forth issue then in copious golden jets,
Sparkles from the wheel.

The scene and all its belongings, how they seize and affect me,
The sad sharp-chinn'd old man with worn clothes and broad shoulder-
    band of leather,
Myself effusing* and fluid, a phantom curiously floating, now here
    absorb'd and arrested,
The group, (an unminded point set in a vast surrounding,)
The attentive, quiet children, the loud, proud, restive base of the
    streets,
The low hoarse purr of the whirling stone, the light-press'd blade,
Diffusing, dropping, sideways-darting, in tiny showers of gold,
Sparkles from the wheel.

TO A PUPIL

Is reform needed? is it through you?
The greater the reform needed, the greater the Personality you need
    to accomplish it.

You! do you not see how it would serve to have eyes, blood, com-
    plexion, clean and sweet?
Do you not see how it would serve to have such a body and soul that
    when you enter the crowd an atmosphere of desire and com-
    mand enters with you, and every one is impress'd with your
    Personality?

O the magnet! the flesh over and over!
Go, dear friend, if need be give up all else, and commence to-day to
    inure° yourself to pluck, reality, self-esteem, definiteness,
    elevatedness,
Rest not till you rivet and publish yourself of your own Personality.

UNFOLDED OUT OF THE FOLDS

Unfolded out of the folds of the woman man comes unfolded, and is
always to come unfolded,
Unfolded only out of the superbest woman of the earth is to come the
superbest man of the earth,
Unfolded out of the friendliest woman is to come the friendliest man,
Unfolded only out of the perfect body of a woman can a man be
form'd of perfect body,
Unfolded only out of the inimitable poems of woman can come the
poems of man, (only thence have my poems come;)
Unfolded out of the strong and arrogant woman I love, only thence
can appear the strong and arrogant man I love,
Unfolded by brawny embraces from the well-muscled woman I love,
only thence come the brawny embraces of the man,
Unfolded out of the folds of the woman's brain come all the folds of
the man's brain, duly obedient,
Unfolded out of the justice of the woman all justice is unfolded,
Unfolded out of the sympathy of the woman is all sympathy;
A man is a great thing upon the earth and through eternity, but every
jot of the greatness of man is unfolded out of woman;
First the man is shaped in the woman, he can then be shaped in him-
self.

WHAT AM I AFTER ALL

What am I after all but a child, pleas'd with the sound of my own
name? repeating it over and over;
I stand apart to hear—it never tires me.

To you your name also;
Did you think there was nothing but two or three pronunciations in
the sound of your name?

KOSMOS*

Who includes diversity and is Nature,
Who is the amplitude of the earth, and the coarseness and sexuality
of the earth, and the great charity of the earth, and the equilibrium also,
Who has not look'd forth from the windows the eyes for nothing, or
whose brain held audience with messengers for nothing,
Who contains believers and disbelievers, who is the most majestic
lover,
Who holds duly his or her triune proportion of realism, spiritualism,
and of the æsthetic or intellectual,

Who having consider'd the body finds all its organs and parts good,
Who, out of the theory of the earth and of his or her body under-
stands by subtle analogies all other theories,
The theory of a city, a poem, and of the large politics of these States;
Who believes not only in our globe with its sun and moon, but in
other globes with their suns and moons,
Who, constructing the house of himself or herself, not for a day but
for all time, sees races, eras, dates, generations,
The past, the future, dwelling there, like space, inseparable together.

OTHERS MAY PRAISE WHAT THEY LIKE

Others may praise what they like;
But I, from the banks of the running Missouri, praise nothing in art
or aught else,
Till it has well inhaled the atmosphere of this river, also the western
prairie-scent,
And exudes it all again.

WHO LEARNS MY LESSON COMPLETE?

Who learns my lesson complete?
Boss, journeyman, apprentice, churchman and atheist,
The stupid and the wise thinker, parents and offspring, merchant,
clerk, porter and customer,
Editor, author, artist, and schoolboy—draw nigh and commence,
It is no lesson—it lets down the bars to a good lesson,
And that to another, and every one to another still.

The great laws take and effuse* without argument,
I am of the same style, for I am their friend,
I love them quits and quits, I do not halt and make salaams.

I lie abstracted and hear beautiful tales of things and the reasons of
things,
They are so beautiful I nudge myself to listen.

I cannot say to any person what I hear—I cannot say it to myself—
it is very wonderful.

It is no small matter, this round and delicious globe moving so exactly
in its orbit for ever and ever, without one jolt or the untruth
of a single second,
I do not think it was made in six days, nor in ten thousand years,
nor ten billions of years,
Nor plann'd and built one thing after another as an architect plans
and builds a house.

I do not think seventy years is the time of a man or woman,
Nor that seventy millions of years is the time of a man or woman,
Nor that years will ever stop the existence of me, or any one else.

Is it wonderful that I should be immortal? as every one is immortal;
I know it is wonderful, but my eyesight is equally wonderful, and
    how I was conceived in my mother's womb is equally wonder-
    ful,
And pass'd from a babe in the creeping trance of a couple of summers
    and winters to articulate and walk—all this is equally wonder-
    ful.

And that my soul embraces you this hour, and we affect each other
    without ever seeing each other, and never perhaps to see each
    other, is every bit as wonderful.

And that I can think such thoughts as these is just as wonderful,
And that I can remind you, and you think them and know them to
    be true, is just as wonderful.

And that the moon spins round the earth and on with the earth, is
    equally wonderful,
And that they balance themselves with the sun and stars is equally
    wonderful.

TESTS

All submit to them where they sit, inner, secure, unapproachable to
    analysis in the soul,
Not traditions, not the outer authorities are the judges,
They are the judges of outer authorities and of all traditions,
They corroborate as they go only whatever corroborates themselves,
    and touches themselves;
For all that, they have it forever in themselves to corroborate far and
    near without one exception.

THE TORCH

On my Northwest coast in the midst of the night a fishermen's group
    stands watching,
Out on the lake that expands before them, others are spearing salmon,
The canoe, a dim shadowy thing, moves across the black water,
Bearing a torch ablaze at the prow.

O STAR OF FRANCE
1870-71

O star of France,
The brightness of thy hope and strength and fame,
Like some proud ship that led the fleet so long,

Beseems to-day a wreck driven by the gale, a mastless hulk,
And 'mid its teeming madden'd half-drown'd crowds,
Nor helm nor helmsman.

Dim smitten star,
Orb not of France alone, pale symbol of my soul, its dearest hopes,
The struggle and the daring, rage divine for liberty,
Of aspirations toward the far ideal, enthusiast's dreams of brother-
        hood,
Of terror to the tyrant and the priest.

Star crucified—by traitors sold,
Star panting o'er a land of death, heroic land,
Strange, passionate, mocking, frivolous land.

Miserable! yet for thy errors, vanities, sins, I will not now rebuke thee,
Thy unexampled woes and pangs have quell'd them all,
And left thee sacred.

In that amid thy many faults thou ever aimedst highly,
In that thou wouldst not really sell thyself however great the price,
In that thou surely wakedst weeping from thy drugg'd sleep,
In that alone among thy sisters thou, giantess, didst rend the ones that
        shamed thee,
In that thou couldst not, wouldst not, wear the usual chains,
This cross, thy livid face, thy pierced hands and feet,
The spear thrust in thy side.

O star! O ship of France, beat back and baffled long!
Bear up O smitten orb! O ship continue on!

Sure as the ship of all, the Earth itself,
Product of deathly fire and turbulent chaos,
Forth from its spasms of fury and its poisons,
Issuing at last in perfect power and beauty,
Onward beneath the sun following its course,
So thee O ship of France!

Finish'd the days, the clouds dispel'd,
The travail o'er, the long-sought extrication,
When lo! reborn, high o'er the European world,
(In gladness answering thence, as face afar to face, reflecting ours
        Columbia,)
Again thy star O France, fair lustrous star,
In heavenly peace, clearer, more bright than ever,
Shall beam immortal.

THE OX-TAMER

In a far-away northern county in the placid pastoral region,
Lives my farmer friend, the theme of my recitative, a famous tamer of oxen,
There they bring him the three-year-olds and the four-year-olds to break them,
He will take the wildest steer in the world and break him and tame him,
He will go fearless without any whip where the young bullock chafes up and down the yard,
The bullock's head tosses restless high in the air with raging eyes,
Yet see you! how soon his rage subsides—how soon this tamer tames him;
See you! on the farms hereabouts a hundred oxen young and old, and he is the man who has tamed them,
They all know him, all are affectionate to him,
See you! some are such beautiful animals, so lofty looking;
Some are buff-color'd, some mottled, one has a white line running along his back, some are brindled,
Some have wide flaring horns (a good sign)—see you! the bright hides,
See, the two with stars on their foreheads—see, the round bodies and broad backs,
How straight and square they stand on their legs—what fine sagacious eyes!
How they watch their tamer—they wish him near them—how they turn to look after him!
What yearning expression! how uneasy they are when he moves away from them;
Now I marvel what it can be he appears to them, (books, politics, poems, depart—all else departs,)
I confess I envy only his fascination—my silent, illiterate friend,
Whom a hundred oxen love there in his life on farms,
In the northern county far, in the placid pastoral region.

AN OLD MAN'S THOUGHT OF SCHOOL

For the Inauguration of a Public School, Camden, New Jersey, 1874

An old man's thought of school,
An old man gathering youthful memories and blooms that youth itself cannot.

Now only do I know you,
O fair auroral skies—O morning dew upon the grass!

And these I see, these sparkling eyes,
These stores of mystic meaning, these young lives,
Building, equipping like a fleet of ships, immortal ships,
Soon to sail out over the measureless seas,
On the soul's voyage.

Only a lot of boys and girls?
Only the tiresome spelling, writing, ciphering classes?
Only a public school?

Ah more, infinitely more;
(As George Fox rais'd his warning cry, "Is it this pile of brick and
    mortar, these dead floors, windows, rails, you call the church?
Why this is not the church at all—the church is living, ever living
    souls.")

And you America,
Cast you the real reckoning for your present?
The lights and shadows of your future, good or evil?
To girlhood, boyhood look, the teacher and the school.

WANDERING AT MORN

Wandering at morn,
Emerging from the night from gloomy thoughts, thee in my thoughts,
Yearning for thee harmonious Union! thee, singing bird divine!
Thee coil'd in evil times my country, with craft and black dismay,
    with every meanness, treason thrust upon thee,
This common marvel I beheld—the parent thrush I watch'd feeding
    its young,
The singing thrush whose tones of joy and faith ecstatic,
Fail not to certify and cheer my soul.

There ponder'd, felt I,
If worms, snakes, loathsome grubs, may to sweet spiritual songs be
    turn'd,
If vermin so transposed, so used and bless'd may be,
Then may I trust in you, your fortunes, days, my country;
Who knows but these may be the lessons fit for you?
From these your future songs may rise with joyous trills,
Destin'd to fill the world.

ITALIAN MUSIC IN DAKOTA
("The Seventeenth—the finest Regimental Band I ever heard.")

Through the soft evening air enwinding all,
Rocks, woods, fort, cannon, pacing sentries, endless wilds,
In dulcet streams, in flutes' and cornets' notes,

Electric, pensive, turbulent, artificial,
(Yet strangely fitting even here, meanings unknown before,
Subtler than ever, more harmony, as if born here, related here,
Not to the city's fresco'd rooms, not to the audience of the opera house,
Sounds, echoes, wandering strains, as really here at home,
Sonnambula's innocent love, trios with *Norma's* anguish,
And thy ecstatic chorus *Poliuto;*)
Ray'd in the limpid yellow slanting sundown,
Music, Italian music in Dakota.

While Nature, sovereign of this gnarl'd realm,
Lurking in hidden barbaric grim recesses,
Acknowledging rapport° however far remov'd,
(As some old root or soil of earth its last-born flower or fruit,)
Listens well-pleas'd.

WITH ALL THY GIFTS

With all thy gifts America,
Standing secure, rapidly tending, overlooking the world,
Power, wealth, extent, vouchsafed to thee—with these and like of
    these vouchsafed to thee,
What if one gift thou lackest? (the ultimate human problem never
    solving,)
The gift of perfect women fit for thee—what if that gift of gifts thou
    lackest?
The towering feminine of thee? the beauty, health, completion, fit for
    thee?
The mothers fit for thee?

MY PICTURE-GALLERY

In a little house keep I pictures suspended, it is not a fix'd house,
It is round, it is only a few inches from one side to the other;
Yet behold, it has room for all the shows of the world, all memories!
Here the tableaus of life, and here the groupings of death;
Here, do you know this? this is cicerone himself,
With finger rais'd he points to the prodigal pictures.

THE PRAIRIE STATES

A newer garden of creation, no primal solitude,
Dense, joyous, modern, populous millions, cities and farms,
With iron interlaced, composite, tied, many in one,
By all the world contributed—freedom's and law's and thrift's society,
The crown and teeming paradise, so far, of time's accumulations,
To justify the past.

PROUD MUSIC OF THE STORM

1

Proud music of the storm,
Blast that careers so free, whistling across the prairies,
Strong hum of forest tree-tops—wind of the mountains,
Personified dim shapes—you hidden orchestras,
You serenades of phantoms with instruments alert,
Bending with Nature's rhythmus all the tongues of nations;
You chords left as by vast composers—you choruses,
You formless, free, religious dances—you from the Orient,
You undertone of rivers, roar of pouring cataracts,
You sounds from distant guns with galloping cavalry,
Echoes of camps with all the different bugle-calls,
Trooping tumultuous, filling the midnight late, bending me powerless,
Entering my lonesome slumber-chamber, why have you seiz'd me?

2

Come forward O my soul, and let the rest retire,
Listen, lose not, it is toward thee they tend,
Parting the midnight, entering my slumber-chamber,
For thee they sing and dance O soul.

A festival song,
The duet of the bridegroom and the bride, a marriage-march,
With lips of love, and hearts of lovers fill'd to the brim with love,
The red-flush'd cheeks and perfumes, the cortege swarming full of
      friendly faces young and old,
To flutes' clear notes and sounding harps' cantabile.

Now loud approaching drums,
Victoria! see'st thou in powder-smoke the banners torn but flying?
      the rout of the baffled?
Hearest those shouts of a conquering army?

(Ah soul, the sobs of women, the wounded groaning in agony,
The hiss and crackle of flames, the blacken'd ruins, the embers ot
      cities,
The dirge and desolation of mankind.)

Now airs antique and mediæval fill me,
I see and hear old harpers with their harps at Welsh festivals,
I hear the minnesingers singing their lays of love,
I hear the minstrels, gleemen, troubadours, of the middle ages.

Now the great organ sounds,
Tremulous, while underneath, (as the hid footholds of the earth.
On which arising rest, and leaping forth depend,

All shapes of beauty, grace, and strength, all hues we know,
Green blades of grass and warbling birds, children that gambol and
       play, the clouds of heaven above,)
The strong base stands, and its pulsations intermits not,
Bathing, supporting, merging all the rest, maternity of all the rest,
And with it every instrument in multitudes,
The players playing, all the world's musicians,
The solemn hymns and masses rousing adoration,
All passionate heart-chants, sorrowful appeals,
The measureless sweet vocalists of ages,
And for their solvent setting earth's own diapason,
Of winds and woods and mighty ocean waves,
A new composite orchestra, binder of years and climes, ten-fold
      renewer,
As of the far-back days the poets tell, the Paradiso,
The straying hence, the separation long, but now the wandering done,
The journey done, the journeyman come home,
And man and art with Nature fused again.

Tutti! for earth and heaven;
(The Almighty leader now for once has signal'd with his wand.)

The manly strophe of the husbands of the world,
And all the wives responding.

The tongues of violins,
(I think O tongues ye tell this heart, that cannot tell itself,
This brooding yearning heart, that cannot tell itself.)

3

Ah from a little child,
Thou knowest soul how to me all sounds became music,
My mother's voice in lullaby or hymn,
(The voice, O tender voices, memory's loving voices,
Last miracle of all, O dearest mother's, sister's, voices;)
The rain, the growing corn, the breeze among the long-leav'd corn,
The measur'd sea-surf beating on the sand,
The twittering bird, the hawk's sharp scream,
The wild-fowl's notes at night as flying low migrating north or south,
The psalm in the country church or mid the clustering trees, the open
      air camp-meeting,
The fiddler in the tavern, the glee, the long-strung sailor-song,
The lowing cattle, bleating sheep, the crowing cock at dawn.

All songs of current lands come sounding round me,
The German airs of friendship, wine and love,
Irish ballads, merry jigs and dances, English warbles,
Chansons of France, Scotch tunes, and o'er the rest,
Italia's peerless compositions.

Across the stage with pallor on her face, yet lurid passion,
Stalks Norma brandishing the dagger in her hand.

I see poor crazed Lucia's eyes' unnatural gleam,
Her hair down her back falls loose and dishevel'd.

I see where Ernani walking the bridal garden,
Amid the scent of night-roses, radiant, holding his bride by the hand,
Hears the infernal call, the death pledge of the horn.

To crossing swords and gray hairs bared to heaven,
The clear electric base and baritone of the world,
The trombone duo, Libertad* forever!

From Spanish chestnut trees' dense shade,
By old and heavy convent walls a wailing song,
Song of lost love, the torch of youth and life quench'd in despair,
Song of the dying swan, Fernando's heart is breaking.

Awaking from her woes at last retriev'd Amina sings,
Copious as stars and glad as morning light the torrents of her joy.

(The teeming lady comes,
The lustrous orb, Venus contralto, the blooming mother,
Sister of loftiest gods, Alboni's self I hear.)

4

I hear those odes, symphonies, operas,
I hear in the *William Tell* the music of an arous'd and angry people,
I hear Meyerbeer's *Huguenots,* the *Prophet,* or *Robert,*
Gounod's *Faust,* or Mozart's *Don Juan.*

I hear the dance-music of all nations,
The waltz, some delicious measure, lapsing, bathing me in bliss,
The bolero to tinkling guitars and clattering castanets.

I see religious dances old and new,
I hear the sound of the Hebrew lyre,
I see the crusaders marching bearing the cross on high, to the martial
    clang of cymbals,
I hear dervishes monotonously chanting, interspers'd with frantic
    shouts, as they spin around turning always towards Mecca,
I see the rapt religious dances of the Persians and the Arabs,
Again, at Eleusis, home of Ceres, I see the modern Greeks dancing,
I hear them clapping their hands as they bend their bodies,
I hear the metrical shuffling of their feet.

I see again the wild old Corybantian dance, the performers wounding
    each other,

I see the Roman youth to the shrill sound of flageolets throwing and
      catching their weapons,
As they fall on their knees and rise again.

I hear from the Mussulman mosque the muezzin calling,
I see the worshippers within, nor form nor sermon, argument nor word,
But silent, strange, devout, rais'd, glowing heads, ecstatic faces.

I hear the Egyptian harp of many strings,
The primitive chants of the Nile boatmen,
The sacred imperial hymns of China,
To the delicate sounds of the king, (the stricken wood and stone,)
Or to Hindu flutes and the fretting twang of the vina,
A band of bayaderes.°

5

Now Asia, Africa leave me, Europe seizing inflates me,
To organs huge and bands I hear as from vast concourses of voices,
Luthers' strong hymn *Eine feste Burg ist unser Gott*,
Rossini's *Stabat Mater dolorosa*,
Or floating in some high cathedral dim with gorgeous color'd windows,
The passionate *Agnus Dei* or *Gloria in Excelsis*.

Composers! mighty maestros!
And you, sweet singers of old lands, soprani, tenori, bassi!
To you a new bard caroling in the West,
Obeisant sends his love.

(Such led to thee O soul,
All senses, shows and objects, lead to thee,
But now it seems to me sound leads o'er all the rest.)

I hear the annual singing of the children in St. Paul's cathedral,
Or, under the high roof of some colossal hall, the symphonies, ora-
      torios of Beethoven, Handel, or Haydn,
The *Creation* in billows of godhood laves me.

Give me to hold all sounds, (I madly struggling cry,)
Fill me with all the voices of the universe,
Endow me with their throbbings, Nature's also,
The tempests, waters, winds, operas and chants, marches and dances,
Utter, pour in, for I would take them all!

6

Then I woke softly,
And pausing, questioning awhile the music of my dream,
And questioning all those reminiscences, the tempest in its fury,
And all the songs of sopranos and tenors,
And those rapt oriental dances of religious fervor,

And the sweet varied instruments, and the diapason of organs,
And all the artless plaints of love and grief and death,
I said to my silent curious soul out of the bed of the slumber-chamber,
Come, for I have found the clew I sought so long,
Let us go forth refresh'd amid the day,
Cheerfully tallying life, walking the world, the real,
Nourish'd henceforth by our celestial dream.

And I said, moreover,
Haply what thou hast heard O soul was not the sound of winds,
Nor dream of raging storm, nor sea-hawk's flapping wings nor harsh
    scream,
Nor vocalism of sun-bright Italy,
Nor German organ majestic, nor vast concourse of voices, nor layers
    of harmonies,
Nor strophes of husbands and wives, nor sound of marching soldiers,
Nor flutes, nor harps, nor the bugle-calls of camps,
But to a new rhythmus fitted for thee,
Poems bridging the way from Life to Death, vaguely wafted in night
    air, uncaught, unwritten,
Which let us go forth in the bold day and write.

PASSAGE TO INDIA

1

Singing my days,
Singing the great achievements of the present,
Singing the strong light works of engineers,
Our modern wonders, (the antique ponderous Seven outvied,)
In the Old World the east the Suez canal,
The New by its mighty railroad spann'd,
The seas inlaid with eloquent gentle wires;
Yet first to sound, and ever sound, the cry with thee O soul,
The Past! the Past! the Past!

The Past—the dark unfathom'd retrospect!
The teeming gulf—the sleepers and the shadows!
The past—the infinite greatness of the past!
For what is the present after all but a growth out of the past?
(As a projectile form'd, impell'd, passing a certain line, still keeps on,
So the present, utterly form'd, impell'd by the past.)

2

Passage O soul to India!
Eclaircise* the myths Asiatic, the primitive fables.

Not you alone proud truths of the world,
Nor you alone ye facts of modern science,
But myths and fables of eld,* Asia's, Africa's fables,
The far-darting beams of the spirit, the unloos'd dreams,
The deep diving bibles and legends,
The daring plots of the poets, the elder religions;
O you temples fairer than lilies pour'd over by the rising sun!
O you fables spurning the known, eluding the hold of the known,
    mounting to heaven!
You lofty and dazzling towers, pinnacled, red as roses, burnish'd with
    gold!
Towers of fables immortal fashion'd from mortal dreams!
You too I welcome and fully the same as the rest!
You too with joy I sing.

Passage to India!
Lo, soul, seest thou not God's purpose from the first?
The earth to be spann'd, connected by network,
The races, neighbors, to marry and be given in marriage,
The oceans to be cross'd, the distant brought near,
The lands to be welded together.

A worship new I sing,
You captains, voyagers, explorers, yours,
You engineers, you architects, machinists, yours,
You, not for trade or transportation only,
But in God's name, and for thy sake O soul.

3

Passage to India!
Lo soul for thee of tableaus twain,
I see in one the Suez canal initiated, open'd,
I see the procession of steamships, the Empress Eugenie's leading the
    van,
I mark from on deck the strange landscape, the pure sky, the level sand
    in the distance,
I pass swiftly the picturesque groups, the workmen gather'd,
The gigantic dredging machines.

In one again, different, (yet thine, all thine, O soul, the same,)
I see over my own continent the Pacific railroad surmounting every
    barrier,
I see continual trains of cars winding along the Platte carrying freight
    and passengers,
I hear the locomotives rushing and roaring, and the shrill steam-
    whistle,
I hear the echoes reverberate through the grandest scenery in the
    world,
I cross the Laramie plains, I note the rocks in grotesque shapes, the
    buttes,
I see the plentiful larkspur and wild onions, the barren, colorless,
    sage-deserts,
I see in glimpses afar or towering immediately above me the great
    mountains, I see the Wind river and the Wahsatch mountains,
I see the Monument mountain and the Eagle's Nest, I pass the Promon-
    tory, I ascend the Nevadas,
I scan the noble Elk mountain and wind around its base,
I see the Humboldt range, I thread the valley and cross the river,
I see the clear waters of lake Tahoe, I see forests of majestic pines,
Or crossing the great desert, the alkaline plains, I behold enchanting
    mirages of waters and meadows,
Marking through these and after all, in duplicate slender lines,
Bridging the three or four thousand miles of land travel,
Tying the Eastern to the Western sea,
The road between Europe and Asia.

(Ah Genoese thy dream! thy dream!
Centuries after thou art laid in thy grave,
The shore thou foundest verifies thy dream.)

4

Passage to India!
Struggles of many a captain, tales of many a sailor dead,
Over my mood stealing and spreading they come,
Like clouds and cloudlets in the unreach'd sky.

Along all history, down the slopes,
As a rivulet running, sinking now, and now again to the surface rising,
A ceaseless thought, a varied train—lo, soul, to thee, thy sight, they
        rise,
The plans, the voyages again, the expeditions,
Again Vasco de Gama sails forth,
Again the knowledge gain'd, the mariner's compass,
Lands found and nations born, thou born America,
For purpose vast, man's long probation fill'd,
Thou rondure of the world at last accomplish'd.

5

O vast Rondure, swimming in space,
Cover'd all over with visible power and beauty,
Alternate light and day and the teeming spiritual darkness,
Unspeakable high processions of sun and moon and countless stars
        above,
Below, the manifold grass and waters, animals, mountains, trees,
With inscrutable purpose, some hidden prophetic intention,
Now first it seems my thought begins to span thee.

Down from the gardens of Asia descending radiating,
Adam and Eve appear, then their myriad progeny after them,
Wandering, yearning, curious, with restless explorations,
With questionings, baffled, formless, feverish, with never-happy hearts,
With that sad incessant refrain, *Wherefore unsatisfied soul?* and
        Whither O mocking life?

Ah who shall soothe these feverish children?
Who justify these restless explorations?
Who speak the secret of impassive earth?
Who bind it to us? what is this separate Nature so unnatural?
What is this earth to our affections? (unloving earth, without a throb
        to answer ours,
Cold earth, the place of graves.)

Yet soul be sure the first intent remains, and shall be carried out,
Perhaps even now the time has arrived.

After the seas are all cross'd, (as they seem already cross'd,)
After the great captains and engineers have accomplish'd their work,
After the noble inventors, after the scientists, the chemist, the geolo-
        gist, ethnologist,

Finally shall come the poet worthy that name,
The true son of God shall come singing his songs.

Then not your deeds only O voyagers, O scientists and inventors, shall
    be justified,
All these hearts as of fretted children shall be sooth'd,
All affection shall be fully responded to, the secret shall be told,
All these separations and gaps shall be taken up and hook'd and
    link'd together,
The whole earth, this cold, impassive, voiceless earth, shall be com-
    pletely justified,
Trinitas divine shall be gloriously accomplish'd and compacted by the
    true son of God, the poet,
(He shall indeed pass the straits and conquer the mountains,
He shall double the cape of Good Hope to some purpose,)
Nature and Man shall be disjoin'd and diffused no more,
The true son of God shall absolutely fuse them.

6

Year at whose wide-flung door I sing!
Year of the purpose accomplish'd!
Year of the marriage of continents, climates and oceans!
(No mere doge of Venice now wedding the Adriatic,)
I see O year in you the vast terraqueous globe given and giving all,
Europe to Asia, Africa join'd, and they to the New World,
The lands, geographies, dancing before you, holding a festival garland,
As brides and bridegrooms hand in hand.

Passage to India!
Cooling airs from Caucasus far, soothing cradle of man,
The river Euphrates flowing, the past lit up again.

Lo soul, the retrospect brought forward,
The old, most populous, wealthiest of earth's lands,
The streams of the Indus and the Ganges and their many affluents,
(I my shores of America walking to-day behold, resuming all,)
The tale of Alexander on his warlike marches suddenly dying,
On one side China and on the other side Persia and Arabia,
To the south the great seas and the bay of Bengal,
The flowing literatures, tremendous epics, religions, castes,
Old occult Brahma interminably far back, the tender and junior
    Buddha,
Central and southern empires and all their belongings, possessors,
The wars of Tamerlane, the reign of Aurungzebe,
The traders, rulers, explorers, Moslems, Venetians, Byzantium, the
    Arabs, Portuguese,
The first travelers famous yet, Marco Polo, Batouta the Moor,
Doubts to be solv'd, the map incognita, blanks to be fill'd,
The foot of man unstay'd, the hands never at rest,
Thyself O soul that will not brook a challenge.

The mediæval navigators rise before me,
The world of 1492, with its awaken'd enterprise,
Something swelling in humanity now like the sap of the earth in spring,
The sunset splendor of chivalry declining.

And who art thou sad shade?
Gigantic, visionary, thyself a visionary,
With majestic limbs and pious beaming eyes,
Spreading around with every look of thine a golden world,
Enhuing it with gorgeous hues.

As the chief histrion,*
Down to the footlights walks in some great scena,
Dominating the rest I see the Admiral himself,
(History's type of courage, action, faith,)
Behold him sail from Palos leading his little fleet,
His voyage behold, his return, his great fame,
His misfortunes, calumniators, behold him a prisoner, chain'd,
Behold his dejection, poverty, death.

(Curious in time I stand, noting the efforts of heroes,
Is the deferment long? bitter the slander, poverty, death?
Lies the seed unreck'd for centuries in the ground? lo, to God's due
        occasion,
Uprising in the night, it sprouts, blooms,
And fills the earth with use and beauty.)

7

Passage indeed O soul to primal thought,
Not lands and seas alone, thy own clear freshness,
The young maturity of brood and bloom,
To realms of budding bibles.

O soul, repressless, I with thee and thou with me,
Thy circumnavigation of the world begin,
Of man, the voyage of his mind's return,
To reason's early paradise,
Back, back to wisdom's birth, to innocent intuitions,
Again with fair creation.

8

O we can wait no longer,
We too take ship O soul,
Joyous we too launch out on trackless seas,
Fearless for unknown shores on waves of ecstasy to sail,
Amid the wafting winds, (thou pressing me to thee, I thee to me, O
        soul,)
Caroling free, singing our song of God,
Chanting our chant of pleasant exploration.

With laugh and many a kiss,
(Let others deprecate, let others weep for sin, remorse, humiliation,)
O soul, thou pleasest me, I thee.

Ah more than any priest O soul we too believe in God,
But with the mystery of God we dare not dally.

O soul thou pleasest me, I thee,
Sailing these seas or on the hills, or waking in the night,
Thoughts, silent thoughts, of Time and Space and Death, like waters
      flowing,
Bear me indeed as through the regions infinite,
Whose air I breathe, whose ripples hear, lave me all over,
Bathe me O God in thee, mounting to thee,
I and my soul to range in range of thee.

O Thou transcendent,
Nameless, the fibre and the breath,
Light of the light, shedding forth universes, thou centre of them,
Thou mightier centre of the true, the good, the loving,
Thou moral, spiritual fountain—affection's source—thou reservoir,
(O pensive soul of me—O thirst unsatisfied—waitest not there?
Waitest not haply for us somewhere there the Comrade perfect?)
Thou pulse—thou motive of the stars, suns, systems,
That, circling, move in order, safe, harmonious,
Athwart the shapeless vastnesses of space,
How should I think, how breathe a single breath, how speak, if, out
      of myself,
I could not launch, to those, superior universes?

Swiftly I shrivel at the thought of God,
At Nature and its wonders, Time and Space and Death,
But that I, turning, call to thee O soul, thou actual Me,
And lo, thou gently masterest the orbs,
Thou matest Time, smilest content at Death,
And fillest, swellest full the vastnesses of Space.

Greater than stars or suns,
Bounding O soul thou journeyest forth;
What love than thine and ours could wider amplify?
What aspirations, wishes, outvie thine and ours O soul?
What dreams of the ideal? what plans of purity, perfection, strength,
What cheerful willingness for others' sake to give up all?
For others' sake to suffer all?

Reckoning ahead O soul, when thou, the time achiev'd,
The seas all cross'd, weather'd the capes, the voyage done,
Surrounded, copest, frontest God, yieldest, the aim attain'd,
As fill'd with friendship, love complete, the Elder Brother found,
The Younger melts in fondness in his arms.

9

Passage to more than India!
Are thy wings plumed indeed for such far flights?
O soul, voyagest thou indeed on voyages like those?
Disportest thou on waters such as those?
Soundest below the Sanscrit and the Vedas?
Then have thy bent* unleash'd.

Passage to you, your shores, ye aged fierce enigmas!
Passage to you, to mastership of you, ye strangling problems!
You, strew'd with the wrecks of skeletons, that, living, never reach'd
    you.

Passage to more than India!
O secret of the earth and sky!
Of you O waters of the sea! O winding creeks and rivers!
Of you O woods and fields! of you strong mountains of my land!
Of you O prairies! of you gray rocks!
O morning red! O clouds! O rain and snows!
O day and night, passage to you!

O sun and moon and all you stars! Sirius and Jupiter!
Passage to you!

Passage, immediate passage! the blood burns in my veins!
Away O soul! hoist instantly the anchor!
Cut the hawsers—haul out—shake out every sail!
Have we not stood here like trees in the ground long enough?
Have we not grovel'd here long enough, eating and drinking like mere
    brutes?
Have we not darken'd and dazed ourselves with books long enough?

Sail forth—steer for the deep waters only,
Reckless O soul, exploring, I with thee, and thou with me,
For we are bound where mariner has not yet dared to go,
And we will risk the ship, ourselves and all.

O my brave soul!
O farther farther sail!
O daring joy, but safe! are they not all the seas of God?
O farther, farther, farther sail!

PRAYER OF COLUMBUS

A batter'd, wreck'd old man,
Thrown on this savage shore, far, far from home,
Pent by the sea and dark rebellious brows, twelve dreary months,
Sore, stiff with many toils, sicken'd and nigh to death,
I take my way along the island's edge,
Venting a heavy heart.

I am too full of woe!
Haply I may not live another day;
I cannot rest O God, I cannot eat or drink or sleep,
Till I put forth myself, my prayer, once more to Thee,
Breathe, bathe myself once more in Thee, commune with Thee,
Report myself once more to Thee.

Thou knowest my years entire, my life,
My long and crowded life of active work, not adoration merely;
Thou knowest the prayers and vigils of my youth,
Thou knowest my manhood's solemn and visionary meditations,
Thou knowest how before I commenced I devoted all to come to Thee,
Thou knowest I have in age ratified all those vows and strictly kept
    them,
Thou knowest I have not once lost nor faith nor ecstasy in Thee,
In shackles, prison'd, in disgrace, repining not,
Accepting all from Thee, as duly come from Thee.

All my emprises* have been fill'd with Thee,
My speculations, plans, begun and carried on in thoughts of Thee,
Sailing the deep or journeying the land for Thee;
Intentions, purports, aspirations mine, leaving results to Thee.

O I am sure they really came from Thee,
The urge, the ardor, the unconquerable will,
The potent, felt, interior command, stronger than words,
A message from the Heavens whispering to me even in sleep,
These sped me on.

By me and these the work so far accomplish'd,
By me earth's elder cloy'd and stifled lands uncloy'd, unloos'd,
By me the hemispheres rounded and tied, the unknown to the known.

The end I know not, it is all in Thee,
Or small or great I know not—haply what broad fields, what lands,
Haply the brutish measureless human undergrowth I know,
Transplanted there may rise to stature, knowledge worthy Thee,

Haply the swords I know may there indeed be turn'd to reaping-tools,
Haply the lifeless cross I know, Europe's dead cross, may bud and
  blossom there.

One effort more, my altar this bleak sand;
That Thou O God my life hast lighted,
With ray of light, steady, ineffable, vouchsafed of Thee,
Light rare untellable, lighting the very light,
Beyond all signs, descriptions, languages;
For that O God, be it my latest word, here on my knees,
Old, poor, and paralyzed, I thank Thee.

My terminus near,
The clouds already closing in upon me,
The voyage balk'd, the course disputed, lost,
I yield my ships to Thee.

My hands, my limbs grow nerveless,
My brain feels rack'd, bewilder'd,
Let the old timbers part, I will not part,
I will cling fast to Thee, O God, though the waves buffet me,
Thee, Thee at least I know.

Is it the prophet's thought I speak, or am I raving?
What do I know of life? what of myself?
I know not even my own work past or present,
Dim ever-shifting guesses of it spread before me,
Of newer better worlds, their mighty parturition,
Mocking, perplexing me.

And these things I see suddenly, what mean they?
As if some miracle, some hand divine unseal'd my eyes,
Shadowy vast shapes smile through the air and sky,
And on the distant waves sail countless ships,
And anthems in new tongues I hear saluting me.

THE SLEEPERS

1

I wander all night in my vision,
Stepping with light feet, swiftly and noiselessly stepping and stop-
 ping,
Bending with open eyes over the shut eyes of sleepers,
Wandering and confused, lost to myself, ill-assorted, contradictory,
Pausing, gazing, bending, and stopping.

How solemn they look there, stretch'd and still,
How quiet they breathe, the little children in their cradles.

The wretched features of ennuyés,* the white features of corpses, the
 livid faces of drunkards, the sick-gray faces of onanists,
The gash'd bodies on battle-fields, the insane in their strong-door'd
 rooms, the sacred idiots, the new-born emerging from gates,
 and the dying emerging from gates,
The night pervades them and infolds them.

The married couple sleep calmly in their bed, he with his palm on
 the hip of the wife, and she with her palm on the hip of the
 husband,
The sisters sleep lovingly side by side in their bed,
The men sleep lovingly side by side in theirs,
And the mother sleeps with her little child carefully wrapt.

The blind sleep, and the deaf and dumb sleep,
The prisoner sleeps well in the prison, the runaway son sleeps,
The murderer that is to be hung next day, how does he sleep?
And the murder'd person, how does he sleep?

The female that loves unrequited sleeps,
And the male that loves unrequited sleeps,
The head of the money-maker that plotted all day sleeps,
And the enraged and treacherous dispositions, all, all sleep.

I stand in the dark with drooping eyes by the worst-suffering and the
 most restless,
I pass my hands soothingly to and fro a few inches from them,
The restless sink in their beds, they fitfully sleep.

Now I pierce the darkness, new beings appear,
The earth recedes from me into the night,
I saw that it was beautiful, and I see that what is not the earth is
 beautiful.

I go from bedside to bedside, I sleep close with the other sleepers each
    in turn,
I dream in my dream all the dreams of the other dreamers,
And I become the other dreamers.

I am a dance—play up there! the fit is whirling me fast!

I am the ever-laughing—it is new moon and twilight,
I see the hiding of douceurs,* I see nimble ghosts whichever way I
    look,
Cache and cache again deep in the ground and sea, and where it is
    neither ground nor sea.

Well do they do their jobs those journeymen divine,
Only from me can they hide nothing, and would not if they could,
I reckon I am their boss and they make me a pet besides,
And surround me and lead me and run ahead when I walk,
To lift their cunning covers to signify me with stretch'd arms, and
    resume the way;
Onward we move, a gay gang of blackguards! with mirth-shouting
    music and wild-flapping pennants of joy!

I am the actor, the actress, the voter, the politician,
The emigrant and the exile, the criminal that stood in the box,
He who has been famous and he who shall be famous after to-day,
The stammerer, the well-formed person, the wasted or feeble person.

I am she who adorn'd herself and folded her hair expectantly,
My truant lover has come, and it is dark.

Double yourself and receive me darkness,
Receive me and my lover too, he will not let me go without him.

I roll myself upon you as upon a bed, I resign myself to the dusk.

He whom I call answers me and takes the place of my lover,
He rises with me silently from the bed.

Darkness, you are gentler than my lover, his flesh was sweaty and
    panting,
I feel the hot moisture yet that he left me.

My hands are spread forth, I pass them in all directions,
I would sound up the shadowy shore to which you are journeying.

Be careful darkness! already what was it touch'd me?
I thought my lover had gone, else darkness and he are one,
I hear the heart-beat, I follow, I fade away.

2

I descend my western course, my sinews are flaccid,
Perfume and youth course through me and I am their wake.

It is my face yellow and wrinkled instead of the old woman's,
I sit low in a straw-bottom chair and carefully darn my grandson's
    stockings.

It is I too, the sleepless widow looking out on the winter midnight,
I see the sparkles of starshine on the icy and pallid earth.

A shroud I see and I am the shroud, I wrap a body and lie in the
    coffin,
It is dark here under ground, it is not evil or pain here, it is blank
    here, for reasons.

(It seems to me that every thing in the light and air ought to be happy,
Whoever is not in his coffin and the dark grave let him know he has
    enough.)

3

I see a beautiful gigantic swimmer swimming naked through the
    eddies of the sea,
His brown hair lies close and even to his head, he strikes out with
    courageous arms, he urges himself with his legs,

I see his white body, I see his undaunted eyes,
I hate the swift-running eddies that would dash him head-foremost
    on the rocks.

What are you doing you ruffianly red-trickled waves?
Will you kill the courageous giant? will you kill him in the prime of
    his middle age?

Steady and long he struggles,
He is baffled, bang'd, bruis'd, he holds out while his strength holds out,
The slapping eddies are spotted with his blood, they bear him away,
    they roll him, swing him, turn him,
His beautiful body is borne in the circling eddies, it is continually
    bruis'd on rocks,
Swiftly and out of sight is borne the brave corpse.

4

I turn but do not extricate myself,
Confused, a past-reading, another, but with darkness yet.

The beach is cut by the razory ice-wind, the wreck-guns sound,
The tempest lulls, the moon comes floundering through the drifts.

I look where the ship helplessly heads end on, I hear the burst as she
      strikes, I hear the howls of dismay, they grow fainter and
      fainter.

I cannot aid with my wringing fingers,
I can but rush to the surf and let it drench me and freeze upon me.

I search with the crowd, not one of the company is wash'd to us alive,
In the morning I help pick up the dead and lay them in rows in a barn.

5

Now of the older war-days, the defeat at Brooklyn,
Washington stands inside the lines, he stands on the intrench'd hills
      amid a crowd of officers,
His face is cold and damp, he cannot repress the weeping drops,
He lifts the glass perpetually to his eyes, the color is blanch'd from his
      cheeks,
He sees the slaughter of the southern braves confided to him by their
      parents.

The same at last and at last when peace is declared,
He stands in the room of the old tavern, the well-belov'd soldiers all
      pass through,
The officers speechless and slow draw near in their turns,
The chief encircles their necks with his arm and kisses them on the
      cheek,
He kisses lightly the wet cheeks one after another, he shakes hands
      and bids good-by to the army.

6

Now what my mother told me one day as we sat at dinner together,
Of when she was a nearly grown girl living home with her parents on
      the old homestead.

A red squaw came one breakfast-time to the old homestead,
On her back she carried a bundle of rushes for rush-bottoming chairs,
Her hair, straight, shiny, coarse, black, profuse, half-envelop'd her
      face,
Her step was free and elastic, and her voice sounded exquisitely as
      she spoke.

My mother look'd in delight and amazement at the stranger,
She look'd at the freshness of her tall-borne face and full and pliant
      limbs,
The more she look'd upon her she loved her,
Never before had she seen such wonderful beauty and purity,
She made her sit on a bench by the jamb of the fireplace, she cook'd
      food for her,
She had no work to give her, but she gave her remembrance and
      fondness.

The red squaw staid all the forenoon, and toward the middle of the
    afternoon she went away,
O my mother was loth* to have her go away,
All the week she thought of her, she watch'd for her many a month,
She remember'd her many a winter and many a summer,
But the red squaw never came nor was heard of there again.

7

A show of the summer softness—a contact of something unseen—an
    amour of the light and air,
I am jealous and overwhelm'd with friendliness,
And will go gallivant* with the light and air myself.

O love and summer, you are in the dreams and in me,
Autumn and winter are in the dreams, the farmer goes with his thrift,
The droves and crops increase, the barns are well-fill'd.

Elements merge in the night, ships make tacks in the dreams,
The sailor sails, the exile returns home,
The fugitive returns unharm'd, the immigrant is back beyond months
    and years,
The poor Irishman lives in the simple house of his childhood with the
    well-known neighbors and faces,
They warmly welcome him, he is barefoot again, he forgets he is well
    off,
The Dutchman voyages home, and the Scotchman and Welshman
    voyage home, and the native of the Mediterranean voyages
    home,
To every port of England, France, Spain, enter well-fill'd ships,
The Swiss foots it toward his hills, the Prussian goes his way, the
    Hungarian his way, and the Pole his way,
The Swede returns, and the Dane and Norwegian return.

The homeward bound and the outward bound,
The beautiful lost swimmer, the ennuyé, the onanist, the female that
    loves unrequited, the money-maker,
The actor and actress, those through with their parts and those wait-
    ing to commence,
The affectionate boy, the husband and wife, the voter, the nominee
    that is chosen and the nominee that has fail'd,
The great already known and the great any time after to-day,
The stammerer, the sick, the perfect-form'd, the homely,
The criminal that stood in the box, the judge that sat and sentenced
    him, the fluent lawyers, the jury, the audience,
The laugher and weeper, the dancer, the midnight widow, the red
    squaw,
The consumptive, the erysipalite, the idiot, he that is wrong'd,
The antipodes, and every one between this and them in the dark,
I swear they are averaged now—one is no better than the other,
The night and sleep have liken'd them and restored them.

I swear they are all beautiful,
Every one that sleeps is beautiful, every thing in the dim light is
    beautiful,
The wildest and bloodiest is over, and all is peace.

Peace is always beautiful,
The myth of heaven indicates peace and night.

The myth of heaven indicates the soul,
The soul is always beautiful, it appears more or it appears less, it
    comes or it lags behind,
It comes from its embower'd garden and looks pleasantly on itself and
    encloses the world,
Perfect and clean the genitals previously jetting,° and perfect and
    clean the womb cohering,
The head well-grown proportion'd and plumb, and the bowels and
    joints proportion'd and plumb.

The soul is always beautiful,
The universe is duly in order, every thing is in its place,
What has arrived is in its place and what waits shall be in its place,
The twisted skull waits, the watery or rotten blood waits,
The child of the glutton or venerealee waits long, and the child of
    the drunkard waits long, and the drunkard himself waits long,
The sleepers that lived and died wait, the far advanced are to go on
    in their turns, and the far behind are to come on in their turns,
The diverse shall be no less diverse, but they shall flow and unite—
    they unite now.

8

The sleepers are very beautiful as they lie unclothed,
They flow hand in hand over the whole earth from east to west as
    they lie unclothed,
The Asiatic and African are hand in hand, the European and American
    are hand in hand,
Learn'd and unlearn'd are hand in hand, and male and female are
    hand in hand,
The bare arm of the girl crosses the bare breast of her lover, they
    press close without lust, his lips press her neck,
The father holds his grown or ungrown son in his arms with measure-
    less love, and the son holds the father in his arms with measure-
    less love,
The white hair of the mother shines on the white wrist of the daughter,
The breath of the boy goes with the breath of the man, friend is in-
    arm'd by friend,
The scholar kisses the teacher and the teacher kisses the scholar, the
    wrong'd is made right,
The call of the slave is one with the master's call, and the master
    salutes the slave,

The felon steps forth from the prison, the insane becomes sane, the
  suffering of sick persons is reliev'd,
The sweatings and fevers stop, the throat that was unsound is sound,
  the lungs of the consumptive are resumed, the poor distress'd
  head is free,
The joints of the rheumatic move as smoothly as ever, and smoother
  than ever,
Stiflings and passages open, the paralyzed become supple,
The swell'd and convuls'd and congested awake to themselves in
  condition,
They pass the invigoration of the night and the chemistry of the
  night, and awake.

I too pass from the night,
I stay a while away O night, but I return to you again and love you.

Why should I be afraid to trust myself to you?
I am not afraid, I have been well brought forward by you,
I love the rich running day, but I do not desert her in whom I lay so
  long,
I know not how I came of you and I know not where I go with you,
  but I know I came well and shall go well.

I will stop only a time with the night, and rise betimes,
I will duly pass the day O my mother, and duly return to you.

TRANSPOSITIONS

Let the reformers descend from the stands where they are forever
  bawling—let an idiot or insane person appear on each of the
  stands;
Let judges and criminals be transposed—let the prison-keepers be put
  in prison—let those that were prisoners take the keys;
Let them that distrust birth and death lead the rest.

TO THINK OF TIME

1

To think of time—of all that retrospection,
To think of to-day, and the ages continued henceforward.

Have you guess'd you yourself would not continue?
Have you dreaded these earth-beetles?
Have you fear'd the future would be nothing to you?

Is to-day nothing? is the beginningless past nothing?
If the future is nothing they are just as surely nothing.

To think that the sun rose in the east—that men and women were
     flexible, real, alive—that every thing was alive,
To think that you and I did not see, feel, think, nor bear our part,
To think that we are now here and bear our part.

2

Not a day passes, not a minute or second without an accouchement,*
Not a day passes, not a minute or second without a corpse.

The dull nights go over and the dull days also,
The soreness of lying so much in bed goes over,
The physician after long putting off gives the silent and terrible look
     for an answer,
The children come hurried and weeping, and the brothers and sisters
     are sent for,
Medicines stand unused on the shelf, (the camphor-smell has long
     pervaded the rooms,)
The faithful hand of the living does not desert the hand of the dying,
The twitching lips press lightly on the forehead of the dying,
The breath ceases and the pulse of the heart ceases,
The corpse stretches on the bed and the living look upon it,
It is palpable as the living are palpable.

The living look upon the corpse with their eyesight,
But without eyesight lingers a different living and looks curiously on
     the corpse.

3

To think the thought of death merged in the thought of materials,
To think of all these wonders of city and country, and others taking
     great interest in them, and we taking no interest in them.

To think how eager we are in building our houses,
To think others shall be just as eager, and we quite indifferent.

(I see one building the house that serves him a few years, or seventy
    or eighty years at most,
I see one building the house that serves him longer than that.)

Slow-moving and black lines creep over the whole earth—they never
    cease—they are the burial lines,
He that was President was buried, and he that is now President shall
    surely be buried.

4

A reminiscence of the vulgar fate,
A frequent sample of the life and death of workmen,
Each after his kind.

Cold dash of waves at the ferry-wharf, posh* and ice in the river, half-
    frozen mud in the streets,
A gray discouraged sky overhead, the short last daylight of December,
A hearse and stages, the funeral of an old Broadway stage-driver, the
    cortege mostly drivers.

Steady the trot to the cemetery, duly rattles the death-bell,
The gate is pass'd, the new-dug grave is halted at, the living alight,
    the hearse uncloses,
The coffin is pass'd out, lower'd and settled, the whip is laid on the
    coffin, the earth is swiftly shovel'd in,
The mound above is flatted with the spades—silence,
A minute—no one moves or speaks—it is done,
He is decently put away—is there any thing more?

He was a good fellow, free-mouth'd, quick-temper'd, not bad-looking,
Ready with life or death for a friend, fond of women, gambled, ate
    hearty, drank hearty,
Had known what it was to be flush, grew low-spirited toward the last,
    sicken'd, was help'd by a contribution,
Died, aged forty-one years—and that was his funeral.

Thumb extended, finger uplifted, apron, cape, gloves, strap, wet-
    weather clothes, whip carefully chosen,
Boss, spotter, starter, hostler, somebody loafing on you, you loafing on
    somebody, headway, man before and man behind,
Good day's work, bad day's work, pet stock, mean stock, first out, last
    out, turning-in at night,
To think that these are so much and so nigh to other drivers, and he
    there takes no interest in them.

5

The markets, the government, the working-man's wages, to think what
    account they are through our nights and days,
To think that other working-men will make just as great account of
    them, yet we make little or no account.

The vulgar and the refined, what you call sin and what you call good-
    ness, to think how wide a difference,
To think the difference will still continue to others, yet we lie beyond
    the difference.

To think how much pleasure there is,
Do you enjoy yourself in the city? or engaged in business? or planning
    a nomination and election? or with your wife and family?
Or with your mother and sisters? or in womanly housework? or the
    beautiful maternal cares?
These also flow onward to others, you and I flow onward,
But in due time you and I shall take less interest in them.

Your farm, profits, crops—to think how engross'd you are,
To think there will still be farms, profits, crops, yet for you of what
    avail?

6

What will be will be well, for what is is well,
To take interest is well, and not to take interest shall be well.

The domestic joys, the daily housework or business, the building of
    houses, are not phantasms, they have weight, form, location,
Farms, profits, crops, markets, wages, government, are none of them
    phantasms,
The difference between sin and goodness is no delusion,
The earth is not an echo, man and his life and all the things of his
    life are well-consider'd.

You are not thrown to the winds, you gather certainly and safely
    around yourself,
Yourself! yourself! yourself, for ever and ever!

7

It is not to diffuse you that you were born of your mother and father,
    it is to identify you,
It is not that you should be undecided, but that you should be decided,
Something long preparing and formless is arrived and form'd in you,
You are henceforth secure, whatever comes or goes.

The threads that were spun are gather'd, the weft crosses the warp,
    the pattern is systematic.

The preparations have every one been justified,
The orchestra have sufficiently tuned their instruments, the baton has
    given the signal.

The guest that was coming, he waited long, he is now housed,
He is one of those who are beautiful and happy, he is one of those
    that to look upon and be with is enough.

The law of the past cannot be eluded,
The law of the present and future cannot be eluded,
The law of the living cannot be eluded, it is eternal,
The law of promotion and transformation cannot be eluded,
The law of heroes and good-doers cannot be eluded,
The law of drunkards, informers, mean persons, not one iota thereof
    can be eluded.

8

Slow moving and black lines go ceaselessly over the earth,
Northerner goes carried and Southerner goes carried, and they on the
    Atlantic side and they on the Pacific,
And they between, and all through the Mississippi country, and all
    over the earth.

The great masters and kosmos° are well as they go, the heroes and
    good-doers are well,
The known leaders and inventors and the rich owners and pious and
    distinguish'd may be well,
But there is more account than that, there is strict account of all.

The interminable hordes of the ignorant and wicked are not nothing,
The barbarians of Africa and Asia are not nothing,
The perpetual successions of shallow people are not nothing as they go.

Of and in all these things,
I have dream'd that we are not to be changed so much, nor the law of
    us changed,
I have dream'd that heroes and good-doers shall be under the present
    and past law,
And that murderers, drunkards, liars, shall be under the present and
    past law,
For I have dream'd that the law they are under now is enough.

And I have dream'd that the purpose and essence of the known life,
    the transient,
Is to form and decide identity for the unknown life, the permanent.

If all came but to ashes of dung,
If maggots and rats ended us, then Alarum! for we are betray'd,
Then indeed suspicion of death.

Do you suspect death? if I were to suspect death I should die now,
Do you think I could walk pleasantly and well-suited toward annihila-
    tion?

Pleasantly and well-suited I walk,
Whither I walk I cannot define, but I know it is good,
The whole universe indicates that it is good,
The past and the present indicate that it is good.

How beautiful and perfect are the animals!
How perfect the earth, and the minutest thing upon it!
What is called good is perfect, and what is called bad is just as perfect,
The vegetables and minerals are all perfect, and the imponderable fluids perfect;
Slowly and surely they have pass'd on to this, and slowly and surely they yet pass on.

I swear I think now that every thing without exception has an eternal soul!
The trees have, rooted in the ground! the weeds of the sea have! the animals!

I swear I think there is nothing but immortality!
That the exquisite scheme is for it, and the nebulous float° is for it, and the cohering is for it!
And all preparation is for it—and identity is for it—and life and materials are altogether for it!

WHISPERS OF HEAVENLY DEATH

DAREST THOU NOW O SOUL

Darest thou now O soul,
Walk out with me toward the unknown region,
Where neither ground is for the feet nor any path to follow?

No map there, nor guide,
Nor voice sounding, nor touch of human hand,
Nor face with blooming flesh, nor lips, nor eyes, are in that land.

I know it not O soul,
Nor dost thou, all is a blank before us,
All waits undream'd of in that region, that inaccessible land.

Till when the ties loosen,
All but the ties eternal, Time and Space,
Nor darkness, gravitation, sense, nor any bounds bounding us.

Then we burst forth, we float,
In Time and Space O soul, prepared for them,
Equal, equipt at last, (O joy! O fruit of all!) them to fulfil O soul.

WHISPERS OF HEAVENLY DEATH

Whispers of heavenly death murmur'd I hear,
Labial gossip of night, sibilant chorals,
Footsteps gently ascending, mystical breezes wafted soft and low,
Ripples of unseen rivers, tides of a current flowing, forever flowing,
(Or is it the plashing of tears? the measureless waters of human tears?)

I see, just see skyward, great cloud-masses,
Mournfully slowly they roll, silently swelling and mixing,
With at times a half-dimm'd sadden'd far-off star,
Appearing and disappearing.

(Some parturition rather, some solemn immortal birth;
On the frontiers to eyes impenetrable,
Some soul is passing over.)

CHANTING THE SQUARE DEIFIC

1

Chanting the square deific, out of the One advancing, out of the sides,
Out of the old and new, out of the square entirely divine,
Solid, four-sided, (all the sides needed,) from this side Jehovah am I,

Old Brahm I, and I Saturnius am;
Not Time affects me—I am Time, old, modern as any,
Unpersuadable, relentless, executing righteous judgments,
As the Earth, the Father, the brown old Kronos, with laws,
Aged beyond computation, yet ever new, ever with those mighty laws
    rolling,
Relentless I forgive no man—whoever sins dies—I will have that man's
    life;
Therefore let none expect mercy—have the seasons, gravitation, the
    appointed days, mercy? no more have I,
But as the seasons and gravitation, and as all the appointed days that
    forgive not,
I dispense from this side judgments inexorable without the least
    remorse.

2

Consolator most mild, the promis'd one advancing,
With gentle hand extended, the mightier God am I,
Foretold by prophets and poets in their most rapt prophecies and
    poems,
From this side, lo! the Lord Christ gazes—lo! Hermes I—lo! mine is
    Hercules' face,
All sorrow, labor, suffering, I, tallying it, absorb in myself,
Many times have I been rejected, taunted, put in prison, and cruci-
    fied, and many times shall be again,
All the world have I given up for my dear brothers' and sisters' sake,
    for the soul's sake,
Wending my way through the homes of men, rich or poor, with the
    kiss of affection,
For I am affection, I am the cheer-bringing God, with hope and all-
    enclosing charity,
With indulgent words as to children, with fresh and sane words, mine
    only,
Young and strong I pass knowing well I am destin'd myself to an
    early death;
But my charity has no death—my wisdom dies not, neither early nor
    late,
And my sweet love bequeath'd here and elsewhere never dies.

3

Aloof, dissatisfied, plotting revolt,
Comrade of criminals, brother of slaves,
Crafty, despised, a drudge, ignorant,
With sudra° face and worn brow, black, but in the depths of my heart,
    proud as any,
Lifted now and always against whoever scorning assumes to rule me,
Morose, full of guile, full of reminiscences, brooding, with many wiles,
(Though it was thought I was baffled and dispel'd, and my wiles done,
    but that will never be,)

Defiant, I, Satan, still live, still utter words, in new lands duly appear-
ing, (and old ones also,)
Permanent here from my side, warlike, equal with any, real as any,
Nor time nor change shall ever change me or my words.

4

Santa Spirita, breather, life,
Beyond the light, lighter than light,
Beyond the flames of hell, joyous, leaping easily above hell,
Beyond Paradise, perfumed solely with mine own perfume,
Including all life on earth, touching, including God, including Saviour
and Satan,
Ethereal, pervading all, (for without me what were all? what were
God?)
Essence of forms, life of the real identities, permanent, positive,
(namely the unseen,)
Life of the great round world, the sun and stars, and of man, I, the
general soul,
Here the square finishing, the solid, I the most solid,
Breathe my breath also through these songs.

OF HIM I LOVE DAY AND NIGHT

Of him I love day and night I dream'd I heard he was dead,
And I dream'd I went where they had buried him I love, but he was
not in that place,
And I dream'd I wander'd searching among burial-places to find him,
And I found that every place was a burial-place;
The houses full of life were equally full of death, (this house is now,)
The streets, the shipping, the places of amusement, the Chicago,
Boston, Philadelphia, the Mannahatta,* were as full of the dead
as of the living,
And fuller, O vastly fuller of the dead than of the living;
And what I dream'd I will henceforth tell to every person and age,
And I stand henceforth bound to what I dream'd,
And now I am willing to disregard burial-places and dispense with
them,
And if the memorials of the dead were put up indifferently every-
where, even in the room where I eat or sleep, I should be satis-
fied,
And if the corpse of any one I love, or if my own corpse, be duly ren-
der'd to powder and pour'd in the sea, I shall be satisfied,
Or if it be distributed to the winds I shall be satisfied.

YET, YET, YE DOWNCAST HOURS

Yet, yet, ye downcast hours, I know ye also,
Weights of lead, how ye clog and cling at my ankles,

Earth to a chamber of mourning turns—I hear the o'erweening, mocking voice,
Matter is conqueror—matter, triumphant only, continues onward.

Despairing cries float ceaselessly toward me,
The call of my nearest lover, putting forth, alarm'd, uncertain,
The sea I am quickly to sail, come tell me,
Come tell me where I am speeding, tell me my destination.

I understand your anguish, but I cannot help you,
I approach, hear, behold, the sad mouth, the look out of the eyes, your
    mute inquiry,
Whither I go from the bed I recline on, come tell me;
Old age, alarm'd, uncertain—a young woman's voice, appealing to me
    for comfort;
A young man's voice, *Shall I not escape?*

AS IF A PHANTOM CARESS'D ME

As if a phantom caress'd me,
I thought I was not alone walking here by the shore;
But the one I thought was with me as now I walk by the shore, the
    one I loved that caress'd me,
As I lean and look through the glimmering light, that one has utterly
    disappear'd,
And those appear that are hateful to me and mock me.

ASSURANCES

I need no assurances, I am a man who is pre-occupied of his own soul;
I do not doubt that from under the feet and beside the hands and face
        I am cognizant of, are now looking faces I am not cognizant
        of, calm and actual faces,
I do not doubt but the majesty and beauty of the world are latent in
        any iota of the world,
I do not doubt I am limitless, and that the universes are limitless, in
        vain I try to think how limitless,
I do not doubt that the orbs and the systems of orbs play their swift
        sports through the air on purpose, and that I shall one day be
        eligible to do as much as they, and more than they,
I do not doubt that temporary affairs keep on and on millions of
        years,
I do not doubt interiors have their interiors, and exteriors have their
        exteriors, and that the eyesight has another eyesight, and the
        hearing another hearing, and the voice another voice,
I do not doubt that the passionately-wept deaths of young men are
        provided for, and that the deaths of young women and the
        deaths of little children are provided for,

(Did you think Life was so well provided for, and Death, the purport
of all Life, is not well provided for?)
I do not doubt that wrecks at sea, no matter what the horrors of them,
no matter whose wife, child, husband, father, lover, has gone
down, are provided for, to the minutest points,
I do not doubt that whatever can possibly happen anywhere at any
time, is provided for in the inherences* of things,
I do not think Life provides for all and for Time and Space, but I believe Heavenly Death provides for all.

QUICKSAND YEARS

Quicksand years that whirl me I know not whither,
Your schemes, politics, fail, lines give way, substances mock and elude
me,
Only the theme I sing, the great and strong-possess'd soul, eludes not,
One's-self must never give way—that is the final substance—that out
of all is sure,
Out of politics, triumphs, battles, life, what at last finally remains?
When shows break up what but One's-Self is sure?

THAT MUSIC ALWAYS ROUND ME

That music always round me, unceasing, unbeginning, yet long
untaught I did not hear,
But now the chorus I hear and am elated,
A tenor, strong, ascending with power and health, with glad notes of
daybreak I hear,
A soprano at intervals sailing buoyantly over the tops of immense
waves,
A transparent base shuddering lusciously under and through the universe,
The triumphant tutti, the funeral wailings with sweet flutes and violins,
all these I fill myself with,
I hear not the volumes of sound merely, I am moved by the exquisite
meanings,
I listen to the different voices winding in and out, striving, contending
with fiery vehemence to excel each other in emotion;
I do not think the performers know themselves—but now I think I
begin to know them.

WHAT SHIP PUZZLED AT SEA

What ship puzzled at sea, cons for the true reckoning?
Or coming in, to avoid the bars and follow the channel a perfect pilot
needs?
Here, sailor! here, ship! take aboard the most perfect pilot,
Whom, in a little boat, putting off and rowing, I hailing you offer.

A NOISELESS PATIENT SPIDER

A noiseless patient spider,
I mark'd where on a little promontory it stood isolated,
Mark'd how to explore the vacant vast surrounding,
It launch'd forth filament, filament, filament, out of itself,
Ever unreeling them, ever tirelessly speeding them.

And you O my soul where you stand,
Surrounded, detached, in measureless oceans of space,
Ceaselessly musing, venturing, throwing, seeking the spheres to con-
nect them,
Till the bridge you will need be form'd, till the ductile anchor hold,
Till the gossamer thread you fling catch somewhere, O my soul.

O LIVING ALWAYS, ALWAYS DYING

O living always, always dying!
O the burials of me past and present,
O me while I stride ahead, material, visible, imperious as ever;
O me, what I was for years, now dead, (I lament not, I am content;)
O to disengage myself from those corpses of me, which I turn and look
at where I cast them,
To pass on, (O living! always living!) and leave the corpses behind.

TO ONE SHORTLY TO DIE

From all the rest I single out you having a message for you,
You are to die—let others tell you what they please, I cannot
prevaricate,
I am exact and merciless, but I love you—there is no escape for you.

Softly I lay my right hand upon you, you just feel it,
I do not argue, I bend my head close and half envelop it,
I sit quietly by, I remain faithful,
I am more than nurse, more than parent or neighbor,
I absolve you from all except yourself spiritual bodily, that is eternal,
you yourself will surely escape,
The corpse you will leave will be but excrementitious.

The sun bursts through in unlooked-for directions,
Strong thoughts fill you and confidence, you smile,
You forget you are sick, as I forget you are sick,
You do not see the medicines, you do not find the weeping friends,
I am with you,
I exclude others from you, there is nothing to be commiserated,
I do not commiserate, I congratulate you.

NIGHT ON THE PRAIRIES

Night on the prairies,
The supper is over, the fire on the ground burns low,
The wearied emigrants sleep, wrapt in their blankets;
I walk by myself—I stand and look at the stars, which I think now I
    never realized before.

Now I absorb immortality and peace,
I admire death and test propositions.

How plenteous! how spiritual! how resumé!
The same old man and soul—the same old aspirations, and the same
    content.

I was thinking the day most splendid till I saw what the not-day
    exhibited,
I was thinking this globe enough till there sprang out so noiseless
    around me myriads of other globes.

Now while the great thoughts of space and eternity fill me I will
    measure myself by them,
And now touch'd with the lives of other globes arrived as far along as
    those of the earth,
Or waiting to arrive, or pass'd on farther than those of the earth,
I henceforth no more ignore them than I ignore my own life,
Or the lives of the earth arrived as far as mine, or waiting to arrive.

O I see now that life cannot exhibit all to me, as the day cannot,
I see that I am to wait for what will be exhibited by death.

THOUGHT

As I sit with others at a great feast, suddenly while the music is play-
    ing,
To my mind, (whence it comes I know not,) spectral in mist of a
    wreck at sea,
Of certain ships, how they sail from port with flying streamers and
    wafted kisses, and that is the last of them,
Of the solemn and murky mystery about the fate of the President,
Of the flower of the marine science of fifty generations founder'd off
    the Northeast coast and going down—of the steamship Arctic
    going down,
Of the veil'd tableau—women gather'd together on deck, pale, heroic,
    waiting the moment that draws so close—O the moment!
A huge sob—a few bubbles—the white foam spirting* up—and then
    the women gone,

Sinking there while the passionless wet flows on—and I now ponder-
    ing, Are those women indeed gone?
Are souls drown'd and destroy'd so?
Is only matter triumphant?

THE LAST INVOCATION

At the last, tenderly,
From the walls of the powerful fortress'd house,
From the clasp of the knitted locks, from the keep of the well-closed
    doors,
Let me be wafted.

Let me glide noiselessly forth;
With the key of softness unlock the locks—with a whisper,
Set ope the doors O soul.

Tenderly—be not impatient,
(Strong is your hold O mortal flesh,
Strong is your hold O love.)

AS I WATCH'D THE PLOUGHMAN PLOUGHING

As I watch'd the ploughman ploughing,
Or the sower sowing in the fields, or the harvester harvesting,
I saw there too, O life and death, your analogies;
(Life, life is the tillage, and Death is the harvest according.)

PENSIVE AND FALTERING

Pensive and faltering,
The words *the Dead* I write,
For living are the Dead,
(Haply the only living, only real,
And I the apparition, I the spectre.)

THOU MOTHER WITH THY
EQUAL BROOD

1

Thou Mother with thy equal brood,
Thou varied chain of different States, yet one identity only,
A special song before I go I'd sing o'er all the rest,
For thee, the future.

I'd sow a seed for thee of endless Nationality,
I'd fashion thy ensemble including body and soul,
I'd show away ahead thy real Union, and how it may be accomplish'd.

The paths to the house I seek to make,
But leave to those to come the house itself.

Belief I sing, and preparation;
As Life and Nature are not great with reference to the present only,
But greater still from what is yet to come,
Out of that formula for thee I sing.

2

As a strong bird on pinions free,
Joyous, the amplest spaces heavenward cleaving,
Such be the thought I'd think of thee America,
Such be the recitative I'd bring for thee.

The conceits of the poets of other lands I'd bring thee not,
Nor the compliments that have served their turn so long,
Nor rhyme, nor the classics, nor perfume of foreign court or indoor
    library;
But an odor I'd bring as from forests of pine in Maine, or breath of an
        Illinois prairie,
With open airs of Virginia or Georgia or Tennessee, or from Texas
        uplands, or Florida's glades,
Or the Saguenay's black stream, or the wide blue spread of Huron,
With presentment of Yellowstone's scenes, or Yosemite,
And murmuring under, pervading all, I'd bring the rustling sea-sound,
That endlessly sounds from the two Great Seas of the world.

And for thy subtler sense subtler refrains dread Mother,
Preludes of intellect tallying these and thee, mind-formulas fitted for
        thee, real and sane and large as these and thee,
Thou! mounting higher, diving deeper than we knew, thou transcen-
        dental Union!
By thee fact to be justified, blended with thought,
Thought of man justified, blended with God,

Through my idea, lo, the immortal reality!
Through thy reality, lo, the immortal idea!

3

Brain of the New World, what a task is thine,
To formulate the Modern—out of the peerless grandeur of the modern,
Out of thyself, comprising science, to recast poems, churches, art,
(Recast, maybe discard them, end them—maybe their work is done,
    who knows?)
By vision, hand, conception, on the background of the mighty past,
    the dead,
To limn with absolute faith the mighty living present.

And yet thou living present brain, heir of the dead, the Old World
    brain,
Thou that lay folded like an unborn babe within its folds so long,
Thou carefully prepared by it so long—haply thou but unfoldest it,
    only maturest it,
It to eventuate in thee—the essence of the by-gone time contain'd in
    thee,
Its poems, churches, arts, unwitting to themselves, destined with
    reference to thee;
Thou but the apples, long, long, long a-growing,
The fruit of all the Old ripening to-day in thee.

4

Sail, sail thy best, ship of Democracy,
Of value is thy freight, 'tis not the Present only,
The Past is also stored in thee,
Thou holdest not the venture of thyself alone, not of the Western
    continent alone,
Earth's *résumé* entire floats on thy keel O ship, is steadied by thy
    spars,
With thee Time voyages in trust, the antecedent nations sink or swim
    with thee,
With all their ancient struggles, martyrs, heroes, epics, wars, thou
    bear'st the other continents,
Theirs, theirs as much as thine, the destination-port triumphant;
Steer then with good strong hand and wary eye O helmsman, thou
    carriest great companions,
Venerable priestly Asia sails this day with thee,
And royal feudal Europe sails with thee.

5

Beautiful world of new superber birth that rises to my eyes,
Like a limitless golden cloud filling the western sky,
Emblem of general maternity lifted above all,
Sacred shape of the bearer of daughters and sons,

Out of thy teeming womb thy giant babes in ceaseless procession
    issuing,
Acceding from such gestation, taking and giving continual strength
    and life,
World of the real—world of the twain in one,
World of the soul, born by the world of the real alone, led to identity,
    body, by it alone,
Yet in beginning only, incalculable masses of composite precious ma-
    terials,
By history's cycles forwarded, by every nation, language, hither sent,
Ready, collected here, a freer, vast, electric world, to be constructed
    here,
(The true New World, the world of orbic science, morals, literatures
    to come,)
Thou wonder world yet undefined, unform'd, neither do I define thee,
How can I pierce the impenetrable blank of the future?
I feel thy ominous greatness evil as well as good,
I watch thee advancing, absorbing the present, transcending the past,
I see thy light lighting, and thy shadow shadowing, as if the entire
    globe,
But I do not undertake to define thee, hardly to comprehend thee,
I but thee name, thee prophesy, as now,
I merely thee ejaculate!

Thee in thy future,
Thee in thy only permanent life, career, thy own unloosen'd mind,
    thy soaring spirit,
Thee as another equally needed sun, radiant, ablaze, swift-moving
    fructifying all,
Thee risen in potent cheerfulness and joy, in endless great hilarity,
Scattering for good the cloud that hung so long, that weigh'd so long
    upon the mind of man,
The doubt, suspicion, dread, of gradual, certain decadence of man;
Thee in thy all-supplying, all-enclosing worship—thee in no single
    moral, spiritual, South, North, West, East,
(To thy immortal breasts, Mother of All, thy every daughter, son,
    endear'd alike, forever equal,)
Thee in thy own musicians, singers, artists, unborn yet, but certain,
Thee in thy moral wealth and civilization, (until which thy proudest
    material civilization must remain in vain,)
Thee in thy all-supplying, all-enclosing worship—thee in no single
    bible saviour, merely,
Thy saviours, countless, latent within thyself, thy bibles incessant
    within thyself, equal to any, divine as any,
(Thy soaring course thee formulating, not in thy two great wars, nor
    in thy century's visible growth,
But far more in these leaves and chants, thy chants, great Mother!)
Thee in an education grown of thee, in teachers, studies, students,
    born of thee,

Thee in thy democratic fêtes en-masse,* thy high original festivals, operas, lecturers, preachers,

Thee in thy ultimata, (the preparations only now completed, the edifice on sure foundations tied,)

Thee in thy pinnacles, intellect, thought, thy topmost rational joys, thy love and godlike aspiration,

In thy resplendent coming literati, thy full-lung'd orators, thy sacerdotal bards, kosmic savans,*

These! these in thee, (certain to come,) to-day I prophesy.

6

Land tolerating all, accepting all, not for the good alone, all good for thee,

Land in the realms of God to be a realm unto thyself,

Under the rule of God to be a rule unto thyself.

(Lo, where arise three peerless stars,

To be thy natal stars my country, Ensemble, Evolution, Freedom,

Set in the sky of Law.)

Land of unprecedented faith, God's faith,

Thy soil, thy very subsoil, all upheav'd,

The general inner earth so long so sedulously draped over, now hence for what it is boldly laid bare,

Open'd by thee to heaven's light for benefit or bale.

Not for success alone,

Not to fair-sail unintermitted always,

The storm shall dash thy face, the murk of war and worse than war shall cover thee all over,

(Wert capable of war, its tug and trials? be capable of peace, its trials,

For the tug and mortal strain of nations come at last in prosperous peace, not war;)

In many a smiling mask death shall approach beguiling thee, thou in disease shalt swelter,

The livid cancer spread its hideous claws, clinging upon thy breasts, seeking to strike thee deep within,

Consumption of the worst, moral consumption, shall rouge thy face with hectic,*

But thou shalt face thy fortunes, thy diseases, and surmount them all,

Whatever they are to-day and whatever through time they may be,

They each and all shall lift and pass away and cease from thee,

While thou, Time's spirals rounding, out of thyself, thyself still extricating, fusing,

Equable, natural, mystical Union thou, (the mortal with immortal blent,)

Shalt soar toward the fulfilment of the future, the spirit of the body and the mind,

The soul, its destinies.

The soul, its destinies, the real real,
(Purport of all these apparitions of the real;)
In thee America, the soul, its destinies,
Thou globe of globes! thou wonder nebulous!
By many a throe of heat and cold convuls'd, (by these thyself
    solidifying,)
Thou mental, moral orb—thou New, indeed new, Spiritual World!
The Present holds thee not—for such vast growth as thine,
For such unparallel'd flight as thine, such brood as thine,
The FUTURE only holds thee and can hold thee.

A PAUMANOK * PICTURE

Two boats with nets lying off the sea-beach, quite still,
Ten fishermen waiting—they discover a thick school of mossbonkers*—
    they drop the join'd seine-ends in the water,
The boats separate and row off, each on its rounding course to the
    beach, enclosing the mossbonkers,
The net is drawn in by a windlass by those who stop ashore,
Some of the fishermen lounge in their boats, others stand ankle-deep
    in the water, pois'd on strong legs,
The boats partly drawn up, the water slapping against them,
Strew'd on the sand in heaps and windrows, well out from the water,
    the green-back'd spotted mossbonkers.

FROM NOON TO STARRY NIGHT

THOU ORB ALOFT FULL-DAZZLING

Thou orb aloft full-dazzling! thou hot October noon!
Flooding with sheeny* light the gray beach sand,
The sibilant near sea with vistas far and foam,
And tawny streaks and shades and spreading blue;
O sun of noon refulgent! my special word to thee.

Hear me illustrious!
Thy lover me, for always I have loved thee,
Even as basking babe, then happy boy alone by some wood edge,
    thy touching-distant beams enough,
Or man matured, or young or old, as now to thee I launch my invoca-
    tion.

(Thou canst not with thy dumbness me deceive,
I know before the fitting man all Nature yields,
Though answering not in words, the skies, trees, hear his voice—and
    thou O sun,
As for thy throes, thy perturbations,* sudden breaks and shafts of
    flame gigantic,
I understand them, I know those flames, those perturbations well.)

Thou that with fructifying heat and light,
O'er myriad farms, o'er lands and waters North and South,
O'er Mississippi's endless course, o'er Texas' grassy plains, Kanada's
    woods,
O'er all the globe that turns its face to thee shining in space,
Thou that impartially infoldest all, not only continents, seas,
Thou that to grapes and weeds and little wild flowers givest so liberally,
Shed, shed thyself on mine and me, with but a fleeting ray out of thy
    million millions,
Strike through these chants.

Nor only launch thy subtle dazzle and thy strength for these,
Prepare the later afternoon of me myself—prepare my lengthening
    shadows,
Prepare my starry nights.

FACES

1

Sauntering the pavement or riding the country by-road, lo, such faces!
Faces of friendship, precision, caution, suavity, ideality,
The spiritual-prescient face, the always welcome common benevolent
    face,

The face of the singing of music, the grand faces of natural lawyers
    and judges broad at the back-top,
The faces of hunters and fishers bulged at the brows, the shaved
    blanch'd faces of orthodox citizens,
The pure, extravagant, yearning questioning artist's face,
The ugly face of some beautiful soul, the handsome detested or
    despised face,
The sacred faces of infants, the illuminated face of the mother of
    many children,
The face of an amour, the face of veneration,
The face as of a dream, the face of an immobile rock,
The face withdrawn of its good and bad, a castrated face,
A wild hawk, his wings clipp'd by the clipper,
A stallion that yielded at last to the thongs and knife of the gelder.

Sauntering the pavement thus, or crossing the ceaseless ferry, faces
    and faces and faces,
I see them and complain not, and am content with all.

2

Do you suppose I could be content with all if I thought them their
    own finalè?

This now is too lamentable a face for a man,
Some abject louse asking leave to be, cringing for it,
Some milk-nosed maggot blessing what lets it wrig to its hole.

This face is a dog's snout sniffing for garbage,
Snakes nest in that mouth, I hear the sibilant threat.

This face is a haze more chill than the arctic sea,
Its sleepy and wabbling* icebergs crunch as they go.

This is a face of bitter herbs, this an emetic, they need no label,
And more of the drug-shelf, laudanum, caoutchouc, or hog's-lard.

This face is an epilepsy, its wordless tongue gives out the unearthly
    cry,
Its veins down the neck distend, its eyes roll till they show nothing
    but their whites,
Its teeth grit, the palms of the hands are cut by the turn'd-in nails,
The man falls struggling and foaming to the ground, while he specu-
    lates well.

This face is bitten by vermin and worms,
And this is some murderer's knife with a half-pull'd scabbard.

This face owes to the sexton his dismalest fee,
An unceasing death-bell tolls there.

3

Features of my equals would you trick me with your creas'd and
    cadaverous march?
Well, you cannot trick me.

I see your rounded never-erased flow,
I see 'neath the rims of your haggard and mean disguises.

Splay and twist as you like, poke with the tangling fores of fishes
    or rats,
You'll be unmuzzled, you certainly will.

I saw the face of the most smear'd and slobbering idiot they had at
    the asylum,
And I knew for my consolation what they knew not,
I knew of the agents that emptied and broke my brother,
The same wait to clear the rubbish from the fallen tenement,
And I shall look again in a score or two of ages,
And I shall meet the real landlord perfect and unharm'd, every inch
    as good as myself.

4

The Lord advances, and yet advances,
Always the shadow in front, always the reach'd hand bringing up
    the laggards.

Out of this face emerge banners and horses—O superb! I see what
    is coming,
I see the high pioneer-caps, see staves of runners clearing the way,
I hear victorious drums.

This face is a life-boat,
This is the face commanding and bearded, it asks no odds of the rest,
This face is flavor'd fruit ready for eating,
This face of a healthy honest boy is the programme of all good.

These faces bear testimony slumbering or awake,
They show their descent from the Master himself.

Off the word I have spoken I except not one—red, white, black, are
    all deific,
In each house is the ovum, it comes forth after a thousand years.

Spots or cracks at the windows do not disturb me,
Tall and sufficient stand behind and make signs to me,
I read the promise and patiently wait.

This is a full-grown lily's face,
She speaks to the limber-hipp'd man near the garden pickets,
Come here she blushingly cries, *Come nigh to me limber-hipp'd man,*
Stand at my side till I lean as high as I can upon you,
Fill me with albescent honey, bend down to me,
Rub to me with your chafing beard, rub to my breast and shoulders.

5

The old face of the mother of many children,
Whist! I am fully content.

Lull'd and late is the smoke of the First-day morning,
It hangs low over the rows of trees by the fences,
It hangs thin by the sassafras and wild-cherry and cat-brier under
     them.
I saw the rich ladies in full dress at the soiree,
I heard what the singers were singing so long,
Heard who sprang in crimson youth from the white froth and the
     water-blue.

Behold a woman!
She looks out from her quaker cap, her face is clearer and more
     beautiful than the sky.

She sits in an armchair under the shaded porch of the farmhouse,
The sun just shines on her old white head.

Her ample gown is of cream-hued linen,
Her grandsons raised the flax, and her grand-daughters spin it with
     the distaff and the wheel.

The melodious character of the earth,
The finish beyond which philosophy cannot go and does not wish
     to go,
The justified mother of men.

THE MYSTIC TRUMPETER

1

Hark, some wild trumpeter, some strange musician,
Hovering unseen in air, vibrates capricious tunes to-night.

I hear thee trumpeter, listening alert I catch thy notes,
Now pouring, whirling like a tempest round me,
Now low, subdued, now in the distance lost.

2

Come nearer bodiless one, haply in thee resounds
Some dead composer, haply thy pensive life

Was fill'd with aspirations high, unform'd ideals,
Waves, oceans musical, chaotically surging,
That now ecstatic ghost, close to me bending, thy cornet echoing,
    pealing,
Gives out to no one's ears but mine, but freely gives to mine,
That I may thee translate.

3

Blow trumpeter free and clear, I follow thee,
While at thy liquid prelude, glad, serene,
The fretting world, the streets, the noisy hours of day withdraw,
A holy calm descends like dew upon me,
I walk in cool refreshing night the walks of Paradise,
I scent° the grass, the moist air and the roses;
Thy song expands my numb'd imbonded spirit, thou freest,
    launchest me,
Floating and basking upon heaven's lake.

4

Blow again trumpeter! and for my sensuous eyes,
Bring the old pageants, show the feudal world.

What charm thy music works! thou makest pass before me,
Ladies and cavaliers long dead, barons are in their castle halls, the
    troubadours are singing,
Arm'd knights go forth to redress wrongs, some in quest of the
    holy Graal;
I see the tournament, I see the contestants incased in heavy armor
    seated on stately champing horses,
I hear the shouts, the sounds of blows and smiting steel;
I see the Crusaders' tumultuous armies—hark, how the cymbals
    clang,
Lo, where the monks walk in advance, bearing the cross on high.

5

Blow again trumpeter! and for thy theme,
Take now the enclosing theme of all, the solvent and the setting,
Love, that is pulse of all, the sustenance and the pang,
The heart of man and woman all for love,
No other theme but love—knitting, enclosing, all-diffusing love.

O how the immortal phantoms crowd around me!
I see the vast alembic° ever working, I see and know the flames that
    heat the world,
The glow, the blush, the beating hearts of lovers,
So blissfully happy some, and some so silent, dark, and nigh to death;
Love, that is all the earth to lovers—love, that mocks time and space,
Love, that is day and night—love, that is sun and moon and stars,
Love, that is crimson, sumptuous, sick with perfume,
No other words but words of love, no other thought but love.

6

Blow again trumpeter—conjure war's alarums.

Swift to thy spell a shuddering hum like distant thunder rolls,
Lo, where the arm'd men hasten—lo, mid the clouds of dust the glint
    of bayonets,
I see the grime-faced cannoneers, I mark the rosy flash amid the
    smoke, I hear the cracking of the guns;
Nor war alone—thy fearful music-song, wild prayer, brings every
    sight of fear,
The deeds of ruthless brigands, rapine, murder—I hear the cries for
    help!
I see ships foundering at sea, I behold on deck and below deck the
    terrible tableaus.

7

O trumpeter, methinks I am myself the instrument thou playest,
Thou melt'st my heart, my brain—thou movest, drawest, changest
    them at will;
And now thy sullen notes send darkness through me,
Thou takest away all cheering light, all hope,
I see the enslaved, the overthrown, the hurt, the opprest of the whole
    earth,
I feel the measureless shame and humiliation of my race, it becomes
    all mine,
Mine too the revenges of humanity, the wrongs of ages, baffled feuds
    and hatreds,
Utter defeat upon me weighs—all lost—the foe victorious,
(Yet 'mid the ruins Pride colossal stands unshaken to the last,
Endurance, resolution to the last.)

8

Now trumpeter for thy close,
Vouchsafe a higher strain than any yet,
Sing to my soul, renew its languishing faith and hope,
Rouse up my slow belief, give me some vision of the future,
Give me for once its prophecy and joy.

O glad, exulting, culminating song!
A vigor more than earth's is in thy notes,
Marches of victory—man disenthral'd—the conqueror at last,
Hymns to the universal God from universal man—all joy!
A reborn race appears—a perfect world, all joy!
Women and men in wisdom innocence and health—all joy!
Riotous laughing bacchanals fill'd with joy!
War, sorrow, suffering gone—the rank earth purged—nothing but joy
    left!
The ocean fill'd with joy—the atmosphere all joy!

Joy! joy! in freedom, worship, love! joy in the ecstasy of life!
Enough to merely be! enough to breathe!
Joy! joy! all over joy!

TO A LOCOMOTIVE IN WINTER

Thee for my recitative,
Thee in the driving storm even as now, the snow, the winter-day
    declining,
Thee in thy panoply, thy measur'd dual throbbing and thy beat
    convulsive,
Thy black cylindric body, golden brass and silvery steel,
Thy ponderous side-bars, parallel and connecting rods, gyrating,
    shuttling at thy sides,
Thy metrical, now swelling pant and roar, now tapering in the
    distance,
Thy great protruding head-light fix'd in front,
Thy long, pale, floating vapor-pennants, tinged with delicate purple,
The dense and murky clouds out-belching from thy smoke-stack,
Thy knitted frame, thy springs and valves, the tremulous twinkle of
    thy wheels,
Thy train of cars behind, obedient, merrily following,
Through gale or calm, now swift, now slack, yet steadily careering;
Type of the modern—emblem of motion and power—pulse of the
    continent,
For once come serve the Muse and merge in verse, even as here I
    see thee,
With storm and buffeting gusts of wind and falling snow,
By day thy warning ringing bell to sound its notes,
By night thy silent signal lamps to swing.

Fierce-throated beauty!
Roll through my chant with all thy lawless music, thy swinging lamps
    at night,
Thy madly-whistled laughter, echoing, rumbling like an earthquake,
    rousing all,
Law of thyself complete, thine own track firmly holding,
(No sweetness debonair of tearful harp or glib piano thine,)
Thy trills of shrieks by rocks and hills return'd,
Launch'd o'er the prairies wide, across the lakes,
To the free skies unpent and glad and strong.

O MAGNET-SOUTH

O magnet-South! O glistening perfumed South! my South!
O quick mettle, rich blood, impulse and love! good and evil! O all
    dear to me!

O dear to me my birth-things—all moving things and the trees where
    I was born—the grains, plants, rivers,
Dear to me my own slow sluggish rivers where they flow, distant,
    over flats of silvery sands or through swamps,
Dear to me the Roanoke, the Savannah, the Altamahaw, the Pedee,
    the Tombigbee, the Santee, the Coosa, and the Sabine,
O pensive, far away wandering, I return with my soul to haunt their
    banks again,
Again in Florida I float on transparent lakes, I float on the Okeechobee,
    I cross the hummock-land or through pleasant openings or
    dense forests,
I see the parrots in the woods, I see the papaw-tree and the blossom-
    ing titi;
Again, sailing in my coaster on deck, I coast off Georgia, I coast up
    the Carolinas,
I see where the live-oak is growing, I see where the yellow-pine, the
    scented bay-tree, the lemon and orange, the cypress, the grace-
    ful palmetto,
I pass rude sea-headlands and enter Pamlico sound through an inlet,
    and dart my vision inland;
O the cotton plant! the growing fields of rice, sugar, hemp!
The cactus guarded with thorns, the laurel-tree with large white
    flowers,
The range afar, the richness and barrenness, the old woods charged
    with mistletoe and trailing moss,
The piney odor and the gloom, the awful natural stillness, (here in
    these dense swamps the freebooter carries his gun, and the
    fugitive has his conceal'd hut;)
O the strange fascination of these half-known half-impassable swamps,
    infested by reptiles, resounding with the bellow of the alligator,
    the sad noises of the night-owl and the wild-cat, and the whirr
    of the rattlesnake,
The mocking-bird, the American mimic, singing all forenoon, singing
    through the moon-lit night,
The humming-bird, the wild turkey, the raccoon, the opossum;
A Kentucky corn-field, the tall, graceful, long-leav'd corn, slender,
    flapping, bright green, with tassels, with beautiful ears each
    well-sheath'd in its husk;
O my heart! O tender and fierce pangs, I can stand them not, I will
    depart;
O to be a Virginian where I grew up! O to be a Carolinian!
O longings irrepressible! O I will go back to old Tennessee and never
    wander more.

MANNAHATTA*

I was asking for something specific and perfect for my city,
Whereupon lo! upsprang the aboriginal name.

Now I see what there is in a name, a word, liquid, sane, unruly,
    musical, self-sufficient,
I see that the word of my city is that word from of old,
Because I see that word nested in nests of water-bays, superb,
Rich, hemm'd thick all around with sailships and steamships, an island
    sixteen miles long, solid-founded,
Numberless crowded streets, high growths of iron, slender, strong,
    light, splendidly uprising toward clear skies.
Tides swift and ample, well-loved by me, toward sundown,
The flowing sea-currents, the little islands, larger adjoining islands,
    the heights, the villas,
The countless masts, the white shore-steamers, the lighters, the ferry-
    boats, the black sea-steamers well-model'd,
The down-town streets, the jobbers' houses of business, the houses
    of business of the ship-merchants and money-brokers, the
    river-streets,
Immigrants arriving, fifteen or twenty thousand in a week,
The carts hauling goods, the manly race of drivers of horses, the
    brown-faced sailors,
The summer air, the bright sun shining, and the sailing clouds aloft,
The winter snows, the sleigh-bells, the broken ice in the river, passing
    along up or down with the flood-tide or ebb-tide,
The mechanics of the city, the masters, well-form'd, beautiful-faced,
    looking you straight in the eyes,
Trottoirs° throng'd, vehicles, Broadway, the women, the shops and
    shows,
A million people—manners free and superb—open voices—hospitality
    —the most courageous and friendly young men,
City of hurried and sparkling waters! city of spires and masts!
City nested in bays! my city!

ALL IS TRUTH

O me, man of slack faith so long,
Standing aloof, denying portions so long,
Only aware to-day of compact all-diffused truth,
Discovering to-day there is no lie or form of lie, and can be none, but
    grows as inevitably upon itself as the truth does upon itself,
Or as any law of the earth or any natural production of the earth does.

(This is curious and may not be realized immediately, but it must be
    realized,
I feel in myself that I represent falsehoods equally with the rest,
And that the universe does.)

Where has fail'd a perfect return indifferent of lies or the truth?
Is it upon the ground, or in water or fire? or in the spirit of man?
    or in the meat and blood?

Meditating among liars and retreating sternly into myself, I see that
    there are really no liars or lies after all,
And that nothing fails its perfect return, and that what are called lies
    are perfect returns,
And that each thing exactly represents itself and what has preceded it,
And that the truth includes all, and is compact just as much as space
    is compact,
And that there is no flaw or vacuum in the amount of the truth—but
    that all is truth without exception;
And henceforth I will go celebrate any thing I see or am,
And sing and laugh and deny nothing.

A RIDDLE SONG

That which eludes this verse and any verse,
Unheard by sharpest ear, unform'd in clearest eye or cunningest mind,
Nor lore nor fame, nor happiness nor wealth,
And yet the pulse of every heart and life throughout the world in-
    cessantly,
Which you and I and all pursuing ever miss,
Open but still a secret, the real of the real, an illusion,
Costless, vouchsafed to each, yet never man the owner,
Which poets vainly seek to put in rhyme, historians in prose,
Which sculptor never chiseled yet, nor painter painted,
Which vocalist never sung, nor orator nor actor ever utter'd,
Invoking here and now I challenge for my song.

Indifferently, 'mid public, private haunts, in solitude,
Behind the mountain and the wood,
Companion of the city's busiest streets, through the assemblage,
It and its radiations constantly glide.

In looks of fair unconscious babes,
Or strangely in the coffin'd dead,
Or show of breaking dawn or stars by night,
As some dissolving delicate film of dreams,
Hiding yet lingering.

Two little breaths of words comprising it,
Two words, yet all from first to last comprised in it.

How ardently for it!
How many ships have sail'd and sunk for it!
How many travelers started from their homes and ne'er return'd!
How much of genius boldly staked and lost for it!
What countless stores of beauty, love, ventur'd for it!
How all superbest deeds since Time began are traceable to it—and
    shall be to the end!

How all heroic martyrdoms to it!
How, justified by it, the horrors, evils, battles of the earth!
How the bright fascinating lambent* flames of it, in every age and
    land, have drawn men's eyes,
Rich as a sunset on the Norway coast, the sky, the islands, and the
    cliffs,
Or midnight's silent glowing northern lights unreachable.

Haply God's riddle it, so vague and yet so certain,
The soul for it, and all the visible universe for it,
And heaven at last for it.

EXCELSIOR

Who has gone farthest? for I would go farther,
And who has been just? for I would be the most just person of the
    earth,
And who most cautious? for I would be more cautious,
And who has been happiest? O I think it is I—I think no one was
    ever happier than I,
And who has lavish'd all? for I lavish constantly the best I have,
And who proudest? for I think I have reason to be the proudest son
    alive—for I am the son of the brawny and tall-topt city,
And who has been bold and true? for I would be the boldest and
    truest being of the universe,
And who benevolent? for I would show more benevolence than all
    the rest,
And who has receiv'd the love of the most friends? for I know what
    it is to receive the passionate love of many friends,
And who possesses a perfect and enamour'd body? for I do not believe
    any one possesses a more perfect or enamour'd body than mine,
And who thinks the amplest thoughts? for I would surround those
    thoughts,
And who has made hymns fit for the earth? for I am mad with
    devouring ecstasy to make joyous hymns for the whole earth.

AH POVERTIES, WINCINGS, AND SULKY RETREATS

Ah poverties, wincings, and sulky retreats,
Ah you foes that in conflict have overcome me,
(For what is my life or any man's life but a conflict with foes, the old,
    the incessant war?)
You degradations, you tussle with passions and appetites,
You smarts from dissatisfied friendships, (ah wounds the sharpest of
    all!)
You toil of painful and choked articulations, you meannesses,
You shallow tongue-talks at tables, (my tongue the shallowest of any;)

You broken resolutions, you racking angers, you smother'd ennuis!
Ah think not you finally triumph, my real self has yet to come forth,
It shall yet march forth o'ermastering, till all lies beneath me,
It shall yet stand up the soldier of ultimate victory.

THOUGHTS

Of public opinion,
Of a calm and cool fiat sooner or later, (how impassive! how certain
and final!)
Of the President with pale face asking secretly to himself, *What will
the people say at last?*
Of the frivolous Judge—of the corrupt Congressman, Governor, Mayor
—of such as these standing helpless and exposed,
Of the mumbling and screaming priest, (soon, soon deserted,)
Of the lessening year by year of venerableness, and of the dicta of
officers, statutes, pulpits, schools,
Of the rising forever taller and stronger and broader of the intuitions
of men and women, and of Self-esteem and Personality;
Of the true New World—of the Democracies resplendent en-masse,*
Of the conformity of politics, armies, navies, to them,
Of the shining sun by them—of the inherent light, greater than the
rest,
Of the envelopment of all by them, and the effusion* of all from them.

MEDIUMS

They shall arise in the States,
They shall report Nature, laws, physiology, and happiness,
They shall illustrate Democracy and the kosmos,*
They shall be alimentive,* amative,* perceptive,
They shall be complete women and men, their pose brawny and
supple, their drink water, their blood clean and clear,
They shall fully enjoy materialism and the sight of products, they
shall enjoy the sight of the beef, lumber, bread-stuffs, of
Chicago the great city,
They shall train themselves to go in public to become orators and
oratresses,
Strong and sweet shall their tongues be, poems and materials of poems
shall come from their lives, they shall be makers and finders,
Of them and of their works shall emerge divine conveyers, to convey
gospels,
Characters, events, retrospections, shall be convey'd in gospels, trees,
animals, waters, shall be convey'd,
Death, the future, the invisible faith, shall all be convey'd.

WEAVE IN, MY HARDY LIFE

Weave in, weave in, my hardy life,
Weave yet a soldier strong and full for great campaigns to come,
Weave in red blood, weave sinews in like ropes, the senses, sight
    weave in,
Weave lasting sure, weave day and night the weft, the warp, in-
    cessant weave, tire not,
(We know not what the use O life, nor know the aim, the end, nor
    really aught we know,
But know the work, the need goes on and shall go on, the death-
    envelop'd march of peace as well as war goes on,)
For great campaigns of peace the same the wiry threads to weave,
We know not why or what, yet weave, forever weave.

SPAIN, 1873-74

Out of the murk of heaviest clouds,
Out of the feudal wrecks and heap'd-up skeletons of kings,
Out of that old entire European debris, the shatter'd mummeries,
Ruin'd cathedrals, crumble of palaces, tombs of priests,
Lo, Freedom's features fresh undimm'd look forth—the same immortal
    face looks forth;
(A glimpse as of thy Mother's face Columbia,
A flash significant as of a sword,
Beaming towards thee.)

Nor think we forget thee maternal;
Lag'd'st° thou so long? shall the clouds close again upon thee?
Ah, but thou hast thyself now appear'd to us—we know thee,
Thou hast given us a sure proof, the glimpse of thyself,
Thou waitest there as everywhere thy time.

BY BROAD POTOMAC'S SHORE

By broad Potomac's shore, again old tongue,
(Still uttering, still ejaculating, canst never cease this babble?)
Again old heart so gay, again to you, your sense, the full flush spring
    returning,
Again the freshness and the odors, again Virginia's summer sky,
    pellucid blue and silver,
Again the forenoon purple of the hills,
Again the deathless grass, so noiseless soft and green,
Again the blood-red roses blooming.

Perfume this book of mine O blood-red roses!
Lave subtly with your waters every line Potomac!
Give me of you O spring, before I close, to put between its pages!
O forenoon purple of the hills, before I close, of you!
O deathless grass, of you!

FROM FAR DAKOTA'S CAÑONS
June 25, 1876

From far Dakota's cañons,
Lands of the wild ravine, the dusky Sioux, the lonesome stretch, the
      silence,
Haply to-day a mournful wail, haply a trumpet-note for heroes.

The battle-bulletin,
The Indian ambuscade, the craft, the fatal environment,
The cavalry companies fighting to the last in sternest heroism,
In the midst of their little circle, with their slaughter'd horses for
      breast-works,
The fall of Custer and all his officers and men.

Continues yet the old, old legend of our race,
The loftiest of life upheld by death,
The ancient banner perfectly maintain'd,
O lesson opportune, O how I welcome thee!

As sitting in dark days,
Lone, sulky, through the times thick murk looking in vain for light,
      for hope,
From unsuspected parts a fierce and momentary proof,
(The sun there at the centre though conceal'd,
Electric life forever at the centre,)
Breaks forth a lightning flash.

Thou of the tawny flowing hair in battle,
I erewhile saw, with erect head, pressing ever in front, bearing a
      bright sword in thy hand,
Now ending well in death the splendid fever of thy deeds,
(I bring no dirge for it or thee, I bring a glad triumphal sonnet,)
Desperate and glorious, aye in defeat most desperate, most glorious,
After thy many battles in which never yielding up a gun or a color,
Leaving behind thee a memory sweet to soldiers,
Thou yieldest up thyself.

OLD WAR-DREAMS

In midnight sleep of many a face of anguish,
Of the look at first of the mortally wounded, (of that indescribable
      look,)

Of the dead on their backs with arms extended wide,
      I dream, I dream, I dream.

Of scenes of Nature, fields and mountains,
Of skies so beauteous after a storm, and at night the moon so un-
      earthly bright,
Shining sweetly, shining down, where we dig the trenches and gather
      the heaps,
      I dream, I dream, I dream.

Long have they pass'd, faces and trenches and fields,
Where through the carnage I moved with a callous composure, or
      away from the fallen,
Onward I sped at the time—but now of their forms at night,
      I dream, I dream, I dream.

THICK-SPRINKLED BUNTING

Thick-sprinkled bunting! flag of stars!
Long yet your road, fateful flag—long yet your road, and lined with
      bloody death,
For the prize I see at issue at last is the world,
All its ships and shores I see interwoven with your threads greedy
      banner;
Dream'd again the flags of kings, highest borne, to flaunt unrival'd?
O hasten flag of man—O with sure and steady step, passing highest
      flags of kings,
Walk supreme to the heavens mighty symbol—run up above them all,
Flag of stars! thick-sprinkled bunting!

WHAT BEST I SEE IN THEE
To U.S.G. return'd from his World's Tour

What best I see in thee,
Is not that where thou mov'st down history's great highways,
Ever undimm'd by time shoots warlike victory's dazzle,
Or that thou sat'st where Washington sat, ruling the land in peace,
Or thou the man whom feudal Europe fêted, venerable Asia swarm'd
      upon,
Who walk'd with kings with even pace the round world's promenade:
But that in foreign lands, in all thy walks with kings,
Those prairie sovereigns of the West, Kansas, Missouri, Illinois,
Ohio's, Indiana's millions, comrades, farmers, soldiers, all to the front,
Invisibly with thee walking with kings with even pace the round
      world's promenade,
Were all so justified.

SPIRIT THAT FORM'D THIS SCENE
Written in Platte Cañon, Colorado

Spirit that form'd this scene,
These tumbled rock-piles grim and red,
These reckless heaven-ambitious peaks,
These gorges, turbulent-clear streams, this naked freshness,
These formless wild arrays, for reasons of their own,
I know thee, savage spirit—we have communed together,
Mine too such wild arrays, for reasons of their own;
Was't charged against my chants they had forgotten art?
To fuse within themselves its rules precise and delicatesse?*
The lyrist's measur'd beat, the wrought-out temple's grace—column
     and polish'd arch forgot?
But thou that revelest here—spirit that form'd this scene,
They have remember'd thee.

AS I WALK THESE BROAD MAJESTIC DAYS

As I walk these broad majestic days of peace,
(For the war, the struggle of blood finish'd, wherein, O terrific Ideal,
Against vast odds erewhile having gloriously won,
Now thou stridest on, yet perhaps in time toward denser wars,
Perhaps to engage in time in still more dreadful contests, dangers,
Longer campaigns and crises, labors beyond all others,)
Around me I hear that eclat of the world, politics, produce,
The announcements of recognized things, science,
The approved growth of cities and the spread of inventions.

I see the ships, (they will last a few years,)
The vast factories with their foremen and workmen,
And hear the indorsement of all, and do not object to it.

But I too announce solid things,
Science, ships, politics, cities, factories, are not nothing,
Like a grand procession to music of distant bugles pouring, triumph-
     antly moving, and grander heaving in sight,
They stand for realities—all is as it should be.

Then my realities;
What else is so real as mine?
Libertad* and the divine average, freedom to every slave on the face
     of the earth,
The rapt promises and luminè* of seers, the spiritual world, these
     centuries-lasting songs,

And our visions, the visions of poets, the most solid announcements
   of any.

A CLEAR MIDNIGHT

This is thy hour O Soul, thy free flight into the wordless,
Away from books, away from art, the day erased, the lesson done,
Thee fully forth emerging, silent, gazing, pondering the themes thou
   lovest best,
Night, sleep, death and the stars.

SONGS OF PARTING

AS THE TIME DRAWS NIGH

As the time draws nigh glooming a cloud,
A dread beyond of I know not what darkens me.

I shall go forth,
I shall traverse the States awhile, but I cannot tell whither or how long,
Perhaps soon some day or night while I am singing my voice will
suddenly cease.

O book, O chants! must all then amount to but this?
Must we barely arrive at this beginning of us?—and yet it is enough,
O soul;
O soul, we have positively appear'd—that is enough.

YEARS OF THE MODERN

Years of the modern! years of the unperform'd!
Your horizon rises, I see it parting away for more august dramas,
I see not America only, not only Liberty's nation but other nations
preparing,
I see tremendous entrances and exits, new combinations, the solidarity
of races,
I see that force advancing with irresistible power on the world's stage,
(Have the old forces, the old wars, played their parts? are the acts
suitable to them closed?)
I see Freedom, completely arm'd and victorious and very haughty,
with Law on one side and Peace on the other,
A stupendous trio all issuing forth against the idea of caste;
What historic denouements are these we so rapidly approach?
I see men marching and countermarching by swift millions,
I see the frontiers and boundaries of the old aristocracies broken,
I see the landmarks of European kings removed,
I see this day the People beginning their landmarks, (all others give
way;)
Never were such sharp questions ask'd as this day,
Never was average man, his soul, more energetic, more like a God,
Lo, how he urges and urges, leaving the masses no rest!
His daring foot is on land and sea everywhere, he colonizes the
Pacific, the archipelagoes,
With the steamship, the electric telegraph, the newspaper, the whole-
sale engines of war,
With these and the world-spreading factories he interlinks all geog-
raphy, all lands;

What whispers are these O lands, running ahead of you, passing
  under the seas?
Are all nations communing? is there going to be but one heart to the
  globe?
Is humanity forming en-masse? for lo, tyrants tremble, crowns grow
  dim,
The earth, restive, confronts a new era, perhaps a general divine war,
No one knows what will happen next, such portents fill the days and
  nights;
Years prophetical! the space ahead as I walk, as I vainly try to pierce
  it, is full of phantoms,
Unborn deeds, things soon to be, project their shapes around me,
This incredible rush and heat, this strange ecstatic fever of dreams
  O years!
Your dreams O years, how they penetrate through me! (I know not
  whether I sleep or wake;)
The perform'd America and Europe grow dim, retiring in shadow
  behind me,
The unperform'd, more gigantic than ever, advance, advance upon me.

ASHES OF SOLDIERS

Ashes of soldiers South or North,
As I muse retrospective murmuring a chant in thought,
The war resumes, again to my sense your shapes,
And again the advance of the armies.

Noiseless as mists and vapors,
From their graves in the trenches ascending,
From cemeteries all through Virginia and Tennessee,
From every point of the compass out of the countless graves,
In wafted clouds, in myriads large, or squads of twos or threes or single
  ones they come,
And silently gather round me.

Now sound no note O trumpeters,
Not at the head of my cavalry parading on spirited horses,
With sabres drawn and glistening, and carbines by their thighs, (ah
  my brave horsemen!
My handsome tan-faced horseman! what life, what joy and pride,
With all the perils were yours.)

Nor you drummers, neither at reveillé at dawn,
Nor the long roll alarming the camp, nor even the muffled beat for a
  burial,
Nothing from you this time O drummers bearing my warlike drums.

But aside from these and the marts of wealth and the crowded
      promenade,
Admitting around me comrades close unseen by the rest and voiceless,
The slain elate° and alive again, the dust and debris alive,
I chant this chant of my silent soul in the name of all dead soldiers.

Faces so pale with wondrous eyes, very dear, gather closer yet,
Draw close, but speak not.

Phantoms of countless lost,
Invisible to the rest henceforth become my companions,
Follow me ever—desert me not while I live.

Sweet are the blooming cheeks of the living—sweet are the musical
      voices sounding,
But sweet, ah sweet, are the dead with their silent eyes.

Dearest comrades, all is over and long gone,
But love is not over—and what love, O comrades
Perfume from battle-fields rising, up from the fœtor° arising.

Perfume therefore my chant, O love, immortal love,
Give me to bathe the memories of all dead soldiers,
Shroud them, embalm them, cover them all over with tender pride.

Perfume all—make all wholesome,
Make these ashes to nourish and blossom,
O love, solve all, fructify all with the last chemistry.

Give me exhaustless, make me a fountain,
That I exhale love from me wherever I go like a moist perpetual dew,
For the ashes of all dead soldiers South or North.

THOUGHTS

1

Of these years I sing,
How they pass and have pass'd through convuls'd pains, as through
      parturitions,
How America illustrates birth, muscular youth, the promise, the sure
      fulfilment, the absolute success, despite of people—illustrates
      evil as well as good,
The vehement struggle so fierce for unity in one's-self;
How many hold despairingly yet to the models departed, caste, myths,
      obedience, compulsion, and to infidelity,
How few see the arrived models, the athletes, the Western States, or
      see freedom or spirituality, or hold any faith in results,
(But I see the athletes, and I see the results of the war glorious and
      inevitable, and they again leading to other results.)

How the great cities appear—how the Democratic masses, turbulent,
wilful, as I love them,
How the whirl, the contest, the wrestle of evil with good, the sounding
and resounding, keep on and on,
How society waits unform'd, and is for a while between things ended
and things begun,
How America is the continent of glories, and of the triumph of freedom
and of the Democracies, and of the fruits of society, and of
all that is begun,
And how the States are complete in themselves—and how all triumphs
and glories are complete in themselves, to lead onward,
And how these of mine and of the States will in their turn be convuls'd, and serve other parturitions and transitions,
And how all people, sights, combinations, the democratic masses too,
serve—and how every fact, and war itself, with all its horrors,
serves,
And how now or at any time each serves the exquisite transition of
death.

2

Of seeds dropping into the ground, of births,
Of the steady concentration of America, inland, upward, to impreg-
nable and swarming places,
Of what Indiana, Kentucky, Arkansas, and the rest, are to be,
Of what a few years will show there in Nebraska, Colorado, Nevada,
and the rest,
(Or afar, mounting the Northern Pacific to Sitka or Aliaska,)
Of what the feuillage* of America is the preparation for—and of what
all sights, North, South, East and West, are,
Of this Union welded in blood, of the solemn price paid, of the un-
named lost ever present in my mind;
Of the temporary use of materials for identity's sake,
Of the present, passing, departing—of the growth of completer men
than any yet,
Of all sloping down there where the fresh free giver the mother, the
Mississippi flows,
Of mighty inland cities yet unsurvey'd and unsuspected,
Of the new and good names, of the modern developments, of inalien-
able homesteads,
Of a free and original life there, of simple diet and clean and sweet
blood,
Of litheness, majestic faces, clear eyes, and perfect physique there,
Of immense spiritual results future years far West, each side of the
Anahuacs,
Of these songs, well understood there, (being made for that area,)
Of the native scorn of grossness and gain there,
(O it lurks in me night and day—what is gain after all to savageness
and freedom?)

SONG AT SUNSET

Splendor of ended day floating and filling me,
Hour prophetic, hour resuming the past,
Inflating my throat, you divine average,
You earth and life till the last ray gleams I sing.

Open mouth of my soul uttering gladness,
Eyes of my soul seeing perfection,
Natural life of me faithfully praising things,
Corroborating forever the triumph of things

Illustrious every one!
Illustrious what we name space, sphere of unnumber'd spirits,
Illustrious the mystery of motion in all beings, even the tiniest insect,
Illustrious the attribute of speech, the senses, the body,
Illustrious the passing light—illustrious the pale reflection on the new
       moon in the western sky,
Illustrious whatever I see or hear or touch, to the last.

Good in all,
In the satisfaction and aplomb of animals,
In the annual return of the seasons,
In the hilarity of youth,
In the strength and flush of manhood,
In the grandeur and exquisiteness of old age,
In the superb vistas of death.

Wonderful to depart!
Wonderful to be here!
The heart, to jet the all-alike and innocent blood!
To breathe the air, how delicious!
To speak—to walk—to seize something by the hand!
To prepare for sleep, for bed, to look on my rose-color'd flesh!
To be conscious of my body, so satisfied, so large!
To be this incredible God I am!
To have gone forth among other Gods, these men and women I love.

Wonderful how I celebrate you and myself!
How my thoughts play subtly at the spectacles around!
How the clouds pass silently overhead!
How the earth darts on and on! and how the sun, moon, stars, dart on
       and on!
How the water sports and sings! (surely it is alive!)
How the trees rise and stand up, with strong trunks, with branches
       and leaves!
(Surely there is something more in each of the trees, some living soul.)

O amazement of things—even the least particle!
O spirituality of things!
O strain musical flowing through ages and continents, now reaching
    me and America!
I take your strong chords, intersperse them, and cheerfully pass them
    forward.

I too carol the sun, usher'd or at noon, or as now, setting,
I too throb to the brain and beauty of the earth and of all the growths
    of the earth,
I too have felt the resistless call of myself.

As I steam'd down the Mississippi,
As I wander'd over the prairies,
As I have lived, as I have look'd through my windows my eyes,
As I went forth in the morning, as I beheld the light breaking in the
    east,
As I bathed on the beach of the Eastern Sea, and again on the beach
    of the Western Sea,
As I roam'd the streets of inland Chicago, whatever streets I have
    roam'd,
Or cities or silent woods, or even amid the sights of war,
Wherever I have been I have charged myself with contentment and
    triumph.

I sing to the last the equalities modern or old,
I sing the endless finalés of things,
I say Nature continues, glory continues,
I praise with electric voice,
For I do not see one imperfection in the universe,
And I do not see one cause or result lamentable at last in the uni-
    verse.

O setting sun! though the time has come,
I still warble under you, if none else does, unmitigated adoration.

AS AT THY PORTALS ALSO DEATH

As at thy portals also death,
Entering thy sovereign, dim, illimitable grounds,
To memories of my mother, to the divine blending, maternity,
To her, buried and gone, yet buried not, gone not from me,
(I see again the calm benignant face fresh and beautiful still,
I sit by the form in the coffin,
I kiss and kiss convulsively again the sweet old lips, the cheeks, the
    closed eyes in the coffin;)
To her, the ideal woman, practical, spiritual, of all of earth, life, love,
    to me the best,
I grave a monumental line, before I go, amid these songs,
And set a tombstone here.

MY LEGACY

The business man the acquirer vast,
After assiduous years surveying results, preparing for departure,
Devises houses and lands to his children, bequeaths stocks, goods,
    funds for a school or hospital,
Leaves money to certain companions to buy tokens, souvenirs of gems
    and gold.

But I, my life surveying, closing,
With nothing to show to devise from its idle years,
Nor houses nor lands, nor tokens of gems or gold for my friends,
Yet certain remembrances of the war for you, and after you,
And little souvenirs of camps and soldiers, with my love,
I bind together and bequeath in this bundle of songs.

PENSIVE ON HER DEAD GAZING

Pensive on her dead gazing I heard the Mother of All,
Desperate on the torn bodies, on the forms covering the battle-fields
    gazing,
(As the last gun ceased, but the scent of the powder-smoke linger'd,)
As she call'd to her earth with mournful voice while she stalk'd,
Absorb them well O my earth, she cried, I charge you lose not my
    sons, lose not an atom,
And you streams absorb them well, taking their dear blood,
And you local spots, and you airs that swim above lightly impalpable,
And all you essences of soil and growth, and you my rivers' depths,
And you mountain sides, and the woods where my dear children's blood
    trickling redden'd,
And you trees down in your roots to bequeath to all future trees,
My dead absorb or South or North—my young men's bodies absorb,
    and their precious precious blood,
Which holding in trust for me faithfully back again give me many a
    year hence,
In unseen essence and odor of surface and grass, centuries hence,
In blowing airs from the fields back again give me my darlings, give
    my immortal heroes,
Exhale me them centuries hence, breathe me their breath, let not an
    atom be lost,
O years and graves! O air and soil! O my dead, an aroma sweet!
Exhale them perennial sweet death, years, centuries hence.

CAMPS OF GREEN

Not alone those camps of white, old comrades of the wars,
When as order'd forward, after a long march,
Footsore and weary, soon as the light lessens we halt for the night,

Some of us so fatigued carrying the gun and knapsack, dropping
    asleep in our tracks,
Others pitching the little tents, and the fires lit up begin to sparkle,
Outposts of pickets posted surrounding alert through the dark,
And a word provided for countersign, careful for safety,
Till to the call of the drummers at daybreak loudly beating the drums,
We rise up refresh'd, the night and sleep pass'd over, and resume our
    journey,
Or proceed to battle.

Lo, the camps of the tents of green,
Which the days of peace keep filling, and the days of war keep filling,
With a mystic army, (is it too order'd forward? is it too only halting
    awhile,
Till night and sleep pass over?)

Now in those camps of green, in their tents dotting the world,
In the parents, children, husbands, wives, in them, in the old and
    young,
Sleeping under the sunlight, sleeping under the moonlight, content
    and silent there at last,
Behold the mighty bivouac-field and waiting-camp of all,
Of the corps and generals all, and the President over the corps and
    generals all,
And of each of us O soldiers, and of each and all in the ranks we
    fought,
(There without hatred we all, all meet.)

For presently O soldiers, we too camp in our place in the bivouac-
    camps of green,
But we need not provide for outposts, nor word for the counter-sign,
Nor drummer to beat the morning drum.

THE SOBBING OF THE BELLS
(Midnight, Sept. 19-20, 1881)

The sobbing of the bells, the sudden death-news everywhere,
The slumbers rouse, the rapport of the People,
(Full well they know that message in the darkness,
Full well return, respond within their breasts, their brains, the sad
    reverberations,)
The passionate toll and clang—city to city, joining, sounding, passing,
Those heart-beats of a Nation in the night.

AS THEY DRAW TO A CLOSE

As they draw to a close,
Of what underlies the precedent songs—of my aims in them,
Of the seed I have sought to plant in them,

Of joy, sweet joy, through many a year, in them,
(For them, for them have I lived, in them my work is done,)
Of many an aspiration fond, of many a dream and plan;
Through Space and Time fused in a chant, and the flowing eternal
    identity,
To Nature encompassing these, encompassing God—to the joyous,
    electric all,
To the sense of Death, and accepting exulting in Death in its turn the
    same as life,
The entrance of man to sing;
To compact you, ye parted, diverse lives,
To put rapport the mountains and rocks and streams,
And the winds of the north, and the forests of oak and pine,
With you O soul.

JOY, SHIPMATE, JOY!

Joy, shipmate, joy!
(Pleas'd to my soul at death I cry,)
Our life is closed, our life begins,
The long, long anchorage we leave,
The ship is clear at last, she leaps!
She swiftly courses from the shore,
Joy, shipmate, joy!

THE UNTOLD WANT

The untold want by life and land ne'er granted,
Now voyager sail thou forth to seek and find.

PORTALS

What are those of the known but to ascend and enter the Unknown?
And what are those of life but for Death?

THESE CAROLS

These carols sung to cheer my passage through the world I see,
For completion I dedicate to the Invisible World.

NOW FINALÈ TO THE SHORE

Now finalè to the shore,
Now land and life finalè and farewell,
Now Voyager depart, (much, much for thee is yet in store,)
Often enough hast thou adventur'd o'er the seas,

Cautiously cruising, studying the charts,
Duly again to port and hawser's tie returning;
But now obey thy cherish'd secret wish,
Embrace thy friends, leave all in order,
To port and hawser's tie no more returning,
Depart upon thy endless cruise old Sailor.

SO LONG!*

To conclude, I announce what comes after me.

I remember I said before my leaves sprang at all,
I would raise my voice jocund and strong with reference to consummations.

When America does what was promis'd,
When through these States walk a hundred millions of superb persons,
When the rest part away for superb persons and contribute to them,
When breeds of the most perfect mothers denote America,
Then to me and mine our due fruition.

I have press'd through in my own right,
I have sung the body and the soul, war and peace have I sung, and the songs of life and death,
And the songs of birth, and shown that there are many births.

I have offer'd my style to every one, I have journey'd with confident step;
While my pleasure is yet at the full I whisper *So long!*
And take the young woman's hand and the young man's hand for the last time.

I announce natural persons to arise,
I announce justice triumphant,
I announce uncompromising liberty and equality,
I announce the justification of candor and the justification of pride.

I announce that the identity of these States is a single identity only,
I announce the Union more and more compact, indissoluble,
I announce splendors and majesties to make all the previous politics of the earth insignificant.

I announce adhesiveness,* I say it shall be limitless, unloosen'd,
I say you shall yet find the friend you were looking for.

I announce a man or woman coming, perhaps you are the one, (*So long!*)
I announce the great individual, fluid as Nature, chaste, affectionate, compassionate, fully arm'd.

I announce a life that shall be copious, vehement, spiritual, bold,
I announce an end that shall lightly and joyfully meet its translation.

I announce myriads of youths, beautiful, gigantic, sweet-blooded,
I announce a race of splendid and savage old men.

O thicker and faster—(*So long!*)
O crowding too close upon me,
I foresee too much, it means more than I thought,
It appears to me I am dying.

Hasten throat and sound your last,
Salute me—salute the days once more. Peal the old cry once more.

Screaming electric, the atmosphere using,
At random glancing, each as I notice absorbing,
Swiftly on, but a little while alighting,
Curious envelop'd messages delivering,
Sparkles hot, seed ethereal down in the dirt dropping,
Myself unknowing, my commission obeying, to question it never daring,
To ages and ages yet the growth of the seed leaving,
To troops out of the war arising, they the tasks I have set promulging,
To women certain whispers of myself bequeathing, their affection me more clearly explaining,
To young men my problems offering—no dallier I—I the muscle of their brains trying,
So I pass, a little time vocal, visible, contrary,
Afterward a melodious echo, passionately bent for, (death making me really undying,)
The best of me then when no longer visible, for toward that I have been incessantly preparing.

What is there more, that I lag* and pause and crouch extended with unshut mouth?
Is there a single final farewell?

My songs cease, I abandon them,
From behind the screen where I hid I advance personally solely to you.

Camerado,* this is no book,
Who touches this touches a man,
(Is it night? are we here together alone?)
It is I you hold and who holds you,
I spring from the pages into your arms—decease calls me forth.

O how your fingers drowse me,
Your breath falls around me like dew, your pulse lulls the tympans of
    my ears,
I feel immerged from head to foot,
Delicious, enough.

Enough O deed impromptu and secret,
Enough O gliding present—enough O summ'd-up past.

Dear friend whoever you are take this kiss,
I give it especially to you, do not forget me,
I feel like one who has done work for the day to retire awhile,
I receive now again of my many translations, from my avataras°
    ascending, while others doubtless await me,
An unknown sphere more real than I dream'd, more direct, darts
    awakening rays about me, *So long!*
Remember my words, I may again return,
I love you, I depart from materials,
I am as one disembodied, triumphant, dead.

SANDS AT SEVENTY

(First Annex)

MANNAHATTA*

My city's fit and noble name resumed,
Choice aboriginal name, with marvelous beauty, meaning,
A *rocky founded island—shores where ever gayly dash the coming,
going, hurrying sea waves.*

PAUMANOK*

Sea-beauty! stretch'd and basking!
One side thy inland ocean laving, broad, with copious commerce,
    steamers, sails,
And one the Atlantic's wind caressing, fierce or gentle—mighty hulls
    dark-gliding in the distance.
Isle of sweet brooks of drinking-water—healthy air and soil!
Isle of the salty shore and breeze and brine!

FROM MONTAUK POINT

I stand as on some mighty eagle's beak,
Eastward the sea absorbing, viewing, (nothing but sea and sky,)
The tossing waves, the foam, the ships in the distance,
The wild unrest, the snowy, curling caps—that inbound urge and
    urge of waves,
Seeking the shores forever.

TO THOSE WHO'VE FAIL'D

To those who've fail'd, in aspiration vast,
To unnam'd soldiers fallen in front on the lead,
To calm, devoted engineers—to over-ardent travelers—to pilots on
    their ships,
To many a lofty song and picture without recognition—I'd rear a
    laurel-cover'd monument,
High, high above the rest—To all cut off before their time,
Possess'd by some strange spirit of fire,
Quench'd by an early death.

A CAROL CLOSING SIXTY-NINE

A carol closing sixty-nine—a *résumé*—a repetition,
My lines in joy and hope continuing on the same,
Of ye, O God, Life, Nature, Freedom, Poetry;
Of you, my Land—your rivers, prairies, States—you, mottled Flag I
    love,
Your aggregate retain'd entire—Of north, south, east and west, your
    items all;
Of me myself—the jocund heart yet beating in my breast,
The body wreck'd, old, poor and paralyzed—the strange inertia falling
    pall-like round me,
The burning fires down in my sluggish blood not yet extinct,
The undiminish'd faith—the groups of loving friends.

THE BRAVEST SOLDIERS

Brave, brave were the soldiers (high named to-day) who lived
    through the fight;
But the bravest press'd to the front and fell, unnamed, unknown.

A FONT OF TYPE

This latent mine—these unlaunch'd voices—passionate powers,
Wrath, argument, or praise, or comic leer, or prayer devout,
(Not nonpareil, brevier, bourgeois, long primer merely,)
These ocean waves arousable to fury and to death,
Or sooth'd to ease and sheeny° sun and sleep,
Within the pallid slivers slumbering.

AS I SIT WRITING HERE

As I sit writing here, sick and grown old,
Not my least burden is that dulness of the years, querilities,
Ungracious glooms, aches, lethargy, constipation, whimpering *ennui*,
May filter in my daily songs.

MY CANARY BIRD

Did we count great, O soul, to penetrate the themes of mighty books,
Absorbing deep and full from thoughts, plays, speculations?
But now from thee to me, caged bird, to feel thy joyous warble,
Filling the air, the lonesome room, the long forenoon,
Is it not just as great, O soul?

QUERIES TO MY SEVENTIETH YEAR

Approaching, nearing, curious,
Thou dim, uncertain spectre—bringest thou life or death?
Strength, weakness, blindness, more paralysis and heavier?
Or placid skies and sun? Wilt stir the waters yet?
Or haply cut me short for good? Or leave me here as now,
Dull, parrot-like and old, with crack'd voice harping, screeching?

THE WALLABOUT MARTYRS

(In Brooklyn, in an old vault, mark'd by no special recognition, lie huddled at this moment the undoubtedly authentic remains of the stanchest and earliest Revolutionary patriots from the British prison ships and prisons of the times of 1776-83, in and around New York, and from all over Long Island; originally buried—many thousands of them—in trenches in the Wallabout sands.)

Greater than memory of Achilles or Ulysses,
More, more by far to thee than tomb of Alexander,
Those cart loads of old charnel ashes, scales and splints of mouldy
      bones,
Once living men—once resolute courage, aspiration, strength,
The stepping stones to thee to-day and here, America.

THE FIRST DANDELION

Simple and fresh and fair from winter's close emerging,
As if no artifice of fashion, business, politics, had ever been,
Forth from its sunny nook of shelter'd grass—innocent, golden, calm
      as the dawn,
The spring's first dandelion shows its trustful face.

AMERICA

Centre of equal daughters, equal sons,
All, all alike endear'd, grown, ungrown, young or old,
Strong, ample, fair, enduring, capable, rich,
Perennial with the Earth, with Freedom, Law and Love,
A grand, sane, towering, seated Mother,
Chair'd in the adamant of Time.

MEMORIES

How sweet the silent backward tracings!
The wanderings as in dreams—the meditation of old times resumed—
      their loves, joys, persons, voyages.

TO-DAY AND THEE

The appointed winners in a long-stretch'd game;
The course of Time and nations—Egypt, India, Greece and Rome;
The past entire, with all its heroes, histories, arts, experiments,
Its store of songs, inventions, voyages, teachers, books,
Garner'd for now and thee—To think of it!
The heirdom all converged in thee!

AFTER THE DAZZLE OF DAY

After the dazzle of day is gone,
Only the dark, dark night shows to my eyes the stars;
After the clangor of organ majestic, or chorus, or perfect band,
Silent, athwart my soul, moves the symphony true.

ABRAHAM LINCOLN, BORN FEB. 12, 1809
(Publish'd Feb. 12, 1888)

To-day, from each and all, a breath of prayer—a pulse of thought,
To memory of Him—to birth of Him.

OUT OF MAY'S SHOWS SELECTED

Apple orchards, the trees all cover'd with blossoms;
Wheat fields carpeted far and near in vital emerald green;
The eternal, exhaustless freshness of each early morning;
The yellow, golden, transparent haze of the warm afternoon sun;
The aspiring lilac bushes with profuse purple or white flowers.

HALCYON DAYS

Not from successful love alone,
Nor wealth, nor honor'd middle age, nor victories of politics or war;
But as life wanes, and all the turbulent passions calm,
As gorgeous, vapory, silent hues cover the evening sky,
As softness, fulness, rest, suffuse the frame, like fresher, balmier air,
As the days take on a mellower light, and the apple at last hangs
        really finish'd and indolent-ripe on the tree,
Then for the teeming quietest, happiest days of all!
The brooding and blissful halcyon days!

FANCIES AT NAVESINK

The Pilot in the Mist

Steaming the northern rapids—(an old St. Lawrence reminiscence,
A sudden memory-flash comes back, I know not why,
Here waiting for the sunrise, gazing from this hill;) †
Again 'tis just at morning—a heavy haze contends with daybreak,
Again the trembling, laboring vessel veers me—I press through foam-
    dash'd rocks that almost touch me,
Again I mark where aft the small thin Indian helmsman
Looms in the mist, with brow elate* and governing hand.

Had I the Choice

Had I the choice to tally greatest bards,
To limn their portraits, stately, beautiful, and emulate at will,
Homer with all his wars and warriors—Hector, Achilles, Ajax,
Or Shakspere's woe-entangled Hamlet, Lear, Othello—Tennyson's
    fair ladies,
Metre or wit the best, or choice conceit to wield in perfect rhyme,
    delight of singers;
These, these, O sea, all these I'd gladly barter,
Would you the undulation of one wave, its trick to me transfer,
Or breathe one breath of yours upon my verse,
And leave its odor there.

You Tides with Ceaseless Swell

You tides with ceaseless swell! you power that does this work!
You unseen force, centripetal, centrifugal, through space's spread,
Rapport* of sun, moon, earth, and all the constellations,
What are the messages by you from distant stars to us? what Sirius'?
    what Cappella's?
What central heart—and you the pulse—vivifies all? what boundless
    aggregate of all?
What subtle indirection and significance in you? what clue to all in
    you? what fluid, vast identity,
Holding the universe with all its parts as one—as sailing in a ship?

Last of Ebb, and Daylight Waning

Last of ebb, and daylight waning,
Scented sea-cool landward making, smells of sedge and salt incoming,
With many a half-caught voice sent up from the eddies,

† Navesink — a sea-side mountain, lower entrance of New York Bay.

Many a muffled confession—many a sob and whisper'd word,
As of speakers far or hid.

How they sweep down and out! how they mutter!
Poets unnamed—artists greatest of any, with cherish'd lost designs,
Love's unresponse—a chorus of age's complaints—hope's last words,
Some suicide's despairing cry, *Away to the boundless waste, and never
again return.*

On to oblivion then!
On, on, and do your part, ye burying, ebbing tide!
On for your time, ye furious debouché!*

And Yet Not You Alone

And yet not you alone, twilight and burying ebb,
Nor you, ye lost designs alone—nor failures, aspirations;
I know, divine deceitful ones, your glamour's seeming;
Duly by you, from you, the tide and light again—duly the hinges
turning,
Duly the needed discord-parts offsetting, blending,
Weaving from you, from Sleep, Night, Death itself,
The rhythmus of Birth eternal.

Proudly the Flood Comes In

Proudly the flood comes in, shouting, foaming, advancing,
Long it holds at the high, with bosom broad outswelling,
All throbs, dilates—the farms, woods, streets of cities—workmen at
work,
Mainsails, topsails, jibs, appear in the offing—steamers' pennants of
smoke—and under the forenoon sun,
Freighted with human lives, gaily the outward bound, gaily the
inward bound,
Flaunting from many a spar the flag I love.

By That Long Scan of Waves

By that long scan of waves, myself call'd back, resumed upon myself,
In every crest some undulating light or shade—some retrospect,
Joys, travels, studies, silent panoramas—scenes, ephemeral,
The long past war, the battles, hospital sights, the wounded and the
dead,
Myself through every by-gone phase—my idle youth—old age at hand,
My three-score years of life summ'd up, and more, and past,
By any grand ideal tried, intentionless, the whole a nothing,
And haply yet some drop within God's scheme's ensemble—some
wave, or part of wave,
Like one of yours, ye multitudinous ocean.

Then Last of All

Then last of all, caught from these shores, this hill,
Of you O tides, the mystic human meaning;
Only by law of you, your swell and ebb, enclosing me the same,
The brain that shapes, the voice that chants this song.

ELECTION DAY, NOVEMBER, 1884

If I should need to name, O Western World, your powerfulest scene
    and show,
'Twould not be you, Niagara—nor you, ye limitless prairies—nor your
    huge rifts of canyons, Colorado,
Nor you, Yosemite—nor Yellowstone, with all its spasmic geyser loops
    ascending to the skies, appearing and disappearing,
Nor Oregon's white cones—nor Huron's belt of mighty lakes—nor
    Mississippi's stream:
—This seething hemisphere's humanity, as now, I'd name—*the still
    small voice* vibrating—America's choosing day,
(The heart of it not in the chosen—the act itself the main, the quad-
    rennial choosing,)
The stretch of North and South arous'd—sea-board and inland—
    Texas to Maine—the Prairie States—Vermont, Virginia, Cali-
    fornia,
The final ballot-shower from East to West—the paradox and conflict,
The countless snow-flakes falling—(a swordless conflict,
Yet more than all Rome's wars of old, or modern Napoleon's:) the
    peaceful choice of all,
Or good or ill humanity—welcoming the darker odds, the dross:
—Foams and ferments the wine? it serves to purify—while the heart
    pants, life glows:
These stormy gusts and winds waft precious ships,
Swell'd Washington's, Jefferson's, Lincoln's sails.

WITH HUSKY-HAUGHTY LIPS, O SEA!

With husky-haughty lips, O sea!
Where day and night I wend thy surf-beat shore,
Imaging to my sense thy varied strange suggestions,
(I see and plainly list thy talk and conference here,)
Thy troops of white-maned racers racing to the goal,
Thy ample, smiling face, dash'd with the sparkling dimples of the sun,
Thy brooding scowl and murk—thy unloos'd hurricanes,
Thy unsubduedness, caprices, wilfulness;
Great as thou art above the rest, thy many tears—a lack from all
    eternity in thy content,

(Naught but the greatest struggles, wrongs, defeats, could make thee
       greatest—no less could make thee,)
Thy lonely state—something thou ever seek'st and seek'st, yet never
       gain'st,
Surely some right withheld—some voice, in huge monotonous rage,
       of freedom-lover pent,
Some vast heart, like a planet's, chain'd and chafing in those breakers,
By lengthen'd swell, and spasm, and panting breath,
And rhythmic rasping of thy sands and waves,
And serpent hiss, and savage peals of laughter,
And undertones of distant lion roar,
(Sounding, appealing to the sky's deaf ear—but now, rapport for once,
A phantom in the night thy confidant for once,)
The first and last confession of the globe,
Outsurging, muttering from thy soul's abysms,
The tale of cosmic elemental passion,
Thou tellest to a kindred soul.

DEATH OF GENERAL GRANT

As one by one withdraw the lofty actors,
From that great play on history's stage eterne,
That lurid, partial act of war and peace—of old and new contending,
Fought out through wrath, fears, dark dismays, and many a long
       suspense;
All past—and since, in countless graves receding, mellowing,
Victor's and vanquish'd—Lincoln's and Lee's—now thou with them,
Man of the mighty days—and equal to the days!
Thou from the prairies!—tangled and many-vein'd and hard has been
       thy part,
To admiration has it been enacted!

RED JACKET (FROM ALOFT)

*(Impromptu on Buffalo City's monument to, and re-burial of the old
Iroquois orator, October 9, 1884)*

Upon this scene, this show,
Yielded to-day by fashion, learning, wealth,
(Not in caprice alone—some grains of deepest meaning,)
Haply, aloft, (who knows?) from distant sky-clouds' blended shapes,
As some old tree, or rock or cliff, thrill'd with its soul,
Product of Nature's sun, stars, earth direct—a towering human form,
In hunting-shirt of film, arm'd with the rifle, a half-ironical smile
      curving its phantom lips,
Like one of Ossian's ghosts looks down.

WASHINGTON'S MONUMENT, FEBRUARY, 1885

Ah, not this marble, dead and cold:
Far from its base and shaft expanding—the round zones circling,
    comprehending,
Thou, Washington, art all the world's, the continents' entire—not yours
    alone, America,
Europe's as well, in every part, castle of lord or laborer's cot,
Or frozen North, or sultry South—the African's—the Arab's in his tent,
Old Asia's there with venerable smile, seated amid her ruins;
(Greets the antique the hero new? 'tis but the same—the heir legiti-
    mate, continued ever,
The indomitable heart and arm—proofs of the never-broken line,
Courage, alertness, patience, faith, the same—e'en in defeat defeated
    not, the same:)
Wherever sails a ship, or house is built on land, or day or night,
Through teeming cities' streets, indoors or out, factories or farms,
Now, or to come, or past—where patriot wills existed or exist,
Wherever Freedom, pois'd by Toleration, sway'd by Law,
Stands or is rising thy true monument.

OF THAT BLITHE THROAT OF THINE

(*More than eighty-three degrees north — about a good day's steaming
distance to the Pole by one of our fast oceaners in clear water — Greely the
explorer heard the song of a single snow-bird merrily sounding over the
desolation.*)

Of that blithe throat of thine from arctic bleak and blank,
I'll mind the lesson, solitary bird—let me too welcome chilling drifts,
E'en the profoundest chill, as now—a torpid pulse, a brain unnerv'd,
Old age land-lock'd within its winter bay—(cold, cold, O cold!)
These snowy hairs, my feeble arm, my frozen feet,
For them thy faith, thy rule I take, and grave it to the last;
Not summer's zones alone—not chants of youth, or south's warm tides
    alone,
But held by sluggish floes, pack'd in the northern ice, the cumulus of
    years,
These with gay heart I also sing.

BROADWAY

What hurrying human tides, or day or night?
What passions, winnings, losses, ardors, swim thy waters!
What whirls of evil, bliss and sorrow, stem thee!
What curious questioning glances—glints of love!

Leer, envy, scorn, contempt, hope, aspiration!
Thou portal—thou arena—thou of the myriad long-drawn lines and
    groups!
(Could but thy flagstones, curbs, façades, tell their inimitable tales;
Thy windows rich, and huge hotels—thy side-walks wide;)
Thou of the endless sliding, mincing, shuffling feet!
Thou, like the parti-colored world itself—like infinite, teeming, mock-
    ing life!
Thou visor'd, vast, unspeakable show and lesson!

TO GET THE FINAL LILT OF SONGS

To get the final lilt of songs,
To penetrate the inmost lore of poets—to know the mighty ones,
Job, Homer, Eschylus, Dante, Shakspere, Tennyson, Emerson;
To diagnose the shifting-delicate tints of love and pride and doubt—
    to truly understand,
To encompass these, the last keen faculty and entrance-price,
Old age, and what it brings from all its past experiences.

OLD SALT KOSSABONE

Far back, related on my mother's side,
Old Salt Kossabone, I'll tell you how he died:
(Had been a sailor all his life—was nearly 90—lived with his married
    grandchild, Jenny;
House on a hill, with view of bay at hand, and distant cape, and stretch
    to open sea;)
The last of afternoons, the evening hours, for many a year his regular
    custom,
In his great arm chair by the window seated,
(Sometimes, indeed, through half the day,)
Watching the coming, going of the vessels, he mutters to himself—
    And now the close of all:
One struggling outbound brig, one day, baffled for long—cross-tides
    and much wrong going,
At last at nightfall strikes the breeze aright, her whole luck veering,
And swiftly bending round the cape, the darkness proudly entering,
    cleaving, as he watches,
"She's free—she's on her destination"—these the last words—when
    Jenny came, he sat there dead,
Dutch Kossabone, Old Salt, related on my mother's side, far back.

THE DEAD TENOR

As down the stage again,
With Spanish hat and plumes, and gait inimitable,
Back from the fading lessons of the past, I'd call, I'd tell and own,

How much from thee! the revelation of the singing voice from thee!
(So firm—so liquid-soft—again that tremulous, manly timbre!
The perfect singing voice—deepest of all to me the lesson—trial and
      test of all:)
How through those strains distill'd—how the rapt ears, the soul of me,
      absorbing
Fernando's heart, *Manrico's* passionate call, *Ernani's*, sweet *Gennaro's*,
I fold thenceforth, or seek to fold, within my chants transmuting,
Freedom's and Love's and Faith's unloos'd cantabile,
(As perfume's, color's, sunlight's correlation:)
From these, for these, with these, a hurried line, dead tenor,
A wafted autumn leaf, dropt in the closing grave, the shovel'd earth,
To memory of thee.

CONTINUITIES

(From a talk I had lately with a German spiritualist)
Nothing is ever really lost, or can be lost,
No birth, identity, form—no object of the world,
Nor life, nor force, nor any visible thing;
Appearance must not foil, nor shifted sphere confuse thy brain,
Ample are time and space—ample the fields of Nature.
The body, sluggish, aged, cold—the embers left from earlier fires,
The light in the eye grown dim, shall duly flame again;
The sun now low in the west rises for mornings and for noons continual;
To frozen clods ever the spring's invisible law returns,
With grass and flowers and summer fruits and corn.

YONNONDIO

(The sense of the word is lament for the aborigines. *It is an Iroquois
term: and has been used for a personal name.)*

A song, a poem of itself—the word itself a dirge,
Amid the wilds, the rocks, the storm and wintry night,
To me such misty, strange tableaux the syllables calling up;
Yonnondio—I see, far in the west or north, a limitless ravine, with
      plains and mountains dark,
I see swarms of stalwart chieftains, medicine-men, and warriors,
As flitting by like clouds of ghosts, they pass and are gone in the
      twilight,
(Race of the woods, the landscapes free, and the falls!
No picture, poem, statement, passing them to the future:)
Yonnondio! Yonnondio!—unlimn'd they disappear;
To-day gives place, and fades—the cities, farms, factories fade;
A muffled sonorous sound, a wailing word is borne through the air for
      a moment,
Then blank and gone and still, and utterly lost.

LIFE

Ever the undiscouraged, resolute, struggling soul of man;
(Have former armies fail'd? then we send fresh armies—and fresh
    again;)
Ever the grappled mystery of all earth's ages old or new;
Ever the eager eyes, hurrahs, the welcome-clapping hands, the loud
    applause;
Ever the soul dissatisfied, curious, unconvinc'd at last;
Struggling to-day the same—battling the same.

"GOING SOMEWHERE"

My science-friend, my noblest woman-friend,
(Now buried in an English grave—and this a memory-leaf for her dear
    sake,)
Ended our talk—"The sum, concluding all we know of old or modern
    learning, intuitions deep,
"Of all Geologies—Histories—of all Astronomy—of Evolution, Meta-
    physics all,
"Is, that we all are onward, onward, speeding slowly, surely bettering,
"Life, life an endless march, an endless army, (no halt, but it is duly
    over,)
"The world, the race, the soul—in space and time the universes,
"All bound as is befitting each—all surely going somewhere."

SMALL THE THEME OF MY CHANT
(From the 1867 edition of "L. of G.")

Small the theme of my Chant, yet the greatest—namely, One's-Self—
    a simple, separate person. That, for the use of the New World,
    I sing.
Man's physiology complete, from top to toe, I sing. Not physiognomy
    alone, nor brain alone, is worthy for the Muse;—I say the Form
    complete is worthier far. The Female equally with the Male,
    I sing.
Nor cease at the theme of One's-Self. I speak the word of the modern,
    the word En-Masse.°
My Days I sing, and the Lands—with interstice° I knew of hapless
    War,
(O friend, whoe'er you are, at last arriving hither to commence, I feel
    through every leaf the pressure of your hand, which I return.
And thus upon our journey, footing the road, and more than once,
    and link'd together let us go.)

TRUE CONQUERORS

Old farmers, travelers, workmen (no matter how crippled or bent,)
Old sailors, out of many a perilous voyage, storm and wreck,
Old soldiers from campaigns, with all their wounds, defeats and scars;
Enough that they've survived at all—long life's unflinching ones!
Forth from their struggles, trials, fights, to have emerged at all—in that
    alone,
True conquerors o'er all the rest.

THE UNITED STATES TO OLD WORLD CRITICS

Here first the duties of to-day, the lessons of the concrete,
Wealth, order, travel, shelter, products, plenty;
As of the building of some varied, vast, perpetual edifice,
Whence to arise inevitable in time, the towering roofs, the lamps,
The solid-planted spires tall shooting to the stars.

THE CALMING THOUGHT OF ALL

That coursing on, whate'er men's speculations,
Amid the changing schools, theologies, philosophies,
Amid the bawling presentations new and old,
The round earth's silent vital laws, facts, modes continue.

THANKS IN OLD AGE

Thanks in old age—thanks ere I go,
For health, the midday sun, the impalpable air—for life, mere life,
For precious ever-lingering memories, (of you my mother dear—you
    father—you, brothers, sisters, friends,)
For all my days—not those of peace alone—the days of war the same,
For gentle words, caresses, gifts from foreign lands,
For shelter, wine and meat—for sweet appreciation,
(You distant, dim unknown—or young or old—countless, unspecified,
    readers belov'd,
We never met, and ne'er shall meet—and yet our souls embrace, long,
    close and long;)
For beings, groups, love, deeds, words, books—for colors, forms,
For all the brave strong men—devoted, hardy men—who've forward
    sprung in freedom's help, all years, all lands,
For braver, stronger, more devoted men—(a special laurel ere I go, to
    life's war's chosen ones,

The cannoneers of song and thought—the great artillerists—the fore-
    most leaders, captains of the soul:)
As soldier from an ended war return'd—As traveler out of myriads, to
    the long procession retrospective,
Thanks—joyful thanks!—a soldier's, traveler's thanks.

LIFE AND DEATH

The two old, simple problems ever intertwined,
Close home, elusive, present, baffled, grappled.
By each successive age insoluble, pass'd on,
To ours to-day—and we pass on the same.

THE VOICE OF THE RAIN

And who art thou? said I to the soft-falling shower,
Which, strange to tell, gave me an answer, as here translated:
I am the Poem of Earth, said the voice of the rain,
Eternal I rise impalpable out of the land and the bottomless sea,
Upward to heaven, whence, vaguely form'd, altogether changed, and
    yet the same,
I descend to lave the drouths, atomies,* dust-layers of the globe,
And all that in them without me were seeds only, latent, unborn;
And forever, by day and night, I give back life to my own origin and
    make pure and beautify it;
(For song, issuing from its birth-place, after fulfilment, wandering,
Reck'd or unreck'd, duly with love returns.)

SOON SHALL THE WINTER'S FOIL BE HERE

Soon shall the winter's foil be here;
Soon shall these icy ligatures unbind and melt—A little while,
And air, soil, wave, suffused shall be in softness, bloom and growth—
    a thousand forms shall rise
From these dead clods and chills as from low burial graves.
Thine eyes, ears—all thy best attributes—all that takes cognizance of
    natural beauty,
Shall wake and fill. Thou shalt perceive the simple shows, the delicate
    miracles of earth,
Dandelions, clover, the emerald grass, the early scents and flowers,
The arbutus under foot, the willow's yellow-green, the blossoming plum
    and cherry;
With these the robin, lark and thrush, singing their songs—the flitting
    bluebird;
For such the scenes the annual play brings on.

WHILE NOT THE PAST FORGETTING
(Publish'd May 30, 1888)

While not the past forgetting,
To-day, at least, contention sunk entire—peace, brotherhood uprisen;
For sign reciprocal our Northern, Southern hands,
Lay on the graves of all dead soldiers, North or South,
(Nor for the past alone—for meanings to the future,)
Wreaths of roses and branches of palm.

THE DYING VETERAN
(A Long Island incident—early part of the nineteenth century)

Amid these days of order, ease, prosperity,
Amid the current songs of beauty, peace, decorum,
I cast a reminiscence—(likely 'twill offend you,
I heard it in my boyhood;)—More than a generation since,
A queer old savage man, a fighter under Washington himself,
(Large, brave, cleanly, hot-blooded, no talker, rather spiritualistic,
Had fought in the ranks—fought well—had been all through the
          Revolutionary war,)
Lay dying—sons, daughters, church-deacons, lovingly tending him,
Sharping their sense, their ears, towards his murmuring, half-caught
          words:
"Let me return again to my war-days,
To the sights and scenes—to forming the line of battle,
To the scouts ahead reconnoitering,
To the cannons, the grim artillery,
To the galloping aids, carrying orders,
To the wounded, the fallen, the heat, the suspense,
The perfume strong, the smoke, the deafening noise;
Away with your life of peace!—your joys of peace!
Give me my old wild battle-life again!"

STRONGER LESSONS

Have you learn'd lessons only of those who admired you, and were
          tender with you, and stood aside for you?
Have you not learn'd great lessons from those who reject you, and brace
          themselves against you? or who treat you with contempt, or
          dispute the passage with you?

A PRAIRIE SUNSET

Shot gold, maroon and violet, dazzling silver, emerald, fawn,
The earth's whole amplitude and Nature's multiform power consign'd
          for once to colors;

The light, the general air possess'd by them—colors till now unknown,
No limit, confine—not the Western sky alone—the high meridian—
    North, South, all,
Pure luminous color fighting the silent shadows to the last.

TWENTY YEARS

Down on the ancient wharf, the sand, I sit, with a new-comer chatting:
He shipp'd as green-hand boy, and sail'd away, (took some sudden,
    vehement notion;)
Since, twenty years and more have circled round and round,
While he the globe was circling round and round,—and now returns:
How changed the place—all the old land-marks gone—the parents
    dead;
(Yes, he comes back *to lay in port for good—to settle*—has a well-fill'd
    purse—no spot will do but this;)
The little boat that scull'd him from the sloop, now held in leash I see,
I hear the slapping waves, the restless keel, the rocking in the sand,
I see the sailor kit, the canvas bag, the great box bound with brass,
I scan the face all berry-brown and bearded—the stout-strong frame,
Dress'd in its russet suit of good Scotch cloth
(Then what the told-out story of those twenty years? What of the
    future?)

ORANGE BUDS BY MAIL FROM FLORIDA

    (*Voltaire closed a famous argument by claiming that a ship of war
and the grand opera were proofs enough of civilization's and France's
progress, in his day.*)

A lesser proof than old Voltaire's, yet greater,
Proof of this present time, and thee, thy broad expanse, America,
To my plain Northern hut, in outside clouds and snow,
Brought safely for a thousand miles o'er land and tide,
Some three days since on their own soil live-sprouting,
Now here their sweetness through my room unfolding,
A bunch of orange buds by mail from Florida.

TWILIGHT

The soft voluptuous opiate shades,
The sun just gone, the eager light dispell'd—(I too will soon be gone,
    dispell'd,)
A haze—nirwana—rest and night—oblivion.

YOU LINGERING SPARSE LEAVES OF ME

You lingering sparse leaves of me on winter-nearing boughs,
And I some well-shorn tree of field or orchard-row;
You tokens diminute° and lorn—(not now the flush of May, or July
    clover-bloom—no grain of August now;)
You pallid banner-staves—you pennants valueless—you overstay'd of
    time,
Yet my soul-dearest leaves confirming all the rest,
The faithfulest—hardiest—last.

NOT MEAGRE, LATENT BOUGHS ALONE

Not meagre, latent boughs alone, O songs! (scaly and bare, like
    eagles' talons,)
But haply for some sunny day (who knows?) some future spring, some
    summer—bursting forth,
To verdant leaves, or sheltering shade—to nourishing fruit,
Apples and grapes—the stalwart limbs of trees emerging—the fresh,
    free, open air,
And love and faith, like scented roses blooming.

THE DEAD EMPEROR
(Publish'd March 10, 1888)

To-day, with bending head and eyes, thou, too, Columbia,
Less for the mighty crown laid low in sorrow—less for the Emperor,
Thy true condolence breathest, sendest out o'er many a salt sea mile,
Mourning a good old man—a faithful shepherd, patriot.

AS THE GREEK'S SIGNAL FLAME
(For Whittier's eightieth birthday, December 17, 1887)

As the Greek's signal flame, by antique records told,
Rose from the hill-top, like applause and glory,
Welcoming in fame some special veteran, hero,
With rosy tinge reddening the land he'd served,
So I aloft from Mannahatta's ship-fringed shore,
Lift high a kindled brand for thee, Old Poet.

THE DISMANTLED SHIP

In some unused lagoon, some nameless bay,
On sluggish, lonesome waters, anchor'd near the shore,
An old, dismasted, gray and batter'd ship, disabled, done,

After free voyages to all the seas of earth, haul'd up at last and
    hawser'd tight,
Lies rusting, mouldering.

NOW PRECEDENT SONGS, FAREWELL

Now precedent songs, farewell—by every name farewell,
(Trains of a staggering line in many a strange procession, waggons,
From ups and downs—with intervals—from elder years, mid-age, or
    youth,)
"In Cabin'd Ships," or "Thee Old Cause" or "Poets to Come"
Or "Paumanok," "Song of Myself," "Calamus," or "Adam,"
Or "Beat! Beat! Drums" or "To the Leaven'd Soil they Trod,"
Or "Captain! My Captain!" "Kosmos," "Quicksand Years," or
    "Thoughts,"
"Thou Mother with thy Equal Brood," and many, many more un-
    specified,
From fibre heart of mine—from throat and tongue—(My life's hot
    pulsing blood,
The personal urge and form for me—not merely paper, automatic type
    and ink,)
Each song of mine—each utterance in the past—having its long, long
    history,
Of life or death, or soldier's wound, of country's loss or safety,
(O heaven! what flash and started endless train of all! compared
    indeed to that!
What wretched shred e'en at the best of all!)

AN EVENING LULL

After a week of physical anguish,
Unrest and pain, and feverish heat,
Toward the ending day a calm and lull comes on,
Three hours of peace and soothing rest of brain.†

OLD AGE'S LAMBENT PEAKS

The touch of flame—the illuminating fire—the loftiest look at last,
O'er city, passion, sea—o'er prairie, mountain, wood—the earth itself;
The airy, different, changing hues of all, in falling twilight,

†The two songs on page 321 ["Now Precedent Songs, Farewell" and "an Evening
Lull"] are eked out during an afternoon, June, 1888, in my seventieth year, at a
critical spell of illness. Of course no reader and probably no human being at any
time will ever have such phases of emotional and solemn action as these involve to
me. I feel in them an end and close of all.

Objects and groups, bearings, faces, reminiscences;
The calmer sight—the golden setting, clear and broad:
So much i' the atmosphere, the points of view, the situations whence
    we scan,
Bro't out by them alone—so much (perhaps the best) unreck'd
    before;
The lights indeed from them—old age's lambent* peaks.

AFTER THE SUPPER AND TALK

After the supper and talk—after the day is done,
As a friend from friends his final withdrawal prolonging,
Good-bye and Good-bye with emotional lips repeating,
(So hard for his hand to release those hands—no more will they meet,
No more for communion of sorrow and joy, of old and young,
A far-stretching journey awaits him, to return no more,)
Shunning, postponing severance—seeking to ward off the last word
    ever so little,
E'en at the exit-door turning—charges superfluous calling back—e'en
    as he descends the steps,
Something to eke out a minute additional—shadows of nightfall
    deepening,
Farewells, messages lessening—dimmer the forthgoer's visage and
    form,
Soon to be lost for aye in the darkness—loth,* O so loth to depart!
Garrulous to the very last.

PREFACE NOTE TO 2d ANNEX
Concluding L. of G.—1891

Had I not better withhold (in this old age and paralysis of me) such little tags and fringe-dots (maybe specks, stains,) as follow a long dusty journey, and witness it afterward? I have probably not been enough afraid of careless touches, from the first—and am not now—nor of parrot-like repetitions—nor platitudes and the commonplace. Perhaps I am too democratic for such avoidances. Besides, is not the verse-field, as originally plann'd by my theory, now sufficiently illustrated—and full time for me to silently retire?—(indeed amid no loud call or market for my sort of poetic utterance).

In answer, or rather defiance, to that kind of well-put interrogation, here comes this little cluster, and conclusion of my preceding clusters. Though not at all clear that, as here collated, it is worth printing (certainly I have nothing fresh to write)—I while away the hours of my 72d year—hours of forced confinement in my den—by putting in shape this small old age collation:

Last droplets of and after spontaneous rain,
From many limpid distillations and past showers;
(Will they germinate anything? mere exhalations as they all are — the land's
    and sea's — America's;
Will they filter to any deep emotion? any heart and brain?)

However that may be, I feel like improving to-day's opportunity and wind up. During the last two years I have sent out, in the lulls of illness and exhaustion, certain chirps—lingering-dying ones probably (undoubtedly)—which now I may as well gather and put in fair type while able to see correctly—(for my eyes plainly warn me they are dimming, and my brain more and more palpably neglects or refuses, month after month, even slight tasks or revisions).

In fact, here I am these current years 1890 and '91, (each successive fortnight getting stiffer and stuck deeper) much like some hard-cased dilapidated grim ancient shell-fish or time-bang'd conch (no legs, utterly non-locomotive) cast up high and dry on the shore-sands, helpless to move anywhere—nothing left but behave myself quiet, and while away the days yet assign'd, and discover if there is anything for the said grim and time-bang'd conch to be got at last out of inherited good spirits and primal buoyant centre-pulses down there deep somewhere within his gray-blurr'd old shell. . . . (Reader, you must allow a little fun here—for one reason there are too many of the following poemets about death, &c., and for another the passing hours (July 5, 1890) are so sunny-fine. And old as I am I feel to-day almost a part of some frolicsome wave, or for sporting yet like a kid or kitten—probably a streak of physical adjustment and perfection here and now. I believe I have it in me perennially anyhow.)

Then behind all, the deep down consolation (it is a glum one, but I dare not be sorry for the fact of it in the past, nor refrain from dwelling, even vaunting here at the end) that this late-years palsied old shorn and shell-fish condition of me is the indubitable outcome and growth, now near for 20 years along, of too over-zealous, over-continued bodily and emotional excitement and action through the times of 1862, '3, '4, and '5, visiting and waiting on wounded and sick army volunteers, both sides, in campaigns or contests, or after them, or in hospitals or fields south of Washington City, or in that place and elsewhere—those hot, sad, wrenching times—the army volunteers, all States—or North or South—the wounded, suffering, dying—the exhausting, sweating summers, marches, battles, carnage—those trenches hurriedly heap'd by the corpse-thousands, mainly unknown—Will the America of the future—will this vast rich Union ever realize what itself cost, back there after all?—those hecatombs of battle-deaths— Those times of which, O faroff reader, this whole book is indeed finally but a reminiscent memorial from thence by me to you?

GOOD-BYE MY FANCY
(Second Annex)

SAIL OUT FOR GOOD, EIDÓLON YACHT!

Heave the anchor short!
Raise main-sail and jib—steer forth,
O little white-hull'd sloop, now speed on really deep waters,
(I will not call it our concluding voyage,
But outset and sure entrance to the truest, best, maturest;)
Depart, depart from solid earth—no more returning to these shores,
Now on for aye our infinite free venture wending,
Spurning all yet tried ports, seas, hawsers, densities, gravitation,
Sail out for good, eidólon° yacht of me!

LINGERING LAST DROPS

And whence and why come you?

We know not whence, (was the answer,)
We only know that we drift here with the rest,
That we linger'd and lagg'd°—but were wafted at last, and are now
    here,
To make the passing shower's concluding drops.

GOOD-BYE MY FANCY

Good-bye† my fancy—(I had a word to say,
But 'tis not quite the time—The best of any man's word or say,
Is when its proper place arrives—and for its meaning,
I keep mine till the last.)

ON, ON THE SAME, YE JOCUND TWAIN!

On, on the same, ye jocund twain!
My life and recitative, containing birth, youth, mid-age years,

† Behind a Good-bye there lurks much of the salutation of another beginning —
to me, Development, Continuity, Immortality, Transformation, are the chiefest
life-meanings of Nature and Humanity, and are the *sine qua non* of all facts, and
each fact.
    Why do folks dwell so fondly on the last words, advice, appearance. of the depart-
ing? Those last words are not samples of the best, which involve vitality at its full,
and balance, and perfect control and scope. But they are valuable beyond measure
to confirm and endorse the varied train, facts, theories and faith of the whole preceding
life.

Fitful as motley-tongues of flame, inseparably twined and merged in
one—combining all,
My single soul—aims, confirmations, failures, joys—Nor single soul
alone,
I chant my nation's crucial stage, (America's, haply humanity's)—the
trial great, the victory great,
A strange *éclaircissement** of all the masses past, the eastern world,
the ancient, medieval,
Here, here from wanderings, strayings, lessons, wars, defeats—here at
the west a voice triumphant—justifying all,
A gladsome pealing cry—a song for once of utmost pride and satis-
faction;
I chant from it the common bulk, the general average horde, (the
best no sooner than the worst)—And now I chant old age,
(My verses, written first for forenoon life, and for the summer's, au-
tumn's spread,
I pass to snow-white hairs the same, and give to pulses winter-cool'd
the same;)
As here in careless trill, I and my recitatives, with faith and love,
Wafting to other work, to unknown songs, conditions,
On, on, ye jocund twain! continue on the same!

MY 71ST YEAR

After surmounting three-score and ten,
With all their chances, changes, losses, sorrows,
My parents' deaths, the vagaries of my life, the many tearing passions
of me, the war of '63 and '4,
As some old broken soldier, after a long, hot, wearying march, or haply
after battle,
To-day at twilight, hobbling, answering company roll-call, *Here,* with
vital voice,
Reporting yet, saluting yet the Officer over all.

APPARITIONS

A vague mist hanging 'round half the pages:
(Sometimes how strange and clear to the soul,
That all these solid things are indeed but apparitions, concepts, non-
realities.)

THE PALLID WREATH

Somehow I cannot let it go yet, funeral though it is,
Let it remain back there on its nail suspended,
With pink, blue, yellow, all blanch'd, and the white now gray and
ashy,

One wither'd rose put years ago for thee, dear friend;
But I do not forget thee. Hast thou then faded?
Is the odor exhaled? Are the colors, vitalities, dead?
No, while memories subtly play—the past vivid as ever;
For but last night I woke, and in that spectral ring saw thee,
Thy smile, eyes, face, calm, silent, loving as ever;
So let the wreath hang still awhile within my eye-reach,
It is not yet dead to me, nor even pallid.

AN ENDED DAY

The soothing sanity and blitheness of completion,
The pomp and hurried contest-glare and rush are done;
Now triumph! transformation! jubilate! †

OLD AGE'S SHIP & CRAFTY DEATH'S

From east and west across the horizon's edge,
Two mighty masterful vessels sailers steal upon us:
But we'll make race a-time upon the sea—a battle-contest yet! bear
        lively there!
(Our joys of strife and derring-do to the last!)
Put on the old ship all her power to-day!
Crowd top-sail, top-gallant and royal studding-sails,

† Note. — *Summer country life.* — *Several years.* — In my rambles and explorations I found a woody place near the creek, where for some reason the birds in happy mood seem'd to resort in unusual numbers. Especially at the beginning of the day, and again at the ending, I was sure to get there the most copious bird-concerts. I repair'd there frequently at sunrise — and also at sunset, or just before. . . . Once the question arose in me: Which is the best singing, the first or the lattermost? The first always exhilarated, and perhaps seem'd more joyous and stronger; but I always felt the sunset or late afternoon sounds more penetrating and sweeter — seem'd to touch the soul — often the evening thrushes, two or three of them, responding and perhaps blending. Though I miss'd some of the mornings, I found myself getting to be quite strictly punctual at the evening utterances.

Another Note. — "He went out with the tide and the sunset," was a phrase I heard from a surgeon describing an old sailor's death under peculiarly gentle conditions.

During the Secession War, 1863 and '4, visiting the Army Hospitals around Washington, I form'd the habit, and continued it to the end, whenever the ebb or flood tide began the latter part of the day, of punctually visiting those at that time populous wards of suffering men. Somehow (or I thought so) the effect of the hour was palpable. The badly wounded would get some ease, and would like to talk a little, or be talk'd to. Intellectual and emotional natures would be at their best: Deaths were always easier; medicines seem'd to have better effect when given then, and a lulling atmosphere would pervade the wards.

Similar influences, similar circumstances and hours, day-close, after great battles, even with all their horrors. I had more than once the same experience on the fields cover'd with fallen or dead.

Out challenge and defiance—flags and flaunting pennants added,
As we take to the open! take to the deepest, freest waters.

TO THE PENDING YEAR

Have I no weapon-word for thee—some message brief and fierce?
(Have I fought out and done indeed the battle?) Is there no shot left,
For all thy affectations, lisps, scorns, manifold silliness?
Not for myself—my own rebellious self in thee?

Down, down, proud gorge!—though choking thee;
Thy bearded throat and high-borne forehead to the gutter;
Crouch low thy neck to eleemosynary gifts.

SHAKSPERE-BACON'S CIPHER

I doubt it not—then more, far more;
In each old song bequeath'd—in every noble page or text,
(Different—something unreck'd before—some unsuspected author,)
In every object, mountain, tree, and star—in every birth and life,
As part of each—evolv'd from each—meaning, behind the ostent,°
A mystic cipher waits infolded.

LONG, LONG HENCE

After a long, long course, hundreds of years, denials,
Accumulations, rous'd love and joy and thought,
Hopes, wishes, aspirations, ponderings, victories, myriads of readers,
Coating, compassing, covering—after ages' and ages' encrustations,
Then only may these songs reach fruition.

BRAVO, PARIS EXPOSITION!

Add to your show, before you close it, France,
With all the rest, visible, concrete, temples, towers, goods, machines
    and ores,
Our sentiment wafted from many million heart-throbs, ethereal but
    solid,
(We grand-sons and great-grand-sons do not forget your grand-sires,)
From fifty Nations and nebulous Nations, compacted, sent oversea
    to-day,
America's applause, love, memories and good-will.

INTERPOLATION SOUNDS

(*General Philip Sheridan was buried at the Cathedral, Washington, D. C., August, 1888, with all the pomp, music, and ceremonies of the Roman Catholic service.*)

Over and through the burial chant,
Organ and solemn service, sermon, bending priests,
To me come interpolation sounds not in the show—plainly to me,
    crowding up the aisle and from the window,
Of sudden battle's hurry and harsh noises—war's grim game to sight
    and ear in earnest;
The scout call'd up and forward—the general mounted and his aids
    around him—the new-brought word—the instantaneous order
    issued;
The rifle crack—the cannon thud—the rushing forth of men from their
    tents;
The clank of cavalry—the strange celerity of forming ranks—the
    slender bugle note;
The sound of horses' hoofs departing—saddles, arms, accoutrements.†

TO THE SUN-SET BREEZE

Ah, whispering, something again, unseen,
Where late this heated day thou enterest at my window, door,
Thou, laving, tempering all, cool-freshing, gently vitalizing
Me, old, alone, sick, weak-down, melted-worn with sweat;
Thou, nestling, folding close and firm yet soft, companion better than
    talk, book, art,
(Thou hast, O Nature! elements! utterance to my heart beyond the
    rest—and this is of them,)
So sweet thy primitive taste to breathe within—thy soothing fingers
    on my face and hands,

† Note. — Camden, N. J., August 7, 1888. — Walt Whitman asks the *New York Herald* "to add his tribute to Sheridan":

"In the grand constellation of five or six names, under Lincoln's Presidency, that history will bear for ages in her firmament as marking the last life-throbs of secession, and beaming on its dying gasps, Sheridan's will be bright. One consideration rising out of the now dead soldier's example as it passes my mind, is worth taking notice of. If the war had continued any long time these States, in my opinion, would have shown and proved the most conclusive military talents ever evinced by any nation on earth. That they possess'd a rank and file ahead of all other known in points of quality and limitlessness of number are easily admitted. But we have, too, the eligibility of organizing, handling and officering equal to the other. These two, with modern arms, transportation, and inventive American genius, would make the United States, with earnestness, not only able to stand the whole world, but conquer that world united against us."

Thou, messenger-magical strange bringer to body and spirit of me,
(Distances balk'd—occult medicines penetrating me from head to
    foot,)
I feel the sky, the prairies vast—I feel the mighty northern lakes,
I feel the ocean and the forest—somehow I feel the globe itself swift-
    swimming in space;
Thou blown from lips so loved, now gone—haply from endless store,
    God-sent,
(For thou art spiritual, Godly, most of all known to my sense,)
Minister to speak to me, here and now, what word has never told, and
    cannot tell,
Art thou not universal concrete's distillation? Law's, all Astronomy's
    last refinement?
Hast thou no soul? Can I not know, identify thee?

OLD CHANTS

An ancient song, reciting, ending,
Once gazing toward thee, Mother of All,
Musing, seeking themes fitted for thee,
Accept for me, thou saidst, *the elder ballads,*
And name for me before thou goest each ancient poet.

(Of many debts incalculable,
Haply our New World's chieftest debt is to old poems.)

Ever so far back, preluding thee, America,
Old chants, Egyptian priests, and those of Ethiopia,
The Hindu epics, the Grecian, Chinese, Persian,
The Biblic books and prophets, and deep idyls of the Nazarene,
The Iliad, Odyssey, plots, doings, wanderings of Eneas,
Hesiod, Eschylus, Sophocles, Merlin, Arthur,
The Cid, Roland at Roncesvalles, the Nibelungen,
The troubadours, minstrels, minnesingers, skalds,
Chaucer, Dante, flocks of singing birds,
The Border Minstrelsy, the bye-gone ballads, feudal tales, essays,
    plays,
Shakspere, Schiller, Walter Scott, Tennyson,
As some vast wondrous weird dream-presences,
The great shadowy groups gathering around,
Darting their mighty masterful eyes forward at thee,
Thou! with as now thy bending neck and head, with courteous hand
    and word, ascending,
Thou! pausing a moment, drooping thine eyes upon them, blent with
    their music,
Well pleased, accepting all, curiously prepared for by them,
Thou enterest at thy entrance porch.

A CHRISTMAS GREETING

(From a Northern Star-Group to a Southern, 1889-90)

Welcome, Brazilian brother—thy ample place is ready;
A loving hand—a smile from the north—a sunny instant hail!
(Let the future care for itself, where it reveals its troubles, impedimentas,
Ours, ours the present throe, the democratic aim, the acceptance and the faith;)
To thee to-day our reaching arm, our turning neck—to thee from us the expectant eye,
Thou cluster free! thou brilliant lustrous one! thou, learning well,
The true lesson of a nation's light in the sky,
(More shining than the Cross, more than the Crown,)
The height to be superb humanity.

SOUNDS OF THE WINTER

Sounds of the winter too,
Sunshine upon the mountains—many a distant strain
From cheery railroad train—from nearer field, barn, house,
The whispering air—even the mute crops, garner'd apples, corn,
Children's and women's tones—rhythm of many a farmer and of flail,
An old man's garrulous lips among the rest, *Think not we give out yet,*
Forth from these snowy hairs we keep up yet the lilt.

A TWILIGHT SONG

As I sit in twilight late alone by the flickering oak-flame,
Musing on long-pass'd war scenes—of the countless buried unknown soldiers,
Of the vacant names, as unindented air's and sea's—the unreturn'd,
The brief truce after battle, with grim burial-squads, and the deep-fill'd trenches
Of gather'd dead from all America, North, South, East, West, whence they came up,
From wooded Maine, New-England's farms, from fertile Pennsylvania, Illinois, Ohio,
From the measureless West, Virginia, the South, the Carolinas, Texas,
(Even here in my room-shadows and half-lights in the noiseless flickering flames,
Again I see the stalwart ranks on-filing, rising—I hear the rhythmic tramp of the armies;)
You million unwrit names all, all—you dark bequest from all the war,

A special verse for you—a flash of duty long neglected—your mystic
    roll strangely gather'd here,
Each name recall'd by me from out the darkness and death's ashes,
Henceforth to be, deep, deep within my heart recording, for many a
    future year,
Your mystic roll entire of unknown names, or North or South,
Embalm'd with love in this twilight song.

WHEN THE FULL-GROWN POET CAME

When the full-grown poet came,
Out spake pleased Nature (the round impassive globe, with all its
    shows of day and night,) saying, *He is mine;*
But out spake too the Soul of man, proud, jealous and unreconciled,
    Nay, he is mine alone;
—Then the full-grown poet stood between the two, and took each by
    the hand;
And to-day and ever so stands, as blender, uniter, tightly holding
    hands,
Which he will never release until he reconciles the two,
And wholly and joyously blends them.

OSCEOLA

*(When I was nearly grown to manhood in Brooklyn, New York (middle
of 1838), I met one of the return'd U. S. Marines from Fort Moultrie,
S. C., and had long talks with him — learn'd the occurrence below described
— death of Osceola. The latter was a young, brave, leading Seminole,
in the Florida war of that time — was surrender'd to our troops, imprison'd,
and literally died of "a broken heart," at Fort Moultrie. He sicken'd of his
confinement — the doctor and officers made every allowance and kindness
possible for him; then the close.)*

When his hour for death had come,
He slowly rais'd himself from the bed on the floor,
Drew on his war-dress, shirt, leggings, and girdled the belt around his
    waist,
Call'd for vermilion paint (his looking-glass was held before him,)
Painted half his face and neck, his wrists, and back-hands,
Put the scalp-knife carefully in his belt—then lying down, resting a
    moment,
Rose again, half sitting, smiled, gave in silence his extended hand to
    each and all,
Sank faintly low to the floor (tightly grasping the tomahawk handle,)
Fix'd his look on wife and little children—the last:
(And here a line in memory of his name and death.)

A VOICE FROM DEATH
(The Johnstown, Penn., cataclysm, May 31, 1889)

A voice from Death, solemn and strange, in all his sweep and power,
With sudden, indescribable blow—towns drown'd—humanity by
    thousands slain,
The vaunted work of thrift, goods, dwellings, forge, street, iron bridge,
Dash'd pell-mell by the blow—yet usher'd life continuing on,
(Amid the rest, amid the rushing, whirling, wild debris,
A suffering woman saved—a baby safely born!)

Although I come and unannounc'd, in horror and in pang,
In pouring flood and fire, and wholesale elemental crash, (this voice
    so solemn, strange,)
I too a minister of Deity.

Yea, Death, we bow our faces, veil our eyes to thee,
We mourn the old, the young untimely drawn to thee,
The fair, the strong, the good, the capable,
The household wreck'd, the husband and the wife, the engulf'd forger
    in his forge,
The corpses in the whelming waters and the mud,
The gather'd thousands to their funeral mounds, and thousands never
    found or gather'd.

Then after burying, mourning the dead,
(Faithful to them found or unfound, forgetting not, bearing the past,
    here new musing,)
A day—a passing moment or an hour—America itself bends low,
Silent, resign'd, submissive.

War, death, cataclysm like this, America,
Take deep to thy proud prosperous heart.

E'en as I chant, lo! out of death, and out of ooze and slime,
The blossoms rapidly blooming, sympathy, help, love,
From West and East, from South and North and over sea,
Its hot-spurr'd hearts and hands humanity to human aid moves on;
And from within a thought and lesson yet.

Thou ever-darting Globe! through Space and Air!
Thou waters that encompass us!
Thou that in all the life and death of us, in action or in sleep!
Thou laws invisible that permeate them and all,
Thou that in all, and over all, and through and under all, incessant!

Thou! thou! the vital, universal, giant force resistless, sleepless, calm,
Holding Humanity as in thy open hand, as some ephemeral toy,
How ill to e'er forget thee!

For I too have forgotten,
(Wrapt in these little potencies of progress, politics, culture, wealth,
      inventions, civilization,)
Have lost my recognition of your silent ever-swaying power, ye
      mighty, elemental throes,
In which and upon which we float, and every one of us is buoy'd.

A PERSIAN LESSON

For his o'erarching and last lesson the greybeard sufi,*
In the fresh scent of the morning in the open air,
On the slope of a teeming Persian rose-garden,
Under an ancient chestnut-tree wide spreading its branches,
Spoke to the young priests and students.

"Finally my children, to envelop each word, each part of the rest,
Allah is all, all, all—is immanent in every life and object,
May-be at many and many-a-more removes—yet Allah, Allah, Allah
      is there.

"Has the estray* wander'd far? Is the reason-why strangely hidden?
Would you sound below the restless ocean of the entire world?
Would you know the dissatisfaction? the urge and spur of every life;
The something never still'd—never entirely gone? the invisible need
      of every seed?

"It is the central urge in every atom,
(Often unconscious, often evil, downfallen,)
To return to its divine source and origin, however distant,
Latent the same in subject and in object, without one exception."

THE COMMONPLACE

The commonplace I sing;
How cheap is health! how cheap nobility!
Abstinence, no falsehood, no gluttony, lust;
The open air I sing, freedom, toleration,
(Take here the mainest lesson—less from books—less from the
      schools,)
The common day and night—the common earth and waters,
Your farm—your work, trade, occupation,
The democratic wisdom underneath, like solid ground for all.

"THE ROUNDED CATALOGUE DIVINE COMPLETE"

(*Sunday ——— — ———. — Went this forenoon to church. A college professor, Rev. Dr. ———, gave us a fine sermon, during which I caught the above words; but the minister included in his "rounded catalogue" letter and spirit, only the esthetic things, and entirely ignored what I name in the following:*)

The devilish and the dark, the dying and diseas'd,
The countless (nineteen-twentieths) low and evil, crude and savage,
The crazed prisoners in jail, the horrible, rank, malignant,
Venom and filth, serpents, the ravenous sharks, liars, the dissolute;
(What is the part the wicked and the loathsome bear within earth's
orbic scheme?)
Newts, crawling things in slime and mud, poisons,
The barren soil, the evil men, the slag and hideous rot.

MIRAGES

(*Noted verbatim after a supper-talk out doors in Nevada with two old
miners*)

More experiences and sights, stranger, than you'd think for;
Times again, now mostly just after sunrise or before sunset,
Sometimes in spring, oftener in autumn, perfectly clear weather, in
plain sight,
Camps far or near, the crowded streets of cities and the shop-fronts,
(Account for it or not—credit or not—it is all true,
And my mate there could tell you the like—we have often confab'd
about it,)
People and scenes, animals, trees, colors and lines, plain as could be,
Farms and dooryards of home, paths border'd with box, lilacs in
corners,
Weddings in churches, thanksgiving dinners, returns of long-absent
sons,
Glum funerals, the crape-veil'd mother and the daughters,
Trials in courts, jury and judge, the accused in the box,
Contestants, battles, crowds, bridges, wharves,
Now and then mark'd faces of sorrow or joy,
(I could pick them out this moment if I saw them again,)
Show'd to me just aloft to the right in the sky-edge,
Or plainly there to the left on the hill-tops.

L. OF G.'S PURPORT

Not to exclude or demarcate, or pick out evils from their formidable
masses (even to expose them,)
But add, fuse, complete, extend—and celebrate the immortal and the
good.

Haughty this song, its words and scope,
To span vast realms of space and time,
Evolution—the cumulative—growths and generations.

Begun in ripen'd youth and steadily pursued,
Wandering, peering, dallying with all—war, peace, day and night
      absorbing,
Never even for one brief hour abandoning my task,
I end it here in sickness, poverty, and old age.

I sing of life, yet mind me well of death:
To-day shadowy Death dogs my steps, my seated shape, and has for
      years—
Draws sometimes close to me, as face to face.

THE UNEXPRESS'D

How dare one say it?
After the cycles, poems, singers, plays,
Vaunted Ionia's, India's—Homer, Shakspere—the long, long times,
      thick dotted roads, areas,
The shining clusters and the Milky Ways of stars—Nature's pulses
      reap'd,
All retrospective passions, heroes, war, love, adoration,
All ages' plummets dropt to their utmost depths,
All human lives, throats, wishes, brains—all experiences' utterance;
After the countless songs, or long or short, all tongues, all lands,
Still something not yet told in poesy's voice or print—something lack-
      ing,
(Who knows? the best yet unexpress'd and lacking.)

GRAND IS THE SEEN

Grand is the seen, the light, to me—grand are the sky and stars,
Grand is the earth, and grand are lasting time and space,
And grand their laws, so multiform, puzzling, evolutionary;
But grander far the unseen soul of me, comprehending, endowing all
      those,
Lighting the light, the sky and stars, delving the earth, sailing the sea,
(What were all those, indeed, without thee, unseen soul? of what
      amount without thee?)
More evolutionary, vast, puzzling, O my soul!
More multiform far—more lasting thou than they.

UNSEEN BUDS

Unseen buds, infinite, hidden well,
Under the snow and ice, under the darkness, in every square or cubic
    inch,
Germinal, exquisite, in delicate lace, microscopic, unborn,
Like babes in wombs, latent, folded, compact, sleeping;
Billions of billions, and trillions of trillions of them waiting,
(On earth and in the sea—the universe—the stars there in the heavens,)
Urging slowly, surely forward, forming endless,
And waiting ever more, forever more behind.

GOOD-BYE MY FANCY!

Good-bye my Fancy!
Farewell dear mate, dear love!
I'm going away, I know not where,
Or to what fortune, or whether I may ever see you again,
So Good-bye my Fancy.

Now for my last—let me look back a moment;
The slower fainter ticking of the clock is in me,
Exit, nightfall, and soon the heart-thud stopping.

Long have we lived, joy'd, caress'd together;
Delightful!—now separation—Good-bye my Fancy,

Yet let me not be too hasty,
Long indeed have we lived, slept, filter'd, become really blended into
    one;
Then if we die we die together, (yes, we'll remain one,)
If we go anywhere we'll go together to meet what happens,
May-be we'll be better off and blither, and learn something,
May-be it is yourself now really ushering me to the true songs, (who
    knows?)
May-be it is you the mortal knob really undoing, turning—so now
    finally,
Good-bye—and hail! my Fancy.

AN EXECUTOR'S DIARY NOTE, 1891

[To Old Age Echoes]

I said to W. W. today: "Though you have put the finishing touches on the *Leaves*, closed them with your good-by, you will go on living a year or two longer and writing more poems. The question is, what will you do with these poems when the time comes to fix their place in the volume?" "Do with them? I am not unprepared—I have even contemplated that emergency—I have a title in reserve: Old Age Echoes—applying not so much to things as to echoes of things, reverberant, an aftermath." "You have dropt enough by the roadside, as you went along, from different editions, to make a volume. Some day the world will demand to have that put together somewhere." "Do you think it?" "Certainly. Should you put it under ban?" "Why should I—how could I? So far as you may have anything to do with it I place upon you the injunction that whatever may be added to the *Leaves* shall be supplementary, avowed as such, leaving the book complete as I left it, consecutive to the point I left off, marking always an unmistakable, deep down, unobliterable division line. In the long run the world will do as it pleases with the book. I am determined to have the world know what I was pleased to do."

Here is a late personal note from W. W.: "My tho't is to collect a lot of prose and poetry pieces—small or smallish mostly, but a few larger —appealing to the good will, the heart—sorrowful ones not rejected— but no morbid ones given."

There is no reason for doubt that "A Thought of Columbus," closing "Old Age Echoes," was W. W.'s last deliberate composition, dating December, 1891.

OLD AGE ECHOES

(*Posthumous Additions*)

TO SOAR IN FREEDOM AND IN FULLNESS OF POWER

I have not so much emulated the birds that musically sing,
I have abandon'd myself to flights, broad circles,
The hawk, the seagull, have far more possess'd me than the canary or
      mocking-bird,
I have not felt to warble and trill, however sweetly,
I have felt to soar in freedom and in the fullness of power, joy, volition.

THEN SHALL PERCEIVE

In softness, languor, bloom, and growth,
Thine eyes, ears, all thy sense—thy loftiest attribute—all that takes
      cognizance of beauty,
Shall rouse and fill—then shall perceive!

THE FEW DROPS KNOWN

Of heroes, history, grand events, premises, myths, poems,
The few drops known must stand for oceans of the unknown,
On this beautiful and thick peopl'd earth, here and there a little
      specimen put on record,
A little of Greeks and Romans, a few Hebrew canticles, a few death
      odors as from graves, from Egypt—
What are they to the long and copious retrospect of antiquity?

ONE THOUGHT EVER AT THE FORE

One thought ever at the fore—
That in the Divine Ship, the World, breasting Time and Space,
All Peoples of the globe together sail, sail the same voyage, are bound
      to the same destination.

WHILE BEHIND ALL FIRM AND ERECT

While behind all, firm and erect as ever,
Undismay'd amid the rapids—amid the irresistible and deadly urge,
Stands a helmsman, with brow elate* and strong hand.

A KISS TO THE BRIDE
Marriage of Nelly Grant, May 21, 1874

Sacred, blithesome, undenied,
With benisons from East and West,
And salutations North and South,
Through me indeed to-day a million hearts and hands,
Wafting a million loves, a million soulfelt prayers;
—Tender and true remain the arm that shields thee!
Fair winds always fill the ship's sails that sail thee!
Clear sun by day, and light stars at night, beam on thee!
Dear girl—through me the ancient privilege too,
For the New World, through me, the old, old wedding greeting:
O youth and health! O sweet Missouri rose! O bonny bride!
Yield thy red cheeks, thy lips, to-day,
Unto a Nation's loving kiss.

NAY, TELL ME NOT TO-DAY THE PUBLISH'D SHAME
Winter of 1873, Congress in Session

Nay, tell me not to-day the publish'd shame,
Read not to-day the journal's crowded page,
The merciless reports still branding forehead after forehead,
The guilty column following guilty column.

To-day to me the tale refusing,
Turning from it—from the white capitol turning,
Far from these swelling domes, topt with statues,
More endless, jubilant, vital visions rise
Unpublish'd, unreported.

Through all your quiet ways, or North or South, you Equal States,
     you honest farms,
Your million untold manly healthy lives, or East or West, city or
     country,
Your noiseless mothers, sisters, wives, unconscious of their good,
Your mass of homes nor poor nor rich, in visions rise—(even your
     excelient poverties,)
Your self-distilling, never-ceasing virtues, self-denials, graces,
Your endless base of deep integrities within, timid but certain,
Your blessings steadily bestow'd, sure as the light, and still,
(Plunging to these as a determin'd diver down the deep hidden
     waters,)
These, these to-day I brood upon—all else refusing, these will I con,
To-day to these give audience.

SUPPLEMENT HOURS

Sane, random, negligent hours,
Sane, easy, culminating hours,
After the flush, the Indian summer, of my life,
Away from Books—away from Art—the lesson learn'd, pass'd o'er,
Soothing, bathing, merging all—the sane, magnetic,
Now for the day and night themselves—the open air,
Now for the fields, the seasons, insects, trees—the rain and snow,
Where wild bees flitting hum,
Or August mulleins grow, or winter's snowflakes fall,
Or stars in the skies roll round—
The silent sun and stars.

OF MANY A SMUTCH'D DEED REMINISCENT

Full of wickedness, I—of many a smutch'd deed reminiscent—of worse
    deeds capable,
Yet I look composedly upon nature, drink day and night the joys of
    life, and await death with perfect equanimity,
Because of my tender and boundless love for him I love and because
    of his boundless love for me.

TO BE AT ALL
(Cf. Stanza 27, "Song of Myself")

To be at all—what is better than that?
I think if there were nothing more developed, the clam in its callous
    shell in the sand were august enough.
I am not in any callous shell;
I am cased with supple conductors, all over,
They take every object by the hand, and lead it within me;
They are thousands, each one with his entry to himself;
They are always watching with their little eyes, from my head to my
    feet;
One no more than a point lets in and out of me such bliss and magni-
    tude,
I think I could lift the girder of the house away if it lay between me
    and whatever I wanted.

DEATH'S VALLEY
To accompany a picture; by request. "The Valley of the Shadow of
Death," from the painting by George Inness.

Nay, do not dream, designer dark,
Thou hast portray'd or hit thy theme entire;

I, hoverer of late by this dark valley, by its confines, having glimpses
      of it,
Here enter lists with thee, claiming my right to make a symbol too.
For I have seen many wounded soldiers die,
After dread suffering—have seen their lives pass off with smiles;
And I have watch'd the death-hours of the old; and seen the infant
      die;
The rich, with all his nurses and his doctors;
And then the poor, in meagerness and poverty;
And I myself for long, O Death, have breath'd my every breath
Amid the nearness and the silent thought of thee.

And out of these and thee,
I make a scene, a song (not fear of thee,
Nor gloom's ravines, nor bleak, nor dark—for I do not fear thee,
Nor celebrate the struggle, or contortion, or hard-tied knot,)
Of the broad blessed light and perfect air, with meadows, rippling
      tides, and trees and flowers and grass,
And the low hum of living breeze—and in the midst God's beautiful
      eternal right hand,
Thee, holiest minister of Heaven—thee, envoy, usherer, guide at last
      of all,
Rich, florid, loosener of the stricture-knot call'd life,
Sweet, peaceful, welcome Death.

ON THE SAME PICTURE
Intended for first stanza of "Death's Valley"

Aye, well I know 'tis ghastly to descend that valley:
Preachers, musicians, poets, painters, always render it,
Philosophs exploit—the battlefield, the ship at sea, the myriad beds,
      all lands,
All, all the past have enter'd, the ancientest humanity we know,
Syria's, India's, Egypt's, Greece's, Rome's;
Till now for us under our very eyes spreading the same to-day,
Grim, ready, the same to-day, for entrance, yours and mine,
Here, here 'tis limn'd.

A THOUGHT OF COLUMBUS

The mystery of mysteries, the crude and hurried ceaseless flame,
      spontaneous, bearing on itself.
The bubble and the huge, round, concrete orb!
A breath of Deity, as thence the bulging universe unfolding!
The many issuing cycles from their precedent minute!
The eras of the soul incepting in an hour,
Haply the widest, farthest evolutions of the world and man.

Thousands and thousands of miles hence, and now four centuries back,
A mortal impulse thrilling its brain cell,
Reck'd or unreck'd, the birth can no longer be postpon'd:
A phantom of the moment, mystic, stalking, sudden,
Only a silent thought, yet toppling down of more than walls of brass
    or stone.
(A flutter at the darkness' edge as if old Time's and Space's secret
    near revealing.)
A thought! a definite thought works out in shape.
Four hundred years roll on.
The rapid cumulus—trade, navigation, war, peace, democracy, roll on;
The restless armies and the fleets of time following their leader—the
    old camps of ages pitch'd in newer, larger areas,
The tangl'd, long-deferr'd éclaircissement* of human life and hopes
    boldly begins untying,
As here to-day up-grows the Western World.

(An added word yet to my song, far Discoverer, as ne'er before sent
    back to son of earth—
If still thou hearest, hear me,
Voicing as now—lands, races, arts, bravas to thee,
O'er the long backward path to thee—one vast consensus north, south,
    east, west,
Soul plaudits! acclamation! reverent echoes!
One manifold, huge memory to thee! oceans and lands!
The modern world to thee and thought of thee!)

REJECTED POEMS

GREAT ARE THE MYTHS
1855-1876 †

1

Great are the myths — I too delight in them;
Great are Adam and Eve — I too look back and accept them;
Great the risen and fallen nations, and their poets, women, sages, inventors,
    rulers, warriors, and priests.

Great is Liberty! great is Equality! I am their follower;
Helmsmen of nations, choose your craft! where you sail, I sail,
I weather it out with you, or sink with you.

Great is Youth — equally great is Old Age — great are the Day and Night;
Great is Wealth — great is Poverty — great is Expression — great is Silence.

Youth, large, lusty, loving — Youth, full of grace, force, fascination!
Do you know that Old Age may come after you, with equal grace, force,
    fascination?

Day, full-blown and splendid — Day of the immense sun, action, ambition,
    laughter,
The Night follows close, with millions of suns, and sleep, and restoring
    darkness.

Wealth, with the flush hand, fine clothes, hospitality;
But then the Soul's wealth, which is candor, knowledge, pride, enfolding
    love;
(Who goes for men and women showing Poverty richer than wealth?)

Expression of speech! in what is written or said, forget not that Silence is
    also expressive,
That anguish as hot as the hottest, and contempt as cold as the coldest, may
    be without words.

† Following the titles in this section are dates of first and last appearances of
poems in *Leaves of Grass.* — Ed. Note.

2

Great is the Earth, and the way it became what it is;
Do you imagine it has stopt at this? the increase abandon'd?
Understand then that it goes as far onward from this, as this is from the
    times when it lay in covering waters and gases, before man had
    appear'd.

Great is the quality of Truth in man;
The quality of truth in man supports itself through all changes,
It is inevitably in the man — he and it are in love, and never leave each
    other.

The truth in man is no dictum, it is vital as eyesight;
If there be any Soul, there is truth — if there be man or woman there is
    truth — if there be physical or moral, there is truth;
If there be equilibrium or volition, there is truth — if there be things at all
    upon the earth, there is truth.

O truth of the earth! I am determin'd to press my way toward you;
Sound your voice! I scale mountains, or dive in the sea after you.

3

Great is Language — it is the mightiest of the sciences,
It is the fulness, color, form, diversity of the earth, and of men and women,
    and of all qualities and processes;
It is greater than wealth — it is greater than buildings, ships, religions,
    paintings, music.

Great is the English speech — what speech is so great as the English?
Great is the English brood — what brood has so vast a destiny as the English?
It is the mother of the brood that must rule the earth with the new rule;
The new rule shall rule as the Soul rules, and as the love, justice, equality
    in the Soul rule.

Great is Law — great are the few old land-marks of the law,
They are the same in all times, and shall not be disturb'd.

4

Great is Justice!
Justice is not settled by legislators and laws — it is in the Soul;
It cannot be varied by statutes, any more than love, pride, the attraction
    of gravity, can;
It is immutable — it does not depend on majorities — majorities or what
    not, come at last before the same passionless and exact tribunal.

For justice are the grand natural lawyers, and perfect judges — it is in
    their Souls;
It is well assorted — they have not studied for nothing — the great includes
    the less;
They rule on the highest grounds — they oversee all eras, states, adminis-
    trations.

The perfect judge fears nothing — he could go front to front before God;
Before the perfect judge all shall stand back — life and death shall stand
    back — heaven and hell shall stand back.

5

Great is Life, real and mystical, wherever and whoever;
Great is Death — sure as life holds all parts together, Death holds all parts
    together.

Has Life much purport? — Ah, Death has the greatest purport.

POEM OF REMEMBRANCE FOR A GIRL OR A BOY OF THESE STATES
1856-1860

You just maturing youth! You male or female!
Remember the organic compact of These States,
Remember the pledge of the Old Thirteen thenceforward to the rights,
    life, liberty, equality of man,
Remember what was promulged by the founders, ratified by The States,
    signed in black and white by the Commissioners, and read by Wash-
    ington at the head of the army,
Remember the purposes of the founders, — Remember Washington;
Remember the copious humanity streaming from every direction toward
    America;
Remember the hospitality that belongs to nations and men; (Cursed be
    nation, woman, man, without hospitality!)
Remember, government is to subserve individuals,
Not any, not the President, is to have one jot more than you or me,
Not any habitan of America is to have one jot less than you or me.

Anticipate when the thirty or fifty millions, are to become the hundred
    or two hundred millions, of equal freemen and freewomen, amicably
    joined.

Recall ages — One age is but a part — ages are but a part;
Recall the angers, bickerings, delusions, superstitions, of the idea of caste,
Recall the bloody cruelties and crimes.

Anticipate the best women;
I say an unnumbered new race of hardy and well-defined women are to
    spread through all These States,
I say a girl fit for These States must be free, capable, dauntless, just the
    same as a boy.

Anticipate your own life — retract with merciless power,
Shirk nothing — retract in time — Do you see those errors, diseases, weak-
    nesses, lies, thefts?
Do you see that lost character? — Do you see decay, consumption, rum-
    drinking, dropsy, fever, mortal cancer or inflammation?
Do you see death, and the approach of death?

THINK OF THE SOUL
1856-1871

Think of the Soul;
I swear to you that body of yours gives proportions to your Soul somehow
    to live in other spheres;
I do not know how, but I know it is so.

Think of loving and being loved;
I swear to you, whoever you are, you can interfuse yourself with such
    things that everybody that sees you shall look longingly upon you.

Think of the past;
I warn you that in a little while others will find their past in you and your
    times.

The race is never separated — nor man nor woman escapes;
All is inextricable — things, spirits, Nature, nations, you too — from prece-
    dents you come.

Recall the ever-welcome defiers, (The mothers precede them;)
Recall the sages, poets, saviors, inventors, lawgivers, of the earth;
Recall Christ, brother of rejected persons — brother of slaves, felons, idiots,
    and of insane and diseas'd persons.

Think of the time when you were not yet born;
Think of times you stood at the side of the dying;
Think of the time when your own body will be dying.

Think of spiritual results,
Sure as the earth swims through the heavens, does every one of its objects
    pass into spiritual results.

Think of manhood, and you to be a man;
Do you count manhood, and the sweet of manhood, nothing?

Think of womanhood, and you to be a woman;
The creation is womanhood;
Have I not said that womanhood involves all?
Have I not told how the universe has nothing better than the best
    womanhood?

RESPONDEZ!
1856-1876

Respondez! Respondez!
(The war is completed — the price is paid — the title is settled beyond
    recall;)
Let every one answer! let those who sleep be waked! let none evade!
Must we still go on with our affections and sneaking?

Let me bring this to a close — I pronounce openly for a new distribution of roles;

Let that which stood in front go behind; and let that which was behind advance to the front and speak;

Let murderers, bigots, fools, unclean persons, offer new propositions!

Let the old propositions be postponed!

Let faces and theories be turn'd inside out! let meanings be freely criminal, as well as results!

Let there be no suggestion above the suggestion of drudgery!

Let none be pointed toward his destination! (Say! do you know your destination?)

Let men and women be mock'd with bodies and mock'd with Souls!

Let the love that waits in them, wait! let it die, or pass still-born to other spheres!

Let the sympathy that waits in every man, wait! or let it also pass, a dwarf, to other spheres!

Let contradictions prevail! let one thing contradict another! and let one line of my poems contradict another!

Let the people sprawl with yearning, aimless hands! let their tongues be broken! let their eyes be discouraged! let none descend into their hearts with the fresh lusciousness of love!

(Stifled, O days! O lands! in every public and private corruption!

Smother'd in thievery, impotence, shamelessness, mountain-high;

Brazen effrontery, scheming, rolling like ocean's waves around and upon you, O my days! my lands!

For not even those thunderstorms, nor fiercest lightnings of the war, have purified the atmosphere;)

— Let the theory of America still be management, caste, comparison! (Say! what other theory would you?)

Let them that distrust birth and death still lead the rest! (Say! why shall they not lead you?)

Let the crust of hell be neared and trod on! let the days be darker than the nights! let slumber bring less slumber than waking time brings!

Let the world never appear to him or her for whom it was all made!

Let the heart of the young man still exile itself from the heart of the old man! and let the heart of the old man be exiled from that of the young man!

Let the sun and moon go! let scenery take the applause of the audience! let there be apathy under the stars!

Let freedom prove no man's inalienable right! every one who can tyrannize, let him tyrannize to his satisfaction!

Let none but infidels be countenanced!

Let the eminence of meanness, treachery, sarcasm, hate, greed, indecency, impotence, lust, be taken for granted above all! let writers, judges, governments, households, religions, philosophies, take such for granted above all!

Let the worst men beget children out of the worst women!

Let the priest still play at immortality!

Let death be inaugurated!

Let nothing remain but the ashes of teachers, artists, moralists, lawyers, and learn'd and polite persons!

Let him who is without my poems be assassinated!

Let the cow, the horse, the camel, the garden-bee — let the mud-fish, the lobster, the mussel, eel, the sting-ray, and the grunting pig-fish —

let these, and the like of these, be put on a perfect equality with man and woman!

Let churches accommodate serpents, vermin, and the corpses of those who have died of the most filthy of diseases!

Let marriage slip down among fools, and be for none but fools!

Let men among themselves talk and think forever obscenely of women! and let women among themselves talk and think obscenely of men!

Let us all, without missing one, be exposed in public, naked, monthly, at the peril of our lives! let our bodies be freely handled and examined by whoever chooses!

Let nothing but copies at second hand be permitted to exist upon the earth!

Let the earth desert God, nor let there ever henceforth be mention'd the name of God!

Let there be no God!

Let there be money, business, imports, exports, custom, authority, precedents, pallor, dyspepsia, smut, ignorance, unbelief!

Let judges and criminals be transposed! let the prison-keepers be put in prison! let those that were prisoners take the keys! (Say! why might they not just as well be transposed?)

Let the slaves be masters! let the masters become slaves!

Let the reformers descend from the stands where they are forever bawling! let an idiot or insane person appear on each of the stands!

Let the Asiatic, the African, the European, the American, and the Australian, go armed against the murderous stealthiness of each other! let them sleep armed! let none believe in good will!

Let there be no unfashionable wisdom! let such be scorn'd and derided off from the earth!

Let a floating cloud in the sky — let a wave of the sea — let growing mint, spinach, onions, tomatoes — let these be exhibited as shows, at a great price for admission!

Let all the men of These States stand aside for a few smouchers!° let the few seize on what they choose! let the rest gawk, giggle, starve, obey!

Let shadows be furnish'd with genitals! let substances be deprived of their genitals!

Let there be wealthy and immense cities — but still through any of them, not a single poet, savior, knower, lover!

Let the infidels of These States laugh all faith away!

If one man be found who has faith, let the rest set upon him!

Let them affright faith! let them destroy the power of breeding faith!

Let the she-harlots and the he-harlots be prudent! let them dance on, while seeming lasts! (O seeming! seeming! seeming!)

Let the preachers recite creeds! let them still teach only what they have been taught!

Let insanity still have charge of sanity!

Let books take the place of trees, animals, rivers, clouds!

Let the daub'd portraits of heroes supersede heroes!

Let the manhood of man never take steps after itself!

Let it take steps after eunuchs, and after consumptive and genteel persons!

Let the white person again tread the black person under his heel! (Say! which is trodden under heel, after all?)

Let the reflections of the things of the world be studied in mirrors! let the things themselves still continue unstudied!

Let a man seek pleasure everywhere except in himself!

Let a woman seek happiness everywhere except in herself!
(What real happiness have you had one single hour through your whole
    life?)
Let the limited years of life do nothing for the limitless years of death!
    (What do you suppose death will do, then?)

APOSTROPH
1860

O mater! O fils!
O brood continental!
O flowers of the prairies!
O space boundless! O hum of mighty products!
O you teeming cities! O so invincible, turbulent, proud!
O race of the future! O women!
O fathers! O you men of passion and the storm!
O native power only! O beauty!
O yourself! O God! O divine average!
O you bearded roughs! O bards! O all those slumberers!
O arouse! the dawn-bird's throat sounds shrill! Do you not hear the cock
    crowing?
O, as I walk'd the beach, I heard the mournful notes foreboding a tempest —
    the low, oft-repeated shriek of the diver, the long-lived loon;
O I heard, and yet hear, angry thunder; — O you sailors! O ships! make
    quick preparation!
O from his masterful sweep, the warning cry of the eagle!
(Give way there, all! It is useless! Give up your spoils;)
O sarcasms! Propositions! (O if the whole world should prove indeed a
    sham, a sell!)
O I believe there is nothing real but America and freedom!
O to sternly reject all except Democracy!
O imperator! O who dare confront you and me?
O to promulgate our own! O to build for that which builds for mankind!
O feuillage!° O North! O the slope drained by the Mexican sea!
O all, all inseparable — ages, ages, ages!
O a curse on him that would dissever this Union for any reason whatever!
O climate, labors! O good and evil! O death!
O you strong with iron and wood! O Personality!
O the village or place which has the greatest man or woman! even if it
    be only a few ragged huts;
O the city where women walk in public processions in the streets, the same
    as the men;
O a wan and terrible emblem, by me adopted!
O shapes arising! shapes of the future centuries!
O muscle and pluck forever for me!
O workmen and workwomen forever for me!
O farmers and sailors! O drivers of horses forever for me!
O I will make the new bardic list of trades and tools!
O you coarse and wilful! I love you!
O South! O longings for my dear home! O soft and sunny airs.
O pensive! O I must return where the palm grows and the mocking-bird
    sings, or else I die!
O equality! O organic compacts! I am come to be your born poet!

O whirl, contest, sounding and resounding! I am your poet, because I am
    part of you;
O days by-gone! Enthusiasts! Antecedents!
O vast preparations for These States! O years!
O what is now being sent forward thousands of years to come!
O mediums! O to teach! to convey the invisible faith!
To promulge ° real things! to journey through all The States!
O creation! O to-day! O laws! O unmitigated adoration!
O for mightier broods of orators, artists, and singers!
O for native songs! carpenter's, boatman's, ploughman's songs! shoemaker's
    songs!
O haughtiest growth of time! O free and extatic!
O what I, here, preparing, warble for!
O you hastening light! O the sun of the world will ascend, dazzling, and
    take his height — and you too will ascend;
O so amazing and so broad! up there resplendent, darting and burning;
O prophetic! O vision staggered with weight of light! with pouring glories!
O copious! O hitherto unequalled!
O Libertad! ° O compact! O union impossible to dissever!
O my Soul! O lips becoming tremulous, powerless!
O centuries, centuries yet ahead!
O voices of greater orators! I pause — I listen for you!
O you States! Cities! defiant of all outside authority! I spring at once into
    your arms! you I most love!
O you grand Presidentiads! I wait for you!
New history! New heroes! I project you!
Visions of poets! only you really last! O sweep on! sweep on!
O Death! O you striding there! O I cannot yet!
O heights! O infinitely too swift and dizzy yet!
O purged lumine! ° you threaten me more than I can stand!
O present! I return while yet I may to you!
O poets to come, I depend upon you!

O SUN OF REAL PEACE
1860-1876

O sun of real peace! O hastening light!
O free and extatic! O what I here, preparing, warble for!
O the sun of the world will ascend, dazzling, and take his height — and
    you too, O my Ideal will surely ascend!
O so amazing and broad — up there resplendent, darting and burning!
O vision prophetic, stagger'd with weight of light! with pouring glories!
O lips of my soul, already becoming powerless!
O ample and grand Presidentiads! Now the war, the war is over!
New history! new heroes! I project you!
Visions of poets! only you really last! sweep on! sweep on!
O heights too swift and dizzy yet!
O purged and luminous! you threaten me more than I can stand!
(I must not venture — the ground under my feet menaces me — it will not
    support me:
O future too immense,) — O present, I return, while yet I may, to you.

[SO FAR AND SO FAR, AND ON TOWARD THE END]
1860

So far, and so far, and on toward the end,
Singing what is sung in this book, from the irresistible impulses of me;
But whether I shall continue beyond this book, to maturity,
Whether I shall dart forth the true rays, the ones that wait unfired,
(Did you think the sun was shining its brightest?
No — it has not yet fully risen;)
Whether I shall complete what is here started,
Whether I shall attain my own height, to justify these, yet unfinished,
Whether I shall make THE POEM OF THE NEW WORLD, transcending all
    others — depends, rich persons, upon you,
Depends, whoever you are now filling the current Presidentiad, upon you,
Upon you, Governor, Mayor, Congressman,
And you. contemporary America.

IN THE NEW GARDEN, IN ALL THE PARTS
1860

In the new garden, in all the parts,
In cities now, modern, I wander,
Though the second or third result, or still further, primitive yet,
Days, places, indifferent — though various, the same,
Time, Paradise, the Mannahatta, the prairies, finding me unchanged,
Death indifferent — Is it that I lived long since? Was I buried very long
    ago?
For all that, I may now be watching you here, this moment;
For the future, with determined will, I seek — the woman of the future,
You, born years, centuries after me, I seek.

[STATES!]
1860

States!
Were you looking to be held together by the lawyers?
By an agreement on a paper? Or by arms?

Away!
I arrive, bringing these, beyond all the forces of courts and arms,
These! to hold you together as firmly as the earth itself is held together.

The old breath of life, ever new,
Here! I pass it by contact to you, America.

O mother! have you done much for me?
Behold, there shall from me be much done for you.

There shall from me be a new friendship — It shall be called after my name,
It shall circulate through The States, indifferent of place,

It shall twist and intertwist them through and around each other —
      Compact shall they be, showing new signs,
Affection shall solve every one of the problems of freedom,
Those who love each other shall be invincible,
They shall finally make America completely victorious, in my name.

One from Massachusetts shall be a comrade to a Missourian,
One from Maine or Vermont, and a Carolinian and an Oregonese, shall be
      friends triune, more precious to each other than all the riches of the
      earth.

To Michigan shall be wafted perfume from Florida,
To the Mannahatta from Cuba or Mexico,
Not the perfume of flowers, but sweeter, and wafted beyond death.

No danger shall balk Columbia's lovers,
If need be, a thousand shall sternly immolate themselves for one,
The Kanuck shall be willing to lay down his life for the Kansian, and the
      Kansian for the Kanuck, on due need.

It shall be customary in all directions, in the houses and streets, to see
      manly affection,
The departing brother or friend shall salute the remaining brother or friend
      with a kiss.

There shall be innovations,
There shall be countless linked hands — namely, the Northeasterner's, and
      the Northwesterner's and the Southwesterner's, and those of the
      interior and all their brood,
These shall be masters of the world under a new power,
They shall laugh to scorn the attacks of all the remainder of the world.

The most dauntless and rude shall touch face to face lightly,
The dependence of Liberty shall be lovers,
The continuance of Equality shall be comrades.

These shall tie and band stronger than hoops of iron,
I, extatic, O partners! O lands! henceforth with the love of lovers tie you.

[LONG I THOUGHT THAT KNOWLEDGE]
1860

Long I thought that knowledge alone would suffice me — O if I could but
      obtain knowledge!
Then my lands engrossed me — Lands of the prairies, Ohio's land, the
      southern savannas, engrossed me — For them I would live — I
      would be their orator;
Then I met the examples of old and new heroes — I heard of warriors,
      sailors, and all dauntless persons — And it seemed to me that I too
      had it in me to be as dauntless as any — and would be so;
And then, to enclose all, it came to me to strike up the songs of the New
      World — And then I believed my life must be spent in singing;

But now take notice, land of the prairies, land of the south savannas, Ohio's
    land,
Take notice, you Kanuck woods — and you Lake Huron — and all that
    with you roll toward Niagara — and you Niagara also,
And you, Californian mountains — That you each and all find somebody
    else to be your singer of songs,
For I can be your singer of songs no longer — One who loves me is jealous
    of me, and withdraws me from all but love,
With the rest I dispense — I sever from what I thought would suffice me,
    for it does not — it is now empty and tasteless to me,
I heed knowledge, and the grandeur of The States, and the example of
    heroes, no more,
I am indifferent to my own songs — I will go with him I love,
It is to be enough for us that we are together — We never separate again.

[HOURS CONTINUING LONG, SORE AND HEAVY-HEARTED]
1860

Hours continuing long, sore and heavy-hearted,
Hours of the dusk, when I withdraw to a lonesome and unfrequented spot,
    seating myself, leaning my face in my hands;
Hours sleepless, deep in the night, when I go forth, speeding swiftly the
    country roads, or through the city streets, or pacing miles and miles,
    stifling plaintive cries;
Hours discouraged, distracted — for the one I cannot content myself with-
    out, soon I saw him content himself without me;
Hours when I am forgotten, (O weeks and months are passing, but I
    believe I am never to forget!)
Sullen and suffering hours! (I am ashamed — but it is useless — I am
    what I am;)
Hours of my torment — I wonder if other men ever have the like, out of
    the like feelings?
Is there even one other like me — distracted — his friend, his lover, lost
    to him?
Is he too as I am now? Does he still rise in the morning, dejected, thinking
    who is lost to him? and at night, awaking, think who is lost?
Does he too harbor his friendship silent and endless? harbor his anguish
    and passion?
Does some stray reminder, or the casual mention of a name, bring the fit
    back upon him, taciturn and deprest?
Does he see himself reflected in me? In these hours, does he see the face
    of his hours reflected?

[WHO IS NOW READING THIS?]
1860

Who is now reading this?

May-be one is now reading this who knows some wrong-doing of my past life,
Or may-be a stranger is reading this who has secretly loved me,
Or may-be one who meets all my grand assumptions and egotisms with
    derision,
Or may-be one who is puzzled at me.

As if I were not puzzled at myself!
Or as if I never deride myself! (O conscience-struck! O self-convicted!)
Or as if I do not secretly love strangers! (O tenderly, a long time, and never
    avow it;)
Or as if I did not see, perfectly well, interior in myself, the stuff of wrong-
    doing,
Or as if it could cease transpiring from me until it must cease.

TO YOU
1860-1867

Let us twain walk aside from the rest;
Now we are together privately, do you discard ceremony,
Come! vouchsafe to me what has yet been vouchsafed to none — Tell me
    the whole story,
Tell me what you would not tell your brother, wife, husband, or physician.

[OF THE VISAGES OF THINGS]
1860-1867

Of the visages of things — And of piercing through to the accepted hells
    beneath;
Of ugliness — To me there is just as much in it as there is in beauty — And
    now the ugliness of human beings is acceptable to me;
Of detected persons — To me, detected persons are not, in any respect,
    worse than undetected persons — and are not in any respect worse
    than I am myself;
Of criminals — To me, any judge, or any jurior, is equally criminal — and
    any reputable person is also — and the President is also.

SAYS
1860-1867

1

I say whatever tastes sweet to the most perfect person, that is finally right.

2

I say nourish a great intellect, a great brain;
If I have said anything to the contrary, I hereby retract it.

3

I say man shall not hold property in man;
I say the least developed person on earth is just as important and sacred
    to himself or herself, as the most developed person is to himself
    or herself.

4

I say where liberty draws not the blood out of slavery, there slavery draws
    the blood out of liberty,
I say the word of the good old cause in These States, and resound it hence
    over the world.

5

I say the human shape or face is so great, it must never be made ridiculous;
I say for ornaments nothing outre can be allowed,
And that anything is most beautiful without ornament,
And that exaggerations will be sternly revenged in your own physiology, and
    in other persons' physiology also;
And I say that clean-shaped children can be jetted* and conceived only
    where natural forms prevail in public, and the human face and form
    are never caricatured;
And I say that genius need never more be turned to romances,
(For facts properly told, how mean appear all romances.)

6

I say the word of lands fearing nothing — I will have no other land;
I say discuss all and expose all — I am for every topic openly;
I say there can be no salvation for These States without innovators —
    without free tongues, and ears willing to hear the tongues;
And I announce as a glory of These States, that they respectfully listen to
    propositions, reforms, fresh views and doctrines, from successions of
    men and women,
Each age with its own growth.

7

I have said many times that materials and the Soul are great, and that all
    depends on physique;
Now I reverse what I said, and affirm that all depends on the aesthetic or
    intellectual,
And that criticism is great — and that refinement is greatest of all;
And I affirm now that the mind governs — and that all depends on the mind.

8

With one man or woman — (no matter which one — I even pick out the
    lowest,)
With him or her I now illustrate the whole law;
I say that every right, in politics or what-not, shall be eligible to that one
    man or woman, on the same terms as any.

DEBRIS
1860

He is wisest who has the most caution,
He only wins who goes far enough.

Any thing is as good as established, when that is established that will
    produce and continue it.

What General has a good army in himself, has a good army;
He happy in himself, or she happy in herself, is happy,
But I tell you you cannot be happy by others, any more than you can beget
    or conceive a child by others.

One sweeps by, attended by an immense train,
All emblematic of peace — not a soldier or menial among them.

One sweeps by, old, with black eyes, and profuse white hair,
He has the simple magnificence of health and strength,
His face strikes as with flashes of lightning whoever it turns toward.

Three old men slowly pass, followed by three others, and they by three others,
They are beautiful — the one in the middle of each group holds his companions by the hand,
As they walk, they give out perfume wherever they walk.

What weeping face is that looking from the window?
Why does it stream those sorrowful tears?
Is it for some burial place, vast and dry?
Is it to wet the soil of graves?

I will take an egg out of the robin's nest in the orchard,
I will take a branch of gooseberries from the old bush in the garden, and go and preach to the world;
You shall see I will not meet a single heretic or scorner,
You shall see how I stump clergymen, and confound them,
You shall see me showing a scarlet tomato, and a white pebble from the beach.

Behavior — fresh, native, copious, each one for himself or herself,
Nature and the Soul expressed — America and freedom expressed — in it the finest art,
In it pride, cleanliness, sympathy, to have their chance,
In it physique, intellect, faith — in it just as much as to manage an army or a city, or to write a book — perhaps more,
The youth, the laboring person, the poor person, rivalling all the rest — perhaps outdoing the rest,
The effects of the universe no greater than its;
For there is nothing in the whole universe that can be more effective than a man's or a woman's daily behavior can be,
In any position, in any one of These States.

I thought I was not alone, walking here by the shore,
But the one I thought was with me, as now I walk by the shore,
As I lean and look through the glimmering light — that one has utterly disappeared,
And those appear that perplex me.

THOUGHT
1860-1876

Of what I write from myself — As if that were not the resumé;
Of Histories — As if such, however complete, were not less complete than the preceding poems;
As if those shreds, the records of nations, could possibly be as lasting as the preceding poems;
As if here were not the amount of all nations, and of all the lives of heroes.

SOLID, IRONICAL, ROLLING ORB
1865-1876

Solid, ironical, rolling orb!
Master of all, and matter of fact! — at last I accept your terms;
Bringing to practical, vulgar tests, of all my ideal dreams,
And of me, as lover and hero.

BATHED IN WAR'S PERFUME
1865-1876

Bathed in war's perfume — delicate flag!
(Should the days needing armies, needing fleets, come again,)
O to hear you call the sailors and the soldiers! flag like a beautiful woman!
O to hear the tramp, tramp, of a million answering men! O the ships they
    arm with joy!
O to see you leap and beckon from the tall masts of ships!
O to see you peering down on the sailors on the decks!
Flag like the eyes of women.

NOT MY ENEMIES EVER INVADE ME
1865

Not my enemies ever invade me — no harm to my pride from them I fear;
But the lovers I recklessly love — lo! how they master me!
Lo! me, ever open and helpless, bereft of my strength!
Utterly abject, grovelling on the ground before them.

THIS DAY, O SOUL
1865-1876

This day, O Soul, I give you a wondrous mirror;
Long in the dark, in tarnish and cloud it lay — But the cloud has pass'd,
    and the tarnish gone;
. . . Behold, O Soul! it is now a clean and bright mirror,
Faithfully showing you all the things of the world.

LESSONS
1871

There are who teach only the sweet lessons of peace and safety;
But I teach lessons of war and death to those I love,
That they readily meet invasions, when they come.

ONE SONG, AMERICA, BEFORE I GO
1872

One song, America, before I go,
I'd sing, o'er all the rest, with trumpet sound,
For thee — the Future.

I'd sow a seed for thee of endless Nationality;
I'd fashion thy Ensemble, including Body and Soul;
I'd show, away ahead, the real Union, and how it may be accomplish'd

(The paths to the House I seek to make,
But leave to those to come, the House itself.)

Belief I sing — and Preparation;
As Life and Nature are not great with reference to the Present only,
But greater still from what is to come,
Out of that formula for Thee I sing.

AFTER AN INTERVAL
1876
(*Nov. 22, 1875, midnight — Saturn and Mars in conjunction*)

After an interval, reading, here in the midnight,
With the great stars looking on — all the stars of Orion looking,
And the silent Pleiades — and the duo looking of Saturn and ruddy Mars;
Pondering, reading my own songs, after a long interval, (sorrow and death
    familiar now,)
Ere closing the book, what pride! what joy! to find them,
Standing so well the test of death and night!
And the duo of Saturn and Mars!

THE BEAUTY OF THE SHIP
1876

When, staunchly entering port,
After long ventures, hauling up, worn and old,
Battered by sea and wind, torn by many a fight,
With the original sails all gone, replaced, or mended,
I only saw, at last, the beauty of the Ship.

TWO RIVULETS
1876

Two Rivulets side by side,
Two blended, parallel, strolling tides,
Companions, travelers, gossiping as they journey.

For the Eternal Ocean bound,
These ripples, passing surges, streams of Death and Life,
Object and Subject hurrying, whirling by,
The Real and Ideal,

Alternate ebb and flow the Days and Nights,
(Strands of a Trio twining, Present, Future, Past.)

In You, whoe'er you are, my book perusing,
In I myself—in all the World—these ripples flow,
All, all, toward the mystic Ocean tending.

(O yearnful waves! the kisses of your lips!
Your breasts so broad, with open arms, O firm, expanded shore!)

OR, FROM THAT SEA OF TIME
1876

1

Or, from that Sea of Time,
Spray, blown by the wind—a double winrow-drift of weeds and shells;
(O little shells, so curious-convolute! so limpid-cold and voiceless!
Yet will you not, to the tympans of temples held,
Murmurs and echoes still bring up—Eternity's music, faint and far,
Wafted inland, sent from Atlantica's rim—strains for the Soul of the Prairies,
Whisper'd reverberations—chords for the ear of the West, joyously sounding
Your tidings old, yet ever new and untranslatable;)
Infinitessimals out of my life, and many a life,
(For not my life and years alone I give—all, all I give;)
These thoughts and Songs—waifs from the deep—here, cast high and dry,
Wash'd on America's shores.

2

Currents of starting a Continent new,
Overtures sent to the solid out of the liquid,
Fusion of ocean and land—tender and pensive waves,
(Not safe and peaceful only—waves rous'd and ominous too,
Out of the depths, the storm's abysms—who knows whence? Death's waves,
Raging over the vast, with many a broken spar and tatter'd sail.)

FROM MY LAST YEARS
1876

From my last years, last thoughts I here bequeath,
Scatter'd and dropt, in seeds, and wafted to the West,
Through moisture of Ohio, prairie soil of Illinois—through Colorado, California air,
For Time to germinate fully.

IN FORMER SONGS
1876

1

In former songs Pride have I sung, and Love, and passionate, joyful Life,
But here I twine the strands of Patriotism and Death.

And now, Life, Pride, Love, Patriotism and Death,
To you, O FREEDOM, purport of all!
(You that elude me most—refusing to be caught in songs of mine,)
I offer all to you.

2

'Tis not for nothing, Death,
I sound out you, and words of you, with daring tone—embodying you,
In my new Democratic chants—keeping you for a close,
For last impregnable retreat—a citadel and tower,
For my last stand—my pealing, final cry.

SELECTED PROSE

Whitman's prose is represented in the following pages by the complete prefaces and by the long, celebrated work, *Democratic Vistas*.

The word "prefaces" is a slight misnomer for the four prose works here collected under that title. Only one, the 1855 Preface, ever really stood at the beginning of *Leaves of Grass*, and then only for one—the first—edition. The 1872 Preface stood at the beginning of a separate publication of *As a Strong Bird on Pinions Free* (later incorporated in *Leaves of Grass* as "Thou Mother with Thy Equal Brood"). The 1876 Preface appeared not in the *Leaves of Grass* volume but in the *Two Rivulets* volume of the Centennial Edition. "A Backward Glance O'er Travel'd Roads" was first published separately in 1888 and, when included in the deathbed edition, was placed not at the beginning but at the end of the volume, after the annexes. (All of them were considerably altered when reprinted in Whitman's *Complete Prose*.) Nevertheless these prose works may be read as successive prefaces revealing Whitman's changing and shifting plans and purposes as well as his expanding poetic vision. The first and the last, one looking to the future, the other to the past, are no doubt the most valuable; though the other two, written in mid-career, give us extraordinary glimpses into the poet's development.

Democratic Vistas appeared first as a whole work in 1871 (parts had been published earlier in periodicals). Examining in turn the idea of political democracy, the philosophy of personalism, and the nature of literature, Whitman stresses throughout the urgent need for great, archetypal literature if democracy is to fulfill its function of producing great persons and a great people.

The complete prefaces together with *Democratic Vistas* constitute Whitman's poetics for democracy and, at the same time, reveal his hopes and dreams for his own *Leaves of Grass*.

PREFACES

PREFACE TO 1855 EDITION OF "LEAVES OF GRASS"

America does not repel the past or what it has produced under its forms or amid other politics or the idea of castes or the old religions . . . accepts the lesson with calmness . . . is not so impatient as has been supposed that the slough still sticks to opinions and manners and literature while the life which served its requirements has passed into the new life of the new forms . . . perceives that the corpse is slowly borne from the eating and sleeping rooms of the house . . . perceives that it waits a little while in the door . . . that it was fittest for its days . . . that its action has descended to the stalwart and wellshaped heir who approaches . . . and that he shall be fittest for his days.

The Americans of all nations at any time upon the earth have probably the fullest poetical nature. The United States themselves are essentially the greatest poem. In the history of the earth hitherto the largest and most stirring appear tame and orderly to their ampler largeness and stir. Here at last is something in the doings of man that corresponds with the broadcast doings of the day and night. Here is not merely a nation but a teeming nation of nations. Here is action untied from strings necessarily blind to particulars and details magnificently moving in vast masses. Here is the hospitality which forever indicates heroes. . . . Here are the roughs and beards and space and ruggedness and nonchalance that the soul loves. Here the performance disdaining the trivial unapproached in the tremendous audacity of its crowds and groupings and the push of its perspective spreads with crampless and flowing breath and showers its prolific and splendid extravagance. One sees it must indeed own the riches of the summer and winter, and need never be bankrupt while corn grows from the ground or the orchards drop apples or the bays contain fish or men beget children upon women.

Other states indicate themselves in their deputies . . . but the genius of the United States is not best or most in its executives or legislatures, nor in its ambassadors or authors or colleges or churches or parlors, nor even in its newspapers or inventors . . . but always most in the common people. Their manners speech dress friendships —the freshness and candor of their physiognomy—the picturesque looseness of their carriage . . . their deathless attachment to freedom—their aversion to anything indecorous or soft or mean—the practical acknowledgment of the citizens of one state by the citizens of all other states—the fierceness of their roused resentment—their curiosity and welcome of novelty—their self-esteem and wonderful sympathy—their susceptibility to a slight—the air they have of persons who never knew how it felt to stand in the presence of superiors—the fluency of their speech—their delight in music, the sure symptom of manly tenderness and native elegance of soul . . . their good temper and openhandedness—the terrible significance of their elections—the President's taking off his hat to them not they to him—these too are unrhymed poetry. It awaits the gigantic and generous treatment worthy of it.

The largeness of nature or the nation were monstrous without a corresponding largeness and generosity of the spirit of the citizen. Not nature nor swarming states nor streets and steamships nor prosperous business nor farms nor capital nor learning may suffice for the ideal of man . . . nor suffice the poet. No reminiscences may suffice either. A live nation can always cut a deep mark and can have the best authority the cheapest . . . namely from its own soul. This is the sum of the profitable uses of individuals or states and of present action and grandeur and of the subjects of poets.—As if it were necessary to trot back generation after generation to the eastern records! As if the beauty and sacredness of the demonstrable must fall behind that of the mythical! As if men do not make their mark out of any times! As if the opening of the western continent by discovery and what has transpired since in North and South America were less than the small theatre of the antique or the aimless sleepwalking of the middle ages! The pride of the United States leaves the wealth and finesse of the cities and all returns of commerce and agriculture and all the magnitude of geography or shows of exterior victory to enjoy the breed of fullsized men or one full sized man unconquerable and simple.

The American poets are to enclose old and new for America is the race of races. Of them a bard is to be commensurate with a people. To him the other continents arrive as contributions . . . he gives them reception for their sake and his own sake. His spirit responds to his country's spirit . . . he incarnates its geography and natural life and rivers and lakes. Mississippi with annual freshets and changing chutes, Missouri and Columbia and Ohio and Saint Lawrence with the falls and beautiful masculine Hudson, do not embouchure where they spend themselves more than they embouchure into him. The blue breadth over the inland sea of Virginia and Maryland and the sea off Massachusetts and Maine and over Manhattan bay and over Champlain and Erie and over Ontario and Huron and Michigan and Superior, and over the Texan and Mexican and Floridian and Cuban seas and over the seas off California and Oregon, is not tallied by the blue breadth of the waters below more than the breadth of above and below is tallied by him. When the long Atlantic coast stretches longer and the Pacific coast stretches longer he easily stretches with them north or south. He spans between them also from east to west and reflects what is between them. On him rise solid growths that offset the growths of pine and cedar and hemlock and liveoak and locust and chestnut and cypress and hickory and limetree and cotton-wood and tuliptree and cactus and wildvine and tamarind and persimmon . . . and tangles as tangled as any canebreak or swamp . . . and forests coated with transparent ice and icicles hanging from the boughs and crackling in the wind . . . and sides and peaks of mountains . . . and pasturage sweet and free as savannah or upland or prairie . . . with flights and songs and screams that answer those of the wildpigeon and highhold and orchard-oriole and coot and surf-duck and redshouldered-hawk and fish-hawk and white-ibis and indian-hen and cat-owl and water-pheasant and qua-bird and pied-sheldrake and blackbird and mockingbird and buzzard and condor and night-heron and eagle. To him the hereditary countenance descends both mother's and father's. To him enter the essences of the real things and past and present events—of the enormous diversity of temperature and agriculture and mines—the tribes of red aborigines—the weather-beaten vessels entering new ports or making landings on rocky coasts—the first settlements north or south—the rapid stature and muscle—the haughty defiance of '76, and the war and peace and formation of the constitution . . . the union always surrounded by blatherers and always calm and impregnable—the perpetual coming of immigrants—the wharf-hemm'd cities and superior marine—the unsurveyed interior—the loghouses and clearings and wild animals and hunters and trappers . . . the free commerce—the fisheries and whaling and gold-digging—the endless gestation of new states—the convening of Congress every December, the members duly coming up from all climates and the uttermost parts . . . the noble character of the young mechanics and of all free American workmen and workwomen . . . the general ardor and friendliness and enterprise—the perfect equality of the female with the male . . . the large amativeness—the fluid movement of the population—the factories and mercantile life and labor-saving machinery—the Yankee swap—the New-York firemen and the target excursion—the southern plantation life—the character of the northeast and of the northwest and southwest—slavery and the tremulous spreading of hands to protect it, and the stern opposition to it which shall never cease till it ceases or the speaking of tongues and the moving of lips cease. For such the expression of the American poet is to be transcendant and new. It is to be indirect and not direct or descriptive or epic. Its quality goes through these to much more. Let the age and wars of other nations be chanted and their eras and characters be illustrated and that finish the verse. Not so the great psalm of the republic. Here the theme is creative and has vista. Here comes one among the well-beloved stonecutters and plans with decision and science and sees the solid and beautiful forms of the future where there are now no solid forms.

Of all nations the United States with veins full of poetical stuff most need poets and will doubtless have the greatest and use them the greatest. Their Presidents shall not be their common referee so much as their poets shall. Of all mankind the great poet is the equable man. Not in him but off from him things are grotesque or eccentric or fail of their sanity. Nothing out of its place is good and nothing in its place is bad. He bestows on every object or quality its fit proportions neither more nor less. He is the arbiter of the diverse and he is the key. He is the equalizer of his age and land . . . he supplies what wants supplying and checks what wants checking. If peace is the routine out of him speaks the spirit of peace, large, rich, thrifty, building vast and populous cities, encouraging agriculture and the arts and commerce—lighting the study of man, the soul, immortality—federal, state, or municipal government, marriage, health, free trade, intertravel by land and sea . . . nothing too close, nothing too far off . . . the stars not too far off. In war he is the most deadly force of the war. Who recruits him recruits horse and foot . . . he fetches parks of artillery the best that engineer ever knew. If the time becomes slothful and heavy he knows how to arouse it . . . he can make every word he speaks draw blood. Whatever stagnates in the flat of custom or obedience or legislation he never stagnates. Obedience does not master him, he masters it. High up out of reach he stands turning a concentrated light . . . he turns the pivot with his finger . . . he baffles the swiftest runners as he stands and easily overtakes and envelops them. The time straying toward infidelity and confections and persiflage he withholds by his steady faith . . . he spreads out his dishes . . . he offers the sweet firmfibred meat that grows men and women. His brain is the ultimate brain. He is no arguer . . . he is judgment. He judges not as the judge judges but as the sun falling around a helpless thing. As he sees the farthest he has the most faith. His thoughts are the hymns of the praise of things. In the talk on the soul and eternity and God off of his equal plane he is silent. He sees eternity less like a play with a prologue and denouement . . . he sees eternity in men and women . . . he does not see men and women as dreams or dots. Faith is the antiseptic of the soul . . . it pervades the common people and preserves them . . . they never give up believing and expecting and trusting. There is that indescribable freshness and unconsciousness about an illiterate person that humbles and mocks the power of the noblest expressive genius. The poet sees for a certainty how one not a great artist may be just as sacred as the greatest artist. . . . The power to destroy or remould is freely used by him but never the power of attack. What is past is past. If he does not expose superior models and prove himself by every step he takes he is not what is wanted. The presence of the greatest poet conquers . . . not parleying or struggling or any prepared attempts. Now he has passed that way see after him! there is not left any vestige of despair or misanthropy or cunning or exclusiveness or the ignominy of a nativity or color or delusion of hell or the necessity of hell . . . and no man thenceforward shall be degraded for ignorance or weakness or sin.

The greatest poet hardly knows pettiness or triviality. If he breathes into any thing that was before thought small it dilates with the grandeur and life of the universe. He is a seer . . . he is individual . . . he is complete in himself . . . the others are as good as he, only he sees it and they do not. He is not one of the chorus . . . he does not stop for any regulations . . . he is the president of regulation. What the eyesight does to the rest he does to the rest. Who knows the curious mystery of the eyesight? The other senses corroborate themselves, but this is removed from any proof but its own and foreruns the identities of the spiritual world. A single glance of it mocks all the investigations of man and all the instruments and books of the earth and all reasoning. What is marvelous? what is unlikely? what is impossible or baseless or vague? after you have once just opened the space of a peachpit and given audience to far and near and to the sunset and had all things enter with electric swiftness softly and duly without confusion or jostling or jam.

The land and sea, the animals fishes and birds, the sky of heaven and the orbs, the forests mountains and rivers, are not small themes . . . but folks expect of the poet to indicate more than the beauty and dignity which always attach to dumb real objects . . . they expect him to indicate the path between reality and their souls. Men and women perceive the beauty well enough . . . probably as well as he. The passionate tenacity of hunters, woodmen, early risers, cultivators of gardens and orchards and fields, the love of healthy women for the manly form, seafaring persons, drivers of horses, the passion for light and the open air, all is an old varied sign of the unfailing perception of beauty and of a residence of the poetic in outdoor people. They can never be assisted by poets to perceive . . . some may but they never can. The poetic quality is not marshalled in rhyme or uniformity or abstract addresses to things nor in melancholy complaints or good precepts, but is the life of these and much else and is in the soul. The profit of rhyme is that it drops seeds of a sweeter and more luxuriant rhyme, and of uniformity that it conveys itself into its own roots in the ground out of sight. The rhyme and uniformity of perfect poems show the free growth of metrical laws and bud from them as unerringly and loosely as lilacs or roses on a bush, and take shapes as compact as the shapes of chestnuts and oranges and melons and pears, and shed the perfume impalpable to form. The fluency and ornaments of the finest poems or music or orations or recitations are not independent but dependent. All beauty comes from beautiful blood and a beautiful brain. If the greatnesses are in conjunction in a man or woman it is enough . . . the fact will prevail through the universe . . . but the gaggery and gilt of a million years will not prevail. Who troubles himself about his ornaments or fluency is lost. This is what you shall do: Love the earth and sun and the animals, despise riches, give alms to every one that asks, stand up for the stupid and crazy, devote your income and labor to others, hate tyrants, argue not concerning God, have patience and indulgence toward the people, take off your hat to nothing known or unknown or to any man or number of men, go freely with powerful uneducated persons and with the young and with the mothers of families, read these leaves in the open air every season of every year of your life, re-examine all you have been told at school or church or in any book, dismiss whatever insults your own soul, and your very flesh shall be a great poem and have the richest fluency not only in its words but in the silent lines of its lips and face and between the lashes of your eyes and in every motion and joint of your body. . . . The poet shall not spend his time in unneeded work. He shall know that the ground is always ready plowed and manured . . . others may not know it but he shall. He shall go directly to the creation. His trust shall master the trust of everything he touches . . . and shall master all attachment.

The known universe has one complete lover and that is the greatest poet. He consumes an eternal passion and is indifferent which chance happens and which possible contingency of fortune or misfortune and persuades daily and hourly his delicious pay. What balks or breaks others is fuel for his burning progress to contact and amorous joy. Other proportions of the reception of pleasure dwindle to nothing to his proportions. All expected from heaven or from the highest he is rapport with in the sight of the daybreak or a scene of the winterwoods or the presence of children playing or with his arm round the neck of a man or woman. His love above all love has leisure and expanse . . . he leaves room ahead of himself. He is no irresolute or suspicious lover . . . he is sure . . . he scorns intervals. His experience and the showers and thrills are not for nothing. Nothing can jar him . . . suffering and darkness cannot—death and fear cannot. To him complaint and jealousy and envy are corpses buried and rotten in the earth . . . he saw them buried. The sea is not surer of the shore or the shore of the sea than he is of the fruition of his love and of all perfection and beauty.

The fruition of beauty is no chance of hit or miss . . . it is inevitable as life . . . it is exact and plumb as gravitation. From the eyesight proceeds another eyesight and from the hearing proceeds another hearing and from the voice proceeds another voice eternally curious of the harmony of things with man. To these respond perfections not only in the committees that were supposed to stand for the rest but in the rest themselves just the same. These understand the law of perfection in masses and floods . . . that its finish is to each for itself and onward from itself . . . that it is profuse and impartial . . . that there is not a minute of the light or dark nor an acre of the earth or sea without it—nor any direction of the sky nor any trade or employment nor any turn of events. This is the reason that about the proper expression of beauty there is precision and balance . . . one part does not need to be thrust above another.

The best singer is not the one who has the most lithe and powerful organ . . . the pleasure of poems is not in them that take the handsomest measure and similes and sound.

Without effort and without exposing in the least how it is done the greatest poet brings the spirit of any or all events and passions and scenes and persons some more and some less to bear on your individual character as you hear or read. To do this well is to compete with the laws that pursue and follow time. What is the purpose must surely be there and the clue of it must be there . . . and the faintest indication is the indication of the best and then becomes the clearest indication. Past and present and future are not disjoined but joined. The greatest poet forms the consistence of what is to be from what has been and is. He drags the dead out of their coffins and stands them again on their feet . . . he says to the past, Rise and walk before me that I may realize you. He learns the lesson . . . he places himself where the future becomes present. The greatest poet does not only dazzle his rays over character and scenes and passions . . . he finally ascends and finishes all . . . he exhibits the pinnacles that no man can tell what they are for or what is beyond . . . he glows a moment on the extremest verge. He is most wonderful in his last half-hidden smile or frown . . . by that flash of the moment of parting the one that sees it shall be encouraged or terrified afterwards for many years. The greatest poet does not moralize or make applications of morals . . . he knows the soul. The soul has that measureless pride which consists in never acknowledging any lessons but its own. But it has sympathy as measureless as its pride and the one balances the other and neither can stretch too far while it stretches in company with the other. The inmost secrets of art sleep with the twain. The greatest poet has lain close betwixt both and they are vital in his style and thoughts.

The art of art, the glory of expression and the sunshine of the light of letters is simplicity. Nothing is better than simplicity . . . nothing can make up for excess or for the lack of definiteness. To carry on the heave of impulse and pierce intellectual depths and give all subjects their articulations are powers neither common nor very uncommon. But to speak in literature with the perfect rectitude and insouciance of the movements of animals and the unimpeachableness of the sentiment of trees in the woods and grass by the roadside is the flawless triumph of art. If you have looked on him who has achieved it you have looked on one of the masters of the artists of all nations and times. You shall not contemplate the flight of the graygull over the bay or the mettlesome action of the blood horse or the tall leaning of sunflowers on their stalk or the appearance of the sun journeying through heaven or the appearance of the moon afterward with any more satisfaction than you shall contemplate him. The greatest poet has less a marked style and is more the channel of thoughts and things without increase or diminution, and is the free channel of himself. He swears to his art, I will not be meddlesome, I will not have in my writing any elegance or effect or originality to hang in the way between me and the rest like curtains. I will have nothing hang in the way, not the richest curtains. What I tell I tell for precisely what it is. Let who may exalt or startle or fascinate or sooth I will have purposes as health or heat or snow has and be as regardless of observation. What I experience or portray shall go from my composition without a shred of my composition. You shall stand by my side and look in the mirror with me.

The old red blood and stainless gentility of great poets will be proved by their unconstraint. A heroic person walks at his ease through and out of that custom or precedent or authority that suits him not. Of the traits of the brotherhood of writers savans musicians inventors and artists nothing is finer than silent defiance advancing from new free forms. In the need of poems philosophy politics mechanism science behaviour, the craft of art, an appropriate native grand-opera, shipcraft, or any craft, he is greatest forever and forever who contributes the greatest original practical example. The cleanest expression is that which finds no sphere worthy of itself and makes one.

The messages of great poets to each man and woman are, Come to us on equal terms, Only then can you understand us, We are no better than you, What we enclose you enclose, What we enjoy you may enjoy. Did you suppose there could be only one Supreme? We affirm there can be unnumbered Supremes, and that one does not countervail another any more than one eyesight countervails another . . . and that men can be good or grand only of the consciousness of their supremacy within them. What do you think is the grandeur of storms and dismemberments and the deadliest battles and wrecks and the wildest fury of the elements and the power of the sea and the motion of nature and of the throes of human desires and dignity and hate and love? It is that something in the soul which says, Rage on, Whirl on, I tread master here and everywhere, Master of the spasms of the sky and of the shatter of the sea, Master of nature and passion and death, And of all terror and all pain.

The American bards shall be marked for generosity and affection and for encouraging competitors. . . . They shall be kosmos . . . without monopoly or secresy . . . glad to pass any thing to any one . . . hungry for equals night and day. They shall not be careful of riches and privilege they shall be riches and privilege . . . they shall perceive who the most affluent man is. The most affluent man is he that confronts all the shows he sees by equivalents out of the stronger wealth of himself. The American bard shall delineate no class of persons nor one or two out of the strata of interests nor love most nor truth most nor the soul most nor the body most . . . and not be for the eastern states more than the western or the northern states more than the southern.

Exact science and its practical movements are no checks on the greatest poet but always his encouragement and support. The outset and remembrance are there . . . there are the arms that lifted him first and brace him best . . . there he returns after all his goings and comings. The sailor and traveler . . . the atomist chemist

astronomer geologist phrenologist spiritualist mathematician historian
and lexicographer are not poets, but they are the lawgivers of poets
and their construction underlies the structure of every perfect poem.
No matter what rises or is uttered they sent the seed of the conception of it . . . of them and by them stand the visible proofs of
souls . . . always of their fatherstuff must be begotten the sinewy
races of bards. If there shall be love and content between the father
and the son and if the greatness of the son is the exuding of the
greatness of the father there shall be love between the poet and the
man of demonstrable science. In the beauty of poems are the tuft and
final applause of science.

Great is the faith of the flush of knowledge and of the investigation of the depths of qualities and things. Cleaving and circling here
swells the soul of the poet yet is president of itself always. The depths
are fathomless and therefore calm. The innocence and nakedness are
resumed . . . they are neither modest nor immodest. The whole
theory of the special and supernatural and all that was twined with it
or educed out of it departs as a dream. What has ever happened
. . . what happens and whatever may or shall happen, the vital
laws enclose all . . . they are sufficient for any case and for all
cases . . . none to be hurried or retarded . . . any miracle of affairs
or persons inadmissible in the vast clear scheme where every motion
and every spear of grass and the frames and spirits of men and
women and all that concerns them are unspeakably perfect miracles
all referring to all and each distinct and in its place. It is also not
consistent with the reality of the soul to admit that there is anything
in the known universe more divine than men and women.

Men and women and the earth and all upon it are simply to be
taken as they are, and the investigation of their past and present and
future shall be unintermitted and shall be done with perfect candor.
Upon this basis philosophy speculates ever looking toward the poet,
ever regarding the eternal tendencies of all toward happiness never
inconsistent with what is clear to the senses and to the soul. For the
eternal tendencies of all toward happiness make the only point of
sane philosophy. Whatever comprehends less than that . . . whatever is less than the laws of light and of astronomical motion . . .
or less than the laws that follow the thief the liar the glutton and
the drunkard through this life and doubtless afterward . . . or less
than vast stretches of time or the slow formation of density or the
patient upheaving of strata—is of no account. Whatever would put
God in a poem or system of philosophy as contending against some
being or influence, is also of no account. Sanity and ensemble
characterise the great master . . . spoilt in one principle all is spoilt.
The great master has nothing to do with miracles. He sees health
for himself in being one of the mass . . . he sees the hiatus in
singular eminence. To the perfect shape comes common ground. To
be under the general law is great for that is to correspond with it.
The master knows that he is unspeakably great and that all are unspeakably great . . . that nothing for instance is greater than to

conceive children and bring them up well . . . that to be is just as great as to perceive or tell.

In the make of the great masters the idea of political liberty is indispensable. Liberty takes the adherence of heroes wherever men and women exist . . . but never takes any adherence or welcome from the rest more than from poets. They are the voice and exposition of liberty. They out of ages are worthy the grand idea . . . to them it is confided and they must sustain it. Nothing has precedence of it and nothing can warp or degrade it. The attitude of great poets is to cheer up slaves and horrify despots. The turn of their necks, the sound of their feet, the motions of their wrists, are full of hazard to the one and hope to the other. Come nigh them awhile and though they neither speak or advise you shall learn the faithful American lesson. Liberty is poorly served by men whose good intent is quelled from one failure or two failures or any number of failures, or from the casual indifference or ingratitude of the people, or from the sharp show of the tushes of power, or the bringing to bear soldiers and cannon or any penal statutes. Liberty relies upon itself, invites no one, promises nothing, sits in calmness and light, is positive and composed, and knows no discouragement. The battle rages with many a loud alarm and frequent advance and retreat . . . the enemy triumphs . . . the prison, the handcuffs, the iron necklace and anklet, the scaffold, garrote and leadballs do their work . . . the cause is asleep . . . the strong throats are choked with their own blood . . . the young men drop their eyelashes toward the ground when they pass each other . . . and is liberty gone out of that place? No never. When liberty goes it is not the first to go nor the second nor third to go . . . it waits for all the rest to go . . . it is the last. . . . When the memories of the old martyrs are faded utterly away . . . when the large names of patriots are laughed at in the public halls from the lips of the orators . . . when the boys are no more christened after the same but christened after tyrants and traitors instead . . . when the laws of the free are grudgingly permitted and laws for informers and blood-money are sweet to the taste of the people . . . when I and you walk abroad upon the earth stung with compassion at the sight of numberless brothers answering our equal friendship and calling no man master—and when we are elated with noble joy at the sight of slaves . . . when the soul retires in the cool communion of the night and surveys its experience and has much extasy over the word and deed that put back a helpless innocent person into the gripe of the gripers or into any cruel inferiority . . . when those in all parts of these states who could easier realize the true American character but do not yet—when the swarms of cringers, suckers, doughfaces, lice of politics, planners of sly involutions for their own preferment to city offices or state legislatures or the judiciary or congress or the presidency, obtain a response of love and natural deference from the people whether they get the offices or no . . . when it is better to be a bound booby and rogue in office at a high salary than the poorest free mechanic or farmer with his hat removed from his head and firm eyes, and a candid and generous heart . . . and when servility by town or state or the federal government or any oppression on a large scale or small scale can be tried on without its own punishment following duly after in exact proportion against the smallest chance of escape . . . or rather when all life and all the souls of men and women are discharged from any part of the earth—then only shall the instinct of liberty be discharged from that part of the earth.

As the attributes of the poets of the kosmos concentre in the real body and soul and in the pleasure of things they possess the superiority of genuineness over all fiction and romance. As they emit themselves facts are showered over with light . . . the daylight is lit with more volatile light . . . also the deep between the setting and rising sun goes deeper many fold. Each precise object or condition or combination or process exhibits a beauty . . . the multiplication table its —old age its—the carpenter's trade its—the grand-opera its . . . the hugehulled cleanshaped New-York clipper at sea under steam or full sail gleams with unmatched beauty . . . the American circles and large harmonies of government gleam with theirs . . . and the commonest definite intentions and actions with theirs. The poets of the kosmos advance through all interpositions and coverings and turmoils and stratagems to first principles. They are of use . . . they dissolve poverty from its need and riches from its conceit. You large proprietor they say shall not realize or perceive more than any one else. The owner of the library is not he who holds a legal title to it having bought and paid for it. Any one and every one is owner of the library who can read the same through all the varieties of tongues and subjects and styles, and in whom they enter with ease and take residence and force toward paternity and maternity, and make supple and powerful and rich and large. . . . These American states strong and healthy and accomplished shall receive no pleasure from violations of natural models and must not permit them. In paintings or mouldings or carvings in mineral or wood, or in the illustrations of books or newspapers, or in any comic or tragic prints, or in the patterns of woven stuffs or anything to beautify rooms or furniture or costumes, or to put upon cornices or monuments or on the prows or sterns of ships, or to put anywhere before the human eye indoors or out, that which distorts honest shapes or which creates unearthly beings or places or contingencies is a nuisance and revolt. Of the human form especially it is so great it must never be made ridiculous. Of ornaments to a work nothing outre can be allowed . . . but those ornaments can be allowed that conform to the perfect facts of the open air and that flow out of the nature of the work and come irrepressibly from it and are necessary to the completition of the work. Most works are most beautiful without ornament. . . . Exaggerations will be revenged in human physiology. Clean and vigorous children are jetted and conceived only in those communities where the models of natural forms are public every day. . . . Great genius and the people of these states must never be demeaned to romances. As soon as histories are properly told there is no more need of romances.

The great poets are also to be known by the absence in them of tricks and by the justification of perfect personal candor. Then folks echo a new cheap joy and a divine voice leaping from their brains: How beautiful is candor! All faults may be forgiven of him who has perfect candor. Henceforth let no man of us lie, for we have seen that openness wins the inner and outer world and that there is no single exception, and that never since our earth gathered itself in a mass have deceit or subterfuge or prevarication attracted its smallest particle or the faintest tinge of a shade—and that through the enveloping wealth and rank of a state or the whole republic of states a sneak or sly person shall be discovered and despised . . . and that the soul has never been once fooled and never can be fooled . . . and thrift without the loving nod of the soul is only a fœtid puff . . . and there never grew up in any of the continents of the globe nor upon any planet or satellite or star, nor upon the asteroids, nor in any part of ethereal space, nor in the midst of density, nor under the fluid wet of the sea, nor in the condition which precedes the birth of babes, nor at any time during the changes of life, nor in that condition that follows what we term death, nor in any stretch of abeyance or action afterward of vitality, nor in any process of formation or reformation anywhere, a being whose instinct hated the truth.

Extreme caution or prudence, the soundest organic health, large hope and comparison and fondness for women and children, large alimentiveness and destructiveness and causality, with a perfect sense of the oneness of nature and the propriety of the same spirit applied to human affairs . . . these are called up of the float of the brain of the world to be parts of the greatest poet from his birth out of his mother's womb and from her birth out of her mother's. Caution seldom goes far enough. It has been thought that the prudent citizen was the citizen who applied himself to solid gains and did well for himself and his family and completed a lawful life without debt or crime. The greatest poet sees and admits these economies as he sees the economies of food and sleep, but has higher notions of prudence than to think he gives much when he gives a few slight attentions at the latch of the gate. The premises of the prudence of life are not the hospitality of it or the ripeness and harvest of it. Beyond the independence of a little sum laid aside for burial-money, and of a few clapboards around and shingles overhead on a lot of American soil owned, and the easy dollars that supply the year's plain clothing and meals, the melancholy prudence of the abandonment of such a great being as a man is to the toss and pallor of years of moneymaking with all their scorching days and icy nights and all their stifling deceits and underhanded dodgings, or infinitessimals of parlors, or shameless stuffing while others starve . . . and all the loss of the bloom and odor of the earth and of the flowers and atmosphere and of the sea and of the true taste of the women and men you pass or have to do with in youth or middle age, and the issuing sickness and desperate revolt at the close of a life without elevation or naivete, and the ghastly chatter of a death without serenity or majesty, is the great fraud upon modern civilization and forethought, blotching the surface and system which civilization undeniably drafts, and moistening with tears the immense features it spreads and spreads with such velocity before the reached kisses of the soul. . . . Still the right explanation remains to be made about prudence. The prudence of the mere wealth and respectability of the most esteemed life appears too faint for the eye to observe at all when little and large alike drop quietly aside at the thought of the prudence suitable for immortality. What is wisdom that fills the thinness of a year or seventy or eighty years to wisdom spaced out by ages and coming back at a certain time with strong reinforcements and rich presents and the clear faces of wedding-guests as far as you can look in every direction running gaily toward you? Only the soul is of itself . . . all else has reference to what ensues. All that a person does or thinks is of consequence. Not a move can a man or woman make that affects him or her in a day or a month or any part of the direct lifetime or the hour of death but the same affects him or her onward afterward through the indirect lifetime. The indirect is always as great and real as the direct. The spirit receives from the body just as much as it gives to the body. Not one name of word or deed . . . not of venereal sores or discolorations . . . not the privacy of the onanist . . . not of the putrid veins of gluttons or rum-drinkers . . . not peculation or cunning or betrayal or murder . . . no serpentine poison of those that seduce women . . . not the foolish yielding of women . . . not prostitution . . . not of any depravity of young men . . . not of the attainment of gain by discreditable means . . . not any nastiness of appetite . . . not any harshness of officers to men or judges to prisoners or fathers to sons or sons to fathers or husbands to wives or bosses to their boys . . . not of greedy looks or malignant wishes . . . nor any of the wiles practised by people upon themselves . . . ever is or ever can be stamped on the programme but it is duly realized and returned, and that returned in further performances . . . and they returned again. Nor can the push of charity or personal force ever be any thing else than the profoundest reason, whether it brings arguments to hand or no. No specification is necessary . . . to add or subtract or divide is in vain. Little or big, learned or unlearned, white or black, legal or illegal, sick or well, from the first inspiration down the windpipe to the last expiration out of it, all that a male or female does that is vigorous and benevolent and clean is so much sure profit to him or her in the unshakable order of the universe and through the whole scope of it forever. If the savage or felon is wise it is well . . . if the greatest poet or savan is wise it is simply the same . . . if the President or chief justice is wise it is the same . . . if the young mechanic or farmer is wise it is no more or less . . . if the prostitute is wise it is no more nor less. The interest will come round . . . all will come round. All the best ac-

tions of war and peace . . . all help given to relatives and strangers
and the poor and old and sorrowful and young children and widows
and the sick, and to all shunned persons . . . all furtherance of
fugitives and of the escape of slaves . . . all the self-denial that stood
steady and aloof on wrecks and saw others take the seats of the boats
. . . all offering of substance or life for the good old cause, or for a
friend's sake or opinion's sake . . . all pains of enthusiasts scoffed at
by their neighbors . . . all the vast sweet love and precious suffering of mothers . . . all honest men baffled in strifes recorded or unrecorded . . . all the grandeur and good of the few ancient nations
whose fragments of annals we inherit . . . and all the good of the
hundreds of far mightier and more ancient nations unknown to us
by name or date or location . . . all that was ever manfully begun,
whether it succeeded or not . . . all that has at any time been well
suggested out of the divine heart of man or by the divinity of his
mouth or by the shaping of his great hands . . . and all that is well
thought or done this day on any part of the surface of the globe . . .
or on any of the wandering stars or fixed stars by those there as we are
here . . . or that is henceforth to be well thought or done by you
whoever you are, or by any one—these singly and wholly inured at
their time and inure now and will inure always to the identities from
which they sprung or shall spring. . . . Did you guess any of them
lived only its moment? The world does not so exist . . . no parts
palpable or impalpable so exist . . . no result exists now without being from its long antecedent result, and that from its antecedent, and
so backward without the farthest mentionable spot coming a bit
nearer to the beginning than any other spot. . . . What ever satisfies
the soul is truth. The prudence of the greatest poet answers at last the
craving and glut of the soul, is not contemptuous of less ways of prudence if they conform to its ways, puts off nothing, permits no let-up
for its own case or any case, has no particular sabbath or judgment-
day, divides not the living from the dead or the righteous from the
unrighteous, is satisfied with the present, matches every thought or
act by its correlative, knows no possible forgiveness or deputed atonement . . . knows that the young man who composedly periled his
life and lost it has done exceeding well for himself, while the man
who has not periled his life and retains it to old age in riches and ease
has perhaps achieved nothing for himself worth mentioning . . .
and that only that person has no great prudence to learn who has
learnt to prefer real longlived things, and favors body and soul the
same, and perceives the indirect assuredly following the direct, and
what evil or good he does leaping onward and waiting to meet him
again—and who in his spirit in any emergency whatever neither
hurries or avoids death.

The direct trial of him who would be the greatest poet is today. If
he does not flood himself with the immediate age as with vast oceanic
tides . . . and if he does not attract his own land body and soul to
himself and hang on its neck with incomparable love and plunge his
semitic muscle into its merits and demerits . . . and if he be not

himself the age transfigured . . . and if to him is not opened the
eternity which gives similitude to all periods and locations and processes and animate and inanimate forms, and which is the bond of
time, and rises up from its inconceivable vagueness and infiniteness
in the swimming shape of today, and is held by the ductile anchors
of life, and makes the present spot the passage from what was to what
shall be, and commits itself to the representation of this wave of an
hour and this one of the sixty beautiful children of the wave—let him
merge in the general run and wait his development. . . . Still the
final test of poems or any character or work remains. The prescient
poet projects himself centuries ahead and judges performer or performance after the changes of time. Does it live through them? Does
it still hold on untired? Will the same style and the direction of
genius to similar points be satisfactory now? Has no new discovery in
science or arrival at superior planes of thought and judgment and behaviour fixed him or his so that either can be looked down upon?
Have the marches of tens and hundreds and thousands of years made
willing detours to the right hand and the left hand for his sake? Is he
beloved long and long after he is buried? Does the young man think
often of him? and the young woman think often of him? and do the
middle-aged and the old think of him?

A great poem is for ages and ages in common and for all degrees
and complexions and all departments and sects and for a woman as
much as a man and a man as much as a woman. A great poem is no
finish to a man or woman but rather a beginning. Has any one
fancied he could sit at last under some due authority and rest satisfied
with explanations and realize and be content and full? To no such
terminus does the greatest poet bring . . . he brings neither cessation or sheltered fatness and ease. The touch of him tells in action.
Whom he takes he takes with firm sure grasp into live regions previously unattained . . . thenceforward is no rest . . . they see the
space and ineffable sheen that turn the old spots and lights into dead
vacuums. The companion of him beholds the birth and progress of
stars and learns one of the meanings. Now there shall be a man
cohered out of tumult and chaos . . . the elder encourages the
younger and shows him how . . . they two shall launch off fear-
lessly together till the new world fits an orbit for itself and looks
unabashed on the lesser orbits of the stars and sweeps through the
ceaseless rings and shall never be quiet again.

There will soon be no more priests. Their work is done. They may
wait awhile . . . perhaps a generation or two . . . dropping off by
degrees. A superior breed shall take their place . . . the gangs of
kosmos and prophets en masse shall take their place. A new order
shall arise and they shall be the priests of man, and every man shall
be his own priest. The churches built under their umbrage shall be
the churches of men and women. Through the divinity of themselves
shall the kosmos and the new breed of poets be interpreters of men
and women and of all events and things. They shall find their inspiration in real objects today, symptoms of the past and future . . .

They shall not deign to defend immortality or God or the perfection of things or liberty or the exquisite beauty and reality of the soul. They shall arise in America and be responded to from the remainder of the earth.

The English language befriends the grand American expression . . . it is brawny enough and limber and full enough. On the tough stock of a race who through all change of circumstances was never without the idea of political liberty, which is the animus of all liberty, it has attracted the terms of daintier and gayer and subtler and more elegant tongues. It is the powerful language of resistance . . . it is the dialect of common sense. It is the speech of the proud and melancholy races and of all who aspire. It is the chosen tongue to express growth faith self-esteem freedom justice equality friendliness amplitude prudence decision and courage. It is the medium that shall well nigh express the inexpressible.

No great literature nor any like style of behaviour or oratory or social intercourse or household arrangements or public institutions or the treatment by bosses of employed people, nor executive detail or detail of the army or navy, nor spirit of legislation or courts or police or tuition or architecture or songs or amusements or the costumes of young men, can long elude the jealous and passionate instinct of American standards. Whether or no the sign appears from the mouths of the people, it throbs a live interrogation in every freeman's and freewoman's heart after that which passes by or this built to remain. Is it uniform with my country? Are its disposals without ignominious distinctions? Is it for the evergrowing communes of brothers and lovers, large, well-united, proud beyond the old models, generous beyond all models? Is it something grown fresh out of the fields or drawn from the sea for use to me today here? I know that what answers for me an American must answer for any individual or nation that serves for a part of my materials. Does this answer? or is it without reference to universal needs? or sprung of the needs of the less developed society of special ranks? or old needs of pleasure overlaid by modern science and forms? Does this acknowledge liberty with audible and absolute acknowledgment, and set slavery at naught for life and death? Will it help breed one goodshaped and wellhung man, and a woman to be his perfect and independent mate? Does it improve manners? Is it for the nursing of the young of the republic? Does it solve readily with the sweet milk of the nipples of the breasts of the mother of many children? Has it too the old ever-fresh forbearance and impartiality? Does it look with the same love on the last born and those hardening toward stature, and on the errant, and on those who disdain all strength of assault outside of their own?

The poems distilled from other poems will probably pass away. The coward will surely pass away. The expectation of the vital and great can only be satisfied by the demeanor of the vital and great. The swarms of the polished deprecating and reflectors and the polite float off and leave no remembrance. America prepares with composure and goodwill for the visitors that have sent word. It is not intellect that is to be their warrant and welcome. The talented, the artist, the ingenious, the editor, the statesman, the erudite . . . they are not unappreciated . . . they fall in their place and do their work. The soul of the nation also does its work. No disguise can pass on it . . . no disguise can conceal from it. It rejects none, it permits all. Only toward as good as itself and toward the like of itself will it advance half-way. An individual is as superb as a nation when he has the qualities which make a superb nation. The soul of the largest and wealthiest and proudest nation may well go half-way to meet that of its poets. The signs are effectual. There is no fear of mistake. If the one is true the other is true. The proof of a poet is that his country absorbs him as affectionately as he has absorbed it.

PREFACE, 1872

To *As a Strong Bird on Pinions Free*

The impetus and ideas urging me, for some years past, to an utterance, or attempt at utterance, of New World songs, and an epic of Democracy, having already had their published expression, as well as I can expect to give it, in LEAVES OF GRASS, the present and any future pieces from me are really but the surplusage forming after that Volume, or the wake eddying behind it. I fulfilled in that an imperious conviction, and the commands of my nature as total and irresistible as those which make the sea flow, or the globe revolve. But of this Supplementary Volume, I confess I am not so certain. Having from early manhood abandoned the business pursuits and applications usual in my time and country, and obediently yielded myself up ever since to the impetus mentioned, and to the work of expressing those ideas, it may be that mere habit has got dominion of me, when there is no real need of saying anything further. . . . But what is life but an experiment? and mortality but an exercise? with reference to results beyond. And so shall my poems be. If incomplete here, and superfluous there, *n'importe*—the earnest trial and persistent exploration shall at least be mine, and other success failing, shall be success enough. I have been more anxious, anyhow, to suggest the songs of vital endeavor and manly evolution, and furnish something for races of outdoor athletes, than to make perfect rhymes, or reign in the parlors. I ventured from the beginning, my own way, taking chances —and would keep on venturing.

I will therefore not conceal from any persons, known or unknown to me, who take interest in the matter, that I have the ambition of devoting yet a few years to poetic composition. . . . The mighty present age! To absorb, and express in poetry, any thing of it—of its world—America—cities and States—the years, the events of our Nineteenth Century—the rapidity of movement—the violent contrasts, fluctuations of light and shade, of hope and fear—the entire revolution made by science in the poetic method—these great new underlying facts and new ideas rushing in and spreading everywhere;—Truly a mighty age! As if in some colossal drama, acted again like those of old, under the open sun, the Nations of our time, and all the characteristics of Civilization, seem hurrying, stalking across, flitting from wing to wing, gathering, closing up, toward some long-prepared, most tremendous denouement. Not to conclude the infinite scenas of the race's life and toil and happiness and sorrow, but haply that the boards be cleared from oldest, worst incumbrances, accumulations, and Man resume the eternal play anew, and under happier, freer auspices. . . . To me, the United States are important because, in this colossal drama, they are unquestionably designated for the leading parts, for many a century to come. In them History and Humanity seem to seek to culminate. Our broad areas are even now the busy theatre of plots, passions, interests, and suspended problems, compared to which the intrigues of the past of Europe, the wars of dynasties, the scope of kings and kingdoms, and even the development of peoples, as hitherto, exhibit scales of measurement comparatively narrow and trivial. And on these areas of ours, as on a stage, sooner or later, something like an *eclaircissement* of all the past civilization of Europe and Asia is probably to be evolved.

The leading parts. . . . Not to be acted, emulated here, by us again, that role till now foremost in History—Not to become a conqueror nation, or to achieve the glory of mere military, or diplomatic, or commercial superiority—but to become the grand Producing Land of nobler Men and Women—of copious races, cheerful, healthy, tolerant, free—To become the most friendly Nation, (the United States indeed,)—the modern composite Nation, formed from all, with room for all, welcoming all immigrants—accepting the work of our own interior development, as the work fitly filling ages and ages to come;—the leading Nation of peace, but neither ignorant nor incapable of being the leading Nation of war;—not the Man's Nation only, but the Woman's Nation—a land of splendid mothers, daughters, sisters, wives.

Our America to-day I consider in many respects as but indeed a vast seething mass of *materials,* ampler, better, (worse also,) than previously known—eligible to be used to carry toward its crowning stage, and build for good the great Ideal Nationality of the future, the Nation of the Body and the Soul.†—no limit here to land, help, opportunities, mines, products, demands, supplies, &c.;—with (I think) our political organization, National, State, and Municipal, permanently established, as far ahead as we can calculate—but, so far, no social, literary, religious, or esthetic organizations, consistent with our politics, or becoming to us—which organizations can only come, in time, through native schools or teachers of great Democratic Ideas, Religion—through Science, which now, like a new sunrise, ascending, begins to illuminate all—and through our own begotten Poets and Literatures. . . . (The moral of a late well-written book on Civilization seems to be that the only real foundation-walls and basis—and also *sine qua non* afterward—of true and full Civilization, is the eligibility and certainty of boundless products for feeding, clothing, sheltering every body—perennial fountains of physical and domestic comfort, with intercommunication, and with civil and ecclesiastical freedom—and that then the esthetic and mental business will take

† The problems of the achievements of this crowning stage through future first-class National Singers, Orators, Artists, and others — of creating in literature an *imaginative* New World, the correspondent and counterpart of the current Scientific and Political New Worlds — and the perhaps distant, but still delightful prospect, (for our children, if not in our own day,) of delivering America, and, indeed, all Christian lands everywhere, from the thin, moribund, and watery, but appallingly extensive nuisance of conventional poetry — by putting something really alive and substantial in its place — I have undertaken to grapple with, and argue, in Demo-cratic Vistas.

care of itself . . . Well, the United States have established this basis,
and upon scales of extent, variety, vitality, and continuity, rivaling
those of Nature; and have now to proceed to build an Edifice upon
it. I say this Edifice is only to be fitly built by new Literatures, especially the Poetic. I say a modern Image-Making creation is indispensable to fuse and express modern Political and Scientific creations
—and then the Trinity will be complete.)

When I commenced, years ago, elaborating the plan of my poems,
and continued turning over that plan, and shifting it in my mind
through many years, (from the age of twenty-eight to thirty-five,)
experimenting much, and writing and abandoning much, one deep
purpose underlay the others, and has underlain it and its execution
ever since—and that has been the Religious purpose. Amid many
changes, and a formulation taking far different shape from what I
at first supposed, this basic purpose has never been departed from in
the composition of my verses. Not of course to exhibit itself in the
old ways, as in writing hymns or psalms with an eye to the church-
pew, or to express conventional pietism, or the sickly yearnings of
devotees, but in new ways, and aiming at the widest sub-bases and
inclusions of Humanity, and tallying the fresh air of sea and land.
I will see, (said I to myself,) whether there is not, for my purposes
as poet, a Religion, and a sound Religious germenancy in the average
Human Race, at least in their modern development in the United
States, and in the hardy common fiber and native yearnings and elements, deeper and larger, and affording more profitable returns, than
all mere sects or churches—as boundless, joyous, and vital as Nature
itself—A germenancy that has too long been unencouraged, unsung,
almost unknown. . . . With Science, the Old Theology of the East,
long in its dotage, begins evidently to die and disappear. But (to my
mind) Science—and may be such will prove its principal service—as
evidently prepares the way for One indescribably grander—Time's
young but perfect offspring—the New Theology—heir of the West—
lusty and loving, and wondrous beautiful. For America, and for to-
day, just the same as any day, the supreme and final Science is the
Science of God—what we call science being only its minister—as
Democracy is or shall be also. And a poet of America (I said) must
fill himself with such thoughts, and chant his best out of them. . . .
And as those were the convictions and aims, for good or bad, of
LEAVES OF GRASS, they are no less the intention of this Volume. As
there can be, in my opinion, no sane and complete Personality, nor
any grand and electric Nationality, without the stock element of Religion imbuing all the other elements, (like heat in chemistry, invisible itself, but the life of all visible life,) so there can be no
Poetry worthy the name without that element behind all. . . . The
time has certainly come to begin to discharge the idea of Religion, in
the United States, from mere ecclesiasticism, and from Sundays and
churches and church-going, and assign it to that general position,
chiefest, most indispensable, most exhilarating, to which the others

are to be adjusted, inside of all human character, and education, and affairs. The people, especially the young men and women of America, must begin to learn that Religion, (like Poetry,) is something far, far different from what they supposed. It is, indeed, too important to the power and perpetuity of the New World to be consigned any longer to the churches, old or new, Catholic or Protestant—Saint this, or Saint that. . . . It must be consigned henceforth to Democracy *en masse,* and to Literature. It must enter into the Poems of the Nation. It must make the Nation.

The Four Years' War is over—and in the peaceful, strong, exciting, fresh occasions of To-day, and of the Future, that strange, sad war is hurrying even now to be forgotten. The camp, the drill, the lines of sentries, the prisons, the hospitals—(ah! the hospitals!)—all have passed away—all seem now like a dream. A new race, a young and lusty generation, already sweeps in with oceanic currents, obliterating the war, and all its scars, its mounded graves, and all its reminiscences of hatred, conflict, death. So let it be obliterated. I say the life of the present and the future makes undeniable demands upon us each and all, South, North, East, West. . . . To help put the United States (even if only in imagination) hand in hand, in one unbroken circle in a chant—To rouse them to the unprecedented grandeur of the part they are to play, and are even now playing—to the thought of their great Future, and the attitude conformed to it—especially their great Esthetic, Moral, Scientific future, (of which their vulgar material and political present is but as the preparatory tuning of instruments by an orchestra,) these, as hitherto, are still, for me, among my hopes, ambitions.

Leaves of Grass, already published, is, in its intentions, the song of a great composite *Democratic Individual,* male or female. And following on and amplifying the same purpose, I suppose I have in my mind to run through the chants of this Volume, (if ever completed,) the thread-voice, more or less audible, of an aggregated, inseparable, unprecedented, vast, composite, electric *Democratic nationality.*

Purposing, then, to still fill out, from time to time through years to come, the following Volume, (unless prevented,) I conclude this Preface to the first instalment of it, penciled in the open air, on my fifty-third birthday, by wafting to you, dear Reader, whoever you are, (from amid the fresh scent of the grass, the pleasant coolness of the forenoon breeze, the lights and shades of tree-boughs silently dappling and playing around me, and the notes of the cat-bird for undertone and accompaniment,) my true good-will and love.

W. W.

Washington, D.C., May 31, 1872.

PREFACE, 1876

To Volume II of the Centennial Edition, *Two Rivulets*

At the eleventh hour, under grave illness, I gather up the pieces of Prose and Poetry left over since publishing, a while since, my first and main volume, LEAVES OF GRASS—pieces, here, some new, some old—nearly all of them (sombre as many are, making this almost Death's book) composed in by-gone atmosphere of perfect health— and, preceded by the freshest collection, the little TWO RIVULETS, and by this rambling Prefatory gossip,† now send them out, embodied in the present Melange, partly as my contribution and outpouring to celebrate, in some sort, the feature of the time, the first Centennial of our New World Nationality—and then as chyle and nutriment to that moral Indissoluble Union, equally representing All, and the mother of many coming Centennials.

And e'en for flush and proof of our America—for reminder, just as much, or more, in moods of towering pride and joy, I keep my special chants of Death and Immortality‡ to stamp the coloring-finish of all,

---

† This Preface is not only for the present collection, but, in a sort of all my writings, both Volumes.

‡ PASSAGE TO INDIA. — As in some ancient legend-play, to close the plot and the hero's career, there is a farewell gathering on ship's deck and on shore, a loosing of hawsers and ties, a spreading of sails to the wind — a starting out on unknown seas, to fetch up no one knows whither — to return no more — And the curtain falls, and there is the end of it — So I have reserv'd that Poem, with its cluster, to finish and explain much that, without them, would not be explain'd, and to take leave, and escape for good, from all that has preceded them. (Then probably *Passage to India*, and its cluster, are but freer vent and fuller expression to what, from the first, and so on throughout, more or less lurks in my writings, underneath every page, every line, everywhere.)

I am not sure but the last inclosing sublimation of Race or Poem is, What it thinks of Death. . . . After the rest has been comprehended and said, even the grandest — After those contributions to mightiest Nationality, or to sweetest Song, or to the best Personalism, male or female, have been glean'd from the rich and varied themes of tangible life, and have been fully accepted and sung, and the pervading fact of visible existence, with the duty it devolves, is rounded and apparently completed, it still remains to be really completed by suffusing through the whole and several, that other pervading invisible fact, so large a part, (is it not the largest part?) of life here, combining the rest, and furnishing, for Person or State, the only permanent and unitary meaning to all, even the meanest life, consistently with the dignity of the Universe, in Time. . . . As, from the eligibility to this thought, and the cheerful conquest of this fact, flash forth the first distinctive proofs of the Soul, so to me, (extending it only a little further,) the ultimate Democratic purports, the ethereal and spiritual ones, are to concentrate here, and as fixed stars, radiate hence. For, in my opinion, it is no less than this idea of Immortality, above all other ideas, that is to enter into, and vivify, and give crowning religious stamp, to Democracy in the New World.

present and past. For terminus and temperer to all, they were originally written, and that shall be their office at the last.

For some reason—not explainable or definite to my own mind, yet secretly pleasing and satisfactory to it—I have not hesitated to embody in, and run through the Volume, two altogether distinct veins, or strata—Politics for one, and for the other, the pensive thought of Immortality. . . . Thus, too, the prose and poetic, the dual forms of the present book. The pictures from the Hospitals during the War, in *Memoranda*, I have also decided to include. Though they differ in character and composition from the rest of my pieces, yet I feel that they ought to go with them, and must do so. . . . The present Volume, therefore, after its minor episodes, probably divides into these Two, at first sight far diverse, veins of topic and treatment. One will be found in the prose part of Two RIVULETS, in *Democratic Vistas*,

---

It was originally my intention, after chanting in LEAVES OF GRASS the songs of the Body and Existence, to then compose a further, equally needed Volume, based on those convictions of perpetuity and conservation which, enveloping all precedents, make the unseen Soul absolutely at last. I meant, while in a sort continuing the theme of my first chants, to then shift the slides, and exhibit the problem and paradox of the same ardent and fully appointed Personality entering the sphere of the resistless gravitation of Spiritual Law, and with cheerful face estimating Death, not at all as the cessation, but as somehow what I feel it must be, the entrance upon by far the greatest part of existence, and something that Life is at least as much for, as it is for itself.

But the full construction of such a work (even if I lay the foundation, or give impetus to it) is beyond my powers, and must remain for some bard in the future. The physical and the sensuous, in themselves or in their immediate continuations, retain holds upon me which I think are never entirely releas'd; and those holds I have not only not denied, but hardly wish'd to weaken.

Meanwhile, not entirely to give the go-by to my original plan, and far more to avoid a mark'd hiatus in it, than to entirely fulfil it, I end my books with thoughts, or radiations from thoughts, on Death, Immortality, and a free entrance into the Spiritual world. In those thoughts, in a sort, I make the first steps or studies toward the mighty theme, from the point of view necessitated by foregoing poems, and by Modern Science. In them I also seek to set the keystone to my Democracy's enduring arch. I re-collate them now, for the press, (much the same, I transcribe my *Memoranda* following, of gloomy times out of the War, and Hospitals) in order to partially occupy and off-set days of strange sickness, and the heaviest affliction and bereavement of my life; and I fondly please myself with the notion of leaving that cluster to you, O unknown Reader of the future, as 'something to remember me by,' more especially than all else. Written in former days of perfect health, little did I think the pieces had the purport that now, under present circumstances, opens to me.

[As I write these lines, May 31, 1875, it is again early summer — again my birthday — now my fifty-sixth. Amid the outside beauty and freshness, the sunlight and verdure of the delightful season, O how different the moral atmosphere amid which I now revise this Volume, from the jocund influence surrounding the growth and advent of LEAVES OF GRASS. I occupy myself, arranging these pages for publication, still envelopt in thoughts of the death two years since of my dear Mother, the most perfect and magnetic character, the rarest combination of practical, moral and spiritual, and the least selfish, of all and any I have ever known — and by me O so much the most deeply loved — and also under the physical affliction of a tedious attack of paralysis, obstinately lingering and keeping its hold upon me, and quite suspending all

in the Preface to *As a Strong Bird*, and in the concluding Notes to *Memoranda* of the Hospitals. The other, wherein the all-enclosing thought and fact of Death is admitted, (not for itself so much as a powerful factor in the adjustments of Life,) in the realistic pictures of *Memoranda*, and the free speculations and ideal escapades of *Passage to India*.

Has not the time come, indeed, in the development of the New World, when its Politics should ascend into atmospheres and regions hitherto unknown—(far, far different from the miserable business that of late and current years passes under that name)—and take rank with Science, Philosophy and Art? . . . Three points, in especial, have become very dear to me, and all through I seek to make them again and again, in many forms and repetitions, as will be seen: 1. That the true growth-characteristics of the Democracy of the New World are henceforth to radiate in superior Literary, Artistic and Religious Expressions, far more than in its Republican forms, universal suffrage, and frequent elections, (though these are unspeakably important). . . . 2. That the vital political mission of The United States is, to practically solve and settle the problem of two sets of rights—the fusion, thorough compatibility and junction of individual State prerogatives, with the indispensable necessity of centrality and Oneness—the National Identity power—the sovereign Union, relentless, permanently comprising all, and over all, and in that never yielding an inch . . . then 3d. Do we not, amid a general malaria of Fogs and Vapors, our day, unmistakably see two Pillars of Promise, with grandest, indestructible indications—One, that the morbid facts of American politics and society everywhere are but passing incidents and flanges of our unbounded impetus of growth—weeds, annuals of the rank, rich soil—not central, enduring, perennial things? The Other, that all the hitherto experience of The States, their first Century, has been but preparation, adolescence—and that This Union is only now and henceforth (*i. e.* since the Secession war) to enter on its full Democratic career?

Of the whole, Poems and Prose, (not attending at all to chronological order, and with original dates and passing allusions in the heat and impression of the hour, left shuffled in, and undisturb'd,)

---

bodily activity and comfort . . . I see now, much clearer than ever — perhaps these experiences were needed to show — how much my former poems, the bulk of them, are indeed the expression of health and strength, the sanest, joyfullest life.]

Under these influences, therefore, I still feel to keep *Passage to India* for last words even to this Centennial dithyramb. Not as, in antiquity, at highest festival of Egypt, the noisome skeleton of Death was also sent on exhibition to the revelers, for zest and shadow to the occasion's joy and light — but as the perfect marble statue of the normal Greeks at Elis, suggesting death in the form of a beautiful and perfect young man, with closed eyes, leaning on an inverted torch — emblem of rest and aspiration after action — of crown and point which all lives and poems should steadily have reference to, namely, the justified and noble termination of our identity, this grade of it, and outlet-preparation to another grade.

the chants of LEAVES OF GRASS, my former Volume, yet serve as the indispensable deep soil, or basis, out of which, and out of which only, could come the roots and stems more definitely indicated by these later pages. (While that Volume radiates Physiology alone, the present One, though of the like origin in the main, more palpably doubtless shows the Pathology which was pretty sure to come in time from the other.)

In that former and main Volume, composed in the flush of my health and strength, from the age of 30 to 50 years, I dwelt on Birth and Life, clothing my ideas in pictures, days, transactions of my time, to give them positive place, identity—saturating them with that vehemence of pride and audacity of freedom necessary to loosen the mind of still-to-be-form'd America from the accumulated folds, the superstitions, and all the long, tenacious and stifling anti-democratic authorities of the Asiatic and European past—my enclosing purport being to express, above all artificial regulation and aid, the eternal Bodily Character of One's-Self.†

The varieties and phases, (doubtless often paradoxical, contradic-

---

† LEAVES OF GRASS. — Namely, a character, making most of common and normal elements, to the superstructure of which not only the precious accumulations of the learning and experiences of the Old World, and the settled social and municipal necessities and current requirements, so long a-building, shall still faithfully contribute, but which, at its foundations and carried up thence, and receiving its impetus from the Democratic spirit, and accepting its gauge, in all departments, from the Democratic formulas, shall again directly be vitalized by the perennial influences of Nature at first hand, and the old heroic stamina of Nature, the strong air of prairie and mountain, the dash of the briny sea, the primary antiseptics — of the passions, in all their fullest heat and potency, of courage, rankness, amativeness, and of immense pride. . . . Not to lose at all, therefore, the benefits of artificial progress and civilization, but to re-occupy for Western tenancy the oldest though ever-fresh fields, and reap from them the savage and sane nourishment indispensable to a hardy nation, and the absence of which, threatening to become worse and worse, is the most serious lack and defect to-day of our New World literature.

Not but what the brawn of LEAVES OF GRASS is, I think, thoroughly spiritualized everywhere, for final estimate, but, from the very subjects, the direct effect is a sense of the Life, as it should be, of flesh and blood, and physical urge, and animalism. . . . While there are other themes, and plenty of abstract thoughts and poems in the Volume — While I have put in it (supplemented in the present Work by my prose *Memoranda*,) passing and rapid but actual glimpses of the great struggle between the Nation and the Slavepower, (1861-'65,) as the fierce and bloody panorama of that contest unroll'd itself — While the whole Book, indeed, revolves around that Four Years' War, which, as I was in the midst of it, becomes, in *Drum-Taps*, pivotal to the rest entire — follow'd by *Marches now the War is Over* — and here and there, before and afterward, not a few episodes and speculations — *that* — namely, to make a type-portrait for living, active, worldly, healthy Personality, objective as well as subjective, joyful and potent, and modern and free, distinctively for the use of the United States, male and female, through the long future — has been, I say, my general object. (Probably, indeed, the whole of these varied songs, and all my writings, both Volumes, only ring changes in some sort, on the ejaculation, How vast, how eligible, how joyful, how real, is a Human Being, himself or herself.)

Though from no definite plan at the time, I see now that I have unconsciously

tory,) of the two Volumes, of Leaves, and of these Rivulets, are
ultimately to be considered as One in structure, and as mutually ex-
planatory of each other—as the multiplex results, like a tree, of series
of successive growths, (yet from one central or seed-purport)—there
having been five or six such cumulative issues, editions, commencing
back in 1855 and thence progressing through twenty years down to
date, (1875-76)—some things added or re-shaped from time to time,
as they were found wanted, and other things represt. Of the former
Book, more vehement, and perhaps pursuing a central idea with
greater closeness—join'd with the present One, extremely varied in
theme—I can only briefly reiterate here, that all my pieces, alternated
through Both, are only of use and value, if any, as such an interpene-
trating, composite, inseparable Unity.

Two of the pieces in this Volume were originally Public Recita-

---

sought by indirections at least as much as directions, to express the whirls and
rapid growth and intensity of the United States, the prevailing tendency and events
of the Nineteenth Century, and largely the spirit of the whole current World, my
time; for I feel that I have partaken of that spirit, as I have been deeply interested
in all those events, the closing of long-stretch'd eras and ages, and, illustrated in the
history of the United States, the opening of larger ones. (The death of President
Lincoln, for instance, fitly, historically closes, in the Civilization of Feudalism, many
old influences — drops on them, suddenly, a vast, gloomy, as it were, separating
curtain. The world's entire dramas afford none more indicative — none with folds
more tragic, or more sombre or far spreading.)

Since I have been ill, (1873-74-75,) mostly without serious pain, and with plenty
of time and frequent inclination to judge my poems, (never composed with eye on the
book-market, nor for fame, nor for any pecuniary profit,) I have felt temporary
depression more than once, for fear that in Leaves of Grass the *moral* parts were
not sufficiently pronounc'd. But in my clearest and calmest moods I have realized
that as those Leaves, all and several, surely prepare the way for, and necessitate
Morals, and are adjusted to them, just the same as Nature does and is, they are what,
consistently with my plan, they must and probably should be. . . . (In a certain
sense, while the Moral is the purport and last intelligence of all Nature, there is
absolutely nothing of the moral in the works, or laws, or shows of Nature. Those
only lead inevitably to it — begin and necessitate it.)

Then I meant Leaves of Grass, as publish'd, to be the Poem of Identity, (of
Yours, whoever you are, now reading these lines.) . . . For genius must realize that,
precious as it may be, there is something far more precious, namely, simple Identity,
One's-self. A man is not greatest as victor in war, nor inventor or explorer, nor even
in science, or in his intellectual or artistic capacity, or exemplar in some vast
benevolence. To the highest Democratic view, man is most acceptable in living well
the average, practical life and lot which happens to him as ordinary farmer, sea-farer,
mechanic, clerk, laborer, or driver — upon and from which position as a central basis
or pedestal, while performing its labors, and his duties as citizen, son, husband,
father and employed person, he preserves his physique, ascends, developing, radiating
himself in other regions — and especially where and when, (greatest of all, and
nobler than the proudest mere genius or magnate in any field,) he fully realizes the
Conscience, the Spiritual, the divine faculty, cultivated well, exemplified in all his
deeds and words, through life, uncompromising to the end — a flight loftier than any
of Homer's or Shakspere's — broader than all poems and bibles — namely, Nature's

tions—the College Commencement Poem, *As a Strong Bird*—and
then the *Song of the Exposition*, to identify these great Industrial
gatherings, the majestic outgrowths of the Modern Spirit and Practice—and now fix'd upon, the grandest of them, for the Material event
around which shall be concentrated and celebrated, (as far as any one
event can combine them,) the associations and practical proofs of the
Hundred Years' life of the Republic. The glory of Labor, and the
bringing together not only representatives of all the trades and products, but, fraternally, of all the Workmen of all the Nations of the
World, (for this is the Idea behind the Centennial at Philadelphia,)
is, to me, so welcome and inspiring a theme, that I only wish I were
a younger and a fresher man, to attempt the enduring Book, of poetic
character, that ought to be written about it.

The arrangement in print of Two Rivulets—the indirectness of

---

own, and in the midst of it, Yourself, your own Identity, body and soul. (All serves,
helps — but in the centre of all, absorbing all, giving, for your purpose, the only
meaning and vitality to all, master or mistress of all, under the law, stands Yourself.)
. . . To sing the Song of that divine law of Identity, and of Yourself, consistently
with the Divine Law of the Universal, is a main intention of those Leaves.

Something more may be added — for, while I am about it, I would make a full
confession. I also sent out Leaves of Grass to arouse and set flowering in men's
and women's hearts, young and old, (my present and future readers,) endless streams
of living, pulsating love and friendship, directly from them to myself, now and
ever. To this terrible, irrepressible yearning, (surely more or less down underneath in
most human souls,) — this never-satisfied appetite for sympathy, and this boundless
offering of sympathy — this universal democratic comradeship — this old, eternal, yet
ever-new interchange of adhesiveness, so fitly emblematic of America — I have given
in that book, undisguisedly, declaredly, the openest expression. . . . Poetic literature
has long been the formal and conventional tender of art and beauty merely, and of a
narrow, constipated, special amativeness. I say, the subtlest, sweetest, surest tie between me and Him or Her, who, in the pages of *Calamus* and other pieces realizes
me — though we never see each other or through ages and ages hence — must, in this
way, be personal affection. And those — be they few, or be they many — are at any
rate *my readers* in a sense that belongs not, and can never belong, to better, prouder
poems.

Besides, important as they are in my purpose as emotional expressions for humanity,
the special meaning of the *Calamus* cluster of Leaves of Grass, (and more or less
running through that book, and cropping out in *Drum-Taps*,) mainly resides in its
Political significance. In my opinion it is by a fervent, accepted development of
Comradeship, the beautiful and sane affection of man for man, latent in all the
young fellows, North and South, East and West — it is by this, I say, and by what
goes directly and indirectly along with it, that the United States of the future, (I
cannot too often repeat,) are to be most effectually welded together, intercalated,
anneal'd into a Living Union.

Then, for enclosing clue of all, it is imperatively and ever to be borne in mind that
Leaves of Grass entire is not to be construed as an intellectual or scholastic effort
or Poem mainly, but more as a radical utterance out of the abysms of the Soul, the
Emotions and the Physique — an utterance adjusted to, perhaps born of, Democracy
and Modern Science, and in its very nature regardless of the old conventions, and,
under the great Laws, following only its own impulses.

the name itself, (suggesting meanings, the start of other meanings, for the whole Volume) are but parts of the Venture which my Poems entirely are. For really they have all been Experiments, under the urge of powerful, quite irresistible, perhaps wilful influences, (even escapades,) to see how such things will eventually turn out—and have been recited, as it were, by my Soul, to the special audience of Myself, far more than to the world's audience. (See, further on,† Preface of *As a Strong Bird,* &c., 1872.) Till now, by far the best part of the whole business is, that, these days, in leisure, in sickness and old age, my Spirit, by which they were written or permitted erewhile, does not go back on them, but still and in cabinet hours, fully, deliberately allows them.

Estimating the American Union as so far and for some time to come, in its yet formative condition, I therefore now bequeath Poems and Essays as nutriment and influences to help truly assimilate and harden, and especially to furnish something toward what The States most need of all, and which seems to me yet quite unsupplied in literature, namely, to show them, or begin to show them, Themselves distinctively, and what They are for. For though perhaps the main points of all ages and nations are points of resemblance, and, even while granting evolution, are substantially the same, there are some vital things in which this Republic, as to its individualities, and as a compacted Nation, is to specially stand forth, and culminate modern humanity. And these are the very things it least morally and mentally knows—(though, curiously enough, it is at the same time faithfully acting upon them.)

I count with such absolute certainty on the Great Future of The United States—different from, though founded on, the past—that I have always invoked that Future, and surrounded myself with it, before or while singing my Songs. . . . (As ever, all tends to followings—America, too, is a prophecy. What, even of the best and most successful, would be justified by itself alone? by the present, or the material ostent alone? Of men or States, few realize how much they live in the future. That, rising like pinnacles, gives its main significance to all You and I are doing to-day. Without it, there were little meaning in lands or poems—little purport in human lives. . . . All ages, all Nations and States, have been such prophecies. But where any former ones with prophecy so broad, so clear, as our times, our lands—as those of the West?)

Without being a Scientist, I have thoroughly adopted the conclusions of the great Savans and Experimentalists of our time, and of the last hundred years, and they have interiorly tinged the chyle of all my verse, for purposes beyond. Following the Modern Spirit, the real Poems of the Present, ever solidifying and expanding into the Future, must vocalize the vastness and splendor and reality with which

† Pages 429–432 of the present volume. — Ed. Note.

Scientism has invested Man and the Universe, (all that is called Creation,) and must henceforth launch Humanity into new orbits, consonant with that vastness, splendor, and reality, (unknown to the old poems,) like new systems of orbs, balanced upon themselves, revolving in limitless space, more subtle than the stars. Poetry, so largely hitherto and even at present wedded to children's tales, and to mere amorousness, upholstery and superficial rhyme, will have to accept, and, while not denying the Past, nor the Themes of the past, will be revivified by this tremendous inovation, the Kosmic Spirit, which must henceforth, in my opinion, be the background and underlying impetus, more or less visible, of all first-class Songs.

Only, (for me, at any rate, in all my Prose and Poetry,) joyfully accepting Modern Science, and loyally following it without the slightest hesitation, there remains ever recognized still a higher flight, a higher fact, the Eternal Soul of Man, (of all Else too,) the Spiritual, the Religious—which it is to be the greatest office of Scientism, in my opinion, and of future Poetry also, to free from fables, crudities and superstitions, and launch forth in renewed Faith and Scope a hundred fold. To me, the worlds of Religiousness, of the conception of the Divine, and of the Ideal, though mainly latent, are just as absolute in Humanity and the Universe as the world of Chemistry, or anything in the objective worlds. To me,

> The prophet and the Bard,
> Shall yet maintain themselves—in higher circles yet,
> Shall mediate to the Modern, to Democracy—interpret yet to them,
> God and Eidólons.

To me, the crown of Savantism is to be, that it surely opens the way for a more splendid Theology, and for ampler and diviner Songs. No year, or even century, will settle this. There is a phase of the Real, lurking behind the Real, which it is all for. There is also in the Intellect of man, in time, far in prospective recesses, a judgment, a last appellate court, which will settle it.

In certain parts, in these flights, or attempting to depict or suggest them, I have not been afraid of the charge of obscurity, in either of my Two Volumes—because human thought, poetry or melody, must leave dim escapes and outlets—must possess a certain fluid, aërial character, akin to space itself, obscure to those of little or no imagination, but indispensable to the highest purposes. Poetic style, when address'd to the Soul, is less definite form, outline, sculpture, and becomes vista, music, half-tints, and even less than half-tints. True, it may be architecture, but again it may be the forest wild-wood, or the best effects thereof, at twilight, the waving oaks and cedars in the wind, and the impalpable odor.

Finally, as I have lived in fresh lands, inchoate, and in a revolutionary age, future-founding, I have felt to identify the points of that age, these lands, in my recitatives, altogether in my own way.

Thus my form has strictly grown from my purports and facts, and is the analogy of them. . . . Within my time the United States have emerg'd from nebulous vagueness and suspense, to full orbic, (though varied,) decision—have done the deeds and achiev'd the triumphs of half a score of centuries—and are henceforth to enter upon their real history—the way being now, (*i. e.* since the result of the Secession War,) clear'd of death-threatening impedimenta, and the free areas around and ahead of us assured and certain, which were not so before—(the past century being but preparations, trial-voyages and experiments of the Ship, before her starting out upon deep water.)

In estimating my Volumes, the world's current times and deeds, and their spirit, must be first profoundly estimated. Out of the Hundred Years just ending, (1776-1876,) with their genesis of inevitable wilful events, and new introductions, and many unprecedented things of war and peace, (to be realized better, perhaps only realized, at the remove of a Century hence)—Out of that stretch of time, and especially out of the immediately preceding Twenty-Five Years, (1850-75,) with all their rapid changes, innovations, and audacious movements—and bearing their own inevitable wilful birth-marks—my Poems too have found genesis. W. W.

A BACKWARD GLANCE O'ER
TRAVEL'D ROADS

[Preface to *November Boughs*, 1888]

Perhaps the best of songs heard, or of any and all true love, or life's fairest episodes, or sailors', soldiers' trying scenes on land or sea, is the *résumé* of them, or any of them, long afterwards, looking at the actualities away back past, with all their practical excitations gone. How the soul loves to float amid such reminiscences!

So here I sit gossiping in the early candle-light of old age—I and my book—casting backward glances over our travel'd road. After completing, as it were, the journey—(a varied jaunt of years, with many halts and gaps of intervals—or some lengthen'd ship-voyage, wherein more than once the last hour had apparently arrived, and we seem'd certainly going down—yet reaching port in a sufficient way through all discomfitures at last)—After completing my poems, I am curious to review them in the light of their own (at the time unconscious, or mostly unconscious) intentions, with certain unfoldings of the thirty years they seek to embody. These lines, therefore, will probably blend the weft of first purposes and speculations, with the warp of that experience afterwards, always bringing strange developments.

Result of seven or eight stages and struggles extending through nearly thirty years, (as I nigh my three-score-and-ten I live largely on memory,) I look upon "Leaves of Grass," now finish'd to the end of its opportunities and powers, as my definitive *carte visite* to the coming generations of the New World,† if I may assume to say so. That I have not gain'd the acceptance of my own time, but have fallen back on fond dreams of the future—anticipations—("still lives the song, though Regnar dies")—That from a worldly and business point of view "Leaves of Grass" has been worse than a failure—that public criticism on the book and myself as author of it yet shows mark'd anger and contempt more than anything else—("I find a solid line of enemies to you everywhere,"—letter from W. S. K., Boston, May 28, 1884)—And that solely for publishing it I have been the object of two or three pretty serious special official buffetings—is all probably no more than I ought to have expected. I had my choice when I commenc'd. I bid neither for soft eulogies, big money returns, nor the approbation of existing schools and conventions. As fulfill'd or partially fulfill'd, the best comfort of the whole business (after a small band of the dearest friends and upholders ever vouchsafed to man or cause—doubtless all the more faithful and uncompromising

---

† When Champollion, on his death-bed, handed to the printer the revised proof of his "Egyptian Grammar," he said gayly, "Be careful of this — it is my *carte de visite* to posterity."

—this little phalanx!—for being so few) is that, unstopp'd and un-warp'd by any influence outside the soul within me, I have had my say entirely my own way, and put it unerringly on record—the value thereof to be decided by time.

In calculating that decision, William O'Connor and Dr. Bucke are far more peremptory than I am. Behind all else that can be said, I consider "Leaves of Grass" and its theory experimental—as, in the deepest sense, I consider our American republic itself to be, with its theory. (I think I have at least enough philosophy not to be too absolutely certain of anything, or any results.) In the second place, the volume is a *sortie*—whether to prove triumphant, and conquer its field of aim and escape and construction, nothing less than a hun-dred years from now can fully answer. I consider the point that I have positively gain'd a hearing, to far more than make up for any and all other lacks and withholdings. Essentially, *that* was from the first, and has remain'd throughout, the main object. Now it seems to be achiev'd, I am certainly contented to waive any otherwise mo-mentous drawbacks, as of little account. Candidly and dispassionately reviewing all my intentions, I feel that they were creditable—and I accept the result, whatever it may be.

After continued personal ambition and effort, as a young fellow, to enter with the rest into competition for the usual rewards, business, political, literary, &c.—to take part in the great *mêlée*, both for vic-tory's prize itself and to do some good—After years of those aims and pursuits, I found myself remaining possess'd, at the age of thirty-one to thirty-three, with a special desire and conviction. Or rather, to be quite exact, a desire that had been flitting through my previous life, or hovering on the flanks, mostly indefinite hitherto, had steadily advanced to the front, defined itself, and finally dominated every-thing else. This was a feeling or ambition to articulate and faithfully express in literary or poetic form, and uncompromisingly, my own physical, emotional, moral, intellectual, and æsthetic Personality, in the midst of, and tallying, the momentous spirit and facts of its im-mediate days, and of current America—and to exploit that Personality, identified with place and date, in a far more candid and compre-hensive sense than any hitherto poem or book.

Perhaps this is in brief, or suggests, all I have sought to do. Given the Nineteenth Century, with the United States, and what they furnish as area and points of view, "Leaves of Grass" is, or seeks to be, simply a faithful and doubtless self-will'd record. In the midst of all, it gives one man's—the author's—identity, ardors, observations, faiths, and thoughts, color'd hardly at all with any decided coloring from other faiths or other identities. Plenty of songs had been sung—beautiful, matchless songs—adjusted to other lands than these—another spirit and stage of evolution; but I would sing, and leave out or put in, quite solely with reference to America and to-day. Modern science and democracy seem'd to be throwing out their challenge to poetry to put them in its statements in contradistinction to the songs and myths of the past. As I see it now (perhaps too late,) I have unwittingly taken up that challenge and made an attempt at such statements—which I certainly would not assume to do now, knowing more clearly what it means.

For grounds for "Leaves of Grass" as a poem, I abandon'd the conventional themes, which do not appear in it: none of the stock ornamentation, or choice plots of love or war, or high, exceptional personages of Old-World song; nothing, as I may say, for beauty's sake—no legend, or myth, or romance, nor euphemism, nor rhyme. But the broadest average of humanity and its identities in the now ripening Nineteenth Century, and especially in each of their countless examples and practical occupations in the United States to-day.

One main contrast of the ideas behind every page of my verses, compared with establish'd poems, is their different relative attitude towards God, towards the objective universe, and still more (by reflection, confession, assumption, &c.) the quite changed attitude of the ego, the one chanting or talking, towards himself and towards his fellow-humanity. It is certainly time for America, above all, to begin this readjustment in the scope and basic point of view of verse; for everything else has changed. As I write, I see in an article on Wordsworth, in one of the current English magazines, the lines, "A few weeks ago an eminent French critic said that, owing to the special tendency to science and to its all-devouring force, poetry would cease to be read in fifty years." But I anticipate the very contrary. Only a firmer, vastly broader, new area begins to exist—nay, is already form'd —to which the poetic genius must emigrate. Whatever may have been the case in years gone by, the true use for the imaginative faculty of modern times is to give ultimate vivification to facts, to science, and to common lives, endowing them with the glows and glories and final illustriousness which belong to every real thing, and to real things only. Without that ultimate vivification—which the poet or other artist alone can give—reality would seem incomplete, and science, democracy, and life itself, finally in vain.

Few appreciate the moral revolutions, our age, which have been profounder far than the material or inventive or war-produced ones. The Nineteenth Century, now well towards its close (and ripening into fruit the seeds of the two preceding centuries †)—the uprisings of national masses and shiftings of boundary-lines—the historical and other prominent facts of the United States—the war of attempted Secession—the stormy rush and haste of nebulous forces—never can future years witness more excitement and din of action—never completer change of army front along the whole line, the whole civilized world. For all these new and evolutionary facts, meanings, purposes, new poetic messages, new forms and expressions, are inevitable.

† The ferment and germination even of the United States to-day, dating back to and in my opinion mainly founded on, the Elizabethan age in English history, the age of Francis Bacon and Shakspere. Indeed, when we pursue it, what growth or advent is there that does not date back, back, until lost — perhaps its most tantalizing clues lost — in the receded horizons of the past?

My Book and I—what a period we have presumed to span! those thirty years from 1850 to '80—and America in them! Proud, proud indeed may we be, if we have cull'd enough of that period in its own spirit to worthily waft a few live breaths of it to the future!

Let me not dare, here or anywhere, for my own purposes, or any purposes, to attempt the definition of Poetry, nor answer the question what it is. Like Religion, Love, Nature, while those terms are indispensable, and we all give a sufficiently accurate meaning to them, in my opinion no definition that has ever been made sufficiently encloses the name Poetry; nor can any rule or convention ever so absolutely obtain but some great exception may arise and disregard and overturn it.

Also it must be carefully remember'd that first-class literature does not shine by any luminosity of its own; nor do its poems. They grow of circumstances, and are evolutionary. The actual living light is always curiously from elsewhere—follows unaccountable sources, and is lunar and relative at the best. There are, I know, certain controling themes that seem endlessly appropriated to the poets—as war, in the past—in the Bible, religious rapture and adoration—always love, beauty, some fine plot, or pensive or other emotion. But, strange as it may sound at first, I will say there is something striking far deeper and towering far higher than those themes for the best elements of modern song.

Just as all the old imaginative works rest, after their kind, on long trains of presuppositions, often entirely unmention'd by themselves, yet supplying the most important bases of them, and without which they could have had no reason for being, so "Leaves of Grass," before a line was written, presupposed something different from any other, and, as it stands, is the result of such presupposition. I should say, indeed, it were useless to attempt reading the book without first carefully tallying that preparatory background and quality in the mind. Think of the United States to-day—the facts of these thirty-eight or forty empires solder'd in one—sixty or seventy millions of equals, with their lives, their passions, their future—these incalculable, modern, American, seething multitudes around us, of which we are inseparable parts! Think, in comparison, of the petty environage and limited area of the poets of past or present Europe, no matter how great their genius. Think of the absence and ignorance in all cases hitherto, of the multitudinousness, vitality, and the unprecedented stimulants of to-day and here. It almost seems as if a poetry with cosmic and dynamic features of magnitude and limitlessness suitable to the human soul, were never possible before. It is certain that a poetry of absolute faith and equality for the use of the democratic masses never was.

In estimating first-class song, a sufficient Nationality, or, on the other hand, what may be call'd the negative and lack of it (as in Goethe's case, it sometimes seems to me,) is often, if not always, the first element. One needs only a little penetration to see, at more or less removes, the material facts of their country and radius, with the coloring of the moods of humanity at the time, and its gloomy or hopeful prospects, behind all poets and each poet, and forming their birthmarks. I know very well that my "Leaves" could not possibly have emerged or been fashion'd or completed, from any other era than the latter half of the Nineteenth Century, nor any other land than democratic America, and from the absolute triumph of the National Union arms.

And whether my friends claim it for me or not, I know well enough, too, that in respect to pictorial talent, dramatic situations, and especially in verbal melody and all the conventional technique of poetry, not only the divine works that to-day stand ahead in the world's reading, but dozens more, transcend (some of them immeasurably transcend) all I have done, or could do. But it seem'd to me, as the objects in Nature, the themes of æstheticism, and all special exploitations of the mind and soul, involve not only their own inherent quality, but the quality, just as inherent and important, of *their point of view*,† the time had come to reflect all themes and things, old and new, in the lights thrown on them by the advent of America and democracy—to chant those themes through the utterance of one, not only the grateful and reverent legatee of the past, but the born child of the New World—to illustrate all through the genesis and ensemble of to-day; and that such illustration and ensemble are the chief demands of America's prospective imaginative literature. Not to carry out, in the approved style, some choice plot of fortune or misfortune, or fancy, or fine thoughts, or incidents, or courtesies—all of which has been done overwhelmingly and well, probably never to be excell'd—but that while in such æsthetic presentation of objects, passions, plots, thoughts, &c., our lands and days do not want, and probably will never have, anything better than they already possess from the bequests of the past, it still remains to be said that there is even towards all those a subjective and contemporary point of view appropriate to ourselves alone, and to our new genius and environments, different from anything hitherto; and that such conception of current or gone-by life and art is for us the only means of their assimilation consistent with the Western world.

Indeed, and anyhow, to put it specifically, has not the time arrived when, (if it must be plainly said, for democratic America's sake, if for no other) there must imperatively come a readjustment of the whole theory and nature of Poetry? The question is important, and I may turn the argument over and repeat it: Does not the best thought of our day and Republic conceive of a birth and spirit of song superior to anything past or present? To the effectual and moral consolidation of our lands (already, as materially establish'd, the greatest factors in known history, and far, far greater through what they prelude and necessitate, and are to be in future)—to conform with and build on the concrete realities and theories of the universe furnish'd by sci-

---

† According to Immanuel Kant, the last essential reality, giving shape and significance to all the rest.

ence, and henceforth the only irrefragable basis for anything, verse included—to root both influences in the emotional and imaginative action of the modern time, and dominate all that precedes or opposes them—is not either a radical advance and step forward, or a new verteber of the best song indispensable?

The New World receives with joy the poems of the antique, with European feudalism's rich fund of epics, plays, ballads—seeks not in the least to deaden or displace those voices from our ear and area—holds them indeed as indispensable studies, influences, records, comparisons. But though the dawn-dazzle of the sun of literature is in those poems for us of to-day—though perhaps the best parts of current character in nations, social groups, or any man's or woman's individuality, Old World or New, are from them—and though if I were ask'd to name the most precious bequest to current American civilization from all the hitherto ages, I am not sure but I would name those old and less old songs ferried hither from east and west—some serious words and debits remain; some acrid considerations demand a hearing. Of the great poems receiv'd from abroad and from the ages, and to-day enveloping and penetrating America, is there one that is consistent with these United States, or essentially applicable to them as they are and are to be? Is there one whose underlying basis is not a denial and insult to democracy? What a comment it forms, anyhow, on this era of literary fulfillment, with the splendid day-rise of science and resuscitation of history, that our chief religious and poetical works are not our own, nor adapted to our light, but have been furnish'd by far-back ages out of their arriere and darkness, or, at most, twilight dimness! What is there in those works that so imperiously and scornfully dominates all our advanced civilization, and culture?

Even Shakspere, who so suffuses current letters and art (which indeed have in most degrees grown out of him,) belongs essentially to the buried past. Only he holds the proud distinction for certain important phases of that past, of being the loftiest of the singers life has yet given voice to. All, however, relate to and rest upon conditions, standards, politics, sociologies, ranges of belief, that have been quite eliminated from the Eastern hemisphere, and never existed at all in the Western. As authoritative types of song they belong in America just about as much as the persons and institutes they depict. True, it may be said, the emotional, moral, and æsthetic natures of humanity have not radically changed—that in these the old poems apply to our times and all times, irrespective of date; and that they are of incalculable value as pictures of the past. I willingly make those admissions and to their fullest extent; then advance the points herewith as of serious, even paramount importance.

I have indeed put on record elsewhere my reverence and eulogy for those never-to-be-excell'd poetic bequests and their indescribable preciousness as heirlooms for America. Another and separate point must now be candidly stated. If I had not stood before those poems with uncover'd head, fully aware of their colossal grandeur and

beauty of form and spirit, I could not have written "Leaves of Grass."
My verdict and conclusions as illustrated in its pages are arrived at
through the temper and inculcation of the old works as much as
through anything else—perhaps more than through anything else. As
America fully and fairly construed is the legitimate result and evolutionary outcome of the past, so I would dare to claim for my verse.
Without stopping to qualify the averment, the Old World has had
the poems of myths, fictions, feudalism, conquest, caste, dynastic
wars, and splendid exceptional characters and affairs, which have
been great; but the New World needs the poems of realities and
science and of the democratic average and basic equality, which shall
be greater. In the centre of all, and object of all, stands the Human
Being, towards whose heroic and spiritual evolution poems and everything directly or indirectly tend, Old World or New.

Continuing the subject, my friends have more than once suggested
—or may be the garrulity of advancing age is possessing me—some
further embryonic facts of "Leaves of Grass," and especially how I
enter'd upon them. Dr. Bucke has, in his volume, already fully and
fairly described the preparation of my poetic field, with the particular
and general plowing, planting, seeding, and occupation of the ground,
till everything was fertilized, rooted, and ready to start its own
way for good or bad. Not till after this, did I attempt any serious
acquaintance with poetic literature. Along in my sixteenth year I
had become possessor of a stout, well-cramm'd one thousand page
octavo volume (I have it yet,) containing Walter Scott's poetry entire
—an inexhaustible mine and treasury of poetic forage (especially the
endless forests and jungles of notes)—has been so to me for fifty years,
and remains so to this day.†

Later, at intervals, summers and falls, I used to go off, sometimes
for a week at a stretch, down in the country, or to Long Island's seashores—there, in the presence of outdoor influences, I went over
thoroughly the Old and New Testaments, and absorb'd (probably to
better advantage for me than in any library or indoor room—it makes
such difference *where* you read,) Shakspere, Ossian, the best translated versions I could get of Homer, Eschylus, Sophocles, the old
German Nibelungen, the ancient Hindoo poems, and one or two
other masterpieces, Dante's among them. As it happen'd, I read the
latter mostly in an old wood. The *Iliad* (Buckley's prose version) I
read first thoroughly on the peninsula of Orient, northeast end of
Long Island, in a shelter'd hollow of rocks and sand, with the sea on

† Sir Walter Scott's *COMPLETE POEMS;* especially including BORDER MINS-
TRELSY; then Sir Tristrem; Lay of the Last Minstrel; Ballads from the German;
Marmion; Lady of the Lake; Vision of Don Roderick; Lord of the Isles; Rokeby;
Bridal of Triermain; Field of Waterloo; all the Dramas; Harold the Dauntless;
various Introductions, endless interesting Notes, and Essays on Poetry, Romance, Etc.
  Lockhart's 1833 (or '34) edition with Scott's latest and copious revisions and
annotations. (All the poems were thoroughly read by me, but the ballads of the
Border Minstrelsy over and over again.)

each side. (I have wonder'd since why I was not overwhelm'd by those mighty masters. Likely because I read them, as described, in the full presence of Nature, under the sun, with the far-spreading landscape and vistas, or the sea rolling in.)

Toward the last I had among much else look'd over Edgar Poe's poems—of which I was not an admirer, tho' I always saw that beyond their limited range of melody (like perpetual chimes of music bells, ringing from lower *b* flat up to *g*) they were melodious expressions, and perhaps never excell'd ones, of certain pronounc'd phases of human morbidity. (The Poetic area is very spacious—has room for all —has so many mansions!) But I was repaid in Poe's prose by the idea that (at any rate for our occasions, our day) there can be no such thing as a long poem. The same thought had been haunting my mind before, but Poe's argument, though short, work'd the sum and proved it to me.

Another point had an early settlement, clearing the ground greatly. I saw, from the time my enterprise and questionings positively shaped themselves (how best can I express my own distinctive era and surroundings, America, Democracy?) that the trunk and centre whence the answer was to radiate, and to which all should return from straying however far a distance, must be an identical body and soul, a personality—which personality, after many considerations and ponderings I deliberately settled should be myself—indeed could not be any other. I also felt strongly (whether I have shown it or not) that to the true and full estimate of the Present both the Past and the Future are main considerations.

These, however, and much more might have gone on and come to naught (almost positively would have come to naught,) if a sudden, vast, terrible, direct and indirect stimulus for new and national declamatory expression had not been given to me. It is certain, I say, that, although I had made a start before, only from the occurrence of the Secession War, and what it show'd me as by flashes of lightning, with emotional depths it sounded and arous'd (of course, I don't mean in my own heart only, I saw it just as plainly in others, in millions)—that only from the strong flare and provocation of that war's sights and scenes the final reasons-for-being of an autochthonic and passionate song definitely came forth.

I went down to the war fields in Virginia (end of 1862,) lived thenceforward in camp—saw great battles and the days and nights afterward—partook of all the fluctuations, gloom, despair, hopes again arous'd, courage evoked—death readily risk'd—*the cause,* too—along and filling those agonistic and lurid following years, 1863-'64-'65— the real parturition years (more than 1776-'83) of this henceforth homogeneous Union. Without those three or four years and the experiences they gave, "Leaves of Grass" would not now be existing.

But I set out with the intention also of indicating or hinting some point-characteristics which I since see (though I did not then, at least not definitely) were bases and object-urgings toward those

"Leaves" from the first. The word I myself put primarily for the description of them as they stand at last, is the word Suggestiveness. I round and finish little, if anything; and could not, consistently with my scheme. The reader will always have his or her part to do, just as much as I have had mine. I seek less to state or display any theme or thought, and more to bring you, reader, into the atmosphere of the theme or thought—there to pursue your own flight. Another impetus-word is Comradeship as for all lands, and in a more commanding and acknowledg'd sense than hitherto. Other word signs would be Good Cheer, Content, and Hope.

The chief trait of any given poet is always the spirit he brings to the observation of Humanity and Nature—the mood out of which he contemplates his subjects. What kind of temper and what amount of faith report these things? Up to how recent a date is the song carried? What the equipment, and special raciness of the singer— what his tinge of coloring? The last value of artistic expressers, past and present—Greek æsthetes, Shakspere—or in our own day Tennyson, Victor Hugo, Carlyle, Emerson—is certainly involv'd in such questions. I say the profoundest service that poems or any other writings can do for their reader is not merely to satisfy the intellect, or supply something polish'd and interesting, nor even to depict great passions, or persons or events, but to fill him with vigorous and clean manliness, religiousness, and give him *good heart* as a radical possession and habit. The educated world seems to have been growing more and more ennuyed for ages, leaving to our time the inheritance of it all. Fortunately there is the original inexhaustible fund of buoyancy, normally resident in the race, forever eligible to be appeal'd to and relied on.

As for native American individuality, though certain to come, and on a large scale, the distinctive and ideal type of Western character (as consistent with the operative political and even money-making features of United States' humanity in the Nineteenth Century as chosen knights, gentlemen and warriors were the ideals of the centuries of European feudalism) it has not yet appear'd. I have allow'd the stress of my poems from beginning to end to bear upon American individuality and assist it—not only because that is a great lesson in Nature, amid all her generalizing laws, but as counterpoise to the leveling tendencies of Democracy—and for other reasons. Defiant of ostensible literary and other conventions, I avowedly chant "the great pride of man in himself," and permit it to be more or less a *motif* of nearly all my verse. I think this pride indispensable to an American. I think it not inconsistent with obedience, humility, deference, and self-questioning.

Democracy has been so retarded and jeopardized by powerful personalities, that its first instincts are fain to clip, conform, bring in stragglers, and reduce everything to a dead level. While the ambitious thought of my song is to help the forming of a great aggregate Nation, it is, perhaps, altogether through the forming of myriads of fully develop'd and enclosing individuals. Welcome as are equality's and fraternity's doctrines and popular education, a certain liability accompanies them all, as we see. That primal and interior something in man, in his soul's abysms, coloring all, and, by exceptional fruitions, giving the last majesty to him—something continually touch'd upon and attain'd by the old poems and ballads of feudalism, and often the principal foundation of them—modern science and democracy appear to be endangering, perhaps eliminating. But that forms an appearance only; the reality is quite different. The new influences, upon the whole, are surely preparing the way for grander individualities than ever. To-day and here personal force is behind everything, just the same. The times and depictions from the Iliad to Shakspere inclusive can happily never again be realized—but the elements of courageous and lofty manhood are unchanged.

Without yielding an inch the working-man and working-woman were to be in my pages from first to last. The ranges of heroism and loftiness with which Greek and feudal poets endow'd their god-like or lordly born characters—indeed prouder and better based and with fuller ranges than those—I was to endow the democratic averages of America. I was to show that we, here and to-day, are eligible to the grandest and the best—more eligible now than any times of old were. I will also want my utterances (I said to myself before beginning) to be in spirit the poems of the morning. (They have been founded and mainly written in the sunny forenoon and early midday of my life.) I will want them to be the poems of women entirely as much as men. I have wish'd to put the complete Union of the States in my songs without any preference or partiality whatever. Henceforth, if they live and are read, it must be just as much South as North—just as much along the Pacific as Atlantic—in the valley of the Mississippi, in Canada, up in Maine, down in Texas, and on the shores of Puget Sound.

From another point of view "Leaves of Grass" is avowedly the song of Sex and Amativeness, and even Animality—though meanings that do not usually go along with those words are behind all, and will duly emerge; and all are sought to be lifted into a different light and atmosphere. Of this feature, intentionally palpable in a few lines, I shall only say the espousing principle of those lines so gives breath of life to my whole scheme that the bulk of the pieces might as well have been left unwritten were those lines omitted. Difficult as it will be, it has become, in my opinion, imperative to achieve a shifted attitude from superior men and women towards the thought and fact of sexuality, as an element in character, personality, the emotions, and a theme in literature. I am not going to argue the question by itself; it does not stand by itself. The vitality of it is altogether in its relations, bearings, significance—like the clef of a symphony. At last analogy the lines I allude to, and the spirit in which they are spoken, permeate all "Leaves of Grass," and the work must stand or fall with them, as the human body and soul must remain as an entirety.

Universal as are certain facts and symptoms of communities or individuals all times, there is nothing so rare in modern conventions and poetry as their normal recognizance. Literature is always calling in the doctor for consultation and confession, and always giving evasions and swathing suppressions in place of that "heroic nudity"† on which only a genuine diagnosis of serious cases can be built. And in respect to editions of "Leaves of Grass" in time to come (if there should be such) I take occasion now to confirm those lines with the settled convictions and deliberate renewals of thirty years, and to hereby prohibit, as far as word of mine can do so, any elision of them.

Then still a purpose enclosing all, and over and beneath all. Ever since what might be call'd thought, or the budding of thought, fairly began in my youthful mind, I had had a desire to attempt some worthy record of that entire faith and acceptance ("to justify the ways of God to man" is Milton's well-known and ambitious phrase) which is the foundation of moral America. I felt it all as positively then in my young days as I do now in my old ones; to formulate a poem whose every thought or fact should directly or indirectly be or connive at an implicit belief in the wisdom, health, mystery, beauty of every process, every concrete object, every human or other existence, not only consider'd from the point of view of all, but of each.

While I cannot understand it or argue it out, I fully believe in a clue and purpose in Nature, entire and several; and that invisible spiritual results, just as real and definite as the visible, eventuate all concrete life and all materialism, through Time. My book ought to emanate buoyancy and gladness legitimately enough, for it was grown out of those elements, and has been the comfort of my life since it was originally commenced.

One main genesis-motive of the "Leaves" was my conviction (just as strong to-day as ever) that the crowning growth of the United States is to be spiritual and heroic. To help start and favor that growth—or even to call attention to it, or the need of it—is the beginning, middle and final purpose of the poems. (In fact, when really cipher'd out and summ'd to the last, plowing up in earnest the interminable average fallows of humanity—not "good government" merely, in the common sense—is the justification and main purpose of these United States.)

Isolated advantages in any rank or grace or fortune—the direct or indirect threads of all the poetry of the past—are in my opinion distasteful to the republican genius, and offer no foundation for its fitting verse. Establish'd poems, I know, have the very great advantage of chanting the already perform'd, so full of glories, reminiscences dear to the minds of men. But my volume is a candidate for the future. "All original art," says Taine, anyhow, "is self-regulated, and no original art can be regulated from without; it carries its own counterpoise, and does not receive it from elsewhere—lives on its own blood"—a solace to my frequent bruises and sulky vanity.

As the present is perhaps mainly an attempt at personal statement or illustration, I will allow myself as further help to extract the fol-

† "Nineteenth Century," July, 1883.

lowing anecdote from a book, "Annals of Old Painters," conn'd by me in youth. Rubens, the Flemish painter, in one of his wanderings through the galleries of old convents, came across a singular work. After looking at it thoughtfully for a good while, and listening to the criticisms of his suite of students, he said to the latter, in answer to their questions, (as to what school the work implied or belong'd,) "I do not believe the artist, unknown and perhaps no longer living, who has given the world this legacy, ever belong'd to any school, or ever painted anything but this one picture, which is a personal affair —a piece out of a man's life."

"Leaves of Grass" indeed (I cannot too often reiterate) has mainly been the outcropping of my own emotional and other personal nature —an attempt, from first to last, to put *a Person,* a human being (myself, in the latter half of the Nineteenth Century, in America,) freely, fully and truly on record. I could not find any similar personal record in current literature that satisfied me. But it is not on "Leaves of Grass" distinctively as *literature,* or a specimen thereof, that I feel to dwell, or advance claims. No one will get at my verses who insists upon viewing them as a literary performance, or attempt at such performance, or as aiming mainly toward art or æstheticism.

I say no land or people or circumstances ever existed so needing a race of singers and poems differing from all others, and rigidly their own, as the land and people and circumstances of our United States need such singers and poems to-day, and for the future. Still further, as long as the States continue to absorb and be dominated by the poetry of the Old World, and remain unsupplied with autochthonous song, to express, vitalize and give color to and define their material and political success, and minister to them distinctively, so long will they stop short of first-class Nationality and remain defective.

In the free evening of my day I give to you, reader, the foregoing garrulous talk, thoughts, reminiscences,

> As idly drifting down the ebb,
> Such ripples, half-caught voices, echo from the shore.

Concluding with two items for the imaginative genius of the West, when it worthily rises—First, what Herder taught to the young Goethe, that really great poetry is always (like the Homeric or Biblical canticles) the result of a national spirit, and not the privilege of a polish'd and select few; Second, that the strongest and sweetest songs yet remain to be sung.

DEMOCRATIC VISTAS

As the greatest lessons of Nature through the universe are perhaps the lessons of variety and freedom, the same present the greatest lessons also in New World politics and progress. If a man were ask'd, for instance, the distinctive points contrasting modern European and American political and other life with the old Asiatic cultus, as lingering-bequeath'd yet in China and Turkey, he might find the amount of them in John Stuart Mill's profound essay on Liberty in the future, where he demands two main constituents, or sub-strata, for a truly grand nationality—1st, a large variety of character—and 2nd, full play for human nature to expand itself in numberless and even conflicting directions—(seems to be for general humanity much like the influences that make up, in their limitless field, that perennial health-action of the air we call the weather—an infinite number of currents and forces, and contributions, and temperatures, and cross purposes, whose ceaseless play of counterpart upon counterpart brings constant restoration and vitality). With this thought—and not for itself alone, but all it necessitates, and draws after it—let me begin my speculations.

America, filling the present with greatest deeds and problems, cheerfully accepting the past, including feudalism (as, indeed, the present is but the legitimate birth of the past, including feudalism), counts, as I reckon, for her justification and success (for who, as yet, dare claim success?) almost entirely on the future. Nor is that hope unwarranted. Today, ahead, though dimly yet, we see, in vistas, a copious, sane, gigantic offspring. For our New World I consider far less important for what it has done, or what it is, than for results to come. Sole among nationalities, these States have assumed the task to put in forms of lasting power and practicality, on areas of amplitude rivaling the operations of the physical kosmos, the moral political speculations of ages, long, long deferr'd, the democratic republican principle, and the theory of development and perfection by voluntary standards, and self-reliance. Who else, indeed, except the United States, in history, so far, have accepted in unwitting faith, and, as we now see, stand, act upon, and go security for, these things?

But preluding no longer, let me strike the keynote of the following strain. First premising that, though the passages of it have been written at widely different times (it is, in fact, a collection of memoranda, perhaps for future designers, comprehenders), and though it may be open to the charge of one part contradicting another—for there are opposite sides to the great question of democracy, as to every great question—I feel the parts harmoniously blended in my own realization and convictions, and present them to be read only in such oneness, each page and each claim and assertion modified and temper'd by the others. Bear in mind, too, that they are not the result of studying up in political economy, but of the ordinary sense, observing, wandering among men, these States, these stirring years of war and peace. I will not gloss over the appaling dangers of universal suffrage in the United States. In fact, it is to admit and face these dangers I am writing. To him or her within whose thought rages the battle, advancing, retreating, between democracy's convictions, aspirations, and the people's crudeness, vice, caprices, I mainly write this essay. I shall use the words America and democracy as convertible terms. Not an ordinary one is the issue. The United States are destined either to surmount the gorgeous history of feudalism, or else prove the most tremendous failure of time. Not the least doubtful am I on any prospects of their material success. The triumphant future of their business, geographic and productive departments, on larger scales and in more varieties than ever, is certain. In those respects the republic must soon (if she does not already) outstrip all examples hitherto afforded, and dominate the world.†

Admitting all this, with the priceless value of our political institutions, general suffrage (and fully acknowledging the latest, widest opening of the doors), I say that, far deeper than these, what finally and only is to make of our Western world a nationality superior to any hitherto known, and outtopping the past, must be vigorous, yet unsuspected Literatures, perfect personalities and sociologies, original, transcendental, and expressing (what, in highest sense, are not yet express'd at all) democracy and the modern. With these, and out of these, I promulge new races of Teachers, and of perfect Women, indispensable to endow the birth-stock of a New World. For feudalism, caste, the ecclesiastic traditions, though palpably retreating from political institutions, still hold essentially, by their spirit, even in this coun-

---

† "From a territorial area of less than nine hundred thousand square miles, the Union has expanded into over four millions and a half — fifteen times larger than that of Great Britain and France combined — with a shore-line, including Alaska, equal to the entire circumference of the earth, and with a domain within these lines far wider than that of the Romans in their proudest days of conquest and renown. With a river, lake, and coastwise commerce estimated at over two thousand millions of dollars per year; with a railway traffic of four to six thousand millions per year, and the annual domestic exchanges of the country running up to nearly ten thousand millions per year; with over two thousand millions of dollars invested in manufacturing, mechanical, and mining industry; with over five hundred millions of acres of land in actual occupancy, valued, with their appurtenances, at over seven thousand millions of dollars, and producing annually crops valued at over three thousand millions of dollars; with a realm which, if the density of Belgium's population were possible, would be vast enough to include all the present inhabitants of the world; and with equal rights guaranteed to even the poorest and humblest of our forty millions of people — we can, with a manly pride akin to that which distinguish'd the palmiest

try, entire possession of the more important fields, indeed the very subsoil, of education, and of social standards and literature.

I say that democracy can never prove itself beyond cavil, until it founds and luxuriantly grows its own forms of art, poems, schools, theology, displacing all that exists, or that has been produced anywhere in the past, under opposite influences. It is curious to me that while so many voices, pens, minds, in the press, lecture rooms, in our Congress, etc., are discussing intellectual topics, pecuniary dangers, legislative problems, the suffrage, tariff and labor questions, and the various business and benevolent needs of America, with propositions, remedies, often worth deep attention, there is one need, a hiatus the profoundest, that no eye seems to perceive, no voice to state. Our fundamental want today in the United States, with closest, amplest reference to present conditions, and to the future, is of a class, and the clear idea of a class, of native authors, literatuses, far different, far higher in grade, than any yet known, sacerdotal, modern, fit to cope with our occasions, lands, permeating the whole mass of American mentality, taste, belief, breathing into it a new breath of life, giving it decision, affecting politics far more than the popular superficial suffrage, with results inside and underneath the elections of Presidents or Congresses—radiating, begetting appropriate teachers, schools, manners, and, as its grandest result, accomplishing (what neither the schools nor the churches and their clergy have hitherto accomplish'd, and without which this nation will no more stand, permanently, soundly, than a house will stand without a sub-stratum), a religious and moral character beneath the political and productive and intellectual bases of the States. For know you not, dear, earnest reader, that the people of our land may all read and write, and may all possess the right to vote—and yet the main things may be entirely lacking?—(and this to suggest them).

View'd, today, from a point of view sufficiently over-arching, the problem of humanity all over the civilized world is social and religious, and is to be finally met and treated by literature. The priest departs, the divine literatus comes. Never was anything more wanted than,

_____

days of Rome, claim," etc., etc., etc. — *Vice President Colfax's Speech, July 4, 1870.*
Later — *London "Times" (Weekly), June 23, '82*

"The wonderful wealth-producing power of the United States defies and sets at naught the grave drawbacks of a mischievous protective tariff, and has already obliterated, almost wholly, the traces of the greatest of modern civil wars. What is especially remarkable in the present development of American energy and success is its wide and equable distribution. North and south, east and west, on the shores of the Atlantic and the Pacific, along the chain of the great lakes, in the valley of the Mississippi, and on the coasts of the Gulf of Mexico, the creation of wealth and the increase of population are signally exhibited. It is quite true, as has been shown by the recent apportionment of population in the House of Representatives, that some sections of the Union have advanced, relatively to the rest, in an extraordinary and unexpected degree. But this does not imply that the States which have gained no additional representatives or have actually lost some have been stationary or have receded. The fact is that the present tide of prosperity has risen so high that it has overflowed all barriers, and has fill'd up the backwaters, and established something like an approach to uniform success."

today, and here in the States, the poet of the modern is wanted, or the great literatus of the modern. At all times, perhaps, the central point in any nation, and that whence it is itself really sway'd the most, and whence it sways others, is its national literature, especially its archetypal poems. Above all previous lands, a great original literature is surely to become the justification and reliance (in some respects the sole reliance of American democracy).

Few are aware how the great literature penetrates all, gives hue to all, shapes aggregates and individuals, and, after subtle ways, with irresistible power, constructs, sustains, demolishes at will. Why tower, in reminiscence, above all the nations of the earth, two special lands, petty in themselves, yet inexpressibly gigantic, beautiful, columnar? Immortal Judah lives, and Greece immortal lives, in a couple of poems.

Nearer than this. It is not generally realized, but it is true, as the genius of Greece, and all the sociology, personality, politics, and religion of those wonderful states, resided in their literature or æsthetics, that what was afterwards the main support of European chivalry, the feudal, ecclesiastical, dynastic world over there—forming its osseous structure, holding it together for hundreds, thousands of years, preserving its flesh and bloom, giving it form, decision, rounding it out, and so saturating it in the conscious and unconscious blood, breed, belief, and intuitions of men, that it still prevails powerful to this day, in defiance of the mighty changes of time—was its literature, permeating to the very marrow, especially that major part, its enhancing songs, ballads, and poems.†

To the ostent of the senses and eyes, I know, the influences which stamp the world's history are wars, uprisings or downfalls of dynasties, changeful movement of trade, important inventions, navigation, military or civil governments, advent of powerful personalities, conquerors, etc. These of course play their part; yet, it may be, a single new thought, imagination, abstract principle, even literary style, fit for the time, put in shape by some great literatus, and projected among mankind, may duly cause changes, growths, removals, greater than the longest and bloodiest war, or the most stupendous merely political dynastic, or commercial overturn.

In short, as though it may not be realized, it is strictly true, that a few first-class poets, philosophs, and authors have substantially settled and given status to the entire religion, education, law, sociology, etc.,

---

† See, for hereditaments, specimens, Walter Scott's Border Minstrelsy, Percy's collection, Ellis's early English Metrical Romances, the European continental poems of Walter of Aquitania, and the Nibelungen, of pagan stock, but monkish-feudal redaction; the history of the Troubadours, by Fauriel; even the far-back cumbrous old Hindu epics, as indicating the Asian eggs out of which European chivalry was hatch'd; Ticknor's chapters on the Cid, and on the Spanish poems and poets of Calderon's time. Then always, and, of course, as the superbest poetic culmination-expression of feudalism, the Shaksperean dramas, in the attitudes, dialogue, characters, etc., of the princes, lords, and gentlemen, the pervading atmosphere, the implied and express'd standard of manners, the high port and proud stomach, the regal embroidery of style, etc.

of the hitherto civilized world, by tingeing and often creating the atmospheres out of which they have arisen, such also must stamp, and more than ever stamp, the interior and real democratic construction of this American continent, today, and days to come. Remember also this fact of difference, that, while through the antique and through the mediæval ages, highest thoughts and ideals realized themselves, and their expression made its way by other arts, as much as, or even more than by, technical literature (not open to the mass of persons, or even to the majority of eminent persons), such literature in our day and for current purposes is not only more eligible than all the other arts put together, but has become the only general means of morally influencing the world. Painting, sculpture, and the dramatic theatre, it would seem, no longer play an indispensable or even important part in the workings and mediumship of intellect, utility, or even high æsthetics. Architecture remains, doubtless with capacities, and a real future. Then music, the combiner, nothing more spiritual, nothing more sensuous, a god, yet completely human, advances, prevails, holds highest place; supplying in certain wants and quarters what nothing else could supply. Yet in the civilization of today it is undeniable that, over all the arts, literature dominates, serves beyond all—shapes the character of church and school—or, in any rate, is capable of doing so. Including the literature of science, its scope is indeed unparallel'd.

Before proceeding further, it were perhaps well to discriminate on certain points. Literature tills its crops in many fields, and some may flourish, while others lag. What I say in these Vistas has its main bearing on imaginative literature, especially poetry, the stock of all. In the department of science, and the specialty of journalism, there appear, in these States, promises, perhaps fulfillments, of highest earnestness, reality and life. These, of course, are modern. But in the region of imaginative, spinal and essential attributes, something equivalent to creation is, for our age and lands, imperatively demanded. For not only is it not enough that the new blood, new frame of democracy shall be vivified and held together merely by political means, superficial suffrage, legislation, etc., but it is clear to me that, unless it goes deeper, gets at least as firm and as warm a hold in men's hearts, emotions and belief, as, in their days, feudalism or ecclesiasticism, and inaugurates its own perennial sources, welling from the center forever, its strength will be defective, its growth doubtful, and its main charm wanting. I suggest, therefore, the possibility, should some two or three really original American poets (perhaps artists or lecturers) arise, mounting the horizon like planets, stars of the first magnitude, that, from their eminence, fusing contributions, races, far localities, etc., together, they would give more compaction and more moral identity (the quality to-day most needed) to these States, than all its Constitutions, legislative and judicial ties, and all its hitherto political, warlike, or materialistic experiences. As, for instance, there could hardly happen anything that would more serve the States, with all their variety of origins, their diverse climes, cities, standards, etc., than possessing an aggregate of heroes, characters, exploits, sufferings, prosperity or misfortune, glory or disgrace, common to all, typical of it all—no less, but even greater would it be to possess the aggregation of a cluster of mighty poets, artists, teachers, fit for us, national expressers, comprehending and effusing for the men and women of the States, what is universal, native, common to all, inland and seaboard, northern and southern. The historians say of ancient Greece, with her ever-jealous autonomies, cities and states, that the only positive unity she ever own'd or receiv'd, was the sad unity of a common subjection, at the last, to foreign conquerors. Subjection, aggregation of that sort, is impossible to America; but the fear of conflicting and irreconcilable interiors, and the lack of a common skeleton, knitting all close, continually haunts me. Or, if it does not, nothing is plainer than the need, a long period to come, of a fusion of the States into the only reliable identity, the moral and artistic one. For, I say, the true nationality of the States, the genuine union, when we come to a mortal crisis, is, and is to be, after all, neither the written law, nor (as is generally supposed) either self-interest, or common pecuniary or material objects—but the fervid and tremendous IDEA, melting everything else with resistless heat, and solving all lesser and definite distinctions in vast, indefinite, spiritual, emotional power.

It may be claim'd (and I admit the weight of the claim) that common and general worldly prosperity, and a populace well-to-do, and with all life's material comforts, is the main thing, and is enough. It may be argued that our republic is, in performance, really enacting today the grandest arts, poems, etc., by beating up the wilderness into fertile farms, and in her railroads, ships, machinery, etc. And it may be ask'd, Are these not better, indeed, for America, than any utterances even of greatest rhapsode, artist, or literatus?

I too hail those achievements with pride and joy: then answer that the soul of man will not with such only—nay, not with such at all—be finally satisfied; but needs what, (standing on these and on all things, as the feet stand on the ground), is addressed to the loftiest, to itself alone.

Out of such considerations, such truths, arises for treatment in these Vistas the important question of character, of an American stock-personality, with literatures and arts for outlets and return-expressions, and, of course, to correspond, within outlines common to all. To these, the main affair, the thinkers of the United States, in general so acute, have either given feeblest attention, or have remain'd, and remain, in a state of somnolence.

For my part, I would alarm and caution even the political and business reader, and to the utmost extent, against the prevailing delusion that the establishment of free political institutions, and plentiful intellectual smartness, with general good order, physical plenty, industry, etc. (desirable and precious advantages as they all are), do, of themselves, determine and yield to our experiment of democracy the fruitage of success. With such advantages at present fully, or almost fully, possess'd—the Union just issued, victorious, from the struggle with the only foes it need ever fear (namely, those within itself, the

interior ones), and with unprecedented materialistic advancement—
society, in these States, is canker'd, crude, superstitious and rotten.
Political, or law-made society is, and private, or voluntary society, is
also. In any vigor, the element of the moral conscience, the most important, the verteber to State or man, seems to me either entirely
lacking, or seriously enfeebled or ungrown.

I say we had best look our times and lands searchingly in the face,
like a physician diagnosing some deep disease. Never was there, perhaps, more hollowness at heart than at present, and here in the United
States. Genuine belief seems to have left us. The underlying principles
of the States are not honestly believ'd in (for all this hectic glow, and
these melodramatic screamings), nor is humanity itself believ'd in.
What penetrating eye does not everywhere see through the mask?
The spectacle is appalling. We live in an atmosphere of hypocrisy
throughout. The men believe not in the women, nor the women in
the men. A scornful superciliousness rules in literature. The aim of all
the *littérateurs* is to find something to make fun of. A lot of churches,
sects, etc., the most dismal phantasms I know, usurp the name of religion. Conversation is a mass of badinage. From deceit in the spirit,
the mother of all false deeds, the offspring is already incalculable. An
acute and candid person, in the revenue department in Washington,
who is led by the course of his employment to regularly visit the cities,
north, south, and west, to investigate frauds, has talked much with
me about his discoveries. The depravity of the business classes of our
country is not less than has been supposed, but infinitely greater. The
official services of America, national, state, and municipal, in all their
branches and departments, except the judiciary, are saturated in corruption, bribery, falsehood, maladministration; and the judiciary is
tainted. The great cities reek with respectable as much as non-respect-
able robbery and scoundrelism. In fashionable life, flippancy, tepid
amours, weak infidelism, small aims, or no aims at all, only to kill
time. In business (this all-devouring modern word, business), the one
sole object is, by any means, pecuniary gain. The magician's serpent
in the fable ate up all the other serpents; and moneymaking is our
magician's serpent, remaining today sole master of the field. The best
class we show, is but a mob of fashionably dress'd speculators and
vulgarians. True, indeed, behind this fantastic farce, enacted on the
visible stage of society, solid things and stupendous labors are to be
discover'd, existing crudely and going on in the background, to advance and tell themselves in time. Yet the truths are none the less
terrible. I say that our New World democracy, however great a success
in uplifting the masses out of their sloughs, in materialistic development, products, and in a certain highly deceptive superficial popular
intellectuality, is, so far, an almost complete failure in its social aspects,
and in really grand religious, moral, literary, and æsthetic results. In
vain do we march with unprecedented strides to empire so colossal,
outvying the antique, beyond Alexander's, beyond the proudest sway
of Rome. In vain have we annex'd Texas, California, Alaska, and reach
north for Canada and south for Cuba. It is as if we were somehow

being endow'd with a vast and more and more thoroughly appointed body, and then left with little or no soul.

Let me illustrate further, as I write, with current observation, localities, etc. The subject is important, and will bear repetition. After an absence, I am now again (September, 1870) in New York City and Brooklyn, on a few weeks' vacation. The splendor, picturesqueness, and oceanic amplitude and rush of these great cities, the unsurpassed situation, rivers and bay, sparkling sea-tides, costly and lofty new buildings, façades of marble and iron, of original grandeur and elegance of design, with the masses of gay color, the preponderance of white and blue, the flags flying, the endless ships, the tumultuous streets, Broadway, the heavy, low, musical roar, hardly ever intermitted, even at night; the jobbers' houses, the rich shops, the wharves, the great Central Park, and the Brooklyn Park of hills (as I wander among them this beautiful fall weather, musing, watching, absorbing)—the assemblages of the citizens in their groups, conversations, trades, evening amusements, or along the by-quarters—these, I say, and the like of these, completely satisfy my senses of power, fullness, motion, etc., and give me, through such senses and appetites, and through my æsthetic conscience, a continued exaltation and absolute fulfillment. Always and more and more, as I cross the East and North rivers, the ferries, or with the pilots in their pilot-houses, or pass an hour in Wall Street, or the Gold Exchange, I realize (if we must admit such partialisms) that not Nature alone is great in her fields of freedom and the open air, in her storms, the shows of night and day, the mountains, forests, sea—but in the artificial, the work of man too is equally great—in this profusion of teeming humanity—in these ingenuities, streets, goods, houses, ships—these hurrying, feverish, electric crowds of men, their complicated business genius (not least among the geniuses), and all this mighty, many-threaded wealth and industry concentrated here.

But sternly discarding, shutting our eyes to the glow and grandeur of the general superficial effect, coming down to what is of the only real importance, Personalities, and examining minutely, we question, we ask, Are there, indeed, *men* here worthy the name? Are there athletes? Are there perfect women, to match the generous material luxuriance? Is there a pervading atmosphere of beautiful manners? Are there crops of fine youths, and majestic old persons? Are there arts worthy freedom and a rich people? Is there a great moral and religious civilization—the only justification of a great material one? Confess that to severe eyes, using the moral microscope upon humanity, a sort of dry and flat Sahara appears, these cities, crowded with petty grotesques, malformations, phantoms, playing meaningless antics. Confess that everywhere, in shop, street, church, theatre, barroom, official chair, are pervading flippancy and vulgarity, low cunning, infidelity—everywhere the youth puny, impudent, foppish, prematurely ripe—everywhere an abnormal libidinousness, unhealthy forms, male, female, painted, padded, dyed, chignon'd, muddy complexions, bad blood, the capacity for good motherhood deceasing or deceas'd, shallow notions of beauty, with a range of manners, or rather lack of manners (considering the advantages enjoy'd), probably the meanest to be seen in the world.†

Of all this, and these lamentable conditions, to breathe into them the breath recuperative of sane and heroic life, I say a new-founded literature, not merely to copy and reflect existing surfaces, or pander to what is called taste—not only to amuse, pass away time, celebrate the beautiful, the refined, the past, or exhibit technical, rhythmic, or grammatical dexterity—but a literature underlying life, religious, consistent with science, handling the elements and forces with competent power, teaching and training men—and, as perhaps the most precious of its results, achieving the entire redemption of woman out of these incredible holds and webs of silliness, millinery, and every kind of dyspeptic depletion—and thus insuring to the States a strong and sweet Female Race, a race of perfect Mothers—is what is needed.

And now, in the full conception of these facts and points, and all that they infer, pro and con—with yet unshaken faith in the elements of the American masses, the composites, of both sexes, and even consider'd as individuals—and ever recognizing in them the broadest bases of the best literary and æsthetic appreciation—I proceed with my speculations, Vistas.

First, let us see what we can make out of a brief, general, sentimental consideration of political democracy, and whence it has arisen, with regard to some of its current features, as an aggregate, and as the basic structure of our future literature and authorship. We shall, it is true, quickly and continually find the origin-idea of the singleness of man, individualism, asserting itself, and cropping forth, even from the opposite ideas. But the mass, or lump character, for imperative reasons, is to be ever carefully weigh'd, borne in mind, and provided for. Only from it, and from its proper regulation and potency, comes the other, comes the chance of individualism. The two are contradictory, but our task is to reconcile them.‡

---

† Of these rapidly sketch'd hiatuses, the two which seem to be most serious are, for one, the condition, absence, or perhaps the singular abeyance, of moral conscientious fiber all through American society; and, for another, the appaling depletion of women in their powers of sane athletic maternity, their crowning attribute, and ever making the woman, in loftiest spheres, superior to the man.

I have sometimes thought, indeed, that the sole avenue and means of a reconstructed sociology depended, primarily, on a new birth, elevation, expansion, invigoration of woman, affording, for races to come (as the conditions that antedate birth are indispensable), a perfect motherhood. Great, great, indeed, far greater than they know, is the sphere of women. But doubtless the question of such new sociology all goes together, includes many varied and complex influences and premises, and the man as well as the woman, and the woman as well as the man.

‡The question hinted here is one which time only can answer. Must not the virtue of modern Individualism, continually enlarging, usurping all, seriously affect, perhaps keep down entirely, in America, the like of the ancient virtue of Patriotism, the fervid and absorbing love of general country? I have no doubt myself that the two will merge, and will mutually profit and brace each other, and that from them a greater product, a third will arise. But I feel that at present they and their oppositions form a serious problem and paradox in the United States.

The political history of the past may be summ'd up as having grown out of what underlies the words, order, safety, caste, and especially out of the need of some prompt deciding authority, and of cohesion at all cost. Leaping time, we come to the period within the memory of people now living, when, as from some lair where they had slumber'd long, accumulating wrath, sprang up and are yet active (1790, and on even to the present, 1870) those noisy eructations, destructive iconoclasms, a fierce sense of wrongs, amid which moves the form, well known in modern history, in the Old World, stain'd with much blood, and mark'd by savage reactionary clamors and demands. These bear, mostly, as on one inclosing point of need.

For after the rest is said—after the many time-honor'd and really true things for subordination, experience, rights of property, etc., have been listen'd to and acquiesced in—after the valuable and well-settled statement of our duties and relations in society is thoroughly conn'd over and exhausted—it remains to bring forward and modify everything else with the idea of that Something a man is (last precious consolation of the drudging poor), standing apart from all else, divine in his own right, and a woman in hers, sole and untouchable by any canons of authority, or any rule derived from precedent, state-safety, the acts of legislatures, or even from what is called religion, modesty, or art. The radiation of this truth is the key of the most significant doings of our immediately preceding three centuries, and has been the political genesis and life of America. Advancing visibly, it still more advances invisibly. Underneath the fluctuations of the expressions of society, as well as the movements of the politics of the leading nations of the world, we see steadily pressing ahead and strengthening itself, even in the midst of immense tendencies toward aggregation, this image of completeness in separatism, of individual personal dignity, of a single person, either male or female, characterized in the main, not from extrinsic acquirements or position, but in the pride of himself or herself alone; and, as an eventual conclusion and summing up (or else the entire scheme of things is aimless, a cheat, a crash), the simple idea that the last, best dependence is to be upon humanity itself, and its own inherent, normal, full-grown qualities without any superstitious support whatever. This idea of perfect individualism it is indeed that deepest tinges and gives character to the idea of the aggregate. For it is mainly or altogether to serve independent separatism that we favor a strong generalization, consolidation. As it is to give the best vitality and freedom to the rights of the States (every bit as important as the right of nationality, the union), that we insist on the identity of the Union at all hazards.

The purpose of democracy—supplanting old belief in the necessary absoluteness of establish'd dynastic rulership, temporal, ecclesiastical, and scholastic, as furnishing the only security against chaos, crime, and ignorance—is, through many transmigrations and amid endless ridicules, arguments, and ostensible failures, to illustrate, at all hazards, this doctrine or theory that man, properly train'd in sanest, highest freedom, may and must become a law, and series of laws, unto himself, surrounding and providing for, not only his own personal control, but all his relations to other individuals, and to the State; and that, while other theories, as in the past histories of nations, have proved wise enough, and indispensable perhaps for their conditions, *this*, as matters now stand in our civilized world, is the only scheme worth working from, as warranting results like those of Nature's laws, reliable, when once establish'd, to carry on themselves.

The argument of the matter is extensive, and, we admit, by no means all on one side. What we shall offer will be far, far from sufficient. But while leaving unsaid much that should properly even prepare the way for the treatment of this many-sided question of political liberty, equality, or republicanism—leaving the whole history and consideration of the feudal plan and its products, embodying humanity, its politics and civilization, through the retrospect of past time (which plan and products, indeed, make up all of the past, and a large part of the present)—leaving unanswer'd, at least by any specific and local answer, many a well-wrought argument and instance, and many a conscientious declamatory cry and warning—as, very lately, from an eminent and venerable person abroad †—things, problems, full of doubt, dread, suspense (not new to me, but old occupiers of many an anxious hour in city's din, or night's silence), we still may give a page or so, whose drift is opportune. Time alone can finally answer these things. But as a substitute in passing, let us, even if fragmentarily, throw forth a short direct or indirect suggestion of the premises of that other plan, in the new spirit, under the new forms, started here in our America.

As to the political section of Democracy, which introduces and breaks ground for further and vaster sections, few probably are the minds, even in these republican States, that fully comprehend the aptness of that phrase, "the government of the people, by the people, for the people," which we inherit from the lips of Abraham Lincoln; a formula whose verbal shape is homely wit, but whose scope includes both the totality and all minutiæ of the lesson.

The People! Like our huge earth itself, which, to ordinary scansion, is full of vulgar contradictions and offence, man, viewed in the lump, displeases, and is a constant puzzle and affront to the merely educated classes. The rare, cosmical, artist-mind, lit with the Infinite, alone confronts his manifold and oceanic qualities—but taste, intelligence and culture (so-called), have been against the masses, and remain so. There is plenty of glamour about the most damnable crimes and hoggish

---

† "Shooting Niagara."—I was at first roused to much anger and abuse by this essay from Mr. Carlyle, so insulting to the theory of America—but happening to think afterwards how I had more than once been in the like mood, during which his essay was evidently cast, and seen persons and things in the same light (indeed, some might say there are signs of the same feeling in these Vistas)—I have since read it again, not only as a study, expressing as it does certain judgments from the highest feudal point of view, but have read it with respect as coming from an earnest soul, and as contributing certain sharp-cutting metallic grains, which, if not gold or silver, may be good, hard, honest iron.

meannesses, special and general, of the feudal and dynastic world over there, with its *personnel* of lords and queens and courts, so well dress'd and so handsome. But the People are ungrammatical, untidy, and their sins gaunt and ill bred.

Literature, strictly consider'd, has never recognized the People, and, whatever may be said, does not today. Speaking generally, the tendencies of literature, as hitherto pursued, have been to make mostly critical and querulous men. It seems as if, so far, there were some natural repugnance between a literary and professional life, and the rude rank spirit of the democracies. There is, in later literature, a treatment of benevolence, a charity business, rife enough it is true; but I know nothing more rare, even in this country, than a fit scientific estimate and reverent appreciation of the People—of their measureless wealth of latent power and capacity, their vast, artistic contrasts of lights and shades—with, in America, their entire reliability in emergencies, and a certain breadth of historic grandeur, of peace or war, far surpassing all the vaunted samples of book-heroes, or any *haut ton* coteries, in all the records of the world.

The movements of the late Secession War, and their results, to any sense that studies well and comprehends them, show that popular democracy, whatever its faults and dangers, practically justifies itself beyond the proudest claims and wildest hopes of its enthusiasts. Probably no future age can know, but I well know, how the gist of this fiercest and most resolute of the world's warlike contentions resided exclusively in the unnamed, unknown rank and file; and how the brunt of its labor of death was, to all essential purposes, volunteered. The People, of their own choice, fighting, dying for their own idea, insolently attack'd by the secession-slave-power, and its very existence imperil'd. Descending to detail, entering any of the armies, and mixing with the private soldiers, we see and have seen august spectacles. We have seen the alacrity with which the American-born populace, the peaceablest and most good-natured race in the world, and the most personally independent and intelligent, and the least fitted to submit to the irksomeness and exasperation of regimental discipline, sprang, at the first tap of the drum, to arms—not for gain, nor even glory, nor to repel invasion—but for an emblem, a mere abstraction—for the life, *the safety of the flag*. We have seen the unequal'd docility and obedience of these soldiers. We have seen them tried long and long by hopelessness, mismanagement, and by defeat; have seen the incredible slaughter toward or through which the armies (as at first Fredericksburg, and afterward at the Wilderness), still unhesitatingly obey'd orders to advance. We have seen them in trench, or crouching behind breastwork, or tramping in deep mud, or amid pouring rain or thick-falling snow, or under forced marches in hottest summer (as on the road to get to Gettysburg—vast suffocating swarms, divisions, corps, with every single man so grimed and black with sweat and dust, his own mother would not have known him—his clothes all dirty, stain'd and torn, with sour, accumulated sweat for perfume—many a comrade, perhaps a brother, sun-struck, staggering out, dying, by the roadside, of exhaustion—yet the great bulk bearing steadily on, cheery enough, hollow-bellied from hunger, but sinewy with unconquerable resolution.

We have seen this race proved by wholesale, by drearier, yet more fearful tests—the wound, the amputation, the shatter'd face or limb, the slow hot fever, long impatient anchorage in bed, and all the forms of maiming, operation, and disease. Alas! America have we seen, though only in her early youth, already to hospital brought. There have we watch'd these soldiers, many of them only boys in years— mark'd their decorum, their religious nature and fortitude, and their sweet affection. Wholesale, truly. For at the front, and through the camps, in countless tents, stood the regimental, brigade, and division hospitals; while everywhere amid the land, in or near cities, rose clusters of huge, whitewash'd, crowded, one-story wooden barracks; and there ruled agony with bitter scourge, yet seldom brought a cry; and there stalk'd death by day and night along the narrow aisles between the rows of cots, or by the blankets on the ground, and touch'd lightly many a poor sufferer, often with blessed, welcome touch.

I know not whether I shall be understood, but I realize that it is finally from what I learn'd personally mixing in such scenes that I am now penning these pages. One night in the gloomiest period of the war, in the Patent Office hospital in Washington city, as I stood by the bedside of a Pennsylvania soldier, who lay, conscious of quick approaching death, yet perfectly calm, and with noble, spiritual manner, the veteran surgeon, turning aside, said to me, that though he had witness'd many, many deaths of soldiers, and had been a worker at Bull Run, Antietam, Fredericksburg, etc., he had not seen yet the first case of man or boy that met the approach of dissolution with cowardly qualms or terror. My own observation fully bears out the remark.

What have we here, if not, towering above all talk and argument, the plentifully supplied, last-needed proof of democracy, in its personalities? Curiously enough, too, the proof on this point comes, I should say, every bit as much from the south, as from the north. Although I have spoken only of the latter, yet I deliberately include all. Grand, common stock! to me the accomplish'd and convincing growth, prophetic of the future; proof undeniable to sharpest sense, of perfect beauty, tenderness and pluck, that never feudal lord, nor Greek, nor Roman breed, yet rival'd. Let no tongue ever speak in disparagement of the American races, north or south, to one who has been through the war in the great army hospitals.

Meantime, general humanity (for to that we return, as, for our purposes, what it really is, to bear in mind), has always, in every department, been full of perverse maleficence, and is so yet. In downcast hours the soul thinks it always will be—but soon recovers from such sickly moods. I myself see clearly enough the crude, defective streaks in all the strata of the common people; the specimens and vast collections of the ignorant, the credulous, the unfit and uncouth, the incapable, and the very low and poor. The eminent person just men-tion'd sneeringly asks whether we expect to elevate and improve a nation's politics by absorbing such morbid collections and qualities therein. The point is a formidable one, and there will doubtless always be numbers of solid and reflective citizens who will never get over it. Our answer is general, and is involved in the scope and letter of this essay. We believe the ulterior object of political and all other govern-ment (having, of course, provided for the police, the safety of life, property, and for the basic statute and common law, and their ad-ministration, always first in order), to be among the rest, not merely to rule, to repress disorder, etc., but to develop, to open up to cultiva-tion, to encourage the possibilities of all beneficent and manly out-croppage, and of that aspiration for independence, and the pride and self-respect latent in all characters. (Or, if there be exceptions, we cannot, fixing our eyes on them alone, make theirs the rule for all.)

I say the mission of government, henceforth, in civilized lands, is not repression alone, and not authority alone, not even of law, nor by that favorite standard of the eminent writer, the rule of the best men, the born heroes and captains of the race (as if such ever, or one time out of a hundred, get into the big places, elective or dynastic)—but higher than the highest arbitrary rule, to train communities through all their grades, beginning with individuals and ending there again, to rule themselves. What Christ appear'd for in the moral-spiritual field for human-kind, namely, that in respect to the absolute soul, there is in the possession of such by each single individual, something so transcendent, so incapable of gradations (like life), that, to that extent, it places all beings on a common level, utterly regardless of the distinctions of intellect, virtue, station, or any height or lowliness what-ever—is tallied in like manner, in this other field, by democracy's rule that men, the nation, as a common aggregate of living identities, affording in each a separate and complete subject for freedom, worldly thrift and happiness, and for a fair chance for growth, and for protec-tion in citizenship, etc., must, to the political extent of the suffrage or vote, if no further, be placed, in each and in the whole, on one broad, primary, universal, common platform.

The purpose is not altogether direct; perhaps it is more indirect. For it is not that democracy is of exhaustive account in itself. Perhaps, indeed, it is (like Nature), of no account in itself. It is that, as we see, it is the best, perhaps only, fit and full means, formulater, general caller-forth, trainer, for the million, not for grand material personali-ties only, but for immortal souls. To be a voter with the rest is not so much; and this, like every institute, will have its imperfections. But to become an enfranchised man, and now, impediments removed, to stand and start without humiliation, and equal with the rest; to commence, or have the road clear'd to commence, the grand experi-ment of development, whose end (perhaps requiring several genera-tions), may be the forming of a full-grown man or woman—that *is* something. To ballast the State is also secured, and in our times is to be secured, in no other way.

We do not (at any rate I do not), put it either on the ground that the People, the masses, even the best of them, are, in their latent or exhibited qualities, essentially sensible and good—nor on the ground of their rights; but that good or bad, rights or no rights, the democratic formula is the only safe and preservative one for coming times. We endow the masses with the suffrage for their own sake, no doubt; then, perhaps still more, from another point of view, for community's sake. Leaving the rest to the sentimentalists, we present freedom as sufficient in its scientific aspect, cold as ice, reasoning, deductive, clear and passionless as crystal.

Democracy too is law, and of the strictest, amplest kind. Many suppose (and often in its own ranks the error), that it means a throwing aside of law, and running riot. But, briefly, it is the superior law, not alone that of physical force, the body, which, adding to, it supersedes with that of the spirit. Law is the unshakable order of the universe forever; and the law over all, and law of laws, is the law of successions; that of the superior law, in time, gradually supplanting and overwhelming the inferior one. (While, for myself, I would cheerfully agree—first covenanting that the formative tendencies shall be administered in favor, or at least not against it, and that this reservation be closely construed—that until the individual or community show due signs, or be so minor and fractional as not to endanger the State, the condition of authoritative tutelage may continue, and self-government must abide its time.) Nor is the æsthetic point, always an important one, without fascination for highest aiming souls. The common ambition strains for elevations, to become some privileged exclusive. The master sees greatness and health in being part of the mass; nothing will do as well as common ground. Would you have in yourself the divine, vast, general law? Then merge yourself in it.

And, topping democracy, this most alluring record, that it alone can bind, and ever seeks to bind, all nations, all men, of however various and distant lands, into a brotherhood, a family. It is the old, yet ever-modern dream of earth, out of her eldest and her youngest, her fond philosophers and poets. Not that half only, individualism, which isolates. There is another half, which is adhesiveness or love, that fuses, ties, and aggregates, making the races comrades, and fraternizing all. Both are to be vitalized by religion (sole worthiest elevator of man or State), breathing into the proud, material tissues, the breath of life. For I say at the core of democracy, finally, is the religious element. All the religions, old and new, are there. Nor may the scheme step forth, clothed in resplendent beauty and command, till these, bearing the best, the latest fruit, the spiritual, shall fully appear.

A portion of our pages we might indite with reference toward Europe, especially the British part of it, more than our own land, perhaps not absolutely needed for the home reader. But the whole question hangs together, and fastens and links all peoples. The liberalist of today has this advantage over antique or medieval times, that his doctrine seeks not only to individualize but to universalize.

The great word Solidarity has arisen. Of all dangers to a nation, as things exist in our day, there can be no greater one than having certain portions of the people set off from the rest by a line drawn —they not privileged as others, but degraded, humiliated, made of no account. Much quackery teems, of course, even on democracy's side, yet does not really affect the orbic quality of the matter. To work in, if we may so term it, and justify God, His divine aggregate, the People (or, the veritable horned and sharp-tailed Devil, *His* aggregate, if there be who convulsively insist upon it)—this, I say, is what democracy is for; and this is what our America means, and is doing —may I not say, has done? If not, she means nothing more, and does nothing more, than any other land. And, as by virtue of its cosmical, antiseptic power, Nature's stomach is fully strong enough not only to digest the morbific matter always presented, not to be turn'd aside, and perhaps, indeed, intuitively gravitating thither—but even to change such contributions into nutriment for highest use and life—so American democracy's. That is the lesson we, these days, send over to European lands by every western breeze.

And truly, whatever may be said, in the way of abstract argument, for or against the theory of a wider democratizing of institutions in any civilized country, much trouble might well be saved to all European lands by recognizing this palpable fact (for a palpable fact it is), that some form of such democratizing is about the only resource now left. *That*, or chronic dissatisfaction continued, mutterings which grow annually louder and louder, till, in due course, and pretty swiftly in most cases, the inevitable crisis, dynastic ruin. Anything worthy to be call'd statesmanship in the Old World, I should say, among the advanced students, adepts, or men of any brains, does not debate today whether to hold on, attempting to lean back and monarchize, or to look forward and democratize—but *how,* and in what degree and part, most prudently to democratize.

The eager and often inconsiderate appeals of reformers and revolutionists are indispensable, to counterbalance the inertness and fossilism making so large a part of human institutions. The latter will always take care of themselves—the danger being that they rapidly tend to ossify us. The former is to be treated with indulgence, and even with respect. As circulation to air, so is agitation and a plentiful degree of speculative license to political and moral sanity. Indirectly, but surely, goodness, virtue, law (of the very best), follow freedom. These, to democracy, are what the keel is to the ship, or saltness to the ocean.

The true gravitation-hold of liberalism in the United States will be a more universal ownership of property, general homesteads, general comfort—a vast, intertwining reticulation of wealth. As the human frame, or, indeed, any object in this manifold universe, is best kept together by the simple miracle of its own cohesion, and the necessity, exercise, and profit thereof, so a great and varied nationality, occupying millions of square miles, were firmest held and knit by the principle of the safety and endurance of the aggregate of its middling property owners. So that, from another point of view, ungracious as it may sound, and a paradox after what we have been saying, democracy looks with suspicion, ill-satisfied eye upon the very poor, the ignorant, and on those out of business. She asks for men and women with occupations, well-off, owners of houses and acres, and with cash in the bank—and with some cravings for literature, too; and must have them, and hastens to make them. Luckily, the seed is already well sown, and has taken ineradicable root.†

Huge and mighty are our days, our republican lands—and most in their rapid shiftings, their changes, all in the interest of the cause. As I write this particular passage (November 1868), the din of disputation rages around me. Acrid the temper of the parties, vital the pending questions. Congress convenes; the President sends his message; reconstruction is still in abeyance; the nomination and the contest for the twenty-first Presidential draw close, with loudest threat and bustle. Of these, and all the like of these, the eventuations I know not; but well I know that behind them, and whatever their eventuations, the vital things remain safe and certain, and all the needed work goes on. Time, with soon or later superciliousness, disposes of Presidents, Congressmen, party platforms, and such. Anon, it clears the stage of each and any mortal shred that thinks itself so potent to its day; and at and after which (with precious, golden exceptions once or twice in a century), all that relates to sir potency is flung to molder in a burial-vault, and no one bothers himself the least bit about it afterwards. But the People ever remain, tendencies continue, and all the idiocratic transfers in unbroken chain go on.

In a few years the dominion-heart of America will be far inland, toward the West. Our future national capital may not be where the present one is. It is possible, nay likely, that in less than fifty years, it will migrate a thousand or two miles, will be refounded, and everything belonging to it made on a different plan, original, far more superb. The main social, political, spine-character of the States will probably run along the Ohio, Missouri and Mississippi rivers, and west and north of them, including Canada. Those regions, with the group of powerful brothers toward the Pacific (destined to the mastership of that sea and its countless paradises of islands), will compact and settle the traits of America, with all the old retain'd, but more expanded, grafted on newer, hardier, purely native stock. A

---

† For fear of mistake, I may as well distinctly specify, as cheerfully included in the model and standard of these Vistas, a practical, stirring, worldly, moneymaking, even materialistic character. It is undeniable that our farms, stores, offices, dry goods, coal and groceries, enginery, cash accounts, trades, earnings, markets, etc., should be attended to in earnest, and actively pursued, just as if they had a real and permanent existence. I perceive clearly that the extreme business energy, and this almost maniacal appetite for wealth prevalent in the United States, are parts of amelioration and progress, indispensably needed to prepare the very results I demand. My theory includes riches, and the getting of riches, and the amplest products, power, activity, inventions, movements, etc. Upon them, as upon sub-strata, I raise the edifice design'd in these Vistas.

giant growth, composite from the rest, getting their contribution, absorbing it, to make it more illustrious. From the north, intellect, the sun of things, also the idea of unswayable justice, anchor amid the last, the wildest tempests. From the south the living soul, the animus of good and bad, haughtily admitting no demonstration but its own. While from the west itself comes solid personality, with blood and brawn, and the deep quality of all-accepting fusion.

Political democracy, as it exists and practically works in America, with all its threatening evils, supplies a training school for making first-class men. It is life's gymnasium, not of good only, but of all. We try often, though we fall back often. A brave delight, fit for freedom's athletes, fills these arenas, and fully satisfies, out of the action in them, irrespective of success. Whatever we do not attain, we at any rate attain the experiences of the fight, the hardening of the strong campaign, and throb with currents of attempt at least. Time is ample. Let the victors come after us. Not for nothing does evil play its part among us. Judging from the main portions of the history of the world, so far, justice is always in jeopardy, peace walks amid hourly pitfalls, and of slavery, misery, meanness, the craft of tyrants and the credulity of the populace, in some of the protean forms, no voice can at any time say. They are not. The clouds break a little, and the sun shines out—but soon and certain the lowering darkness falls again, as if to last forever. Yet is there an immortal courage and prophecy in every sane soul that cannot, must not, under any circumstances, capitulate. *Vive,* the attack—the perennial assault! *Vive,* the unpopular cause—the spirit that audaciously aims—the never-abandon'd efforts, pursued the same amid opposing proofs and precedents.

Once, before the war (alas! I dare not say how many times the mood has come!) I, too, was fill'd with doubt and gloom. A foreigner, an acute and good man, had impressively said to me, that day—putting in form, indeed, my own observations: "I have travel'd much in the United States, and watch'd their politicians, and listen'd to the speeches of the candidates, and read the journals, and gone into the public-houses, and heard the unguarded talk of men. And I have found your vaunted America honey-comb'd from top to toe with infidelism, even to itself and its own programme. I have mark'd the brazen hell-faces of secession and slavery gazing defiantly from all the windows and doorways. I have everywhere found, primarily, thieves and scalliwags arranging the nominations to offices, and sometimes filling the offices themselves. I have found the north just as full of bad stuff as the south. Of the holders of public office in the Nation or the States or their municipalities, I have found that not one in a hundred has been chosen by any spontaneous selection of the outsiders, the people, but all have been nominated and put through by little or large caucuses of the politicians, and have got in by corrupt rings and electioneering, not capacity or desert. I have noticed how the millions of sturdy farmers and mechanics are thus the helpless supple-jacks of comparatively few politicians. And I have noticed more and more, the alarming spectacle of parties usurping the government, and openly and shamelessly wielding it for party purposes."

Sad, serious, deep truths. Yet are there other, still deeper, amply confronting, dominating truths. Over those politicians and great and little rings, and over all their insolence and wiles, and over the powerfullest parties, looms a power, too sluggish maybe, but ever holding decisions and decrees in hand, ready, with stern process, to execute them as soon as plainly needed—and at times, indeed, summarily crushing to atoms the mightiest parties, even in the hour of their pride.

In saner hours far different are the amounts of other things from what, at first sight, they appear. Though it is no doubt important who is elected governor, mayor, or legislator (and full of dismay when incompetent or vile ones get elected, as they sometimes do), there are other, quieter contingencies, infinitely more important. Shams, etc., will always be the show, like ocean's scum; enough, if waters deep and clear make up the rest. Enough, that while the piled embroider'd shoddy gaud and fraud spreads to the superficial eye, the hidden warp and weft are genuine, and will wear forever. Enough, in short, that the race, the land which could raise such as the late rebellion, could also put it down.

The average man of a land at last only is important. He, in these States, remains immortal owner and boss, deriving good uses, somehow, out of any sort of servant in office, even the basest (certain universal requisites, and their settled regularity and protection, being first secured); a nation like ours, in a sort of geological formation state, trying continually new experiments, choosing new delegations, is not served by the best men only, but sometimes more by those that provoke it—by the combats they arouse. Thus national rage, fury, discussion, etc., better than content. Thus, also, the warning signals, invaluable for after times.

What is more dramatic than the spectacle we have seen repeated, and doubtless long shall see—the popular judgment taking the successful candidates on trial in the offices—standing off, as it were, and observing them and their doings for a while, and always giving, finally, the fit, exactly due reward? I think, after all, the sublimest part of political history, and its culmination, is currently issuing from the American people. I know nothing grander, better exercise, better digestion, more positive proof of the past, the triumphant result of faith in human-kind, than a well-contested American national election.

Then still the thought returns (like the thread-passage in overtures), giving the key and echo to these pages. When I pass to and fro, different latitudes, different seasons, beholding the crowds of the great cities, New York, Boston, Philadelphia, Cincinnati, Chicago, St. Louis, San Francisco, New Orleans, Baltimore—when I mix with these interminable swarms of alert, turbulent, good-natured, independent citizens, mechanics, clerks, young persons—at the idea of this mass of men, so fresh and free, so loving and so proud, a singular awe falls upon me. I feel, with dejection and amazement, that among our geniuses and talented writers or speakers, few or none have yet really spoken to this people, created a single image-making work for them, or absorb'd the central spirit and the idiosyncrasies which are theirs—and which, thus, in highest ranges, so far remain entirely uncelebrated, unexpress'd.

Dominion strong is the body's; dominion stronger is the mind's. What has fill'd, and fills today our intellect, our fancy, furnishing the standards therein, is yet foreign. The great poems, Shakspere included, are poisonous to the idea of the pride and dignity of the common people, the lifeblood of democracy. The models of our literature, as we get it from other lands, ultramarine, have had their birth in courts, and bask'd and grown in castle sunshine; all smells of princes' favors. Of workers of a certain sort, we have, indeed, plenty, contributing after their kind; many elegant, many learn'd, all complacent. But touch'd by the national test, or tried by the standards of democratic personality, they wither to ashes. I say I have not seen a single writer, artist, lecturer, or what not, that has confronted the voiceless but ever erect and active, pervading, underlying will and typic aspiration of the land, in a spirit kindred to itself. Do you call those genteel little creatures American poets? Do you term that perpetual, pistareen, paste-pot work, American art, American drama, taste, verse? I think I hear, echoed as from some mountaintop afar in the west, the scornful laugh of the Genius of these States.

Democracy, in silence, biding its time, ponders its own ideals, not of literature and art only—not of men only, but of women. The idea of the women of America (extricated from this daze, this fossil and unhealthy air which hangs about the word *lady*) develop'd, raised to become the robust equals, workers, and, it may be, even practical and political deciders with the men—greater than man, we may admit, through their divine maternity, always their towering, emblematical attribute—but great, at any rate, as man, in all departments; or, rather, capable of being so, soon as they realize it, and can bring themselves to give up toys and fictions, and launch forth, as men do, amid real, independent, stormy life.

Then, as toward our thought's finalè (and, in that, over-arching the true scholar's lesson), we have to say there can be no complete or epical presentation of democracy in the aggregate, or anything like it, at this day, because its doctrines will only be effectually incarnated in any one branch, when, in all, their spirit is at the root and center. Far, far, indeed, stretch, in distance, our Vistas! How much is still to be disentangled, freed! How long it takes to make this American world see that it is, in itself, the final authority and reliance!

Did you, too, O friend, suppose democracy was only for elections, for politics, and for a party name? I say democracy is only of use there that it may pass on and come to its flower and fruits in manners, in the highest forms of interaction between men, and their beliefs— in religion, literature, colleges, and schools—democracy in all public and private life, and in the army and navy.† I have intimated that, as a paramount scheme, it has yet few or no full realizers and believers. I do not see, either, that it owes any serious thanks to noted propagandists or champions, or has been essentially help'd, though often harm'd, by them. It has been and is carried on by all the moral forces, and by trade, finance, machinery, intercommunications, and, in fact, by all the developments of history, and can no more be stopp'd than the tides, or the earth in its orbit. Doubtless, also, it resides, crude and latent, well down in the hearts of the fair average of the American-born people, mainly in the agricultural regions. But it is not yet, there or anywhere, the fully receiv'd, the fervid, the absolute faith.

I submit, therefore, that the fruition of democracy, on aught like a grand scale, resides altogether in the future. As, under any profound and comprehensive view of the gorgeous-composite feudal world, we see in it, through the long ages and cycles of ages, the results of a deep, integral, human and divine principle, or fountain, from which issued laws, ecclesia, manners, institutes, costumes, personalities, poems (hitherto unequal'd), faithfully partaking of their source, and indeed only arising either to betoken it, or to furnish parts of that varied-flowing display, whose center was one and absolute—so, long ages hence, shall the due historian or critic make at least an equal retrospect, an equal history for the democratic principle. It too must be adorn'd, credited with its results—then, when it, with imperial power, through amplest time, has dominated mankind—has been the source and test of all the moral, æsthetic, social, political, and religious expressions and institutes of the civilized world —has begotten them in spirit and in form, and has carried them to its own unprecedented heights—has had (it is possible) monastics and ascetics, more numerous, more devout than the monks and priests of all previous creeds—has sway'd the ages with a breadth and rectitude tallying Nature's own—has fashion'd, systematized, and triumphantly finish'd and carried out, in its own interest, and with unparallel'd success, a new earth and a new man.

Thus we presume to write, as it were, upon things that exist not, and travel by maps yet unmade, and a blank. But the throes of birth are upon us; and we have something of this advantage in seasons of strong formations, doubts, suspense—for then the afflatus of such themes haply may fall upon us, more or less; and then, hot from surrounding war and revolution, our speech, though without polish'd coherence, and a failure by the standard called criticism, comes forth, real at least as the lightnings.

And maybe we, these days, have, too, our own reward—(for there

† The whole present system of the officering and personnel of the army and navy of these States, and the spirit and letter of their trebly-aristocratic rules and regulations, is a monstrous exotic, a nuisance and revolt, and belong here just as much as orders of nobility, or the Pope's council of cardinals. I say if the present theory of our army and navy is sensible and true, then the rest of America is an unmitigated fraud.

are yet some, in all lands, worthy to be so encouraged). Though not for us the joy of entering at the last the conquered city—not ours the chance ever to see with our own eyes the peerless power and splendid *éclat* of the democratic principle, arriv'd at meridian, filling the world with effulgence and majesty far beyond those of past history's kings, or all dynastic sway—there is yet, to whoever is eligible among us, the prophetic vision, the joy of being toss'd in the brave turmoil of these times—the promulgation and the path, obedient, lowly reverent to the voice, the gesture of the god, or holy ghost, which others see not, hear not—with the proud consciousness that amid whatever clouds, seductions, or heart-wearying postponements, we have never deserted, never despair'd, never abandon'd the faith.

So much contributed, to be conn'd well, to help prepare and brace our edifice, our plann'd Idea—we still proceed to give it in another of its aspects—perhaps the main, the high façade of all. For to democracy, the leveler, the unyielding principle of the average, is surely join'd another principle, equally unyielding, closely tracking the first, indispensable to it, opposite (as the sexes are opposite), and whose existence, confronting and ever modifying the other, often clashing, paradoxical, yet neither of highest avail without the other, plainly supplies to these grand cosmic politics of ours, and to the launch'd forth mortal dangers of republicanism, today, or any day, the counterpart and offset whereby Nature restrains the deadly original relentlessness of all her first-class laws. This second principle is individuality, the pride and centripetal isolation of a human being in himself—identity—personalism. Whatever the name, its acceptance and thorough infusions through the organizations of political commonalty now shooting Aurora-like about the world, are of utmost importance, as the principle itself is needed for very life's sake. It forms, in a sort, or is to form, the compensating balance-wheel of the successful working machinery of aggregate America.

And, if we think of it, what does civilization itself rest upon—and what object has it, with its religions, arts, schools, etc., but rich, luxuriant, varied personalism? To that, all bends; and it is because toward such result democracy alone, on anything like Nature's scale, breaks up the limitless fallows of human-kind, and plants the seed, and gives fair play, that its claims now precede the rest. The literature, songs, æsthetics, etc., of a country are of importance principally because they furnish the materials and suggestions of personality for the women and men of that country, and enforce them in a thousand effective ways.† As the topmost claim of a strong consolidating of

---

† After the rest is satiated, all interest culminates in the field of persons, and never flags there. Accordingly in this field have the great poets and literatuses signally toiled. They too, in all ages, all lands, have been creators, fashioning, making types of men and women, as Adam and Eve are made in the divine fable. Behold, shaped, bred by orientalism, feudalism, through their long growth and culmination, and breeding back in return — (when shall we have an equal series, typical of democracy?) — behold, commencing in primal Asia (apparently formulated, in what beginning we

the nationality of these States, is, that only by such powerful compaction can the separate States secure that full and free swing within their spheres, which is becoming to them, each after its kind, so will individuality, with unimpeded branchings, flourish best under imperial republican forms.

Assuming Democracy to be at present in its embryo condition, and that the only large and satisfactory justification of it resides in the future, mainly through the copious production of perfect characters among the people, and through the advent of a sane and pervading religiousness, it is with regard to the atmosphere and spaciousness fit for such characters, and of certain nutriment and cartoon-draftings proper for them, and indicating them for New World purposes, that I continue the present statement—an exploration, as of new ground, wherein, like other primitive surveyors, I must do the best I can, leaving it to those who come after me to do much better. (The service, in fact, if any, must be to break a sort of first path or track, no matter how rude and ungeometrical.)

We have frequently printed the word Democracy. Yet I cannot too often repeat that it is a word the real gist of which still sleeps, quite unawaken'd, notwithstanding the resonance and the many angry tempests out of which its syllables have come, from pen or tongue. It is a great word, whose history, I suppose, remains unwritten, because that history has yet to be enacted. It is, in some sort, younger brother of another great and often-used word, Nature, whose history also waits unwritten. As I perceive, the tendencies of our day, in the States (and I entirely respect them), are toward those vast and sweeping movements, influences, moral and physical, of humanity, now and always current over the planet, on the scale of the impulses of the elements. Then it is also good to reduce the whole matter to the consideration of a single self, a man, a woman, on permanent grounds. Even for the treatment of the universal, in politics, metaphysics, or anything, sooner or later we come down to one single, solitary soul.

There is, in sanest hours, a consciousness, a thought that rises, independent, lifted out from all else, calm, like the stars, shining

---

know, in the gods of the mythologies, and coming down thence), a few samples out of the countless product, bequeath'd to the moderns, bequeath'd to America as studies. For the men, Yudishtura, Rama, Arjuna, Solomon, most of the Old and New Testament characters; Achilles, Ulysses, Theseus, Prometheus, Hercules, Aeneas, Plutarch's heroes; the Merlin of Celtic bards; the Cid, Arthur and his knights, Siegfried and Hagen in the Nibelungen; Roland and Oliver; Roustam in the Shah-Nemah; and so on to Milton's Satan, Cervantes' Don Quixote, Shakspere's Hamlet, Richard II, Lear, Marc Antony, etc., and the modern Faust. These, I say, are models, combined, adjusted to other standards than America's, but of priceless value to her and hers.

Among women, the goddesses of the Egyptian, Indian, and Greek mythologies, certain Bible characters, especially the Holy Mother; Cleopatra, Penelope; the portraits of Brunhelde and Chriemhilde in the Nibelungen; Oriana, Una, etc.; the modern Consuelo, Walter Scott's Jeanie and Effie Deans, etc., etc. (Yet woman portrayed or outlin'd at her best, or as perfect human mother, does not hitherto, it seems to me, fully appear in literature.)

eternal. This is the thought of identity—yours for you, whoever you are, as mine for me. Miracle of miracles, beyond statement, most spiritual and vaguest of earth's dreams, yet hardest basic fact, and only entrance to all facts. In such devout hours, in the midst of the significant wonders of heaven and earth (significant only because of the Me in the center), creeds, conventions, fall away and become of no account before this simple idea. Under the luminousness of real vision, it alone takes possession, takes value. Like the shadowy dwarf in the fable, once liberated and look'd upon, it expands over the whole earth, and spreads to the roof of heaven.

The quality of BEING, in the object's self, according to its own central idea and purpose, and of growing therefrom and thereto—not criticism by other standards, and adjustments thereto—is the lesson of Nature. True, the full man wisely gathers, culls, absorbs; but if, engaged disproportionately in that, he slights or overlays the precious idiocrasy and special nativity and intention that he is, the man's self, the main thing, is a failure, however wide his general cultivation. Thus, in our times, refinement and delicatesse are not only attended to sufficiently, but threaten to eat us up, like a cancer. Already, the democratic genius watches, ill-pleased, these tendencies. Provision for a little healthy rudeness, savage virtue, justification of what one has in one's self, whatever it is, is demanded. Negative qualities, even deficiencies, would be a relief. Singleness and normal simplicity and separation, amid this more and more complex, more and more artificialized state of society—how pensively we yearn for them! how we would welcome their return!

In some such direction, then—at any rate enough to preserve the balance—we feel called upon to throw what weight we can, not for absolute reasons, but current ones. To prune, gather, trim, conform, and ever cram and stuff, and be genteel and proper, is the pressure of our days. While aware that much can be said even in behalf of all this, we perceive that we have not now to consider the question of what is demanded to serve a half-starved and barbarous nation, or set of nations, but what is most applicable, most pertinent, for numerous congeries of conventional, over-corpulent societies, already becoming stifled and rotten with flatulent, infidelistic literature, and polite conformity and art. In addition to establish'd sciences, we suggest a science as it were of healthy average personalism, on original-universal grounds, the object of which should be to raise up and supply through the States a copious race of superb American men and women, cheerful, religious, ahead of any yet known.

America has yet morally and artistically originated nothing. She seems singularly unaware that the models of persons, books, manners, etc., appropriate for former conditions and for European lands, are but exiles and exotics here. No current of her life, as shown on the surfaces of what is authoritatively called her society, accepts or runs into social or æsthetic democracy; but all the currents set squarely against it. Never, in the Old World, was thoroughly upholster'd exterior appearance and show, mental and other, built entirely on the idea of caste, and on the sufficiency of mere outside acquisition—never were glibness, verbal intellect more the test, the emulation—more loftily elevated as head and sample—than they are on the surface of our republican States this day. The writers of a time hint the mottoes of its gods. The word of the modern, say these voices, is the word Culture.

We find ourselves abruptly in close quarters with the enemy. This word Culture, or what it has come to represent, involves, by contrast, our whole theme, and has been, indeed, the spur, urging us to engagement. Certain questions arise. As now taught, accepted and carried out, are not the processes of culture rapidly creating a class of supercilious infidels, who believe in nothing? Shall a man lose himself in countless masses of adjustments, and be so shaped with reference to this, that, and the other, that the simply good and healthy and brave parts of him are reduced and clipp'd away, like the bordering of box in a garden? You can cultivate corn and roses and orchards—but who shall cultivate the mountain peaks, the ocean, and the tumbling gorgeousness of the clouds? Lastly—is the readily given reply that culture only seeks to help, systematize, and put in attitude, the elements of fertility and power, a conclusive reply?

I do not so much object to the name, or word, but I should certainly insist, for the purposes of these States, on a radical change of category, in the distribution of precedence. I should demand a programme of culture, drawn out, not for a single class alone, or for the parlors or lecture rooms, but with an eye to practical life, the west, the workingmen, the facts of farms and jackplanes and engineers, and of the broad range of the women also of the middle and working strata, and with reference to the perfect equality of women, and of a grand and powerful motherhood. I should demand of this programme or theory a scope generous enough to include the widest human area. It must have for its spinal meaning the formation of a typical personality of character, eligible to the uses of the high average of men—and *not* restricted by conditions ineligible to the masses. The best culture will always be that of the manly and courageous instinct, and loving perceptions, and of self-respect—aiming to form, over this continent, an idiocrasy of universalism, which, true child of America, will bring joy to its mother, returning to her in her own spirit, recruiting myriads of offspring, able, natural, perceptive, tolerant, devout believers in her, America, and with some definite instinct why and for what she has arisen, most vast, most formidable of historic births, and is, now and here, with wonderful step, journeying through Time.

The problem, as it seems to me, presented to the New World, is, under permanent law and order, and after preserving cohesion (ensemble-Individuality), at all hazards, to vitalize man's free play of special Personalism, recognizing in it something that calls ever more to be consider'd, fed, and adopted as the sub-stratum for the best that belongs to us (government indeed is for it), including the new æsthetics of our future.

To formulate beyond this present vagueness—to help line and put before us the species, or a specimen of the species, of the democratic ethnology of the future, is a work toward which the genius of our land, with peculiar encouragement, invites her well-wishers. Already certain limnings, more or less grotesque, more or less fading and watery, have appear'd. We too (repressing doubts and qualms) will try our hand.

Attempting, then, however crudely, a basic model or portrait of personality for general use for the manliness of the State (and doubtless that is most useful which is most simple and comprehensive for all, and toned low enough), we should prepare the canvas well beforehand. Parentage must consider itself in advance. (Will the time hasten when fatherhood and motherhood shall become a science—and the noblest science?) To our model, a clear-blooded, strong-fibered physique is indispensable; the questions of food, drink, air, exercise, assimilation, digestion, can never be intermitted. Out of these we descry a well-begotten selfhood—in youth, fresh, ardent, emotional, aspiring, full of adventure; at maturity, brave, perceptive, under control, neither too talkative nor too reticent, neither flippant nor somber; of the bodily figure, the movements easy, the complexion showing the best blood, somewhat flush'd, breast expanded, an erect attitude, a voice whose sound outvies music, eyes of calm and steady gaze, yet capable also of flashing—and a general presence that holds its own in the company of the highest. (For it is native personality, and that alone, that endows a man to stand before presidents or generals, or in any distinguished collection, with *aplomb*—and *not* culture, or any knowledge or intellect whatever.)

With regard to the mental-educational part of our model, enlargement of intellect, stores of cephalic knowledge, etc., the concentration thitherward of all the customs of our age, especially in America, is so overweening, and provides so fully for that part, that important and necessary as it is, it really needs nothing from us here—except, indeed, a phrase of warning and restraint. Manners, costumes, too, though important, we need not dwell upon here. Like beauty, grace of motion, etc., they are results. Causes, original things, being attended to, the right manners unerringly follow. Much is said, among artists, of "the grand style," as if it were a thing by itself. When a man, artist or whoever, has health, pride, acuteness, noble aspirations, he has the motive-elements of the grandest style. The rest is but manipulation (yet that is no small matter).

Leaving still unspecified several sterling parts of any model fit for the future personality of America, I must not fail, again and ever, to pronounce myself on one, probably the least attended to in modern times—a hiatus, indeed, threatening its gloomiest consequences after us. I mean the simple, unsophisticated Conscience, the primary moral element. If I were asked to specify in what quarter lie the grounds of darkest dread, respecting the America of our hopes, I should have to point to this particular. I should demand the invariable application to individuality, this day and any day, of that old, ever-true plumb-rule of persons, eras, nations. Our triumphant modern civilizee, with his all-schooling and his wondrous appliances, will still show himself but an amputation while this deficiency remains. Beyond (assuming a more hopeful tone), the vertebration of the manly and womanly personalism of our Western world, can only be, and is, indeed, to be (I hope), its all penetrating Religiousness.

The ripeness of Religion is doubtless to be looked for in this field of individuality, and is a result that no organization or church can ever achieve. As history is poorly retain'd by what the technists call history, and is not given out from their pages, except the learner has in himself the sense of the well-wrapt, never yet written, perhaps impossible to be written, history—so Religion, although casually arrested, and, after a fashion, preserv'd in the churches and creeds, does not depend at all upon them, but is a part of the identified soul, which, when greatest, knows not bibles in the old way, but in new ways—the identified soul, which can really confront Religion when it extricates itself entirely from the churches, and not before.

Personalism fuses this, and favors it. I should say, indeed, that only in the perfect uncontamination and solitariness of individuality may the spirituality of religion positively come forth at all. Only here, and on such terms, the meditation, the devout ecstasy, the soaring flight. Only here, communion with the mysteries, the eternal problems, whence? whither? Alone, and identity, and the mood—and the soul emerges, and all statements, churches, sermons, melt away like vapors. Alone, and silent thought and awe, and aspiration—and then the interior consciousness, like a hitherto unseen inscription, in magic ink, beams out its wondrous lines to the sense. Bibles may convey, and priests expound, but it is exclusively for the noiseless operation of one's isolated Self, to enter the pure ether of veneration, reach the divine levels, and commune with the unutterable.

To practically enter into politics is an important part of American personalism. To every young man, north and south, earnestly studying these things, I should here, as an offset to what I have said in former pages, now also say, that maybe to views of very large scope, after all, perhaps the political (perhaps the literary and sociological) America goes best about its development its own way—sometimes, to temporary sight, appalling enough. It is the fashion among dillettants and fops (perhaps I myself am not guiltless), to decry the whole formulation of the active politics of America, as beyond redemption, and to be carefully kept away from. See you that you do not fall into this error. America, it may be, is doing very well upon the whole, notwithstanding these antics of the parties and their leaders, these half-brain'd nominees, and many ignorant ballots, and many elected failures and blatherers. It is the dillettants, and all who shirk their duty, who are not doing well. As for you, I advise you to enter more strongly yet into politics. I advise every young man to do so. Always inform yourself; always do the best you can; always vote. Disengage yourself from parties. They have been useful, and to some extent remain so; but the floating, uncommitted electors, farmers, clerks, mechanics, the masters of parties—watching aloof, inclining victory this side or that side—such are the ones most needed, present and future. For America, if eligible at all to downfall and ruin, is eligible within herself, not without; for I see clearly that the combined foreign world could not beat her down. But these savage, wolfish parties alarm me. Owning no law but their own will, more and more combative, less and less tolerant of the idea of ensemble and of equal brotherhood, the perfect equality of the States, the ever-overarching American ideas, it behooves you to convey yourself implicitly to no party, nor submit blindly to their dictators, but steadily hold yourself judge and master over all of them.

So much (hastily toss'd together, and leaving far more unsaid), for an ideal, or intimations of an ideal, toward American manhood. But the other sex, in our land, requires at least a basis of suggestion.

I have seen a young American woman, one of a large family of daughters, who, some years since, migrated from her meager country home to one of the northern cities, to gain her own support. She soon became an expert seamstress, but finding the employment too confining for health and comfort, she went boldly to work for others, to housekeep, cook, clean, etc. After trying several places, she fell upon one where she was suited. She has told me that she finds nothing degrading in her position; it is not inconsistent with personal dignity, self-respect, and the respect of others. She confers benefits and receives them. She has good health; her presence itself is healthy and bracing; her character is unstain'd; she has made herself understood, and preserves her independence, and has been able to help her parents, and educate and get places for her sisters; and her course of life is not without opportunities for mental improvement, and of much quiet, uncosting happiness and love.

I have seen another woman who, from taste and necessity conjoin'd, has gone into practical affairs, carries on a mechanical business, partly works at it herself, dashes out more and more into real hardy life, is not abash'd by the coarseness of the contact, knows how to be firm and silent at the same time, holds her own with unvarying coolness and decorum, and will compare, any day, with superior carpenters, farmers, and even boatmen and drivers. For all that, she has not lost the charm of the womanly nature, but preserves and bears it fully, though through such rugged presentation.

Then there is the wife of a mechanic, mother of two children, a woman of merely passable English education, but of fine wit, with all her sex's grace and intuitions, who exhibits, indeed, such a noble female personality, that I am fain to record it here. Never abnegating her own proper independence, but always genially preserving it, and what belongs to it—cooking, washing, child-nursing, house-tending—she beams sunshine out of all these duties, and makes them illustrious. Physiologically sweet and sound, loving work, practical, she yet knows that there are intervals, however few, devoted to recreation, music, leisure, hospitality—and affords such intervals. Whatever she does and wherever she is, that charm, that indescribable, perfume of genuine womanhood attends her, goes with her, exhales from her, which belongs of right to all the sex, and is, or ought to be, the invariable atmosphere and common aureola of old as well as young.

My dear mother once described to me a resplendent person, down on Long Island, whom she knew in early days. She was known by the name of the Peacemaker. She was well toward eighty years old, of happy and sunny temperament, had always lived on a farm, and was very neighborly, sensible and discreet, an invariable and welcom'd favorite, especially with young married women. She had numerous children and grandchildren. She was uneducated, but possess'd a native dignity. She had come to be a tacitly agreed upon domestic regulator, judge, settler of difficulties, shepherdess, the reconciler in the land. She was a sight to draw near and look upon, with her large figure, her profuse snow-white hair (uncoif'd by any headdress or cap), dark eyes, clear complexion, sweet breath, and peculiar personal magnetism.

The foregoing portraits, I admit, are frightfully out of line from these imported models of womanly personality—the stock feminine characters of the current novelists, or of the foreign court poems (Ophelias, Enids, princesses, or ladies of one thing or another), which fill the envying dreams of so many poor girls, and are accepted by our men, too, as supreme ideals of feminine excellence to be sought after. But I present mine just for a change.

Then there are mutterings (we will not now stop to heed them here, but they must be heeded), of something more revolutionary. The day is coming when the deep questions of woman's entrance amid the arenas of practical life, politics, the suffrage, etc., will not only be argued all around us, but may be put to decision, and real experiment.

Of course, in these States, for both man and woman, we must entirely recast the types of highest personality from what the oriental, feudal, ecclesiastical worlds bequeath us, and which yet possess the imaginative and æsthetic fields of the United States, pictorial and melodramatic, not without use as studies, but making sad work, and forming a strange anachronism upon the scenes and exigencies around us. Of course, the old undying elements remain. The task is, to successfully adjust them to new combinations, our own days. Nor is this so incredible. I can conceive a community, today and here, in which, on a sufficient scale, the perfect personalities, without noise meet; say in some pleasant western settlement or town, where a couple of hundred best men and women, of ordinary worldly status, have by luck been drawn together, with nothing extra of genius or wealth, but virtuous, chaste, industrious, cheerful, resolute, friendly and devout. I can conceive such a community organized in running order, powers judiciously delegated—farming, building, trade, courts, mails, schools, elections, all attended to; and then the rest of life, the main thing, freely branching and blossoming in each individual, and bearing golden fruit. I can see there, in every young and old man, after his kind, and in every woman after hers, a true personality, develop'd, exercised proportionately in body, mind, and spirit. I can imagine this case as one not necessarily rare or difficult, but in buoyant accordance with the municipal and general requirements of our times. And I can realize in it the culmination of something better than any stereotyped *éclat* of history or poems. Perhaps unsung, undramatized, unput in essays or biographies—perhaps even some such community already exists, in Ohio, Illinois, Missouri, or somewhere, practically fulfilling itself, and thus outvying, in cheapest vulgar life, all that has been hitherto shown in best ideal pictures.

In short, and to sum up, America, betaking herself to formative action (as it is about time for more solid achievement, and less windy promise), must, for her purposes, cease to recognize a theory of character grown of feudal aristocracies, or form'd by merely literary standards, or from any ultramarine full-dress formulas of culture, polish, caste, etc., and must sternly promulgate her own new standard, yet old enough, and accepting the old, the perennial elements, and combining them into groups, unities, appropriate to the modern, the democratic, the west, and to the practical occasions and needs of our own cities, and of the agricultural regions. Ever the most precious in the common. Ever the fresh breeze of field, or hill or lake, is more than any palpitation of fans, though of ivory, and redolent with perfume; and the air is more than the costliest perfumes.

And now, for fear of mistake, we may not intermit to beg our absolution from all that genuinely is, or goes along with, even Culture. Pardon us, venerable shade! if we have seem'd to speak lightly of your office. The whole civilization of the earth, we know, is yours, with all the glory and the light thereof. It is, indeed, in your own spirit, and seeking to tally the loftiest teachings of it, that we aim these poor utterances. For you, too, mighty minister! know that there is something greater than you, namely, the fresh, eternal qualities of Being. From them, and by them, as you, at your best, we too evoke the last, the needed help, to vitalize our country and our days. Thus we pronounce not so much against the principle of culture; we only supervise it, and promulgate along with it, as deep, perhaps a deeper, principle. As we have shown the New World including in itself the all-leveling aggregate of democracy, we show it also including the all-varied, all-permitting, all-free theorem of individuality, and erecting therefor a lofty and hitherto unoccupied framework or platform, broad enough for all, eligible to every farmer and mechanic—to the female equally with the male—a towering selfhood, not physically perfect only—not satisfied with the mere mind's and learning's stores, but religious, possessing the idea of the infinite (rudder and compass sure amid this troublous voyage, o'er darker, wildest wave, through stormiest wind, of man's or nation's progress)—realizing, above the rest, that known humanity, in deepest sense, is fair adhesion to itself, for purposes beyond—and that, finally, the personality of mortal life is most important with reference to the immortal, the unknown, the spiritual, the only permanently real, which as the ocean waits for and receives the rivers, waits for us each and all.

Much is there, yet, demanding line and outline in our Vistas, not only on these topics, but others quite unwritten. Indeed, we could talk the matter, and expand it, through lifetime. But it is necessary to return to our original premises. In view of them, we have again pointedly to confess that all the objective grandeurs of the world, for highest purposes, yield themselves up, and depend on mentality alone. Here, and here only, all balances, all rests. For the mind, which alone builds the permanent edifice, haughtily builds it to itself. By it, with what follows it, are convey'd to mortal sense the culminations of the materialistic, the known, and a prophecy of the unknown. To take expression, to incarnate, to endow a literature with grand and archetypal models—to fill with pride and love the utmost capacity, and to achieve spiritual meanings, and suggest the future—these, and these only, satisfy the soul. We must not say one word against real materials; but the wise know that they do not become real till touched by emotions, the mind. Did we call the latter imponderable? Ah, let us rather proclaim that the slightest song-tune, the countless ephemera of passions aroused by orators and tale-tellers, are more dense, more weighty than the engines there in the great factories, or the granite blocks in their foundations.

Approaching thus the momentous spaces, and considering with reference to a new and greater personalism, the needs and possibilities of American imaginative literature, through the medium-light of what we have already broach'd, it will at once be appreciated that a vast gulf of difference separates the present accepted condition of these spaces, inclusive of what is floating in them, from any condition adjusted to, or fit for, the world, the America, there sought to be indicated, and the copious races of complete men and women, along these Vistas crudely outlined. It is, in some sort, no less a difference than lies between that long-continued nebular state and vagueness of the astronomical worlds, compared with the subsequent state, the definitely-form'd worlds themselves, duly compacted, clustering in systems, hung up there, chandeliers of the universe, beholding and mutually lit by each other's lights, serving for ground of all substantial foothold, all vulgar uses—yet serving still more as an undying chain and echelon of spiritual proofs and shows. A boundless field to fill! A new creation, with needed orbic works launch'd forth, to revolve in free and lawful circuits—to move, self-poised, through the ether, and shine like heaven's own suns! With such, and nothing less, we suggest that New World literature, fit to rise upon, cohere, and signalize in time, these States.

What, however, do we more definitely mean by New World literature? Are we not doing well enough here already? Are not the United States this day busily using, working, more printer's type, more presses, than any other country? uttering and absorbing more publications than any other? Do not our publishers fatten quicker and deeper? (helping themselves, under shelter of a delusive and sneaking law, or rather absence of law, to most of their forage, poetical, pictorial, historical, romantic, even comic, without money and without price—and fiercely resisting the timidest proposal to pay for it). Many will come under this delusion—but my purpose is to dispel it. I say that a nation may hold and circulate rivers and oceans of very readable print, journals, magazines, novels, library books, "poetry," etc.—such as the States today possess and circulate—of unquestionable aid and value—hundreds of new volumes annually composed and brought out here, respectable enough, indeed unsurpass'd in smartness and erudition—with further hundreds, or rather millions (as by free forage or theft aforementioned), also thrown into the market—and yet, all the while, the said nation, land, strictly speaking, may possess no literature at all.

Repeating our inquiry, what, then, do we mean by real literature? especially the democratic literature of the future? Hard questions to meet. The clues are inferential, and turn us to the past. At best, we can only offer suggestions, comparisons, circuits.

It must still be reiterated, as, for the purpose of these memoranda, the deep lesson of history and time, that all else in the contributions of a nation or age, through its politics, materials, heroic personalities, military *éclat*, etc., remains crude, and defers, in any close and thoroughgoing estimate, until vitalized by national, original achetypes in literature. They only put the nation in form, finally tell anything—prove, complete anything—perpetuate anything. Without doubt, some of the richest and most powerful and populous communities of the antique world, and some of the grandest personalities and events, have, to after and present times, left themselves entirely unbequeath'd. Doubtless, greater than any that have come down to us, were among those lands, heroisms, persons, that have not come down to us at all, even by name, date, or location. Others have arrived safely, as from voyages over wide, century-stretching seas. The little ships, the miracles that have buoy'd them, and by incredible chances safely convey'd them (or the best of them, their meaning and essence) over long wastes, darkness, lethargy, ignorance, etc., have been a few inscriptions —a few immortal compositions, small in size, yet compassing what measureless values of reminiscence, contemporary portraitures, manners, idioms, and beliefs, with deepest inference, hint, and thought, to tie and touch forever the old, new body, and the old, new soul! These! and still these! bearing the freight so dear—dearer than pride—dearer than love. All the best experience of humanity, folded, saved, freighted to us here. Some of these tiny ships we call Old and New Testament, Homer, Eschylus, Plato, Juvenal, etc. Precious minims! I think, if we were forced to choose, rather than have you, and the likes of you, and what belongs to, and has grown of you, blotted out and gone, we could better afford, appalling as that would be, to lose all actual ships, this day fasten'd by wharf, or floating on wave, and see them, with all their cargoes, scuttled and sent to the bottom.

Gathered by geniuses of city, race or age, and put by them in highest of art's forms, namely, the literary form, the peculiar combinations and the outshows of that city, age, or race, its particular modes of the universal attributes and passions, its faiths, heroes, lovers and gods, wars, traditions, struggles, crimes, emotions, joys (or the subtle spirit of these), having been pass'd on to us to illumine our own selfhood, and its experiences—what they supply, indispensable and highest, if taken away, nothing else in all the world's boundless storehouses could make up to us, or ever again return.

For us, along the great highways of time, those monuments stand

—those forms of majesty and beauty. For us those beacons burn through all the nights. Unknown Egyptians, graving hieroglyphs; Hindus, with hymn and apothegm and endless epic; Hebrew prophet, with spirituality, as in flashes of lightning, conscience like red-hot iron, plaintive songs and screams of vengeance for tyrannies and enslavement; Christ, with bent head, brooding love and peace, like a dove; Greek, creating eternal shapes of physical and æsthetic proportion; Roman, lord of satire, the sword, and the codex;—of the figures, some far off and veil'd, others nearer and visible; Dante, stalking with lean form, nothing but fiber, not a grain of superfluous flesh; Angelo, and the great painters, architects, musicians; rich Shakspere, luxuriant as the sun, artist and singer of feudalism in its sunset, with all the gorgeous colors, owner thereof, and using them at will; and so to such as German Kant and Hegel, where they, though near us, leaping over the ages, sit again, impassive, imperturbable, like the Egyptian gods. Of these, and the like of these, is it too much, indeed, to return to our favorite figure, and view them as orbs and systems of orbs, moving in free paths in the spaces of that other heaven, the kosmic intellect, the soul?

Ye powerful and resplendent ones! ye were, in your atmospheres, grown not for America, but rather for her foes, the feudal and the old—while our genius is democratic and modern. Yet could ye, indeed, but breathe your breath of life into our New World's nostrils—not to enslave us, as now, but, for our needs, to breed a spirit like your own—perhaps (dare we to say it?) to dominate, even destroy, what you yourselves have left! On your plane, and no less, but even higher and wider, must we mete and measure for today and here. I demand races of orbic bards, with unconditional, uncompromising sway. Come forth, sweet democratic despots of the west!

By points like these we, in reflection, token what we mean by any land's or people's genuine literature. And thus compared and tested, judging amid the influence of loftiest products only, what do our current copious fields of print, covering in manifold forms, the United States, better, for an analogy, present, than, as in certain regions of the sea, those spreading, undulating masses of squid, through which the whale swimming, with head half out, feeds?

Not but that doubtless our current so-called literature (like an endless supply of small coin) performs a certain service, and maybe too, the service needed for the time, (the preparation-service, as children learn to spell). Everybody reads, and truly nearly everybody writes, either books, or for the magazines or journals. The matter has magnitude, too, after a sort. But is it really advancing? or, has it advanced for a long while? There is something impressive about the huge editions of the dailies and weeklies, the mountain-stacks of white paper piled in the press-vaults, and the proud, crashing, ten-cylinder presses, which I can stand and watch any time by the half hour. Then (though the States in the field of imagination present not a single first-class work, not a single great literatus), the main objects, to amuse, to titillate, to pass away time, to circulate the news, and rumors of news, to rhyme, and read rhyme, are yet attain'd, and on a scale of infinity. Today, in books, in the rivalry of writers, especially novelists, success (so-called) is for him or her who strikes the mean flat average, the sensational appetite for stimulus, incident, persiflage, etc., and depicts, to the common caliber, sensual, exterior life. To such, or the luckiest of them, as we see, the audiences are limitless and profitable; but they cease presently. While this day, or any day, to workmen portraying interior or spiritual life, the audiences were limited, and often laggard—but they last forever.

Compared with the past, our modern science soars, and our journals serve—but ideal and even ordinary romantic literature, does not, I think, substantially advance. Behold the prolific brood of the contemporary novel, magazine tale, theatre play, etc. The same endless thread of tangled and superlative love story, inherited, apparently from the Amadises and Palmerins of the 13th, 14th, and 15th centuries over there in Europe. The costumes and associations brought down to date, the seasoning hotter and more varied, the dragons and ogres left out—but the *thing*, I should say, has not advanced—is just as sensational, just as strain'd—remains about the same, nor more, nor less.

What is the reason our time, our lands, that we see no fresh local courage, sanity, of our own—the Mississippi, stalwart Western men, real mental and physical facts, Southerners, etc., in the body of our literature? especially the poetic part of it. But always, instead, a parcel of dandies and ennuyees, dapper little gentlemen from abroad, who flood us with their thin sentiment of parlors, parasols, piano songs, tinkling rhymes, the five-hundredth importation—or whimpering and crying about something, chasing one aborted conceit after another, and forever occupied in dyspeptic amours with dyspeptic women. While, current and novel, the grandest events and revolutions, and stormiest passions of history, are crossing today with unparalleled rapidity and magnificence over the stages of our own and all the continents, offering new materials, opening new vistas, with largest needs, inviting the daring launching forth of conceptions in literature, inspired by them, soaring in highest regions, serving art in its highest (which is only the other name for serving God, and serving humanity), where is the man of letters, where is the book, with any nobler aim than to follow in the old track, repeat what has been said before—and, as its utmost triumph, sell well, and be erudite or elegant?

Mark the roads, the processes, through which these States have arrived, standing easy, henceforth ever-equal, ever-compact, in their range today. European adventures? the most antique? Asiatic or African? old history—miracles—romances? Rather, our own unquestion'd facts. They hasten, incredible, blazing bright as fire. From the deeds and days of Columbus down to the present, and including the present—and especially the late Secession War—when I con them, I feel, every leaf, like stopping to see if I have not made a mistake, and fall'n on the splendid figments of some dream. But it is no dream. We stand, live, move, in the huge flow of our age's materialism—in its spirituality. We have founded for us the most positive of lands. The

founders have pass'd to other spheres—but what are these terrible
duties they have left us?

Their policies the United States have, in my opinion, with all their
faults, already substantially establish'd, for good, on their own native,
sound, long-vista'd principles, never to be overturn'd, offering a sure
basis for all the rest. With that, their future religious forms, sociology,
literature, teachers, schools, costumes, etc., are of course to make a
compact whole, uniform, on tallying principles. For how can we
remain, divided, contradicting ourselves this way?† I say we can
only attain harmony and stability by consulting ensemble and the
ethic purports, and faithfully building upon them. For the New
World, indeed, after two grand stages of preparation-strata, I perceive
that now a third stage, being ready for (and without which the
other two were useless), with unmistakable signs appears. The First
stage was the planning and putting on record the political foundation rights of immense masses of people—indeed all people—in the
organization or republican National, State, and municipal governments, all constructed with reference to each, and each to all. This
is the American programme, not for classes, but for universal man,
and is embodied in the compacts of the Declaration of Independence,
and, as it began and has now grown, with its amendments, the
Federal Constitution—and in the State governments, with all their
interiors, and with general suffrage; those having the sense not only
of what is in themselves, but that their certain several things started,
planted, hundreds of others in the same direction duly arise and
follow. The Second stage relates to material prosperity, wealth, produce, laborsaving machines, iron, cotton, local, State, and continental
railways, intercommunication and trade with all lands, steamships,
mining, general employment, organization of great cities, cheap
appliances for comfort, numberless technical schools, books, newspapers, a currency for money circulation, etc. The Third stage, rising
out of the previous ones, to make them and all illustrious, I, now,
for one, promulge, announcing a native expression-spirit, getting into
form, adult, and through mentality, for these States, self-contain'd,
different from others, more expansive, more rich and free, to be
evidenced by original authors and poets to come, by American personalities, plenty of them, male and female, traversing the States, none
excepted—and by native superber tableaux and growths of language,
songs, operas, orations, lectures, architecture—and by a sublime and
serious Religious Democracy sternly taking command, dissolving the
old, sloughing off surfaces, and from its own interior and vital principles, reconstructing, democratizing society.

† Note, today, an instructive, curious spectacle and conflict. Science (twin, in its
fields, of Democracy in its) — Science, testing absolutely all thoughts, all works,
has already burst well upon the world — a sun, mounting, most illuminating, most
glorious — surely never again to set. But against it, deeply entrench'd, holding possession, yet remains (not only through the churches and schools, but by imaginative
literature, and unregenerate poetry), the fossil theology of the mythic-materialistic,
superstitious, untaught and credulous, fable-loving, primitive ages of humanity.

For America, type of progress, and of essential faith in man, above all his errors and wickedness—few suspect how deep, how deep it really strikes. The world evidently supposes, and we have evidently supposed so too, that the States are merely to achieve the equal franchise, an elective government—to inaugurate the respectability of labor, and become a nation of practical operatives, law-abiding, orderly, and well-off. Yes, those are indeed parts of the task of America; but they not only do not exhaust the progressive conception, but rather arise, teeming with it, as the mediums of deeper, higher progress. Daughter of a physical revolution—mother of the true revolutions, which are of the interior life, and of the arts. For so long as the spirit is not changed, any change of appearance is of no avail.

The old men, I remember as a boy, were always talking of American independence. What is independence? Freedom from all laws or bonds except those of one's own being, control'd by the universal ones. To lands, to man, to woman, what is there at last to each, but the inherent soul, nativity, indiosyncrasy, free, highest poised, soaring its own flight, following out itself?

At present, these States, in their theology and social standards (of greater importance than their political institutions) are entirely held possession of by foreign lands. We see the sons and daughters of the New World, ignorant of its genius, not yet inaugurating the native, the universal, and the near still importing the distant, the partial, and the dead. We see London, Paris, Italy—not original, superb, as where they belong—but second-hand here, where they do not belong. We see the shreds of Hebrews, Romans, Greeks; but where, on her own soil, do we see, in any faithful, highest, proud expression, America herself? I sometimes question whether she has a corner in her own house.

Not but that in one sense, and a very grand one, good theology, good art, or good literature, has certain features shared in common. The combination fraternizes, ties the races—is, in many particulars, under laws applicable indifferently to all, irrespective of climate or date, and, from whatever source, appeals to emotions, pride, love, spirituality, common to human-kind. Nevertheless, they touch a man closest (perhaps only actually touch him), even in these, in their expression through autochthonic lights and shades, flavors, fondnesses, aversions, specific incidents, illustrations, out of his own nationality, geography, surroundings, antecedents, etc. The spirit and the form are one, and depend far more on association, identity, and place, than is supposed. Subtly interwoven with the materiality and personality of a land, a race—Teuton, Turk, Californian, or what not—there is always something—I can hardly tell what it is—history but describes the results of it—it is the same as the untellable look of some human faces. Nature, too, in his stolid forms, is full of it—but to most it is there a secret. This something is rooted in the invisible roots, the profoundest meanings of that place, race, or nationality; and to absorb and again effuse it, uttering words and products as from its midst, and carrying it into highest regions, is the work, or a main part of the work, of any country's true author, poet, historian, lecturer, and perhaps even priest and philosoph. Here, and here only, are the foundations for our really valuable and permanent verse, drama, etc.

But at present (judged by any higher scale than that which finds the chief ends of existence to be to feverishly make money during one half of it, and by some "amusement," or perhaps foreign travel, flippantly kill time, the other half), and considered with reference to purposes of patriotism, health, a noble personality, religion, and the democratic adjustments, all these swarms of poems, literary magazines, dramatic plays, resultant so far from American intellect, and the formation of our best ideas, are useless and a mockery. They strengthen and nourish no one, express nothing characteristic, give decision and purpose to no one, and suffice only the lowest level of vacant minds.

Of what is called the drama, or dramatic presentation in the United States, as now put forth at the theatres, I should say it deserves to be treated with the same gravity, and on a par with the questions of ornamental confectionery at public dinners, or the arrangement of curtains and hangings in a ballroom—nor more, nor less. Of the other, I will not insult the reader's intelligence (once really entering into the atmosphere of these Vistas), by supposing it necessary to show, in detail, why the copious dribble, either of our little or well-known rhymesters, does not fulfill, in any respect, the needs and august occasions of this land. America demands a poetry that is bold, modern, and all-surrounding and kosmical, as she is herself. It must in no respect ignore science or the modern, but inspire itself with science and the modern. It must bend its vision toward the future, more than the past. Like America, it must extricate itself from even the greatest models of the past, and, while courteous to them, must have entire faith in itself, and the products of its own democratic spirit only. Like her, it must place in the van, and hold up at all hazards, the banner of the divine pride of man in himself (the radical foundation of the new religion). Long enough have the People been listening to poems in which common humanity, deferential, bends low, humiliated, acknowledging superiors. But America listens to no such poems. Erect, inflated, and fully self-esteeming be the chant; and then America will listen with pleased ears.

Nor may the genuine gold, the gems, when brought to light at last, be probably usher'd forth from any of the quarters currently counted on. Today, doubtless, the infant genius of American poetic expression (eluding those highly refined imported and gilt-edged themes, and sentimental and butterfly flights, pleasant to orthodox publishers—causing tender spasms in the coteries, and warranted not to chafe the sensitive cuticle of the most exquisitely artificial gossamer delicacy), lies sleeping far away, happily unrecognized and uninjur'd by the coteries, the art-writers, the talkers and critics of the saloons, or the lecturers in the colleges—lies sleeping, aside, unrecking itself, in some western idiom, or native Michigan or Tennessee repartee, or stump speech—or in Kentucky or Georgia, or the Carolinas—or in some slang

or local song or allusion of the Manhattan, Boston, Philadelphia, or
Baltimore mechanic—or up in the Maine woods—or off in the hut of
the California miner, or crossing the Rocky Mountains, or along the
Pacific railroad—or on the breasts of the young farmers of the northwest, or Canada, or boatmen of the lakes. Rude and coarse nursing
beds, these; but only from such beginnings and stocks, indigenous
here, may haply arrive, be grafted, and sprout in time, flowers of
genuine American aroma, and fruits truly and fully our own.

I say it were a standing disgrace to these States—I say it were a
disgrace to any nation, distinguish'd above others by the variety and
vastness of its territories, its materials, its inventive activity, and the
splendid practicality of its people, not to rise and soar above others,
also in its original styles in literature and art, and its own supply of
intellectual and æsthetic masterpieces, archetypal, and consistent with
itself. I know not a land except ours that has not, to some extent, however small, made its title clear. The Scotch have their born ballads,
subtly expressing their past and present, and expressing character.
The Irish have theirs. England, Italy, France, Spain, theirs. What has
America? With exhaustless mines of the richest ore of epic, lyric, tale,
tune, picture, etc., in the Four Years' War; with, indeed, I sometimes
think, the richest masses of material ever afforded a nation, more
variegated, and on a larger scale—the first sign of proportionate, native,
imaginative Soul, and first-class works to match, is (I cannot too often
repeat), so far wanting.

Long ere the second centennial arrives, there will be some forty to
fifty great States, among them Canada and Cuba. When the present
century closes, our population will be sixty or seventy millions. The
Pacific will be ours, and the Atlantic mainly ours. There will be daily
electric communication with every part of the globe. What an age!
What a land! Where, elsewhere, one so great? The individuality of
one nation must then, as always, lead the world. Can there be any
doubt who the leader ought to be? Bear in mind, though, that nothing
less than the mightiest original non-subordinated SOUL has ever really,
gloriously led, or ever can lead. (This Soul—its other name, in these
Vistas, is LITERATURE.)

In fond fancy leaping those hundred years ahead let us survey
America's works, poems, philosophies, fulfilling prophecies, and giving
form and decision to best ideals. Much that is now undream'd of, we
might then perhaps see establish'd, luxuriantly cropping forth, richness,
vigor of letters and of artistic expression, in whose products character
will be a main requirement, and not merely erudition or elegance.

Intense and loving comradeship, the personal and passionate attachment of man to man—which, hard to define, underlies the lessons
and ideals of the profound saviors of every land and age, and which
seems to promise, when thoroughly develop'd, cultivated, and recognized in manners and literature, the most substantial hope and safety
of the future of these States, will then be fully express'd.†

† It is to the development, identification, and general prevalence of that fervid
comradeship (the adhesive love, at least rivaling the amative love hitherto possessing

A strong-fibered joyousness and faith, and the sense of health *al fresco,* may well enter into the preparation of future noble American authorship. Part of the test of a great literatus shall be the absence in him of the idea of the covert, the lurid, the maleficent, the devil, the grim estimates inherited from the Puritans, hell, natural depravity, and the like. The great literatus will be known, among the rest, by his cheerful simplicity, his adherence to natural standards, his limitless faith in God, his reverence, and by the absence in him of doubt, ennui, burlesque, persiflage, or any strained and temporary fashion.

Nor must I fail, again and yet again, to clinch, reiterate more plainly still (O that indeed such survey as we fancy may show in time this part completed also!) the lofty aim, surely the proudest and the purest, in whose service the future literatus, of whatever field, may gladly labor. As we have intimated, offsetting the material civilization of our race, our nationality, its wealth, territories, factories, population, products, trade, and military and naval strength, and breathing breath of life into all these, and more, must be its moral civilization—the formulation, expression, aidancy whereof, is the very highest height of literature. The climax of this loftiest range of civilization, rising above all the gorgeous shows and results of wealth, intellect, power, and art, as such—above even theology and religious fervor—is to be its development, from the eternal bases, and the fit expression, of absolute Conscience, moral soundness, Justice. Even in religious fervor there is a touch of animal heat. But moral conscientiousness, crystalline, without flaw, not Godlike only, entirely human, awes and enchants forever. Great is emotional love, even in the order of the rational universe. But, if we must make gradations, I am clear there is something greater. Power, love, veneration, products, genius, æsthetics, tried by subtlest comparisons, analyses, and in serenest moods, somewhere fail, somehow become vain. Then noiseless, with flowing steps, the lord, the sun, the last ideal comes. By the names right, justice, truth, we suggest, but do not describe it. To the world of men it remains a dream, an idea as they call it. But no dream is it to the wise—but the proudest, almost only solid lasting thing of all. Its analogy in the material universe is what holds together this world, and every object upon it, and carries its dynamics on forever sure and safe. Its lack, and the persistent shirking of it, as in life, sociology, literature, politics,

---

imaginative literature, if not going beyond it), that I look for the counterbalance and offset of our materialistic and vulgar American democracy, and for the spiritualization thereof. Many will say it is a dream, and will not follow my inferences; but I confidently expect a time when there will be seen, running like a half-hid warp through all the myriad audible and visible worldly interests of America, threads of manly friendship, fond and loving, pure and sweet, strong and life-long, carried to degrees hitherto unknown — not only giving tone to individual character, and making it unprecedently emotional, muscular, heroic, and refined, but having the deepest relations to general politics. I say democracy infers such loving comradeship, as its most inevitable twin or counterpart, without which it will be incomplete, in vain, and incapable of perpetuating itself.

business, and even sermonizing these times, or any times, still leaves the abysm, the mortal flaw and smutch, mocking civilization today, with all its unquestion'd triumphs, and all the civilization so far known.†

Present literature, while magnificently fulfilling certain popular demands, with plenteous knowledge and verbal smartness, is profoundly sophisticated, insane, and its very joy is morbid. It needs tally and express Nature, and the spirit of Nature, and to know and obey the standards. I say the question of Nature, largely considered, involves the questions of the æsthetic, the emotional, and the religious—and involves happiness. A fitly born and bred race, growing up in right conditions of outdoor as much as indoor harmony, activity and development, would probably, from and in those conditions, find it enough merely *to live*—and would, in their relations to the sky, air, water, trees, etc., and to the countless common shows, and in the fact of life itself, discover and achieve happiness—with Being suffused night and day by wholesome extasy, surpassing all the pleasures that wealth, amusement, and even gratified intellect, erudition, or the sense of art, can give.

In the prophetic literature of these States (the reader of my speculations will miss their principal stress unless he allows well for the point that a new Literature, perhaps a new Metaphysics, certainly a new Poetry, are to be, in my opinion, the only sure and worthy supports and expressions of the American Democracy), Nature, true Nature, and the true idea of Nature, long absent, must, above all, become fully restored, enlarged, and must furnish the pervading atmosphere to poems, and the test of all high literary and æsthetic compositions. I do not mean the smooth walks, trimm'd hedges, poseys and nightingales of the English poets, but the whole orb, with its geologic history, the kosmos, carrying fire and snow, that rolls through the illimitable areas, light as a feather, though weighing billions of tons. Furthermore, as by what we now partially call Nature is intended, at most, only what is entertainable by the physical conscience, the sense of matter, and of good animal health—on these it must be distinctly

† I am reminded as I write that out of this very conscience, or idea of conscience, of intense moral right, and in its name and strain'd construction, the worst fanaticisms, wars, persecutions, murders, etc., have yet, in all lands, in the past, been broach'd and have come to their devilish fruition. Much is to be said, but I may say here, and in response, that side by side with the unflagging stimulation of the elements of religion and conscience must henceforth move with equal sway, science, absolute reason, and the general proportionate development of the whole man. These scientific facts, deductions, are divine too — precious counted parts of moral civilization, and, with physical health, indispensable to it, to prevent fanaticism. For abstract religion, I perceive, is easily led astray, ever credulous, and is capable of devouring, remorseless like fire and flame. Conscience, too, isolated from all else, and from the emotional nature, may but attain the beauty and purity of glacial, snowy ice. We want, for these States, for the general character, a cheerful, religious fervor, endued with the ever-present modifications of the human emotions, friendship, benevolence, with a fair field for scientific inquiry, the right of individual judgment, and always the cooling influences of material Nature.

accumulated, incorporated, that man, comprehending these, has, in towering superaddition, the moral and spiritual consciences, indicating his destination beyond the ostensible, the mortal.

To the heights of such estimate of Nature indeed ascending, we proceed to make observations for our Vistas, breathing rarest air. What is I believe called Idealism seems to me to suggest (guarding against extravagance, and ever modified even by its opposite) the course of inquiry and desert of favor for our New World metaphysics, their foundation of and in literature, giving hue to all.†

The elevating and etherealizing ideas of the unknown and of unreality must be brought forward with authority, as they are the legitimate heirs of the known, and of reality, and at least as great as

---

† The culmination and fruit of literary artistic expression, and its final fields of pleasure for the human soul, are in metaphysics, including the mysteries of the spiritual world, the soul itself, and the question of the immortal continuation of our identity. In all ages, the mind of man has brought up here—and always will. Here, at least, of whatever race or era, we stand on common ground. Applause, too, is unanimous, antique or modern. These authors who work well in this field — though their reward, instead of a handsome percentage, or royalty, may be but simply the laurel crown of the victors in the great Olympic games — will be dearest to humanity, and their works, however æsthetically defective, will be treasur'd forever. The altitude of literature and poetry has always been religion — and always will be. The Indian Vedas, the Nackas of Zoroaster, the Talmud of the Jews, the Old Testament, the Gospel of Christ and His disciples, Plato's works, the Koran of Mohammed, the Edda of Snorro, and so on toward our own day, to Swedenborg, and to the invaluable contributions of Leibnitz, Kant, and Hegel — these, with such poems only in which (while singing well of persons and events, of the passions of man, and the shows of the material universe), the religious tone, the consciousness of mystery, the recognition of the future, of the unknown, of Deity over and under all, and of the divine purpose, are never absent, but indirectly give tone to all — exhibit literature's real heights and elevations, towering up like the great mountains of the earth.

Standing on this ground — the last, the highest, only permanent ground — and sternly criticizing, from it, all works, either of the literary, or any art, we have peremptorily to dismiss every pretensive production, however fine its æsthetic or intellectual points, which violates or ignores, or even does not celebrate, the central divine idea of All, suffusing universe, of eternal trains of purpose, in the development, by however slow degrees, of the physical, moral, and spiritual kosmos. I say he has studied, meditated to no profit, whatever may be his mere erudition, who has not absorb'd this simple consciousness and faith. It is not entirely new — but it is for Democracy to elaborate it, and look to build upon and expand from it, with uncompromising reliance. Above the doors of teaching the inscription is to appear, Though little or nothing can be absolutely known, perceived, except from a point of view which is evanescent, yet we know at least one permanency, that Time and Space, in the will of God, furnish successive chains, completions of material births and beginnings, solve all discrepancies, fears and doubts, and eventually fulfill happiness — and that the prophecy of those births, namely spiritual results, throws the true arch over all teaching, all science. The local considerations of sin, disease, deformity, ignorance, death, etc., and their measurement by the superficial mind, and ordinary legislation and theology, are to be met by science, boldly accepting, promulging this faith, and planting the seeds of superber laws — of the explication of the physical universe through the spiritual — and clearing the way for a religion, sweet and unimpugnable alike to little child or great savan.

their parents. Fearless of scoffing, and of the ostent, let us take our stand, our ground, and never desert it, to confront the growing excess and arrogance of realism. To the cry, now victorious—the cry of sense, science, flesh, incomes, farms, merchandise, logic, intellect, demonstrations, solid perpetuities, buildings of brick and iron, or even the facts of the shows of trees, earth, rocks, etc., fear not, my brethren, my sisters, to sound out with equally determin'd voice, that conviction brooding within the recesses of every envision'd soul—illusions! apparitions! figments all! True, we must not condemn the show, neither absolutely deny it, for the indispensability of its meanings; but how clearly we see that, migrate in soul to what we can already conceive of superior and spiritual points of view, and palpable as it seems under present relations, it all and several might, nay certainly would, fall apart and vanish.

I hail with joy the oceanic, variegated, intense practical energy, the demand for facts, even the business materialism of the current age, our States. But woe to the age and land in which these things, movements, stopping at themselves, do not tend to ideas. As fuel to flame, and flame to the heavens, so much wealth, science, materialism—even this democracy of which we make so much—unerringly feed the highest mind, the soul. Infinitude the flight: fathomless the mystery. Man, so diminutive, dilates beyond the sensible universe, competes with, outcopes space and time, meditating even one great idea. Thus, and thus only, does a human being, his spirit, ascend above, and justify, objective Nature, which, probably nothing in itself, is incredibly and divinely serviceable, indispensable, real, here. And as the purport of objective Nature is doubtless folded, hidden, somewhere here—as somewhere here is what this globe and its manifold forms, and the light of day, and night's darkness, and life itself, with all its experiences, are for—it is here the great literature, especially verse, must get its inspiration and throbbing blood. Then may we attain to a poetry worthy the immortal soul of man, and which, while absorbing materials, and, in their own sense, the shows of Nature, will, above all, have, both directly and indirectly, a freeing, fluidizing, expanding, religious character, exulting with science, fructifying the moral elements, and stimulating aspirations, and meditations on the unknown.

The process, so far, is indirect and peculiar, and though it may be suggested, cannot be defined. Observing, rapport, and with intuition, the shows and forms presented by Nature, the sensuous luxuriance, the beautiful in living men and women, the actual play of passions, in history and life—and, above all, from those developments either in Nature or human personality in which power (dearest of all to the sense of the artist) transacts itself—out of these, and seizing what is in them, the poet, the æsthetic worker in any field, by the divine magic of his genius, projects them, their analogies, by curious removes, indirections, in literature and art. (No useless attempt to repeat the material creation, by daguerrotyping the exact likeness by mortal mental means.) This is the image-making faculty, coping with material creation, and rivaling, almost triumphing over it. This alone, when all the other parts of a specimen of literature or art are ready and waiting, can breathe into it the breath of life, and endow it with identity.

"The true question to ask," says the Librarian of Congress in a paper read before the Social Science Convention at New York, October 1869, "The true question to ask respecting a book, is, *has it help'd any human soul?*" This is the hint, statement, not only of the great literatus, his book, but of every great artist. It may be that all works of art are to be first tried by their art qualities, their image-forming talent, and their dramatic, pictorial, plot-constructing, euphonious and other talents. Then, whenever claiming to be first-class works, they are to be strictly and sternly tried by their foundation in, and radiation, in the highest sense and always indirectly, of, the ethic principles and eligibility to free, arouse, dilate.

As, within the purposes of the kosmos, and vivifying all meteorology, and all the congeries of the mineral, vegetable and animal worlds—all the physical growth and development of man, and all the history of the race of politics, religions, wars, etc., there is a moral purpose, a visible or invisible intention, certainly underlying it all—its results and proof needing to be patiently waited for—needing intuition, faith, idiosyncrasy, to its realization, which many, and especially the intellectual, do not have—so in the product, or congeries of the product, of the greatest literatus. This is the last, profoundest measure and test of a first-class literary or æsthetic achievement, and when understood and put in force must fain, I say, lead to works, books, nobler than any hitherto known. Lo! Nature (the only complete, actual poem), existing calmly in the divine scheme, containing all, content, careless of the criticisms of a day, or these endless and wordy chatterers. And lo! to the consciousness of the soul, the permanent identity, the thought, the something, before which the magnitude even of democracy, art, literature, etc., dwindles, becomes partial, measurable—something that fully satisfies (which those do not). That something is the All, and the idea of All, with the accompanying idea of eternity, and of itself, the soul, buoyant, indestructible, sailing space forever, visiting every region, as a ship the sea. And again lo! the pulsations in all matter, all spirit, throbbing forever—the eternal beats, eternal systole and diastole of life in things—wherefrom I feel and know that death is not the ending, as was thought, but rather the real beginning—and that nothing ever is or can be lost, nor ever die, nor soul, nor matter.

In the future of these States must arise poets immenser far, and make great poems of death. The poems of life are great, but there must be the poems of the purports of life, not only in itself, but beyond itself. I have eulogized Homer, the sacred bards of Jewry, Eschylus, Juvenal, Shakspere, etc., and acknowledged their inestimable value. But (with perhaps the exception, in some, not all respects, of the second mention'd) I say there must, for future and democratic purposes, appear poets (dare I to say so?) of higher class even than any of those—poets not only possess'd of the religious fire and abandon of Isaiah, luxuriant in the epic talent of Homer, or for proud characters as in Shakspere, but consistent with the Hegelian formulas, and consistent with modern science. America needs, and the world needs, a class of bards who will, now and ever, so link and tally the rational physical being of man, with the ensembles of time and space, and with this vast and multiform show, Nature, surrounding him, ever tantalizing him, equally a part, and yet not a part of him, as to essentially harmonize, satisfy, and put at rest. Faith, very old, now scared away by science, must be restored, brought back by the same power that caused her departure—restored with new sway, deeper, wider, higher than ever. Surely, this universal ennui, this coward fear, this shuddering at death, these low, degrading views, are not always to rule the spirit pervading future society, as it has the past, and does the present. What the Roman Lucretius sought most nobly, yet all too blindly, negatively and seeking to do for his age and its successors, must be done positively by some great coming literatus, especially poet, who, while remaining fully poet, will absorb whatever science indicates, with spiritualism, and out of them, and out of his own genius, will compose the great poem of death. Then will man indeed confront Nature, and confront time and space, both with science, and *con amore*, and take his right place, prepared for life, master of fortune and misfortune. And then that which was long wanted will be supplied, and the ship that had it not before in all her voyages, will have an anchor.

There are still other standards, suggestions, for products of high literatuses. That which really balances and conserves the social and political world is not so much legislation, police, treaties, and dread of punishment, as the latent eternal intuitional sense, in humanity, of fairness, manliness, decorum, etc. Indeed, this perennial regulation, control, and oversight, by self-suppliance, is *sine qua non* to democracy; and a highest, widest aim of democratic literature may well be to bring forth, cultivate, brace, and strengthen this sense, in individuals and society. A strong mastership of the general inferior self by the superior self, is to be aided, secured, indirectly, but surely, by the literatus, in his works, shaping, for individual or aggregate democracy, a great passionate body, in and along with which goes a great masterful spirit.

And still, providing for contingencies, I fain confront the fact, the need of powerful native philosophs and orators and bards, these States, as rallying points to come, in times of danger, and to fend off ruin and defection. For history is long, long, long. Shift and turn the combinations of the statement as we may, the problem of the future of America is in certain respects as dark as it is vast. Pride, competition, segregation, vicious wilfulness, and license beyond example, brood already upon us. Unwieldly and immense, who shall hold in behemoth? who bridle leviathan? Flaunt it as we choose, athwart and over the roads of our progress loom huge uncertainty, and dreadful, threatening gloom. It is useless to deny it: Democracy grows rankly up the thickest, noxious, deadliest plants and fruits of all—brings worse and worse invaders—needs newer, larger, stronger, keener compensations and compellers.

Our lands, embracing so much (embracing indeed the whole, rejecting none), hold in their breast that flame also, capable of consuming
themselves, consuming us all. Short as the span of our national life has
been, already have death and downfall crowded close upon us—and
will again crowd close, no doubt, even if warded off. Ages to come
may never know, but I know, how narrowly during the late Secession
War—and more than once, and more than twice or thrice—our Nationality (wherein bound up, as in a ship in a storm, depended, and yet
depend, all our best life, all hope, all value), just grazed, just by a hair
escaped destruction. Alas! to think of them! the agony and bloody
sweat of certain of those hours! those cruel, sharp, suspended crises!

Even today, amid these whirls, incredible flippancy, and blind fury
of parties, infidelity, entire lack of first-class captains and leaders, added
to the plentiful meanness and vulgarity of the ostensible masses—that
problem, the labor question, beginning to open like a yawning gulf,
rapidly widening every year—what prospect have we? We sail a
dangerous sea of seething currents, cross and undercurrents, vortices—
all so dark, untried—and whither shall we turn? It seems as if the
Almighty had spread before this nation charts of imperial destinies,
dazzling as the sun, yet with many a deep intestine difficulty, and human aggregate of cankerous imperfection—saying, lo! the roads, the
only plans of development, long and varied with all terrible balks and
ebullitions. You said in your soul, I will be empire of empires, over-
shadowing all else, past and present, putting the history of Old-World
dynasties, conquests behind me, as of no account—making a new
history, a history of democracy, making old history a dwarf—I alone
inaugurating largeness, culminating time. If these, O lands of America,
are indeed the prizes, the determination of your soul, be it so. But
behold the cost, and already specimens of the cost. Thought you greatness was to ripen for you like a pear? If you would have greatness,
know that you must conquer it through ages, centuries—must pay for
it with a proportionate price. For you too, as for all lands, the struggle,
the traitor, the wily person in office, scrofulous wealth, the surfeit of
prosperity, the demonism of greed, the hell of passion, the decay of
faith, the long postponement, the fossil-like lethargy, the ceaseless need
of revolutions, prophets, thunderstorms, deaths, births, new projections and invigorations of ideas and men.

Yet I have dream'd, merged in that hidden-tangled problem of our
fate, whose long unraveling stretches mysteriously through time—
dream'd out, portray'd, hinted already—a little or a larger band—a
band of brave and true, unprecedented yet—arm'd and equipt at every
point—the members separated, it may be, by different dates and States,
or south, or north, or east, or west—Pacific, Atlantic, Southern, Cana-
dian—a year, a century here, and other centuries there—but always
one, compact in soul, conscience-conserving, God-inculcating, inspired
achievers, not only in literature, the greatest art, but achievers in all
art—a new, undying order, dynasty, from age to age transmitted—a
band, a class, at least as fit to cope with current years, our dangers,
needs, as those who, for their times, so long, so well, in armor or in

cowl, upheld and made illustrious, that far-back feudal, priestly world. To offset chivalry, indeed, those vanish'd countless knights, old altars, abbeys, priests, ages and strings of ages, a knightlier and more sacred cause today demands, and shall supply, in a New World, to larger, grander work, more than the counterpart and tally of them.

Arrived now, definitely, at an apex for these Vistas, I confess that the promulgation and belief in such a class or institution—a new and greater literatus order—its possibility (nay certainty), underlies these entire speculations—and that the rest, the other parts, as superstructures, are all founded upon it. It really seems to me the condition, not only of our future national and democratic development, but of our perpetuation. In the highly artificial and materialistic bases of modern civilization, with the corresponding arrangements and methods of living, the force-infusion of intellect alone, the depraving influences of riches just as much as poverty, the absence of all high ideals in character—with the long series of tendencies, shapings, which few are strong enough to resist, and which now seem, with steam-engine speed, to be everywhere turning out the generations of humanity like uniform iron castings—all of which, as compared with the feudal ages, we can yet do nothing better than accept, make the best of, and even welcome, upon the whole, for their oceanic practical grandeur, and their restless wholesale kneading of the masses—I say of all this tremendous and dominant play of solely materialistic bearings upon current life in the United States, with the results as already seen, accumulating, and reaching far into the future, that they must either be confronted and met by at least an equally subtle and tremendous force-infusion for purposes of spiritualization, for the pure conscience, for genuine æsthetics, and for absolute and primal manliness and womanliness—or else our modern civilization, with all its improvements, is in vain, and we are on the road to a destiny, a status, equivalent, in its real world, to that of the fabled damned.

Prospecting thus the coming unsped days, and that new order in them—marking the endless train of exercise, development, unwind, in nation as in man, which life is for—we see, fore-indicated, amid these prospects and hopes, new law-forces of spoken and written language—not merely the pedagogue-forms, correct, regular, familiar with precedents, made for matters of outside propriety, fine words, thoughts definitely told out—but a language fann'd by the breath of Nature, which leaps overhead, cares mostly for impetus and effects, and for what it plants and invigorates to grow—tallies life and character, and seldomer tells a thing than suggests or necessitates it. In fact, a new theory of literary composition for imaginative works of the very first class, and especially for highest poems, is the sole course open to these States. Books are to be call'd for, and supplied, on the assumption that the process of reading is not a half-sleep, but, in highest sense, an exercise, a gymnast's struggle; that the reader is to do something for himself, must be on the alert, must himself or herself construct indeed the poem, argument, history, metaphysical essay—the text furnishing the hints, the clue, the start or framework. Not the book needs so much to be the complete thing, but the reader of the book does. That were to make a nation of supple and athletic minds, well-train'd, intuitive, used to depend on themselves, and not on a few coteries of writers.

Investigating here, we see, not that it is a little thing we have, in having the bequeath'd libraries, countless shelves of volumes, records, etc.; yet how serious the danger, depending entirely on them, of the bloodless vein, the nerveless arm, the false application, at second or third hand. We see that the real interest of this people of ours in the theology, history, poetry, politics, and personal models of the past (the British islands, for instance, and indeed all the past), is not necessarily to mold ourselves or our literature upon them, but to attain fuller, more definite comparisons, warnings, and the insight to ourselves, our own present, and our own far grander, different, future history), religion, social customs, etc. We see that almost everything that has been written, sung, or stated, of old, with reference to humanity under the feudal and oriental institutes, religions, and for other lands, needs to be rewritten, resung, restated, in terms consistent with the institution of these States, and to come in range and obedient uniformity with them.

We see, as in the universes of the material kosmos, after meteorological, vegetable, and animal cycles, man at last arises, born through them, to prove them, concentrate them, to turn upon them with wonder and love—to command them, adorn them, and carry them upward into superior realms—so, out of the series of the preceding social and political universes, now arise these States. We see that while many were supposing things established and completed, really the grandest things always remain; and discover that the work of the New World is not ended, but only fairly begun.

We see our land, America, her literature, æsthetics, etc., as, substantially, the getting in form, or effusement and statement, of deepest basic elements and loftiest final meanings, of history and man—and the portrayal (under the eternal laws and conditions of beauty) of our own physiognomy, the subjective tie and expression of the objective, as from our own combination, continuation, and points of view—and the deposit and record of the national mentality, character, appeals, heroism, wars, and even liberties—where these, and all, culminate in native literary and artistic formulation, to be perpetuated; and not having which native, first-class formulation, she will flounder about, and her other, however imposing, eminent greatness, prove merely a passing gleam; but truly having which, she will understand herself, live nobly, nobly contribute, emanate, and, swinging, poised safely on herself, illumin'd and illuming, become a full-form'd world, and divine Mother not only of material but spiritual worlds, in ceaseless succession through time—the main thing being the average, the bodily, the concrete, the democratic, the popular, on which all the superstructures of the future are to permanently rest.

GLOSSARY

OF DIFFICULT TERMS

ACCOUCHE! ACCOUCHEZ!   French: be delivered (of child); in Whitman, produce or create.

ACCOUCHEUR   A medical man who attends childbirth cases.

ACCOUCHEMENT   Childbirth.

ADHESIVENESS   From phrenology: a mental faculty manifested in lasting friendship, fraternity, companionship.

ADMIRANT   French: admiring, regarding with wonder.

AFFETTUOSO   Italian: affected, pathetic; affectionate.

AFFLATUS   An impelling mental force acting from within; poetic inspiration.

ALEMBIC   A still; a container formerly used for distillation, usually made of glass or copper.

ALIMENT   That which nourishes or sustains; food; nutriment.

ALIMENTIVE   From phrenology: inclined to eat and drink; to seek or take nourishment.

ALLONS   French: let us go.

AMATIVE   Disposed to loving.

AMATIVENESS   From phrenology: propensity to love, or sexual passion.

AMBULANZA   Whitman: an army ambulance; Italian: a field hospital.

AMIES   French: friends; lovers.

APEX   The tip of anything; in botany, the tip of a young plant shoot.

ARRIERE   (preceded by *in*) Behind, toward the rear.

ASKANT   Adjective: mistrustful, faithless. Adverb: with mistrust.

ATELIER   French: workshop; studio.

ATOMIES   Dust motes.

AVATARA   Sanskrit: incarnation.

BARNEGAT   An inlet and bay along the coast of New Jersey.

BATTUE   Wholesale slaughter of unresisting crowds.

BAYADERE   French: Hindu dancing girl.

BENT   Impetus, concentrated energy.

BLAB   Verb: to talk indiscreetly. Noun: indiscreet talk.

BLATHERER   One who makes vapid or noisy talk, or voluble non-sense.

BON-MOT   Clever saying.

BONZE   Buddhist monk of Japan.

BURIN'D   Engraved on copper.

BUSTARD   A goose-like bird.

CALAMUS   Whitman writes: "Calamus is the very large and aroma-tic grass, or rush, growing about water ponds in the valleys — spears about three feet high; often called Sweet Flag; grows all over the Northern and Middle States. The recherché or ethereal sense of the term, as used in my book, arises probably from the actual Cala-mus presenting the biggest and hardiest kind of spears of grass, and their fresh, aquatic, pungent bouquet."

CAMERADO   A close companion; one who shares all. From 16th-century Spanish *Camarada:* chambermate.

CANISTER   Canister-shot; a collection of small projectiles in a case, to be fired from a cannon.

CANTABILE   Smooth flow.

CANTATRICE   A female professional singer.

CARLACUE   Slang for curlicue; a fancy curve or flourish.

CARTOUCHE   Oval or oblong figure in Egyptian hieroglyphics, in-closing characters expressing royal or divine names or titles.

CHANSONNIER   French: song writer.

CHEF-D'OEUVRE   French: masterpiece.

CHUFF   A cheek swollen or puffed with fat. In Whitman, probably the fleshy part, or cheek, of the hand.

CLINCH   Noun: a clinching together. Verb: to fasten securely, es-pecially by flattening the point which has passed through a plank or plate; to take a strong hold.

COLTER   An iron blade attached to the front of a plowshare.

COMITY   Courteous and friendly understanding.

COMPEND   Compendium; a summary, an epitome.

COMPLAISANCE   French: obligingness, deference to the wishes of others.

CONJOINT   Joined together, united.

CONTRARIETY   Opposition of one thing to another in nature, qual-ity, or action; diametrical difference.

DEBOUCH   To issue from a narrow place into a wider place.

DEBOUCHÉ   French: outlet, opening.

DELICATESSE   French: delicacy.

DEMESNE   Territory of a state or nation; domain.

DIMINUTE   Diminished, lessened.

DISSEVER'D   Separated, disunited.

DOLCE   Italian: agreeable, gentle.

DOUCEURS   English (18th c.): bribes (from French: sweets).

DRIB   To fall in drops.

ECLAIRCISE   To clear up, enlighten.

ÉCLAIRCISSEMENT   French: an explanation, enlightenment.

EFFULGENTLY   Resplendently, radiantly.

EFFUSE   To pour out.

EFFUSION   A pouring forth.

EIDOLON   An image; especially in Whitman, the spiritual counterpart of a physical object or manifestation.

ELATE   Proud, exalted.

ELD   Antiquity, the olden time.

ELEVE   French: pupil.

EMBOUCHURE   The part of a musical instrument applied to the mouth. In "By Blue Ontario's Shore" probably the literal French meaning: put into the mouth or discharge by a mouth.

EMPRISE   An undertaking of an adventurous nature.

EMULOUS   Closely resembling, imitative of.

EN-MASSE   French: all together, as a whole.

ENNUYÉ   French: person affected with boredom or annoyance.

ESTRAY   A stray animal.

EVEN   (be even) to have settled accounts; to be square.

EXALTÉ   French: uplifted, ennobled.

EXURGE   To rise up, start out.

FEMME   *See* MA FEMME.

FETCH   Nautical: to arrive at, come to, reach.

FETICH   Fetish: an inanimate object worshipped by savages, as having inherent magical powers or being animated by a spirit.

FEUILLAGE   French: foliage, leaves. In Whitman, clusters of leaves, related to grass as a universal symbol.

FEUILLAGÉ   In leaf.

FLOAT   The action of being suspended in water or air; the flux or flood of the tide; a floating object.

FOETOR   Fetor; an offensive smell.

FORETRUCK   Nautical: a cap of wood fixed on the head of a fore-mast; a foretop.

FORMULE   French: set form of words; formula.

FRIENDLILY   In a friendly manner, like a friend.

GALLIVANT   To gad about in a showy fashion; flirt.

GAMUT   The whole musical scale.

GRAPE   Grape-shot; a cluster of small cast-iron balls used as a charge for a cannon.

GYMNOSOPHIST   Ancient Hindu philosopher of ascetic habits.

HABITAN   Old French: inhabitant, resident.

HACKMATACK   The American Larch or Tamarack, a tree found in northern swamps.

HAP   An event which befalls one; a chance, happening, accident.

HARBINGE   To announce beforehand.

HECTIC   The flush of a consumptive fever.

HEFT   Mass, bulk, main part.

HIGGLING   Striving for petty advantages in bargaining.

HISTRION   A stage-player, actor.

HOPPLE   Leg iron, fetter.

HYMEN   Marriage; wedlock; wedding nuptials. *Hymenee* is probably a Whitman coinage: a partner in marriage. Cf. employ, employee. In "O Hymen! O Hymenee!" Whitman's specific meaning is clearly sexual.

IMPERTURBE   Apparently original with Whitman from *imperturbable:* undisturbed, calm, unruffled.

INHERENCE   Existence of permanent attribute or quality within something; indwelling.

INSPIRE   Breathe in, inhale.

INTERSTICE   A narrow opening or chink.

INURE TO   To toughen or harden by exercise; deaden the sensibility of; accustom, habituate.

IRRUPTIONS   Violent entries or invasions.

JET   Noun: a stream of liquid spurting forth from a small orifice. Verb: to spurt forth. In Whitman, used for the male orgasm.

Jour   Colloquial abbreviation for journeyman, a man who has learned his trade but works for wages rather than on his own account.

Kelson   A line of jointed timbers in a ship laid on the middle of the floor-timbers over the keel, fastened with long bolts and clinched.

Knees   Pieces of timber naturally bent, used to secure parts of a ship together.

Koboo   A low form of humanity. Whitman writes: "Brutish human beings, wild men, the 'Koboo.' Elias Pierson (June '57) describes to me a very low kind of human beings he saw in one of the Ladrone islands, they were quite hairy, had a few rags for clothing and lived in earthen shelters, something like ovens, into which they crawled."

Kosmos   The universe as a harmoniously ordered system.

Lag   (v) To fall behind; loiter; linger.

Lambent   Shining with a soft clear light without fierce heat.

Libertad   Spanish: liberty, freedom; privilege, immunity; independence. In Whitman, the personification of these concepts, or the man who enjoys them.

Lictors   Officers who attended upon a magistrate and executed sentence of judgment upon offenders.

Life-car   A water-tight vessel moved by rope, by means of which persons can be brought ashore from wrecked ships through heavy seas.

Limpsy   Limp, wanting in stiffness.

Literat   Whitman's variant of literate: a learned or literary man.

Longeve   Long-lived, long-lasting.

Loth   Loath: averse, disinclined, unwilling, reluctant.

Loup-lump   A mass of iron in a pasty condition ready for the rolls.

Luminè   Whitman coinage probably from French *luminaire:* luminary, light; star, sun.

Ma femme   My woman, my wife. In Whitman refers to personification of Democracy.

Mannahatta   Indian name for Manhattan. Whitman appears to use the two names interchangeably.

Maya   Illusion; a prominent term of Hindu philosophy.

Melange   French: mixing, blending, mingling.

Morbific   Producing or causing disease.

Mortise   *See* Tenon.

MOSSBONKER   Menhaden, a fish of the herring family common on the east coast of the United States.

NIPHON   Japan.

OBI   An amulet or charm.

OMNES   Latin: all (pl.).

OMNIFIC   Making all things; all-creating.

OMNIGENOUS   Of all kinds.

ORDURE   Filth, dirt; excrement.

OSTENT   Sign, portent, wonder, prodigy.

PAUMANOK   Indian name for Long Island.

PERTURBATIONS   Disturbances of the regular order or course; the deviations of heavenly bodies from theoretically regular orbit.

PISMIRE   An ant.

PLENUM   A condition of fullness.

POSH   A soft mass; slush.

PRESIDENTIAD   Apparently a Whitman coinage: a presidential term of office.

PROMULGE   To expose to public view; to set forth or declare publicly.

RAPPORT   Relation, connection; relations, intercourse.

RECK   To care, be troubled, concern oneself.

RECONNOISSANCE   Recognition, acknowledgment.

ROMANZA   Italian: a melody, air; a romance.

SAUROIDS   Large extinct lizard-like animals such as the ichthyosaurus, plesiosaurus, etc.

SAVAN   Savant; a man of learning or science.

SAVANTISM   Apparently a Whitman coinage: the qualities of a savant.

SCARF'D   Bound up with a scarf.

SCENT   To inhale the smell of, to smell at.

SCOOT   To flow with force.

SCRAGGED   Scraggy, ragged, stunted or scanty in growth.

SCUD   Ocean foam or spray driven by the wind; light wind-driven clouds. Other meanings may be applicable to "last scud of day."

SCUM   Froth; figuratively, unnecessary trimming.

SCUTTLE   An opening in a building's roof or wall closed with a shutter or a lid.

SHEENY   Full of brightness; having a bright, shiny surface.

SIDLE   A sidling movement; edging along in a unobtrusive manner.

SIMILITUDE   A counterpart or equal; resemblance, similarity, likeness.

SMOUCHER   One who deceives, cheats, or pilfers.

SO LONG!   Whitman's comment: "a delicious American-New York-idiomatic phrase at parting — equivalent to 'good bye' 'adieu' etc."

SOMNAMBULE   French: sleep-walker.

SPIRT   Noun: a sudden outbreak or brief spell of activity. Verb: to send out or to issue in a jet.

SPORADES   Possibly a Whitman coinage from *sporadic:* things occuring singly, separate, scattered; or a figurative allusion to the Sporades, two groups of Greek islands in the Aegean.

STONECROP   The common name of *Sedum,* an herb which grows in masses on rocks, old walls, etc.

SUDRA   Pertaining to a Sudra, a member of the lowest of the Hindu castes.

SUFI   One of a sect of Mohammedan ascetic mystics.

SWASH   Wet refuse; or the splashing sound.

TENON AND MORTISE   A tenon, a projection formed on the end of a piece of wood, fits into a mortise, or corresponding cavity in another piece of wood, to form a close joint.

TEOKALLI   Teocalli: an ancient Mexican or Central American temple, usually built on a truncated pyramid.

THEWS   The bodily powers or forces of a man, might, strength, vigor; muscles or tendons.

TILTH   Cultivation.

TROTTOIR   French: sidewalk, paved footway.

TUFT   Whitman's exact meaning here is difficult to ascertain. Suggestions: a cluster of short-stalked leaves or flowers growing from a common point; ornamental tassel on academic cap.

UNRIPT   Laid open, disclosed.

VASTING   Laying waste, destroying.

WABBLING   Wobbling; moving unsteadily from side to side or with uncertain direction.

WILT   To lose energy or vigor.

YAWP   A loud cry or yell.

TITLE INDEX

511

RIVERSIDE EDITIONS

* In preparation